CRIMINAL CAREERS AND "CAREER CRIMINALS"

VOLUME II

Alfred Blumstein, Jacqueline Cohen,
Jeffrey A. Roth, and Christy A. Visher, *editors*

Panel on Research on Criminal Careers

Committee on Research on Law Enforcement and the Administration of Justice

Commission on Behavioral and Social Sciences and Education

National Research Council

NATIONAL ACADEMY PRESS
Washington, D.C. 1986

NATIONAL ACADEMY PRESS 2101 CONSTITUTION AVENUE NW WASHINGTON, DC 20418

NOTICE: The project that is the subject of this report was approved by the Governing Board of the National Research Council, whose members are drawn from the councils of the National Academy of Sciences, the National Academy of Engineering, and the Institute of Medicine. The members of the committee responsible for the report were chosen for their special competences and with regard for appropriate balance.

This report has been reviewed by a group other than the authors according to procedures approved by a Report Review Committee consisting of members of the National Academy of Sciences, the National Academy of Engineering, and the Institute of Medicine.

The National Research Council was established by the National Academy of Sciences in 1916 to associate the broad community of science and technology with the Academy's purposes of furthering knowledge and of advising the federal government. The Council operates in accordance with general policies determined by the Academy under the authority of its congressional charter of 1863, which establishes the Academy as a private, nonprofit, self-governing membership corporation. The Council has become the principal operating agency of both the National Academy of Sciences and the National Academy of Engineering in the conduct of their services to the government, the public, and the scientific and engineering communities. It is administered jointly by both Academies and the Institute of Medicine. The National Academy of Engineering and the Institute of Medicine were established in 1964 and 1970, respectively, under the charter of the National Academy of Sciences.

This project was sponsored by the National Institute of Justice, U.S. Department of Justice, under Contract No. 83-IJ-CX-0010. The contents do not necessarily reflect the views or policies of the grantor agency.

Library of Congress Cataloging-in-Publication Data

Criminal careers and "career criminals."

Bibliography: v. 1, p.
Includes index.
1. Crime analysis—United States. 2. Crime and criminals—United States. 3. Criminal behavior, Prediction of. I. Blumstein, Alfred. II. National Research Council (U.S.). Panel on Research on Criminal Careers.
HV7936.C88C75 1986 364.3'0973 86-18282
ISBN 0-309-03684-4 (v. 1)
ISBN 0-309-03683-6 (v. 2)

Printed in the United States of America

NATIONAL ACADEMY PRESS

The National Academy Press was created by the National Academy of Sciences to publish the reports issued by the Academy and by the National Academy of Engineering, the Institute of Medicine, and the National Research Council, all operating under the charter granted to the National Academy of Sciences by the Congress of the United States.

Panel on Research on Criminal Careers

ALFRED BLUMSTEIN (*Chair*), School of Urban and Public Affairs, Carnegie-Mellon University
ALLEN H. ANDREWS, JR., Superintendent of Police, City of Peoria, Illinois
DELBERT S. ELLIOTT, Department of Sociology and Behavioral Research Institute, University of Colorado
DAVID P. FARRINGTON, Institute of Criminology, Cambridge University, England
JOHN KAPLAN, School of Law, Stanford University
ROLF LOEBER, Western Psychiatric Institute and Clinic, University of Pittsburgh
CHARLES F. MANSKI, Department of Economics, University of Wisconsin
NORVAL MORRIS, School of Law, University of Chicago
ALBERT J. REISS, JR., Department of Sociology, Yale University
LEE ROBINS, Washington University Medical School, St. Louis, Missouri
HAROLD ROSE, Department of Urban Affairs, University of Wisconsin at Milwaukee
DANIEL S. SMITH, Department of History, University of Illinois at Chicago
ANDREW L. SONNER, State's Attorney for Montgomery County, Maryland
REGGIE B. WALTON, Associate Judge, Superior Court of the District of Columbia
JAMES Q. WILSON, Department of Government, Harvard University, and Graduate School of Management, University of California at Los Angeles
MARVIN E. WOLFGANG, Sellin Center for Studies in Criminology and Criminal Law, University of Pennsylvania

JEFFREY A. ROTH, *Study Director*
CHRISTY A. VISHER, *Research Associate*
GAYLENE J. DUMOUCHEL, *Administrative Secretary*
JACQUELINE COHEN, *Consultant*, School of Urban and Public Affairs, Carnegie-Mellon University

Committee on Research on Law Enforcement and the Administration of Justice

Contents

Contents, Volume I

Preface

In 1983, when the Panel on Research on Criminal Careers was convened, the U.S. prison population had experienced a rapid growth—more than doubling from 196,000 in 1972 to 437,000 in 1983—and the crime rate had just passed its 1980 peak of 13 million reported index crimes, or almost 6,000 crimes per 100,000 population. There was strong policy interest in finding alternatives to rapidly escalating imprisonment costs and what was perceived as relatively ineffective crime control.

One approach that was widely considered was to direct attention at "career criminals," high-rate or long-duration offenders who contribute most to total crime rates. Research at the Rand Corporation had highlighted the extreme variability in individual rates of riminal activity: in surveys of prisoners, the worst 10 percent of offenders reported committing more than 50 robberies or 200 burglaries per year, but half the prisoners reported committing fewer than 5 burglaries or robberies per year. This extreme variation enhanced the appeal of being able to distinguish high-rate from low-rate offenders. To this end, a number of prediction scales have been proposed to distinguish the high-rate offenders from the more numerous ordinary offenders.

Any prediction of an individual's future offending must draw on research on criminal careers, the characterization of the sequence of individual criminal activity: initiation of criminal activity, variation over the career in the frequency of offending and in the kinds of crimes committed, and, finally, termination of criminal activity. Any attempt to identify the *career criminals* in a population requires examination of the *criminal careers* of all offenders to find the characteristics that distinguish the most serious offenders: those having the longest remaining careers, the highest frequencies of offending, and committing the most serious kinds of offenses.

The panel was convened to evaluate the feasibility of predicting the future course of criminal careers, to assess the effects of prediction instruments in reducing crime through incapacitation (usually by incarceration), and to review the contribution of research on criminal careers to the development of fundamental knowledge about crime and criminals. Ultimately, such knowledge is necessary for understanding the dimensions of the crime problem, for isolating factors that contribute to criminality, and for developing effective crime control strategies. In particular, many commonly held perceptions of correlates of crime that derive from aggregate or macroanalysis do not hold at the individual or micro level. As knowledge about criminal careers develops, the insights into individual offending that emerge will certainly stimulate refinements to criminological theory. They will also lead to improved criminal justice decisions, both by drawing attention to some variables that are not adequately appreciated and by directing attention away from other variables that are incorrectly perceived as important. Criminal career information is also necessary for estimating the effects of changes in incarceration policy on crime and on prison populations.

In reviewing the scientific evidence on criminal careers, the panel members were in general agreement about the findings and conclusions, but there were, however, divergent views on the ethics of how such information should be used in dealing with offenders. At one end of a spectrum is the view that no actions taken by the criminal justice system should take any account of individual differences in anticipated future offending; from this perspective, any use of predictive information would be objectionable. At the other end of the spectrum is a desire to see even weak results put to use as quickly as possible; advocates of this position point to the shortcomings of current decisions and emphasize that any contribution could improve the quality of decisions and thereby reduce crime. In the middle, most panel members view prediction of future offending as a legitimate consideration in criminal justice decisions, particularly since it is currently being done implicitly at some level in practice. This view also maintains, however, that the role of prediction must be rigorously constrained and, in particular, that it not result in punishments or restraints that are unjust in terms of the offense committed. Although the panel viewed the making of pronouncements on ethical issues as outside its role, we did devote considerable attention to ethical considerations to be sure that our conclusions were sensitive to them. The scientific concern that is central to the panel's role is that any use of prediction be based on correct information intelligently used. We found a number of instances in which prediction rules were naively generated, with poor methods, or violated fundamental tenets of validity testing. Thus, it became important to call attention to more appropriate methods and to identify useful information—both information that contributes to identifying career criminals as well as information that is frequently used but should not be used.

Many aspects of the work of the panel can be viewed as a follow-up to earlier work by the Panel on Research on Deterrent and Incapacitative Effects, whose report was published in 1978. That report noted that any assessment of incapacitative effects or improvement of them was severely handicapped by the paucity of substantive research findings on individual offending patterns that could contribute to estimates of the magnitude of incapacitative effects. That panel thus recommended that priority be assigned to research on criminal careers and that "the most immediate empirical investigation should be directed at estimating the individual crime rate and the length of a criminal career."

Pursuit of these issues has been a major feature of the Crime Control Theory Research Program of the National Institute of Justice, directed by Richard Linster and Joel Garner. It is always disappointing to find that knowledge does not accumulate as fast as one would like and that the measurements of those criminal career parameters are still short of definitive. In the context of the earlier review, however, it is impressive how much additional research has accumulated that provides internally consistent measurement of the key dimensions of criminal careers and of their relationships to other relevant variables.

Criminal justice is a field of social science research that is heavily beset by ideological considerations. In such a setting, any individual study is properly met with some skepticism and concern about the author's particular ideological bent and the degree to which that perspective may have had an excessive influence in shaping the results. A panel such as this one, which brings together individuals with a full array of the requisite disciplinary perspectives and technical skills, and with a diversity of ideological stances, thus represents an important vehicle for assessing the current evidence in the field and for identifying promising research directions.

Given its charge to assess the evidence on criminal careers and to point to future research directions, the panel pursued two intensive efforts. First, the panel's staff reviewed the relevant literature, and these reviews are included as appendices in Volume I: Appendix A by Christy Visher and Jeffrey Roth reviews the literature on participation in criminal careers; Appendix B by Jacqueline Cohen reviews the literature on the individual frequency of offending and on the mix of offense types by active offenders.

Second, the panel commissioned a number of papers that were presented and discussed at a workshop in Woods Hole, Massachusetts, on July 23–25, 1984 (see Appendix C in Volume I for the program and list of participants). Several of the papers review major bodies of literature: on prediction and its uses (by Stephen and Don Gottfredson); on the influence on criminal careers of alcohol (by James Collins) and of drugs (by Eric Wish and Bruce Johnson); and on group patterns in offending (by Albert J. Reiss). Because of the considerable interest generated by the Rand Second Inmate Survey, the panel also asked Christy Visher to undertake a reanalysis of the data from that survey. Two commissioned papers, one by Joseph Weis and another by John Copas and Roger Tarling, address methodological and measurement issues; a paper by

Mark Moore addresses relevant normative issues; and two papers introduce new models of criminal careers that derive from recent advances in economics (by Christopher Flinn) and in stochastic processes (by John Lehoczky). These papers constitute this volume. They are the responsibility of their authors and do not necessarily represent the views of the panel, but they were valuable resources for the panel in its discussions and represent important contributions to the literature on criminal careers.

The panel members represent a diverse group (see biographical sketches in Appendix D in Volume I). The panel benefited particularly from the sensitivity, sophistication, and challenges offered by the practitioners, who conveyed insights about the current state of their professions—needs, strengths, shortcomings—and the operational constraints that limit the application of research findings. The academic members of the panel are all distinguished researchers. Some are working in areas related to criminal careers, while others brought specialized expertise in particular disciplines, methodologies, jurisprudence, or policy analysis. Discussions at panel meetings were always lively, full of interesting ideas; disagreements were consistently isolated and dealt with directly. It was indeed a pleasure working with so able and committed a group.

The dedicated efforts of the staff have been central to the work of the panel. Jeffrey Roth was the study director from the inception of the panel and contributed considerably in terms of managing the affairs of the panel, in drafting significant segments of the report, and in his careful review of all materials. Christy Visher began her association with the panel as a National Research Council Fellow, undertook the review of the Rand Second Inmate Survey, and brought significant criminological background and experience to the work of the panel in its review of the literature and in drafting and editing major sections of the report. Jacqueline Cohen of Carnegie-Mellon University built on her experience as a consultant to the prior Panel on Research on Deterrent and Incapacitative Effects, her extensive research on criminal careers and incapacitation, and her extensive knowledge of the related literature; her diligent contributions to all aspects of the work of the panel, especially in reviewing the literature and in drafting major portions of the report, are very much appreciated. The task of editing the large volume of material assembled by the panel has been considerable. Eugenia Grohman, the associate director for reports of the Commission on Behavioral and Social Sciences and Education, not only sharpened our language but also challenged our assertions when they were insufficiently developed or documented, and so she made an excellent and important contribution to the report of the panel. Jean Shirhall was also very effective in editing the appendices to Volume I and the papers in this volume.

The panel has benefited considerably from the administrative and secretarial work of Gaylene Dumouchel at the National Research Council and Elizabeth Kiselev at Carnegie-Mellon University.

An important feature of the panel's work has been the support and encouragement of the sponsor, the National Institute of Justice. Richard Linster kept in close touch with the panel throughout its work, and James Stewart, the director of the National Institute of Justice, provided the kind of encouragement and support that has characterized his stewardship of the institute's research program.

ALFRED BLUMSTEIN, *Chair*
Panel on Research on Criminal Careers

1

Issues in the Measurement of Criminal Careers

Joseph G. Weis

Between 1850 and 1900, each decennial census in the United States included a question on mortality that simply asked the respondent to report the number of household members who had died during the past year. One would assume that a death in one's family would be of sufficient significance and salience that it would be reported accurately. However, a comparison of the census estimates of mortality with the number of deaths officially registered showed an "underestimation of deaths amounting to over 50 percent" (Shryock, Siegel, and Associates, 1975:392). The survey estimate of mortality was considered so flawed and unreliable that the practice was discontinued at the turn of the century.[1] About 70 years later questions that asked whether a respondent had been the victim of a variety of crimes were added to census surveys. The earliest pilot national victimization survey reported that more than 50 percent of victimizations are not reported to the police, which suggests that the official records of crime underestimate the volume of crime (Ennis, 1967).

The juxtaposition of the two underestimations highlights two major issues in the measurement of crime—the adequacy of official records as measures of phenomena and the apparent discrepancy in estimates of the amount and distribution of crime generated by different measurement methods. The resolution of these issues in the measurement of crime has not been as easily accomplished as in the

Joseph G. Weis is director of the Center for Law and Justice and associate professor of sociology, University of Washington.

The author is grateful to Jeanne Kleyn, Margie Ramsdell, George Bridges, Elizabeth Loftus, Lynn Frandsen, Kris Jones, and James McCann for their suggestions, assistance, and support in preparing this paper.

[1]Improved record-keeping and survey techniques have reduced the rate of underreporting, but there remain substantial differences between survey and official-record estimates of mortality. For example, a one-time 1962 comparison of the number of deaths reported in a quarterly census household survey and the number of officially registered deaths shows survey underreports of approximately 21 percent ± 7 (Shryock, Siegel, and Associates, 1975:392).

measurement of mortality. For example, the substantially lower estimates of mortality produced by using survey techniques were identified as the source of discrepancy and the survey was abandoned because of confidence in the relatively complete sample of deaths contained in official mortality records. But the substantially higher estimates of crime generated by victimization surveys, as well as by self-reports of criminal involvement, have not been attributed solely to the survey measures because of the selective sample of crimes and criminals represented (i.e., underrepresented) in official crime records. In fact, instead of one measure being considered clearly superior to another, the different measures of crime have come to be viewed by many as competing approaches, and each has its champions. Some see the potential for complementary measures of crime, each tapping somewhat different but overlapping domains of the phenomenon.

To date, this battleground of competing perspectives has been confined almost exclusively to research on juvenile delinquency, which has been characterized by cross-section designs and local samples within which serious offenders, minorities, and the economically disadvantaged are underrepresented. With the recent interest in the extent to which criminal career research can inform crime control policy, the field of controversy has been broadened. The basic facts of criminal careers are either unknown or unclear. The parameters of criminal involvement over time—prevalence, individual offending rates, patterns of criminal behavior, and duration of involvement—and the correlates of those parameters have not been specified, due in part to the paucity of rigorous research in the area and the concomitant unresolved measurement issues. All the problems regarding the validity and reliability of measures of crime apply to criminal career research, but they are complicated and exacerbated by temporal change and the apparently unique characteristics of serious, chronic offenders. Unfortunately, only one study has addressed the validity and reliability of measures in research on criminal careers (among a sample of adult prisoners) and that compared two methods of measuring criminal behavior, official records and self-reports (Marquis and Ebener, 1981). There is not a rich literature available on alternative approaches to measuring individual offending patterns or on ways to resolve apparent discrepancies among measures in estimates of criminal career parameters or their correlates.

The purposes of this paper are, first, to describe briefly the alternative approaches to the measurement of criminal careers, particularly self-reports and official records; second, to discuss the actual and potential sources of bias and distortion in the measures of parameters and correlates and their effects on the convergence or discrepancy of estimates; and, third, to propose some research strategies for improving the measurement of criminal careers to increase the convergent validity among the different measures of individual offending patterns and to improve their capacity for reciprocal adjustment or calibration. Theory construction, policymaking, and program implementation and evaluation can be better informed by convergent than discrepant sources of information on the basic facts of crime.

ALTERNATIVE MEASUREMENT APPROACHES

Five basic alternative approaches to the measurement of crime produce data that may be useful, directly or indirectly, in measuring individual offending patterns: official crime records, self-reports of criminal behavior, reports of personal victimization, direct observations, and informant reports. It is clear that the most viable and useful alternatives for measuring individual offending patterns are official records and self-reports. One group of criminal career researchers considers both as necessary, and self-reports, in particular, as "essential" (Greenwood, 1979:43–44) for measuring the frequency of individual criminal involvement and the relationship between offenses committed and offenses that result in criminal justice system processing.

Victimization, observation, and informant measures of crime are more indirect in their generation of estimates than the two other measures and have limited applications in criminal career research. In general, they tend not to measure the parameters and correlates of criminal behavior as comprehensively or directly, and they suffer from having somewhat unique or narrow sample characteristics. Victimization surveys are victim based, rather than offender based, and consequently provide only indirect estimates of parameters and correlates at the aggregate level for a small subset of basically personal crimes and an even smaller subset of victimizer (or offender) characteristics (Hindelang, Gottfredson, and Garofalo, 1978). Perhaps most important, the fact that the results of victimization surveys cannot be compared with other data sources at the individual-offender level is the most critical weakness of using victimization surveys in criminal career research. Direct observation studies, on the other hand, particularly if done within a prospective longitudinal design and carried out for a number of years, are better able to measure individual-level parameters and correlates than victimization surveys. But, unfortunately, they typically use small, selective samples of high-risk juvenile subjects whose behavior is not representative of serious crime happening in natural settings or out "on the street." As for informant reports, the most severe limitation is that informants can only report on others whom they know and observe directly or hear about indirectly. The sample, therefore, is very limited and selective.

Official-record data are adequate for estimates of *official* prevalence and individual offending rates, patterns, and duration. In fact, as a measure of crime mix, crime switching, and duration, official records are probably more useful than self-reports, primarily because time markers are incorporated in the records, which permits relatively accurate estimation of official onset and termination and of the sequence of changes in offenses of record. However, official data are not as adequate as measures of the correlates and determinants of parameters, simply because many of the important pieces of information on the social, demographic, economic, and psychological characteristics of offenders are not routinely, systematically, or accurately collected. This, however, is one of the strengths of self-report surveys, which can collect a great variety of rich etiological and descriptive information along with the reports of personal involvement in criminal behavior. Self-reports are also more adequate measures of prevalence and individual offending rates than official data but are weakest as a basis for studying patterns of involvement and duration, particularly within the typical cross-section study design. Respondents have difficulty in remembering and dating onset, termination is (by definition) almost immeasurable, and respondents have even more difficulty recalling the sequences of a variety of offenses.

Official records are necessary to those agencies responsible for crime control; they constitute the standard external validation criterion to which other measures are compared and are the only continuous, lifelong record of criminal involvement. Self-reports typically cover much shorter time spans than official records, although they provide the potential for long-term measurement of a variety of samples. More importantly, they provide more detailed and richer information on an individual offender's involvement in crime and on other characteristics of descriptive and etiological interest.

In sum, official and self-report measures best meet the needs of criminal career research. They measure more comprehensively and systematically the parameters and correlates of individual offending patterns over time for serious crimes (e.g., robbery, burglary, assault, drug dealing, auto theft, larceny), can be compared more easily and directly with each other on an individual-offender basis, and, therefore, inform crime control policy regarding the serious, chronic offender. Taken together, they are at the heart of the controversy over the question of convergence and discrepancy in estimates of correlates of crime produced by different measurement approaches. The issue is whether official records and self-reports of criminal behavior generate similar distributions and correlates of crime. Are the two measures consistent or inconsistent in their representations of the general characteristics of crime and criminals?

The answers to the questions above are very important for two reasons. First, the implications for theory, policy, and programs will reflect the convergence or discrepancy of crime measures—discrepant correlates suggest different strategies, while convergent correlates support complementary strategies and confirm information on the facts of crime. Second, as the convergence in the estimates of correlates approaches unity, one measure can be substituted for the other (Nettler, 1974:89–90). Of course, this is unlikely, but if there is "apparent" and "sufficient" convergence, the correlates—or characteristics of offenders and offenses—could be taken into account to estimate parameters of criminal careers, particularly prevalence and individual offending rates (Chaiken, Rolph, and Houchens, 1981: 14). That is, the use of one measure to calibrate the other is enhanced with convergence.

CONVERGENCE OR DISCREPANCY IN ESTIMATES

In general, there is surprising consistency in the descriptions of the most important correlates of crime based on official crime records and self-reports of criminal involvement. Indeed, there are fewer discrepancies than one might expect, given the severe criticisms that have been leveled against each method of measurement. In fact, among the major sociodemographic and etiological correlates of crime, only one is clearly discrepant in its correlation with the two measures—race—and one may or may not be discrepant—social class. The only other apparently discrepant correlation is for a variable that has not been treated in theory or research as a major correlate—pulse rate (Farrington, 1983).[2] The remainder of the major correlates are con-

[2]Farrington (1983:15) reports that convicted youths tend to have low pulse rates, especially if they are violent offenders, but that low pulse rate does not predict high rates of self-reported violent behavior, even though convictions and self-reports of violence are significantly related. A possible explanation of this discrepancy could be that convicted juvenile criminals, particularly those convicted for serious crimes of violence, are more cool and callous than other respondents, who may not be as hardened by experience with the criminal justice system. They may simply be more likely to deceive and underreport involvement in crimes of violence and, therefore, attenuate the correlation. The situation may be somewhat analogous to the cool, hardened criminal "beating" a lie-detector test. And we know from empirical research that those who are most involved in the most serious crimes and who have official records are most likely to give invalid responses and underreport (Hindelang, Hirschi, and Weis, 1981:212–214).

vergent or very similar in their relation to official and self-report measures (Hindelang, Hirschi, and Weis, 1981).

Only a limited number of studies allow the kinds of direct comparisons of official and self-report data on individuals in the same sample that are necessary to address adequately the issue of convergence or discrepancy in the correlates of crime. However, among those studies, the estimates produced by official or self-report measures are largely consistent for sex (see Hindelang, Hirschi, and Weis, 1981: 137–155 for an extensive review), age (Farrington, 1983; Langan and Farrington, 1983:530–531), school performance and achievement, intellectual ability and general competence, delinquency of friends or peers, poor family supervision, and other major correlates that have been identified as etiologically important (West and Farrington, 1977; Hindelang, Hirschi, and Weis, 1981:199–207; Farrington, 1982).[3] The two major correlates about which there is some controversy, social class and race, provide clues about the differential validity and reliability that may be responsible for the discrepant and, hence, divergent estimates of criminal career parameters.

[3]For each of the major correlates for which there is no apparent discrepancy in the correlation between itself and official and self-report measures of crime, there may be inconsistencies in correlations across but, typically, not within subgroups of respondents. For example, the relation of school performance, whether measured by official grade average, achievement test, or self-report of performance, is consistently inverse with official and self-reported crime (see Glueck and Glueck, 1950; Jensen, 1976; Hindelang, Hirschi, and Weis, 1981:199–202). However, for some respondents, specifically black, male official delinquents, even though there is an inverse relation between self-reports of grades and official and self-reported delinquency, both correlations are lower than should be expected. They are not discrepant by method of measurement, but the correlations produced by each are lower than expected because of the apparent diminished validity of self-reports, for both grades and delinquent behavior, among members of this subgroup.

Social Class

Most research on the relation between social class and crime does not assess the issue. Rather, it assumes that there is a strong inverse relation between class and "official" delinquency and then compares self-report estimates with this established "thoroughly documented" fact (see Gordon, 1976). This relationship was established with ecological correlations, which, as is well known, tend to overestimate individual-level correlations substantially—the "ecological fallacy" (Robinson, 1950; Hannan, 1971). In addition, most of the studies relied on one measure of crime, either official data or self-reports, which precludes a direct comparative assessment of the correlations generated by each method of measurement.

The finding of no important relationship between individual-level measures of class and self-reported crime is also a well-established and thoroughly documented fact, one that has been replicated by many self-report studies (Short and Nye, 1958; Akers, 1964; Gold, 1970; Hindelang, Hirschi, and Weis, 1981). Given the different facts about social class and crime that are generated by official and self-report measures, there are logically only two ways to bring them into convergence. The first approach implies that, since there is little doubt about the inverse relationship between official crime and class, self-reports are defective and, if improved technically, would also show an inverse relationship with class (Elliott and Ageton, 1980), hence convergence. The second approach implies that, since there is little doubt about the finding of no important relationship between self-reported crime and class, official measures are suspect but, if the problem was corrected, they would also show no relationship with crime (Hindelang, Hirschi, and Weis, 1979), hence convergence. The relevant empirical question, then, is: what is the individual-level relationship between social class and official and self-reported crime?

Two meta-analyses of the class-crime relationship come to opposite conclusions regarding the correlation between class and official crime measures. Tittle, Villemez, and Smith (1978) report no important relationship, claiming it to be a myth in criminology. In a later review Braithwaite (1981) concludes that there is some evidence to support an official crime-class correlation. Examining those studies that use individual-level official data only (Havighurst, 1962; Hathaway and Monachesi, 1963; Polk, Frease, and Richmond, 1974) shows that the relationship between social class and official delinquency is weakly negative to nonexistent (Hindelang, Hirschi, and Weis, 1981:187–188). A more recent longitudinal study of a cohort of 7,719 boys in Stockholm (Janson, 1982) also reports no important individual-level relationship between a "family's social position" and a boy's having a police record.

Many, many more self-report studies typically also report no significant relationship between self-reported crime and class (e.g., Dentler and Monroe, 1961; Akers, 1964; Hindelang, 1973; Bachman, O'Malley, and Johnston, 1978). However, there is a major exception to the apparent consensus of self-report studies, and that is the recent work of Elliott and Ageton (1980) and Elliott and Huizinga (1983). Based on analyses of the National Youth Survey[4] probability sample of approximately 1,500 youths, they report that there is a moderate inverse relationship between class and serious "person crimes" and serious "property crimes," particularly for person crimes among black youths of low socioeconomic status (Elliott and Ageton, 1980). Later analyses of the national youth panel for 1976–1980 show small-to-moderate class differences in prevalence and incidence for serious crimes, and the relationship is stronger for incidence than prevalence scales (Elliott and Huizinga, 1983). Official data have also been collected on the national youth sample, but they have not yet been reported in the literature in a direct assessment of discrepancy or convergence.

Of the five major studies reviewed by Hindelang, Hirschi, and Weis (1981: 188–193) that have both official and self-report measures on an individual level for the same sample, all showed convergent estimates of the correlation between social class and official self-reported crime (Reiss and Rhodes, 1961; Hirschi, 1969; Williams and Gold, 1972; Wolfgang, Figlio, and Sellin, 1972; Elliott and Voss, 1974). Only one of the studies showed convergent estimates of a small inverse relationship (Reiss and Rhodes, 1961). Another study, based on the Cambridge (England) Study in Delinquent Development, found an inverse relationship between social class at age 14 and having an official conviction record at age 17–20, but no relation to self-reported crime at age 18 (Farrington, 1979; 1982:17).[5] This discrepancy is only one among a much broader pattern of finding no important differences between estimates of a vari-

[4]In 1967 the National Institute of Mental Health sponsored the first of a relatively regular series of national youth surveys of a representative sample of juveniles for the purpose of estimating the extent and nature of delinquency and substance abuse in the United States. The survey was repeated in 1972, and in 1976 the National Institute for Juvenile Justice and Delinquency Prevention became a cosponsor of an annual survey of the self-reported and official delinquency of a national probability panel of youths aged 11–17 in 1976.

[5]European, primarily British, studies of the class-crime relationship tend to find an inverse relationship no matter what the measure, in good part because of the more differentiated, structured, and rigid class structure that exists in Britain, so that this finding of "discrepancy" is somewhat unusual within the British context (see Belson, 1968; McDonald, 1969; Bytheway and May, 1971).

ety of correlates based on self-reports and official records. This apparent discrepancy may be interpretable in light of an important reanalysis of the follow-up interview data from the Philadelphia cohort study (Wolfgang, Figlio, and Sellin, 1972). Thornberry and Farnworth (1982) found no important relationship between status, as measured primarily by educational attainment, and criminal involvement, whether measured by self-report interviews or police arrest data, when the cohort members were juveniles. However, there was a significant inverse relationship between status and both official and self-reported crime when the cohort members were adults. That is, convergent estimates of the status-crime relationship are produced for juveniles and adults, even though they are in different directions. The findings for adults are particularly important for criminal career research, because among serious, chronic offenders the relationships between parameters and correlates are apparently different during different stages in career development. In other words, the operation of social class is not the same at age 12 as it is at age 25.

Another major study shows that there is a very weak to nonexistent relationship between social class and official and self-reported juvenile crime. More importantly, the study attempts to identify and test the substantive and methodological sources of discrepancy, not only for social class, but for a number of other variables that have some empirical and theoretical importance (Hindelang, Hirschi, and Weis, 1975, 1978, 1979, 1981; Weis, 1983b). Hindelang, Hirschi, and Weis (1975, 1979) propose that the apparent discrepancy between self-report and official measures for social class, as well as for gender and race, becomes "illusory" when standard but critical methodological considerations are taken into account, particularly comparisons of results by level of measurement and by the domain (variety), type, and seriousness of criminal behavior. They contend that, if the data are properly analyzed by comparing individual-level measures of both official and self-reported crime with individual-level measures of class, and the types and seriousness of crimes in both are the same, the alleged discrepancy for social class is resolved.[6] Simply put, one should not compare apples with oranges. Elliott and Ageton (1980) have recommended basically the same methodological adjustments; in addition they suggest that the proper analysis of self-report data should include more attention to scoring and scaling of items. Specifically, they suggest that the reported frequency of illegal acts should not be restricted in the scoring of individual incidence of involvement (which is preferred to prevalence) and that the unique properties and contributions of individual crimes that may be related to social class (or other variables) should not be lost in global scales of delinquency.

Hindelang, Hirschi, and Weis (1981: 181–198) discovered in a comprehensive empirical test of these hypotheses that there is a weak, insignificant, or nonexistent relationship with socioeconomic status when one controls for level of measurement and compares individual-level data on both variables. It seems that no matter how one measures, scales, or scores the data, there are small, typically negative relations between social class and juvenile delinquency. The correlations (γ) range from $-.01$ to $-.08$ between occupation of principal wage earner and the self-report delinquency scales (prevalence scales for total, serious, general,

[6]The same logic, of course, can be applied to other correlates and has been by Hindelang, Hirschi, and Weis (1981); only race proved not to be amenable to these methodological discrepancy-resolution strategies and procedur

drug, family-school offense indexes) and the total official offenses index (Hindelang, Hirschi, and Weis, 1981:196). These findings also hold when the additional suggestions of Elliott and Ageton (1980) are incorporated in the analysis: that is, one still finds consistently weak-to-nonexistent relations that at times are in the wrong direction when one (1) uses their self-report scales scored for incidence or the total unrestricted frequency within the past year; (2) examines each of the three official delinquency indexes (police contacts ever, police contacts past year, juvenile court referral ever); (3) does an item-by-item analysis of their 69 self-report items; and (4) examines each of their (1, 2, 3) relationships separately with a variety of indicators of socioeconomic status, including father's education, father's occupation, mother's education, mother's occupation, father employed, mother employed, father's socioeconomic index, and mother's socioeconomic index (Weis, 1981, 1986).

These results are perplexing because some rigorous studies report a moderate inverse relation between social class and self-reported crime (e.g., Elliott and Ageton, 1980; Elliott and Huizinga, 1983), while other rigorous studies show an absent-to-weak inverse relation for both self-report and official measures (e.g., Hindelang, Hirschi, and Weis, 1981; Thornberry and Farnworth, 1982). Given that there are no published or otherwise available results on a convergent inverse relationship, except for Reiss and Rhodes (1961), the conclusion for now is that there is much more evidence, across a variety of some of the most important data sets compiled on juvenile crime (e.g., National Youth Survey: Gold, 1970, and Williams and Gold, 1972; Richmond youth project: Hirschi, 1969; Philadelphia birth cohort study: Thornberry and Farnworth, 1982; Seattle youth study: Hindelang, Hirschi, and Weis, 1981) that convergence is more likely to show that there is a weak negative-to-nonexistent relation between social class and both official and self-report measures of crime. However, what is disturbing is that the agreed standard methodological adjustments that should be applied to these data comparisons (same level of measurement, same domain of criminal acts, more sensitive scoring and scaling procedures) do not go far enough in creating some kind of apparent consensus on the issue of convergent validity.

Race

Race is the only major correlate (Wolfgang and Ferracuti, 1967; Wolfgang, Figlio, and Sellin, 1972; Curtis, 1974; Hindelang, 1978; Blumstein, 1982) for which the methodological adjustments proposed by Hindelang, Hirschi, and Weis (1979), particularly the controls for type and seriousness of offense (especially violence), do not make the official and self-report relations consistent in the way they do for sex, social class, and other important correlates of crime. Official data historically have implied that blacks are "more criminal" than whites simply by virtue of their overrepresentation in the criminal justice system and official records. Self-reports, on the other hand, suggest that there is less difference in both prevalence and incidence of crime (e.g., Gold, 1970; Chaiken and Chaiken, 1982). The discrepancy is so large that "the range of ratios in self-report samples restricted to a single sex . . . *does not overlap* with the range of ratios found in official data. . . . The *very strong* relation between race and delinquency in official data is not present in self-report data. In fact, the self-report relation would have to be characterized as *weak* or *very weak*, with a mean black-to-white ratio of less than 1.1:1 expected on the basis of previous research" (Hindelang, Hirschi, and Weis, 1981:159; emphasis in original).

Contrary to expectations that comparing the more serious and violent crimes would show race differences of a magnitude similar to those represented in official records, the race differences for both self-report serious-delinquency scales and individual items are not very large or significant. Hindelang, Hirschi, and Weis (1981) report white-to-black ratios that approximate 1 for the total prevalence scale; paradoxically, for the frequency or incidence scales the ratios are less than 1 on five of their six scales, which implies more white than black involvement in crime. These ratios approach unity as one moves from the less to more serious offenses but do not, as the official-data ratios would suggest, exceed 1. The overall 2:1 black-to-white ratio in the Seattle study's official-record data is approximated by prevalence ratios for self-reports of some types of face-to-face violence, for example, carrying a weapon, hitting a teacher, using a club, gun, or other weapon to get something, beating someone seriously enough to send them to the hospital, robbery, and jumping and beating someone, as well as for official reaction, probation, and school suspension (Hindelang, Hirschi, and Weis, 1981:166–169). One might interpret this to mean that there may be violent-offense specialization by race, but the frequency estimates do not support this, for either scales or individual items; it seems that either the criminal justice system discriminates substantially against blacks, particularly males, or that blacks may be underreporting the extent of their involvement in crime.

Other research on juveniles and, more surprisingly, on adult prisoners supports these findings regarding apparent underreporting by blacks, particularly males with official criminal records. Shannon (1982, 1983) reports that in the Racine, Wisconsin, cohort study of the relationship between juvenile and adult criminal careers, self-reports of delinquency had little relationship to race, but there was a disproportionate representation of blacks with official records of police contact. Black males had the most contacts and most extensive, serious involvement with the police—75 percent of the black males had a police contact while a juvenile, compared with 50 percent of the white males. It appears that juvenile black males may be underreporting their criminal involvement because "while 80 percent of the whites in each cohort either reported their number of police contacts consistently with police records or overestimated them, only half the blacks reported the number of contacts consistently with the records and the other half reported fewer contacts in comparison with official records" (Shannon, 1982:1, 10). Other studies on juvenile crime also suggest underreporting and potential validity problems among black respondents, particularly males with official records (Chambliss and Nagasawa, 1969; Gould, 1969; Hirschi, 1969).[7]

Intriguing corroborative findings are also reported on male adult prisoners, including serious, chronic offenders, in the first (Peterson, Braiker, and Polich, 1981) and second (Marquis and Ebener, 1981; Chaiken and Chaiken, 1982) Rand surveys of incarcerated felons. Peterson, Braiker, and Polich (1981:xxii–xxiii, 60–65) report that the results of an anonymous survey of California prisoners generated "complex" results on race. The self-reports showed that black inmates were "less active and dangerous criminals" than white inmates—they were involved in the smallest variety of crimes and at the lowest reported rates compared with whites and Chicanos. They also reported less involvement in crimes of violence. Even when corrections are made

[7]In a personal communication, Delbert Elliott indicates that similar underreporting and potential validity problems among this subgroup were also appearing in ongoing analyses of the National Youth Survey data.

for different apparent probabilities of arrest and estimated offense rates by race (the model of street offenders developed by Chaiken), differences remain, with the exception that blacks are shown to be more involved in crime than Chicanos. The interpretation of these differences by race in self-reports and official records, particularly the apparent underreporting by black prisoners, is considered "somewhat ambiguous" and two possibilities are offered—either blacks do, indeed, commit fewer crimes and less frequently or the criminal justice system is more likely to imprison blacks, particularly low-rate, occasional criminals. A third source of the differences is only alluded to in a footnote—the differential reliability and validity of self-report responses by race.

Unfortunately, the first Rand inmate survey was anonymous, so the self-reports and official records could not be validated reciprocally at the individual level (Peterson, Braiker, and Polich, 1981:25–26, 90). However, Chaiken and Chaiken (1982:226, 244, 245, 247) and Chaiken, Chaiken, and Peterson (1982:17) suggest that there may have been underreporting among some subgroups of prisoners in the second Rand inmate survey, particularly among blacks and the less educated.[8] For example, there is the "puzzling finding" that blacks report much lower rates of assault than whites; but it is also reported that the responses of blacks are less reliable, i.e., have "substantially worse internal quality," and that "respondents whose survey responses have poor internal quality tend to report low crime commission rates for the crimes they report committing." There seems to be consistency in both inmate surveys regarding the underreporting of some subgroups, particularly black inmates, leading to lower-than-expected individual offending rates when self-reports are compared with official records.

In short, a number of studies of juvenile and adult offenders report a discrepancy between race and self-reported and official crime data, and the discrepancy is likely explained by underreporting on the self-report instrument rather than by race discrimination within the criminal justice system. Therefore, attention needs to be turned to the connection between self-reports and official records and possible racial and other differences in the link between the two. In this regard the next section addresses two questions: What is the nature of the reliability and validity of the two measures? How do they affect estimates of parameters and correlates and, ultimately, the convergence of the estimates generated by the two approaches to measuring individual offending patterns?

EFFECTS OF RELIABILITY AND VALIDITY ON ESTIMATES

Given the apparent underreporting of criminal involvement in self-report surveys that was identified in a number of studies and its possible contribution to discrepant correlations, the focus here is on the effects of the differential reliability and validity of measurement approaches on estimates. Of particular interest are "response effects" (Sudman and Bradburn, 1974) in self-report surveys as possible sources of bias.[9] A brief discussion

[8]It is interpreted here as a "suggestion" because the data on individual offending rates by race could not be found in Chaiken and Chaiken (1982). Relations between race and other variables, including "internal quality" and "external reliability" of measures, are reported extensively, but the distribution of self-reported individual offending by offense and race could not be found.

[9]Given the focus of most of the research in this area and space limitations, other sources of error and bias, such as processing, sampling, and design, are

of the current state of the reliability and validity of self-reports of crime precedes a more detailed treatment of some of the more important sources of apparent and potential distortion and response bias in self-report measures.

Reliability of Self-Reports of Crime

Although Reiss (1975) is correct that few self-report researchers have assessed the reliability of instruments, the evidence shows that the self-report method is very reliable, and that if there is a problem with this type of measure it is more likely in the area of validity (Hindelang, Hirschi, and Weis, 1981:84). In terms of internal consistency, both self-reports of juvenile crime (Hindelang, Hirschi, and Weis, 1981:81) and of crime among adult prisoners (Marquis and Ebener, 1981; Chaiken and Chaiken, 1982) show "impressive reliability," although there is some evidence of systematic variation in internal consistency by respondent subgroups among adult prisoners. For example, inmates convicted of drug dealing "left significantly more questions blank," and inmates who saw themselves as a "thief, player, or alcoholic/drunk" did significantly worse on the internal consistency of responses. In addition, even though there did not seem to be much difference in external reliability (validity) among whites, blacks, or Hispanics (although it was still lower, on the average, than internal consistency), the "summary measure ('percent of bad internal quality indicators') was worse than average for black repondents" (Chaiken and Chaiken, 1982:226, 244).

Test-retest reliability of self-report data is also quite good, both for reports of criminal behavior and for independent variables. A small number of studies on juvenile delinquency have reported high test-retest reliability coefficients; the time between administration of the self-report instrument ranged from a couple of hours (Hindelang, Hirschi, and Weis, 1981: 81–82) to a number of years (Farrington, 1973; Bachman, O'Malley, and Johnston, 1978). These and other studies (Dentler and Monroe, 1961; Clark and Tifft, 1966; Belson, 1968; Kulik, Stein, and Sarbin, 1968) show that there is substantial consistency in self-reports of the same criminal acts, but reliability diminishes with time. In general, the test-retest reliability coefficients are higher for criminal behavior items than for other items (Elliott and Voss, 1974; Bachman, O'Malley, and Johnston, 1978). For example, with a few hours between tests, the coefficients on four independent items (mother's education, grade-point average, parental supervision, and peer delinquency) ranged from 0.4 to 0.9, but the delinquency items varied around 0.9 (Hindelang, Hirschi, and Weis, 1981:82).

The reliability of alternate forms, using split-half coefficients, is also impressive. Elmhorn (1965) reports a coefficient of .86 for 21 delinquency items, and Kulik, Stein, and Sarbin (1968) report coefficients ranging from .70 to .92 for five subscales derived from cluster analysis of 52 delinquency items.

Overall, self-reports are very consistent in the measurement of crime, in terms of internal consistency, test-retest stability, and split-half reliability. There is some evidence, however, that there may be potentially important variation in reliability, particularly internal consistency, by respondent characteristics, with apparently more reliability problems among both black juveniles and adult offenders, the less educated, and those with drug and alcohol abuse in their records. These

---

not addressed directly but only as they relate to response effects. The limitations of official-record measures are discussed later; besides, the issue for official measures is not so much a matter of reliability and validity as it is of utility.

respondent effects on reliability may be related to underreporting of individual criminal involvement, the potential distortion of parameter estimates, and the attenuation of correlations with these respondent characteristics. Threats to validity seem more likely sources of serious measurement problems, particularly among some subgroups of respondents.

Validity of Self-Reports of Crime

There are many types of validity; for example, Costner (1975) has identified eight, ranging from content to face validity.[10] The focus here is on those types of validity that allow empirical assessment of the accuracy of responses. Therefore, the discussion emphasizes different kinds of concurrent validity or the extent to which self-report results are consistent with other concurrent measures of criminal behavior. "Convergent" validity—the extent to which two or more measures intended to measure the same concept (e.g., crime) produce convergent results (Campbell and Fiske, 1959)—is dependent on concurrent validity.

Two types of concurrent validity have been examined in the self-report literature: known group and correlational. In known-group validity, groups known to differ on some dimension, for example, official delinquency, are compared using another measure that is supposed to discriminate between the groups, for example, self-reports of delinquency. The latter is validated to the extent that it shows that known official delinquents differ on self-reports of crime. For example, the original Short and Nye (1958) self-report study included known-group comparisons that showed that their 23-item, self-report checklist could distinguish rather well between boys in state training schools and in high school. These known-group differences in self-reports of crime (Erickson and Empey, 1963; Hindelang, Hirschi, and Weis, 1981:95–96) are evidence of validity, but they do not tell us anything about the magnitude of the relationship between self-report and official measures in more general samples. The degree of validity is better assessed through correlational validation. The question becomes: To what extent are the results of one measurement approach consistent with—or correlated with—those produced by another? The stronger the correlation, the greater the concurrent and convergent validity.

There are a number of measures with which self-reports of criminal behavior can be compared (Hindelang, Hirschi, and Weis, 1981:Figure 5.1, 98): (1) unofficial sources, such as direct observation or the informant reports of peers, teachers, family, and victims; (2) self-reports of official action, such as police contacts, arrests, probation, or incarceration (e.g., Christie, Andenaes, and Skirbekk, 1965; Elmhorn, 1965; Hindelang, Hirschi, and Weis, 1981; Marquis and Ebener, 1981; Chaiken and Chaiken, 1982); (3) official criminal justice records, such as offenses known to the police, court referrals, convictions, and incarceration (Gould, 1969; Erickson, 1972; Elliott and Voss, 1974; Hindelang, Hirschi, and Weis, 1981; Chaiken and Chaiken, 1982); (4) official records from other agencies, such as school, mental health, social service, and drug abuse (Weis, Janvier, and Hawkins, 1982).

Researchers have relied on official measures as the "standard" external validation criteria, because there is substantial evidence and consensus regarding the identification of delinquents and criminals through the official sampling processes of the criminal justice system. Admissions of prior known records are

[10]The eight types of validity are convergent, discriminant, content, face, predictive, concurrent, construct, and factorial (Costner, 1975:2).

particularly important for assessing the degree of reporting accuracy, typically underreporting, and are necessary for at least inferring some degree of accuracy for self-reports of criminal behavior for which there is no record. That is, the apparent validity of those respondents with records who admit to them is extrapolated to their self-reports of criminal behavior, as well as to the self-reports of criminal behavior of those respondents who do not have criminal records. It is typically assumed that the validity of self-reports of criminal record can be extrapolated to self-reports of criminal behavior, but it is not clear that the degree of validity can be transferred from one type of task characteristic (discussed below) or respondent to another. For those respondents who do not have official records of crime, other validation criteria become more critical.

This critical assumption about the validity of self-reports is related to other assumptions that are often made by researchers. One assumption is that the "magnitude" of underreporting of official record can be used as a correction factor, typically involving downward adjustments to self-reports of criminal behavior. A second assumption is that the frequency of self-reported crime and the validity of admissions are related—the higher the self-report estimates, the higher the validity estimates. In other words, the more crime a respondent admits, the more accurate the responses. Third, it is assumed that the validity of measures of crime holds for measures of other variables, particularly those that are more etiological, attitudinal, or descriptive of other respondent characteristics. Fourth, it is assumed that validity is more likely universal in application than differentiated by response effects, whether task, respondent, or interviewer characteristics. There is evidence from correlational validation and reverse-record-check research that these assumptions are questionable and, more likely, not true. Of course, one of the implications is that extrapolation—whether of validity, correction factors, or estimates—from one measure to another is more problematic than perhaps anticipated, at least for now.

The relationships of "self-reports of criminal behavior" and "self-reports of official record" *each* to "official record" are the most important validation correlations to assess. The relationship between self-reports of criminal behavior and having an official record is perplexing. In general, the research evidence suggests that there is a relatively high degree of correlational validity when comparing these two measures, with correlations ranging from .3 to .6 (Hirschi, 1969; Erickson, 1972; Farrington, 1973; Elliott and Voss, 1974). However, one of the few studies to report validity coefficients by subgroup suggests that the validity of self-reports of criminal behavior varies by race, with black (.09) and Asian (.07) juveniles having lower validity coefficients than white juveniles (.34) (Gould, 1969). Hindelang, Hirschi, and Weis (1981:100) also discovered that validity coefficients "vary systematically by race," with black males having much lower validity coefficients (.33 to .42) than white males (.65 to .66) when comparing scores on the total prevalence scale and serious-crimes prevalence scale with three official delinquency measures. This diminished validity translates directly into lower estimates of delinquent involvement among these respondents and the attenuation of the correlation between self-reported delinquency and race.

The relation between self-reports of official records and actual official records is probably the most critical comparison, because it is here that the accuracy of response is put to its most direct and severest test. Even if one disagrees on what an official record "actually" represents, respondents should have direct experience and knowledge of their contact with the criminal justice system and simply need to remember and report it.[11] In general, the validity coefficients are high, in the .8 range—all "juvenile studies show that most of those with official records can be identified through self-reports" of records (Hindelang, Hirschi, and Weis, 1981:104). In fact, the correlations (gammas) between the three official crime indexes and three self-report indicators of official action range between .6 and .8; the highest average validity coefficients are for self-reports of court referral (.8) and the lowest for police contact (.6) (Hindelang, Hirschi, and Weis, 1981:104–105). The lower validity for the police measure is also evident in research among adult offenders. Marquis and Ebener (1981:viii, 13–14) report that the accuracy of reports of arrest is "uncertain" in comparison with self-reports of convictions among a prisoner sample, and they suggest that this is attributable to apparent face-validity problems because arrest can mean several things on the rap sheets. This same kind of face-validity effect could be responsible for the lower validity coefficient for the item in the Seattle youth study that asked respondents whether they had been "picked up by the police."

Overall, the correlational evidence supports relatively high validity for both self-reports and indicators of official contact. However, the sources of imperfect correlation remain unclear.

Reverse Record Checks

The use of record checks facilitates a more rigorous investigation and assessment of the sources of diminished validity, as well as of the magnitude of the problem. Having prior knowledge of a respondent's official record allows the researcher to assess directly the accuracy of responses regarding the existence of the record, as well as to compare self-reported crimes with official offenses of record. Reverse record checks,[12] whereby respondents in a study are sampled using

[11] In a personal communication, Delbert Elliott has indicated that some respondents in the National Youth Survey who denied they committed crimes of record claimed that the police were simply harassing them and the records represented these "bum raps." There are rare examples of arrested or convicted "innocents," but it is clear that those with records have very likely committed a crime, in some cases many, many more than result in official action, whether juvenile (Erickson and Empey, 1963) or adult (Peterson, Braiker, and Polich, 1981:55–65) offenders. And the great majority of official offenders do not deny their guilt but readily confess to their crime. Wolfgang, Figlio, and Sellin (1972) report that 90 percent of the juveniles who had police contacts confessed to the police on apprehension. It is possible that once in a while the criminal justice system errs and "gets the wrong person" (Voss, 1963), that an offender may report harassment by local law enforcement officials that leads to discriminatory and empty arrests, and that criminal justice system records are incomplete and, therefore, claimed to be inadequate as a standard external validation criterion. However, the possibilities—or facts, if you wish—do not negate the fact that criminal justice system record data are as good as any standard external validation criterion in the social sciences, probably better than most. Compared with the other alternatives, it is clearly the best, and one needs to remember that the validation of two measures is reciprocal by definition, so if concurrent, convergent validity is demonstrated for self-reports and arrests, both are validated and by the "relationship" between the two. And, finally, there is no such thing as a "perfect" external validation criterion to which the relative validity of another measure can be established.

[12] "Reverse" record check is used here by convention to indicate only that information in records is checked with information reported by a respondent. It does not necessarily mean that a sample was selected from a population of potential subjects who have records. Marquis (1980) and Marquis and Ebener (1981) have pointed out that this kind of sampling design, called a "partial" design, can only account for underreports, simply because there is no respondent without a record who could report having one.

the existence of record as a sampling criterion, have been used in health surveys (e.g., Cannell and Fowler, 1963; Marquis, 1978, 1980), victimization surveys (Law Enforcement Assistance Administration, 1972), crime surveys (Erickson and Empey, 1963; Blackmore, 1974; Hardt and Peterson-Hardt, 1977; Bridges, 1981; Hindelang, Hirschi, and Weis, 1981), studies of drinking and alcoholics (Sobell and Sobell, 1978), and research on drug addicts (Ball, 1967). In general, the majority of respondents with official records will report having them; in one instance 100 percent of a group of juveniles who had court records admitted the fact (Erickson and Empey, 1963:459).

There is not a random distribution of the underreporters but, rather, apparent systematic bias in the accuracy of responses to queries about one's official record. In the delinquency literature, the rate of underreporting seems to vary between 5 and 60 percent of the samples (Gibson, Morrison, and West, 1970; Hardt and Peterson-Hardt, 1977; Hindelang, Hirschi, and Weis, 1981), depending on the official criterion and seriousness of the crime. What is perhaps the only data set on crime that has a record check built into the study design that allows sex and race comparisons shows no sex difference but an apparent race difference in the underreporting of official contact, which averages about 10 percent for white males and 30 percent for black males (Hindelang, Hirschi, and Weis, 1981:122–124). For the serious crime index (burglary, robbery, vehicle theft, person crime, weapon offense), 20 percent of the white males but 57 percent of the black males underreported official contacts. The difference is even greater for some of the individual serious offenses, for example, 67 percent nonreporting for burglary and 62 percent for weapon offenses among black males, compared with 18 and 22 percent, respectively, for white males (Hindelang, Hirschi, and Weis, 1981:172).[13] It is clear that black male respondents are much less likely to report crimes that fit the offense category of their crime(s) of record.

Among general adult samples, as well as different kinds of offender subgroups, the nature of the response bias is more ambiguous. Bridges (1983:571), for example, reports that among the follow-up interview sample of the Philadelphia cohort study, the "respondents uniformly overstated the number of offenses resulting in arrest, ages at the time of offenses, the seriousness of offense, and the number of others arrested." But Sobell and Sobell (1978) find that alcoholics and ex-alcoholics tend to underreport their felony arrests. Finally, separate analyses of the Rand inmate surveys (Marquis and Ebener, 1981; Chaiken and Chaiken, 1982) indicate that there is either no response bias or, in some cases, overreporting of arrests and convictions.

One of the limitations that these studies of adults share with some of the studies of juvenile response bias (e.g., Erickson and Empey, 1963) is that the

[13]Contrary to what Elliott (1982) has suggested, the differences among the four sex-race groups do not show that white males are atypical and that black males, white females, and black females are in line with other estimates of nonreporting. If one looks at the total number of offenses and the per-serious-crime index category, one discovers that among black females there are only 22 serious offenses, that in four of the five offense categories there are only two offenses each, and that the three 100 percent nonreports fall within those categories, all of which contribute to an artificially high and undependable estimate of the nonreporting rate for black females. For white females the situation is the same—with a total of only 16 offenses, one category with no offenses and another with one offense, the percentages are misleading as a consequence. In short, for the serious crimes in particular, the ones of most concern in the Seattle youth study and here, the data for female offenders do not provide a sufficient basis for concluding much at all about the effects of their nonreporting on validity.

respondent knows that the researcher has had access to his official records and, therefore, can verify or disconfirm responses. This undoubtedly contributes to greater agreement and, perhaps, overreporting. Another problem is the very long reference period for responses, e.g., adults may be asked to report events that occurred during their juvenile years, perhaps more than 10 years earlier. In the only "double blind" study of self-reports of official record, i.e., the questionnaire administrators did not know if the respondent had a record and the respondent did not know that official criminal status was used as a sampling criterion and was, therefore, known to project management, there was variable and systematic underreporting (Hindelang, Hirschi, and Weis, 1981).

In short, there is evidence from research on both adults and juveniles that there is important variation by subgroups in the accuracy of responses regarding official records. There seems to be differential validity by respondent characteristics, specifically and perhaps most importantly by race. In the next section the types of apparent or potential respondent effects are examined in more detail, particularly as they and other task and interviewer sources of response effects may compromise validity and reliability and, therefore, affect estimates of prevalence, incidence, and correlates.

SOURCES OF RESPONSE EFFECTS ON VALIDITY AND RELIABILITY

The somewhat ambiguous and sometimes conflicting findings regarding response patterns to questions about having official contact with the criminal justice system, as noted, suggest some kind of systematic response bias. If this is so, there is the possibility that diminished validity may also extend to respondents' self-reports of criminal behavior. There may be generalized systematic error in the reports of certain subgroups of respondents for the whole range of crime, particularly for the most serious offenses. Obviously, this could distort self-report scores for the very offenses that might resolve discrepancy between self-report and official measures—the more serious crimes, which are the concern of the criminal justice system.

There are many real and potential distorting effects on responses to survey questions—"response effects"—that could be related to the validity and reliability of self-reports of crime and, therefore, to estimates of criminal career parameters. However, the evidence from general survey research indicates that some kinds of response effects may be more important than others, particularly when "threatening," "anxiety arousing," or "dangerous" questions are asked. Additionally, some response effects may be more important than others to validity and reliability in research on serious crime and chronic offenders, at least according to the scant direct research evidence on these types of behaviors and respondents. Consequently, a selective subset of response effects and their apparent or potential impact on self-reports of individual offending patterns are the focus of discussion in this section.

There are three major sources of response effects on the accuracy and consistency of answers to survey questions—interviewer, task, and respondent characteristics (Sudman and Bradburn, 1974; Bradburn and Sudman, 1979; Dijkstra and van der Zouwen, 1982; Bradburn and Danis, 1984). Interviewer characteristics are either "role independent" attributes, such as gender, race, age, and personal biography, or "role restricted," such as interviewing style, competence, experience, and interviewer's expectations of respondents or responses (see Dijkstra and van der Zouwen, 1982:10–11). Task characteristics describe the survey situation and can be divided roughly into "structural" characteristics, such as method of administration and perceived anonymity, and "question" characteristics, such as wording, length, content, specificity, response categories, threat, salience, and social desirability. Respondent characteristics are the sociodemographic or personal attributes of respondents that affect validity or reliability directly or indirectly through interactions with task and interviewer characteristics.[14]

The very scarce research on response effects in the measurement of crime addresses some of these sources of response bias and shows substantial consistency with findings of survey-methodology research in other substantive areas. There are also some apparent differences, especially regarding the effect of respondent characteristics.

Interviewer Characteristics

It is evident that interviewer characteristics play a minor role in distorting answers to survey questions. Not only does the general literature reach this conclusion (e.g., Sudman and Bradburn, 1974; Brenner, 1982; Hagenaars and Heinen, 1982; Bradburn and Danis, 1984), but also the one study in criminology that can assess interviewer effects within a quasi-experimental design (Hindelang, Hirschi, and Weis, 1981) comes to the same conclusion. The design of that study facilitates a rigorous assessment of interviewer-respondent interaction effects because white male, white female, black male, and black female interviewers were randomly assigned to test conditions and respondents. Therefore, the "role-independent" characteristics of the race and gender of the interviewers and the same sociodemographic characteristics of the respondents could be examined for their interactive effects on the accuracy of responses to questionnaires and in interviews, particularly face-to-face interviews, for which one would hypothesize the largest interviewer effect. Preliminary data analyses suggest that role-independent interviewer effects cannot account for the apparent differential validity associated with black, male, official delinquents because there are no differences in the magnitude or validity of the crime estimates of respondents by interviewer characteristics (Weis, 1983b).

Task Characteristics

Researchers have examined a number of task characteristics that can generate response effects that may have potential implications for research on criminal careers. Structural task characteristics and the characteristics of survey questions are examined below.

Structural Characteristics

Two structural task characteristics, method of administration and anonymity of respondent, have been assessed directly for their effects on the validity and reliability of self-reports of juvenile delin-

[14]There are also four major types of error that are related to response effects (Sudman and Bradburn, 1982:19), particularly task and respondent characteristics and their interactions. The first is memory error, the unintentional forgetting of what happened and when it happened, the consequences being underreporting and telescoping of events, typically forward into the more recent past. The second is motivated error, the intentional underreporting, overreporting, or distortion of responses for positive (e.g., social approval) or negative (e.g., fear of consequences) reasons or motives. The third is communication error, i.e., a respondent does not understand what is being asked and responds idiosyncratically. The fourth is knowledge error, i.e., a respondent may not know the correct or appropriate answer to a question but responds anyway; typically, there is no way for the researcher to measure the lack of knowledge.

quency. Because item threat is so closely related to anonymity, even though it is a question characteristic, it is treated here as well.

It has long been assumed that interviews are better than questionnaires in producing accurate responses and, therefore, are in part responsible for a reported difference in the relation between social class and self-report interview responses (inverse) and questionnaire responses (nonexistent) (Gold, 1966). It has also been assumed that since questions on one's criminal behavior are threatening, anonymity enhances the validity of responses (see Goode and Hatt, 1952; Cannell and Kahn, 1968; Colombotus, 1969; Lin, 1976). However, the Seattle youth study design allows a rigorous examination of the joint effects of method of administration, anonymity of respondent, and threat of item. The results of such an examination show that the effects on both reliability and validity of responses are negligible, which corroborates results from the more general survey-methodology research (e.g., Bradburn and Sudman, 1979:1–13; Fox and Inazu, 1980).

Examining the effects on reliability first, it is clear that method of administration does not affect test-retest consistency in estimates or the internal consistency of responses; nor is there any important variation in any of the subgroups in the sample (Hindelang, Hirschi, and Weis, 1981:119–120). Regarding validity, not one of the six methods of administration that were compared had a significant distorting effect on correlational validity coefficients. There were some minor but unimportant differences by sex and race. For example, questionnaires had higher validity coefficients than interviews for males, and the responses of females under anonymous conditions may have been slightly more valid than those under nonanonymous circumstances. The nonanonymous interview was the least valid of the four conditions among white males, and black males did worst on the anonymous interview and nonanonymous questionnaire (Hindelang, Hirschi, and Weis, 1981:120). Again, these slight and conflicting differences do not portend any systematic or consistent effects of method of administration on correlational validity among any of the respondent subgroups.

The possible effects of method of administration on the results of reverse record checks, particularly on underreporting of criminal record, are a more rigorous test of methods effects.[15] The overall rates of underreporting discussed earlier were basically replicated within each method of administration. Among females the rate of underreporting (22 percent) was identical for each of the two conditions to which they were assigned, the nonanonymous interview and the anonymous questionnaire. Among males the results for the four conditions to which they were assigned are more interesting. White males did more underreporting of official offenses when they were being interviewed (12 percent) or filling out questionnaires (9 percent) under nonanonymous circumstances. Notably, black males, who had an underreporting rate that was about three times the rate for white males, did the least underreporting (22 percent) when they were interviewed under nonanonymous circumstances; their underreporting in the other three methods of administration ranged from 34 to 39 percent (Hindelang, Hirschi, and Weis, 1981:122–123). It

[15]The reader is reminded that both the official offenses of record and the self-reported crimes were grouped because some specific types of crimes were rare, particularly in the official records, as well as being vaguely described and represented in the records of the police department and juvenile court. Therefore, crime-by-offense comparisons could not be made with enough rigor and confidence to justify that type of analysis (see Hindelang, Hirschi, and Weis, 1981).

seems that the standard "face-to-face interview" might be more effective for these types of juvenile offenders.

Criminologists have also used and examined the effects of other, less standard methods of administration, including the randomized response method and the lie detector model. The randomized response method has been used on adult offenders (Tracy and Fox, 1981) and juveniles (Hindelang, Hirschi, and Weis, 1981). In the Seattle youth study, a version of the randomized response method (Warner, 1965) was used with each respondent after he or she had completed the survey under the main method of administration. The results show that the randomized response method is "no more efficient than other traditional techniques of measurement" in estimating the prevalence of juvenile crime as measured by a subset of 8 offenses from the full set of 69 self-reported delinquency items (Weis and van Alstyne, 1979). That is, the prevalence estimates did not vary by method of collecting data, even for one of the most anonymous survey methods that has been developed.[16] In fact, when the randomized response method followed the anonymous interviews, there was "double anonymity" (i.e., of both the respondent and responses), and even this extra degree of anonymity made no difference in prevalence estimates. Apparently, the "threat" of questions about criminal activity did not matter that much to the juvenile respondents in this sample or it mattered to the same extent across a variety of anonymous and nonanonymous methods of administration.

A final method of administration, a variation of the "lie detector" (Clark and Tifft, 1966) or "bogus pipeline" models (Jones and Sigall, 1971), was also partially tested by Hindelang, Hirschi, and Weis (1981:31, 133). After the nonanonymous interview only, respondents were interviewed again about a list of neutral and criminal acts, but the answers were tape-recorded and respondents were informed that a psychological stress evaluator (PSE) would enable the researchers to analyze the tapes and produce graphs that would be read for truthful or dishonest answers. Respondents were shown examples of the graphs and reminded of the lie detector potential of the PSE. Another use, in addition to motivating respondents to be truthful, was direct validation of oral responses with the PSE evaluations of the recorded voice patterns.

Preliminary analyses indicate that on reinterview with the PSE, changes are often made in initial reports, typically increases in reported crime. Approximately 10 percent of the responses among males were changed, and about 90 percent of those changes were from denial to admission of an offense. These percentages were very similar for black and white males (Hindelang, Hirschi, and Weis, 1981:133). Other analyses of these data inform more directly the issue of the validity of this particular method of administration. If deception is related to diminished validity, one can hypothesize that respondents who apparently give less valid responses in general will be more likely to change more of their answers when reinterviewed using the PSE method. However, there was little variation in change scores. Those respondents who may have been generating less valid answers about their criminal involvement under the main test conditions did not have higher change scores. Either the apparently less accurate or less truthful respondents remained consistent in their inaccuracy or deception from the main interview to the PSE interview, regard-

[16] See Tracy and Fox (1981) for a randomized response procedure for estimating incidence in a sample. With refinement, this version of the technique could prove to be more useful in etiological and criminal career research when individual-level measures are necessary.

less of the apparent ability of the researcher to ascertain the truth, or similar change scores reflect similar levels of accuracy and truthfulness (or inaccuracy and dishonesty) across respondent categories (Weis, 1983b).

The standard, direct tests of validity and reliability indicate that no method of administration, whether anonymous or nonanonymous, generates more valid responses than others to questions about criminal behavior. However, more indirect information suggests that there are factors that may be affected by a particular method of administration and that, therefore, inform the overall assessment of validity and reliability. Of obvious interest is the difference in self-report estimates of prevalence and incidence of criminal behavior by method of administration. The research on juvenile delinquency shows the same consistent pattern of no difference in estimates by method of administration, which one might expect if methods do not have any apparent effects on the reliability and validity of responses (Hindelang, Hirschi, and Weis, 1981:124–125). However, there are more omissions and nonresponses on self-administered questionnaires than under other methods of administration, particularly for longer recall periods and relatively nonsalient events (Sudman and Bradburn, 1982:275). For self-reports of juvenile crime, the method of administration is the "best predictor of the number of missing self-report responses, with both questionnaire conditions (anonymous and nonanonymous) contributing about equally" (Hindelang, Hirschi, and Weis, 1981:125), but the nonresponses and missing data are not randomly distributed by method of administration or anonymity. In the anonymous questionnaire condition, 86 percent of the males answered each of the 69 crime items, as did 97 percent in the anonymous interview; in the anonymous questionnaire condition, 90 percent of the females answered all self-report delinquency items, and 96 percent did so in the nonanonymous interview.

The nonresponse rates on past-year frequency were substantially higher, contrary to suggestions that an affirmative answer to an item sets the respondent free to report frequency of involvement with the threat of the item diluted (Sudman and Bradburn, 1982). Seventy-four percent of the males and 79 percent of the females provided past-year frequency reports on all the offenses they admitted to ever committing. In the anonymous interview 92 percent of the males gave all the required frequency estimates, but only 57 percent did so on the anonymous questionnaire. In the nonanonymous interview 94 percent of the females had full response on frequency but only 64 percent did so on the anonymous questionnaire. Both the male and female nonresponse patterns suggest higher nonresponse rates on questionnaires than interviews, particularly the anonymous questionnaire, ironically the favored method of administration in self-report research for the past 30 years. And as reported for general reliability and, especially, validity, it seems that "under all relevant method conditions, court delinquents, blacks, and males had higher rates of nonresponse on the last year frequency items" (Hindelang, Hirschi, and Weis, 1981:126). Of course, depending on how the missing data are managed in analysis, there need not be distortions in relationships, because the answers of these types of respondents are more likely missing from the analysis and, thereby, likely attenuating correlations between crime and other variables.

Finally, method of administration may affect the validity and reliability of responses to variables other than the dependent criterion and, therefore, the relationship between independent and dependent variables. This means that there should be different correlations by method, but the only research on this issue in criminological-methods research concludes that correlations between juvenile crimes and a number of often-used etiological variables (such as parental supervision, respect for the police, and amorality) vary by method, but that no method is consistently better or worse than the others in producing accurate responses to attitude-type items (see Hindelang, Hirschi, and Weis, 1981: 127–128).

There has been more research on method of administration and anonymity than on other task characteristics, but some of the "question-related" sources of response bias apparently contribute more to unreliability and invalidity than the structural task characteristics.

Question Characteristics

In a systematic review of the post-1970 survey-research literature[17] on the response effects of question characteristics, DeLamater (1982) concludes that four aspects of survey questions are potentially more likely to affect respondents' behavior than others: (1) the wording of the question, (2) the salience of the topic addressed by the question, (3) the social desirability of responding one way or another to a question, and (4) the degree to which a question arouses anxiety or is threatening to a respondent. Each of these topics is addressed sequentially in this section, as well as two task characteristics that have been identified as important question-related sources of response bias—response categories and recall period (Bradburn and Danis, 1984). Recognizing that there are important interactions among these sources of error, for example, less salient events have shorter effective recall periods (Cash and Moss, 1972), interactions and other sources of error are also addressed in the discussion.

Question Wording. A major source of response bias can be attributed to communication errors, particularly when questions do not communicate effectively the meaning of an item. Questions may differ in a number of ways that affect response, but three seem particularly important when the questions are about "threatening" behaviors—content, specificity, and length.

The fact that even the slightest changes in the content of a question can substantially alter responses has been thoroughly documented in survey methodology (Schuman and Presser, 1981; Bradburn and Danis, 1984). Changing words in a question can lead to concomitant changes in the meaning attributed by a respondent and, therefore, to different responses. For example, in the measurement of criminal behavior a critical element is "intent," and its inclusion or exclusion can change an item from a crime to a legal act. The question "Have you ever broken a car window?" does not necessarily reflect a crime, and would yield higher estimates than an item that required that it be "on purpose" with the intent to damage it or to enter the car for illegal purposes.

There is evidence from adult-offender samples that question wording is an important source of response effects. Chaiken, Chaiken, and Rolph (1983) have compared the first and second Rand inmate surveys, primarily on differences in question wording and response categories that might be responsible for the "remarkable differences" in prevalence estimates and individual offending rates between the two surveys. They conclude that the "differences between the first and second survey's results for robbery,

[17]Studies appearing before 1970 are reviewed in Sudman and Bradburn (1974).

assault and fraud can be attributed primarily to differences in wording on the survey instrument" and that for some of the crimes for which the wording is "almost identical," differences in wording could "account for substantial disparities in answers for some respondents." For example, on the second survey burglary included breaking into houses, businesses, and cars, but on the first survey it excluded cars and, therefore, affirmative responses on burglary for those who only break into cars (Chaiken, Chaiken, and Rolph, 1983:19, 3).

The specificity of a question may also affect responses, surprisingly leading to typically higher estimates because the question is a better aid to recall (Bradburn and Danis, 1984:15–18). This is shown in a comparison of a general and a specific vandalism item on the same survey for juveniles. The prevalence estimates were more than 10 percent higher on the more specific item, "broken the windows of an empty house or other unoccupied building," than on the more general item, "banged up something that did not belong to you on purpose" (Hindelang, Hirschi, and Weis, 1981:40). It is likely that the higher estimates on the more specific items are an example of "aided recall"—there is more information in the specific question that "aids" or "prompts" or "cues" recall, and it produces a higher rate of response. For prevalence estimates this is an advantage, but for frequency estimates with bounded or specified recall periods, it can cause more telescoping and even higher, although more inaccurate, incidence estimates (Bradburn and Danis, 1984:18).

A final element of question wording that seems to make a difference is the length of the question. According to Tourangeau (1984), the best aid to recognition and recall of a past event is the item itself. Research shows that longer questions reduce the number of omissions and improve recall in a variety of survey settings (Cannell, Marquis, and Laurent, 1977; Cannell, Oksenberg, and Converse, 1977). The longer question is apparently more efficient because of the memory cues that the item provides and the greater length of time it allows the respondent to remember an event; in interview situations, question length is even related to length of reply (Sudman and Bradburn, 1982:50). Unfortunately, there has been no criminological research on the effects of question length, but it seems likely that, in combination with question content and specificity, question length has important effects on responses. In fact, these kinds of question-wording effects are considered sufficiently substantial that Hindelang, Hirschi, and Weis (1981:40) conclude that the "level of self-reported delinquency within a sample appears to fluctuate broadly as a function of apparently minor changes in item content" and that the "magnitude and even the direction of race and sex differences in delinquency are often contingent on item content or wording."

These effects of question wording are primarily attributable to communication errors, which can be corrected in item and instrument construction and testing. Memory errors are less amenable to manipulation and are significant contributors to other sources of response effects, particularly differences in response categories, recall periods, and salience of queried events.

Response Categories. Self-report research on crime began with "closed-ended" questions that used "normative" response categories. The response categories in Short and Nye's original 23 delinquency items, for example, were "very often, several times, once or twice, no" (Nye, 1958:13–14). Some self-report studies have continued to use similar ordinal-level response categories, losing important information in the process and, more importantly, maintaining information that includes considerable error. Normative-response categories make comparisons between respondents difficult and imprecise because one respondent can check "several times" and mean nine times, whereas another may check the same response and mean three times. Each responds according to personal experiences and norms, which are related to personal behavior, as well as to that of peers and reference groups. Unless one "norms" each respondent's answers and thereby standardizes comparisons across response categories (see Bradburn and Sudman, 1979:152–162), accurate comparisons are obviated. The most direct and best solution is to ask the respondent to report the frequency of commission of each crime—more information is preserved and comparisons among respondents are more straightforward and precise, but the question of the validity of the frequency estimates then becomes a critical one.

It has been shown that "open-ended" questions, particularly those that might be regarded as threatening (which might lead to underreporting), are better than closed-ended questions in producing prevalence and, especially, incidence estimates. For example, Bradburn and Sudman (1979) indicate that longer, open-ended questions increased the reported estimates of beer consumption by 60 percent over shorter, closed-ended questions. They also consider the responses to open items more valid (Sudman and Bradburn, 1974), which is the more critical issue. Contrary to what they suggest, higher estimates do not necessarily mean more valid estimates, and if the estimates are not more valid, error is introduced at the high end of the distribution by overreporting. In criminological research, especially research on serious, chronic offenders and on correlations that often depend on the tail end of a distribution, this kind of response bias could be particularly problematic. High-frequency but less valid estimates of criminal involvement could distort correlations, likely amplifying the correlations between crime and other variables.

A good example of the impact of response-category format is the difference in estimates of individual offending within and between the first and second Rand inmate surveys. The first survey used open-ended frequency questions and a modified closed–open-ended format that included four frequency categories (0, 1–2, 3–5, 6–10) and a fifth category that asked for a frequency if the respondent had engaged in the crime 11 or more times. The differences for burglary are substantial; the mean rate from the open-ended, frequency-response format was 16 times the modified categorical rate (Peterson and Braiker, 1980:26). This is also higher than the burglary rate estimates from the second survey, in which two other modified frequency-response formats were used (see Chaiken and Chaiken, 1982:Appendix E, 16, 41). It is also reported that for high-frequency crimes, for example, drug dealing, the frequency reports based on unit of "time on the street" produced even higher estimates than simply asking for a total frequency count over a standard unitary recall period, such as the past year. The implications for validity are not straightforward—the higher estimates could simply reflect even greater inaccuracy of responses. As always, the problem is validating reports of criminal behavior for which no external validation criteria are available. Short of this, what is known about the cognitive psychology of frequency estimates of past events may be helpful in interpreting findings and, ultimately, in developing instruments.

Recall Period and Salience. Since open-ended questions that ask for respondent estimates of "frequency" of criminal behavior are relatively standard in self-report research and are essential for measuring individual offending patterns, the accuracy of reported frequencies becomes a paramount concern. Recalling the frequency of past events is also related to two other question-task characteristics—"recall period" and "salience" of the topic. Hence the discussion turns to the interactions among the three, as well as the contributions of other related sources of memory error, for example, the "similarity" of events, "retroactive interference," and "primacy-recency" effects.

In general, respondents provide more accurate estimates of low-frequency events and much more variable responses for higher frequency events (Loftus, 1980). When the event is criminal behavior and the respondent is asked to locate it within a specified recall period, say the past year, the task becomes much more complex and the sources and magnitude of potential error increase. Two basic sources of memory-performance error are referred to in the criminological literature—"forgetting" what happened (memory decay) and "distortion" of memory by misplacing an event temporally (telescoping), which usually involves remembering it as more recent than it was in actuality (Garofalo and Hindelang, 1977). A third source of memory error, "construction," is usually not considered but is a source of substantial error according to recent research in cognitive psychology (Talland, 1968; Klatzky, 1975; Loftus, 1980, 1982).

Beginning with telescoping and memory decay, there is little doubt that the former occurs in the reporting of victimization and criminal behavior. For example, Garofalo and Hindelang (1977) report that about 20 percent of the victimizations that respondents placed within the recall period actually happened before it, according to police records. Telescoping is one of the consequences of "primacy-recency" effects in memory—we tend to remember best those events that happened recently and worst those that occurred in the distant past, with the qualification that those events at the beginning and end of a series will both be remembered better than those in the middle (a "serial position" effect) (Loftus, 1980:24–25). This means that the longer the recall period, the more criminal acts the respondent will forget, but reporting of the earliest and most recent criminal experiences will probably be most accurate. For example, Bridges (1983) reports that in the Philadelphia cohort follow-up sample, self-reports of the respondent's most recent offense were the most valid and reliable.

The emphasis in criminological research on "memory decay" as the most important source of forgetting and underreporting in both victim and self-report surveys seems misplaced both theoretically and empirically. Forgetting behavioral events such as criminal acts involves the loss of ability to remember information that has been encoded and stored primarily in episodic, long-term memory (Klatzky, 1975:124–127, 178–179). There are two kinds of forgetting: memory decay, which is a passive form of forgetting as a simple function of time passing, and a more active form, interference, which entails one experience interfering with the remembrance of another (Murdock, 1974). "Retroactive" interference and "similarity" interference exert the strongest effects on remembering past events. The former refers to the interference created by subsequent events in remembering prior events, and the latter refers to repeated similar events interfering with the ability to distinguish unique characteristics of any one in a series of similar events (Hunter, 1957:258–268; Murdock, 1974:11–12; Klatzky, 1975:125–127; Loftus, 1980:66–67). In retroactive interference, if there are many interpolated events and they are also similar in their characteristics, the forgetting can be substantial, particularly the ability to distinguish one from another and, therefore, to remember how many discrete events occurred. The primary role of interference and the secondary role of memory decay in forgetting has been highlighted by Murdock's (1974:12) conclusion that perhaps "interference accounts for 85–98 percent of the variance and decay may account for the remainder." In short, frequent, similar retroactive interference is a very potent force in forgetting, even more so when there has been faulty or incomplete encoding and storage of an event to begin with.

The implications for selecting appropriate recall periods for items in a survey are different from an interference versus a memory-decay perspective on forgetting. The recall periods that are typically used are based on the principle that forgetting increases with time, without taking into account other influences on memory, such as "salience" of the question topic, which has demonstrable effects on recall and the perception of time (Bradburn and Danis, 1984:30). The arbitrarily favored recall period is 1 year, on the grounds that longer time periods increase forgetting, frequency estimates, and error, and that shorter time periods might not produce enough reports of low-base-rate behaviors for analytic purposes. Whether 1 year or any recall period is too short or too long is an empirical question, one that is complicated by one of the "most influential of the factors" that affect responses, the salience of the topic (DeLamater, 1982:45). Research shows that salient events, those that are important, relevant, and consequential, are remembered better than those that are not. Cash and Moss (1972) have shown in self-reports of car accidents that the memory of events with high salience was adequate up to about 1 year; the period for intermediate salience was 1–3 months, and for low salience, from 2 weeks to 1 month.

The salience of the event is also related to perceptions of time. Salient events are perceived as more recent than they really are, which means that forward telescoping is more likely for behaviors with high salience (Bradburn and Danis, 1984:300). This, in turn, inflates frequency estimates of the more salient events. Recent events are also perceived as more salient (DeLamater, 1982:22), which has similar effects on respondent's reports of frequency. One of the other characteristics of salient events is that they are usually not relatively frequent within an individual's experience. Behaviors that are more frequent and also similar to each other will also be less salient; in addition they increase retroactive interference, which in turn, decreases the ability to differentiate discrete events and distorts frequency estimates.

In self-reports of criminal behavior, these effects may be problematic for reports of the most serious offenses and for the most serious offenders. For most people, even most offenders, committing a serious crime would be a salient event, relatively easy to remember. In general, one would expect more accurate estimates for serious, less frequent offenses than for less serious, more frequent offenses. However, we know that the majority of serious crimes are committed by a small subgroup of serious, chronic offenders who commit a variety of serious crimes with high frequency—for example, in one study the 10 percent most active incarcerated adult burglars admitted to an average of 232 burglaries per year (Chaiken and Chaiken, 1982:48). For those offenders, burglary is a routine, high-frequency behavior, one much like another. Based on what cognitive psychology and survey methodology suggest about the interactive effects of frequency, salience, recency, similarity, and retroactive interference, one could hypothesize that their estimates of the number of burglaries they commit contain substantial error. The problem is determining the direction of the response bias—the combination of similar, low-salience, high-frequency behaviors could very likely lead to underestimations, although this is hard to believe given the very high frequency estimates that were reported. There is no empirical reason to rule out the possibility that a respondent might overreport for other reasons that have little to do with the cognitive aspects of memory, for example, social approval, deceit, or other motivated sources of error that are more related to respondent characteristics than to question characteristics.

Social Desirability. A question may cause the respondent to consider the social desirability of the response, rather than its accuracy. A respondent may give an answer out of a desire or need for "social approval" or because the question has a "trait desirability" that elicits an approving response (Edwards, 1957). Sudman and Bradburn (1974) report a consistent social-desirability response effect, but one that varies by the nature of the dependent variable and the respondent's sociodemographic characteristics. However, the effect of social desirability on the validity of self-reports of crime among juveniles is not related to apparent differences in the validity of their responses. Since this type of response effect may be more important for respondents who are actively involved in crime and may want to deny it, Hindelang, Hirschi, and Weis (1981) included two desirability variables in their analysis: a five-item acquiescence (yea-saying/nay-saying) scale and a five-item social desirability scale. Within all methods of survey administration and sex, race, and class categories, these social-desirability effects accounted for about 2 percent of the variance in invalidity, as measured by a deceit score that equaled the sums of nonreports across the 13 offense categories identified in a reverse record check (Weis, 1983b). In short, social desirability does not seem to be an important source of response bias in survey questions about crime, at least among juvenile respondents.

Respondent Characteristics

Hindelang, Hirschi, and Weis (1981: 219) have concluded from their analysis of the validity and reliability of self-reports and official records of juvenile crime that "delinquency exists most clearly in the minds of those least likely to engage in it." To the extent that this is true, the implications for research are increasingly important because, as samples become more representative of serious crime and criminals, "measurement problems are intensified." These problems seem to be more related to characteristics of subgroups of respondents and to motivated error than is reported in the literature on general survey methodology.

Of the three major categories of response effects (interviewer, task, and respondent characteristics), the impact of respondent characteristics on answers is probably the most ambiguous. The survey-methodology research on the effects of such sociodemographic attributes as gender, race, and education tends to show no "general effects" (Sudman and Bradburn, 1974; DeLamater, 1982). However, depending on the task, there are observed differences—for example, social-desirability response effects may be greater among women (Clancy and Gove, 1980; Gove, 1982). A variety of factors may be related to respondent effects, but here the discussion focuses on only those that seem particularly pertinent to the potential response bias to questions about crime created by the characteristics of serious, chronic offenders. First the characteristics of these offenders are described briefly, and then the apparent and potential response effects of these respondent characteristics are examined.

Characteristics of Serious, Chronic Offenders

From research on juvenile and adult criminals, there is a relatively clear picture of the small subgroup (between 5 and 10 percent) of offenders who are responsible for committing the majority of serious crimes (Wolfgang, Figlio, and Sellin, 1972; West and Farrington, 1977; Hamparian et al., 1978; Strasburg, 1978; Hindelang, Hirschi, and Weis, 1981; Peterson, Braiker, and Polich, 1981; Chaiken and Chaiken, 1982; Shannon, 1983). In general, both juvenile and adult serious, chronic offenders commit a greater variety of crimes more frequently than other offenders, particularly the more serious crimes and those involving violence (e.g., burglary, robbery, assault, drug dealing, auto theft, grand larceny). They begin their careers at an early age, both committing crimes and being officially sanctioned in their early teenage years. The onset of their criminal behavior typically involves substance abuse, which often becomes a frequent and heavy habit. The early onset and long duration of frequent and serious criminality indicates commitment to a criminal life-style among many of these offenders.

The "violent predators," those inmates who have been identified as the most serious, chronic offenders in the Rand sample, are very young compared with other offenders, are more involved in violence, and, typically, are more serious substance abusers (Chaiken and Chaiken, 1982:64–65, 86–87). In addition to dealing drugs, violent predators started using hard drugs frequently as juveniles and have continued their substance abuse, including heroin addiction, into adulthood. In fact, it is reported that 83 percent of the violent predators were using hard drugs (heroin, barbiturates, amphetamines) in large quantities on an almost daily basis during the measurement period (Chaiken and Chaiken, 1982:65, 155). They are also more likely than other offenders to have heroin habits, although "extreme" polydrug use is more characteristic, especially heroin with amphetamines, barbiturates with alcohol, and barbiturates with amphetamines. As the cost of their abuse increases, so does their criminal activity. Drug use is identified as "one of the major factors in serious high-rate crime" and is associated with "virtually every type of crime" (Chaiken and Chaiken, 1982:155).[18] With the exception of heroin-only addiction, the other combinations of drug use are related to violence.

This symbiotic relationship between substance abuse and crime among many serious, chronic offenders is interwoven into a broader deviant life-style that encompasses cultural norms and values that maintain the relationship and exert additional, independent cultural influences on the offender's behavior (Liebow, 1967; Foster, 1974; Valentine, 1978). Chaiken and Chaiken (1982:176) estimate that "a relatively large fraction of the inmate population, up to 65 percent, may take part in those life-styles."

[18]This is also apparently true among samples of the general youth population; Huizinga and Elliott (1981:80) report that for the majority of young people the use of drugs is not related to criminal behavior, but, that among those who use drugs and do crime, the levels of juvenile criminal involvement are highest among those who use the greatest variety of drugs (alcohol, marijuana, and other drugs) most frequently. In short, more drug use is related to more criminal behavior among juveniles.

Effects of Serious, Chronic Offender Characteristics on Responses

Of interest to most researchers are the effects of offender characteristics on each other, for example, drug use on crime. However, another way to examine the effects of respondent characteristics is on the measurement of criminal behavior, specifically on the validity and reliability of the answers of respondents who possess those attributes. Unfortunately, this has not been the focus of any major research effort, but it is apparent that frequent involvement in serious crime over a long period of time, substance abuse, and engaging in violent acts may have deleterious response effects on self-reports of criminal behavior. As reported earlier, Chaiken and Chaiken (1982: 225–226, 244) concluded that most individual characteristics are not related to the validity ("external reliability") and reliability ("internal quality") of responses of prison inmates, but they did find a few exceptions. For each of the exceptions to respondent effects, what is important is that validity and reliability problems lead to suppression of self-reported individual offending rates. Among an adult-prisoner sample, the evidence suggests blacks, the less educated, drug dealers and users, alcoholics, and life-style criminals probably have less accurate, lower estimates of self-reported criminal involvement. It is hypothesized that the unique characteristics of more serious, chronic offenders contribute to both increased memory error and motivated error in their responses to questions about their official criminal records and criminal behavior.

There is little doubt that drugs, ranging from alcohol to heroin, impair a person's ability to encode and store information about an event during which the person was under the influence of drugs. This diminished capacity to learn and preserve the characteristics of a past event due to intoxication can occur even when moderate amounts have been consumed. Parker and Noble (1977) report that, although the decrements are greatest among heavy drinkers, they are also evident among light drinkers. Encoding and storage are impaired by alcohol, but retrieval is not—that is, if an event occurs while the respondent is in a sober condition, it can be retrieved equally well whether the respondent is sober or intoxicated, unless the respondent is very inebriated. However, if an event occurs during an intoxicated state, the information is less available for retrieval whether the respondent is sober or intoxicated, although there is some research evidence of "state-dependent" recall (Bower, 1970; Birnbuam and Parker, 1977:106; Weingartner and Parker, 1984).

This type of research has typically been carried out with "normal" or "social" drinkers. Among alcohol abusers and alcoholics the effects are even more powerful and dramatic; there may be chronic deficits in storage (Cermak and Butters, 1973) due to heavy episodic consumption or continual intoxication and the influence of the "alcoholic haze" or "blackouts" (Loftus, 1980:93–95). It is possible to forget everything about an event, even a salient one; other events may be remembered only in part and only when reminded of what happened.

The same kinds of effects have been documented for other drugs, including marijuana, PCP, and heroin. There is evidence that PCP drastically impairs learning and memory functions (Perry, 1976). The research on marijuana shows that, like alcohol, there are substantial effects on new learning and storage but not on retrieval (Darley et al., 1973; Loftus, 1980; Wetzel, Janowsky, and Clapton, 1982), and there is evidence that free recall is hampered more than recognition memory (Miller and Cornett, 1978). The research on heroin and polydrug abuse effects is even more interesting because there is some evidence of a racial difference. Penk et al. (1981a,b) report greater decrements in short-term memory among black and Hispanic heroin and polydrug abusers, which suggests that heavy drug abuse may have a more deleterious effect on memory among those groups than among white abusers.

Given that in a typical adult prisoner population about 40 percent were intoxicated daily during the year prior to last arrest, 40 percent of the crimes for which they are incarcerated involved alcohol intoxication, 65 percent of the inmates used other drugs during the year prior to last arrest, and 40 percent of the crimes for which they are incarcerated involved other drugs (Sykes, Roccolo, and Thompson, 1980:60), and, given the sordid drug history of most serious, chronic offenders, it is a short logical leap to the hypothesis that among both juvenile and adult serious, chronic offenders there will be significant memory error in responses to questions about their past criminal behaviors. A substantial proportion of them will be under the influence of drugs at the time of the crime, and this will diminish their ability to encode and store information pertinent to the details and even the essentials of the event. Depending on the amount and kinds of drugs used, and the duration of the drug-using pattern, the completeness and accuracy of recall will vary, but in general the greater the intoxication, the more the memory errors and the lower the estimates of involvement in crime.

The effects of drugs may interact with another factor in forgetting—the nature of the behavior or event. There is evidence that alcoholics "selectively forget" unpleasant events that occur while they are drunk (Jones and Jones, 1977). This tendency to have a poorer memory for bad experiences is characteristic of nonalcoholics as well (Erdelyi and Goldberg, 1979). Events that arouse stress, anxiety, fear, guilt, shame, worry, and other negative emotions and feelings hinder accurate perception and encoding of the details of events, as well as the ability to retrieve and recall what happened (Siegel and Loftus, 1978; Loftus, 1980:77–82). In short, we tend to remember the good and forget the bad. A related factor is the trauma, danger, or violence that is inherent in an event. Loftus and Burns (1982) have demonstrated that the recall of witnessing a violent event—a film of a boy being shot in the face—was substantially inferior to the recall of a nonviolent condition.

Given that serious, chronic offenders engage in serious property and violent crimes, such as robbery and assault, one can hypothesize that the memory of serious criminal acts, and particularly those that involve interpersonal face-to-face confrontations and the threat or actuality of violence, will be impaired significantly. If one also takes into account the probability of drug-intoxication effects, the impairment would be even greater. This memory error shades into motivated error when a respondent consciously wants to forget things that involve pain, acute anxiety, blows to self-esteem, threats to values and norms, feelings of guilt and shame, and so on (Talland, 1968:89–91). An interpersonal crime is likely to include most if not all these elements and, therefore, is a good candidate for being forgotten; at a minimum it is not the kind of behavior that one wants to remember. In some people this desire to forget can make memories more or less unretrievable through "repressive forgetting" (Hunter, 1957:245) and outright "denial" that the event or behavior ever occurred (Talland, 1968:106).

It is also likely that other characteristics of the respondent contribute to the intentional, motivated distortion of memory.

Dishonesty, deceit, and lying may motivate inaccurate responses for a variety of personal and cultural reasons. Any time a past event includes ourselves, there is a tendency to remember the good and forget the bad characteristics of not only the experience but also of ourselves. There is a "self-serving bias" (Nisbett and Ross, 1980) in operation that preserves or enhances our self-esteem, particularly when our role in the event—for example, knifing someone—is not considered a laudable act according to usual cultural standards of propriety. The operation of this bias may lead to lying about what happened. As Loftus (1980:142) has pointed out, in constructive memory "people tend to rewrite history more in line with what they think they ought to have done than what they actually did." If a respondent does not value a behavior and sees it as discrepant with self-image, the response may range from denial to reporting less than actual involvement. On the other hand, if the behavior is valued and enhances self-concept, the response may be inflated. The former condition is considered to typify involvement in and reporting of criminal behavior, but for some criminal respondents the latter condition may be more typical.

What is self-serving, socially desirable, or socially approved will reflect ethnocentric as well as egocentric criteria. For the estimated 65 percent life-style criminals (Chaiken and Chaiken, 1982:176), what is valued will more likely reflect criminal cultural values, making the self-serving bias much more unpredictable in its effects on response accuracy. Another cultural source of response bias may be the black, male, street-corner culture, wherein not cooperating with "the man" has been refined over many years of oppression into a highly functional form of defensive and, more subtly, offensive adaptation. Here anyone, even a black male researcher, is a figure of authority not to be trusted but rather to be hustled and cajoled into believing in the sincerity and veracity of the respondent. These same kinds of attitudes and values exist in white working-class, street-corner cultures (Miller, 1958) and may have similar kinds of effects for those types of offenders.

It is also likely that intellectual competence contributes to unintentional memory error among serious, chronic offenders, more so than among other offenders or nonoffenders. We know that intellectual competence has an important relation to crime in general (Reiss and Rhodes, 1961; Wolfgang, Figlio, and Sellin, 1972; West, 1973; Hirschi and Hindelang, 1977) and an effect on the validity and reliability of self-report responses about criminal behavior among juveniles (Hindelang, Hirschi, and Weis, 1981:202–204) and adult offenders (Chaiken and Chaiken, 1982). The effect is apparently so substantial that it accounts for some of the racial difference in validity discovered in the Seattle youth study. The relation between a 20-item general-knowledge scale and official and self-reported delinquency is negative, as one would expect, but there is apparent underreporting by black males with low knowledge scores. The difference between white and black males in self-reported delinquency is, in part, a consequence of differences in "knowledge." Similar differences are apparent for self-reports of school grades, i.e., relationships between knowledge scores and official and self-reported delinquency indicate differential validity by race, with black males giving the apparently least accurate answers (Hindelang, Hirschi, and Weis, 1981:199–201, 202–204).

Apparently, general cognitive processing, symbol manipulation, problem solving, information processing, and even the capacity for storage are related to measured intelligence (Klatzky, 1975:319–

321). Since many of these processes are activated directly in a survey situation, one should expect more memory errors among respondents with less capacity to perform those processes because of lower intelligence, competence, or knowledge. The evidence among juvenile and adult offenders suggests that this is the case, and one can hypothesize that the effect would be even more acute among a group of serious, chronic offenders.

Another complication is that knowledge errors increase as the ability to count past events diminishes as a function of time and frequency. The respondent is forced to guess more at the high-frequency end of the distribution, claiming knowledge that he does not have, with the result that most respondents will underestimate, but some will overestimate, which contributes to the greater variation and measurement error in high-frequency estimates (Hasher and Chromiak, 1977). This difficulty in recall is evident in the "large disparity" between adult offenders' self-reports of juvenile crime and their official juvenile records (Chaiken and Chaiken, 1982). Many crimes were admitted, but the records showed no criminal involvement. This could be a consequence of forgetfulness and memory distortion among a group of respondents with characteristics that are likely to produce these kinds of response errors. Of course, another possibility is that they did not, indeed, have official contact while juveniles. After all, the odds of being processed by the juvenile justice system are quite low, even among active offenders (Erickson and Empey, 1963; Farrington, 1973).

Obviously, there is another possible explanation. Chaiken and Chaiken (1982: 224) point to the inadequacies of the records available to criminal justice agencies as the source of the disparity. That is, the limitations of official records also contribute to validity and reliability problems in the measurement of crime, including the measurement of individual offending patterns in criminal career research.

LIMITATIONS OF OFFICIAL RECORDS

Most of the major limitations of measures of the amount and distribution of crime based on official records had been identified by the end of the nineteenth century, including the primary problem of the "dark figure" of unknown crime (Sellin and Wolfgang, 1964). Over the years these limitations have been documented repeatedly. For example, Hindelang (1974) discusses 14 and Savitz (1982) 27 limitations of, or problems with, official crime statistics, particularly data from police records and the *Uniform Crime Reports* (*UCR*). These limitations range from differences in counting rules for property and person crimes to comparability difficulties across jurisdictions. However, they are not debilitating limitations—in fact, the validity and reliability of official measures, as evaluated by the standard social-scientific criteria of comparing results over time and with other measures, are quite good. For example, the correlates of offenses known to the police are stable over the 50-year period covered by the *UCR*, and the description of the characteristics, distribution, and correlates of crime is similar to that produced by both victimization and self-report survey measures (Belson, 1968; Hindelang, 1974, 1978; Maltz, 1975; Gordon, 1976; Nettler, 1978; Hindelang, Hirschi, and Weis, 1981; Thornberry and Farnworth, 1982). A number of the limitations of official-record data are discussed briefly below; those problems that have more bearing on criminal career research are discussed in more detail.

Among the variety of official data on crime, "offenses known to the police" are the most widely consulted and utilized, because they are considered closest to the crime itself and in a more constant relationship with crimes committed. The *UCR*, published annually by the FBI, provide statistics on the amount and distribution of crimes known to the police, arrests, and other information about the criminal justice system. A variety of problems with these police data can affect validity and reliability and, therefore, the synthesis of estimates of criminal career parameters produced by offical data and self-reports.

In general, official-record data, whether police, court, or prison data, underestimate the amount and distribution of crime, at both the aggregate and individual level, although here the latter is of more concern and interest.

Individual offenders are differentially vulnerable to acquiring a record, for a variety of reasons, all of which compromise the validity and utility of official-record data for research purposes. First, police practices—for example, arrest policy, number of personnel, allocation of resources, organizational ideology—vary over time and place, which creates potentially different arrest risks and enforcement. Second, laws vary by time and place, and this affects the probabilities of offense and official reaction. Third, changes in local data needs may refocus priorities and resources and lead to different recording practices across and within departments. Fourth, because of agency and jurisdictional differences in policy and practice, the accumulation and comparison of information on an individual who has records from more than one jurisdiction are problematic. Fifth, typically only the most serious offense in a criminal event is recorded; other offenses are not necessarily represented in the official record. Sixth, the number of offenses counted varies by type of crime—for "person" crimes the number of victims in any event equals the number of offenses, while for "property" crimes the event equals the crime. Seventh, most crimes of violence—those that produce bodily injury—are not included in the *UCR* index of crimes and, therefore, are less likely recorded as rigorously by local law enforcement personnel. There are many other methodological and crime-classification problems with official records, as well as other problems that impact the calculation of offense rates, but they will not be addressed here (see Hindelang, 1974; Savitz, 1982). Overall, these general limitations compromise the validity, reliability, and utility of official-record data, especially police statistics, in criminal career research. Other limitations that affect the measurement of criminal careers more directly are the focus of the remainder of this section.

Four limitations of official records—insufficient information, discontinuity, time coding, and sampling[19]—point to the fact that both self-report and official measures have limitations and that official-record data contribute to the apparent validity and reliability problems. In short, the limitations of official-record data make the identification of the serious, chronic offender more difficult, the calibration of official to self-report estimates less precise, and the reciprocal validation comparisons of the two measures more difficult.

Official records are not maintained primarily for research purposes, and consequently, whoever the researcher or whatever the research task, there will be

[19]There are many other problems, but they are not discussed because of space limitations or because they are not considered problematic for criminal career research—for example, the coding and scoring problems that arise when charges, counts, and arrests in police records have to be distinguished by a coder (Marquis and Ebener, 1981). The reader is referred to Savitz (1982) for a treatment of this and other kinds of problems.

insufficient, inadequate, or biased information in the records. This is particularly true for data on individual offenders, simply because official data systems are designed for bookkeeping and the aggregation of data. In trying to identify violent predators from the array of official-record data available, Chaiken and Chaiken (1982:12), for example, concluded that the information that is routinely collected within the criminal justice system cannot be used to make meaningful distinctions between violent predators and other offenders. They consider the validity of the records to be "as suspect as the respondent's veracity: Records are often missing or incomplete" (Chaiken, Chaiken, and Peterson, 1982:9). And those data that are essential for criminal career research—conviction and disposition records—are among the least utilized in the criminal justice system and in research.

Apparently, the information that most accurately predicts high-rate offenders is not available because it is not systematically and routinely collected by the police, courts, or corrections system. For example, in the Rand inmate surveys, only 3 of the 10 variables that predict high-rate robbers are from official records; data for the others were collected in the self-report survey (Chaiken and Chaiken, 1982:86–87). Those offender characteristics found to best distinguish serious, chronic offenders—extensive drug abuse, employment instability, and a record of early juvenile violence—are not easily accessible within the criminal justice system. And the offense-history attributes of these offenders exacerbate the problem—there is greater likelihood of error in their records simply as a function of their more frequent contact with the criminal justice system, more time being covered by the records, more jurisdictions and agencies being involved, more information recorded, more varied and complex cases, more mobility, more discontinuity in record over time and place, and so on. In other words, a long-term, complicated offense history is probably less valid and less reliable than a recent, simple one. One can hypothesize that crime is recorded least accurately in the records of those more involved in crime. The likelihood of more error in the records of serious, chronic offenders will make validation and synthesis with self-reports even more difficult than for less serious offenders.

The problem of incomplete, inadequate information is pervasive, ranging from adult arrest records (Marquis and Ebener, 1981:86) through juvenile records. Paradoxically, automated record systems do not necessarily mean that more complete and adequate information will be provided. In fact, there is a tendency to streamline and economize, to choose a select subset of items that have been collected for entering into the system. This information can be retrieved more easily, but the detailed information that one might need for research purposes is either lost for good because it was not entered or is only available when retrieved manually, just like in the old system.

Juvenile records may present even more problems than adult records, in two ways. First, juvenile police records tend to be less complete and detailed than adult police records, primarily because the rehabilitative ideology of juvenile justice diminishes the importance of and need for good police data. This is particularly so if the juvenile court and police department have a close working relationship, for example, a police juvenile division that works directly with the court-intake system. On the other hand, juvenile court records typically are richer in details about the social, economic, and psychological characteristics of the offender than are adult records, again due primarily to the need for this kind of information in making disposition decisions that may be more therapeutic than punitive. In some juvenile court jurisdictions, this separation in functions may be institutionalized in separate record-keeping systems, a "legal" file for offense-related information and a "social" file for offender-related information.[20] In short, juvenile records, police records in particular, are incomplete and do not represent the seriousness of actual criminal involvement of either those juveniles who do have records or, obviously, the many serious juvenile offenders who do not (Tracy, 1981).

The second way in which juvenile records are problematic reflects the difficulty of accessing information, however incomplete or inadequate, about juvenile criminal activity and other characteristics by adult criminal justice system officials (Chaiken and Chaiken, 1982:224). Given that adult offenders who are most involved in crime began their careers, according to self-reports, before they were 13 years old (Peterson, Braiker, and Polich, 1981:xxix), the unavailability of juvenile record information, particularly on such factors as onset, drug abuse, and violence, is a substantial problem.

This is primarily a problem of continuity between juvenile and adult records, but it also affects the ability to measure change from juvenile to adult status with standard units of comparison measured and recorded in similar ways. Other important official sources of information, and even of correlational validation (see Hindelang, Hirschi, and Weis, 1981:Figure 5.1, 989), are not typically coordinated or integrated with either juvenile or adult criminal justice record systems. Serious, chronic offenders often exhibit early troublesome behavior in or are serviced by the school system (West and Farrington, 1977; Farrington, 1982), mental health system (Cocozza and Steadman, 1974), drug abuse agencies, and other social service institutions. Although at the national level there has been some organized effort to coordinate federal statistics on children, youth, and families, coordination among local agencies, particularly in sharing record information, is rare and certainly not systematic (Zill, Peterson, and Moore, 1984). This kind of information on social, economic, and psychological characteristics would be useful in confirming and supplementing data on current or incipient serious, chronic offenders.

Even though official-record information on temporal sequencing—onset, crime switching, termination—is more trustworthy than self-reports of time, the fact that official records are the only halfway reliable source of time-coding makes error more critical. The dates recorded in criminal history records have been identified as particularly problematic because termination markers, such as "release dates" from institutions, may not be systematically coded and recorded (Greenwood, 1979:41). This means that calculating "time at risk," "street time," or "free time," which is crucial to estimating individual offending rates, is hampered by this source of error. If measuring temporal changes in criminal behavior were not so central to criminal career research, and if respondents' memories for dates and sequential orders were not so unreliable, these time-coding problems would not be considered as critical as they are here. And the problem is not specific to criminal history records; it is a pervasive problem from the point of police contact through discharge from parole.

Finally, there is the issue of sampling,

[20]This discussion is based on the author's research experience with a number of juvenile court and police search systems, particularly the one in King County and Seattle, Washington.

both of offenders and offenses by the juvenile justice and criminal justice systems. Official measures underestimate the actual number of offenders, offenses in the population, and offenses of known offenders. This underestimation is not necessarily a problem if, as Quetelet (1833) suggested, there is a constant ratio between the actual amount of crime and officially recorded crime—the latter then "represents" the former and is an acceptable measure of crime (Weis, 1983a:379). But if the difference in the ratio between unknown and officially known crimes is not due to random error but to systematic bias that cannot be identified, specified, and corrected, the official-record data cannot produce accurate estimates of the actual amount and distribution of crime. Unfortunately, the ratio of unknown to known crime is difficult to specify with precision, and it certainly is not invariable. The criminal justice system may behave in relation to certain offenses and offenders in ways that create differential probabilities of reaction—for example, arrest—that concomitantly produce inconstant ratios between crimes committed and arrests. These may be variations by offense type and seriousness, as well as by offender attribute. The biggest problem with official data is the underreporting by victims to the police. An unknown number of crimes are never discovered, and, of those that are, the majority are not reported to authorities by the victim or other citizens (Skogan, 1977). Unfortunately, this underreporting or nonreporting to the police varies by offense type, victim and offender characteristics, perceptions of police efficiency, and a number of other variables (Hindelang, Hirschi, and Weis, 1978). This variation is not random or predictable in any rigorous, precise way. As with self-reports, there is no way to know or to verify the number of victimizations that "actually" occurred, whether reported on the survey or not.[21]

Of those crimes that are reported to authorities, some may not be recorded, but more likely they will be coded and recorded in such a way that using them for many research purposes is difficult. Among the variety of coding and recording problems (see Savitz, 1982), one is particularly problematic for comparisons of official and self-report data, whatever the purpose. The legal categories that are used to process and code offenses are broad and do not necessarily correspond to the criminal behavior that led to official processing.[22] There may be substantial disparities between the actual criminal behavioral event and the legal category within which it is processed and recorded, as well as substantial variation within the legal category. For example, as a consequence of plea bargaining, the beating of one person by another could be processed, coded, and recorded as disorderly conduct.

If there is disparity, perhaps substantial, between the criminal behavior that an individual commits (and admits on a self-report questionnaire) and the legal designation of the offense of record, the research and measurement problems are significant. Comparisons of self-reports and offenses of record on an individual-offender basis will be problematic. Even for relatively serious offenders, there may be few offenses in the record, which may force aggregation into even broader offense categories to make comparisons

[21]It is also possible that there are differential validity effects by respondent characteristic similar to those observed for self-reports. If so, it makes the victimization data less useful in extrapolating estimates of total crime rates from official records.

[22]Of course, these broad legal categories and what is included in them will also vary over time and across jurisdictions as well, while the behavior can remain invariant.

possible with self-reports (see Hindelang, Hirschi, and Weis, 1981:121). Crime-by-offense-of-record comparisons are difficult unless the sample is very large or very criminal. These disparities would also diminish validity, particularly correlational validity and reverse record checks. The amount of error introduced would likely attenuate correlation coefficients between having an official record and both self-reports of criminal behavior and self-reports of official record. The usual reverse-record-check analysis, wherein the percentage of offenses in police records that are not self-reported is interpreted as an indicator of relative validity, also is affected detrimentally by the error introduced by the noncorrespondence between self-reported criminal behavior and offense of record. One has to make coding decisions about the placement of reported crimes in the available legal offense categories, which is likely to lead to more misclassifications than necessary.

Unfortunately, the sampling process is less amenable to direct modification than some of the other problems with official-record data. As Hindelang, Hirschi, and Weis (1981:21) have concluded, "there is no practical way to directly modify or refine official statistics to compensate for undiscovered, unreported, and unsolved crimes." However, one can study the sampling process more carefully to ascertain its relationship to criminal behavior; for example, differential arrest probabilities can be estimated from self-reports of crime and official records of individual arrest for a subset of those crimes, and changes can be made in administrative and technical aspects of official-record data collection, as well as in the self-report method. These kinds of changes and research are what may be necessary to enhance the validity and reliability of both official and self-report measures, to improve convergence on parameter estimates and their correlates, and, ultimately, to create the best possible combination of measures of individual offending patterns.

RESEARCH STRATEGIES TO IMPROVE MEASUREMENT

Even though official records and self-reports have relatively good general validity and reliability as measures of crime, it is clear that both approaches to measurement are imperfect and have unique problems and limitations. Together, they may provide the most adequate, complementary description of individual offending patterns in criminal career research, particularly if they are both improved and refined to maximize reciprocal validity and reliability and, hence, the prospect for even more convergence than already exists on the representations of the basic characteristics of crime and criminals. Given what we know, what can be done to use official and self-report measures in ways that build on their complementary characteristics to take advantage of their unique strengths and compensate for their weaknesses? What kind of research might improve our knowledge of validity and reliability problems and their effects on estimates of parameters and correlates and, ultimately, the convergence or discrepancy of official and self-report measures of crime?

Many things that can or should be done to improve measurement are simply good research practice. However, there are also many issues, questions, and problems in both official and self-report measurement that require the illumination of empirical research. Four research issues seem particularly important for improving the measurement of individual offending patterns. First is time coding, both in official records (various transaction dates) and in self-reports (recall-period boundaries). Second, the isomorphism of the domains of criminal behavior contained in official records and represented in self-report measures is critical in a variety of ways, ranging from item selection and reverse record checks to attempts to calibrate unknown self-reported crimes to officially known offenses. Third, the method of measurement is probably more critical in research on serious, chronic offenders than on less predatory samples of offenders, and the determination of the most effective way to collect valid and reliable data from these kinds of respondents is critical. Fourth, the potential respondent effects that may be attributed to drug and alcohol abuse, violent criminal behavior, official status as a serious offender, intellectual competence, and race (and their interactions) need to be investigated to determine their actual contribution to response bias.

Given the nascent status of research on the measurement of criminal careers, the development of long-term research strategies is a necessary and logical first step toward achieving greater convergence in the estimates of career parameters produced by different measurement approaches. A strategy, as a "plan" to achieve some end, establishes the boundaries within which more concrete means to that end will be implemented. In the context of this paper, the goal is to achieve synthesis in estimating the parameters of criminal careers. To this end, six "research strategies," of the many possible, are discussed, each of which addresses one or more of the above-identified research issues, as well as other problems, and each of which includes suggestions for the kinds of research and studies that might be incorporated into the longer-range research agenda implied by the strategies.[23]

The research strategies focus on issues in empirical research on the measurement of criminal career parameters and their correlates. It is assumed that the research on measurement issues will lead eventually to the kinds of improvements in criminal career research that will enhance the convergence of estimates and make it more useful for theory, policy, and programs.

1. *Research on the measurement of criminal careers should include a comprehensive, quantitative meta-analysis of the relationship between research methods and findings on parameters and correlates.*

Since research on criminal careers is a relatively new area of concentrated research effort and work on the measurement of criminal careers is rudimentary, organizing and synthesizing the relevant research literature is an essential step in building a better understanding of the effects of research methods on estimates of prevalence, incidence, and correlates of serious, chronic criminal behavior. This type of analysis, whereby published estimates of crime are systematically coded and analyzed statistically, facilitates the investigation of the effects of research methods (independent variables) on, for example, estimates of individual offending rates (dependent variable). By comparing estimates produced by different methods, one can assess convergence and discrepancy (Campbell and Fiske, 1959; Magnusson, 1966) and identify potential sources of error that can be attributed to differences in measurement approaches (Weis and Bridges, 1983: 35–39).

Treating important methodological characteristics of studies as data (see Crain and Mahard, 1983; Bridges, Weis,

[23]This coverage, admittedly, is not comprehensive. Nor does it claim the selection of the four "most important" research issues, or that the six research strategies are the only or preferred ways to address these measurement topics.

and Crutchfield, 1984), one can examine statistical relationships between methodological study characteristics and reported findings on criminal career characteristics, such as involvement in the serious crimes of robbery, assault, and burglary. For example, by including measurement approaches used in a study as a data point (self-report, official records, observation, informant), one can assess the association between type of measure and estimates of prevalence, incidence, and correlates across the sample of studies to determine if there are effects by measurement method. This type of of meta-analysis has been used extensively in educational research, particularly in reviewing and synthesizing experimental research (see Hunter, Schmidt, and Jackson, 1982). These types of meta-analyses are amenable to relatively sophisticated statistical analysis, including regression (e.g., Tittle, Villemez, and Smith, 1978), log linear, and structural equation techniques.

Thus, the potential exists for rigorous synthetic analysis of the relevant literature on measurement in criminal career research. There have been a few recent applications of the approach in criminology. Both Tittle, Villemez, and Smith (1978) and Braithwaite (1981) performed quantitative meta-analyses of the literature on the relationship between social class and crime, treating the published associations as dependent variables and characteristics of the studies as independent variables. A current effort (Weis and Bridges, 1983:35–41, 49–51; Bridges, Weis, and Crutchfield, 1984) that focuses on improving the measurement of violent behavior has direct relevance to measurement issues in criminal career research; it includes as one of four major aims a comprehensive, systematic meta-analysis of the violence literature. The findings and methods of major studies of violence are being analyzed to identify methodological sources of convergence and discrepancy in estimates of prevalence, incidence, and correlates of violence.

2. *Research on the measurement of criminal careers should attempt to specify and estimate the direction and magnitude of response effects in self-report measures.*

No research has focused on response effects on self-reports of criminal behavior, especially among samples that include serious, chronic offenders, whether juvenile or adult. There are isolated examples of research on one or two sources of response bias in the criminological literature (Hindelang, Hirschi, and Weis, 1981; Chaiken and Chaiken, 1982), but only as secondary considerations within broader research efforts. The research on survey methodology includes many studies on response effects and many lists of practical suggestions for reducing them in survey practice (DeLamater, 1982:38–45; Sudman and Bradburn, 1982:36–51, 71–83, 207–208, 229–231; van der Zouwen and Dijkstra, 1982:220). For example, regarding asking threatening questions about behavior, such as criminal activity, the recommendations include, among many more: using open-ended questions; assuring the respondent of anonymity; using competent interviewers; placing the threatening questions toward the middle of the questionnaire; conducting pilot studies when the target population is unique in identifiable ways; using memory aids, such as cued recall; constructing multiple-item measures; measuring social desirability, sensitivity, and other attitudes that may affect response; formulating specific questions; using appropriate recall periods; using longer rather than terse or incomplete questions; phrasing questions in clear, simple language; deliberately loading questions; embedding the most threatening questions first in a list to maximize validity on later questions of interest; making reliability checks; providing full information in introductions; and constructing a logical order of questions.

Many of these suggestions, if implemented in survey-research practice, will probably reduce response effects. But the problem is that the recommendations come out of research on behaviors and samples that are very different from what one finds in criminology, and there remains the need to identify the sources of response bias to estimate direction and magnitude and, ultimately, correct for them in analysis.

Fortunately, a model developed by van der Zouwen and Dijkstra (1982:220–223) for estimating and correcting response effects could facilitate this kind of research. The model specifies the relationship between responses and the characteristics of the task (e.g., anonymity), interviewer (e.g., race), and respondent, as well as the conditions for the occurrence of response effects (e.g., social desirability). Collecting the necessary data to test this model on a sample that includes both juvenile and adult serious, chronic offenders could go far in improving the understanding and correction of response effects in self-reports of criminal behavior and, therefore, the utility of the data for theory, policy, and program purposes.

3. *Research on the measurement of criminal careers should investigate the effects on response bias of respondent characteristics, specifically official criminal status, drug and alcohol abuse, violence, intellectual competence, and race.*

Contrary to findings in survey-methodology research that respondent effects are not substantial in typical research settings with normal samples, evidence in the criminology literature suggests that in self-report surveys of criminal behavior among samples including juvenile and adult offenders, some respondent characteristics are sources and others are potential sources of response bias. In the Seattle youth study, the combination of being a male, black, official delinquent, and having low general knowledge was related to apparent invalidity of responses to self-report items and other etiological questions (Hindelang, Hirschi, and Weis, 1981). In the Rand inmate surveys, the answers to questionnaires among blacks, the less educated, and drug-alcohol abusers were much more internally inconsistent and unreliable, which apparently suppresses estimates of individual criminal involvement. And the research in cognitive psychology suggests that respondents who engage in violent acts or commit crimes while intoxicated on drugs will have impaired memory of the behavior and event (Birnbuam and Parker, 1977; Loftus, 1980). The role of drug abuse as a source of response bias seems particularly significant among serious, chronic offenders, the majority of whom have long-duration, heavy drug-use histories that are related to their involvement in other kinds of crime.

Studying the effects of these respondent characteristics on measurement, specifically on the validity and reliability of responses about criminal behavior, is not the way they are usually examined. However, it seems that the potential for substantial response bias that is attributable to these respondent characteristics warrants serious research consideration. What are their effects on answers to self-report items? How are the effects realized? What are the origins and processes that lead to differential response bias on the basis of these personal attributes?

Answers to these questions may be difficult to get, but a few ways promise at least some illumination of the questions. First, in data sets many of these respondent characteristics are represented in the sample (e.g., Seattle youth study, Rand inmate surveys, Philadelphia cohort study, National Youth Survey, Cambridge Study in Delinquent Development), which would allow reanalyses of validity and reliability taking them into account as covariates.[24] For example, if one hypothesizes lower estimates of individual offending among heavy drug users because of memory impairment, comparing their self-report estimates and validity and reliability scores with those of other respondents should inform the question. Obviously, more complicated multivariate analyses can be performed on as many of these respondent and other characteristics as are available in the respective data set. Second, the experimental research that addresses those personal attributes that affect memory could be replicated with expanded samples that include serious, chronic offenders. This would be a good test and potential confirmation of the hypothesized effects and, therefore, a source of data on the extent of memory decrement that can be attributed to drug histories, violent past, intellectual competence, and so on. Third, given the central role that drug and alcohol abuse plays at the onset and in the development of serious criminal careers and the probable powerful effect it has on memory, research focusing on drugs and crime seems warranted. This is not to suggest that the "relationship" between the two needs to be specified better. Rather, the role of drugs in and during the commission of crimes and the effect on perceiving, encoding, storing, and retrieving the details, and even the essentials, of the event need to be investigated. For examples: What are the effects on recall and response accuracy of respondent intoxication, nodding, or withdrawal—is there uniform impairment or enhanced state-dependent retrieval of information? What kinds of drugs are used during the commission of what kinds of crimes? How much is used per criminal event? Why are drugs used? What is the correspondence between self-reports of drug-crime involvement and official accounts? Fourth, a study could be launched with a simple factorial design that included the necessary sample size and variation on respondent characteristics—official criminal–noncriminal, drug user–nonuser, competent–less competent, black-white, violent–less violent—that would allow a simple assessment of independent and interactive respondent effects. Comparisons on self-reports of individual offending, drug use, official records, and validity and reliability tests could show the hypothesized effects.

[24]These and similar kinds of analyses are currently under way at the University of Washington as part of the reanalysis of data sets on violence in the project "Improving the Measurement of Violent Behavior," sponsored by the National Institute of Mental Health, Center for the Study of Antisocial and Violent Behavior (Weis and Bridges, 1983).

4. *Research on the measurement of criminal careers should include experimental research on the validity and reliability of measurement methods.*

The evidence that exists on the differential validity and reliability of official and self-report methods of measuring crime comes from research on juvenile, general-population samples (e.g., Hindelang, Hirschi, and Weis, 1981). There is a clear need for research on the comparative efficacy of measurement methods for a sample (or samples) that includes adult and serious, chronic offenders. If, indeed, these types of offenders may be more likely to give inaccurate responses, we need to verify that, but, more importantly, we need to identify under what conditions response bias is most likely to occur and in what direction and magnitude. The best way to address this research need is probably with an experimental study that compares two or more approaches to measuring criminal behavior on the same sample. The Seattle youth study (Hindelang, Hirschi, and Weis, 1981) and an extended replication study that focuses on very similar issues in measuring violence among a stratified random sample of criminals, mental patients, and the general population (Weis and Bridges, 1983) are available models for the suggested research. In fact, the latter sample undoubtedly includes a number of serious, chronic offenders in the institutionalized juvenile- and adult-offender subsamples.

What is proposed is that a sufficiently large sample of juvenile and adult serious, chronic offenders be drawn for studying within an experimental design the comparative measurement properties of two self-report methods (the face-to-face interview and the nonanonymous questionnaire) and official-record data. Randomization would be built into the design, each respondent would participate individually (compared with the group administration in the Rand inmate surveys, for example; Chaiken and Chaiken, 1982), and all the suggestions listed above to reduce response effects would be appropriately taken into account.

The face-to-face interview would be the focus of the research, for a number of reasons. First, the information cannot be anonymous for research purposes, and besides anonymity does not seem to affect responses to questions about criminal behavior (Hindelang, Hirschi, and Weis, 1981). Second, there are more nonresponses and missing data on questionnaires than in interviews (Chaiken and Chaiken, 1982; Sudman and Bradburn, 1982). Third, available research evidence suggests that the face-to-face interview may be the most effective method of administration for these types of respondents (Bradburn and Sudman, 1979; Marquis and Ebener, 1981:viii). For example, Hindelang, Hirschi, and Weis (1981) discovered that among those respondents with the highest rate of underreporting—black, male official delinquents—reporting was most accurate during the face-to-face interview. Fourth, an interview setting, with a competent, experienced interviewer, provides a greater degree of control and flexibility in eliciting information from the respondent. For example, to cue recall, test validity of answers, match self-reported crimes to offenses of record, and establish the perception of a "knowing" interviewer, it is recommended that the official record be used (physically, if appropriate) as an integral part of the interview. It can set up "guilty knowledge" questions, i.e., the interviewer refers to offenses of record, for example, three burglaries, and asks about pertinent validating information: Of the three burglaries you were arrested for, how many were of houses or apartments? These kinds of detailed data are extremely difficult to obtain in other ways. This approach can also be used in comparisons of recognition and cued-recall memory of offenses of record.

A "deep probe" would also be part of the interview for four purposes: (1) to collect detailed information on offenses to ascertain face validity and general accuracy of answers; (2) to gather data about other important aspects of the criminal event (e.g., intent, motive, number of crime partners, relationship to victim) that could be compared with official deposition statements for crimes that become offenses of record; this would allow a crude assessment of the disparity between a respondent's memory for details of criminal events and the official version; (3) probing might also be necessary for these kinds of respondents simply to get a relatively normal response pattern (Erickson and Empey, 1963); and (4) as suggested by Hindelang, Hirschi, and Weis (1981), to adjust scores on delinquency items based on corrections made in initial reports as a consequence of probing. The nonanonymous questionnaire and a follow-up randomized response questioning or a real or simulated "lie detector" interview would be included in the design to test these approaches on this type of sample and provide potential alternatives for comparisons; it is less expensive to give respondents a checklist, but the data may not be as complete or useful.

Due to the nature of the sample, this kind of experimental design could also facilitate a more rigorous assessment of the effects of the apparently important respondent characteristics on responses since serious, chronic offenders personify those characteristics. In general, this type of experimental study is the preferred way to determine the best way to collect valid and reliable data from serious, chronic offenders and to validate reciprocally data from official records. Otherwise, we are simply guessing, on the basis of scarce, ancillary evidence, about the most effective method of measurement. This is certainly not a firm foundation on which to build theory, make policy, or design programs.

5. *Research on the measurement of criminal careers should treat the improvement of measurement as a research and development enterprise.*

For a variety of reasons, the preferred research design in criminal career research is the prospective, longitudinal study. Its primary purposes are to observe changes in behavior and correlates in a cohort. However, there is another purpose that should be considered, and that is incorporating into the study design a research and development component on measurement methods. This could be done within an existing longitudinal study or built into one in the future.

There are a number of reasons for proposing that instrument development and validity-reliability research be included in longitudinal studies. First, we simply need to learn more about measuring criminal behavior over time. Knowledge is inadequate and, until necessary improvements are made and we learn more, research is handicapped.

Different measurement approaches are more or less effective at different stages of career development, and some are more rudimentary than others. For example, official records are not very useful as indicators of anything for young children, simply because children do not engage in the criminal behaviors that get them into trouble with the law. On the other hand, direct observations and informant reports (e.g., teachers, parents, peers) are useful approaches in gaining some sense of troublesome behavior among children that might have substantial predictive validity (Farrington, 1982). The application of survey methods to samples of young children is a good example of a standard method of measurement being at a rudimentary stage of development, but having the possibility of improvement if treated as a research and development task incorporated into a longitudinal study design. In fact, self-report surveys of "deviant" behavior and attitudes in a cohort of first graders were defined a priori as a research and development task within a larger prospective longitudinal project on delinquency prevention (Weis, Janvier, and Hawkins, 1982). Each administration of the survey was used to modify and refine the original instrument, increasing internal consistency, variance on items, and efficiency of administration (Weis and Worsley, 1983).

Validity and reliability testing should also be treated as a dynamic process that is built into the research design, rather than something that is attended to after all the data are in and analysis is under way. One should expect validity and reliability to change over time as do the respondents, measures, behaviors, and correlates. And, like the measures, improving the accuracy and quality of the data should be a "given" as a research objective and constantly monitored. For example, what is the differential validity over time of responses based on recognition versus recall memory and how does it affect estimates of criminal career parameters? Or, does the magnitude of response bias by race vary over time, and with what implications for measurement?

If the improvement of measures is treated as a research and development task, it also means that one can "tinker" or try to test different techniques as the project unfolds. For example, respondents could be trained to fill out ledger-type diaries of their activities and, given the design, monitored in the process. One could also use different types of response categories, recall periods, question specificity, and question length in the survey instrument, all with the objective of improving response accuracy over time. Given a cohort sample, the potential effects of "small changes," such as those in question wording, could be directly and accurately assessed. And recall periods could be "bounded" from wave to wave of data collection, making the analysis of temporal changes both easier and more accurate. The time between waves could be varied, covering shorter and longer recall periods, perhaps rotating two or more subsamples to control for testing effects.

Finally, one would have the unique opportunity to observe the development of official records as well. If the research component is designed so that data are collected at relatively frequent intervals from both respondents and records, the capacity to assess reciprocal validity and subjects such as differential arrest probabilities is enhanced substantially. A relatively contemporaneous record check is bound to be more accurate and useful for "triangulation" of results than a reverse record check in which the response interval (the time elapsed between the offense of record and the response to questions about it) is sufficiently long that memory may be faulty or at least not as accurate as it could be.

In sum, treating the improvement of measuring criminal behavior as a research and development task, incorporated in a prospective longitudinal study of the development of criminal careers, would improve substantially the validity and reliability of measures and, ultimately, the ability to describe criminal career parameters and correlates.

6. *Research on the measurement of criminal careers should assess the isomorphism of domains of self-reported crimes and official offenses.*

There is insufficient and inadequate information in official records regarding the characteristics of offenders, as well as the behavioral referents of the legal categories of offense. Offenses of record are the organizational products of a process that transforms initial criminal behavioral events that were detected into sanctioned and, therefore, recorded official offenses (Black, 1970). The problem for research on the measurement of criminal careers is the disparity between the criminal behavior and the official offense. To the extent that there is not a "good fit" behaviorally or conceptually between the two, the implications reverberate throughout research on validity and reliability of both self-report and official measures.

The disparity between what an offender actually did and what is represented in the record can affect all comparative validity tests, including reverse record checks and, ultimately, the convergence or discrepancy of estimates of parameters and correlates. This is not a trivial or esoteric problem, but a very practical problem in comparing the two methods of measurement. If the units of comparison are not the same, comparisons are obviated. We have seen these difficulties in the reverse-record-check comparisons of the Seattle youth study, in which self-reported behaviors were grouped within offense categories to enable comparisons, rather than on the basis of official offenses (Hindelang, Hirschi, and Weis, 1981).

To the extent that there is meaningful disparity, extrapolating from offenses known to total crime, either within a jurisdiction or, more unreliably, across jurisdictions, may be more difficult to do with optimal precision. Even the apparently simple identification of a self-report item that fits an offense category may not be that easy (Hindelang, Hirschi, and Weis, 1981:171–180). In short, the disparity between criminal behavior and legal classification is a critical measurement problem.

To determine the degree of isomorphism between self-report and official domains, one should investigate the structure and content of official records (Marquis and Ebener, 1981:viii). More research is needed on the characteristics of official-record data: What is the domain of criminal behaviors that official records represent? To what extent do the domains of official and self-report data overlap? Is the apparent multidimensionality of criminal behavior in self-report data replicated in official-record data? Answers to some of these questions can be gained through the usual dimensionalizing procedures, for example, factor and cluster analysis of official data. Others require more time-consuming and difficult data collection and analysis. To get closer to the domain of criminal behaviors circumscribed by official records, one needs to delve deeper than the legal categories recorded in the active records of the police department or court. One should go to the offender's case file for the much more detailed information given in depositions by the victim, witnesses, police, and offender. This should enhance the agreement of the two data sources, provide more accurate information from which to select self-report items, increase correlational validity coefficients, make reverse record checks more precise, and so on. In short, more research on the measurement properties of official-record data is needed, particularly on the degree to which the conceptual and behavioral domains of self-report and official measures are isomorphic. To the extent that they are not, the complementarity of the two measures is compromised.

CONCLUSION

Theory, policy, and programs on criminal careers depend on accurate information about the characteristics, distribution, and correlates of criminal behavior over time. Fortunately, the two most viable approaches to measuring the parameters and correlates of criminal careers, self-reports and official records, generally describe the same essential features of crime and criminals. There is much more convergence than discrepancy in their representations of the phenomena. However, research on measurement properties, particularly validity and reliability, shows that both approaches to measuring crime are still plagued by a variety of problems and weaknesses. The improvement of self-report and official measures should be a fixed objective and an ongoing enterprise. The goal should be to maximize the precision and utility of measures of the parameters and correlates of individual offending patterns over time, particularly for serious and violent crimes. In so doing, the refined measurement approaches may generate more similar estimates of parameters but, more likely and more usefully, should produce even more convergent estimates of the correlates of offenses and offenders. With this knowledge about systematic variation, adjustments and fine-tuning are more within the realm of possibility, if not on the basis of current knowledge at least on the basis of future research. A number of research strategies have been described that could improve research on the measurement of criminal careers and, therefore, our ability to understand and address the problem of serious, chronic criminal behavior.

REFERENCES

Akers, Ronald L.
1964 Socio-economic status and delinquent behavior. A retest. *Journal of Research in Crime and Delinquency* 1:38–46.

Bachman, Jerald G., O'Malley, Patrick, and Johnston, Jerome
1978 *Youth in Transition, Vol. VI: Adolescence to Adulthood: Change and Stability in the Lives of Young Men.* Institute for Social Research. Ann Arbor: University of Michigan.

Ball, John C.
1967 The reliability and validity of interview data obtained from 59 narcotics addicts. *American Journal of Sociology* 72:650–654.

Belson, William
1968 *Development of a Procedure for Eliciting Information from Boys about the Nature and Extent of Their Stealing.* Survey Research Centre. London: London School of Economics.

Birnbuam, Isabel M., and Parker, Elizabeth S.
1977 Acute effects of alcohol on storage and retrieval. Pp. 99–108 in Isabel M. Birnbuam and Elizabeth S. Parker, eds., *Alcohol and Human Memory.* New York: John Wiley & Sons.

Black, Donald J.
1970 Production of crime rates. *American Sociological Review* 35:733–748.

Blackmore, Jane
1974 The relationship between self-reported delinquency and official convictions amongst adolescent boys. *British Journal of Criminology* 14:172–176.

Blumstein, Alfred
1982 On the racial disproportionality of United States' prison populations. *Journal of Criminal Law and Criminology* 73:1259–1273.

Bower, Gordon H.
1970 Organizational factors in memory. *Cognitive Psychology* 1:18–46.

Bradburn, Norman M., and Danis, Catalina
1984 Potential contributions of cognitive research to survey questionnaire design. Pp. 101–129 in Thomas B. Jabine, Miron L. Straf, Judith M. Tanur, and Roger Tourangeau, eds., *Cognitive Aspects of Survey Methodology.* Report of the Advanced Research Seminar on Cognitive Aspects of Survey Methodology, Committee on National Statistics, National Research Council. Washington, D.C.: National Academy Press.

Bradburn, Norman M., and Sudman, Seymour
1979 *Improving Interview Method and Questionnaire Design.* San Francisco, Calif.: Jossey-Bass.

Braithwaite, John
1981 The myth of social class and criminality reconsidered. *American Sociological Review* 46:36–57.

Brenner, Michael
1982 Response effects of "role-restricted" characteristics of the interviewer. Pp. 131–165 in Wil Dijkstra and Johannes van der Zouwen, eds., *Response Behavior in the Survey-Interview.* New York: Academic Press.

Bridges, George
1981 Estimating the effects of response errors in self-reports of crime. Pp. 59–76 in James A. Fox, ed., *Methods in Quantitative Criminology.* New York: Academic Press.
1983 An empirical study of error in reports of crime and delinquency. In Marvin E. Wolfgang, Robert M. Figlio, and Terence P. Thornberry, *From Boy to Man, from Delinquency to Crime.* Chicago, Ill.: University of Chicago Press.

Bridges, George, Weis, Joseph G., and Crutchfield, Robert
1984 The Measurement of Violent Behavior: Factors Affecting Estimates of the Prevalence and Correlates of Violent Behavior. Paper presented at the American Sociological Association Meeting, San Antonio, Texas, August.

Bytheway, W. R., and May, D. R.
1971 On fitting the "facts" of social class and criminal behavior: a rejoinder to Box and Ford. *Sociological Review* 19:585–607.

Campbell, Donald T., and Fiske, Donald W.
1959 Convergent and discriminant validation by the multitrait-multimethod matrix. *Psychological Bulletin* 56:81–105.

Cannell, Charles F., and Fowler, Floyd J.
1963 Comparison of a self-enumerative procedure and a personal interview: a validity study. *Public Opinion Quarterly* 27:250–264.

Cannell, Charles F., and Kahn, Robert L.
1968 Interviewing. Pp. 449–487 in Gardner Lindzey and Elliott Aronson, eds., *The Handbook of Social Psychology.* Vol. I. Reading, Mass.: Addison-Wesley.

Cannell, Charles F., Marquis, Kent H., and Laurent, Andre
1977 A summary of studies of interviewing methodology. *Vital and Health Statistics* 69:1–78.

Cannell, Charles F., Oksenberg, Lois, and Converse, Jean M.
1977 Striving for response accuracy: experiments in new interviewing techniques. *Journal of Marketing Research* 14:306–315.

Cash, William S., and Moss, Abigail J.
1972 Optimum recall period for reporting persons injured in motor vehicle accidents. *Vital and Health Statistics* 50:1–33.

Cermak, L., and Butters, N.
1973 Information processing deficits of alcoholic Korsakoff patients. *Quarterly Journal of Studies on Alcohol* 34:1110–1132.

Chaiken, Jan M., and Chaiken, Marcia R.
1982 *Varieties of Criminal Behavior.* Santa Monica, Calif.: Rand Corporation.

Chaiken, Jan M., Chaiken, Marcia R., and Peterson, Joyce E.
1982 *Varieties of Criminal Behavior: Summary and Policy Implications.* Santa Monica, Calif.: Rand Corporation.

Chaiken, Jan M., Chaiken, Marcia R., and Rolph, John E.
1983 *Self Reported Commissions of Crimes: Comparison of Two Questionnaire Formats.* Santa Monica, Calif.: Rand Corporation.

Chaiken, Jan M., Rolph, John E., and Houchens, R. L.
1981 *Methods for Estimating Crime Rates of Individuals: Executive Summary.* Santa Monica, Calif.: Rand Corporation.

Chambliss, William J., and Nagasawa, Richard H.
1969 On the validity of official statistics—a comparative study of white, black, and Japanese high school boys. *Journal of Research in Crime and Delinquency* 6:71–77.

Christie, Nils, Andenaes, Johannes, and Skirbekk, Sigurd
1965 A study of self-reported crime. Pp. 86–116 in Karl O. Christiansen, ed., *Scandinavian Studies in Criminology.* Vol. 1. London: Tavistock.

Clancy, Kevin, and Gove, Walter
1980 Sex diferences in mental illness: an analysis of response bias in self-reports. *American Journal of Sociology* 80:205–216.

Clark, John P., and Tifft, Larry L.
1966 Polygraph and interview validation of self reported delinquent behavior. *American Sociological Review* 31:516–523.

Cocozza, Joseph J., and Steadman, Henry J.
1974 Some refinements in the measurement and prediction of dangerous behavior. *American Journal of Psychiatry* 131(9):1012–1014.

Colombotus, John
1969 Personal vs. telephone interviewers' effect on responses. *Public Health Report* 84:773–782.

Costner, Herbert
1975 The Validity of Indicators. Paper presented at American Sociological Association Meeting, San Francisco, California, August.

Crain, Robert L., and Mahard, Rita E.
1983 The effect of research methodology on desegregation achievement studies: a meta-analysis. *American Journal of Sociology* 88 (5):839–854.

Curtis, Lynn
1974 *Criminal Violence—National Patterns and Behaviors.* Lexington, Mass.: D. C. Heath.

Darley, C. F., Tinklenberg, J. R., Roth, W. T., Hollister, L. E., and Atkinson, R. C.
1973 Influence of marijuana on storage and retrieval processes in memory. *Memory and Cognition* 1:196–200.

DeLamater, John
1982 Response-effects of question content. Pp. 13–48 in Wil Dijkstra and Johannes van der Zouwen, eds., *Response Behavior in the Survey-Interview.* New York: Academic Press.

Dentler, Robert A., and Monroe, Lawrence J.
1961 Social correlates of early adolescent theft. *American Sociological Review* 26:733–743.

Dijkstra, Wil, and van der Zouwen, Johannes
1982 Introduction. Pp. 1–12 in Wil Dijkstra and Johannes van der Zouwen, eds., *Response Behavior in the Survey-Interview.* New York: Academic Press.

Edwards, Allen L.
1957 *The Social Desirability Variable in Personality Assessment and Research.* New York: Dryden.

Elliott, Delbert S.
1982 Review essay on *Measuring Delinquency. Criminology* 20(3–4):527–537.

Elliott, Delbert S., and Ageton, Suzanne
1980 Reconciling race and class differences in self-reported and official estimates of delinquency. *American Sociological Review* 1:95–110.

Elliott, Delbert S., and Huizinga, David
1983 Social class and delinquent behavior in a national youth study. *Criminology* 21:149–177.

Elliott, Delbert S., and Voss, Harwin L.
1974 *Delinquency and Dropout.* Lexington, Mass.: D. C. Heath.

Elmhorn, Kirsten
1965 Study in self report delinquency among school children in Stockholm. Pp. 117–146

in Karl O. Christiansen, ed., *Scandinavian Studies in Criminology*. Vol. 1. London: Tavistock.

Ennis, Philip H.
1967 *Criminal Victimization in the United States: A Report of a National Survey*. National Opinion Research Center. Chicago, Ill.: University of Chicago.

Erdelyi, Matthew H., and Goldberg, Benjamin
1979 Let's not sweep repression under the rug: toward a cognitive psychology of repression. Pp. 365–402 in John Kihlstrom and Frederick J. Evans, eds., *Functional Disorders of Memory*. Hillsdale, N.J.: Lawrence Erlbaum.

Erickson, Maynard
1972 The Changing Relation Between Official and Self-reported Delinquency. Unpublished manuscript. University of Arizona, Tucson.

Erickson, Maynard, and Empey, LaMar T.
1963 Court records, undetected delinquency and decision-making. *Journal of Criminal Law, Criminology, and Police Science* 54:456–469.

Farrington, David
1973 Self-reports of deviant behavior: predictive and stable? *Journal of Criminal Law and Criminology* 64:99–110.
1979 Environmental stress, delinquent behavior, and convictions. Pp. 93–107 in I. G. Sarason and C. D. Spielberger, eds., *Stress and Anxiety*. Vol. 6. Washington, D.C.: Hemisphere.
1982 Stepping Stones to Adult Criminal Careers. Paper presented at Conference on the Development of Antisocial and Prosocial Behavior, Voss, Norway, April.
1983 Executive Summary of Further Analyses of a Longitudinal Survey of Crime and Delinquency. Final Report to the National Institute of Justice. Washington, D.C.: U.S. Department of Justice.

Foster, Herbert L.
1974 *Ribbin', Jivin', and Playin' the Dozens: The Unrecognized Dilemma of Inner City Schools*. Cambridge, Mass.: Ballinger.

Fox, Greer L., and Inazu, Judith K.
1980 Patterns and outcomes of mother-daughter communication about sexuality. *Journal of Social Issues* 36:7–29.

Garofalo, James, and Hindlelang, Michael J.
1977 *An Introduction to the National Crime Survey*. Washington, D.C.: U.S. Department of Justice.

Gibson, H. B., Morrison, Sylvia, and West, D. J.
1970 The confession of known offenses in response to a self-reported delinquency schedule. *British Journal of Criminology* 10:277–280.

Glueck, Sheldon, and Glueck, Eleanor T.
1950 *Unraveling Juvenile Delinquency*. Cambridge, Mass.: Harvard University Press.

Gold, Martin
1966 Undected delinquent behavior. *Journal of Research in Crime and Delinquency* 3:27–46.
1970 *Delinquent Behavior in an American City*. Belmont, Calif.: Brooks/Cole.

Goode, William J., and Hatt, Paul K.
1952 *Methods in Social Research*. New York: McGraw-Hill.

Gordon, Robert A.
1976 Prevalence: the rare datum in delinquency measurement and its implications for the theory of delinquency. Pp. 201–284 in Malcolm W. Klein, ed., *The Juvenile Justice System*. Beverly Hills, Calif.: Sage Publications.

Gould, Leroy C.
1969 Who defines delinquency: a comparison of self-reported and officially reported indices of delinquency for three racial groups. *Social Problems* 16:325–336.

Gove, Walter
1982 Systemic response bias and characteristics of the respondent. Pp. 167–187 in Wil Dijkstra and Johannes van der Zouwen, eds., *Response Behavior in the Survey-Interview*. New York: Academic Press.

Greenwood, Peter
1979 *Rand Research on Criminal Careers: Progress to Date*. Santa Monica, Calif.: Rand Corporation.

Hagenaars, Jacques A., and Heinen, Ton G.
1982 Effects of role-independent interviewer characteristics on responses. Pp. 91–130 in Wil Dijkstra and Johannes van der Zouwen, eds., *Response Behavior in the Survey-Interview*. New York: Academic Press.

Hamparian, Donna M., Schuster, Richard, Dinitz, Simon, and Conrad, John P.
1978 *The Violent Few*. Lexington, Mass.: Lexington.

Hannan, Michael T.
1971 *Aggregation and Disaggregation in Sociology*. Lexington, Mass.: Lexington.

Hardt, Robert H., and Peterson-Hardt, Sandra J.
1977 On determining the quality of the delinquency self-report method. *Journal of Research in Crime and Delinquency* 14:247–261.

Hasher, L., and Chromiak, W.
1977 The processing of frequency information. *Journal of Verbal Learning and Verbal Behavior* 16:173–184.

Hathaway, Starke R., and Monachesi, Elio D.
1963 *Adolescent Personality and Behavior. MMPI Patterns of Normal, Delinquent, Dropout and Other Outcomes*. Minneapolis: University of Minnesota Press.

Havighurst, Robert J.
1962 *Growing Up in River City*. New York: John Wiley & Sons.

Hindelang, Michael J.
1973 Causes of delinquency: a partial replication and extension. *Social Problems* 20:471–487.
1974 *Uniform Crime Reports* revisited. *Journal of Criminal Justice* 2:1–18.
1978 Race and involvement in common law personal crimes. *American Sociological Review* 43:93–109.

Hindelang, Michael J., Gottfredson, Michael R., and Garofalo, James
1978 *Victims of Personal Crime: An Empirical Foundation for a Theory of Personal Victimization*. Cambridge, Mass.: Ballinger.

Hindelang, Michael J., Hirschi, Travis, and Weis, Joseph G.
1975 Self-Reported Delinquency: Methods and Substance. Proposal submitted to the National Institute of Mental Health, Department of Health, Education, and Welfare, MH27778. Department of Sociology, University of Washington.
1978 Social Class, Sex, Race and the Discrepancy between Self-Reported and Official Delinquency. Grant Number MH22778–03. Center for Studies of Crime and Delinquency, National Institute of Mental Health, Department of Health, Education, and Welfare. Department of Sociology, University of Washington.
1979 Correlates of delinquency: the illusion of discrepancy between self-report and official measures. *American Sociological Review* 44:995–1014.
1981 *Measuring Delinquency*. Beverly Hills, Calif.: Sage Publications.

Hirschi, Travis
1969 *Causes of Delinquency*. Berkeley: University of California Press.

Hirschi, Travis, and Hindelang, Michael J.
1977 Intelligence and delinquency: a revisionist review. *American Sociological Review* 42:571–587.

Huizinga, David, and Elliott, Delbert S.
1981 *A Longitudinal Study of Drug Use and Delinquency in a National Sample of Youth: An Assessment of Causal Order*. Boulder, Colo.: Behavioral Research Institute.

Hunter, Ian M. L.
1957 *Memory*. Middlesex, England: Penguin Books.

Hunter, J. E., Schmidt, F. L., and Jackson, G. B.
1982 *Meta-Analysis: Cumulating Research Findings Across Studies*. Beverly Hills, Calif.: Sage Publications.

Janson, Carl-Gunnar
1982 *Delinquency Among Metropolitan Boys*. Department of Sociology. Stockholm: University of Stockholm.

Jensen, Gary F.
1976 Race, achievement and delinquency: a further look at delinquency in a birth cohort. *American Journal of Sociology* 82:379–387.

Jones, Ben M., and Jones, Marilyn K.
1977 Alcohol and memory impairment in male and female social drinkers. Pp. 127–140 in Isabel M. Birnbuam, and Elizabeth S. Parker, eds., *Alcohol and Human Memory*. New York: John Wiley & Sons.

Jones, Edward E., and Sigall, Harold
1971 The bogus pipeline: a new paradigm for measuring affect and attitude. *Psychological Bulletin* 76:349–364.

Klatzky, Roberta L.
1975 *Human Memory: Structures and Processes*. San Francisco, Calif.: W. H. Freeman.

Kulik, James, Stein, Kenneth B., and Sarbin, Theodore R.
1968 Disclosure of delinquent behavior under conditions of anonymity and nonanonymity. *Journal of Consulting and Clinical Psychology* 32:506–509.

Langan, Patrick A., and Farrington, David P.
1983 Two-track or one-track justice? Some evidence from an English longitudinal survey. *Journal of Criminal Law and Criminology* 74:519–546.

Law Enforcement Assistance Administration
1972 *San Jose Methods Test of Known Crime Victims*. Statistics Technical Report No. 1. Washington, D. C.: U.S. Government Printing Office.

Liebow, Elliot
1967 *Tally's Corner: A Study of Negro Street Corner Men*. Boston, Mass.: Little, Brown.

Lin, Nan
1976 *Foundations of Social Research*. New York: McGraw-Hill.

Loftus, Elizabeth F.
1980 *Memory*. Reading, Mass.: Addison-Wesley.
1982 Memory and its distortions. Pp. 123–154 in A. G. Kraut, ed., *The G. Stanley Hall Lecture Series*. Washington, D.C.: American Psychological Association.

Loftus, Elizabeth F., and Burns, T. E.
1982 Mental shock can produce retrograde amnesia. *Memory and Cognition* 10:318–323.

Magnusson, David
1966 *Test Theory*. Boston, Mass.: Addison-Wesley.

Maltz, Michael D.
1975 Crime statistics: a mathematical perspective. *Journal of Criminal Justice* 3:177–193.
Marquis, Kent H.
1978 *Inferring Health Interview Responses from Imperfect Record Checks.* Santa Monica, Calif.: Rand Corporation.
1980 *Hospital Stay Response Error Estimates for the Health Insurance Study's Dayton Baseline Survey.* Santa Monica, Calif.: Rand Corporation.
Marquis, Kent H., and Ebener, Patricia A.
1981 *Quality of Prisoner Self-Reports: Arrest and Conviction Response Errors.* Santa Monica, Calif.: Rand Corporation.
McDonald, Lynn
1969 *Social Class and Delinquency.* London: Faber & Faber.
Miller, Loren L., and Cornett, Teresa L.
1978 Marijuana: dose effects on pulse rate, subjective estimates of intoxication, free recall and recognition memory. *Pharmacology, Biochemistry and Behavior* 9:573–577.
Miller, Walter B.
1958 Lower class culture as a generating milieu of gang delinquency. *Journal of Social Issues* 14:5–19.
Murdock, Bennet B.
1974 *Human Memory: Theory and Data.* Potomac, Md.: Lawrence Erlbaum.
Nettler, Gwynn
1974 *Explaining Crime.* New York: McGraw-Hill.
1978 *Explaining Crime.* 2d edition. New York: McGraw-Hill.
Nisbett, Richard E., and Ross, Lee
1980 *Human Interference: Strategies and Shortcomings of Social Judgment.* Englewood Cliffs, N.J.: Prentice-Hall.
Nye, F. Ivan
1958 *Family Relationships and Delinquent Behavior.* New York: John Wiley & Sons.
Parker, Elizabeth S., and Noble, Ernest P.
1977 Alcohol consumption and cognition filing in social drinkers. *Journal of Studies on Alcohol* 38:1224–1232.
Penk, W. E., Brown, A. S., Roberts, W. R., Dolan, M. P., Atkins, H. G., and Robinowitz, R.
1981a Visual memory for black and white male heroin and nonheroin drug users. *Journal of Abnormal Psychology* 90:486–489.
1981b Visual memory of male Hispanic-American heroin addicts. *Journal of Consulting and Clinical Psychology* 49:771–772.
Perry, D. C.
1976 PCP revisited. *Clinical Toxicology* 9:339–348.
Peterson, Mark A., and Braiker, Harriet B.
1980 *Doing Crime: A Survey of California Prison Inmates.* Santa Monica, Calif.: Rand Corporation.
Peterson, Mark A., and Braiker, Harriet B., with Polich, Suzanne M.
1981 *Who Commits Crimes: A Survey of Prison Inmates.* Cambridge, Mass.: Oelgeschlager, Gunn and Hain.
Polk, Kenneth, Frease, Dean, and Richmond, F. Lynn
1974 Social class, school experience and delinquency. *Criminology* 12:84–96.
Quetelet, Adolphe
1833 *Recherches Sur le Penchant au Crime aux Differens Ages.* 2d edition. Brussels: Hayez.
Reiss, Albert J.
1975 Inappropriate theories and inadequate methods as policy plagues: self-reported delinquency and the law. Pp. 211–222 in N. J. Demerath III, O. Larsen, and K. F. Schuessler, eds., *Social Policy and Sociology.* New York: Academic Press.
Reiss, Albert J., and Rhodes, A. Lewis
1961 The distribution of juvenile delinquency in the social class structure. *American Sociological Review* 26:720–732.
Robinson, W. S.
1950 Ecological correlations and the behavior of individuals. *American Sociological Review* 15:351–357.
Savitz, Leonard
1982 Official statistics. Pp. 3–15 in Leonard Savitz and Norman Johnston, eds., *Contemporary Criminology.* New York: John Wiley & Sons.
Schuman, Howard, and Presser, Stanley
1981 *Questions and Answers in Attitude Surveys.* New York: Academic Press.
Sellin, Thorsten, and Wolfgang, Marvin E.
1964 *The Measurement of Delinquency.* New York: John Wiley & Sons.
Shannon, Lyle W.
1982 *Predicting Adult Criminal Careers from Juvenile Careers.* Iowa Urban Community Research Center. Ames: University of Iowa.
1983 *The Prediction Problem As It Applies to Delinquency and Crime Control.* Iowa Urban Community Research Center. Ames: University of Iowa.
Short, James F., Jr., and Nye, F. Ivan
1958 Events of unrecorded juvenile delinquency: tentative conclusions. *Journal of Criminal Law and Criminology* 49:296–302.
Shryock, Henry S., Siegel, Jacob S., and Associates
1975 *Methods and Materials of Demography.* Rev. edition, Vols. I and II. Washington, D.C.: U. S. Government Printing Office.
Siegel, Judith M., and Loftus, Elizabeth F.
1978 Impact of anxiety and life stress upon eye-

witness testimony. *Bulletin of the Psychonomic Society* 12:479–480.

Skogan, Wesley G.
1977 Dimensions of the dark figure of unreported crime. *Crime and Delinquency* 23:41–50.

Sobell, Mark B., and Sobell, Linda C.
1978 *Behavioral Treatment of Alcohol Problems: Individualized Therapy and Controlled Drinking.* New York: Plenum Press.

Strasburg, Peter A.
1978 *Violent Delinquents.* A Report to the Ford Foundation. New York: Vera Institute of Justice.

Sudman, Seymour, and Bradburn, Norman M.
1974 *Response Effects in Surveys: A Review and Synthesis.* Chicago, Ill.: National Opinion Research Center.
1982 *Asking Questions.* San Francisco, Calif.: Jossey-Bass.

Sykes, Thomas M., Roccolo, Robert L., and Thompson, Joann K.
1980 *An Analysis of Program Needs of Prison Inmates in Washington State.* Olympia, Wash.: Office of Research.

Talland, George A.
1968 *Disorders of Memory and Learning.* Harmondsworth, England: Penguin.

Thornberry, Terence, and Farnworth, Margaret
1982 Social correlates of criminal involvement. *American Sociological Review* 47:505–518.

Tittle, Charles R., Villemez, Wayne J., and Smith, Douglas A.
1978 The myth of social class and criminality: an empirical assessment of the empirical evidence. *American Sociological Review* 43: 643–656.

Tourangeau, Roger
1984 Cognitive sciences and survey methods. Pp. 73–100 in Thomas B. Jabine, Miron L. Straf, Judith M. Tanur, and Roger Tourangeau, eds., *Cognitive Aspects of Survey Methodology.* Report of the Advanced Research Seminar on Cognitive Aspects of Survey Methodology, Committee on National Statistics, National Research Council. Washington, D.C.: National Academy Press.

Tracy, Paul E.
1981 Analysis of the Incidence and Seriousness of Self-reported Delinquency and Crime. Paper presented at the American Society of Criminology Meeting, Washington, D.C., November.

Tracy, Paul E., and Fox, James A.
1981 Validation of randomized response. *American Sociological Review* 2:187–200.

Valentine, Bettylou
1978 *Hustling and Other Hard Work: Life Styles in the Ghetto.* New York: Free Press.

van der Zouwen, Johannes, and Dijkstra, Wil
1982 Conclusions. Pp. 209–222 in Wil Dijkstra and Johannes van der Zouwen, eds., *Response Behavior in the Survey-Interview.* New York: Academic Press.

Voss, Harwin L.
1963 Ethnic differentials in delinquency in Honolulu. *Journal of Criminal Law, Criminology and Police Science* 54:322–327.

Warner, Stanley L.
1965 Randomized response: a survey technique for eliminating evasive answer bias. *Journal of the American Statistical Association* 60:63–69.

Weingartner, Herbert, and Parker, Elizabeth S.
1984 *Memory Consolidation: Psychobiology of Cognition.* Hillsdale, N.J.: Lawrence Erlbaum.

Weis, Joseph G.
1981 One More Time: Social Class and Delinquency. Paper presented at the American Society of Criminology Meeting, Washington, D.C., November.
1983a Crime statistics: reporting systems and methods. Pp. 378–392 in Stanford H. Kadish, ed., *Encyclopedia of Crime and Justice.* New York: Free Press.
1983b Delinquency from the self-report perspective. Pp. 73–88 in Raymond R. Corrado, Marc LeBlanc, and Jean Trepanier, eds., *Current Issues in Juvenile Justice.* Toronto: Butterworths.
1986 The elusive correlation: social class and crime. in Michael R. Gottfredson, ed., *Positive Criminology: Essays in Honor of Michael J. Hindelang.* Beverly Hills, Calif.: Sage.

Weis, Joseph G., and Bridges, George S.
1983 Improving the Measurement of Violent Behavior. Proposal to Center for the Study of Antisocial and Violent Behavior, National Institute of Mental Health. Department of Sociology, University of Washington.
1984 A Meta-analysis of Correlates of Violence. Paper presented at American Society of Criminology Meeting, Cincinnati, Ohio, November.

Weis, Joseph G., and van Alstyne, David
1979 The Measurement of Delinquency by the Randomized Response Method. Paper presented at the American Society of Criminology Meeting, Philadelphia, Pennsylvania, November.

Weis, Joseph G., Janvier, Richard L., and Hawkins, J. David
1982 Delinquent Behavior and Its Prevention: Overview. Washington, D.C.: Office of Juvenile Justice and Delinquency Prevention.

Weis, Joseph G., and Worsley, Katherine
1983 *Measuring Deviant Behavior Among Children.* Washington, D.C.: Office of Juvenile Justice and Delinquency Prevention.

West, Donald J.
1973 *Who Becomes Delinquent?* London: Heinemann.

West, Donald J., and Farrington, David P.
1977 *The Delinquent Way of Life.* London: Heinemann.

Wetzel, C. Douglas, Janowsky, David S., and Clapton, Paul
1982 Remote memory during marijuana intoxication. *Psychopharmacology* 76:278–281.

Williams, Jay R., and Gold, Martin
1972 From delinquent behavior to official delinquency. *Social Problems* 20:209–229.

Wolfgang, Marvin E., and Ferracuti, Franco
1967 *The Subculture of Violence: Toward an Integrated Theory in Criminology.* London: Tavistock.

Wolfgang, Marvin E., Figlio, Robert M., and Sellin, Thorsten
1972 *Delinquency in a Birth Cohort.* Chicago, Ill.: University of Chicago Press.

Zill, Nicholas, Peterson, James L., and Moore, Kristin A.
1984 *Improving National Statistics on Children, Youth, and Families.* Washington, D.C.: Child Trends, Inc.

2

The Impact of Substance Abuse on Criminal Careers

Eric D. Wish and Bruce D. Johnson

OVERVIEW

Approach

This paper reviews what is known about how illicit drug use affects the parameters of criminal careers, especially crime rates, and suggests directions that future research should take to fill the gaps in current knowledge about drug use and crime. To accomplish these goals, we have focused on the small number of studies of drug use that permit the computation of crime rates and that provide important implications for research. We have drawn heavily on our own research and that of our colleagues.

In taking this approach, we have excluded many excellent studies. The interested reader may wish to refer to a number of comprehensive reviews of the drugs and crime literature (Tinklenberg, 1973; McGlothlin, 1979; Weissman, 1979; Gandossy et al., 1980). The reader should also be aware that our selection of studies influences the scope of our discussion and the applicability of our conclusions.

Most of the studies we discuss concern crime among users of heroin and/or cocaine. These two drugs, along with alcohol (which is reviewed separately in this volume), are the drugs that have been most frequently studied in relationship to crime. Although we briefly discuss marijuana and phencyclidine (PCP), relatively few careful studies have been made of the relationship of these drugs to criminal behavior. We also discuss the relationship of barbiturate use and amphetamine use to crime, mainly in the context of studies that have focused on heroin or cocaine use.

In focusing our discussion on studies of heroin and cocaine users, we have thereby limited the types of crimes and the types of populations that we report on. Also, because the use of heroin and

Eric D. Wish and Bruce D. Johnson are research staff members at Narcotic and Drug Research, Inc., New York City. Points of view or opinions in this paper do not necessarily represent the official position or policies of Narcotic and Drug Research, Inc.

The authors would like to thank Lee Robins and Mary Toborg for their comments on earlier drafts of this paper.

cocaine is rare in the general population and in persons under age 17, most of the detailed information about the relationship of these drugs to crime comes from studies of adults who have been processed by the criminal justice system or who have entered publicly funded drug abuse treatment programs. Finally, because men are more likely to be arrested than women, most of the findings refer to them. This is unfortunate in light of growing evidence (Wish, Brady, and Cuadrado, 1984) that drug abuse may be more prevalent and severe among female arrestees than male arrestees.

Much of what we say is largely applicable to the indigent, less educated, adult male drug user who has been arrested. Our discussion is less relevant to the users of heroin and cocaine who are well educated and legitimately employed (Washton and Gold, 1984; Zinberg, 1984); such persons are less likely to be found in state or federally funded treatment programs, from which many researchers select their samples. Little is known about the drug use and criminal behavior of these relatively affluent persons. However, a recent survey of 500 largely employed and educated persons who called a national hotline for help with cocaine-related problems (Washton and Gold, 1984) indicates crimes are less common among these persons than among less affluent users typically studied. Only 12 percent of the sample of mostly chronic cocaine users had been arrested for a cocaine-related crime, and 29 percent indicated stealing from family, friends, or employers to support their habits. The fact that existing research does not permit more extensive discussion of drug use and crime among affluent populations should not hinder us from achieving our main purposes, however, since we are particularly concerned here with how drug use affects the criminal careers of persons processed by the criminal justice system, who are preponderantly not affluent.

Summary of Findings

We summarize here conclusions based on the information presented in this paper. First, studies of persons who have been arrested and processed by the criminal justice system, of unapprehended criminals on the streets, and of persons in drug treatment programs indicate that as levels of illicit drug use (especially of heroin and cocaine) increase so does criminal activity (both drug-distribution offenses and nondrug-related serious offenses). Second, among youths in the general population, the small subset who use cocaine, heroin, or pills for nonmedical reasons account for a disproportionate amount of all juvenile crime. Third, persons in the United States who use these drugs enough to have associated legal problems tend to be so enmeshed in other deviance and adjustment problems as to make attempts to untangle the exact sequence of the onset of drug use and criminal behavior a futile and, perhaps, trivial pursuit. Fourth, chronic users of heroin and/or cocaine who are repeatedly arrested and processed by the criminal justice system typically engage in a variety of drug-distribution activities and other crimes. Fifth, treatment programs can reduce drug abuse and crime if the person remains in treatment. And sixth, urinalysis appears to be an effective tool for identifying drug-using arrestees, but more needs to be learned about how to use this information.

We have also attempted to review a number of topics for which insufficient information was available to draw definitive conclusions. Little is known, for example, about the natural course of drug use and crime among persons processed by the criminal justice system. Does incarceration reduce or only delay drug use and crime? Persons tend to relapse into drug use and crime after release from treatment or detention, but do they make up for lost time? Even persons dependent on heroin have periods in their lives when they reduce or abstain from the use of drugs. More needs to be learned about what brings these periods on and how they might be prolonged.

Drug use appears less prevalent among arrestees over age 35. Is this because drug-abusing criminals drop out of the active criminal population because of early death, incarceration, or institutionalization, or do they turn to alcohol or mature out of their drug use and criminal activities? Or do police avoid arresting older criminals? Or is it that the older criminals, like the rest of the older population, lack opportunities to use illicit drugs? And, do these relationships apply equally to male and female offenders?

Much money and resources are being expended to reduce the supply of illicit drugs in the United States by seizing supplies and asking other governments to reduce poppy and coca plant production in their countries. These efforts assume that by reducing the supply one can reduce the abuse of these drugs and the associated crime. Almost nothing is known, however, about how these efforts actually affect the crime rates of drug abusers. Do the higher prices for illicit drugs that result from a decrease in supply lead to less use and therefore less crime, or does the user merely increase his or her criminal activities to pay the increased prices, or is there no effect because the user turns to more abundant drugs?

More needs to be learned also about how to reduce demand for drugs in offender populations. Which offenders are the best candidates for intervention? Should major efforts go toward deterring the young, drug-using offender at risk of progressing to more serious drug abuse, or toward deterring older persons, who may be more ready to change their ways? There is some evidence that court-ordered treatment may keep persons in treatment longer and, therefore, away from drugs and crime longer. More needs to be learned about how specific types of court-ordered interventions can reduce drug abuse and crime.

The remainder of this paper expands on the points presented above. The paper is divided into two sections and two appendices. In the first section, which is divided into 11 themes, we review the research and draw pertinent conclusions. In the second section, we present suggestions for future research on drug abuse and crime. Appendix A provides a summary of many of the methodologic problems involved in the study of drug use and crime that guided our review of the research. Appendix B provides critical reviews of seven studies from which we have derived many of our conclusions.

CONCLUSIONS FROM THE EMPIRICAL RESEARCH ON DRUG USE AND CRIME

We have reviewed the studies indicated in Appendix B as well as other research bearing on drug abuse and crime and developed a set of themes to categorize the current state of knowledge. Each of these themes is discussed below.

Drug Use and Crime Rates Among Youths and Adults

After reviewing studies of individual crime rates conducted in the mid-1970s, Cohen (1978:229) concluded that, "clearly the most pressing research requirement for estimating the incapacitative effect is to provide adequate estimates of the individual crime rate (λ)." These estimates, she added, should account for variations in λ by crime type, across the criminal population, and during an individual career. This section provides information that shows how an offender's use of hard drugs influences his or her crime rate. Two primary points are stressed:

1. Among youthful and adult offenders, those who use hard drugs, especially if they are daily users, have higher crime rates than those who do not.
2. Studies of these active drug-using offenders that have measured self-reported criminal behavior have produced estimates of crime rates that far exceed estimates based on arrest or conviction records.

Studies of Youths

Information on the crime rates of drug-using youths comes primarily from studies based on data from Elliott and Huizinga's (1984) National Youth Survey (NYS). In assessing the value of such studies one must remember that serious criminal offenses are rare in the general population of youths and that analyses of the most deviant youths are necessarily based on a small number of subjects. Nevertheless, analyses of different types of offenders (e.g., those who limit themselves to minor offenses versus those who commit serious crimes) consistently show that use of serious "hard" drugs (primarily cocaine or heroin) is associated with higher rates of offending.

Johnson, Wish, and Huizinga (1983) used NYS data to assess how rates of juvenile crime change according to the level of drug use and offender type (see also Elliott and Huizinga, 1984). Johnson and colleagues grouped youths into five classes of drug use arranged hierarchically (virtually all users of more serious drugs had used the less serious drugs) in terms of the seriousness of drugs used nonexperimentally in the previous year: (1) no drug or alcohol use (N = 510); (2) alcohol only—used alcohol on four or more occasions (N = 558); (3) marijuana—used on four or more occasions (N = 301); (4) pills—used on three or more occasions (N = 99); (5) cocaine—used on three or more occasions (N = 71, 12 of whom were heroin users). Mean annual crime rates were then calculated for index offenses (rape, robbery, aggravated assault, burglary, larceny, and motor vehicle theft; homicide was excluded), minor offenses (thefts, assaults, vandalism), and drug sales. These findings appear in Table 1.

It is clear from Table 1 that the level of juvenile crime closely parallels the level of drug use. Both nonusers of drugs and alcohol and users of alcohol reported an average of only two or three crimes, most of them minor offenses, in the previous year. Youths who used marijuana had overall rates of crime that were three times higher than the rates for non-drug users or alcohol users. Youths who used pills but not cocaine, in turn, had higher crime rates than the users of marijuana or alcohol, particularly for index offenses and drug sales.

The highest crime rates were found for the youths who reported the use of cocaine. Their rates of index and minor offenses were two to three times those of the pill users, and they had a very high annual rate (48) of drug sales. Separating the youths into offender groups based on the seriousness and number of crimes committed showed that even within these relatively homogeneous groups, youths who used pills or cocaine had the highest crime rates. In fact, one-fourth of the cocaine users had committed three or more index offenses in the previous year. Youths who used cocaine and committed multiple index offenses constituted only 1.3 percent of all youths but accounted for 40 percent of the index crimes reported by the entire sample.

TABLE 1 Mean Annual Rates of Index Offenses, Minor Crimes, and Drug Sales in a National Sample of Youths by Level of Drug Use in the Prior Year (number of cases)

	Youths Who in the Prior Year Used—					
Mean Annual Rate	No Drugs/Alcohol (510)	Alcohol (558)	Marijuana (301)	Pills (99)	Cocaine[a]/Heroin (71)	Total (1,539)
Index offenses	—[b]	—[b]	1	3	9	1
Minor offenses	3	2	6	12	21	5
Drug sales	—[b]	—[b]	1	9	48	3
All offenses	3	2	8	24	78	9

NOTE: Some minor offenses (e.g., running away from home and skipping classes) have been excluded.

[a]Includes 12 who reported using heroin.
[b]Less than one crime per year.

SOURCE: Johnson, Wish, and Huizinga (1983).

Conclusion. These findings from a study of a national sample of youths offer strong support for the hypothesis that serious drug use (especially of cocaine) and criminal offenses tend to be found among the same youths. These findings are also consistent with other widely accepted studies showing that illicit drug use by youths tends to be accompanied by a variety of deviant attitudes and behaviors (Jessor and Jessor, 1977; Robins and Wish, 1977; Kandel, 1978).

Studies of Adults

A study of incarcerated persons in three states (Chaiken and Chaiken, 1982) found that violent predators, i.e., persons who reported committing robbery, assault, and drug dealing and who had very high crime rates, had extensive histories of drug use. Violent predators were more likely than others in the sample to have used hard drugs (including heroin) frequently as a juvenile and to have used drugs daily and in large amounts during the period studied (up to 2 years prior to the current incarceration). It is not clear from the data presented, however, whether drug use is a major factor in differentiating crime rates among offender groups. "Robber-dealers," who committed robbery and drug dealing but not assaults, had lower crime rates than the violent predators but similar drug-use histories (so far as one can tell, given that only significance levels are reported and not actual percentages) (Chaiken and Chaiken, 1982:Table 3.1). The robber-dealers had higher rates of participation for 15 of 19 juvenile and adult drug-use measures. Compared with other inmates, both violent predators and robber-dealers had higher rates of juvenile heroin addiction, use of other hard drugs as a juvenile, daily heroin use costing more than $50, daily barbiturate and amphetamine use (10 or more pills), and combined alcohol and amphetamine use. In the absence of more-detailed information, we have to conclude that the two groups, on the whole, had similar drug abuse histories and that the commission of assaults, not use of drugs, differentiates the two groups.

Further information on this issue is provided by a study (Chaiken, 1983) in which crime rates were computed for these same sample members according to their offender group and level of illicit pill or heroin use during the study period. Table 2 presents the minimum estimates of crime rates for selected nondrug crimes, computed by truncating each person's annual rate for any offense type at

365 (one per day). The findings of this study indicate that for each offender group high-cost heroin users had the highest crime rates. There was no monotonic relationship between drug use and rates of those crimes for other levels of drug use, but this may be because two important drug types (cocaine and marijuana) were not measured. Even the violent predators who did not report drug use had relatively high (156) crime rates, however. The findings indicate that habitual use of heroin does tend to be accompanied by high rates of nondrug crime, regardless of one's overall level or type of offending. On the other hand, the fact that violent predators who did not use drugs had high crime rates, even compared with some groups who were heavy daily heroin users, shows that serious heroin involvement is neither a necessary nor sufficient condition for high crime rates for nondrug crimes. (It should be noted, however, that the data presented in Table 2 omit the high rates of drug-dealing offenses among drug users. Annual rates of drug dealing were generally greater than 1,000 among the high-cost heroin users, and in the 200 to 800 range for the other groups).

Additional evidence for the link between hard-drug use and crime rates is found in a recent study of 201 opiate users in Harlem (Johnson et al., 1985). This study found that crime rates increased with the frequency of self-reported heroin use. Daily heroin users (persons who used heroin 6 or 7 days a week) averaged 1,400 crimes per year; persons who used heroin less than 3 days a week averaged about 500 crimes per year. Although this finding could be affected by respondent-measurement problems, the subjects were interviewed daily for 5 days and then weekly so the recall period was short. If robbery, burglary, shoplifting, and other larcenies are taken as the index crimes, daily heroin users in this study committed 137 such crimes per year, and less regular heroin users committed 47 per year. Other crimes, e.g., forgery, prostitution, pimping, con games, and miscellaneous nondrug crimes, were not related to level of heroin use among this group of users. The annual rates for drug-distribution crimes were much higher than for nondrug crimes, ranging from 245 (for irregular heroin users) to almost 900 (among daily heroin users).

This study (Johnson et al., 1985) also used the offender typology developed by Chaiken and Chaiken (1982) and found

TABLE 2 Annual Crime Rates for Robbery, Assault, Burglary, Theft, and Forgery-Fraud by Drug Use During the Measurement Period

	Drugs Used			
Variety of Offender	No Pills or Heroin[a]	Pills but No Heroin	Low-Cost Heroin Use	Heroin Use Over $50/Day
Violent predator (N)	156 (50)	254 (76)	134 (62)	326 (88)
Robber-dealer	33 (32)	112 (51)	156 (38)	194 (66)
Low-level robber	27 (158)	19 (24)	24 (26)	110 (23)
Burglar-dealer	63 (62)	76 (50)	127 (28)	184 (38)
Low-level burglar	17 (89)	11 (23)	5 (14)	78 (11)
Property-drug offender	67 (52)	6 (21)	104 (31)	204 (29)

NOTE: Measurement period was up to 2 years prior to current incarceration.

[a]Study did not ask about cocaine or marijuana use during this period. Some of these persons could have used these drugs.

SOURCE: Chaiken (1983).

that crime rates were generally high, controlling for offender type, for daily heroin users. These analyses, one should note, did not control for age or other factors that could have affected the crime rates in each group. Table 3 presents the mean annual offense rates, their standard deviations, and the skewness for four offenses, for the 22 robber-dealers in the sample. (Robber-dealers were persons who committed both robbery and drug dealing on 2 percent or more of their days on the street.) The offense-specific crime rates in Table 3 vary considerably. Burglary is a good example because the group was not defined on the basis of burglary rates. Although these 22 robber-dealers, as a whole, had an annual crime rate for burglary of 35.8, 6 of them committed no burglaries, and another 4 committed more than 75. Thus, in computing and analyzing annual crime rates, one must pay special attention to the large variability that can be found even in a somewhat homogeneous group of drug-using offenders.

Some of the variability in individual offense rates may be explained by the finding that persons may have alternating periods of heavy and lesser drug use. One study reported high criminality during runs of narcotics use; when narcotics use declined so did crime rates (McGlothlin, Anglin, and Wilson, 1977). Another study reported that addicts were six times more criminally active during periods of heavy narcotics use than during periods of lesser use (Ball et al., 1981). Both of these studies offer further evidence of a link between heavy narcotics use and higher crime rates.

A study of addicts known to the police in Baltimore (Ball et al., 1981; Ball, Shaffer, and Nurco, 1983) has received considerable public attention because of findings that show the magnitude of the increases in crime rates on days that persons used narcotics heavily, compared with days of less frequent use. The findings of this study are consistent with studies reviewed above that document an increase in crime with increased narcotics use. However, because of problems of ambiguity in the interview questions that measured the frequency of criminal activity (noted in Appendix B), the exact estimates of the increase in criminal behavior should not be used as the basis for policy decisions until this study has been replicated in other sites.

Another study (Wish, Klumpp, et al., 1980; Wish, 1982) analyzed a 6-year recidivism file for 7,087 persons arrested in the District of Columbia. Arrestees detected by urinalysis to be drug users (primarily morphine or phenmetrazine) at any arrest during the period had an average of 4.9 arrests during the 6 years, compared with an average of 2.7 arrests for persons not detected to be drug users. This result could have been observed because persons with multiple arrests probably had more urine tests during the period and thus a greater opportunity to

TABLE 3 Mean Annual Crime Rates Among 22 Robber-Dealers

Offense	Mean Annual Crime Rate	Standard Deviation	Skewness	Range
Robbery	31.3	34.9	2.6	8–155
Burglary	35.8	50.4	2.3	0–212
Shoplifting	48.1	51.1	.9	0–144
Other larcenies	30.2	35.3	1.2	0–122

SOURCE: Johnson et al. (1985).

have a positive specimen and to be classified as a drug user. The researchers continued to find an association between the number of arrests and being a drug user, however, when they controlled for the number of urine test results available for each person. In a related analysis, persons found at an initial arrest to have a positive urine test had rates of multiple rearrest in a 4-year follow-up period that were significantly higher than those found for nonusers, after controlling for age and prior record (Forst and Wish, 1983).

Similar findings were also reported in a study of male arrestees in Manhattan (Wish, Brady, and Cuadrado, 1985). Arrestees with a urine specimen that was positive in tests for any of four drugs (opiates, cocaine, PCP, or methadone; N = 2,647) at the index arrest had an average of 3.5 arrests in a 3-year period, most of which occurred after the index arrest, compared with an average of 1.9 arrests for persons with drug-negative urine at the index arrest (N = 2,089). This higher number of arrests was found among drug-positive arrestees of all ages. In addition, the number of arrests was related to the number of drugs found in a specimen. Arrestees with two or more drugs in their urine (N = 1,081) had an average of 4.6 arrests, compared with an average of 2.8 arrests for persons with one drug (N = 1,566). Thus, arrestees who had recently used multiple hard drugs (usually cocaine and heroin) had the highest number of arrests. Other studies of drug users (Voss, 1976; Inciardi, 1979, 1984; Clayton and Voss, 1981; Collins and Allison, 1983; Johnson et al., 1985) and of the association between the price of heroin and levels of property crimes in the community (Silverman and Spruill, 1977) provide evidence for a link between heroin and cocaine use and criminal activity.

Conclusion. Studies that vary dramatically in the locales and populations sampled, in the measures of crime and drug use, and in the cutting points and classifications of offenders and drug users have consistently found a strong association between the level of cocaine or heroin use and criminal behavior. Among the general population of youths and among adult offenders, users of these drugs have high rates of drug-distribution crimes and serious nondrug crimes, especially those that generate income. Daily users of these drugs tend to have the highest crime rates.

Demonstrating a link between serious drug use and crime is much easier than estimating the actual amount of crime committed by drug abusers, however. Large estimates of the amount of crime attributable to heroin users have been challenged by some as impossible and "mythical" (Singer, 1971; Reuter, 1984).

Diversity of Crimes Among Drug Users

As indicated above, recent research has demonstrated that some offenders who use hard drugs, like the violent predators, may have rates of violent crimes against persons that equal or exceed those found among offenders not using drugs. The analysis of the rates of arrest over a 6-year period for a sample of 7,087 arrestees (Wish, 1982), noted above, found that persons with a positive urinalysis test (at the time of at least one of their arrests) had rates of arrest for bail violations, larceny, robbery, burglary, and drug offenses that were two to three times higher than the rates for persons not detected to be using hard drugs. Drug users' rates of arrest for all other crimes were similar to those found for the nonusers.

Analyses of consecutive arrests among drug users and nonusers from the same study showed a tendency for drug users to be rearrested for property crimes. A sample of all persons who had an arrest in an 8-month panel period were selected for this analysis and all of their rearrests in the following 4 years were tracked. Each of 2,442 arrestees was classified as being drug positive (D+) by urinalysis at the initial arrest or drug negative (D−). The index arrest and the next arrest were classified according to six types of offenses: violent, robbery, property, victimless, drug, and other. The results showed that for D− arrestees the next arrest was most likely to be for the same type of crime as the index arrest. Drug-negative arrestees initially charged with a drug offense were an exception and were more likely to be rearrested for a property crime. All D+ arrestees, however, were more likely to be charged with a property crime at rearrest than any other crime type, regardless of what the charge was at the initial arrest (Wish, Klumpp, et al., 1980:VII-22).

Ethnographic research of indigent drug users in New York shows that the ordinary, high-rate offender may switch from one crime type to another from one day to the next and even on the same day. For example, a person may commit a theft one day, a burglary the next day, several drug sales the next day, and no crimes the next day (Johnson et al., 1985). Other studies of active street hustlers in Harlem have also suggested such a diverse pattern of offending (Strug, Stevie, et al., 1984; Strug, Wish, et al., 1984).

Although ethnographic studies of nonrandom samples of offenders provide findings with unknown representativeness of other offenders, such studies do yield valuable insights into the link between drug use and crime. For example, one of the reasons behind the variety and number of crimes that drug users report may be the rather modest amounts of money they earn from their crimes. Johnson et al. (1985) report that the average nondrug crime committed by the respondents they studied netted the offender only $35 in cash; even the most lucrative nondrug crimes (burglary and robbery) netted an average of only about $80. Estimates of the annual criminal income from both drug and nondrug crimes ranged from $6,000 to $18,000.

Conclusion

Offenders with expensive drug habits clearly commit high rates of income-generating crimes, such as larceny, burglary, and robbery, in addition to high rates of drug-distribution crimes. Evidence from ethnographic studies of indigent street users in New York indicates that these persons earn small amounts of money and, thus, commit numerous crimes to finance their drug use.

Drug Use and Violent Crimes

If one considers robbery to be a violent crime, there is little doubt that drug users commit many violent crimes. However, there has been some controversy in the literature regarding whether drug users commit crimes specifically designed to harm persons (Wish, 1982). Studies of the arrest charges for heroin-using versus nonusing arrestees have uniformly found that the heroin-using arrestees had higher proportions of arrests for property crime and lower proportions of arrests for violent crimes against persons (Kozel and DuPont, 1977). Similarly, inmates with a history of narcotic addiction were only one-third as likely to be serving a sentence for violent crime as were nonusers (Barton, 1976).

In reviewing this topic, McGlothlin (1979:361) cautioned against jumping to the conclusion that such results necessarily mean that heroin users do not commit violent crimes:

> These findings have been loosely interpreted to conclude that narcotic addicts are less likely to commit crimes against persons than are

nonaddict criminals. Actually, the data do not warrant conclusions about the absolute frequency of crimes by the two groups. Addicts exhibit an especially high recidivism rate, and the possibility that they commit many more property crimes, and some more violent crimes, than nonaddict criminals is not inconsistent with the above results.

In recent years the wisdom of this observation has become clear. Analyses of a recidivism file for 7,087 arrestees in the District of Columbia indicated that the percentage of arrest charges for violent crimes against persons for drug users (positive urine test) was lower than that for nonusers (Wish, 1982). However, the rates of arrest for violent crimes for drug-using and nonusing arrestees were equivalent for assaults, sexual assault, and homicide. Rates of arrest among drug users for weapons offenses were higher than those for nonusers. And a study of incarcerated persons (Chaiken and Chaiken, 1982; Chaiken, 1983) found that many of the violent predators, the group defined by drug dealing, assault, and robbery, were heroin users, many of whom had expensive habits.

Drug-using offenders, especially those involved in drug-distribution activities, may be especially prone to commit crimes against persons. Several jurisdictions have recently issued statistics that indicate that between 20 and 30 percent of their homicide cases appear to be "drug related," that is, the victims or perpetrators were either drug users or dealers (Goldstein, 1985; Heffernan, Martin, and Romano, 1982; McBride, 1983). And toxicologic studies of homicide victims in New York have shown a high prevalence of alcohol and drug use by the decedents (Haberman and Baden, 1978).

A rationale for the prevalence of violence among drug abusers has been suggested in terms of a "systemic model" (Goldstein, 1985). This model holds that the drug-distribution system relies mainly on violence and its threat to maintain "order" and to control the sale of these valued, but illegal, substances. A variety of expectations of violence have been developed by higher level dealers to keep lower level distributors "in line." And lower level users-dealers see drug distributors as prime candidates to "rip off" (rob or burglarize). Distributors who have been victimized rarely report such crimes to the police; they settle the matter themselves.

Conclusion

Users of heroin have, in the past, been considered to be unlikely to commit violent crimes against persons. Recent studies suggest that hard-drug users commit violent crimes at least as often as nonusing offenders. The pervasive violence in the drug-distribution system may even increase the likelihood of drug users' becoming perpetrators or victims of violent crimes. More research is needed to clarify the hypothesized link between violent crimes and drug-distribution activities.

Drug-Distribution Activities and the Measurement of Crime Rates

There are a number of reasons for separating drug-related crimes (e.g., possession or sale) from the computation of rates of crime. Drug users, by definition, committed drug-related crimes. However, drug-distribution activities are so much a part of the daily lives of drug-involved offenders that to ignore these activities is to underestimate their crime rates seriously.

Virtually all studies of high-risk populations have found that the rates of drug selling exceed those of any other offense type, especially for users of cocaine or heroin. Chaiken and Chaiken (1982) found that their subjects reported between 90 and 160 drug sales per year. Even among persons who were not daily heroin users, the number of drug sales (about 100) exceeded the number of thefts by a factor of two to five. Drug users in Miami reported two to three drug sales for every theft that they committed (Inciardi, 1979). And others have found that approximately 10 percent of American youths sell drugs in any given year, and a few do so more than 50 times per year (Single and Kandel, 1978; Clayton and Voss, 1981; Johnston, Bachman, and O'Malley, 1982; Elliott et al., 1983). Daily heroin users in East Harlem reported committing an average of 1,000 drug-distribution crimes per person per year (Johnson et al., 1985).

Conclusion

Drug-distribution activities must be taken into consideration when measuring the rates of crime among drug users. These crimes are among the most common committed by drug users, and policies of selective incapacitation or treatment of drug users may have their greatest impact on these crimes.

Onset of Drug Use and Crime: Does It Matter Which Occurred First?

The onset of drug use and crime has been given considerable attention in the research literature. There is often an implicit assumption that knowing when in the life cycle and in what order the two types of behavior first occur may help to resolve two issues: (1) how to intervene in and prevent these behaviors and (2) whether the onset of drug use changes a person's level (or type) of criminal behavior.

Persons who begin to use drugs or alcohol at an early age have a greater likelihood of having problems with substance abuse and alcoholism as adults. The evidence is less definitive on the issue of whether drug use precedes or follows onset of criminal behavior, and it appears that this relationship may depend on the availability of the drug and the conventional age at which its use is initiated.

The typical addict studied before 1950 did not have a prior criminal background (Greenberg and Adler, 1974). These persons, predominantly rural, white southerners, became addicted in their middle twenties, usually as a result of using prescribed drugs. Around 1950 a shift occurred in the type of persons who became heroin addicts. Addicts were now urban blacks and Spanish-speaking males who voluntarily used heroin and who had a history of criminality prior to the beginning of addiction in their teenage years (DuPont and Kozel, 1976). The weight of the evidence seems to support the conclusion that currently most (not all) users of heroin and other hard drugs who eventually come to treatment programs or who are apprehended by the police have deviant or criminal backgrounds that preceded their addiction. Heavy use of heroin and injection of heroin and cocaine tend to begin in the late teens or the early twenties (Inciardi, 1981; Clayton and Voss, 1981). Once addicted, these persons become more involved in drug-distribution activities and other income-generating crimes (McGlothlin, 1979).

Heroin use and, to a lesser degree, cocaine use have a bad reputation in American society, and there is considerable self-selection involved in the use of these drugs. Persons who are deviant in childhood are more likely to use these drugs, and consequently, it is difficult to determine how many crimes committed by users are the result of an underlying disposition toward deviance and criminal behavior. This is a major problem in assessing the *causal* role of drug use in criminal behavior. After considering these issues, Robins (1979:328) concluded,

> Thus, while it is true that the kinds of people who use heroin are also likely to commit crimes, and that committing crimes makes

them especially likely to come to public attention as addicts, the fact that the number of property crimes does seem to fluctuate with the use of heroin makes it highly probable that addiction does directly increase the frequency of theft and other crimes designed to provide money for drugs.

Since Robins's review, a number of studies (Ball et al., 1981; Goldstein, 1981, 1983; Wish, Klumpp, et al., 1981; Chaiken and Chaiken, 1982; Ball, Shaffer, and Nurco, 1983; Chaiken, 1983; Johnson et al., 1985), many of which we have reviewed in this report, have shown the huge repertoire of deviant behaviors in which hard-drug users are involved.

Conclusion

Untangling the causal nexus between drug use and crime is, perhaps, an impossible and unproductive enterprise. Researchers examining this question using information from the National Youth Survey concluded, "the concern over the temporal sequences of these two problems in an effort to determine causal priority is misdirected. If they have a common etiology, either may precede the other with no causal implications" (Elliott and Huizinga, 1984:96). It appears that heavy use of hard drugs is an excellent indicator of persons who have high rates of criminal behavior. Whether they began using drugs before or after they committed their first nondrug crime is probably a function of opportunity and other societal factors. Of more practical consequence is the question of how one might intervene in the process of developing deviant behavior at an early age.

Drug Use Among Arrestees

Studies using urine tests to identify recent drug use provide some indication of the prevalence and development of drug use in offender populations. A study of 57,000 persons arrested in the District of Columbia (Wish, Klumpp, et al., 1980) found that in each of the 5 years from 1973 through 1977 the likelihood of a positive urine test for hard drugs (usually morphine) was low for arrestees below age 20 and peaked for those in their thirties. However, recent research has indicated that the types of urine tests used at that time in the District of Columbia were largely ineffective in detecting cocaine (Wish, Strug, et al., 1983), a drug commonly found among young arrestees.

A study of 110 persons arrested for selling drugs in Harlem (Wish, Anderson, et al., 1984) also found that younger arrestees are unlikely to have test results that are positive for opiates. Urine tests revealed opiate use for 22 percent of the persons aged 18 to 20 and for 33 percent of the persons aged 21 to 25, compared with rates above 55 percent for persons 26 or older. However, cocaine was detected in arrestees of all ages. Injection of cocaine was rare among young arrestees who reported using the drug. Only 15 percent of the cocaine users under 25 who had used cocaine in the 48 hours prior to arrest (N = 42) had injected the drug, compared with 60 percent of persons aged 26 to 30 and 88 percent of those aged 31 to 35.

These age-related trends based on a sample of drug dealers arrested in Harlem were also observed in a study of serious offenders arrested throughout Manhattan (Wish, Brady, et al., 1984). The sample consisted of more than 6,000 men arrested for serious offenses (approximately two-thirds were charged with felony offenses; 20 percent were charged with sale or possession of drugs) and processed in the Manhattan central booking facility between March and October 1984. As one would expect, the prevalence of positive urine tests and self-reported drug use was lower among this population of persons arrested for a variety of offenses than among the drug dealers in Harlem.

Response rates were high in the study (Wish, Brady, et al., 1984). Ninety-five percent of the persons approached agreed to be interviewed about their drug use and treatment histories, and 80 percent of the respondents provided a urine specimen for analysis. The percentage of arrestees at each age level who had a urine test positive for any of four drugs (cocaine, opiates, methadone, and PCP) is shown below:

Age of Arrestee (N)	Percent Drug-Positive
16 (185)	34
17 (179)	36
18 (203)	49
19 (224)	50
20 (254)	47
21 (248)	59
22 (262)	63
23 (238)	63
24 (241)	54
25 (213)	65
26–30 (1,005)	64
31–35 (653)	64
36+ (915)	48

The likelihood of a positive urine test tended to increase with the age of the arrestee, through age 35. A large decline in the rate of positive tests occurred for offenders over age 35.

The age of the arrestee was also related to the type of drug detected. At all age levels, cocaine was the drug most likely to be detected. However, for persons below age 21, opiates and methadone were rarely detected. Between the ages of 16 and 25, PCP was detected at about a uniform rate (mainly between 16 and 25 percent); few arrestees above the age of 25 (12 percent or less) had tests positive for PCP, however. The probability of detecting multiple drugs in the urine increased with age. Between 7 and 10 percent of the arrestees under age 21 had two or more drugs in their urine, compared with between 17 and 32 percent of older arrestees. Arrestees who were between the ages of 25 and 35 had the most drugs in their urine. One-half of their specimens contained cocaine, 30 percent contained opiates, 10 percent methadone, and 10 percent PCP.

The fact that arrestees under age 20 were unlikely to have tests positive for methadone and opiates and were less likely to have multiple drugs in their urine suggests that these persons had less severe drug problems than older arrestees. Information from their interviews indicated that these younger arrestees were less likely to report current dependence on drugs or the need for treatment than were older arrestees. In addition, these youthful users of cocaine were more likely to report that they snorted the drug than older arrestees, who tended to inject cocaine, often with heroin.

The generalizability of these two studies of arrestees in New York City to arrestees in other cities is unknown. Parallel findings are emerging, however, from a comparable ongoing study of urine testing of arrestees in Washington, D.C. (Toborg, 1984). In both sites approximately 56 percent of all tested arrestees have a urine test positive for drugs. The prevalence of tests positive for opiates in the two cities is the same, approximately 20 percent. However, the prevalence of cocaine in Washington is about one-half the prevalence in New York (42 percent), and the prevalence of PCP is more than twice as great in Washington. Thus, the overall level of drug involvement among arrestees in the two cities is the same, although the preferred drugs appear to differ.

Given the caveat regarding their generalizability, these findings raise some interesting points. First, it appears that by the time persons are eligible for arrest as an adult (16 in some jurisdictions, 18 in others), there is almost a 50 percent chance that the person is already using an illicit drug, for example, cocaine or PCP. (These urine test results should probably be considered conservative estimates of drug use, given that many drug-using arrestees probably did not use a drug close enough to the time of arrest to provide a specimen capable of revealing it. The tests can generally detect opiate and cocaine use within 24 to 48 hours and PCP use within five days.) In addition, involvement with serious drugs may be a developmental process, beginning with snorting of drugs, followed by injection of one or more drugs. It is not possible to tell whether the differences in drug use and detection for arrestees at different ages are the result of differences in cohorts or of true developmental stages. The self-report information on the age of initiation of these behaviors among the entire sample can be used to examine this question.

Finally, the findings indicate a decrease in recent drug use by arrestees over the age of 35. Although the idea that persons may mature out of drug addiction has been suggested (Winick, 1962), it is also possible that this decrease in drug users in the population of arrestees could be the result of such things as drug users' avoidance of arrest, imprisonment or institutionalization, death, abstention from drugs, or alcoholism or some other illness. We are aware of no studies of offender populations that indicate which of these factors are pertinent.

Conclusion

Current studies of drug use in two large eastern cities show that a little more than 50 percent of arrestee populations gave evidence of recent illicit drug use. The order of the prevalence of drugs in the two cities differed, however. There was some evidence from two studies that arrestees under age 21 were less involved with opiates and cocaine use by injection than older arrestees. A decrease in the prevalence of recent drug use among arrestees over age 35 raises important questions regarding the ultimate course of serious drug use among offender populations.

Marijuana and Crime—A Weak Link

Research on the relationship between marijuana use and crime has generally found little evidence that the drug induces any type of criminal behavior other than, possibly, selling the drug. Youths have reported that marijuana use reduces their inclination toward violent behavior (Tinklenberg, Roth, et al., 1976; Tinklenberg, Murphy, et al., 1981). And other research has shown that marijuana use takes place as part of an unfolding development of other problems and nonconforming behaviors. In his review of the correlates of marijuana use Jessor (1979: 348) endorses the view that "delinquency and marijuana use are manifestations of the same phenomena—involvement in deviance or problem behavior—and are associated with each other by virtue of a common relationship to social, psychological, and economic etiological variables."

One of the difficulties in assessing the role of marijuana use in crime is that use of other drugs often follows shortly (Kandel, 1984). Studies have shown that marijuana is a "gateway drug"—it opens one up to the use of other drugs (Johnson, 1973; Robins and Wish, 1977; O'Donnell and Clayton, 1981). To be sure, only some marijuana users go on to use harder drugs, but the risk certainly increases with involvement with marijuana. A current study of clients classified by treatment programs as having marijuana as the primary drug of abuse found that, with few exceptions, those persons were using a variety of other drugs, including PCP and cocaine (Kleinman et al., 1984). Because most daily marijuana users also use other drugs, heavy marijuana use and multiple drug use are confounded, and attempts to isolate the impact of marijuana use are next to impossible.

Conclusion

The role of daily marijuana use in serious crime is badly confounded by the use of more serious drugs. Marijuana use may provide an introduction to the illicit drug market and to the use of drugs, such as heroin and cocaine, that have a more direct role in both drug-related and nondrug crime.

PCP and Violent Crime—A Stronger Link

Attempts to measure the prevalence of the use and impact of PCP are hampered by the fact that the substance is often distributed under a variety of names and misrepresented as other drugs. Because marijuana is sometimes laced with PCP, persons may be unaware that they have consumed the latter. Previously, PCP's chief use was in veterinary medicine as an anesthetizing agent, although it was originally synthesized for use with humans (Peterson and Stillman, 1978). It can be taken orally, smoked, snorted, or injected. Phencyclidine is often classified as a hallucinogen, although, because of its diverse actions, there is some disagreement as to how to classify it. Small doses of PCP lead to a drunken state, and larger doses can produce anesthesia, convulsions, and a psychotic-like state.

The available literature on PCP use and crime is sparse and consists mainly of case studies of persons who have committed violent, often bizarre acts (Siegel, 1978, 1980; Fauman and Fauman, 1982). Death from drowning, often in small amounts of water, has been a frequent cause of PCP-related death in California and the media's emphasis on such events helps to give PCP a bad reputation.

Phencyclidine is easily synthesized and inexpensive. One would therefore not expect to find the increases in income-generating crimes with the use of PCP that are found among users of expensive drugs. The potential link between PCP use and violent crimes against persons is based on the idea that some persons become so disoriented when using the drug that they commit acts for which they are not responsible. These assumptions are reflected in the debate regarding the viability of the legal defense of diminished capacity for crimes committed during PCP intoxication (Baxley, 1980). It has been argued that persons who have committed violent crimes while under the influence of PCP are not legally responsible for their acts because they have an inability to have criminal intent. Siegel (1978:285) has concluded,

> The PCP-intoxicated user's orientation toward the immediate present and disregard for long range consequences of his/her behavior would make it difficult for him/her to premeditate criminal acts. But the tendency to react strongly to sensory stimuli in the immediate environment, the inclination to refer everything to oneself that often develops into paranoia, and the need to do something due to intense psychomotor stimulation can all produce an aggression-prone individual. Once again it must be emphasized that emotionally stable people under the influence of low doses of PCP probably will not act in a way very differently from their normal behavior.

Epidemiologic evidence of the percentage of all PCP users who become intoxicated with the drug and commit violent acts is not available. As the statement above implies, one would suspect that only a small minority of PCP users ever reach such a stage. In ongoing studies PCP is the drug that is most likely to be detected in the urine of arrestees in Washington, D.C.—found in 30 percent of male and female arrestees (Toborg,

1984), but it is less prevalent in the urine of arrestees in New York City—12 percent of male arrestees (Wish, 1986). If only 1 percent of these PCP-using arrestees in Washington and New York exhibited the bizarre, violent behavior attributed to PCP-intoxicated persons, our institutions would be overwhelmed with them.

One study of drug use and violence among 112 boys committed to a training school (the average age was 15) did find a strong relationship between PCP abuse and offenses against persons (Simonds and Kashani, 1980). A psychiatrist interviewed each youth and rated each one's abuse of 13 types of drugs. The number of prior offenses against persons (e.g., rape, assault, robbery) and of property offenses was obtained from juvenile records. Abusers of PCP had a greater number of offenses against persons (mean = 15.3 offenses) than abusers of any other drugs. Abusers of barbiturates had the second highest number (mean = 10.0), followed by abusers of amphetamines (mean = 5.2). The level of PCP use was not significantly related to rates of property offenses. Because many of the boys abused multiple drugs and only 17 percent of the offenses against persons were preceded by use of a drug within the prior 24 hours, it was not possible to attribute the violent offenses to the use of any of the drugs.

Conclusion

PCP is used by persons who tend to be multiple drug users. It is one of the more common drugs used by arrestees, although its prevalence varies considerably by jurisdiction. An unknown, but probably very small percentage of users suffer extreme PCP-induced intoxication and disorientation and commit bizarre, often violent acts. Much more research is needed to identify the extent of these problems in users, and to learn how personality, other drug use, and the quality and quantity of PCP ingested contribute to the occurrence of violent behavior.

The Role of Hard-Drug Use in Crime

Despite the strong link between drug use and crime documented in the previous sections of this paper, there is a dearth of literature examining the specific nature of that link. At best, some surveys have asked persons to recall whether they were under the influence of drugs or alcohol at the time they committed a crime. Examples of questions that have not been addressed are: Were you high or experiencing withdrawal symptoms during the crime? When and which substances were taken, and with whom? How did the drug affect the crime? What drugs were taken after the crime, and how soon? The absence of such information may be due to the fact that obtaining such event-specific details requires that persons be interviewed as soon after committing a crime as is possible. Much of the discussion in this section is about recent studies that have used this approach. We look, first, at when the drug use occurs, and then the role of the drugs in the crime.

According to a survey sponsored by the Bureau of Justice Statistics (1983a,b) of 274,564 prisoners in state correctional facilities in 1979, 33 percent reported being under the influence of an illicit drug (includes 8 percent who used marijuana only) at the time they committed the crime for which they were incarcerated. Other studies have asked youths about the commission of delinquent acts and the role of drugs that were used—e.g., Elliott and Huizinga's (1984) National Youth Survey and Tinklenberg and colleagues' study of youths in California (see Tinklenberg and Ochberg, 1981; Tinklenberg, Murphy, et al., 1981). However, because use of hard drugs (cocaine and heroin) and commission of serious crimes are rare in persons under age 18, surveys of the general population can contribute little to an understanding of how often drug use is concurrent with the commission of a crime. To gain information on this topic, one must look at samples of high-risk youths or persons who have had some contact with the criminal justice system. One such study found that juveniles admitted to a training school reported taking drugs, primarily alcohol and marijuana, to give them courage for committing violent crimes (Simonds and Kashani, 1980).

Studies that have tested urine specimens from arrestees in New York City and in Washington, D.C., as noted above, have found that a little more than one-half of all arrestees had recently used an illicit drug (Toborg, 1984; Wish, Brady, et al., 1984). A study of 116 arrestees charged with the possession or sale of illicit drugs found even higher rates of recent drug use (Wish, Anderson, et al., 1984). Eighty percent of the persons interviewed within 1 to 4 hours of arrest had urine specimens that were positive for hard drugs, usually heroin or cocaine, which indicates that the drugs were probably used within the past 24 to 48 hours. There was no indication in either of these studies whether the drug use played a role in the instant arrest.

A number of studies of the role of drug and alcohol use in the crime event have been undertaken by staff at the Interdisciplinary Research Center (IRC) in New York City. These studies used ethnographic techniques to recruit persons in East Harlem who had recently committed a nondrug crime. These studies of unapprehended persons can provide some insight into why and when active criminals take drugs. However, since persons were selected for study with an unknown probability of selection, the generalizability of the findings is unknown.

An IRC study of 59 unapprehended street criminals found that alcohol was frequently taken in large quantities before a crime, often to facilitate the crime by calming nervousness (Strug, Wish, et al., 1984). Cocaine and heroin were also taken for these reasons. These 59 persons reported committing 103 nondrug crimes in the 36 hours prior to their interviews. Theft, robbery, shoplifting, and burglary were the most common crimes. Alcohol was found to be the drug most likely to be used at the time of the crime (in 37 percent of the 103 crimes), and respondents reported that alcohol actually helped them to perform their crimes. Most of these persons had no cocaine or heroin to take before the crime and used their criminal income to purchase drugs and alcohol shortly after the crime.

Conclusion

The evidence is scanty regarding the exact timing of drug use and crime. Information from urine-testing programs tells us only that about one-half of arrestees in two eastern cities had used a drug sometime near the arrest. Whether other cities have this degree of drug use among arrestees is unknown. Findings from studies of active criminal drug users do indicate that alcohol and other drugs may be used to prepare for a crime and are almost surely used after the crime, if money has been obtained. The generalizability of these findings to other offenders is unknown, pending replication of the studies in other sites.

Interventions for Reducing Drug Use and Crime

There is a considerable body of literature on the efficacy of drug abuse treatment programs for reducing clients' crime rates (Sells et al., 1976; Gandossy et al., 1980; Collins, Hubbard, and Rachal, 1985; Collins, Rachal, et al., 1982a,b; Collins and Allison, 1983). To review this literature would be beyond the scope of this paper. However, whether treatment appears to reduce drug abuse and crime has implications for policies that involve involuntary detention for treatment.

By far, the best-designed and best-executed study of a treatment population is the evaluation of the California Civil Addict Program for persons convicted of certain crimes or recommended for treatment by the district attorney (McGlothlin, Anglin, and Wilson, 1977; Anglin and McGlothlin, 1984). Until 1970, this program consisted of a 6-month inpatient period, followed by a 3-year, outpatient drug-treatment period. Inpatient treatments included group therapy, a modified therapeutic-community approach, and educational and vocational training. The outpatient treatments included supervision by a parole agent, weekly counseling, and drug surveillance through urinalysis or naline, an antinarcotic that brings on withdrawal symptoms if the person has been using opiates. If a parolee's whereabouts were unknown for 72 hours, the parole officer issued a warrant for the person's arrest and return to inpatient treatment. In 1970 the inpatient program was eliminated, outpatient treatment was reduced to 2 years, and a methadone outpatient component was instituted.

Using self-report measures and arrest records, it was found that, compared with a group of persons who were released from the program early because of a statutory change, persons who participated in the outpatient program that included strict supervision had a significant reduction in narcotics use while they were in the program. In addition, both self-reports and arrest records confirmed a drop in nondrug criminal activity during this period. Interventions that included supervision with urine testing resulted in lower rates of daily narcotics use, drug dealing, and other criminal activity, and higher rates of employment than did supervision-without-testing or no-supervision statuses. The study concluded that the outpatient program with heavy supervision of parolees was effective because it reduced, not eliminated, the person's daily runs of narcotics use. The report (McGlothlin, Anglin, and Wilson, 1977: 71) states that "a policy of containment aimed at limiting the extremes of narcotic usage and its associated criminal behavior can be successful in minimizing the social costs of addiction, although perhaps not achieving the traditional goal of abstinence."

Because the use of methadone to treat addicts became popular in California during the study period, it was possible to analyze its impact on study members. While almost half the persons used narcotics daily when not receiving methadone, only 6 percent used narcotics daily when they were receiving methadone. A reduction in criminal behavior from 42 to 14 percent was also found for those receiving methadone. Improvement in employment was less marked, and alcohol use was slightly greater while on methadone.

While McGlothlin and colleagues found that methadone-treated clients did as well as those who received the supervision-with-testing treatment, another rigorous study reported less favorable results. For addicts receiving methadone treatment, Lukoff (1974, 1976) reported a great reduction in drug crimes but not in nondrug crimes. Lukoff concluded that more time in treatment was needed to bring about the profound changes in lifestyles and habits needed to produce large reductions in criminal behavior. Another study (Hunt, Lipton, and Spunt, 1984) found that methadone clients committed fewer serious crimes in treatment than did narcotics addicts not in treatment. It may be that differences in types of clients and programs were partially a factor in the different outcomes reported by these studies. As we note in the next section, more research is needed to determine which interventions are effective with particular types of offenders.

Using data from a large study (Treatment Outcomes Prospective Study) of persons entering federally funded treatment programs in 1979 and 1980, another study (Collins and Allison, 1983) also found that the use of legal pressure to induce entry into a treatment program may have beneficial impact on addicts. Collins and Allison studied arrestees who were diverted through the Treatment Alternatives to Street Crime (TASC) program to outpatient drug-free programs and residential treatment programs. Their findings indicate a statistically significant increase in retention in treatment for persons who were referred to treatment by the criminal justice system as opposed to other means. Because legal pressure had a greater impact than other referral methods on persons entering a residential treatment program and because TASC referrals stayed longer than non-TASC criminal justice referrals in outpatient drug-free programs, Collins and Allison (1983:1148) conclude that the findings are consistent with the interpretation that "legal pressure is most effective when accompanied by monitoring or surveillance of clients' behavior."

Conclusion

The studies reviewed indicate that offenders apprehended by the criminal justice system may be helped if they are mandated to participate in treatment that is accompanied by strict supervision and drug surveillance over prolonged periods. More research is needed, however, to determine the types of interventions that work best with particular types of offenders and with persons at arrest, probation, and parole stages.

Identifying High-Rate Drug Users

To intervene with drug-using offenders, it is necessary to identify them. Although self-report information on prior drug use has been shown to be valid in research studies, it is unlikely that arrestees would disclose such self-incriminating information if it were to be used in making decisions regarding their cases. Prior research (Wish, Klumpp, et al., 1980) has underscored the fact that one cannot readily identify drug use by arrestees through self-report in a cell-block interview or by type of arrest charge. In an analysis of 17,000 arrest cases from 1973 and 1974 Wish and colleagues found that only 10 percent of the arrestees who were positive for hard drugs by urinalysis were charged with a drug offense. Other analyses indicated that 50 percent or fewer of the arrestees who were positive by urine test admitted in a cell-block interview that they used hard drugs.

A study of arrestees in Manhattan (Wish, Brady, et al., 1984) has confirmed the findings that compared with their urinalysis results, arrestees greatly underreport their use of PCP, cocaine, and opiates during the 24 to 48 hours prior to arrest. This underreporting occurred despite the fact that the arrestees were told that the research interview was voluntary and anonymous, that it would not affect their cases, and that all information was protected from subpoena and use in civil and criminal proceedings by a Federal Certificate of Confidentiality. When comparable offenders were interviewed in a storefront in East Harlem, the concordance between self-reports and urinalysis results ranged between 70 and 80 percent

(Wish, Strug, et al., 1983; Wish, Brady, and Cuadrado, 1985), and most discrepancies still resulted from underreporting of the drugs that were detected in the specimens.

In another study (Wish, Anderson, et al., 1984) in New York City 116 persons arrested in Harlem, primarily for possession or sale of hard drugs, were interviewed within 2 to 4 hours of arrest and a urine specimen was obtained. The interview information and the urinalysis results indicated considerable drug use and other problems. Almost one-half (46 percent) claimed to have been physically dependent on heroin at one time in their lives. One-quarter reported that they were currently dependent on the drug, and one-third claimed that they needed drug abuse treatment at the time of arrest. The urine tests indicated that almost 80 percent of these persons were using drugs, mainly cocaine and heroin.

Fifty-four of the persons whose cases had been disposed by the time of the analysis had pled guilty, and of the 30 sentenced to some jail time, 76 percent were released immediately for time served or given a sentence of 29 days or less. On release, 43 of the respondents appeared at the research storefront in Harlem to be interviewed in greater detail. (Respondents were paid for their initial interview and urine specimen if they contacted the research staff after release. At that time they were asked to participate in a longer interview and to provide a second specimen.) Compared with the persons who were not reinterviewed, reinterviewees were older and more likely to report that they currently needed treatment for drug or alcohol use (64 versus 27 percent). The educational and ethnic backgrounds of the two groups were the same, as were their reports of daily drug use within the past month.

The follow-up interviews and the urine specimens at the second interview indicated that many of the persons who had been released had returned to drug use and crime almost immediately. Approximately 80 percent of the second specimens were positive for hard drugs, and the majority for more than one drug. These persons had been apprehended and released soon after arrest and there was no systematic attempt by criminal justice system staff to measure or intervene in their drug use.

If all arrestees had the high rates of drug-positive urine tests (heroin or cocaine) that were found among these drug dealers from Harlem, a strategy of using urine tests to flag potentially high-rate offenders would be impossible. (A policy of selective incapacitation is based on the idea that only a small proportion of offenders exhibit very high rates of crime.) Current studies of large numbers of arrestees in New York and Washington indicate that about one-half have positive urine specimens, but only about 20 percent have tests positive for heroin (morphine). In addition, preliminary findings from research in New York City indicate that arrestees with more than one drug in their urine (23 percent of all tested arrestees) at the current arrest have had more arrests over the prior 3 years than persons with only one drug in their urine. Nevertheless, the percentage of arrestees with a positive urine test who are chronic, heavy drug users is still unknown. These issues must be resolved before urine test results can be used effectively to plan interventions for arrestees.

Conclusion

It has been established in studies of arrestees in two large cities that arrestees underreport their recent use of drugs when they are interviewed in criminal justice settings and that drug users cannot be identified readily from the charge at arrest. Urinalysis has been found to detect more drug use than persons admit to in interviews held in criminal justice settings. In addition, there is some indication that urinalysis soon after arrest may provide an indication of the risk of future criminal behavior (Forst and Wish, 1983). More research is needed to determine how best to use urinalysis tests to identify and process drug users.

SUGGESTIONS FOR FUTURE RESEARCH

In this section we present suggestions for future research on the relationship between drug abuse and crime. In the course of writing this paper and in responding to the many questions raised by members of the Panel on Research on Criminal Careers, we have become aware of a number of gaps in the current knowledge about drug use and crime. We discuss below some of the questions that future research should strive to answer. When possible, we have indicated possible strategies for obtaining answers.

Some of the areas that we have chosen to emphasize reflect biases that we wish to make explicit. In our opinion further elaboration and refinement of the "true" rates of crime among drug-using offenders should not be a primary goal of future research. Rather, we believe that future research should build on available findings to determine ways to prevent the development of drug use and crime in persons at high risk for these behaviors, and to develop and assess the impact of interventions that may reduce these behaviors in those who already exhibit them. In accordance with these priorities we recommend that the following questions be addressed.

What Is the Course of Drug Use and Crime in Persons Who Have Been Processed by the Criminal Justice System?

Many studies have investigated how drug abuse treatment affects subsequent drug use and criminal behavior. Far fewer studies have measured the impact of such criminal justice interventions as probation, parole, pretrial diversion, and incarceration on arrestees' drug use and associated crime. Studies are needed of the impact of these conditions, both while the person is in custody or under supervision and after the intervention period has ended. Do these forms of intervention permanently reduce drug use and associated crime or merely postpone them until the person can make up for lost time?

We know of no studies of the natural course of drug use and crime among arrestees. Studies have found that older arrestees are less likely to be using drugs near the time of arrest than are younger arrestees. Have these older arrestees reduced their abuse of drugs, perhaps because of criminal justice interventions or drug abuse treatment? Or have the drug abusers merely matured out of criminal activities or dropped out of the arrestee population because of death or institutionalization? A long-term, prospective study of a cohort of offenders could answer these questions. A quicker and less expensive strategy would be to select a sample of persons arrested in the past and contact each for a research interview; locating and reinterviewing an adequate sample of such persons might be difficult, however.

More information is needed about the types of interventions that are most effective with drug-involved offenders. Experiments with random assignment of persons to specific interventions should be conducted. For example, one study is currently randomly assigning drug-involved persons to drug abuse treatment, to urine surveillance, or to a control group during the pretrial release period (Toborg, 1984). The differences in pretrial rates of rearrest and failure to appear will be measured and compared for each group.

New types of supervised interventions should also be tried. Studies of the California Civil Addict Program (McGlothlin,

Anglin, and Wilson, 1977) indicate that treatment accompanied by supervision was very effective while persons remained in the program. And a large study of treatment outcomes (Collins and Allison, 1983) has reported that persons sent by the court to treatment remained in treatment longer than persons referred by other sources. The traditional view that persons have to enter treatment voluntarily for it to be effective may be inaccurate. Court-ordered interventions accompanied by varying levels of supervision and sanctions should be tested.

Interventions may have to be tailored to the characteristics of the particular offender. Some studies have indicated that younger arrestees may have less severe drug-use patterns than older arrestees. Younger offenders may therefore require interventions designed to deter them from more serious involvement with drugs. Older arrestees with a long history of drug dependence may require treatment that maintains them on a drug such as methadone.

A coordinated intervention strategy that integrates criminal justice sanctions and treatment should be tried. The past practice of placing persons in the hands of criminal justice staff or treatment staff has been inadequate. Programs should offer all the services needed to address the diversity of life problems that offenders who use hard drugs invariably have (Hunt, Lipton, and Spunt, 1984). In addition, special programs that identify and treat the highest risk persons (e.g., violent predators) must be established and evaluated. Successful treatment or incapacitation of these persons may produce the greatest impact on crime rates.

What Impact Does Reducing the Availability of Drugs Have on Drug Use and Crimes?

Behind the government's attempts to reduce the production and importation of illicit drugs is the assumption that these efforts will raise the price of the drugs and thereby deter or reduce their use. The evidence for this is scanty at best and relies primarily on correlations of community-level indicators of drug use and crime. It is possible that higher drug prices may lead persons to commit an increased number of income-generating crimes.

Given the cost of attempting to limit the supply of drugs in this country, a series of experiments should be conducted to determine the impact of such efforts on street-level users. Law enforcement agents could target a location for intensive efforts to reduce the supply of heroin or cocaine. The impact of these activities could then be assessed through a comprehensive set of direct and indirect indicators of drug use and crime in that area. The price and purity of the drugs in the study area could be measured, and criminal activity could be monitored through rates of arrest and reported victimizations. In addition, researchers could interview street-level users about their drug use and crime during the study period and assess whether the local enforcement efforts merely encouraged users to go to other neighborhoods to obtain drugs. Such a study could use a neighboring area as a control group or a design in which the same neighborhood is studied before and after the experiment. Such an experiment would give an indication of the effects of the current multimillion dollar efforts to reduce the supply of drugs in the country.

What Is the Relationship Between Drug Use and Crime Among Females and Do Females Require Specific Types of Interventions?

The overwhelming majority of studies of drug use and crime have concentrated on males. It is true that the criminal justice system processes a much greater number of males than females. However, the magnitude of the drug abuse problem among females, especially those with a history of prostitution, may actually be greater than that found among males. Female arrestees in a number of cities have been found to be more likely to be using drugs at arrest than are males. In a pilot study of females arrested in New York City (Wish, Brady, and Cuadrado, 1984) 84 percent of the females with a history of prostitution who provided a urine specimen shortly after arrest had a positive urinalysis result (almost 80 percent were positive for cocaine). These females also reported a level of drug abuse and associated problems that exceeded those found for male arrestees. Female arrestees with no charge for, or history of, prostitution tended to have rates of recent drug use comparable to those found for the male arrestees.

The types of studies that have already been conducted with male offenders and those that we recommend in this report should be conducted with female offenders. The types of problems female offenders have and the types of interventions that are effective with them should be analyzed.

What Types of Crimes and Associated Problems Are Common to More Affluent Drug Users?

The emergence of cocaine as a commonly used drug throughout American society raises questions about how middle-class users will finance their drug use. Does the use of cocaine and the resulting contact with the illicit drug market increase the likelihood that these persons will use heroin and other drugs? Will it make them more susceptible to violence (both as perpetrators and victims)? Such questions can be answered by conducting interviews with samples of middle-class users who are identified in large-sample drug surveys. Studies of high-risk populations, such as persons who are arrested or who contact service agencies or physicians for assistance, could also offer information on these issues, although such findings would be limited to the type of persons studied.

How Can Offenders Who Are Using Drugs Be Identified?

Thousands of persons are processed by the criminal justice system each year, yet systematic attempts to identify those who are serious drug users are rare. Although urinalysis has shown some promise as a means of detecting persons using hard drugs, more research must be done to determine how current methods of processing and recording information about arrestees can be improved to identify drug users and high-rate offenders. Studies of programs that divert drug users into treatment programs on the basis of a short interview with the arrestee have failed to test systematically the validity of their referral methods. And many questions remain concerning the proper use and administration of the increasingly popular enzyme multiplied immunoassay test (EMIT®) urinalysis techniques (Morgan, 1984). Systematic evaluations of the ability of self-reports, urine tests, and official records to identify drug-using offenders should be conducted. Methods of administering, conducting, and reporting urine test results must be tested and standardized. Confusion in the linking of urine test results with the original donor, for example, could produce disastrous results for the offender and destroy any value of the testing.

Assuming That Drug-Using Offenders Can Be Identified, Can This Information Predict Future Criminal Behavior?

Can identifying drug users at arrest or while on probation or parole permit the differentiation of persons at high risk for future offending? Studies in a few jurisdictions do indicate that drug users appear more recidivistic than other offenders. However, these studies used methods of detection (arrest charge, report of the officer, or urine tests) that have been found to have questionable ability to identify drug users. In addition, the level and types of drugs used by offenders vary from jurisdiction to jurisdiction. Prospective follow-up studies that classify offenders according to current drug use and monitor their future offending, rearrest, and abscondence are needed. These studies should be replicated in many jurisdictions and should be conducted with offenders identified at the point of arrest, probation, and parole. Special emphasis needs to be given to studying the drug use and self-reported crimes of such persons after they have been released (with and without legal supervision). Future research should also examine whether certain types of nonusers are especially good candidates for early release or more lenient treatment.

Assuming That Drug Use by an Offender Is a Good Predictor of Future Criminal Behavior, How Should This Information Be Used in Processing Offenders?

There has been considerable discussion regarding the use of an offender's drug abuse history in making administrative decisions (Feinberg, 1984). The Comprehensive Crime Control Act of 1984 authorized preventive detention for defendants charged with certain federal drug offenses and directed federal judges to consider a variety of factors, including history of drug and alcohol abuse, in setting pretrial release conditions. A number of questions still need to be addressed concerning judicial decision making at the state and local level. Should a person be deprived of pretrial release because of current drug use, even if he or she is charged with a nondrug crime? Should bail be set higher? Are preventive detention statutes needed to permit the use of drug abuse information in setting pretrial release conditions? Should urine surveillance or entry into a treatment program be mandated for all drug users or only for particular types of offenders? Or should urine testing and mandated treatment options be limited to adjudicated persons at the point of the presentence investigation or referral to probation? Research is needed into the views of policymakers, judges, attorneys, and the public on these issues. Aside from the constitutional issues, each jurisdiction may have to decide how to proceed.

How Can We Prevent the Onset of Serious Drug Use and Crime?

The questions above have focused on the many persons who have already developed patterns of hard-drug use and criminal behavior. They are, perhaps, easier to identify, but harder to treat. Identifying youths who are at high risk of developing these behaviors is probably more difficult, but such youths would presumably be easier to treat.

Longitudinal studies of high-risk youths should be conducted. Enough is known to isolate groups of youths containing high-risk persons. Why some of them will cease their deviant behaviors while others continue should be examined. Such studies may not always provide information generalizable to the entire population. However, reduction in serious criminality probably means having an effective strategy for only 2 percent or less of the youth population, anyway.

CONCLUDING COMMENTS

Research into the role of substance abuse in crime has come a long way.

Research questions have been refined to focus on key relationships regarding the role of drugs in the criminal event and to document the diverse patterns of drug use and criminal behaviors among drug-using offenders. Measures of crime and drug use have advanced to the point of classifying types of offenders, assessing their rates of specific offenses in defined time periods, and obtaining information on multiple drug and alcohol use. The research into these issues should continue.

Policymakers must also be informed about current research findings so that policies and solutions reflect the problems and needs of the current drug-abusing offender. A little more than one-half the arrestees studied in Washington, D.C., and New York City had recently used an illicit drug. Such information provides an unusual opportunity to intervene in and treat drug use in the most criminally active population. Yet, with one exception (Washington, D.C.), no jurisdiction in the United States routinely identifies recent drug use in arrestees by urinalysis.

Research can inform policymakers about the effectiveness of possible interventions for identified drug abusers. Strategies are needed for reducing drug abuse and, thereby, crime on a short-term and long-term basis. Selective incapacitation is one alternative that may be useful for the most serious drug-abusing offenders; however, eliminating a person's drug use and offending while he or she is detained is unlikely to lead to a long-term cure. We believe that the greatest chance of success will derive from a coordinated strategy that assesses each offender's diverse set of problems and prepares an integrated solution that draws on a range of available options that extends from mandatory treatment and rehabilitation (Kaplan, 1983), to urine surveillance, daily supervision, and incarceration. It is the challenge of future research to establish how such a strategy can best be implemented.

APPENDIX A

Methodologic Problems in Studying Substance Abuse and Crime

The study of illicit hard-drug use is plagued by many of the same methodologic difficulties that affect the study of other criminal behaviors. Among the most significant problems that must be dealt with are (1) the rarity of hard-drug use in the general population; (2) the validity of self-reports of hard-drug use; (3) the fact that hard-drug use is often episodic; (4) the fact that heavy use of any one drug is usually accompanied by heavy use of other drugs, including alcohol; and (5) the fact that measurement problems may be compounded when both drug use and other criminal behaviors are assessed.

The ways in which these methodologic problems can affect the validity of substance abuse research are discussed below. In Appendix B, these problems are also discussed as they apply to the studies of drug use and crime being reviewed.

Rarity of Hard-Drug Use in the General Population

Surveys of the general population tend to find that use of illicit drugs other than marijuana is relatively rare. One survey (O'Donnell et al., 1976) found that only 100 men in a random sample of 2,510 American men aged 20 to 25 in 1974 had used heroin 10 or more times. In addition, the National Youth Survey (Elliott and Huizinga, 1984), a national probability sample of 1,725 noninstitutionalized youth aged 11 to 17 in 1976, found few users of cocaine or heroin in each of the five waves of interviews from 1976 through 1980. For each year fewer than 1 percent of the sample reported any use of heroin. The prevalence of cocaine use was somewhat greater as the cohort matured, ranging from 1 percent in the 1976 interview sample to 10 percent in the youths reinterviewed in 1980 (Johnston, Bachman, and O'Malley, 1982; Elliott et al., 1983). Use of heroin, cocaine, and PCP, drugs often thought to be associated with criminal behavior, is even less common in the adult population when older persons are included. Because serious criminal behavior is also relatively rare in the general population, studies of heavy drug use and serious crime must necessarily be limited to populations of persons at especially high risk for these behaviors. For example, the National Youth Survey found that only between 1.5 and 2 percent of the sample members were multiple illicit drug users and serious offenders in 1976 or 1980 (Elliott and Huizinga, 1984), yet this group reported a disproportionate share of the crime and drug use found in the whole sample (Johnson, Wish, and Huizinga, 1983).

Thus, much of what is known about hard-drug use and serious crime necessarily comes from studies of adult arrestees or incarcerated persons or from studies of unapprehended persons recruited from communities in which drug use and crime are prevalent. Although such studies cannot provide accurate estimates of drug use and crime relationships in the general society, they do enable researchers to study sufficient numbers of criminally active persons to untangle some of the complex interrelationships between drug use and crime. Nevertheless, the nature of the special populations being studied (e.g., arrestees, incarcerated persons, unapprehended persons) must be considered when assessing to whom the study results may apply.

Given that the focus of the Panel on Research on Criminal Careers is on serious crime and the implications of a selective incapacitation policy, in this appendix we stress studies of high-risk adults and refer only briefly to studies of youth in the general population.

Validating Drug Use

Barring objective observations of another person's taking verified amounts of a known drug in a laboratory or in some other controlled environment, researchers typically measure drug use by the person's self-reports. Cognizant of the fact that study respondents may seek to conceal or underreport their use of illicit drugs, researchers have sought to validate self-reports of recent drug use through urinalysis. By comparing the respondent's reports of drug use with the urinalysis results, one can at least verify the accuracy of the self-reports, assuming that the tests themselves are valid.

There are many reasons why urinalysis may fail to detect drugs that have been taken within the previous 24 to 48 hours, however, including (but not limited to) the fact that the quantity and purity of the substance used and the time since ingestion are usually not known. In addition, a person could accurately report taking a drug that was, in fact, not the drug that he thought he had purchased in the illicit marketplace. Recent work (Wish, Strug, et al., 1983) has indicated, however, that the newer, more sensitive urinalysis (known commercially as EMIT®) can detect the use of street-quality heroin (actually morphine, the metabolite of heroin, is detected), cocaine, and methadone with a high degree of accuracy. The older, widely used mass-screening techniques (thin-layer chromatography) often fail to detect use of illicit, street-quality cocaine and heroin (Wish, Brady, et al., 1984).

Although researchers may find it helpful to test the validity of self-reports of recent drug use through urinalysis, they still face many problems in validating self-reports of drug use. For example, urine tests do not tell us when in the test-sensitive period (approximately 24 to 48 hours for cocaine and heroin) the drug use occurred. One cannot use urine tests to validate reports of drug use several days prior to the collection of the urine specimen. Researchers typically settle for an indication of the veracity of the respondent's answers to questions about drug use from the validation of recent drug use (by urinalysis) and from consistency checks within the interview and between the interview and record information obtained for the respondent.

Episodic Nature of Hard-Drug Use

It is commonly believed that the heavy user of hard drugs, especially of heroin, uses the drug every day. It has become increasingly clear, however, that heroin users go in and out of periods of use even without treatment intervention (McGlothlin, Anglin, and Wilson, 1977; Robins, 1979; Ball et al., 1981; Ball, Shaffer, and Nurco, 1983; Johnson et al., 1985). Studies of active, unapprehended heroin-using offenders in New York City (Johnson, 1984; Johnson et al., 1985) tend to find much polydrug use and drug switching, depending on drug availability and the person's finances and preferences at the time of purchase.

The implications of the episodic nature of drug use for studies of drug use and crime are significant. One must not label a person a drug user over an entire period because the person reports being an addict or heavy user at one time during that period. Measurement of drug use on a daily or weekly basis is needed to relate runs of drug use to changes in criminal behavior (see McGlothlin, Anglin, and Wilson, 1977; Nurco, Cisin, and Balter, 1981a–c).

Polydrug Use Among Heavy Drug Users

Ample evidence exists that the heavier the use of any one drug, the greater the likelihood of use of other drugs. One study (Robins, Helzer, et al., 1980) found that, as the use of alcohol or heroin increased in a sample of veterans, so did the number of other drugs used in the same 2-year period. This study reported that persons addicted to heroin used an average of 10.4 other drugs (out of 20) in a 2-year period after returning to the United States from Vietnam, compared with 7.9 drugs for less regular heroin users. In fact, the authors suggested that knowing how many illicit drugs were used by a person may be as good an indicator of severity of use as knowing which drugs are used. Studies of populations of heroin-using offenders have tended to confirm this high degree of polydrug use (Strug, Stevie, et al., 1984; Strug, Wish, et al., 1984). Both self-reports and urinalysis have indicated that heavy users of any illicit drug use a smorgasbord of drugs, including alcohol, PCP, cocaine, heroin, pills, and illicit methadone—frequently on the same day.

The fact that heavy users of heroin and, indeed, of any illicit psychoactive drug tend to use multiple drugs presents some difficulties for the researcher studying the relationship between drug use and crime. It may be misleading to attribute the criminal behavior of a heroin user to the heroin when that person is probably using a multitude of drugs and alcohol. Studies of drug use and crime must therefore obtain precise information about all substances being used and control for their differential impacts on crime. A good example of this approach appears in the study of veterans cited above (Robins, Helzer, et al., 1980). That study compared the effects of regular use of heroin, amphetamines, marijuana, and barbiturates on social adjustment, after controlling for early predisposing factors as well as other drug use. The authors concluded that the greater social disability found among users of heroin than users of other drugs was probably attributable to the types of persons who use heroin in our society—persons with the greatest predisposition (apparent in their youths) to social problems. Both the use of other drugs and one's disposition toward deviant behaviors must be taken into consideration when ascertaining the impact of a particular drug on one's social adjustment or criminal behavior.

Measuring Drug Use and Crime

We indicated above that persons may tend to underreport their use of illicit drugs and that urine tests can help to detect instances of recent drug use. When one measures both drug use and criminal behaviors by self-reports, however, there is another potential problem. Let us assume that person X is a seasoned drug-abusing offender (perhaps in his late twenties) who is relatively open about his involvement in illicit behaviors. Such a person might report considerable drug use and crime in a research interview. On the other hand, person Y may be younger and as criminally active as person X, but less willing to admit to deviant behaviors. For example, some evidence exists that youthful offenders in Harlem were less likely to admit that they were junkies than were older offenders (Anderson et al., 1984).

Assuming that a sample contains many persons like X and Y, we could find a strong relationship between rates of drug use and crime that would be artifactual, resulting only from the fact that persons willing to disclose one of these behaviors are likely to disclose the others. A similar problem could occur if a respondent tended to view a particular time period to be one of general activity. In such cases he might report a high level of both drug use and crime as a result of this generalized belief about his life at that time.

These biases or distortions in self-reported behaviors could be expected to increase as the time period being recalled gets further away from the time of interview (Bachman and O'Malley, 1981). On the other hand, in our research we have found some indication of underreporting among persons asked to report their drug use in the prior 24 to 48 hours during a research interview held in potentially threatening criminal justice settings. Researchers should, therefore, attempt to test drug and crime associations based on self-reports by comparing them against other information that does not depend solely on self-reports. An example of this strategy is the evaluation of the California Civil Addict Program by McGlothlin, Anglin, and Wilson (1977), in which an association between self-reported reductions in narcotics use and self-reported reductions in crime was verified by a reduction in recorded arrests during the same period.

APPENDIX B

Studies of Drug Abuse and Crime

In this appendix we review studies whose findings greatly influenced our discussion in the body of this paper. We provide a brief summary of the design, major findings, significance, and potential limitations of each study.

Evaluation of the Calfornia Civil Addict Program (McGlothlin, Anglin, and Wilson, 1977)

Sample: Studied 949 men committed to the California Civil Addict Program. Included admissions from 1962–1963, 1964, and 1970. Many sample members entered this program as an alternative to serving time for a crime.

Primary Measures: Self-reports during personal interviews, official arrest records, and urine specimens.

Validity Checks: For criminal behavior, arrest records; for recent drug use, urinalysis.

Study Design: Follow-up study; natural experiment using a comparison group of persons who were released from program early because of a legal technicality; oversampled a group of treatment successes as another comparison group.

Significance of Study: This study is known for its excellent design and execution. Both drug use and crime in specific time periods were measured, and runs of narcotics use were identified. The study indicated that the Civil Addict Program, which consists of inpatient and outpatient periods, was effective while the men were in the program and less effective after termination. Supervision coupled with drug testing (originally with naline and later with urine tests) produced moderate reductions in narcotics use and nondrug crime while the men were in the program. Methadone appeared to have a similar beneficial impact. The study concluded that reductions in daily runs of narcotics use could produce significant reductions in criminal behavior.

Potential Limitations: Sampled only males, largely those convicted of crimes. Applies to persons living in California; impact of methadone use by respondents not totally controlled for in the post-1970 analyses.

Analysis of Drugs and Crime Among Arrestees in the District of Columbia (Wish, Klampp, et al., 1980)

Sample: Consists of 57,944 men and women arrested and adjudicated in the Washington, D.C., Superior Court from 1973 to 1977 and a recidivism file containing 19,277 arrest cases (over a 6-year period) for a sample of 7,087 consecutive persons arrested in an 8-month panel period in 1974–1975.

Primary Measures: Prosecutors' case-processing records (from PROMIS), bail and sentencing information from court records, urinalysis results, and drug abuse treatment records.

Validity Checks: For criminal records, none; for urine test results, some comparison with police officer's perception of arrestee's involvement with narcotics.

Study Design: Cross-section case files of prosecutor's case information and results of a urine test from a specimen taken at arrest were merged for each individual and analyzed; in addition, a person-based file containing arrest cases, urinalysis results, and information on drug treatment for 7,087 persons was constructed and analyzed.

Significance of Study: This study showed that urine test results could identify arrestees at high risk of rearrest in a 4-year follow-up period. Drug-using arrestees in a 6-year period prior to and after the index arrest had higher rates of bail violations and income-generating crimes than nonusers and equivalent rates of arrests for violent crimes. Female arrestees were more likely to be detected to be using drugs at arrest than male arrestees. The report also contains information about the type of victims chosen by drug users and their types of arrest.

Potential Limitations: Study looked only at arrest records and obtained no self-reports of crimes committed. Time at risk was not controlled for, although subsequent analyses indicated that adjustment for time at risk did not alter study findings. Drug use was measured only by urinalysis.

Varieties of Criminal Behavior (Chaiken and Chaiken, 1982)

Sample: Study of 2,190 inmates in prison or jail in Michigan, California, and

Texas. Sample was selected to represent an incoming cohort in the institutions. Analyses were weighted, where necessary.

Primary Measures: Group-administered questionnaires—nonconfidential—to enable linking of information with official records.

Validity Checks: Performed extensive internal and external validity checks. Official records were available only for respondents in prison, however. External validity tests of self-reports versus record information indicated that 23 percent had "bad data" on 31 percent or more of 14 indicators checked. Internal consistency checks showed that between 28 and 32 percent of the respondents had trouble understanding the definition of the 2-year period preceding the primary measurement period. Approximately 17 percent of the sample had bad data on 21 percent or more of the 27 indicators of internal quality that were checked. No systematic relationships were found between the global indices of internal and external validity and personal characteristics or reported crime rates in the measurement period. Official records on drug involvement were so poor that checks of the self-reported information on substance abuse were impossible.

Study Design: One-time, retrospective, self-administered survey questionnaire and available official records were used.

Significance of Study: Study is primarily known for the development of a typology of offenders having different levels of offending rates and for measuring individual offending frequencies (λs) from inmates' self-reports. Self-report information, but not official records, was useful in discriminating high- and low-rate offenders.

Potential Limitations: Used identifiable group-administered questionnaires, rather than personal interviews. Response rates were 50 percent in California and Michigan prisons, 66 percent in California and Michigan jails, and 82 percent in Texas prisons. Measures of drug use were few and simple: did not measure use of marijuana, PCP, or LSD after age 18; did not measure cocaine use at all. Method of drug administration was not measured. Alcohol use was measured by only a single, yes-no question regarding whether the person drank alcohol heavily, got drunk often, or had a drinking problem. The findings may apply to a select population of offenders, given the low probability of incarceration. Respondents' difficulty in differentiating prior time periods places analyses over these periods in doubt. Statistical significance levels were often reported rather than the actual findings, which limits the reader's ability to assess the magnitude of the differences reported.

Criminality Among Heroin Addicts in Baltimore (Ball et al., 1981; Nurco, Cisin, and Balter, 1981a,b,c; Ball, Shaffer, and Nurco, 1983)

Sample: A random sample of 243 male opiate addicts arrested or identified by the Baltimore police department between 1952 and 1971. Sample was stratified by race and time period.

Primary Measures: Personal follow-up interviews and police, juvenile, and FBI records.

Validity Checks: Interview information was checked against record information on date of birth, narcotics use, incarceration and conviction history, and juvenile delinquency history.

Study Design: Follow-up interviews with sample in 1973 and 1974.

Significance of Study: Known for its typology of heroin addicts and for its findings regarding the number of crime days during periods of heavy narcotics use and lesser use.

Potential Limitations: Early papers presented findings for blacks and whites separately, since the sample had been stratified by race to produce nearly equal proportions of whites and blacks. (On original list 77 percent were blacks; in the final sample 57 percent were blacks.) However, research on crime days by Ball et al. (1981) and Ball, Shaffer, and Nurco (1983) pooled blacks and whites without weighting the sample back to its original ethnic composition. Given the many differences found between black and white respondents (Nurco, Cisin, and Balter, 1982), the pooling of all subjects limits the generalizability of results. Because whites were less criminally active than blacks, the disproportionate number of whites in the sample would tend to lower the estimates of crime.

Persons were interviewed as long as 20 years after they had been identified as drug involved by the Baltimore police. Other than verifying that most of these persons were using drugs at about the time they were placed on the list (Bonito, Nurco, and Shaffer, 1976), few checks were made to verify that the behavioral patterns recalled were accurate. This study may also be limited by biases in self-reported behaviors (discussed in Appendix A), which could have produced a strong association between drug use and crime in certain periods as an artifact of the measures. While the number of crime days per year is measured, the study does not report data from which λs may be computed. In addition, the computation of crimes per day is not straightforward, given ambiguity in the way the pertinent questionnaire items were worded.

National Youth Survey (Elliott and Huizinga, 1984)

Sample: Consists of 1,725 youths selected as a representative sample of American youths aged 11 to 17 in 1976. Persons were reinterviewed annually from 1977 to 1981 about their delinquent and drug-using behaviors.

Primary Measures: Self-reports from personal interviews about behaviors during a 12-month period. Also obtained records of arrests.

Validity Checks: For criminal behavior, used arrest records; for recent drug use, used internal consistency checks.

Study Design: Prospective longitudinal design; each year of birth cohort was treated as an independent sample.

Significance of Study: This is the largest and longest study of a national sample of youths that is available. It is recognized for its design and execution. Its reports contain measures of crime rates (routinely reported) for various types of delinquent behavior. It provides the best information available about delinquency in a large, representative sample of youths.

Potential Limitations: The major limitation is the small number of youths reporting extensive delinquency and serious drug use in a national probability sample. Heroin use was almost nonexistent (1 percent or less). While dropouts from the study do not appear to differ substantially from reinterviewees, the loss of even three to five highly delinquent youths could have reduced crime rates.

Economic Behavior of Street Opiate Users (Johnson et al., 1985)

Sample: Consists of 201 heroin and methadone users recruited from the streets of East and Central Harlem in New York City. Subjects were interviewed nine or more times and provided a total of 11,400 person-days of information about their behaviors. Researchers were not successful in developing a sampling frame from which to select persons with a known probability of selection.

Primary Measures: Self-reports covering 33 or more days per person with respect to crimes (type, number, dollar, and drug income), drug patterns (use, purchase, sale), noncriminal income, nondrug expenditures, arrests, and drug treatment.

Validity Checks: For criminal behavior, some observations of subjects committing crime in the streets, internal consistency checks during follow-up interview, reporting of similar crimes during different interviews; occasionally, two or more subjects reported about the same crime event. No arrest records were obtained. Reports of drug use were not validated, although many subjects reporting use appeared intoxicated at the time of interview.

Study Design: Convenience sample of persons encountered on the street who were screened by exaddict field-workers for heroin and methadone use and probable criminal behavior; subjects selected to represent the diversity of drug and criminal life-styles in the neighborhood; subjects reported to storefront research office each day for 5 days and then 1 day per week (for 1 month or longer) to recount prior week's activities.

Significance of Study: This is the first study to compute crime rates from data about self-reported crime for persons while they were active on the streets. It is one of the few studies to present detailed daily and annualized data on the dollar returns from drug use, drug-distribution activities, and other crimes, as well as other economic behaviors. The study presents both quantitative and qualitative information about heroin abusers who are serious and regular criminal offenders.

Potential Limitations: The sample is small and limited in geographical area, and it did not follow accepted sampling procedures. It is unknown how representative the respondents are of other offenders in New York City or in other cities. The λs include numerous small drug-distribution crimes. The analyses seldom control for the effects of demographic characteristics (sex, age, ethnicity, age of onset, education, etc.) on the λs computed.

Studies from the National Institute of Justice–Funded Interdisciplinary Research Center (IRC) for the Study of the Relationship of Drug Use and Crime (Strug, Stevie, et al., 1984; Strug, Wish, et al., 1984; Glassner et al., 1985)

Samples: Three samples: youths in a moderate-size city in New York (N = 100); unapprehended, drug-using adult criminals in East Harlem (N = 179); and adults arrested for possession or sale of drugs in the East Harlem area (N = 116).

Primary Measures: Intensive, open-ended interviews of youths; structured personal interviews and urine tests for apprehended and unapprehended adult criminals.

Validity Checks: Internal checks and some corroboration by other youths; studies of adults checked urine tests against self-reports of recent use of illicit drugs and found considerable concordance.

Study Design: Studies of youths involved three subsamples: a random sample from school lists, a purposive sample based on field observations of deviant youths, and a sample of juveniles adjudicated as delinquent and residing in group homes or detention centers. Youths were interviewed for an average of 4 hours about their drug use, adjustment, and deviance.

Studies of unapprehended and apprehended adults in East Harlem: unapprehended hard-drug users who had recently committed a serious nondrug crime were recruited from the streets and interviewed about the crime event and the role of drug and alcohol use in that event. A comparison group of 116 arrestees were interviewed in a police station (in the same neighborhood as the unapprehended drug users) about their drug-use histories and a urine specimen was obtained. A second follow-up interview was obtained for 43 of these 116 persons after release. The releasees who showed up for reinterview were more indigent and reported more lifetime dependence on drugs than those who did not show up. Their educational and ethnic backgrounds were similar to those who were not reinterviewed, as was their level of recent use of drugs. The follow-up interview was identical to the interview used with unapprehended persons and was followed by collection of a urine specimen.

Significance of Study: Study of youths obtained in-depth information about drugs and crime and successfully oversampled high-risk youths. Studies of adult criminals obtained information about the role of drug and alcohol use in the crime event and examined the criminal justice system's processing of drug-involved arrestees.

Potential Limitations: Study of youths had a small sample and collected much information in a qualitative way that limits quantification and extrapolation to other populations. The studies of unapprehended persons used paid recruiters to find persons who had just committed crimes. The degree to which the study respondents are representative of other addicted offenders is unknown. The comparison group of arrestees does provide some indication of the potential biases in the data from unapprehended respondents. The arrestees in the study were primarily arrested for purchase, sale, or possession of cocaine or heroin, and some findings may not apply to arrestees charged with nondrug crimes or to persons arrested in other jurisdictions in New York City.

Additional Current Studies

Two ongoing studies of urine testing of arrestees, in Washington, D.C., and in New York City, have also influenced the conclusions presented in this paper. The study in Washington (Toborg, 1984) is examining whether it is effective for judges to assign drug-using arrestees to specific pretrial release conditions (treatment and/or urine monitoring) based on the results of a test of a urine specimen obtained shortly after arrest. The study in New York City (Wish, Brady, and Cuadrado, 1984, 1985; Wish, Brady, et al., 1984; Wish, Chedekel, et al., 1985) is examining the feasibility of using urine tests to identify arrestees at high risk of pretrial arrest and failure to appear in court.

REFERENCES

Anderson, Kevin, Wish, Eric, Johnson, Bruce D., Sears, Alton, and Miller, Tom
1984 Living Hard in the City: A Portrait of Ten Young "Hustlers." Paper presented at a meeting of the Academy of Criminal Justice Sciences, Chicago, Illinois, March.

Anglin, M. Douglas, and McGlothlin, William H.
1984 Outcome of narcotic addict treatment in California. Pp. 106–128 in Frank M. Tims and Jacqueline P. Ludford, eds., *Drug Abuse Treatment Evaluation: Strategies, Progress, and Prospects*. Research Monograph 51. Rockville, Md.: National Institute on Drug Abuse.

Bachman, Jerald G., and O'Malley, Patrick M.
1981 When four months equal a year: inconsistencies in student reports of drug use. *Public Opinion Quarterly* 45:536–548.

Ball, John C., Shaffer, John W., and Nurco, David N.
1983 The day-to-day criminality of heroin addicts in Baltimore—a study in the continuity of offense rates. *Drug and Alcohol Dependence* 12:119–142.

Ball, John C., Roxen, Lawrence, Flueck, John A., and Nurco, David N.
1981 The criminality of heroin addicts when addicted and when off opiates. Pp. 39–66 in James A. Inciardi, ed., *The Drugs-Crime Connection*. Beverly Hills, Calif.: Sage Publications.

Barton, William I.
1976 Heroin use and criminality: survey of state correctional facilities, January 1974. Pp. 419–440 in National Institute on Drug Abuse and Research Triangle Institute, *Drug Use and Crime: Report of the Panel on Drug Use and Criminal Behavior*. Appendix. Research Tri-

angle Park, N.C.: Research Triangle Institute.

Baxley, Robert C.
1980 Voluntary intoxication from phencyclidine: will it raise a reasonable doubt of the mental capacity of a person charged with a crime requiring specific intent or mental state? *Journal of Psychedelic Drugs* 12(3–4):330–335.

Bonito, Arthur J., Nurco, David N., and Shaffer, John W.
1976 The veridicality of addicts' self-reports in social research. *International Journal of Addictions* 11(5):719–724.

Bureau of Justice Statistics
1983a *Prisoners and Alcohol.* Washington, D.C.: U.S. Department of Justice.
1983b *Prisoners and Drugs.* Washington, D.C.: U.S. Department of Justice.

Chaiken, Jan, and Chaiken, Marcia
1982 *Varieties of Criminal Behavior.* Santa Monica, Calif.: Rand Corporation.

Chaiken, Marcia
1983 Crime Rates and Substance Abuse Among Types of Offenders. Unpublished paper. Interdisciplinary Research Center, New York City.

Clayton, Richard R., and Voss, Harwin L.
1981 *Young Men and Drugs in Manhattan: A Causal Analysis.* Research Monograph 39. Rockville, Md.: National Institute on Drug Abuse.

Cohen, Jacqueline
1978 The incapacitative effect of imprisonment: a critical review of the literature. Pp. 187–243 in Alfred Blumstein, Jacqueline Cohen, and Daniel Nagin, eds., *Deterrence and Incapacitation: Estimating the Effects of Criminal Sanctions on Crime Rates.* Washington, D.C.: National Academy Press.

Collins, James J., and Allison, Margret
1983 Legal coercion and retention in drug abuse treatment. *Hospital and Community Psychiatry* 14(12):1145–1149.

Collins, James J., Hubbard, Robert, and Rachal, J. Valley
1985 Expensive drug use and illegal income: a test of explanatory hypotheses. *Criminology* 23:743–764.

Collins, James J., Rachal, J. Valley, Hubbard, Robert, Cavanaugh, Elizabeth R., Craddock, S. Gail, and Kristiansen, Patricia L.
1982a *Crime and Crime Indicators in the Treatment Outcome Prospective Study.* Research Triangle Park, N.C.: Research Triangle Institute.
1982b *Criminality in a Drug Treatment Sample: Measurement Issues and Initial Findings.* Research Triangle Park, N.C.: Research Triangle Institute.

DuPont, Robert L., and Kozel, Nicholas J.
1976 Heroin Use and Crime. Paper presented at a meeting of the American Psychiatric Association, Miami Beach, Florida.

Elliott, Delbert S., and Huizinga, David
1984 *The Relationship Between Delinquent Behavior and ADM Problems.* Boulder, Colo.: Behavioral Research Institute.

Elliott, Delbert S., Ageton, Suzanne S., Huizinga, David, Knowles, Brian, and Canter, Rachelle J.
1983 *The Prevalence and Incidence of Delinquent Behavior: 1976–1980.* National Youth Survey Report 26. Boulder, Colo.: Behavioral Research Institute.

Fauman, Beverly J., and Fauman, Michael A.
1982 Phencyclidine abuse and crime: a psychiatric perspective. *Bulletin of the American Academy of Psychiatry and the Law* 10(3):171–176.

Feinberg, Kenneth R.
1984 Selective incapacitation and the effort to improve the fairness of existing sentencing practices. Unpublished paper. Kaye, Scholer, Fierman, Hays, and Handler, Washington, D.C. *Law and Society.*

Forst, Brian, and Wish, Eric
1983 Drug use and crime: providing a missing link. Pp. 84–95 in Kenneth R. Feinberg, ed., *Violent Crime in America.* Washington, D.C.: National Policy Exchange.

Gandossy, Robert P., Williams, Jay R., Cohen, Jo, and Harwood, Henrick J.
1980 *Drugs and Crime: A Survey and Analysis of the Literature.* National Institute of Justice. Washington, D.C.: U.S. Government Printing Office.

Glassner, Barry, Loughlin, Julia, Johnson, Bruce D., Carpenter, Cheryl, Ksander, Margret, Berg, Bruce, and Stuck, Mary
1985 *Drugs and Alcohol in Adolescent Delinquency.* Interdisciplinary Research Center. New York City.

Goldstein, Paul J.
1981 Getting over: economic alternatives to predatory crime among street drug users. Pp. 67–84 in James A. Inciardi, ed., *The Drugs-Crime Connection.* Beverly Hills, Calif.: Sage Publications.
1985 The drugs/violence nexus: a tripartite conceptual framework. *Journal of Drug Issues* 15:493–506.
1983 Drug Related Involvement in Violent Episodes. Proposal to the National Institute on Drug Abuse. New York City: Narcotic and Drug Research, Inc.

Greenberg, Stephanie W., and Adler, Freda
1974 Crime and addiction: an empirical analysis of the literature, 1920–1973. *Contemporary Drug Problems* 3:221–270.

Haberman, Paul, and Baden, Michael
1978 *Alcohol, Other Drugs and Violet Death.* New York: Oxford University Press.

Heffernan, Ronald, Martin, John M., and Romano, Anne T.
1982 Homicides related to drug trafficking. *Federal Probation* September:3–7.

Huizinga, David, and Elliott, Delbert S.
1981 *A Longitudinal Study of Drug Use and Delinquency in a National Sample of Youth: An Assessment of Causal Order.* Boulder, Colo.: Behavioral Research Institute.

Hunt, Dana, Lipton, Douglas S., and Spunt, Barry
1984 Patterns of criminal activity among methadone clients and current narcotics users not in treatment. *Journal of Drug Issues* 14:687–702.

Inciardi, James A.
1979 Heroin use and street crime. *Crime and Delinquency* July:335–346.
1981 *The Drugs-Crime Connection.* Beverly Hills, Calif.: Sage Publications.
1984 *Criminal Justice.* Orlando, Fla.: Academic Press.

Jessor, Richard
1979 Marihuana: a review of recent psychosocial research. Pp. 337–355 in Robert L. Dupont, Avram Goldstein, and John O'Donnell, eds., *Handbook on Drug Abuse.* Rockville, Md.: National Institute on Drug Abuse.

Jessor, Richard, and Jessor, Shirley
1977 *Problem Behavior and Psychosocial Development: A Longitudinal Study of Youth.* New York: Academic Press.

Johnson, Bruce D.
1973 *Marijuana Users and Drug Subcultures.* New York: John Wiley & Sons.
1984 Empirical patterns of heroin consumption among selected street heroin users. Pp. 101–123 in George Serban, ed., *Social and Medical Aspects of Drug Abuse.* Jamaica, N.Y.: Spectrum Publications.

Johnson, Bruce D., Wish, Eric, and Huizinga, David
1983 The Concentration of Delinquent Offending: The Contribution of Serious Drug Involvement to High Rate Delinquency. Paper presented at a meeting of the American Society of Criminology, Denver, November.

Johnson, Bruce D., Goldstein, Paul, Preble, Edward, Schmeidler, James, Lipton, Douglas S., Spunt, Barry, and Miller, Thomas
1985 *Taking Care of Business: The Economics of Crime by Heroin Abusers.* Lexington, Mass.: Lexington Books.

Johnston, Lloyd, Bachman, Jerald G., and O'Malley, Patrick
1982 *Student Drug Use, Attitudes, and Beliefs: 1975–1982.* Rockville, Md.: National Institute on Drug Abuse.

Kandel, Denise B.
1978 *Longitudinal Research on Drug Use.* New York: Halsted Press.
1984 Marijuana users in young adulthood. *Archives of General Psychiatry* 41:200–209.

Kaplan, John
1983 *The Hardest Drug: Heroin and Drug Policy.* Chicago, Ill.: University of Chicago Press.

Kleinman, Paula H., Wish, Eric D., Deren, Sherry, and Rainone, Gregory
1984 The "Pure" Marijuana-using Client: Where? Unpublished paper. Narcotic and Drug Research, Inc., New York.

Kozel, Nicholas J., and DuPont, Robert
1977 *Criminal Charges and Drug Use Patterns of Arrestees in the District of Columbia.* Rockville, Md.: National Institute on Drug Abuse.

Lukoff, Irving F.
1974 Issues in the evaluation of heroin treatment. Pp. 129–157 in Eric Josephson and Eleanor C. Carroll, eds., *Drug Use: Epidemiological and Sociological Approaches.* New York: John Wiley & Sons.
1976 Consequences of use: heroin and other narcotics. Pp. 195–227 in Joan Rittenhouse, ed., *The Epidemiology of Heroin and Other Narcotics.* Research Monograph 16. Rockville, Md.: National Institute on Drug Abuse.

McBride, Duane C.
1983 Homicides and Violence among Miami Drug Dealers. Paper presented at a meeting of the Society for the Study of Social Problems, Detroit, Michigan, August.

McGlothlin, William H.
1979 Drugs and crime. Pp. 357–365 in Robert L. Dupont, Avram Goldstein, and John O'Donnell, eds., *Handbook on Drug Abuse.* Rockville, Md.: National Institute on Drug Abuse.

McGlothlin, William H., Anglin, M. Douglas, and Wilson, Bruce D.
1977 *An Evaluation of the California Civil Addict Program.* Services Research Issues Series. Rockville, Md.: National Institute on Drug Abuse.

Morgan, John P.
1984 Problems of mass screening for misused drugs. *Journal of Psychoactive Drugs* 16(4):305–317.

Nurco, David N., Cisin, Ira H., and Balter, Mitchell B.

1981a Addict careers. I. A new typology. *International Journal of the Addictions* 16(8): 1305–1325.

1981b Addict careers. II. The first ten years. *International Journal of the Addictions* 16(8): 1327–1356.

1981c Addict careers. III. Trends across time. *International Journal of the Addictions* 16(8): 1357–1372.

1982 Trends in the age of onset of narcotic addiction. *Chemical Dependencies: Behavorial and Biomedical Issues* 4(3):221–228.

O'Donnell, John A., and Clayton, Richard R.

1981 The steppingstone hypothesis: a reappraisal. *Chemical Dependencies* 4.

O'Donnell, John A., Voss, Harwin L., Clayton, Richard, Slatin, Gerald T., and Room, Robin G.

1976 *Young Men and Drugs—A Nationwide Survey.* Research Monograph 5. Rockville, Md.: National Institute on Drug Abuse.

Peterson, Robert C., and Stillman, Richard C., eds.

1978 *Phencyclidine (PCP) Abuse: An Appraisal.* Research Monograph 21. Rockville, Md.: National Institute on Drug Abuse.

Reuter, Peter

1984 The (continued) vitality of mythical numbers. *Public Interest* 75:135–147.

Robins, Lee N.

1979 Addict careers. Pp. 325–336 in Robert L. Dupont, Avram Goldstein, and John O'Donnell, eds., *Handbook on Drug Abuse.* Rockville, Md.: National Institute on Drug Abuse.

Robins, Lee N., and Wish, Eric

1977 Development of childhood deviance: a study of 223 urban black men from birth to 18. Pp. 448–473 in Mae F. McMillian and Serrgio Henao, eds., *Child Psychiatry Treatment and Research.* New York: Brunner/Mazel. Also published in *Social Forces* 56(2):448–473.

Robins, Lee N., Davis, Darlene H., and Wish, Eric D.

1977 Detecting predictors of rare events: demographic, family, and personal deviance as predictors of stages in the progression towards narcotic addiction. Pp. 379–406 in J. S. Strauss, H. M. Babigian, and M. Roff, eds., *The Origins and Course of Psychopathology.* New York: Plenum.

Robins, Lee N., Helzer, John E., Hesselbrock, Michie, and Wish, Eric D.

1980 Vietnam veterans three years after Vietnam: how our study changed our view of heroin. In L. Brill and C. Winick, eds., *Yearbook of Substance Abuse.* New York: Human Sciences Press.

Robins, Lee N., Hessellbrock, Michie, Wish, Eric D., and Helzer, John E.

1977 Polydrug and alcohol use by veterans and nonveterans. Pp. 74–90 in David E. Smith, Steven M. Anderson, Millicent Buxton, Nancy Gottlieb, William Harvey, and Tommy Chung, eds., *A Multicultural View of Drug Abuse: Proceedings of the National Drug Abuse Conference, 1977.* Philadelphia, Pa.: Hall and Schenkman.

1978 Alcohol and Crime in Veterans. Paper presented at the National Institute on Law Enforcement and Criminal Justice Colloquium, Washington, D.C.

Sells, Saul B., Stimson, D. D., Joe, G. H., Demaree, R. G., Savage, L. J., and Lloyd, M. R.

1976 A national follow-up study to evaluate the effectiveness of drug abuse treatment: a report on cohort I of DARP five years later. *American Journal of Drug and Alcohol Abuse* 3(4):545–556.

Siegel, Ronald K.

1978 Phencyclidine, criminal behavior, and the defense of diminished capacity. Pp. 272–288 in Robert C. Peterson and Richard C. Stillman, eds., *Phencyclidine (PCP) Abuse: An Appraisal.* Research Monograph 21. Rockville, Md.: National Institute on Drug Abuse.

1980 PCP and violent crime: the people vs. peace. *Journal of Psychedelic Drugs* 12(3–4):317–330.

Silverman, Lester P., and Spruill, Nancy L.

1977 Urban crime and the price of heroin. *Journal of Urban Economics* 4:80–103.

Simonds, John F., and Kashani, Javad

1980 Specific drug use and violence in delinquent boys. *American Journal of Drug and Alcohol Abuse* 7(3&4):305–322.

Singer, Max

1971 The vitality of mythical numbers. *Public Interest* 23:3–9.

Single, Eric, and Kandel, Denise B.

1978 The role of buying and selling in illicit drug use. Pp. 118–128 in Arnold Trebach, ed., *Drugs, Crime, and Politics.* New York: Praeger.

Strug, David, Stevie, B., Wish, Eric, Johnson, Bruce D., Miller, Tom, and Anderson, Kevin

1984 Hustling to Survive: The Role of Drugs, Alcohol, and Crime in the Life of Street Hustlers. Paper presented at a meeting of the Academy of Criminal Justice Sciences, Chicago, March.

Strug, David, Wish, Eric, Johnson, Bruce D., Anderson, Kevin, and Miller, Tom

1984 The role of alcohol in the crimes of heroin

abusers. *Crime and Delinquency* 30(4):551–567.

Tinklenberg, Jared R.
1973 Drugs and crime. Pp. 242–299 in National Commission on Marihuana and Drug Abuse, *Drug Use in America: Problem in Perspective.* Vol. I, Appendix. Washington, D.C.: U.S. Government Printing Office.

Tinklenberg, Jared R., and Ochberg, Frank M.
1981 Patterns of adolescent violence: a California sample. Pp. 121–140 in Jared R. Tinklenberg and Frank M. Ochberg, eds., *Behavioral Aspects of Aggression.* New York: Alan Liss.

Tinklenberg, Jared R., Roth, W. T., Kopell, B. S., and Murphy, P.
1976 Cannabis and alcohol effects on assaultiveness in adolescent delinquents. Pp. 85–94 in *Chronic Cannabis Use. Annals of the New York Academy of Sciences* 282.

Tinklenberg, Jared R., Murphy, Peggy, Murphy, Patricia L., and Pfefferbaum, Arnold
1981 Drugs and criminal assaults by adolescents: a replication study. *Journal of Psychoactive Drugs* 13(3):277–287.

Toborg, Mary
1984 Preliminary Findings on the D.C. Urine Testing Experiment. Paper presented at a Meeting of the American Society of Criminology, Cincinnati.

Voss, Harwin L.
1976 Young men, drugs and crime. Pp. 351–385 in Robert Shellow, ed., *Drug Use andCrime: Appendix, Report of the Panel on Drug Use and Criminal Behavior.* Research Triangle Park, N.C.: Research Triangle Institute.

Washton, Arnold M., and Gold, Mark S.
1984 Chronic cocaine abuse: evidence for adverse effects on health and functioning. *Psychiatric Annals* 14(10):733–743.

Weissman, James C.
1979 Understanding the drugs and crime connection: a systematic examination of drugs and crime relationships. *Journal of Psychedelic Drugs* 10:171–192.

Winick, Charles S.
1962 Maturing out of narcotic addiction. *Bulletin on Narcotics* 14:1–7.

Wish, Eric D.
1982 Are Heroin Users Really Nonviolent? Paper presented at a meeting of the Academy of Criminal Justice Sciences, Louisville, Kentucky, March.
1986 PCP and crime: just another illicit drug? Pp. 174–189 in D. H. Clouet, ed., *Phencyclidine: An Update.* National Institute on Drug Abuse. Research Monograph No. 64. Rockville, Md.: National Institute on Drug Abuse.

Wish, Eric D., Brady, Elizabeth, and Cuadrado, Mary
1984 Female Arrestees: The Most Serious Drug-abusers? Paper presented at the annual meeting of the American Society of Criminology, Cincinnati, Ohio, November.
1985 Drug Use and Crime in Arrestees in Manhattan. Presented at a poster session of the Forty-seventh Annual Scientific Meeting of the Committee on Problems of Drug Dependence, Baltimore, Maryland.

Wish, Eric D., Anderson, Kevin, Miller, Tom, and Johnson, Bruce D.
1984 Drug Use and Abuse in Arrestees: New Findings from a Study of Arrestees in Manhattan. Paper presented at a meeting of the American Criminal Justice Society, Chicago, Illinois, March.

Wish, Eric D., Brady, Elizabeth, Cuadrado, Mary, and Sears, Alton
1984 Preliminary Findings from the "Drug Use as a Predictor of Pretrial Behavior in Arrestees" Project. Paper presented at the annual meeting of the American Society of Criminology, Cincinnati, Ohio, November.

Wish, Eric D., Chedekel, Morris, Brady, Elizabeth, and Cuadrado, Mary
1985 Comparison of the Use of Thin-layer Chromatography and EMIT® for Detecting Recent Drug Use by Arrestees. Paper presented at the annual meeting of the American Academy of Forensic Sciences, Las Vegas, Nevada.

Wish, Eric D., Klumpp, K. A., Moorer, A. H., and Brady, E.
1980 An Analysis of Drugs and Crime Among Arrestees in the District of Columbia. Springfield, Va: National Technical Information Service.
1981 Executive Summary: An Analysis of Drugs and Crime Among Arrestees in the District of Columbia. Washington, D.C.: National Institute on Justice.

Wish, Eric D., Strug, David, Anderson, Kevin, Miller, Tom, and Johnson, Bruce D.
1983 Are Urine Tests Good Indicators of the Validity of Self-Reports of Drug Use? It Depends on the Test. Paper presented at the American Society of Criminology Meeting, Denver, Colorado, November.

Zinberg, Norman
1984 *Drugs, Set, and Setting.* Chicago, Ill.: University of Chicago Press.

3

The Relationship of Problem Drinking to Individual Offending Sequences

James J. Collins

INTRODUCTION

This paper examines the empirical association and etiological relevance of problem drinking to the onset, continuation, and pattern of criminal careers. The main purpose is to determine, based on previous research, what inferences can be made about the relation of problem drinking to serious and repetitious involvement in crimes that victimize persons or property. Hence, the paper is not concerned with crimes that are related to the use or distribution of alcohol. Underage drinking, public drunkenness, the illegal sale of alcoholic beverages, and driving while intoxicated are alcohol-defined offenses and are considered here only if they are relevant to individual offending sequences (criminal careers). Nor is the paper concerned with the influence of alcohol use in particular criminal events. A substantial literature addresses whether drinking precipitates criminal events or changes their character—especially violent events. Some of that literature will be partially relevant here, but the criminal career focus of the paper requires an emphasis on offenders' life cycles and not on particular events. [Reviews of the alcohol-criminal events literature can be found in Roizen and Schneberk (1977) and Collins (1981).]

It is clear that identified offenders are much more likely than the general population to engage in problem drinking. It has not been established, however, that the problem drinking explains serious involvement in crime. Indeed, the fundamental difficulty of this paper will be distinguishing the pervasive use of alcohol among offenders from the explanatory relevance of alcohol use to individual offending sequences. A basic assumption of the paper is that alcohol use is never the sole cause of a criminal career. Alcohol's behavioral effects are filtered through a variety of physiological, psychological, social, and cultural factors. Thus, drawing etiological or causal infer-

James J. Collins is a staff member at the Center for Social Research and Policy Analysis, Research Triangle Institute, Research Triangle Park, North Carolina. The author acknowledges the assistance of Patricia L. Kristiansen and Elizabeth R. Cavanaugh, both of the Research Triangle Institute.

ences will be difficult because of the complexity of the alcohol-behavior relationship and because most of the relevant research has not addressed causal-inference problems.

The ideal research design for making inferences about the effect of alcohol use on individual offending sequences is a longitudinal one that begins to collect data on drinking and criminal behavior before the onset of either behavior. No such research has been done, nor is any planned, so far as this writer is aware. A number of completed or ongoing longitudinal studies have the data with which to analyze the effects of alcohol use on criminal careers, but completed longitudinal analyses have not focused on the role of alcohol. Some researchers have examined the importance of drug use (Johnston, O'Malley, and Eveland, 1976; Elliott, Huizinga, and Ageton, 1982) but they either ignore alcohol use or combine alcohol use with drug use in their analyses. Most of the promise of completed and ongoing longitudinal research to determine whether and how alcohol use affects individual offending sequences remains to be realized.

METHODOLOGICAL ISSUES

Definition and Measurement of Problem Drinking

Problem drinking is the main independent variable in this analysis. The term can have many definitions and is not consistently defined in the literature. Occasional and light or moderate use of alcohol that does not have adverse outcomes is not of interest here. Neither is the focus only on the condition of alcoholism. Problem drinking is interpreted here to include: (1) excessive use of alcohol based on quantity or frequency of intake; (2) adverse consequences of drinking, such as family, job, or health problems; and (3) perceptions of the drinker or others that he or she has a drinking problem. The literature includes work that is not explicit about the definition of drinking problems or alcoholism. In the discussions of individual works that follow, the basis for defining drinking as a problem is made explicit. Usually, the definition relies on some measure of excessive intake or of adverse outcomes of drinking. Sometimes drinking is defined as a problem on the basis of criminal outcomes, such as arrest or violence after drinking. For the purposes of this paper the latter definition confounds independent and dependent variables and inhibits a determination of whether drinking is a causal factor in criminal careers.

Problem drinking is usually measured by records of alcohol-related arrests or alcohol treatment or by self-reports of alcohol-use patterns or problems. Blood alcohol content (BAC) measures, physiological indicators, and use of instruments with known reliabilities are rarely found in the literature. The incompleteness and inaccuracy of public records are well-known problems, and the reliability and validity of self-report data are infrequently discussed in the literature. The discussion below specifies the source of data on problem drinking and discusses those measures when that seems appropriate for methodological or substantive reasons.

If an individual develops a drinking problem, it is very often not permanent. Typical prevalences and types of drinking problems vary by segment of the life cycle, and drinking problems tend to be highest during the young adult years (Cahalan and Room, 1974; Cahalan and Cisin, 1976; Mandell and Ginzburg, 1976; Noble, 1978). There is evidence that problem drinkers often stop having problems through abstinence or controlled drinking (Robins, Bates, and O'Neal, 1962; Fillmore, 1975; Cahalan and Cisin, 1976; Roizen, Cahalan, and Shanks, 1978). The type of drinking problem experienced by an individual also varies by age. For example, Cahalan and Room (1974) show that "police" problems due to drinking are highest between the ages of 21 and 24, but that health problems due to drinking, comparatively low between the ages of 25 and 44, increase after age 44.

An implication of the age-variation and spontaneous-remission evidence is that the lifetime and current prevalences of drinking problems differ. Much of the data in the literature on problem drinking and criminal careers, however, do not distinguish "ever" having drinking problems from "current" problems, nor do they place the drinking problems within a life-cycle segment. This lack of specificity limits the career inferences that can be drawn from the findings. Long-term drinking patterns and the cumulative effects of drinking alcohol over a long period are more relevant to the career focus of this paper than the acute effects of alcohol use in single drinking episodes. This is also consistent with the focus on individual offending sequences rather than particular criminal events.

Some long-term effects of drinking are well known. Misuse of alcohol is associated with liver disease, nutritional deficits, brain dysfunction, cardiovascular problems, and an increased risk of cancer (Eckardt et al., 1981). Much less is known about the long-term behavioral effects of problem drinking. There are empirically unsupported suggestions in the literature that alcohol's chronic effects may cause "irritability," and although the inference must be tentative, chronic alcohol effects may increase individual tendencies toward violence. A more reasonable basis for the pharmacological and physiological effects of alcohol on behavior is through its impact on cognitive capacity. Alcohol use impairs a drinker's ability to perceive, process, assess, and integrate cues from the environment (Pernanen, 1976, 1981).

A distinction is relevant for purposes of this paper, although it is a distinction not usually made in the literature and thus is not sustainable in the analyses that follow. Problematic alcohol use over a long period creates "neuropsychological deficits" in the drinker (Tarter and Alterman, 1984). Presumably, some of those deficits will affect behavior and may explain some criminal behavior. A priori it seems reasonable to expect such criminogenic deficits to impel one to "irrational" (violent) crime rather than to "rational" (acquisitive) crime. A second type of chronic criminogenic effect of problem drinking may be a recurrent effect in individuals who are not necessarily chronic problem drinkers. Examples would be an infrequent drinker who tends to have problems when he or she does drink and a regular drinker who occasionally commits offenses when drinking. Even though these distinctions cannot be made from the existing literature, it is useful to recognize them because of their potential relevance for etiological understanding.

The "eye of the beholder" issue is also an important one for interpreting alcohol use as problematic. Alcohol occupies unique psychological, cultural, moral, and scientific territories in American life. The phenomenological dimension causes definitional and inferential problems, some of which are discussed below. The phenomenological complexities cannot be resolved here, but they are partially addressed through explicit definitions of what is meant by problem drinking.

Definition and Measurement of Criminal Careers

Criminal careers involving "street" crime are of interest here. In general, these are *Uniform Crime Reports* Part I and Part II offenses that involve actual or attempted violence or property loss. This focus excludes two major categories of crime: (1) victimless crime, especially alcohol- and drug-defined crime—including public-order crimes that result from substance abuse (vagrancy, disorderly conduct, et cetera) and (2) white collar crime. The first category is not used to define a criminal career because, as noted, it confounds independent and dependent variables and because interest is in criminal behavior that involves victimization of someone's person or property. It will not always be possible to distinguish the victimless or public-order offenses from other offenses because some studies do not make the distinction.

White collar crime is not considered because almost no information is available on the relationship of alcohol use to such offenses. It is reasonable to infer that white collar criminal careers would be influenced by problem drinking. Alcohol is the principal drug of choice for white collar, psychoactive substance users, and it is known that significant percentages of people of high occupational status are heavy drinkers or have problems with alcohol (Cahalan, Cisin, and Crossley, 1969; Trice and Roman, 1972). The relationship between alcohol problems and white collar crime, however, has not been studied.

Official records and self-report data are used to estimate involvement in crime. Each type of data has its strengths and weaknesses. The most serious problem with using official records to estimate criminal behavior is their incompleteness. Most crimes are not reported to the police (Bureau of Justice Statistics, 1983b). There is also some evidence that alcohol abusers are more likely than nonabusers to be arrested. Petersilia, Greenwood, and Lavin (1978), for example, found that alcohol abusers were arrested for 12.1 percent of the offenses they committed compared with 2 to 3 percent for drug abusers and offenders who were neither drug nor alcohol abusers. If the problem drinker is more likely to be arrested given commission of an offense, it may be a result of the cognitive impairment that results from alcohol use. A drinking offender may be an incompetent offender. If the probability of arrest is higher for problem drinkers than others, official records may overstate the importance of problem drinking to criminal careers.

Self-reports of illegal activity have added an important dimension to the study of criminal careers. The reliability and validity of such data have been examined, and the best general conclusion seems to be that offender reports of illegal involvement represent reasonable approximations of the behaviors in question (Marquis, 1981; Hubbard et al., 1982). The data are likely to contain some systematic error, however. Hubbard et al. (1982) found that the frequency of involvement and length of recall affected the concordance of self-reports of arrest and official records of arrest. Peterson and Braiker (1980) found rapists less willing than other offender types to report the crimes for which they were convicted. Weis (in this volume) discusses other issues relating to self-reports of criminal behavior. Because of the potential for the type of crime data to affect findings in systematic ways, the discussion below specifies the sources of data used in the analyses.

Study Populations

Studies of problem drinking and criminal careers have been carried out on samples of the general population, arrestees or convicted offenders, alcohol abuse and mental-health treatment populations, and prison populations. Studies of the general population are least frequent; studies of prison populations most frequent. Clearly, general-population studies are most generalizable, although such studies are relatively expensive to conduct. Neither a criminal career nor problem drinking is common among the general population, so large samples are required to produce sufficient data for detailed analysis. On the other hand, prison populations have a high prevalence of involvement in criminal activity and problem drinking and are relatively accessible to researchers. The trade-off in using prison samples is limited generalizability. Prisoners are not representative of the general population or of all offenders. Because of the representativeness and generalizability issues, discussions that follow are organized in part by the type of sample studied, i.e., general, alcohol treatment, and criminal justice system samples.

Polydrug Use

It is common for individuals to use multiple psychoactive substances (O'Donnell et al., 1976; Fishburne, Abelson, and Cisin, 1980; Johnston, Bachman, and O'Malley, 1981; Bray, Guess, et al., 1983). This may involve the use of alcohol and other drugs at the same time or within a short time (hours), or different psychoactive substances on different occasions. Polydrug use (including such combinations as alcohol and marijuana, alcohol and barbiturates, heroin and cocaine) has become very common in recent years, and there is evidence that it (including alcohol) is the modal pattern among offenders and treatment populations (Bray, Schlenger, et al., 1982; Chaiken and Chaiken, 1982; Johnson and Goldstein, 1984). Polydrug use creates a complex analytic problem when the behavioral effects of a particular substance are of interest. The behavioral effects of single drugs are not well understood, and, when two or more drugs are used in combination, specific behavioral effects are all but impossible to predict.

Despite the proliferation of polydrug use, most users have a "drug of choice," and individuals who have alcohol or drug problems are usually able to identify the substance that is the primary source of their difficulties. Among 3,325 individuals entering federally funded drug abuse treatment programs in 1979, for example, 87 percent specified a particular substance as being their "primary" problem (Bray, Schlenger, et al., 1982). The separation of individuals into categories based on alcohol or specific-drug problems, however, does oversimplify the reality of substance-use patterns, and individuals may be classified in different categories during different phases of their lives. It is the heuristic assumption of this paper that individuals can be classified accurately as having or not having a drinking problem (lifetime or current). This classification permits examination of the relationship between problem drinking and individual offending sequences.

Because use of hard drugs is usually viewed as a more serious criminogenic factor than alcohol use, there is a tendency among researchers to create hierarchical indices of psychoactive substance use in which the independent effect of alcohol use by drug users is not considered. For example, Johnson, Wish, and Huizinga (1983) analyze the substance use-delinquency relationship for two groups: those who use alcohol only and those who use drugs or drugs and alcohol. This approach assumes, without testing, that drug use is the primary criminogenic effect. The fact that alcohol is a legal drug encourages such a view. It is important, however, to consider separately whether alcohol use, which is often quite heavy among drug users, makes an independent contribution to the occurrence of criminal behavior as part of a polydrug-use pattern.

Gender and Race

The variables of gender and race receive little attention in this paper, mainly because the literature on problem drinking and criminal careers rarely considers gender and race effects. When these variables are included in analyses, the findings are not markedly different for gender or racial groups.

There is evidence that suggests that white-black racial differences in drinking patterns exist and that they have implications for the problem drinking-criminal career relationship. For example, a national survey of state correctional inmates showed a substantial difference by racial group in the percentage of inmates classified as heavy drinkers—50 percent for whites versus 21 percent for blacks (Bureau of Justice Statistics, 1983c). The literature that is relevant to the relation between problem drinking and individual offending sequences, however, does not permit assessment of white-black differences. The same holds for gender; the literature does not address the question of gender effects in the problem drinking-criminal career relationship. Moreover, there seems no reason to believe that problem drinking explains much variation in serious crimes by women. Because women probably commit less than one-fifth of the serious crimes and because the gender variable does not appear to bear on the problem drinking-criminal career relationship, gender is not considered here in any detail.

Making Inferences About Alcohol Effects

Despite years of study, a great deal remains to be understood about the behavioral effects of alcohol use—both acute (short-term) and chronic (long-term) effects. Woods and Mansfield (1983) argue that pharmacological changes in neural functioning brought about by ethanol are "nonspecific." Jones and Vega (1972, 1973) found that a rapid increase in BAC causes behavioral effects. Several researchers report that racial-ethnic groups differ in their reactions to drinking (Wolff, 1972; Fenna et al., 1976; Marco and Randels, 1983); others report that individual psychology influences the effects of alcohol (McCord and McCord, 1962; Zucker, 1968; McClelland et al., 1972). Pernanen (1976, 1981) suggests that the effects of alcohol use on cognition probably interact with environmental cues in complex ways. In sum, the "state of the art" in understanding the behavioral effects of drinking from pharmacologic and psychological perspectives is not far advanced.

Evidence of the complexity of the subject is pointed out by Cordelia (1985). Her analysis suggests that for some types of criminal activity, notably organized crime or planned property crime committed in collaboration with two or more people, problem drinking may act as a bar to criminal activity. Offenders with drinking problems may be viewed as undependable and not recruited into criminal enterprises. This scenario suggests an inverse relationship between problem drinking and organized, rational criminal activity.

In recent years the importance of social and cultural factors in mediating alcohol's behavioral effects, as well as the interpretation of those effects, has been recognized. MacAndrew and Edgerton (1969) generated important insights about the influence of social and cultural factors. They showed how "drunken comportment" was affected by cultural factors and, conversely, how some cultures make provision for untoward behavior after drinking during specified "time out" periods. Room (1983) argues that the causal link between alcohol use and behavior is a sociocultural rather than a pharmacological one.

Three points about sociocultural influences on the alcohol use-behavior interaction are relevant for this paper. These points have to do with expectancy, disavowal, and attribution.

The behavior of individuals after drinking is influenced by effects they expect alcohol to have, quite aside from actual effects attributable to drinking. Lang et al. (1975) found that individuals who had been told they drank alcohol, even though they had not, became more aggressive in controlled laboratory experiments. Tamerin, Weiner, and Mendelson (1970) measured male alcoholics' expectations about how they would feel after drinking and made observations about actual behavior after drinking. Their sample of 13 accurately predicted they would become more aggressive after drinking. However, the subjects inaccurately predicted other effects of drinking (euphoria, sexuality) and their subsequent (after drinking) assessment of their behavior was more concordant with their predrinking predictions than with their actual behavior. Brown et al. (1980) assessed expectancies associated with moderate alcohol consumption among two samples (N = 125 and N = 440). Factor analysis of 216 yes-no items produced six behavioral-expectancy dimensions—one of which was "aggressiveness." Expectancies varied by demographic factors (age, sex) and by drinking experience.

Drinking is sometimes used as an account (Scott and Lyman, 1968) or deviance-disavowal technique. McCaghy (1968) showed how some men convicted of sexual offenses against children used drinking to excuse their behavior. Mosher (1983) points out how recent ABSCAM-convicted offenders have attempted to excuse or justify their behavior by reference to the effects of alcohol. Coleman and Straus (1979) argue that some men drink to give themselves an excuse to beat their wives.

The attribution of blame to alcohol in the absence of clear justification is also observable at the macro level. Gusfield (1963) analyzed the nineteenth century temperance movement and argues that the abolition of alcohol became the subject of a moral crusade as the vehicle for playing out the conflict between competing societal interests. In a review of the family-violence literature Hamilton and Collins (1981) argue that a "malevolence assumption" underlies much of the public debate about alcohol. When alcohol is found to be associated with undesirable events and circumstances, it is assumed to be at fault.

The major points to be made about previous work on the expectancy, disavowal, and attributive aspects of alcohol's effects on behavior are that perceptions and interpretations complicate the causal-inference task and make it difficult to assess the validity of self-perceptions of alcohol's effects. Alcohol occupies unique phenomenological territory, and caution is warranted when attributing effects to its use. There is no doubt that drinking affects behavior. Explaining how that happens is difficult. Moreover, there is a tendency to ascribe blame to drinking without justification.

ASSESSMENT OF THE LITERATURE

This section of the paper reviews the literature on the relation of problem drinking to individual offending sequences. The juvenile, young adult, and later adult life-cycle segments are treated separately. The period that has received most attention by researchers is the young adult period. As will be seen, there are good reasons for this attention.

The separation of the analysis into juvenile, young adult, and later adult periods also reflects society's drinking norms. Most drinking during the juvenile years is illegal and disapproved by adult society.

Nevertheless, drinking is quite common among juveniles. In young adulthood drinking is legally permissible. In fact, heavy drinking accompanied by deviant or disruptive behavior is the norm for young adults in some contexts (for example, in the military or at fraternity parties). Drinking norms shift again for older adults. Family and career responsibilities are expected to mitigate or preclude the heavy use of alcohol, and behavior after drinking is expected to meet a higher level of decorum than is expected in the young adult years.

There is considerable variation around age-graded drinking norms. For example, young adults might be held to higher behavioral standards regarding alcohol use in some contexts, such as at a family reunion. Older adults may be permitted to act like young adults in some situations, such as at a football game. Nonetheless, drinking and its behavioral consequences display age regularities. For this reason, and because the literature itself is roughly organized in this way, the following review is organized around the three life-cycle segments. As mentioned earlier, the reviews will also be roughly organized by sample type (general population, alcohol treatment, and criminal justice) when the literature permits such a separation.

The Juvenile Period

During the juvenile years any consumption of alcohol is a potential problem because drinking is illegal for those under statutory drinking age, which ranges from age 18 to 21. Illegal purchase or consumption of alcoholic beverages, however, is not of interest here unless it is associated with other criminal behavior during the juvenile years or later in the life cycle. Specifically, this review focuses on the following questions: Does the age at which drinking begins have any power to predict involvement in serious crime? Do drinking problems during the juvenile years predict later criminal careers or aspects of individual offending sequences, such as career length or offense specialization? Little previous work has focused on these questions so the answers are necessarily incomplete.

Considerable previous work has focused on drug use during the juvenile years. Most of that work will not be examined here because another paper in this volume (Wish and Johnson) focuses on drug abuse and individual offending sequences. Some work has included alcohol use as an aspect of drug use. More commonly, the literature treats alcohol use, drug use, and other delinquencies (such as truancy, running away from home, and precocious sexual behavior) as aspects of a configuration of problem behaviors (Jessor and Jessor, 1977). This view of juvenile delinquency is a function of the adjudication process for juveniles and of the typical pattern of conduct of delinquents who come to the attention of the juvenile justice system. Juveniles are more likely to be "adjudicated delinquent" than to be convicted of a particular offense, and typically juvenile offenders (like adult offenders) exhibit a mixture of problems and illegal involvements. In comparison with the prevalence of problem behavior and delinquency, involvement in serious crime is low during the juvenile years. It is also low in comparison with the young adult years. Elliott and Huizinga (1983), for example, show how rates of participation in serious crime by youths in a national sample are low in comparison with participation rates for minor crimes and status offenses. Involvement in felony assault, robbery, felony theft, and hard-drug use tends to be lower than involvement in minor assault, minor theft, vandalism, and school delinquency for males and females and across social classes.

General-Population Studies

Alcohol use is very common among high-school-age youths. National surveys conducted in 1974 and 1978 showed that 87 to 89 percent of the tenth through twelfth graders had some experience with alcohol (Rachal et al., 1980). Substantial proportions drank frequently. Twenty-seven to 29 percent in the two surveys drank once a week or more. Heavy drinkers, defined as those drinking at least weekly and taking five or more drinks per drinking occasion, constituted 15 percent of the samples. Based on criteria of frequency of drunkenness and perceived alcohol-related negative consequences, approximately 3 in 10 were classified as misusers of alcohol. Alcohol misusers were significantly more likely than alcohol users to report having trouble with the police; 4.1 percent of male alcohol users and 25.4 percent of male alcohol misusers had trouble with the police because of drinking. The corresponding percentages for female alcohol users and misusers were 2.4 and 11.5, respectively.

The findings from studies of general-population samples of juveniles are that delinquency, as noted above, typically constitutes a varied configuration of problem behaviors. Jessor and Jessor (1977) and Jessor, Chase, and Donovan (1980), analyzing data from the national surveys of high school students referred to above, found that problem drinking was associated with marijuana use and general deviance. Jessor and associates argue further that the different forms of problem behavior develop from common etiological configurations.

Jessor et al. (1968), in a study of a tri-ethnic community, found that different measures of deviance correlate and that theoretical findings were fairly similar across different sex, age, and ethnic groups. White, Johnson, and Garrison (1983), in samples (N = 1,381) of 12-, 15-, and 18-year-olds from New Jersey households, found a "synchronous" development of both substance use (alcohol and drugs) and criminal behavior. The substance-use variable was a stronger predictor of the intensity of delinquent behavior than the reverse.

Rathus, Fox, and Ortins (1980) used a shortened version of the MacAndrew Alcoholism Scale and a self-reported delinquency scale in a study of 786 male and 886 female high school students in a middle-class suburban community. The sample was 97 percent white. The MacAndrew scale was found to predict alcohol abuse successfully, but it also was found to have "global predictive power." The scale predicted some drug use and other delinquency, such as property and personal crimes. The authors interpret this to indicate that problem drinking is part of a general pattern of deviance.

Rydelius (1983a,b) interviewed and collected blood samples in 1980–1981 from 2,300 young men who came to a military recruiting office in Sweden as a result of the compulsory military-service law. Data for 1,004 of the subjects were analyzed. Approximately 99 percent were between 17 and 19 years of age; 93 percent were 18 years old. The amount of pure alcohol consumed within the month prior to the interviews was estimated from self-reports of beer, wine, and spirits consumption. During the interviews, 21 percent admitted minor criminal offenses; 6 percent reported committing theft and burglary; 2 percent reported committing assault and malicious damage; 9 percent had been convicted of crimes; and 5 percent were known for public drunkenness.

Rydelius classified the subjects according to their consumption of pure alcohol and compared high consumers with nonconsumers on a number of dimensions. The high consumers were more likely than the nonconsumers to be drug users and to be involved in other crimes. The percentage of high consumers versus nonconsumers who engaged in various offenses are shown below (from Rydelius, 1983a:Table 7):

Offense	High Consumers versus Nonconsumers (percent)
Pilfering, illegal driving	45 versus 9
Stealing and burglary	38 versus 1
Conviction, any crime	35 versus 3
Known for public drunkenness	35 versus 1
Assault, malicious mischief	14 versus 1

All differences are statistically significant below the .001 level according to the chi-square statistic.

In subsequent psychological testing of 50 high consumers and 50 nonconsumers, the high consumers were found to have psychopathic personality traits and the nonconsumers were found to have normal personalities (Rydelius, 1983b). Differences were found between the two groups on 13 of 15 scales included in the test.

In summary, the evidence from general-population studies of juveniles is that problem drinking covaries with other forms of deviance and with serious criminal behavior. The relationship of problem drinking to deviance and crime is best conceived as one involving a common etiology in the juvenile years.

Delinquent-Population Studies

Studies of delinquent populations also confirm the strong covariation of alcohol use and delinquency. Blane and Hewitt (1977) reviewed a number of studies and concluded that

1. Age at first drink is earlier for delinquents than nondelinquents,
2. Prevalence of drinking is higher among delinquents than among nondelinquents,
3. Drunkenness is more prevalent among delinquents than among nondelinquents,
4. Pathological drinking symptoms are more common among delinquents than among nondelinquents.

Pearce and Garrett (1970) gave a 26–item questionnaire to 292 delinquents from two youth detention homes and 466 nondelinquent high school students in Idaho and Utah. They found the following differences between delinquents and nondelinquents in drinking behavior:

1. Delinquents drank at a younger age;
2. The first drink for delinquents was likely to be with friends; for nondelinquents, it was likely to be at home with parents;
3. Delinquents drank again sooner after the first drink;
4. Drinking prevalence and frequency were higher for delinquents;
5. Delinquents were more likely to have drunk hard liquor.

Bell and Champion (1979), in surveys of general-population and delinquent samples in Great Britain, found that frequent alcohol use was much more common among delinquents than among general-population samples and that the level of alcohol use predicted frequency of delinquency.

Dawkins and Dawkins (1983) examined the relationship between drinking frequency and criminal behavior among 342 residents of a juvenile training school. A questionnaire was administered to collect data about a variety of factors, including drinking frequency and involvement in 21 kinds of nonserious and serious illegal behaviors in the year before entering training school. The authors focused on whether the correlation between drinking frequency and illegal behavior differed for whites, blacks, and Hispanics. Multiple regression analyses revealed that drinking had strong net effects on minor delinquency in each racial group. Drinking frequency was found to explain statistically significant variation in serious and nonserious delinquency for whites and blacks. Drinking frequency did not explain involvement in serious delinquency for Hispanics but was associated with nonserious delinquency for this ethnic group. The authors did not deal with the temporal-order issue, that is, whether frequent drinking preceded, followed, or was coterminous with involvement in illegal behavior. The analyses do show that the empirical association of drinking frequency and criminal behavior was robust among white and black training-school residents.

Vingilis (1981) is not convinced by the evidence on drinking and delinquency because of methodological problems, especially the failure of much research to use control groups. Vingilis appears prepared to acknowledge that delinquents drink more than nondelinquents but thinks that delinquents charged with alcohol-related crimes are similar to delinquents involved in nonalcohol-related crimes. However, use of "alcohol-related trouble with the law" as an indicator of public drinking may not distinguish delinquents in a meaningful way.

Etiology of Drinking and Crime in Juveniles

Evidence on the common etiology of problem drinking and other deviance in the juvenile period and on the covariation of problem drinking and delinquency does not address directly the major issue of this paper: that is, to what extent is problem drinking an important factor in the onset, continuation, and pattern of criminal careers. Two studies give more specific insights about the relationship of problem drinking to individual offending sequences for juveniles.

Virkkunen (1977) studied recidivism among 741 juvenile offenders convicted in 1965 in Finland. He divided the offenders into those with juvenile arrests for drunkenness and those with no such arrests; using the records of Finland's Criminal Register, he examined recidivism for the years 1970–1975 (5 to 10 years after the initial contact). Virkkunen found that those who had juvenile drunkenness arrests were more likely to recidivate and were more likely to have arrests for violent (22 versus 12 percent) and property crimes (47 versus 36 percent), as well as for traffic offenses.

Johnson, Wish, and Huizinga (1983) analyzed National Youth Survey data (Elliott, Huizinga, and Ageton, 1982) with a focus on serious drug use and high-rate, serious delinquency. They created a hierarchical typology of drug users: users of heroin or cocaine (5 percent), users of pills or psychedelics (7 percent), marijuana users (19 percent), alcohol users (29 percent), and non-drug users (41 percent). Users of alcohol in addition to drugs are included in the first three categories. Heavy drug users (heroin, cocaine, pills, psychedelics) were also found to be heavy users of alcohol. Data on criminal activity were collected from self-reports during interviews.

Johnson and colleagues show that among the hierarchical groups those classified as heavy drug users were responsible for a disproportionately large number of index crimes. Those who used only alcohol were comparatively unlikely to commit index offenses or multiple index offenses although they were more likely than nonusers of any drug to commit minor delinquencies. The authors conclude that alcohol use by itself is not associated with either the likelihood or the frequency of involvement in serious crime in the juvenile years. It should be pointed out, however, that this conclusion does not deal fully with the effects of alcohol because alcohol use by those who use other drugs is subsumed in the drug-use categories. The findings do suggest that alcohol use by itself is not important to the occurrence of index offenses during the juvenile years.

Petersilia, Greenwood, and Lavin (1978) interviewed 49 California prison inmates incarcerated for armed robbery. The inmates were asked to reconstruct their criminal careers for their juvenile, young adult, and later adult years. They were also asked about their use of alcohol and drugs and were classified as alcohol involved, drugs involved, involved with both drugs and alcohol, or not involved with either drugs or alcohol. Twenty-five to 30 percent of the inmates were classified as alcohol involved in the three career periods. The major change over the three career segments was an increased tendency toward drug involvement.

Inmates classified as alcohol involved had the lowest median offense rates in each of the three career periods although, as discussed earlier, they were more likely than the three other groups to be arrested for offenses they committed. In terms of specific offense types the alcohol-only offenders had comparatively high rates of aggravated assault and auto theft during the juvenile period and comparatively high rates of burglary and forgery in the young adult period. During the later adult period, the alcohol-only offenders had high forgery and low robbery rates in comparison with the other groups. The offense-specific findings should be viewed as tentative because of sample size (N = 14 alcohol-involved offenders) and because of the challenging cognitive task involved in reconstructing criminal careers over very long periods.

There is more potential in existing longitudinal data on alcohol use and criminal behavior than has thus far been realized. Two examples of fertile data sets for additional study are the National Youth Survey data (Elliott et al., 1983) and the Rutgers Health and Human Development Project data, which are still being accumulated (see White, Johnson, and Garrison, 1983; Pandina, Labouvie, and White, 1984).

Summary: Juveniles

The evidence reviewed here for the juvenile period suggests the following:

1. Drinking problems do not, by themselves, appear to be an important factor in the onset of serious criminal involvement in the juvenile years.
2. Those who drink, drink heavily, or have problems as a result of drinking are more likely to be involved in other forms of deviant behavior. The best current assessment is that there are common etiologies for the juvenile syndrome of problem behavior.
3. Juveniles who are heavy consumers of alcohol have psychopathic personality traits (Rydelius, 1983b).
4. Juvenile offenders with arrests for drunkenness are more likely than juvenile offenders with no drunkenness arrests to have official records of violent and property crime as adults (Virkkunen, 1977).

The Young Adult Period

The young adult period begins between ages 18 and 21 and continues to age 35 or 40. The literature does not distribute neatly into the three life-cycle segments used in this paper, so that some of the work reviewed in this section will cover portions of the juvenile and later adult periods.

Problem drinking is relatively high in

the young adult years—especially among males (Cahalan and Room, 1974; Blane and Hewitt, 1977; Bray, Guess, et al., 1983). The Cahalan and Room national survey of men aged 21 to 59, for example, found that among men aged 21 to 24, 40 percent had experienced at least one alcohol-related problem in the past 3 years; 20 to 22 percent of those between ages 25 and 39 had one or more alcohol-related problems in the past 3 years. Arrest, conviction, and incarceration are also comparatively common in the young adult period (U.S. Department of Justice, 1975; Federal Bureau of Investigation, 1983), although the prevalence of offending appears to be the highest in the juvenile years (Langan and Farrington, 1983; Wolfgang, 1983). Even though both problem drinking and criminal involvement are high in the young adult period, the relationship between the two is not well understood. The following sections summarize what is known.

General-Population Studies of Young Adults

O'Donnell et al. (1976) analyzed data from 1974 interviews with a national sample of 2,510 young men aged 20 to 30. Ninety-two percent of the sample were current alcohol users. During the interviews the young men were asked to report the extent of their alcohol use and also their involvement in 10 categories of crime. The respondents were classified by the extent of their alcohol use: no use, experimental, light, medium, heavy, and very heavy use.

The prevalence of self-reported involvement in crime in the previous year increased with the extent of their alcohol use in the previous year. This was true for the alcohol-related offenses of public intoxication and driving while intoxicated and also for auto theft, breaking and entering, and shoplifting. A direct association between drinking level and crime prevalence was not apparent for armed robbery, stealing face-to-face, gambling, writing bad checks, and forging prescriptions. Respondents were not asked to report their involvement in assaultive offenses.

Bohman et al. (1982) studied the relationship of alcohol abuse and criminality among 862 Swedish men born out of wedlock between 1930 and 1949 in Stockholm, Sweden, and adopted by nonrelatives at an early age. The authors were interested in whether genetic and environmental factors predisposed individuals to adult criminality. The subjects ranged between ages 23 and 43 at the time of last information. Data were obtained from the Excise Board (registration of alcohol abuse) Health Insurance Office records and the Criminal Register. The Excise Board records include a variety of information about alcohol offenses, sanctions, and treatment. Criminal record information included recorded offenses, convictions, and sentences.

Those who had an official criminal record as well as a record of alcohol abuse were more recidivistic, had served longer jail terms, and had committed more violent crimes than criminals without alcohol-abuse records. Criminals without alcohol-abuse records had more often committed property offenses. Bohman and colleagues found that the correlation between age of onset of first alcohol abuse and first crime was .61. In 18 percent of cases the first crime came before first alcohol abuse; in 22 percent of cases, alcohol abuse preceded crime; and in 60 percent of cases the two occurred within 2 years of each other. In summarizing their findings the authors commented on the problem of causal attribution (Bohman et al., 1982:1239):

> Our major conclusion is that different genetic and environmental antecedents influence the development of criminality depending on

whether or not there is associated alcohol abuse. Consequently, it is crucial to distinguish antisocial personality disorders from criminality symptomatic of alcohol abuse in future clinical and etiologic studies. In particular, criminality without alcohol abuse is characterized by petty property offenses whereas alcohol-related criminality is more often violent and highly repetitive.

Robins (1978) examined alcohol use and arrests among a sample of more than 600 Vietnam veterans. The veterans were identified through Army records and interviewed twice. Twenty-three percent of the sample had an arrest in their second or third year back from Vietnam; most arrests were for trivial offenses. Four percent were arrested for property crimes, and 2 percent were arrested for violent crimes. Heavy drinking was common among the veterans, and there was a strong relationship between daily heavy drinking and arrest. When juvenile deviance was controlled, however, the heavy drinking-arrest relationship almost disappeared. Robins concludes that daily heavy drinking does make a significant contribution to arrest but accounts for only about 2 percent of the variance independent of early deviance and drug use.

McCord (1983) examined alcoholism and various criminal career indicators for 400 of the Cambridge Somerville Youth Study subjects. The Cambridge Somerville subjects were youths identified as in need of delinquency prevention services because they were at high risk of becoming delinquents. McCord collected official records of arrest for the subjects in the late 1970s and classified them as alcoholics or nonalcoholics based on interview data about drinking and arrests for alcohol-related offenses. She found the alcoholics had more serious criminal careers than the nonalcoholics. They had significantly more convictions overall and more convictions for crimes against the person.

Robins and her colleagues have analyzed data on alcohol abuse and crime for a sample of 223 black men born in St. Louis between 1930 and 1934 (Robins, Murphy, and Breckenridge, 1968; King et al., 1969; Robins, 1972; Robins and Wish, 1977). The sample was stratified on the basis of the father's presence or absence in the home during childhood, low or high guardian-occupation status, and mild or no school problems versus more serious school problems. A variety of public record systems (school, police, Selective Service, public welfare, prison) were searched for information about each subject, and 223 of the original sample of 235 were interviewed. Sixty-two percent of the sample had a history of heavy drinking. Heavy drinking and recent alcohol problems were associated with arrests for offenses not related to drinking (King et al., 1969). The authors believe alcohol abuse is a crucial intervening variable for a variety of social, economic, and legal troubles.

In two additional articles reporting analyses of the same data, Robins (1972) and Robins and Wish (1977) attempted to deal with the causality issue—that is, does alcohol abuse explain variation in arrest or incarceration independent of other factors and does alcohol abuse exist prior to arrest and incarceration? In the 1972 article Robins uses an actuarial-table technique to analyze the order of onset of alcohol problems and incarceration. Alcohol problems were measured by family complaint, alcohol-related health problems, an arrest for drunkenness, or job-related problems due to drinking. Data were gathered by interview and search of police, court, prison, and parole records. Even though alcohol problems and incarceration correlated 0.24, when other factors and temporal order were controlled, alcohol problems did not predict incarceration.

Robins and Wish (1977) conceptualize

deviance as both quantitative (number of different types of deviance) and qualitative (certain types of deviance are systematically related to other types of deviance) processes. Using the interview and record data for the 223 black men, they analyzed 13 types of deviance by age of onset. One of the variables was drinking before the age of 15; this was one of the strongest predictors of other kinds of deviance, and arrest was one of the outcomes predicted. After the number of earlier types of deviance was controlled, however, early drinking was no longer a significant predictor of arrest, although it appeared to make a contribution to explained variance. These findings indicate, perhaps not surprisingly, that early onset of alcohol use does not by itself explain significant variation in whether an individual eventually gets an arrest record. It is reasonable to think that early drinking effects interact with other factors, such as subsequent drinking behavior.

Alcohol Problems and Criminality in "Captured" Samples of Young Adults

Robins (1966) studied 524 people who had been referred to a guidance clinic in St. Louis as children 30 years before and compared them with a sample of 100 control subjects from the same community 30 years after high school graduation. The subjects were interviewed and a number of public record sources were used to accumulate life histories for the 624 subjects. The study was conceived mainly as a study of sociopathic personality. Robins found that subjects diagnosed as alcoholics during adulthood (but not meeting criteria for sociopathy) were more likely than "well" adults to have an arrest and incarceration history. In this early work Robins did not attempt to control for the temporal order or the confounding effects of other factors. Thus, it is not possible to infer much about the drinking problem-criminal career relationship, except that the two factors appear to covary.

Guze et al. (1962) conducted structured psychiatric interviews in 1960–1961 with 223 offenders who were on probation, on parole, or soon to be discharged from correctional institutions. Forty-three percent had symptoms in three of five symptom groups and were therefore classified as alcoholic. The alcoholic offenders had more arrests than the nonalcoholics; for example, 50 percent of the alcoholics but only 10 percent of the nonalcoholics had 10 or more previous arrests. (Alcohol-related offenses have not been excluded from this comparison.) The alcoholics were significantly more likely than nonalcoholics to be arrested for auto theft, but their arrest rates for robbery, burglary, larceny, forgery, and passing bad checks were not significantly higher than the rates for the nonalcoholics. The alcoholics were more likely to report excessive fighting both before and after age 18. No differences were found in the prevalence of delinquency, antisocial behavior, or crime before the age of 15 for the alcoholic and nonalcoholic groups. A large majority of subjects who reported delinquency or crime before age 15 said their delinquency preceded heavy drinking.

Goodwin, Crane, and Guze (1971) reinterviewed the felons in the Guze et al. (1962) sample, described above, 8 years later. Interviews were conducted with 176 of the original 209 subjects found at follow-up. The alcoholics (N = 118) had many more problems than the nonalcoholics, although a substantial number of the alcoholics were in remission at the time of the interview. The alcoholics who had stopped drinking had fewer arrests and imprisonments than those who had not. Nonetheless, those originally labeled alcoholics were more likely than the nonalcoholics to have arrests and incarcerations for any offense and for fights. Goodwin and colleagues conclude that excessive drinking intensifies or prolongs criminal behavior.

Lindelius and Salum (1973, 1975, 1976) studied samples of men treated for alcoholism in a hospital in Stockholm, Sweden, or registered at the Bureau for Homeless Men in Stockholm. The authors gathered data about criminal careers from the records of the Criminal Register. This central criminal record system permits estimation of a general-population risk of being in the register and, thus, comparison of criminal-record prevalences for the total population and for samples of individuals, such as alcoholics and homeless men.

In the 1973 article, Lindelius and Salum classify 1,026 male alcoholics treated in the hospital between 1956 and 1961 on the basis of the severity of their physical symptoms of alcoholism. Thirty-six percent had tremors without psychosis at admission (group 1); 19 percent had hallucinations with disorientation (group 2); and 45 percent had tremors, hallucinations, and disorientation (group 3). Recorded drinking offenses were examined separately. The alcoholics were more likely to appear in the Criminal Register than the general population, but the severity of alcoholism as measured by medical symptoms did not have much power to explain involvement in serious criminality. Group 3 had a lower percentage (37) of individuals in the Criminal Register than groups 1 and 2 combined (45 percent). An exception to this statement is the finding that assault and battery arrests were high among group 3 alcoholics under age 40 in comparison with this rate for groups 1 and 2. Recidivism was high for all three alcoholic groups but did not differ among the groups.

Lindelius and Salum (1976) compared the officially recorded criminality of the sample of treated alcoholics just described with that for (1) 139 men treated for alcoholism who had no convictions for drunkenness or alcoholism and (2) 202 men registered at Stockholm's Bureau for Homeless Men. The men who had no drunkenness or alcholism record (even though they were treated for alcoholism) were no more likely than the general population to have a criminal record. The official criminal-record rate for the homeless men was highest of the three samples. However, the authors did not control for age in the comparison of the three samples, and the homeless men were older than the other samples. The comparison of the criminal records for the three samples is as follows:

	Alcoholics (no drunk conviction)	Alcoholics (physical withdrawal symptoms)	Homeless men
Mean number of convictions	1.6	3.0	5.3
Percent with violent offense	0	23	35
Percent with property offense	16	17	84
Percent with sexual offense	0	4	7
Percent with driving-under-the-influence offense	0	28	35

The authors conclude that very different findings can result depending on whether one studies the role of alcohol among identified offenders or criminality among alcoholics.

A number of studies of prison samples have examined alcoholism and problem drinking among inmates. These studies find high rates of problem drinking among inmates (Institute for Scientific Analysis, 1978; Crawford et al., 1982; Collins and Schlenger, 1983; Bureau of Justice Statistics, 1983c). Washbrook (1977) is an exception. Without presenting systematic evidence on the point, the author claims that interviews with 5,000 English prisoners showed half to have drunk on the day of the incarceration offense, but that alcohol was relevant to only a small percentage of the offenses, and less than 5 percent of the inmates were alcoholic. (The term "relevant" was not defined.)

More relevant than the alcoholism rate of prisoners for purposes of this paper is whether inmates who are problem drinkers have individual offending patterns that differ from those of offenders who do not have drinking problems. The evidence suggests they do. Five studies show that prisoners with drinking problems have higher assault rates than prisoners without drinking problems.

Mayfield (1976) studied offenders incarcerated in North Carolina prisons for assault offenses. He found that the problem drinkers had more previous arrests for alcohol-related offenses, more nonalcohol-related arrests, and more previous arrests for assault than the incarcerated violent offenders who did not have a drinking problem.

An Institute for Scientific Analysis (1978) report on drinking and criminal career patterns showed that those classified as heavy drinkers were more likely to be incarcerated for a violent offense than for another kind of offense. Data were gathered during interviews of 310 inmates in California, and a quantity-frequency index was used to estimate alcohol consumption.

Barnard, Holzer, and Vera (1979) looked at the history of alcohol use among 88 Florida prisoners who had been charged with rape. Data were collected from informal interviews and institutional records. Twenty-seven percent were classified as alcoholics. The diagnosis was based on the inmate's satisfying any three of six criteria measuring drinking history and consequences of drinking. The alcoholic prisoners had more previous arrests and more previous arrests for violent offenses than the nonalcoholics.

Chaiken and Chaiken (1982) in a study of 2,190 jail and prison inmates in California, Michigan, and Texas found that self-reported problem drinking in the immediate preincarceration period was a strong predictor of self-reported assault rates in the preincarceration period.

Gibbens and Silberman (1970) studied 404 inmates in three London prisons, excluding short-sentence drunkenness offenders. The authors interviewed the inmates and divided them into heavy drinkers and others. (The authors do not clearly describe how the inmates' drinking behavior was classified.) The heavy drinkers were more likely than nondrinkers to have a history of two or more "aggressive" offenses. The heavy drinkers were also more likely to be reconvicted during a 9- to 12-month follow-up period.

Two other studies examined incarcerated samples and considered drinking problems. Myers (1982) interviewed 50 Scottish prisoners incarcerated for violent offenses and 50 prisoners incarcerated for nonviolent offenses. Although the typical drinking levels of the two groups did not differ, the violent prisoners were more likely than the nonviolent prisoners to report drinking at the time of the incarceration offense. Drinking was higher than usual for both groups in the week prior to the incarceration offense.

Edwards, Hensman, and Peto (1971) compared two groups of male prisoners who were incarcerated in 1965. A short-term group (N = 188) was serving sentences of 3 months or less; a long-term group (N = 312) was serving sentences of 1 year or more. The authors collected data using an 80-item semistructured interview. An alcohol-dependence score was constructed on the basis of responses to questions about morning shakes and morning drinking. In the long-term group, those convicted of violent offenses had higher alcohol-dependency scores than those convicted of nonviolent offenses, while the reverse was the case for short-term offenders not incarcerated for a drunkenness offense. Long-term offenders convicted earlier of violent offenses also had elevated alcohol-dependency scores.

Discussion: Young Adults

The evidence cited in the previous two sections suggests the following for the young adult years:

1. Problem drinking covaries directly with self-reported criminality and arrest.
2. Alcohol-treatment samples have higher-than-expected official crime rates, and incarcerated offenders have higher-than-expected problem drinking rates.
3. Problem drinkers have higher-than-expected records of involvement in violent crime and self-report disproportionately high rates of violent behavior.
4. When temporal order and other factors are controlled, the explanatory power of problem drinking for individual offending sequences is reduced or eliminated.

The foregoing and other literature discuss some of the causal aspects of the problem drinking-crime interaction. Three aspects of the etiological issue are discussed briefly below: (1) the relationship of problem drinking and antisocial personality disorder (psychopathic or sociopathic personality), (2) the notion that the temporal order may be crime → problem drinking and not the reverse, and (3) the idea that there are distinct problem drinker-offender types that confound attempts to understand the relationship between problem drinking and individual offending sequences.

Problem Drinking and Antisocial Personality. One way to conceptualize the covariation of problem drinking and criminal behavior is to view each of the factors as aspects of a configuration of behaviors that make up a deviant life-style. In other words, drinking problems and criminal behavior simply represent sets of behaviors that occur together as a result of a common etiology or life orientation. This conception appears to fit the empirical findings fairly well; that is, there is strong covariation between problem drinking and criminal careers, but it is difficult to show the former to be a cause of the latter. But, while this model may fit the facts, it is not helpful for specifying causal factors to guide prevention and treatment strategies.

An analogue of the problem drinking-criminal behavior relationship is that of problem drinking and antisocial personality (ASP) disorder. An ASP disorder is defined, according to the American Psychiatric Association's (1980) *Diagnostic and Statistical Manual of Mental Disorders*, as continuous and chronic antisocial behavior in which the rights of others are violated, including 3 or more of 12 symptoms before age 15 and 4 or more of 9 symptoms after age 18. Alcohol abuse and dependence are commonly found among those diagnosed as ASP (Guze, Goodwin, and Crane, 1969; James, Gregory, and Jones, 1980; Hare, 1983).

Robins (1966:260) asked the question "Are alcoholics mild sociopaths?" She answered the question negatively by suggesting that alcoholics' symptoms are directly attributable to excessive alcohol intake and that it is possible to distinguish the symptoms of the two disorders. The question is important here because it would be helpful to know how drinking problems and ASP disorders are related to each other. If the disorder types are confounded with each other, attempts at etiologic understanding of the problem drinking-individual offending sequences relationship are complicated.

Several writers whose works were reviewed earlier suggest that "psychopathic" personality traits are important to the problem drinking-criminal career relationship (Goodwin, Crane, and Guze, 1971; Lindelius and Salum, 1973, 1975; Bohman et al., 1982; Rydelius, 1983b). Conceptual and empirical refinement of this relationship will serve understanding of the problem drinking-criminal career relationship because it appears that common causal factors may be involved.

Temporal Order of Problem Drinking and Criminal Careers. Some of the empirical evidence indicates that criminal behavior is more likely to precede problem drinking than the reverse (Guze et al., 1962; Robins, Murphy, and Breckenridge, 1968; Lindelius and Salum, 1975). In the Guze et al. research, for example, 66 to 87 percent of those in the sample said their delinquency or crime preceded heavy drinking. In their assessment of the literature, Roizen and Schneberk (1977) argue it is more logical to infer that crime causes "chronic inebriacy" than the reverse. What does seem clear from the literature is that the temporal-order issue is not a simple one. Often crime comes before problem drinking, although the more common pattern appears to be both problem drinking and crime occurring initially within a short time of each other.

A major aspect of this question is how "problem drinking" is defined. Early onset of drinking was a criterion measure used by Robins and Wish (1977). Heavy intake is the measure used by others (Bureau of Justice Statistics, 1983a); still others use physical symptoms or adverse consequences of drinking (Guze et al., 1962; Lindelius and Salum, 1973). With this diversity in the measurement of problem drinking, it is not surprising that findings on the temporal-order issue are not consistent.

It is helpful to distinguish several dimensions of problem drinking: (1) early (age) drinking, (2) heavy intake or symptomatic (binge, morning, et cetera) drinking, (3) problem consequences (family, employment, police problems, et cetera), (4) physical symptoms (tremors, cirrhosis, et cetera), and (5) whether problem drinking is a current problem. These general dimensions can be further refined. For example, heavy drinking can be defined in terms of frequency, number of drinks per drinking occasion, and a quantity-frequency index. A "current" problem can be defined by different periods, such as past year or past 3 years. During the young adult period, measures (2), (3), and (5) above tend to be the most appropriate and frequently used measures of problem drinking. It is also apparent from what is known about the age at which criminal careers start that problem drinking, with the exception of age at first use, often starts after the age at first serious offense. On the surface, this suggests that problem drinking is not etiologically important to the onset of criminal careers.

Although problem drinking may not be important to the onset of criminal careers, that does not mean that it may not be important to the continuation and specific nature of the career. It is this latter point that is the most important general inference to be drawn from the relationship between problem drinking and individual offending sequences in the young adult years. Problem drinking appears to intensify or prolong serious involvement in criminal behavior. Most of the literature reviewed earlier supports such an interpretation.

Problem-Drinker and Offender Types. It may be valid and appropriate to focus scientific and policy attention on subsets of problem drinkers and offender types. The literature does not provide much specific guidance for such a focus, but it does seem clear that some problem-drinker types are more important to individual offending sequences than others. Some of the evidence is noted below.

Roebuck and Johnson (1962) identified the "Negro drinker and assaulter as a criminal type" from an examination of the arrest records of 400 offenders entering the District of Columbia Reformatory in 1954 and 1955. This offender type could also be distinguished from other offender types on the basis of a number of background and socialization factors. McCord (1983) examined adult alcoholism and criminal outcomes for boys rated as "aggressive" by their teachers and found that being so rated was related to later elevated rates of alcoholism and crime.

Coid (1982) and Rydelius (1983b) believe there is an important subgroup of alcohol-abusing offenders that can be distinguished by an underlying personality abnormality. The abnormality is generally described as psychopathy.

Tarter (1983) distinguished type-I (primary) and type-II (secondary) alcoholics. While there is some ambiguity about the exact definition of the two types, it is the type-II alcoholic who is viewed as most likely to engage in criminal behavior related to problem drinking. Type-II alcoholics are male and engage in moderate to heavy drinking. Type-I alcoholics display more severe symptoms of chronic alcoholism. A similar distinction is made by Blane and Chafetz (1979), who talk about two "alcoholics." One type is the traditional clinical, diagnostic, and treatment type. The other, a more transitory type, is characterized by frequent heavy drinking and adverse consequences.

Tarter (1983) compared two groups of primary and secondary alcoholics on a variety of measures and concluded that the primary alcoholic is a valid clinical subtype. Primary alcoholics were more likely than secondary alcoholics to display antecedent minimal brain dysfunction symptoms. Secondary alcoholics were more likely to display symptoms of psychological abnormality. While the importance of age or the number of years of drinking to type-I and type-II alcoholism needs to be assessed, there is the suggestion that types of individuals may be identified who are at high risk of problem drinking and serious criminal involvement.

Finally, after examination of problem drinking remission rates among a group of felons, Goodwin, Crane, and Guze (1971:144) concluded "criminal alcoholics may represent a different variety of alcoholism from that seen in psychiatric private practice or hospital alcoholism wards."

The above evidence suggests that problem drinking is important to individual offending sequences only for some types of people. Stated another way, there appear to be individual characteristics that increase the likelihood that serious criminal behavior related to problem drinking will occur. Additional work should focus more specifically on attempting to identify the antecedent and ongoing individual factors that are related to problem drinking and criminal behavior. Such a focus would be "efficient" from both scientific and policymaking perspectives.

Later Adult Years: Drinking and Crime

The magnitude of the association between problem drinking and individual offending sequences is highest during the young adult years, but it may also be important for a subset of offenders and offenses committed during middle age (approximately ages 35 to 55). Few serious crimes are committed by those over age 55. Past work has often identified the crime problem of old age as one of "chronic inebriacy" (Pittman and Gordon, 1958). Epstein, Mills, and Simon (1970) estimate that four of five arrests of the elderly are for drunkenness. Shichor and Kobrin (1978) make a similar point. Arrest, conviction, and incarceration for alcohol-defined offenses, however, are not of primary interest in this paper.

Middle-aged and older offenders have not received much attention from criminologists or policymakers. The major reason for this is the relatively infrequent arrest of older offenders for serious crimes. Only 11.6 percent of all offenders arrested for index crimes in 1981 were 35 years of age or older (Federal Bureau of Investigation, 1982). Attention to the middle-age or later years has been even less frequent in the study of criminal careers. Some previous work suggests that there may be a relationship between problem drinking and late onset of criminal careers; findings, however, are not consistent.

Edwards, Kyle, and Nicholls (1977) studied a group of 935 male and female alcoholic patients discharged from hospitals in England between 1953 and 1957. The mean age of the sample was 45.2. Scotland Yard criminal records, which usually do not include juvenile or drunkenness offenses, were searched for each of the subjects for the period up to the end of 1957. This included the periods before and after hospitalization.

Thirty-two percent of the men and 17 percent of the women had a conviction record. Mean age at first conviction for the men was 34.9; for the women, it was 37.4. For both sexes, age at first conviction was skewed upward in comparison with general crime statistics. General statistics show that only 21 percent of a group of first offenders were over age 40. In the sample under study 32 percent of the men and 45 percent of the women were aged 40 or older at first conviction. Gibbens and Silberman (1970) also found an excess of alcoholics among those first convicted after age 30. Controlling for age, the alcoholics were also found to have "excess" recidivism rates after hospitalization compared with a control group.

Langan and Greenfeld (Bureau of Justice Statistics, 1983a) studied career patterns in crime using the nationwide survey of state correctional inmates conducted in 1979. The survey includes interviews with a random sample of 11,397 state prison inmates. The authors were interested in studying criminal careers that had spanned a long period, so they limited their analysis to inmates who were at least age 40 at the time of current prison admission. Inmates were classified into four groups according to whether their criminal careers included incarceration between ages 7 and 17 and between ages 18 and 39. Forty-seven percent of the sample of 827 inmates aged 40 or more experienced their first incarceration at age 40 or older (type 4). Almost half of all "incarceration careers" of inmates aged 40 or older did not begin until relatively late. The next largest group (38.2 percent) consisted of those who had no juvenile incarceration but had at least one adult incarceration before age 40 (type 3). Approximately two-thirds of the type-4 offenders were currently incarcerated for a violent crime.

Langan and Greenfeld compared the type-4 inmates with the three other types on the basis of drinking at the time of current incarceration offense, drunk at the time of current incarceration offense, and ever treated for alcohol abuse. The type-4 offender was not more likely than the three other types to have been drinking, drunk, or previously treated for alcohol problems. In fact, the percentages of type-4 inmates in the drinking, drunk, and treated categories were lower than those for the three other types and in some comparisons the type-4 percentages were substantially and significantly lower than those of the three other groups. These findings are not consistent with the findings cited above that showed problem drinkers to be offenders of late onset. The inconsistency is perhaps an example of disparate findings depending on whether alcohol-treatment or criminal-offender samples are studied.

In a study of 187 men identified as "chronic police case inebriates," Pittman and Gordon (1958) constructed criminal career histories from arrest records. Men incarcerated for public intoxication were selected at random from those serving sentences of 30 days or longer in a county prison in Rochester, New York. They averaged 47.7 years of age. The men had to have served at least one previous sentence for public intoxication. The sample is a narrowly defined one, so that generalizability is limited, but the criminal career histories provide some interesting information.

The men in the sample averaged 16.5 recorded arrests for all offenses; the mean number of arrests increases with age from 6.8 for those under 35 to 22.9 for those aged 55 and older. Mean number of arrests for public intoxication was 12.8 for all ages, ranging from 4.1 for those under age 35 to 18.6 for those 55 and older. A total of 22.5 percent of all arrests were for charges other than public intoxication. The mean number of arrests on charges other than public intoxication does not increase significantly with age after 35. The authors (Pittman and Gordon, 1958:261) infer:

> The explanation for the failure of other offenses to increase with age lies in the fact that at the end of the first utilized age period, 35, there is a trend for the inebriates who have been involved in more serious crimes, such as automobile theft or burglary, to cease this type of criminal activity, and for the intoxication pattern of behavior to emerge as an adaptation to the life situation.

Thirty-seven percent of the sample had been arrested on serious charges, but Pittman and Gordon note that those serious offenses tended to occur earlier in the career and reiterate that the "new" pattern of arrest for public drunkenness is a reaction to failed criminal careers. While the "biphasic" criminal career pattern is not inconsistent with this interpretation, the notion of an alcoholic adaption to a failed criminal career by Pittman and Gordon is speculative.

If problem drinkers are late-onset offenders but also have short criminal careers, the above findings may not be inconsistent with each other. In other words, the Edwards, Kyle, and Nicholls (1977) sample may start late and stop quickly. The best tentative conclusion about the effect of problem drinking on serious criminal behavior by those over age 35 is that there is no relationship. The issue needs further study, however, because so little attention has been paid to the question.

SUMMARY, RECOMMENDATIONS, AND IMPLICATIONS

In this section, findings from the three career-segment reviews are summarized, the magnitude of the association between problem drinking and criminal careers is discussed, important methodological issues are noted, and implications for future research are drawn.

Summary of Findings

The best inference regarding the importance of problem drinking to the onset of criminal careers is that of no relationship. Some caution about this conclusion is necessary because age at first drink and the beginning of problem drinking are not adequately distinguished in past work. Drinking at an early age is often viewed as a problem of itself. Most of the available evidence, however, indicates that involvement in crime precedes problem drinking or that the two start at approximately the same time.

A second major inference that is warranted by past research is that there is strong covariation between problem drinking and individual offending sequences. It is not possible to infer confidently that the covariation indicates problem drinking is a causal factor. Common etiologies may be involved. It does appear justified to conclude that individuals who have drinking problems tend, more than individuals without drinking problems, to continue serious criminal activity during young adulthood. Some researchers have seen this as the tendency of problem drinking to extend or intensify the criminal career.

A robust finding justified by the works reviewed and other evidence is that problem drinkers who have criminal careers or offenders with drinking problems are disproportionately likely to have official records for, and to self-report involvement in, violent crime. No fewer than 10 of the studies reviewed showed this pattern, although the finding is most clear among identified criminal justice populations. The connection between problem drinking and violent behavior is considered robust, also, because the finding is replicated in the literature that examines assaultive criminal events. In that literature, alcohol has been found present in the offender, victim, or both offender and victim in very substantial percentages of homicides, forcible rapes, aggravated assaults, and other violent crimes. Recent aggregate-level analyses also find a direct relationship between levels of alcohol consumption and levels of violence (Bielewicz and Mokalewicz, 1982; Lenke, 1982; Olsson and Wikström, 1982) There is little doubt that drinking is etiologically important to the occurrence of some violent behavior.

It is not possible to identify what specific factors combine with alcohol to produce violent behavior. It is clear that some men are at high risk of alcohol-related violence, but the identification of individual risk factors has not progressed beyond the specification of general characteristics, such as aggressiveness or psychopathic personality traits. Correlates of these global descriptions have been noted, but the etiological tie among drinking, violence, and other characteristics has not been made. It may be possible to make some such connections from a meta-analysis of past work, but this has not as yet been accomplished.

Finally, although several researchers have noted a relationship between drinking problems and the late onset of criminal careers, the assessment in this paper does not show that. If late onset of criminal careers is measured by involvement in serious crime, problem drinking has not been shown to be etiologically important. The ambiguity may be related to sample selection or to the failure of past research to separate serious from alcohol-related offenses.

How Much Crime Does Problem Drinking Explain?

At the outset of this paper it was stated that alcohol use is never a sufficient cause of a criminal career. However, the evidence reviewed here, as well as other evidence, demonstrates adequately that problem drinking is associated with criminal behavior, especially violent criminal behavior in the young adult years. The question remains of how much crime is explained by problem drinking. A quantitative answer cannot be provided on the basis of previous work. Individual offending frequencies have not been compared for offenders with and without drinking problems. It is not even possible to compare the explanatory power of problem drinking with that of other independent variables because the alcohol-use variable has rarely been included in relevant multivariate analyses.

Methodological difficulties aside, there are several reasons why the kinds of analyses that would permit a quantitative assessment of problem drinking's contribution to criminal careers have not been undertaken:

1. Alcohol use and problem drinking are common phenomena in the noncriminal population and thus do not stand out as criminogenic factors.
2. Alcohol is an inexpensive drug so that, unlike expensive drugs (such as heroin and cocaine), there is no economic compulsion associated with its heavy use.
3. A theoretical framework for understanding how problem drinking causes criminal behavior does not exist. This lack of theoretical direction, coupled with the fact that drinking is pervasive in offender populations, causes concern that the observed relationship between problem drinking and criminal careers is a spurious one.

The third point is the most important, but it need not be a serious impediment to the development of quantitative estimates of problem drinking's contribution to criminal behavior. Appropriate data and techniques exist to begin development of comparative λs and regression coefficients for problem drinking. These would provide estimates of the magnitude of problem drinking's power to explain criminal careers.

The development of theory has been inhibited by the tendency of criminologists to view explanatory factors in a simplistic way. Thornberry and Christenson (1984) point out that causal conceptions have tended to be unidirectional and that such conceptions do not model criminal behavior very well. They show how unemployment and crime are related to each other in a reciprocal way. Problem drinking is likely to have a similar relationship to criminal behavior. A reciprocal conception may resolve some of the ambiguities in earlier work and lay the foundation for real understanding of the role of alcohol in the etiology of criminal behavior.

Methodological Issues

The single most important methodological aspect of determining whether a causal relationship exists between problem drinking and criminal careers is the nature of the study populations. General-population and captured-sample (i.e., institutional, treatment) study findings are not seriously inconsistent with each other, but differences in findings do exist. Mentioned above was the fact that the problem drinking-violence relationship is strongest among identified criminal justice samples. One possible reason for this finding is related to the probability of arrest. If the findings that suggest that problem drinkers are more likely to be arrested than offenders who do not have a drinking problem are accurate, problem drinkers who are violent offenders may be overrepresented in criminal justice populations.

Measurement of problem drinking needs to be done more carefully in future research. Measures should be quantity-frequency indicators or indicators of specific drinking-related consequences. Arrests for alcohol-related offenses should not be used as an indicator of problem drinking in research to examine the relationship between drinking and crime.

Alcohol use should also be measured and analyzed separately, not as part of an overall drug-use indicator. The latter approach confounds the effects of alcohol and drug use and may mask the effects of alcohol because drug use overrides alcohol use in hierarchically constructed indices. "Current" and "ever" drinking problems also need to be distinguished.

There is a considerable spontaneous remission of problem drinking over the life cycle, and failure to distinguish past and current drinking problems limits inferences that can be drawn about the effects of problem drinking over the life cycle.

Two substantive foci may be helpful to understanding the causal relationship between problem drinking and criminal careers: (1) conceptual and empirical disentanglement of the problem drinker-antisocial personality-criminal career association and (2) development of a problem drinker-offender typology. The first point involves attempting to clarify conceptually and empirically how much overlap exists among the three categories. The ASP disorder designation is a clinical one partially based on criteria that also define criminal behavior. Examples of ASP disorder diagnostic criteria that are also crime categories are assault, theft, vandalism, and driving while intoxicated. Other ASP diagnostic criteria include referral to juvenile court, multiple arrests, and a felony conviction (American Psychiatric Association, 1980). The ASP disorder also includes symptom categories, such as disturbed interpersonal relations and inability to sustain employment—categories that do not necessarily involve antisocial or illegal behavior. However, there is considerable overlap in the factors that define ASP disorder and criminal careers.

The ASP disorder and criminal career concepts also share conceptual and empirical elements in a temporal sense. The criminal career concept implies repetitious involvement in crime over some number of years. The ASP disorder diagnosis requires onset of three or more diagnostic criteria before age 15 and manifestation of at least four specified symptoms subsequent to age 18. Thus, both concepts are consistent with over-time continuity in illegal or deviant behavior.

The ASP disorder and problem-drinking categories tend often to coexist in the same persons, as discussed above and as noted in the APA diagnostic manual. The close association and shared conceptual elements of problem drinking, criminal careers, and ASP disorder suggest the need for careful definition and elaboration of the constructs. With conceptual refinement and subsequent empirical analysis, the causal structure of the association between problem drinking and criminal careers would likely be clarified.

Development of a problem drinker-offender typology is recommended to bring into sharper focus the contribution of individual characteristics (genetic, developmental, psychological, and so on) to the problem drinking-criminal career association. It is clear that problem drinking is not a criminogenic factor for all individuals. It would be helpful if individual risk factors, which could serve as typology dimensions, could be identified. Identification of risk factors serves multiple purposes. Risk factors can provide theoretical direction and, if they are strong predictors, can inform clinical and policy decisions as well.

Recommendations and Implications

The problem drinker-criminal career relationship is worthy of further study. A two-step process is recommended. Some work could start immediately with the use of existing data. Examples of longitudinal data that provide opportunities for relevant analysis are the National Youth Survey (NYS), the Rutgers Health and Human Development data, the 1945 Philadelphia birth cohort data, and the data from three Racine birth cohorts. The data sets provide information about onset, prevalence, and incidence of criminal behavior and include over-time measures. Information about alcohol use is limited in the Philadelphia and Racine cohorts, but both the NYS and the Rutgers' survey include detailed information about alcohol use over time. Thus, models could be developed to trace the covariation and correlates of drinking and crime in the same individuals over time.[1]

The 1979 survey of state correctional inmates (Bureau of Justice Statistics, 1983a) also can address problem drinker-criminal career issues. The inmate survey includes information from more than 10,000 individuals about incarceration, criminal careers, and alcohol use and amount consumed during the year before and at the time of the incarceration offense. Information is also included about drug use. There is considerable potential in the inmate data for modeling the relationship of substance use and crime.

The Treatment Outcomes Prospective Study, which includes data for more than 11,000 individuals who entered publicly funded drug abuse treatment programs in 1979–1981, is also a potentially valuable resource.[2] The data include a retrospective longitudinal dimension and prospective follow-up of a substantial percentage of the 11,000 subjects. Detailed data were collected about alcohol and drug use and self-reported involvement in serious crime. Data on age at first drink and age at first offense(s) provide an opportunity to begin analyses at onset times and to follow subjects over many years.

After the problem drinking-criminal career relationship is further clarified by analyses of existing data, it is likely that new longitudinal research will be advisable. New research could be carefully designed based on what is known and learned in secondary analyses. A focused, well-informed longitudinal design would have a good chance to clarify how problem drinking, by itself or in combination with other factors, contributes to criminal careers.

Few implications for private or public decision making are apparent from the findings of this review. One recommendation echoes Robins and Wish (1977). That recommendation is to attempt to delay the onset of drinking. While the early onset of drinking does not appear to be a sufficient cause of problem drinking or criminal behavior, it does appear to be an important factor. Delaying the start of drinking could have a payoff in terms of preventing crime; this approach, were it to work, would also have the advantage of reducing alcohol-related costs connected with health care, decreased productivity, and motor vehicle accidents.

It is virtually certain that alcohol use is a factor in some violent crime. This review and other evidence support that inference. Violent crime has very high dollar costs and is also responsible for costs not so easily measured, such as altered life-styles due to the fear of crime. Better understanding of the problem drinking-criminal career relationship could set the stage for informed attempts to reduce those costs.

[1]For information on the data bases mentioned, contact the principal investigator, as follows: National Youth Survey, Delbert Elliott, The Behavioral Research Institute, University of Colorado; Rutgers Health and Human Development data, Robert Pandina, Center of Alcohol Studies, Rutgers University; Racine, Wisconsin, birth cohorts, Lyle Shannon, Iowa Urban Community Research Center, University of Iowa; Philadelphia birth cohorts, Marvin E. Wolfgang, Center for Studies in Criminology and Criminal Law, University of Pennsylvania.

[2]For information on this data base, contact the author.

REFERENCES

American Psychiatric Association
1980 *Diagnostic and Statistical Manual of Mental Disorders.* 3d edition. Washington, D.C.: American Psychiatric Association.

Barnard, G., Holzer, C., and Vera, H.
1979 A comparison of alcoholics and non-alcoholics charged with rape. *Bulletin of the American Academy of Psychiatry and the Law* 7:432–440.

Bell, D., and Champion, R.
1979 Deviancy, delinquency and drug use. *British Journal of Psychiatry* 134:269–276.

Bielewicz, A., and Moskalewicz, J.
1982 Temporary prohibition: the Gdansk experience, August, 1980. *Contemporary Drug Problems* Fall:367–381.

Blane, H., and Chafetz, M., eds.
1979 *Youth, Alcohol, and Social Policy.* New York: Plenum Press.

Blane, H., and Hewitt, L.
1977 Alcohol and Youth—An Analysis of the Literature, 1960–1975. Final report prepared for the National Institute on Alcohol Abuse and Alcoholism. University of Pittsburgh, Pittsburgh, Pa.

Bohman, M., Cloninger, C., Sigvardsson, S., and von Knorring, A.
1982 Predisposition to petty criminality in Swedish adoptees. I. Genetic and environmental heterogeneity. *Archives of General Psychiatry* 39:1233–1241.

Bray, R., Schlenger, W., Craddock, S., Hubbard, R., and Rachal, J.
1982 Approaches to the Assessment of Drug Use in the Treatment Outcomes Prospective Study. Research Triangle Institute, Research Triangle Park, N.C.

Bray, R., Guess, L., Mason, R., Hubbard, R., Smith, D., Marsden, M., and Rachal, J.
1983 1982 Worldwide Survey of Alcohol and Nonmedical Drug Use Among Military Personnel. Report prepared for the Department of Defense. Research Triangle Institute, Research Triangle Park, N.C.

Brown, S, Goldman, M., Inn, A., and Anderson, L.
1980 Expectations of reinforcement from alcohol: their domain and relation to drinking patterns. *Journal of Consulting and Clinical Psychology* 48(8):419–426.

Bureau of Justice Statistics
1983a Career patterns and crime. *Bureau of Justice Statistics Special Report.* Washington, D.C.: U.S. Department of Justice.
1983b *Criminal Victimization in the United States, 1981.* Washington, D.C.: U.S. Department of Justice.
1983c Prisoners and alcohol. *Bureau of Justice Statistics Bulletin.* Washington, D.C.: U.S. Department of Justice.

Cahalan, D., and Cisin, I.
1976 Drinking behavior and drinking problems in the United States. In B. Kissin and H. Begleiter, eds., *The Biology of Alcoholism. Vol. 4: Social Aspects of Alcoholism.* New York: Plenum Press.

Cahalan, D., and Room, R.
1974 *Problem Drinking Among American Men.* New Brunswick, N.J.: Rutgers Center of Alcohol Studies.

Cahalan, D., Cisin, S., and Crossley, H.
1969 *American Drinking Practices: A National Study of Drinking Behavior and Attitudes.* New Haven, Conn.: College & University Press.

Chaiken, J., and Chaiken, M.
1982 *Varieties of Criminal Behavior.* Santa Monica, Calif.: Rand Corporation.

Coid, J.
1982 Alcoholism and violence. *Drug and Alcohol Dependence* 9:1–13.

Coleman, D., and Straus, M.
1979 Alcohol Abuse and Family Violence. Paper presented at the annual meeting of the American Sociological Association, Boston, Massachusetts.

Collins, J., ed.
1981 *Drinking and Crime: Perspectives on the Relationship Between Alcohol Consumption and Criminal Behavior.* New York: Guilford Press.

Collins, J., and Schlenger, W.
1983 The Prevalence of Psychiatric Disorder Among Admissions to Prison. Paper presented at the American Society of Criminology 35th Annual Meeting, Denver, Colorado.

Cordelia, A.
1985 Alcohol and property crime: explaining the causal nexus. *Journal of Studies on Alcohol* 46(2):161–171.

Crawford, A., Hinton, J., Docherty, C., Dishman, D., and Mulligan, P.
1982 Alcohol and crime. I. Self-reported alcohol consumption of Scottish prisoners. *Journal of Studies on Alcohol* 43(5):610–613.

Dawkins, R., and Dawkins, M.
1983 Alcohol use and delinquency among black, white, and Hispanic adolescent offenders. *Adolescence* 58(72):799–809.

Eckardt, M., Harford, T., Kaelber, C., Parker, E., Rosenthal, L., Ryback, R., Salmoiraghi, G., Vanderveen, E., and Warren, K.
1981 Health hazards associated with alcohol consumption. *Journal of the American Medical Association* 246(6):648–666.

Edwards, G., Hensman, C., and Peto, J.
1971 Drinking problems among recidivist prisoners. *Psychological Medicine* 1:388–399.

Edwards, G., Kyle, E., and Nicholls, P.
1977 Alcoholics admitted to four hospitals in England. III. Criminal records. *Journal of Studies on Alcohol* 38(9):1648–1664.

Elliott, D., and Huizinga, D.
1983 Social class and delinquent behavior in a national youth panel. *Criminology* 21(2): 149–177.

Elliott, D., Huizinga, D., and Ageton, S.
1982 Explaining Delinquency and Drug Use. The National Youth Survey Project Report No. 21. Report prepared for the Office of Juvenile Justice and Delinquency Prevention, U.S. Department of Justice, and for the Center for Studies of Crime and Delinquency, the National Institute of Mental Health. Behavioral Research Institute, Boulder, Colo.

Elliott, D., Huizinga, D., Knowles, B., and Canter, R.
1983 *The Incidence and Prevalence of Delinquent Behavior: 1976–1980*. Boulder, Colo.: Behavioral Research Institute.

Epstein, L., Mills, C., and Simon, A.
1970 Antisocial behavior of the elderly. *Comprehensive Psychiatry* 11(1):36–42.

Federal Bureau of Investigation
1982 *Uniform Crime Reports, Crime in the United States, 1981*. Washington, D.C.: U.S. Department of Justice.
1983 *Uniform Crime Reports, Crime in the United States, 1982*. Washington, D.C.: U.S. Department of Justice.

Fenna, D., Mix, L., Schaefer, O., and Gilbert, J.
1976 Ethanol metabolism in various racial groups. In M. Everett, J. Waddell, and D. Heath, eds., *Cross-Cultural Approaches to the Study of Alcohol*. The Hague: Mouton Publishers.

Fillmore, K.
1975 Relationship between specific drinking problems in early childhood and middle age: an exploratory 20-year follow-up study. *Quarterly Journal of Studies on Alcohol* 36:819–840.

Fishburne, P., Abelson, H., and Cisin, I.
1980 *National Survey on Drug Abuse: Main Findings, 1979*. National Institute on Drug Abuse. Rockville, Md.: U.S. Department of Health and Human Services.

Gibbens, T., and Silberman, M.
1970 Alcoholism among prisoners. *Psychological Medicine* 1:73–78.

Goodwin, D., Crane, B., and Guze, S.
1971 Felons who drink: an 8-year follow-up. *Quarterly Journal of Studies on Alcohol* 32:136–147.

Gusfield, J.
1963 *Symbolic Crusade*. Urbana: University of Illinois Press.

Guze, S., Goodwin, D., and Crane, J.
1969 Criminality and psychiatric disorder. *Archives of General Psychiatry* 20:583–591.

Guze, S., Tuason, V., Gatfield, P., Stewart, M., and Picken, B.
1962 Psychiatric illness and crime with particular reference to alcoholism: a study of 223 criminals. *Journal of Nervous and Mental Diseases* 134:512–521.

Hamilton, C., and Collins, J.
1981 The role of alcoholism in wife beating and child abuse: a review of the literature. Pp. 253–287 in J. Collins, ed., *Drinking and Crime: Perspectives on the Relationships Between Alcohol Consumption and Criminal Behavior*. New York: Guilford Press.

Hare, R.
1983 Diagnosis of antisocial personality disorder in two prison populations. *American Journal of Psychiatry* 140(7):887–890.

Hubbard, R., Collins, J., Allison, M., Cavanaugh, E., and Rachal, J.
1982 Validity of self-reports of illegal activities and arrests of drug treatment clients. In *Proceedings of the American Statistical Association, 1981*. Washington, D.C.: American Statistical Association.

Institute for Scientific Analysis
1978 Drinking Patterns and Criminal Careers: A Study of 310 Imprisoned Male Felons. Final report prepared for the National Institute on Alcohol Abuse and Alcoholism. Institute for Scientific Analysis, San Francisco, California

James, J., Gregory, D., and Jones, R.
1980 Psychiatric morbidity in prisons. *Hospital and Community Psychiatry* 31(10):674–677.

Jessor, R., and Jessor, S.
1977 *Problem Behavior and Psychosocial Development: A Longitudinal Study of Youth*. New York: Academic Press.

Jessor, R., Chase, J., and Donovan, J.
1980 Psychological correlates of marijuana use and problem drinking in a national sample of adolescents. *American Journal of Public Health* 70(6):604–613.

Jessor, R., Graves, T., Hanson, R., and Jessor, S.
1968 *Society, Personality, and Deviant Behavior: A Study of a Tri-Ethnic Community*. New York: Holt, Rinehart and Winston, Inc.

Johnson, B., and Goldstein, P.
1984 Highlights from the Final Report: Economic Behavior of Street Opiate Users. Narcotic and Drug Research, Inc., and New York State Division of Substance Abuse Services, New York.

Johnson, B., Wish, E., and Huizinga, D.
1983 The Concentration of Delinquent Offending: The Contribution of Serious Drug Involvement to High Rate Delinquency. Report prepared for the National Institute of

Justice and the New York State Division of Substance Abuse Services. Behavioral Research Institute, Boulder, Colorado.

Johnston, L., Bachman, J., and O'Malley, P.
1981 *Student Drug Use in America.* National Institute on Drug Abuse. Rockville, Md.: U.S. Department of Health and Human Services.

Johnston, L., O'Malley, P., and Eveland, L.
1976 Nonaddictive drug use and delinquency: a longitudinal analysis. Pp. 325–350 in Research Triangle Institute, *Appendix to Drug Use and Crime: Report of the Panel on Drug Use and Criminal Behavior.* Report prepared for the National Institute on Drug Abuse. Research Triangle Park, N.C.: Research Triangle Institute.

Jones, B., and Vega, A.
1972 Cognitive performance measured on the ascending and descending limbs of the blood-alcohol curve. *Psychopharmacologia* 23:99–114.
1973 Fast and slow drinkers. Blood-alcohol variables and cognitive performance. *Quarterly Journal of Studies on Alcohol* 34:797–806.

King, L., Murphy, G., Robins, L., and Darvish, H.
1969 Alcohol abuse: a crucial factor in the social problems of Negro men. *American Journal of Psychiatry* 125(12):1682–1690.

Lang, A., Goeckner, D., Adesso, V., and Marlatt, G.
1975 Effects of alcohol on aggression in male social drinkers. *Journal of Abnormal Psychology* 84(5):508–518.

Langan, P., and Farrington, D.
1983 Two-track or one-track justice? Some evidence from an English longitudinal survey. *Journal of Criminal Law & Criminology* 74(2):519–546.

Lenke, T.
1982 Alcohol and crimes of violence: a causal analysis. *Contemporary Drug Problems* Fall:355–365.

Lindelius, R., and Salum, S.
1973 Alcoholism and criminality. *Acta Psychiatrica Scandinavica* 49:306–314.
1975 Alcoholism and crime: a comparative study of three groups of alcoholics. *Journal of Studies on Alcohol* 36(11):1452–1457.
1976 Criminality among homeless men. *British Journal of Addiction* 71:149–153.

MacAndrews, C., and Edgerton, R.
1969 *Drunken Comportment: A Social Explanation.* Chicago, Ill.: Aldine.

Mandell, W., and Ginzburg, H.
1976 Youthful alcohol use, abuse, and alcoholism. Pp. 167–242 in B. Kissin and H. Begleiter, eds., *Social Aspects of Alcoholism. Vol. 4: The Biology of Alcoholism.* New York: Plenum Press.

Marco, L., and Randels, P.
1983 Metabolism and drug interactions of ethanol. Pp. 57–80 in E. Gottheil, K. Druley, T. Skoloda, and H. Waxman, eds., *Etiologic Aspects of Alcohol and Drug-Abuse.* Springfield, Ill.: Charles C Thomas.

Marquis, K.
1981 *Quality of Prisoner Self-Reports: Arrest and Conviction Response Errors.* Report prepared for the National Institute of Justice. Santa Monica, Calif.: Rand Corporation.

Mayfield, D.
1976 Alcoholism, alcohol intoxication, and assaultive behavior. *Diseases of the Nervous System* 37:228–291.

McCaghy, C.
1968 Drinking and deviance disavowal: the case of child molesters. *Social Problems* 16:43–49.

McClelland, D., Davis, W., Kalin, R., and Wanner, E., eds.
1972 *The Drinking Man.* New York: Free Press.

McCord, J.
1983 Alcohol in the service of aggression. Pp. 270–279 in E. Gottheil, K. Druley, T. Skoloda, and H. Waxman, eds., *Alcohol, Drug Abuse and Aggression.* Springfield, Ill.: Charles C Thomas.

McCord, W., and McCord, J.
1962 A longitudinal study of the personality of alcoholics. Pp. 413–430 in D. Pittman and C. Snyder, eds., *Society, Culture, and Drinking Patterns.* New York: John Wiley & Sons.

Mosher, J.
1983 Alcohol: both blame and excuse for criminal behavior. Pp. 437–460 in R. Room and G. Collins, eds., *Alcohol and Disinhibition: Nature and Meaning of the Link.* National Institute on Alcohol Abuse and Alcoholism, Research Monograph No. 12. Rockville, Md.: U.S. Department of Health and Human Services.

Myers, T.
1982 Alcohol and violent crime re-examined: self-reports from two sub-groups of Scottish male prisoners. *British Journal of Addiction* 77:399–413.

Nobel, E., ed.
1978 *Third Special Report to the U.S. Congress on Alcohol and Health.* National Institute on Alcohol Abuse and Alcoholism. Washington, D.C.: U.S. Department of Health, Education, and Welfare.

O'Donnell, J., Voss, H., Clayton, R., Slatin, G., and Room R.
1976 *Young Men and Drugs—A Nationwide Survey.* National Institute on Drug Abuse, Research Monograph 5. Rockville, Md.: U.S. Department of Health, Education, and Welfare.

Olsson, O., and Wikström, P. O. H.
1982 Effects of the experimental Saturday closing of liquor retail stores in Sweden. *Contemporary Drug Problems* Fall:325–353.

Pandina, R., Labouvie, E., and White, H.
1984 Potential contributions of the life span developmental approach to the study of adolescent alcohol and drug use: the Rutgers Health and Human Development Project, a working model. Manuscript submitted for publication to the *Journal of Drug Issues.*

Pearce, J., and Garrett, H.
1970 A comparison of the drinking behavior of delinquent youth versus nondelinquent youth in the states of Idaho and Utah. *Journal of School Health* March:131–135.

Pernanen, K.
1976 Alcohol and crimes of violence. Pp. 351–444 in B. Kissin and H. Begleiter, eds., *Social Aspects of Alcoholism. Vol. 4: The Biology of Alcoholism.* New York: Plenum Press.
1981 Theoretical aspects of the relationship between alcohol use and crime. Pp. 1–69 in J. Collins, ed., *Drinking and Crime: Perspectives on the Relationship Between Alcohol Consumption and Criminal Behavior.* New York: Guilford Press.

Petersilia, J., Greenwood, P., and Lavin, M.
1978 *Criminal Careers of Habitual Felons.* Washington, D.C.: U.S. Government Printing Office.

Peterson, M., and Braiker, H.
1980 *Doing Crime: A Survey of California Prison Inmates.* Santa Monica, Calif.: Rand Corporation.

Pittman, D., and Gordon, C.
1958 Criminal careers of the chronic police case inebriate. *Journal of Studies on Alcohol* 19:255–268.

Rachal, J., Guess, L., Hubbard, R., Maisto, S., Cavanaugh, E., Waddell, R., and Benrud, C.
1980 *Adolescent Drinking Behavior. Vol. I: The Extent and Nature of Adolescent Alcohol and Drug Use: The 1974 and 1978 National Sample.* NTIS No. PB 81–199267. Springfield, Va.: National Technical Information Service.

Rathus, S., Fox, J., and Ortins, J.
1980 The MacAndrew Scale as a measure of substance abuse and delinquency among adolescents. *Journal of Clinical Psychology* 36(2):579–583.

Robins, L.
1966 *Deviant Children Grown Up: A Sociological and Psychiatric Study of Sociopathic Personality.* Baltimore, Md.: Williams & Wilkins.
1972 An actuarial evaluation of the causes and consequences of deviant behavior in young black men. Pp. 137–154 in M. Roff, L. Robins, and M. Pollack, eds., *Life History Research in Psychopathology. Vol. 2.* Minneapolis: University of Minnesota Press.
1978 Alcohol and crime in veterans. Pp. 73–94 in L. Otten, ed., *Colloquium on the Correlates of Crime and the Determinants of Criminal Behavior.* Proceedings. McLean, Va.: Mitre Corporation.

Robins, L., and Wish, E.
1977 Childhood deviance as a developmental process: a study of 223 urban black men from birth to 18. *Social Forces* 56:449–473.

Robins, L., Bates, W., and O'Neal, P.
1962 Adult drinking patterns of former problem children. In D. Pittman and C. Snyder, eds., *Society, Culture and Drinking Patterns.* New York: John Wiley & Sons.

Robins, L., Murphy, G., and Breckenridge, M.
1968 Drinking behavior of young urban Negro men. *Quarterly Journal of Studies on Alcohol* 29:657–683.

Roebuck, J., and Johnson, R.
1962 The Negro drinker and assaulter as a criminal type. *Crime and Delinquency* 8(1):21–33.

Roizen, J., and Schneberk, D.
1977 Alcohol and crime. Pp. 292–422 in M. Aarens, T. Cameron, J. Roizen, R. Roizen, R. Room, D. Schneberk, and D. Wingard, eds., Alcohol, Casualties and Crime. Report prepared for the National Institute on Alcohol Abuse and Alcoholism. Social Research Group, University of California. Berkeley, Calif.

Roizen, R., Cahalan, D., and Shanks, P.
1978 Spontaneous remission among untreated problem drinkers. In D. Kandel, ed., *Longitudinal Research on Drug Abuse.* New York: John Wiley & Sons.

Room, R.
1983 Alcohol and crime: behavioral aspects. *Encyclopedia of Crime and Justice.* New York: MacMillan.

Rydelius, P.
1983a Alcohol-abusing teenage boys: testing a hypothesis on alcohol abuse and personality factors using a personality inventory. *Acta Psychiatrica Scandinavica* 68:381–385.

1983b Alcohol-abusing teenage boys: testing a hypothesis on the relationship between alcohol abuse and social background factors, criminality and personality in teenage boys. *Acta Psychiatrica Scandinavica* 68: 368–380.

Scott, M., and Lyman, S.
1968 Accounts. *American Sociological Review* 33:46–62.

Shichor, D., and Kobrin, S.
1978 Note: criminal behavior among the elderly. *Gerontologist* 18(2):213–218.

Tamerin, J., Weiner, S., and Mendelson, J.
1970 Alcoholics' expectancies and recall of experiences during intoxication. *American Journal of Psychiatry* 126(12):1697–1704.

Tarter, R.
1983 The causes of alcoholism: a biophysical analysis. Pp. 173–201 in E. Gottheil, K. Druley, T. Skoloda, and H. Waxman, eds., *Etiologic Aspects of Alcohol and Drug Abuse.* Springfield, Ill.: Charles C Thomas.

Tarter, R., and Alterman, A.
1984 Neuropsychological deficits in alcoholics: etiological considerations. *Journal of Studies on Alcohol* 45(1):1–9.

Thornberry, T., and Christenson, R.
1984 Unemployment and criminal involvement. *American Sociological Review* 42:298–411.

Trice, H., and Roman, P.
1972 *Spirits and Demons at Work: Alcohol and Other Drugs on the Job.* Ithaca, N.Y.: Hoffman Printing Company.

U.S. Department of Justice
1975 *Surveys of Inmates of State Correctional Facilities—Advance Report.* National Criminal Justice Information and Statistics Service. Washington, D.C.: U.S. Department of Justice.

Vingilis, E.
1981 A literature review of the young drinking offender. Is he a problem drinker? *British Journal of Addiction* 76:27–46.

Virkkunen, M.
1977 Arrests for drunkenness and recidivism in juvenile delinquents. *British Journal of Addiction* 72:201–204.

Washbrook, R.
1977 Alcoholism versus crime in Birmingham, England. *International Journal of Offender Therapy and Comparative Criminology* 21(2):166–173.

White, H., Johnson, V., and Garrison, C.
1983 The Drug-Crime Relationship Among Adolescents and Their Peers. Report prepared for the National Institute on Alcohol Abuse and Alcoholism, the National Institute of Justice, and the National Institute on Drug Abuse. Rutgers University, New Brunswick, N.J.

Wolff, P.
1972 Ethnic differences in alcohol sensitivity. *Science* 175:449–450.

Wolfgang, M.
1983 Delinquency in two birth cohorts. *American Behavioral Scientist* 27(1):75–86.

Woods, S., and Mansfield, J.
1983 Ethanol disinhibition: physiological and behavioral links. Pp. 4–23 in R. Room and G. Collins, eds., *Alcohol and Disinhibition: Nature and Meaning of the Link.* National Institute on Alcohol Abuse and Alcoholism, Research Monograph 12. Rockville, Md.: U.S. Department of Health and Human Services.

Zucker, R.
1968 Sex-role identity patterns and drinking behavior of adolescents. *Quarterly Journal of Studies on Alcohol* 29:868–884.

BIBLIOGRAPHY

Banay, R.
1942 Alcoholism and crime. *Quarterly Journal of Studies on Alcohol* 2:686–716.

Barnard, G., Vera, H., Vera, M., and Newman, G.
1982 Till death do us part: a study of spouse murder. *Bulletin of the American Academy of Psychiatry and the Law* 10(4):271–280.

Bohman, M.
1978 Some genetic aspects of alcoholism and criminality: a population of adoptees. *Archives of General Psychiatry* 35:269–276.

Burt, M., and Biegel, M.
1980 Worldwide Survey of Nonmedical Drug Use and Alcohol Use Among Military Personnel: 1980. Report prepared for the U.S. Department of Defense. Burt Associates, Bethesda, Md.

Cloninger, C. Sigvardsson, S., Bohman, M., and von Knorring, A.
1982 Predisposition to petty criminality in Swedish adoptees. II. Cross-fostering analyses of gene-environment interaction. *Archives of General Psychiatry* 39:1242–1248.

Elliott, D., and Ageton, A.
1976 The relationship between drug use and crime among adolescents. Pp. 297–321 in Research Triangle Institute, *Appendix to Drug Use and Crime: Report of the Panel on Drug Use and Criminal Behavior.* Report prepared for the National Institute on Drug Abuse. Research Triangle Park, N.C.: Research Triangle Institute.

Glueck, S., and Glueck, E.
1937 *Later Criminal Careers*. New York: Commonwealth Fund.

Gottheil, E., Druley, K., Skoloda, T., and Waxman, H.
1983a *Alcohol, Drug Abuse and Aggression*. Springfield, Ill.: Charles C Thomas.
1983b *Etiologic Aspects of Alcohol and Drug Abuse*. Springfield, Ill: Charles C Thomas.

Kandel, D.
1980 Drug and drinking behavior among youth. *Annual Review of Sociology* 6:235–285.

Keller, O., and Vedder, C.
1968 Crimes that old persons commit. *Gerontologist* 8:43–50.

Kissin, B., and Begleiter, H., eds.
1976 *Social Aspects of Alcoholism. Vol. 4: The Biology of Alcoholism*. New York: Plenum Press.

Lang, A.
1983 Drinking and disinhibition: contributions from psychological research. Pp. 48–99 in R. Room and G. Collins, eds., *Alcohol and Disinhibition: Nature and the Meaning of the Link*. National Institute on Alcohol Abuse and Alcoholism, Research Monograph 12. Rockville, Md.: U.S. Department of Health and Human Services.

Lowman, C.
1981 Facts for planning. No. 1: Prevalence of alcohol use among U.S. senior high school students. *Alcohol Health and Research World* 6(1):29–40.

McCord, J.
1981 Alcoholism and criminality: confounding and differentiating factors. *Journal of Studies on Alcohol* 42(9):739–748.

Moberg, D.
1953 Old age and crime. *Journal of Criminal Law* 43:764–776.

National Criminal Justice Information and Statistics Service
1979 *Profile of State Prison Inmates: Sociodemographic Findings from the 1974 Survey of Inmates of State Correctional Facilities*. Washington, D.C.: U.S. Department of Justice.

Otten, L., ed.
1978 *Colloquium on the Correlates of Crime and the Determinants of Criminal Behavior*. Proceedings. McLean, Va.: Mitre Corporation.

Pittman, D., and Snyder, C., eds.
1962 *Society, Culture, and Drinking Patterns*. New York: John Wiley & Sons.

Plant, M.
1979 *Drinking Careers: Occupations, Drinking Habits, and Drinking Problems*. London: Tavistock Publications.

Rachal, J., Williams, J., Brehm, M., Cavanaugh, E., Moore, P., and Eckerman, W.
1975 A National Study of Adolescent Drinking Behavior, Attitudes and Correlates. Report prepared for the National Institute on Alcohol Abuse and Alcoholism. Research Triangle Institute, Research Triangle Park, N.C.

Research Triangle Institute
1976a *Appendix to Drug Use and Crime: Report of the Panel on Drug Use and Criminal Behavior*. Report prepared for the National Institute on Drug Abuse. Research Triangle Park, N.C.: Research Triangle Institute.
1976b *Drug Use and Crime. Report of the Panel on Drug Use and Criminal Behavior*. NTIS No. PB 259–16715. Springfield, Va.: National Technical Information Service.

Shuntich, R., and Taylor, S.
1972 The effects of alcohol on human physical aggression. *Journal of Experimental Research in Personality* 6:34–38.

4

Co-Offender Influences on Criminal Careers

Albert J. Reiss, Jr.

INTRODUCTION

Offender histories ordinarily are characterized by a mix of different types of offenses and by a mix of offenses committed alone and with accomplices. Group or accomplice offending is more characteristic of juvenile than adult careers. This paper reviews the current state of knowledge about co-offending in juvenile and adult criminal careers to illuminate how and when co-offending is relevant to strategies of intervention in criminal careers, particularly strategies to reduce crime rates. The paper begins with a brief description of the major policy questions that will be addressed and then summarizes the knowledge about co-offending that is relevant to them.

Selective Incapacitation of Offenders

One of the major strategies proposed to reduce the crime rate is to incapacitate career criminals selectively, i.e., to remove from society those offenders who have high individual rates of offending. In theory one expects to reduce the number of crimes, and correlatively the number of victims involved in those crimes, by the amount of crime the incapacitated offender would have committed were he or she not incarcerated. Within limits, that seems to be a reasonable presumption, provided the crimes are committed by a single offender. But whether one actually prevents those crimes from occurring when incapacitating an offender will depend also on the group status of the offender and the behavior of co-offenders and their affiliated offending groups. For unless an offender's accomplices are deterred from offending by the offender's incapacitation, no crimes may be saved. The accomplices may continue to commit the offenses alone, with one another, by recruiting new accomplices from within their group, or by recruiting new members to their membership network either as new participants in offending or at increased rates of offending. Group organization and affiliation will facilitate the search for accomplices, and indeed,

Albert J. Reiss, Jr., is the William Graham Sumner professor of sociology and in the Institution for Social and Policy Studies, Yale University, and lecturer in law, Yale Law School. The reader is referred to the Acknowledgments section at the end of this chapter.

Reiss (1980:15–16) has argued that incapacitation can increase the crime rate if it leads to a marginal increase in the number of offenders and their individual rates of offending. It is important, consequently, to know to what extent patterns of recruitment into offending as well as changes in individual rates of offending may limit the capability of an incapacitation policy to reduce the crime rate.

Age of Intervention

It is well known that a substantial proportion of all offending, including offending in serious crimes, occurs at young ages and that the age of onset of offending is quite young. Moreover, a serious juvenile career record appears predictive of high-rate offending in serious crimes as an adult (Chaiken and Chaiken, 1982:87). It is also recognized that, while a great many young people participate in crime, many drop out fairly early in their career (Wolfgang, Figlio, and Sellin, 1972:88), often without any official intervention to deter them from offending. Yet, at an early age a sizable minority of youthful offenders have high individual rates of offending (Wolfgang, Figlio, and Sellin, 1972:104). This raises the question of whether high-rate offenders can be identified at an early age so that they can be selected for special treatment in a juvenile or criminal justice system.

Related to the issue of the early detection and selection of career offenders is whether group affiliation is critical in onset, persistence, and desistance from offending. Of particular interest is the role that groups play in these phases of a juvenile criminal career. Were one able, for example, to identify high-rate offenders who recruited a large number of persons into committing delinquent acts or persons who had a substantial effect on the individual crime rate of a large number of offenders, one might want to select those offender-recruiters for special treatment in a criminal justice system.

Target of Intervention Strategies

Many intervention strategies aim to intervene in the life of an offender to prevent offending either by incapacitating the offender or encouraging desistance when the offender is allowed to remain in the free society. The latter are usually called individual-change strategies. Yet, other strategies are possible, such as altering group and other social structures or intervening in collective activity. If groups are important to the onset, persistence, and desistance from offending, one may want to intervene directly in group relationships or alter group structure so as to reduce the propensity for delinquent or criminal behavior. Or, recognizing that networks facilitate the search for accomplices, one may want to intervene in those networks to increase the costs of search behavior. The discussion that follows of the role of group offending in criminal careers will address the implications for intervention strategies.

THE NATURE OF GROUP OFFENDING

There is no commonly agreed-on definition of a group in research on delinquent and criminal behavior. Offending groups often are treated in writings on delinquency as synonymous with gangs, the gang being a territorially organized, age-graded peer group engaged in a wide range of activities and having a well-defined leadership (Miller, 1975:9). Empirically, most persons who engage in group delinquency are not members of such highly structured groups (Klein and Crawford, 1967; Morash, 1983:329), and in most aggregates of 20 or more peers, persons are only loosely associated with one another, leadership is unclear, and membership turnover is fairly high. Yablonsky (1959) refers to these peer aggregates as "near-groups." Following Lerman (1967:63), group offending is treated in this paper from the perspective of social networks made up of pairs, triads, and constellations of four or more persons. The extent to which networks and relationships within them are bounded organizationally, behaviorally, and territorially is left problematic.

SOME PRELIMINARY ISSUES

Before examining the basic parameters of group offending and their relationship to criminal careers, a few issues that affect concepts and measures of group offending should be considered. These are the relationship of offending to crime events; defining and measuring lone, as contrasted with group, offending; and the effects of criminal justice processing on parameters of group offending.

Crime Incidents, Their Victims, and Their Offenders

Any crime event or incident involves one or more crimes or offenses, one or more offenders, and, consenting and public-order crimes excepted, one or more victims. One expects to find a number of relationships among a population of crime events and their offenses, victims, and offenders. For example, the ratio of victims to events depends on the rate of multiple victimization in events and the rate of victimization of the same person in different events. And the population of offenders relative to the population of events depends on the size of the offending group in an event and individual rates of offending by group members. It is ordinarily assumed, moreover, that the prevalence or participation rate of offenders is well below the aggregate incidence of their offenses and charges and that the differences are due primarily to variation in both individual rates of offending and the size of offending groups in crime events.

The above relationships between offenders and events can be illustrated quite simply using data on residential burglary and robbery. The Peoria (Illinois) Crime Reduction Council (1979), for example, undertook a study of all juveniles taken into custody for residential burglary from 1971 to 1978. There were 467 juveniles who accounted for 306 separate burglaries during this period. The group composition of both the burglary incidents and the offenders involved in them is shown in Table 1.

In regard to burglary offenses committed by apprehended juveniles during this period, single offenders accounted for one-half of all residential burglaries. In regard to offenders involved in these burglaries, however, the one-half of the residential burglaries with two or more offenders involved two-thirds of all offenders, and the great majority of multiple-offender burglaries involved two offenders.

How the size of offending groups affects the size of an offender population is seen even more dramatically for robbery offenses. Just over one-half of all robbery

TABLE 1 Group Composition of Burglary Incidents and Offenders

Group Composition	Number	Percent
Burglary Incidents		
With one offender only	155	50.6
With two or more offenders	151	49.4
Total burglary incidents	306	100.0
Burglary Offenders		
Single offender in incident	155	33.2
Two or more offenders in incident	312	66.8
Total burglary offenders	467	100.0

SOURCE: Peoria Crime Reduction Council (1979).

TABLE 2 Group Composition of Robbery Incidents and Offenders

	Total Number	Percent Distribution by Size of Offending Group			
		One	Two	Three	Four or More
Robbery Incidents	1,149,000	51.5	24.2	14.3	10.0
Robbery Offenders	2,215,272	26.7	25.1	22.3	25.9

SOURCE: Bureau of Justice Statistics (1984:Tables 52 and 62).

victimizations in the United States in 1982 involved a single offender (Bureau of Justice Statistics, 1984:Table 62). Nonetheless, as seen from the distribution in Table 2, only one-fourth of all robbery offenders in those events offended alone, and there were about equal proportions of groups of two, three, and four or more offenders.

Note that for about one-half of all robberies, the *same* robbery is part of the criminal history of more than one offender. Although there are on the average two offenders per robbery, in about one-fourth of all robberies, the same incident enters the criminal history of three or more offenders. If one knows the number of co-offenders in each offense in a criminal history, one can weight offenses accordingly and estimate more precisely the "crimes saved" by incapacitating that offender. The larger the size of any participant's offending group, the less, on the average, that individual's absence should diminish the population of events.

Lone and Group Offenders in Criminal Careers

There is a firmly held view that most offenders are group offenders and that the career lone offender is uncommon. These views are not based on the analysis of criminal careers or histories, however, but rather on the group composition of offending, especially of juvenile offending. The statistical basis for the conclusion ordinarily is the individual and group composition of crime events rather than histories of offending for the offenders involved in those events.

Quite commonly the group-size distribution for a population of events is used to estimate the participation rate of lone offenders in a population. What is reported is a distribution of events by number of offenders, and the proportion of single-offender events is taken as an estimate of the prevalence of lone offenders in a population. Such estimates are misleading because events rather than persons are counted. Corrections can be made by weighting the events by the number of offenders reported for them and using an appropriate population as the base for the rate.

Percentage distributions of the size of offending groups by crime type (the upper halves of Tables 1 and 2) reflect the aggregate risk of being victimized by a group of a given size, including a single individual. By way of contrast, percentage distributions of the number of offenders involved in those incidents by the size of the offending group (the lower halves of Tables 1 and 2) are offender-based statistics and state the probability that a randomly selected offender will commit that crime alone or with a given number of associates. The latter statistics are more appropriate in relating events to criminal careers or to offenders to be processed. When the interest lies in the rate of lone or co-offending crimes, statements should be made about a population of crime events, but when the interest lies in lone- or group-offender participation rates, statements must be made about a population of offenders.

When all the events in a criminal history are considered, a large proportion of offenders exhibit neither exclusively lone nor exclusively group offending. Rather, most offender histories are characterized by a mix of offending alone and with accomplices. Although information on the number of accomplices in each event of an offender's criminal history is generally lacking, some idea of the mix of lone and accomplice offending can be gained by examining the criminal history of the juvenile offenders in the study by the Peoria Crime Reduction Council (1979). The 467 Peoria juveniles apprehended for at least one burglary during a 7.5-year period were involved in 2,820 offenses for which 3,426 charges were filed. Considering only co-offending among the 467 juveniles, 79 (16.9 percent) always committed their offenses without accomplices from the study population, and 91 (19.5 percent) only acted with accomplices from the study population. The large majority (63.6 percent) sometimes acted alone and sometimes with others from the study population.[1]

Unfortunately, good estimates are not available of the variation among criminal histories in the mix of lone and group offenses, of variation in the number of accomplices, and of the consistency and variation of co-offending in an individual's history. With that information, one might weight individual-offender rates by their partial contributions to crime events, especially when estimating the expected crimes saved by incapacitation. One might wish to use such a weighted individual rate as a criterion for selective incapacitation.

Effects of Criminal Justice Processing on Estimates of Group Offending

Self-report studies of male delinquent behavior disclose a higher rate of lone offending than do official records of apprehension for the same offenders (Erikson, 1971; Hindelang, 1971, 1976b). The question arises, therefore, as to whether an apprehension hazard is associated with violating the law with others (Erikson, 1971:121). For if violating in groups increases the likelihood of being apprehended, the prevalence of lone offending will be underrepresented in official records.

Several attempts have been made to test whether there is a group-apprehension hazard by comparing self-reported and officially reported offenses in an offender's history. Erikson (1971:125) concluded that, although there is a greater risk of apprehension for offenses that are officially known rather than self-reported, the selection bias is considerably less for the most serious offenses. Subsequent research by Hindelang (1976b:121) casts doubt on the group-hazard hypothesis. While exclusively group offenders have a higher risk of apprehension per crime than do those who always offend alone, those with a mix of lone and accomplice offending have comparable risks in both types of events.

What does seem apparent from Hindelang's work is that "those engaging in illegal behaviour in groups are likely to engage in this behaviour more frequently than those engaging in the illegal behaviour alone" (1976b:122); indeed, the largest proportion of solitary offenders was found in the group with the lowest

[1]Since the co-offending data in the criminal histories were tabulated only for offenders included in the study population, these are probably underestimates for lone offending.

individual rates of offending and the smallest proportion of solitary offenders in the group with highest individual rates. This supports Erikson's (1971) conclusion that among offending youths, solitary offenders are more likely to engage less frequently in crimes and to commit less serious crimes than group offenders.

Unfortunately, data are unavailable to determine whether adult solitary offenders are also disproportionally involved in the less serious offenses or have lower individual rates of offending. Since major crimes against persons involve higher rates of solitary offending, it is possible that adult solitary offending, in contrast to that of juveniles, is disproportionally concentrated on the more serious offenses.

BASIC PARAMETERS OF GROUP OFFENDING

Despite the fact that a number of major longitudinal studies of criminal careers have followed samples of youths into their adult years (Glueck and Glueck, 1930, 1937, 1940, 1943, 1946; Shannon, 1978; Wolfgang, 1978; Elliott et al., 1983), none has examined patterns of co-offending into adulthood. Thus, this discussion of the parameters of group offending must depend primarily on research on juvenile delinquency. Even that research, however, pays relatively little attention to individual rates of offending or the role of co-offending in careers so that often a single study or source of data must be relied on.

Offending and Group Size

Breckinridge and Abbot (1917) were among the first to point out that most delinquent offenses are committed with at least one other person and that even most youths regarded as lone offenders occasionally engage in delinquency with a companion. Somewhat later, Shaw and Meyer (1929) and Shaw and McKay (1931) estimated in juvenile court samples that less than 20 percent of the juvenile offenders before the court committed offenses alone, that the modal size of an offending group is small (two or three participants), and that most delinquency is not committed by well-organized groups. Shaw and McKay concluded, moreover, that while such offending twosomes and threesomes commonly are combinations from a larger group, a whole group is rarely involved in the same delinquent or criminal act.

Large networks that link by association up to 200 youths ordinarily consist of fewer than 30 or 40 active members organized into smaller cliques of 5–10 members (Klein and Crawford, 1967). In a cohort study of delinquency in a Swedish community, a youth gang was defined as a group of juveniles who were linked together because the police suspected them of committing crimes together (Sarnecki, 1982:144–145).[2] There were well over 100 of these gangs in the study. Membership varied from 2 to 30 boys; the mean size was 5 boys (Sarnecki:151). What was most evident, however, is that groups were constituted by co-offending relationships. These relationships consisted of links of co-offending to form chains of association. One such chain in this Swedish city involved 260 boys and a few girls and constituted about 45 percent of the study population. Together they accounted for 86 percent of the crimes

[2]The study population was located in a southern Swedish industrial community of about 50,000 inhabitants. The records of the local police on all crimes whose suspects were under 15 years old and from the police register (PBR) for all juveniles 15 years and older were the main source of information on offenses. Additional data sources included reports from police hearings, from police interviews with juveniles suspected of crimes, and from social service authorities (Sarnecki, 1982:54–65).

reported during the study period (Sarnecki:144–145).

Although accomplices in delinquency are drawn more often from smaller cliques than from their larger network, the number of accomplices in any delinquent act is much smaller than the number in the clique (Short and Strodtbeck, 1965; Klein and Crawford, 1967). Considering only those offenses committed by two or more offenders, the modal size of an offending group from age 12 onward is two participants. Groups with four or more participants are relatively uncommon after age 14 or 15. The majority of offenders have accomplices until their early 20s, after which the majority commit their offenses alone (Hood and Sparks, 1970:87–88). There is some variation in lone and group offending rates by country and considerable variation by type of offense (Sveri, 1965).

The distribution of group size within an offending history has consequences for intervening in that career. A majority of most common crimes are committed by two or three offenders, and most offenders will have a substantial and continuing history of offenses in which their associates change from crime to crime. The larger the offending group, the more likely it is to be confined to a single event unless the group specializes in specific targets of offending, as in terrorism or in some kinds of white-collar offending in which continuing use of organizational power is integral to committing offenses.

Age of Onset

There is much controversy concerning whether the onset of delinquency is a consequence of induction by co-offenders. Glueck and Glueck (1934a, b, 1937, 1943, 1950) contended that pre-delinquent and delinquent behavior began at an early age in family and school socialization. They claimed that those with delinquent tendencies associate with one another rather than being led into their joint delinquent behavior by their associations. Their definition of delinquency is quite broad and includes behavior labeled as "antisocial" and also "delinquent tendencies" (Glueck and Glueck, 1950:42). Moreover, their conclusion is not based on collecting information about the group composition of specific behavioral acts committed by offenders in their sample. Rather, their contention is based on their observation (Glueck and Glueck, 1950:41) that the onset of delinquency for their institutionalized delinquents occurred before age 10 and consequently, in their view, before the time that groups play a significant role in a boy's life.

Challenging this conclusion, Eynon and Reckless (1961) found that the median age of first contact with juvenile authorities was 13 for incarcerated juvenile offenders and that there were no significant differences in age of onset or the presence or absence of companions at the first officially recorded delinquent act (Eynon and Reckless:169). The median age of onset for the first self-reported delinquent act ranged from 11 to 14 years depending on the type of offense. Self-reports on whether one had companions for each of seven offense types ranged from 56 percent of those who ran away from home to a not surprising 100 percent of those engaging in gang fights (Eynon and Reckless:170). They concluded that the "presence of companions is a major component of male delinquency, regardless of the age of delinquency onset" (Eynon and Reckless:168); companionship is present at early as well as at late onset. But, as they note, what we still lack is information that tells us whether companionship experience relevant to the onset of delinquency causes delinquent behavior (Eynon and Reckless:168).

Most investigators seem to have missed this obvious point—that companionship begins among children at a fairly early age. Although Thrasher (1927), in his classic study of what he called "youth gangs" in Chicago, was well aware of the fact that the kinds of groupings in which he was interested were found at quite young ages, he focused on territorial groupings. Subsequent work focused on "organized gangs" rather than on "companionship." These groups were largely territorially organized and regarded as a phenomenon of adolescent and young adult ages. Recruitment and induction into these peer groups were made problematic but without any explicit attention to prior delinquent histories. This was partly because Thrasher devoted a great deal of attention to official records of delinquency, and a delinquent act was rarely entered as an official record prior to age 12.

In any case, what is at issue is whether the onset of delinquency involves primarily lone offending or whether it is linked primarily to companionship or accomplice relationships. With answers to this key question, one may begin to unravel the problem of the role of groups in launching a continuing offending career, since there must be considerable desistance from offending, even at very early ages.

It is difficult to assess the role that companionship plays in the onset of delinquency because of the weak cross-section designs of most etiological studies and the failure to specify a testable causal model. A longitudinal design that follows members of a birth cohort as well as all their accomplices who are not members of the cohort is necessary to test causal hypotheses about onset. Unfortunately, up to now cohort studies have not examined the role of co-offending in criminal careers. Olson's (1977) multiple regression analysis of the personal interview data for a subset of the Racine birth cohort study (Shannon, 1978) found that first police contact at a very young age was associated only with being male and having friends in trouble with the police. Yet those two variables accounted for at most one-fourth of the variance, indicating that the personal interview variables did not include the most important determinants of age at first police contact (Petersilia, 1980:349).

Group Affiliation and Individual Rates of Offending

Individuals vary considerably in their rates of offending. Most young offenders also have co-offenders in their offending and associate in other group activities with still other offenders. An interesting question is how an individual's rate of offending is related to the offending rate of the affiliated group. Morash (1983:319) concludes that the delinquency rate of one's peers is a strong predictor of an individual's rate of delinquency. Boys who belonged to peer groups with a below-average rate of delinquency had below-average rates of delinquency and boys with peers who had high individual rates of delinquency had an above-average individual rate of delinquency (Morash:321).

Juveniles with high rates of offending typically commit those offenses with a large number of accomplices. Sarnecki (1982) found that the 35 most delinquent juveniles in the Swedish community he studied were linked to one another by membership in the largest gang and two smaller gangs. These were among the most criminally active gangs in the community. The 35 juveniles were involved with 224 accomplices in crime. Almost 3 in 10 of the 799 other delinquents in the community committed at least one crime with 1 of these 35 high-rate offenders (Sarnecki:171,209). The accomplices of these 35 were usually selected from the criminally more active part of the total offending population (Sarnecki:144–145).

High-rate juvenile offenders affiliate

with one another in peer groupings. The 35 most active members were but 6 percent of the delinquents in Sarnecki's study population. They belonged to the three largest membership gangs, in which the mean number of suspected crimes per gang member was 22.3 during a 3-year period—a rate that was three times that of the delinquent population as a whole. The members of the largest gang made up only 13 percent of the population of offenders, yet they accounted for 42 percent of all suspected crime (Sarnecki:174).

Duration of Accomplice Relationships

Most pairings in committing delinquencies are of short duration. Sarnecki (p. 140) found that only 13 percent of the 1,162 juvenile delinquency pairings in an offense in the Swedish community persisted beyond 6 months. Only 4 percent of the pairs were still committing crimes together after 1.5 years, but 1 of the 1,162 offending pairs was committing offenses together after 3.5 years, roughly half the 6 years the study tracked offenders. The short life of any pairing in delinquency partly reflects the fact that most delinquent careers are short. Almost 6 in 10 youths in the Swedish cohort were known to the police during only one 6-month period of the 6-year study (Sarnecki:141). Among those persisting in delinquency, the modal pattern was to change associates in committing offenses.

Sarnecki (pp. 142–143) also found that the most criminally active usually commit their crimes in pairs and that they preserve particular pairings longer than do those who are less active. The most active and seriously delinquent juvenile suspects were 45 times more likely to commit crimes with the same associates than were less active juveniles from the study population.

Quite clearly, accomplices in offending change quite frequently in juvenile careers. The larger the number of offenses committed by an offender, the larger the number of different accomplices linked to that offender's career. One's accomplices as a juvenile are likely to be drawn from cliques or constellations of cliques with which one is affiliated. Ordinarily, these cliques are part of a network. Adults are perhaps more likely than juveniles to be linked in loose networks, ones in which they are linked by weak rather than strong ties (Granovetter, 1973).

Stability of Group Affiliation

An important issue is how shifts among cliques of peers and co-offenders occur and how affiliation with cliques and larger networks is stabilized, on the one hand, and disconnected and terminated, on the other. These issues are not dealt with systematically in the research on crime and delinquency.[3] Thus, empirical studies on delinquent gangs and street-corner groups are used here to explore these issues.

It was quite evident in the Swedish community studied by Sarnecki (1982) that most gangs, as well as pairings, existed for only short periods of time. Only one gang persisted for the entire 6-year period and towards the end of that period it split into two separate groups. Yet a third was spun off in the final 6 months of

---

[3]Similarly, little is known about the stability of group affiliations among a population of nonoffenders. The stability of pair and group affiliations seems to vary by age and to be more stable during the preadolescent than the adolescent years. Still, it seems that all youths frequently change companions for conforming acts, such as walking to school, dating, going to the movies and shopping. Much more needs to be known about pair and group affiliations for nondelinquent or all youths to assess the relative stability of delinquent affiliations. It is possible that delinquent pairings show greater stability than nondelinquent pairings. Choosing different companions for different activities, moreover, may simply be a characteristic of both youthful and adult behavior.

the study. The original gang was still the largest of the three at the close of the study period, however, despite its losing members to form two others (Sarnecki: 153). Although gangs can divide by schism, merge with other gangs, or join a network of gangs, their durability has consequences for individual careers. Career termination may result simply from the short duration of groups and the loose links that bind members, especially for those who rely primarily on group affiliation for accomplices and support in offending.

Suttles's (1968) study of street-corner groups in Chicago allows us to explore the stability of affiliations with offending groups. He identified 32 named street-corner groups in the Addams area of Chicago (Suttles: 157). With one exception, they were made up exclusively of males and averaged from 12 to 15 members in size. Some had as few as 8 members and one had 29. Each of the groups had some members who lived outside the Addams area—ranging from 4 to 17 percent; 12 percent of the members of all the groups lived outside the area (Suttles: 157–167). Outsiders were youths who either formerly lived in the area or were related by kinship to one of the group members (Suttles: 165).

Although Suttles (1968) does not provide detailed information on the duration of the 32 groups, he reports that one lasted but 1 year and that some lasted 2 or 3 years (pp. 161, 166). All were subject to considerable turnover in membership, partly because of residential mobility.[4] Of those known to have quit membership in groups, 41 percent moved to another area of Chicago (Suttles: 167).

One additional fact is worth noting. A substantial proportion of all boys in an area never affiliate with these larger groups (Short and Strodtbeck, 1965:56–57; Suttles: 173). Suttles reports that most of the unaffiliated are boys who regularly "band together" in small cliques (p. 169). Few boys, then, are isolates. The role of affiliation with territorial delinquent groups in accounting for differences in individual rates of offending is unclear, however. Suttles (p. 220) reports that arrest rates were about equal for the affiliated and unaffiliated boys. Yet others, especially Short and Strodtbeck, report much higher individual rates of offending for gang-affiliated boys.

The stability of territorially based groups is threatened by three major contingencies: transiency, incarceration of members, and shifts to conventional careers. Slum neighborhoods especially are characterized by high residential transiency of families. That transiency has three major consequences for territorial youth organizations. For one, it makes the membership of any group volatile. From the perspective of the group, to survive substantial annual turnover in membership, it must obtain new members. From the perspective of the individual member, it means transitory affiliations with some group members and adapting to the exodus of former members and an influx of new members. Recruitment and replacement are age graded, and there is some preference for older rather than younger boys (Suttles: 163). Even associations between gang boys appear age graded. Klein and Crawford (1967:74) report that younger gang members are seldom seen in the company of older gang members.

Another consequence of transiency is that it spreads the network and influence of the group beyond the confines of its

[4]Klein and Crawford (1967) similarly reported high turnover in the black Los Angeles gangs they studied. They reported that "many members affiliate with the group for brief periods of from a few days to a few months, while others move out of the neighborhood or are incarcerated for periods sometimes exceeding a year" (p. 66).

territory, always linking some former residents to it. Chicago appears similar to Sarnecki's (1982) Swedish community in that some youths who move into other areas affiliate with other territorial groups (Keiser, 1969; Short and Moland, 1976:168). Transiency thus both expands the choice of accomplices and links territorially based groups. Just how widely such individual contacts spread across territorially based groups is unclear but some of the most active and serious offenders are transient and use this larger network to search for accomplices.

Transiency also has important consequences for the temporal continuity of territorially based groups. To survive, the group must continually invest in replacing members. The more formally organized a group and the more provision it makes for replacement of members, the more likely it is to survive, as studies of Chicago's black conflict gangs demonstrate. The Vice Lords, which incorporated as a not-for-profit organization, gained as many as 8,000 members in 26 divisions (Sherman, 1970), while the informally organized Nobles barely survived (Short and Moland:168). The higher the residential transiency of an area, the more likely its youths are to be organized into a loose confederation and the fewer and less stringent are the criteria for entry and continuing affiliation with its territorial groups. Moreover, the combination of transiency and the aging of members, with replacement confined to a narrow range of age-mates, suggests that recruitment is limited to newly entering residents or, in a few cases, by mergers among gangs (Sherman, 1970; Short and Moland:168). The combination of these contingencies suggests that unless youth groups are formally structured to deal with turnover, they should have fairly high death rates.

The second important source of instability in gang membership is the rate of incarceration of gang members. The more seriously delinquent the members of a gang, the more likely they are to be incarcerated for substantial periods of time. Short and Moland (p. 168) report that nearly all the Vice Lords had been in correctional institutions at one time or another, and Short and Strodtbeck (1965) draw attention to the disruptions caused by incarcerating gang leaders. Unfortunately, they do not provide estimates of the rate of incarceration for any time interval.

A third important source of turnover in street-corner group membership is the shift to more conventional career affiliations by some members. At least one-half of Suttles's (p. 167) Addams-area group dropouts left because they married, went into the service, joined a job training program, or worked regularly in a job. Relatively few were lost to jail.

The general impression is that delinquents are organized into loose federations rather than highly organized groups. The federation is characterized by loose ties among individuals and cliques or clusters. Members are linked by a variety of activities in addition to delinquent offending. Individuals are not tightly bound either to large groups or to particular pairings within groups. Accomplices change quite frequently. According to Olofsson (1971), Swedish male juvenile delinquents are less selective of companions and their choices are less stable than are those of youths in the general population. It perhaps is reasonable to conclude that, while there are some highly structured territorial gangs that persist for periods of time (Miller, 1958, 1975; Clinard and Ohlin, 1960; Spergel, 1964; Klein and Crawford, 1967), associates in most delinquency offenses are drawn from much less structured networks in which nuclei of offenders are linked as nodes in that network. Territorial gangs (Thrasher, 1927; Whyte, 1943) are perhaps more like nodes in networks than like independent groups in organized conflict relations with others (Bordua, 1961, 1962; Yablonsky, 1962). Over time, networks are durable while particular groups and pairings are transitory and any individual's affiliation is of short duration.

One expects to find a large number of accomplice pairings in any individual's offending history of some duration, but ordinarily the same associates are involved for only a short period of time. Moreover, the higher an individual's rate of offending and the more serious the crimes committed, the more likely that person selects accomplices from a network.

Accepting the importance, even dominance, of networks in delinquent behavior should draw attention to the role of networks in offending and to the role that pairings, as contrasted with individual offending, play in the commission of crime.

PATTERNS IN GROUP OFFENDING

There is considerable variation in the extent to which offenders commit crimes alone and with others when examined in terms of the characteristics of the offense, the offender, and the victim. The bulk of research on the role of groups in offending unfortunately is done only with young offender populations. There are relatively few studies of the group behavior of youths in transition to adult status or of adult offenders at different ages. This makes it necessary to rely on single studies or case studies to infer patterns of group offending for adult offenders.

Sex

Somewhat over 1 in 10 lone offenders in crimes of personal violence in the United States are female offenders (Bureau of Justice Statistics, 1984:Table 40). The proportion of female lone offenders varies by type of violent crime, being negligible for the crime of rape and greatest for the crime of assault. Female offenders in violent crimes select females as their victims far more often than males select males. When females select male victims in violent crimes, they are most likely to assault men and least likely to rob them (Hindelang, 1976a:178).

Participation in most voluntary activities varies by age. Youths are more likely than adults to limit their choices to persons of the same sex. Opportunities for informal contacts with the opposite sex are more limited among youths. Not surprisingly, the associates of young persons in delinquency are almost always of the same sex. Shapland (1978:262) reports that no boy in her sample of 11- and 12-year-olds, when interviewed at age 13 or 14, admitted committing any offense with girls. The pattern is somewhat different when older offenders are included. Among violent, multiple-offender victimizations reported to the National Crime Survey (NCS) in 1982, 19 percent involved women as offenders, either with other women only (7 percent) or with men or men and women (12 percent) (BJS:49).

Only limited data are available to estimate the incidence of lone offending for both personal and property crimes by sex. The Federal Republic of Germany (1982) reports the size of arrested groups for a large number of offenses; the data show that the aggregate male rate of solo offending is somewhat below that of females but that the rate varies by offense. The West German police statistics for 1982 disclose that 68 percent of all males suspected of offenses, compared with 76 percent of all females, were solo offenders. That difference is not large, but women are disproportionally found in offenses that have high proportions of lone offenders, such as assault, shoplifting, prostitution, and petty theft without contact. Moreover, given the low incidence of offending among women and the general absence of organized women's delinquent groups or gangs, it seems reasonable to conclude that women more commonly than men engage in offenses that make them more likely to offend alone. Some confirmation of this is also found in the fact that multiple-offender incidents in which all offenders are female are fewer in absolute numbers and proportionally (7 percent) than are those involving women as lone offenders (13 percent) (compare Tables 40 and 45, BJS: 1984).

Women are less likely to be associated exclusively with other women than they are with men in committing violent crimes. Only 36 percent of the violent criminal victimizations involving one or more female offenders reported to the NCS in 1982 were made up entirely of female offenders; 64 percent involved association with men in the offense (BJS:Table 45). Correlatively, only 12 percent of the violent, multiple-offender incidents involving male offenders also involved female associates.

Women are least likely to offend only with women in the more serious violent crimes of robbery and aggravated assault. Among crimes of violence towards persons, substantial involvement of women offenders with women victims is largely confined to simple assault.

Race

Blacks are somewhat less likely than whites to be solo offenders. Although data are lacking for a population of adult offenders, the NCS data for 1982 disclose that 72 percent of all violent criminal victimizations by whites, compared with 60 percent of those by blacks, were single-offender incidents (BJS:calculated from Tables 44 and 49).

Mixed-race offending is infrequent in multiple-offender victimizations. Less than 6 percent of all 1982 crimes of violence reported to the NCS involved a mix of black, white, or other races of offenders (BJS:Table 49). There was little variation by type of violent crime.

Comparing mixed-sex with mixed-race offending, multiple-offender groups appear about twice as likely to include persons of the opposite sex (12 percent) as another race (6 percent) (BJS:Tables 44 and 49). Thus, accomplices from a different race and sex are uncommon and most accomplices are of the same race and sex.

Age

Group offenders are, in the aggregate, younger than solo offenders (BJS:Tables 41 and 46). In the NCS, offenses in which the offender's age was perceived by victims to be under 21 years were found more often among multiple- than single-offender victimizations (Hindelang, 1976a:172; Bureau of Justice Statistics:Tables 41 and 46).

A study of apprehended burglars in the Thames Valley, England, found that somewhat over three-fourths of the adult burglars, compared with one-half of the juvenile burglars, acted alone in the offense for which they were arrested. Considering only those offenses in which there were accomplices, adult burglars were more likely than juvenile burglars to act in pairs (Macguire and Bennett, 1982: 184).

Information is lacking on the size of offending groups by age for a population of U.S. offenders. Hood and Sparks (1970:87–89), however, report data on size of offending group by age for apprehended offenders in London boroughs and for offenders convicted of theft in Norway. They concluded that, as offenders grow older, they are more likely to be apprehended or convicted for an offense committed alone. Not until the mid-20s, however, are a majority of those apprehended or convicted, lone offenders. The age curve of solo offending is relatively flat until age 16, when the proportion of lone offenders begins to rise rather sharply. This shift is primarily accounted for by a rapid decline in apprehensions involving three or four or more participants, especially the latter. The proportion of apprehensions or convictions involving two participants fluctuates far less over time than does that for lone offenders or for groups with three or more offenders. The proportion with two or more offenders perhaps peaks at ages 16–18, but there is no substantial decline with age. Lone offending exceeds pair offending by the late teens. Older offenders thus ordinarily commit offenses alone or with a single co-offender. Still, at least 1 in 10 offenders in their mid-20s is apprehended or convicted for offending with three or more offenders.

Type of Offense

Certain offenses are identified as typically individual or group offenses. With the exception of robberies and some assaults, the modal size of offending groups reported by victims of major crimes against persons is a single offender; pair offenders are the next most common (Reiss, 1980:Table 1). But, with the exception of homicides and rapes without theft, the majority of *offenders* in crimes against persons commit their offenses with accomplices (Reiss, 1980:Table 2). The mean number of offenders per major common crime is between two and three for robbery and assaults and about one and one-half for all other offenses against the person and property (Reiss, 1980:Table 2).

Self-report studies show considerable variation by types of crime in the proportion of young persons committing offenses alone or with others. Much depends on how the self-report specifies the offense, especially as to the conditions of its occurrence. Shapland (1978:Table 2) found, not surprisingly, that all the 13- and 14-year-olds she studied took money from home as a single offender. At the other extreme, more than 9 of 10 boys said they vandalized public property with others.

Most boys, nonetheless, report acting alone and with others for a variety of offenses. Shapland (1978:262) calculated that the mean percentage involvement in group offending was 59.68 percent (standard deviation of 15.6) for all boys aged 13–14, whereas that for solitary offending was 30.02 percent (standard deviation of 16.4). From this we can conclude that although the typical offender history includes both lone and group offending in the same and different kinds of offenses, the ratio of group to solitary offenses in a youthful offender's career is, on the average, 2:1.

Detailed information on the distribution of solo and group offending for specific offenses is unavailable for the adult offender population of the United States. Although the rate of solo offending appears to be higher for a population of offenders in the Federal Republic of Germany (Kaiser, 1982:103) and the German Democratic Republic (Kraeupl, 1969:63) than in the rest of Europe or in North America, police statistics for adult offenders in West Germany disclose rather marked variation in solo offending by type of offense. Among the major offenses in which at least 8 of every 10 offenders committed the offense alone were murder; sexual offenses, such as exhibitionism and sexual murder; drug abuse involving heroin and cocaine; and the white-collar offenses of embezzlement, forgery, and fraud. By contrast, most of the common crimes had much lower solo offending fractions. At least 8 in every 10 suspects in common thefts, robberies, breakings and enterings, and breaches of the peace had at least one co-offender (Federal Republic of Germany, 1982).

The significance of group affiliation for young offenders is reinforced when the variation in the group composition of offending is examined by age and type of offense. Even for homicide, which in the aggregate is a solo-offender crime and an infrequent offense among young offenders, Zimring (1984:91) found that the younger the homicide offender, the more likely he was to have killed as part of a group and to have done so when engaging in a collateral felony, such as robbery-murder. In brief, young homicide offenders are far less likely than older ones to commit murder and felonious homicide alone.

Relationship Between Victims and Offenders

It is commonly observed that a prior relationship between victims and offenders is more characteristic of some crimes than others. Domestic assaults, for instance, are characterized by cohabitation of victim and offender, whereas assaults involving theft ordinarily occur among strangers. There is a modest relationship between the size of an offending group and the relationship of offenders to their victims (Bureau of Justice Statistics, 1984:Tables 52 and 62). The modal offender in crimes of violence against strangers is a co-offender, whereas single offenders predominate when there is a prior relationship between victim and offender(s). Even the modal offender in robberies of nonstrangers is a lone offender, whereas it is a co-offender in robberies of strangers. The larger the offending group in robberies and assaults of strangers, the more likely victims are to be injured; however, a larger proportion of lone offenders inflict serious injury when the victim is a nonstranger rather than a stranger.

Territorial Concentration

Perhaps the single most noteworthy aspect about common crime is the territorial concentration of offenses, offenders, and, to a substantial degree, victims. A substantial majority of both personal and household crimes occur close to the residences of the offenders and their victims (Reiss, 1967; M. W. Smith, 1972; Pyle et al., 1974).

Juvenile offenders commonly belong to territorially based groups and typically select their co-offenders from those groups or the territory where they reside (Shaw and McKay, 1931; Suttles, 1968; W. G. West, 1974, 1977, 1978; Sarnecki, 1982). Shaw's (1938) tracing of the accomplices in the criminal careers of five Martin brothers illustrates this territorial concentration of career offenders. In the course of their careers these five brothers were implicated in theft with at least 103 other delinquents and criminals. The other offenders resided, for the most part, within seven-tenths of a mile of the Martin residence. Of the 103 co-offenders, 28 were adjudicated in delinquent and criminal proceedings, and all but 3 of the 28 served adult as well as juvenile institutional sentences (Shaw:115–116). The geographic concentration of the Martin brothers' accomplice network was characteristic of both their juvenile and young adult years, although some geographic diversification occurred through accomplices met during periods of incarceration.

Recent work on the neighborhood determinants of criminal victimization sheds additional light on the territorial concentration of offenders and on patterns of group offending. D. Smith (1986) reports that the larger the proportion of single-parent households with children between the ages of 12 and 20 in a neighborhood, the higher the neighborhood's perceived risk and actual rate of victimization by crime. Sampson (1985:25) finds that the greater the proportion of female-headed households and the higher the density of settlement in a neighborhood, the greater the rate of victimization by crime. Sampson (1983:172) similarly finds that juvenile offenders in neighborhoods with both high-density settlement and a large proportion of female-headed households commit a larger proportion of their offenses with others than do juveniles in areas with low density and a small proportion of female-headed households. Sampson's findings hold independent of the racial composition of the neighborhoods.

Additionally, Bottoms and Wyle (1986) report that delinquency rates in public housing projects in English industrial communities are correlated with the degree of concentration of single-parent households with youths of an age to offend. They conclude that high delinquency rates in public housing projects are partly a function of managers' concentrating single-parent households in selected public housing projects.

These studies lend support to the hypothesis that it is the territorial concentration of young males who lack firm controls of parental authority that leads them into a peer-control system that supports co-offending and that simplifies the search for accomplices.

Siblings in Offending

Brothers in Crime, the classic study by Clifford Shaw (1938), traces the criminal careers of five Martin brothers over a period of 15 years. At the close of that time the brothers ranged in age from 25 to 35 years. Four of the five had by then terminated their criminal careers. Shaw (p. 4) describes the crime and criminal justice consequences of their careers in the following way:

> The extent of their participation in delinquent and criminal activities is clearly indicated by the fact that they have served a total of approximately fifty-five years in correctional and penal institutions. They have been picked up and arrested by the police at least 86 times, brought into court seventy times, confined in institutions for forty-two separate periods and placed under supervision of probation and parole officers approximately forty-five times.

These are but the official statistics of their five criminal careers. Autobiographical reports accounted for more than 300 burglaries, the theft of 45 automobiles, and a host of other crimes involving theft, receiving stolen property, and armed robbery (Shaw:5).

The autobiographical accounts of these five brothers offer evidence of older brothers' recruiting their younger brothers into offending, thereby focusing on the role that siblings play in co-offending and how common sibs are as initial and continuing co-offenders. Whether one offends with siblings can be expected to depend on such characteristics as family size and sibling composition by sex and birth order. There is no reliable research on how much the co-offending of siblings accounts for group offending.

We can gain some notion of the role of siblings in criminal events from the Peoria study of residential burglary (Peoria Crime Reduction Council, 1979). Of the 151 burglaries involving two or more offenders for which a juvenile was apprehended, roughly 24 percent involved two or more siblings (and sometimes nonsibling offenders as well). Of these, about two-thirds involved nonsiblings and one-third involved only siblings.

What is apparent from these Peoria data

is that more than 1 in 10 adjudicated burglary events involved at least two members from the same family. Thus, among a population of lone and group offenders in residential burglary, a small proportion of families accounts for a disproportionate amount of the *adjudication decisions*.

Little is known about the transmission of antisocial and criminal behavior within families and across generations of kin. It has been recognized for some time that male delinquents come from larger families than do male nondelinquents of the same age and socioeconomic status (Ferguson, 1952; D. J. West and Farrington, 1973; Blakely, Stephenson, and Nichol, 1974). Jones, Offord, and Abrams (1980) found that, in their comparisons of male probationers and controls, this difference in the size of sibling groups was entirely due to an excess of brothers. Probationers and controls did not differ in number of sisters (Jones, Offord, and Abrams:140).

Of special interest was the finding that the antisocial scores of the brothers of the delinquent male probationers were significantly higher than those of the brothers of their matched controls (Jones, Offord, and Abrams:141). By contrast, among female probationers, both brothers and sisters were more antisocial than the siblings of their control counterparts (Jones, Offord, and Abrams:144).

Even more striking was the discovery that the average antisocial score of the probationers' brothers increased with the number of brothers in the family when the number of sisters was held constant; it decreased with the number of sisters, holding the number of brothers constant (Jones, Offord, and Abrams:142). Jones and his colleagues interpret these results to mean that sisters suppress antisocial behavior in their brothers, whereas brothers respond to one another in ways that stimulate their potential for antisocial behavior, i.e., it is due less to learning antisocial behavior from siblings than to their mutual participation. Evidence on this point appears lacking.

ROLE OF GROUPS IN RECRUITMENT FOR CO-OFFENDING

A substantial proportion of offending involves two or more offenders. There is no evidence that very many offenders, if any, keep the same accomplices over long periods of time. Indeed, quite the opposite appears to characterize the criminal careers of high-rate offenders. Most offenders have a substantial number of different accomplices.

Most offenders appear to select different accomplices, especially as adult offenders. Not too much is known about how and why accomplices are selected. In this section the structure of peer and adult networks that facilitate the search for co-offenders is examined, followed by an examination of what is known about the search for and active recruitment of associates in offending.

Structure of Delinquent Peer Networks

There is some disagreement about how youth groups and their peer networks are structured. Most young males do not appear to belong to tightly bounded groups that have a constant membership and from which they select their accomplices, if indeed selection is the appropriate model for describing how persons come to offend together. This exposition links youths in a web of affiliation or network of contacts and exchanges. Typically, sociometric techniques are used to define a large group that has a much smaller core membership that gathers together with some frequency (Yablonsky, 1962; Short and Strodtbeck, 1965; Gannon, 1966;

TABLE 3 Percentage Comparison of the Types of Group Contacts for Boys in Four Gang Clusters with Different Rates of Delinquency

	Higher Delinquency Clusters		Lower Delinquency Clusters	
Type of Delinquency Contact	A	B	C	D
Percent of all members in cliques	42	43	16	15
Percent of all contacts that are *mutual* contacts among members of their cluster	81	72	20	32
Percent of all contacts that occurred only once	54	35	73	77
Percent of all clique member contacts made within their clique	82	73	47	40

SOURCE: Adapted from Klein and Crawford (1967:Table 2); Hood and Sparks (1970:Table 3:1).

Klein and Crawford, 1967; Sarnecki, 1982). The core of active members within the larger youth group ordinarily is no more than one-fifth the total aggregate of affiliated youths and ranges in size from 20 to 40 or so members (Hood and Sparks, 1970:89–90). That core of firm or active members, in turn, often subdivides into clusters or cliques of 5–10 members (Klein and Crawford, 1967). These aggregations are best described as a loose web of affiliations because most persons have most of their contacts with others in their clique and little, if any, contact with others in the network.

Klein and Crawford (1967) studied the extent to which 32 youths in one gang had contacts with one another during a 6-month period. The observed number of interactions of any member with all others during the 6 months ranged from 1 to 202. Of the 486 possible pair relationships among the 32 members, two-thirds involved no contact and for three-fourths contact was limited to no or only one contact. Most of the contacts occurred within two cliques—one of nine members and the other of five, with the nine-member clique having a much greater frequency of contact than the five-member one (Klein and Crawford:72).

Klein and Crawford (pp. 74–75) divided the gang members into four clusters according to their individual rates of delinquency. Those labeled A and B in Table 3 had relatively higher rates than those labeled C and D. Those in A and B clusters also had continued gang relationships for longer than those in clusters C and D. Higher delinquency group members were more likely to be members of the two major cliques and to have more of their delinquency contacts within the clique, as Table 3 makes readily apparent.

We may conclude from these delinquency and group-affiliation data that delinquent contacts do not result from a stochastic process. Indeed, a substantial amount of delinquency occurs within relatively small clusters that form within a larger network of affiliations. A minority of the contacts, nevertheless, are within the larger network although they occur much less frequently.

Structure of Adult Networks

Surprisingly little is known about how adults make contacts and decide to offend together. Apart from the highly organized criminal activity that is conducted by syndicates, it seems clear that most adult co-offending does not arise from participation in groups of which they are members. Although some adults may form co-offending relationships that are stable over time, the typical co-offending relationship appears to be transitory and there is a continual search for new co-offenders. Among the career thieves studied for the President's Commission on Law Enforcement and the Administration of Justice, the search for opportunities and co-offenders was self-styled as "hustling." Hustling led to "connecting" with other individuals who were similarly searching, "scouting" for opportunities to commit offenses, and looking for buyers for their stolen goods (Gould et al., 1965:25–26). The particular set of accomplices often varies from crime to crime and offenders must work with people according to the requirements of particular crimes. This is especially the case for what Sparks, Greer, and Manning (1982) describe as "crime as work" in "crimes for gain." Gould and his co-workers (pp. 51–52) concluded that

> While a few professional criminals work for extended periods of time with the same accomplices, most work from day to day, or week to week, with whomever they can put together for a particular job. Each job requires different personnel, different plans, different resources, and even a different working schedule.

Searches for accomplices and for means to dispose of illegal gain are facilitated by using networks as well as particular organizations. There are gathering places, organizational settings, and kinds of encounters that facilitate locating accomplices. Additionally, offenders are symbiotically linked to these settings by common residence in a community that is host to these organizations; the accomplice-offenders themselves comprise a loose web of affiliations and a resource for referrals in searches. The local pool halls, bars, and all-night restaurants (Gould et al.:25; Polsky, 1969), the fences (Klockars, 1974), the chop-shops (shops that dismantle motor vehicles), and the legitimate businesses that deal in some stolen goods, such as parts shops, auto dealers, second-hand stores, and pawn shops (Gould et al.:26–27; 37–39) all are points of contact to search for accomplices and to dispose of illegal goods for gain. For some, the syndicate facilitates the search.

What seems to characterize the network among adult offenders is that adult offenders patronize the same places, make the same kinds of transactions, and often reside in the same area. The casual encounter can conclude the search as much as "putting out the word." "Hustling" is not a passive activity but an active search for connections (Gould et al.:25). Indeed, excepting recruitment for the more sophisticated crimes, which require a variety of highly specialized skills, the daily round suffices to select accomplices.

Dual Processes of Recruitment in Groups

Dual processes of recruitment go on in many delinquent and criminal cliques or groups. One process recruits members to a group, either to a loose affiliation with an informal group or, in the limiting case, to a structured position in an organized criminal syndicate. The recruit may be a "raw recruit"—one who is being initiated into delinquent or criminal activity—or more commonly, one who has a history of offending.

A second kind of recruitment process involves group members recruiting accomplices in crimes. Although a member is more likely to recruit an accomplice from among fellow group members than from outside, offenders cross group boundaries to select accomplices.

Recruitment into Offending Groups

Almost all groups that endure for any period of time experience turnover in membership, with some leaving and others joining. Even size of membership ordinarily does not remain constant over time (Suttles:161). Sarnecki (p. 148) concludes that juveniles come into and leave gangs quickly; the boundaries of gangs are quite permeable. Normally, membership is shorter than 6 months, especially for the less delinquent. Members also appear to leave easily, generally without resistance or resentment by the group (Suttles:167). This suggests that there is a kind of sifting and sorting going on in peer groups of delinquents. Yet, it is not necessarily high-rate offenders who remain. A number of studies, e.g., Sarnecki (p. 148), report that a substantial number of high-rate offenders may leave after committing only a few crimes with accomplices drawn from the group. High-rate offenders often have contacts among a number of such groups, recruiting many of their accomplices from outside their own group. The stable core members of a group during the period it persists, thus, are generally neither the highest nor the lowest rate offenders.

Recruitment of Accomplices

Selection of accomplices is facilitated by the fact that some groups are linked with others. Groups with older members, for example, are linked to groups with younger members, and groups of the same ethnic origin are linked with one another. This loose linkage facilitates selection of accomplices from different groups. The most active offenders, moreover, belong to several groups, and so themselves serve as links among their groups. They are the most likely to select accomplices from outside a group in which they may be regarded as a core member. What is not known from any of the studies, however, is whether the highly active members within these groups frequently are selected by others as accomplices. It would appear that they usually are not.

It is no simple matter to disentangle the effect of recruitment on offending rates from the selective recruitment of accomplices on the basis of prior record since longitudinal studies have not addressed recruitment of accomplices. There is no certain answer to the question: How do previously unacquainted offenders find one another and become accomplices? The answer is less obvious than it may seem. Empey (1970), in a postscript to the account of an ex-offender, notes that ex-offenders continue to face blandishments from old friends to return to the old ways since friendship networks are one vehicle for entering into complicity to commit an offense. But he also reports (personal communication) that, when he moved delinquents from one school setting to another to provide them with the anonymity to change to a conventional life-style, within a few weeks they had formed associations with all the "local hoods in the new school." This suggests that active delinquents are continually signaling their interest in locating others with whom they may engage in offending. Such signaling is readily picked up by others who are similarly searching.

We need to understand how people search for accomplices in offending and how successful those searches are, especially among strangers. W. G. West (1974) concluded that local networks that uniquely identify offenders and their skills facilitate recruitment of accomplices in theft. Initial contacts are made when relevant information is passed about a named individual. But just how strangers search out one another to commit an offense is unclear. They may begin, as do detectives, by asking individuals they know to help them find a particular kind of accomplice. However, much searching probably is done by frequenting places where cues direct one to potential accomplices.

From his study of juvenile thieves who were serious offenders, W. G. West (1974, 1977, 1978) reports that it would be an exaggeration to say that most thieves learned how to practice *thieving* as a member of a group into which they were recruited. Rather, based on his interviews and observations of high-rate juvenile thieves, he reports that theft is both endemic to and a highly visible occupation in many lower class or working-class communities. Theft is a readily available activity for almost everyone in the community. Recruitment to high-rate offending in theft takes place, however, in loosely structured peer settings. As described elsewhere in this paper, W. G. West (1978:177–178) reports that

> Groups coalesce and disperse, individuals drift in and out of them, alone or in pairs. Almost all of the neighborhood youths have committed some petty varieties of theft during childhood. They are usually caught and labeled as secondary deviants. A great many teens know of the existence of theft through at least one peer who is thieving as an occupation. The symbiotic relationship between some older and younger clusters facilitates contact between peer groups and the potential recruits are able to meet the already initiated. . . . most teens do not need to befriend somebody to find a "partner in crime": they already have one.

West goes on to describe how serious thieving involves training through repeated contacts with experienced persons in loosely structured social settings or encounters. Some learn by observing older, experienced thieves; for some there is anticipatory apprenticeship by modeling after an older thief and learning his skills. Some may even be self-taught as in the case of one who took a locksmith course by mail and was in demand as an accomplice because he could pick locks. Especially important, W. G. West (1978:179) points out, is the cultivation of contacts and relationships that provide information:

> He needs colleagues, in most cases, who will "cut him in" on jobs, angles, or "hot tips," warn him when "the heat is on," and lend him money when he gets down on his luck. He needs reliable fences and customers, who are aware of constrictions on his work and know how to "play his game" or interact with him to minimize risks and maximize gain.

Many jobs are carried out in partnerships and some require an elementary division of labor (Shover, 1973). All of these rely on supporting contacts and networks.

W. G. West's description can be restated in the following form. Minor delicts and theft are part of class culture and its organization in American society. Hence many youths have engaged in such behavior while growing up. Theft is common among pre-adolescent peer groups as well as adolescent ones. Minor delinquencies, such as truancy, theft, and vandalism, are committed at early ages. What is critical is how some few get channeled into becoming a high-rate or a specialized offender, such as in occupational theft. Loosely structured groups in networks are critical perhaps in leading to high-rate offending careers. To develop an occupational specialization in theft, one needs older offenders who serve as models and who inculcate necessary skills, whether for shoplifting or breaking and entering. Once the skills are acquired, however, whether one commits the offense with accomplices depends on whether a division of labor is required to commit the crime or whether one seeks to reduce risks by taking accomplices. One can shoplift alone, for example, but one's risk may be reduced if an accomplice distracts clerks or is alert to security personnel. On the other hand, accomplices may lower skill levels and increase the risk of apprehension.

From this perspective, the role of groups in recruiting members and inducing persons to offend with them in committing delicts is overstated. For, as W. G. West, Suttles, and others contend, the culture, group organization, and networks that constitute daily life in many neighborhoods create the necessary ecological environment for the development of offending careers.

All too little is known about how individual offending careers intersect one another and how such intersections are determined by individual and collective patterns of group affiliation and recruitment. Studies are needed that examine the intersection of careers for a cohort of offenders to determine the extent to which the members of a group contribute to one another's offending. But, since demographic processes and individual choice lead to selection of accomplices from outside the cohort, to study their contribution to offending, the study population must include all co-offenders of the cohort. Some indication of how substantial that external set of accomplices can be is found in Sarnecki's (1982) Swedish cohort study. The original cohort consisted of all persons born between 1957 and 1968 who were resident in the community and who the police concluded had committed at least one crime in the community between January 1, 1975, and December 31, 1977. There were 575 such individuals in that cohort. But two additional study populations were added as the cohort's offending histories were followed. The first comprised those individuals who were born before 1957 but who police concluded had committed a crime during the study period with someone in the 1957–1968 cohort or who had committed a crime with a juvenile who, in turn, had committed a crime with someone in the original cohort. The second group included persons who police concluded had committed a crime with someone in the 1957–1968 cohort during the follow-up period from January 1, 1978, to December 31, 1980. These two additional populations included 259 individuals, so that the total population studied was 834 individuals (Sarnecki: 50–51).

It may be that high-rate offenders are youths who are highly susceptible to overtures from any offender to join in committing a delinquent act. Their high rate of offending with many different offenders could thus result from their being a "joiner" rather than a recruiter. While further research is needed to explicate the mechanisms of selection of co-offenders, both the Peoria (Peoria Crime Reduction Council, 1979) and the Swedish studies provide some evidence that it is primarily a recruiter effect. It is possible that high-λ offenders who frequently change co-offenders may actually be composed of subpopulations of "joiners" and "recruiters."

Tracing the web of these relationships, Sarnecki (1982) became aware that the high-rate offenders were linked to other offending groups and individuals outside the city as members of groups extended their territorial range in the search for accomplices. He concluded that by age 18–20 the cohort members still active in crime became part of new gangs that represented larger and larger areas and increasingly were composed of more high-rate offenders. The most active juveniles with high rates of offending thus became affiliated with groups whose members encompassed an entire city and, eventually, several cities (Sarnecki: 241). Sarnecki even suggests at one point that were one to trace the web of affiliations over the careers of the most active members of this small group of gangs in one city, one would find that they were linked to a network that encompassed all the major gangs in Sweden. These remarks emphasize again the importance of looking at offending networks and the roles that individuals play in them. Some of the most effective intervention may lie in selecting individuals in terms of their place in offending networks.

Each offender potentially recruits others to offend together in a criminal incident, since each may search for an accomplice. Yet some offenders may be more open to recruitment and others to be recruiters. Below, evidence is examined that strongly suggests that some offenders actively recruit co-offenders. Given their high individual rate of offending, recruiters seem more likely to recruit persons whose individual rate of offending is below theirs. These recruitments may well account for a considerable portion of the recruitee's offending.

Evidence that there are recruiters comes from the Peoria juvenile residential burglary study. Recall that there were 306 residential burglaries, 151 of which involved at least two co-offenders (Peoria Crime Reduction Council, 1979). Of these, 74—or 49 percent—involved at least one offender who was previously apprehended and at least one never previously apprehended. This result is consistent with the view that an experienced offender selects a less-experienced one. These juvenile "recruiters"—the recidivists apprehended with a first-time arrestee—could logically be targets for special treatment.

Substantial evidence that there are recruiters is also found in the study of a Swedish community by Sarnecki (1982). The 35 delinquents with the highest individual rates of offending had a total of 224 accomplices in crime, or one-third of all juveniles in the study population (Sarnecki:209). These high-rate offenders generally did not offend with the same accomplices in very many offenses, which strongly suggests they actively recruited other offenders. Moreover, Sarnecki found that, when high-rate offenders joined less criminally active groups, they recruited members to offending and appeared to introduce new members to a criminal career (Sarnecki: 236). Finally, the most criminally active committed offenses with co-offenders from a larger territorial area (Sarnecki: 171), which suggests that they were recruiting from a larger network.[5]

There is evidence, then, that individuals with high rates of offending often commit offenses with accomplices, most of whom have lower offending rates. Most of these high-rate offenders keep the same accomplice for only a short period of time. Thus, high-rate offenders commit offenses with a substantial number of different accomplices and so must continually search for new accomplices. Still, they are not precluded from also committing some sizable proportion of offenses alone, and that often seems to be the case, increasingly so, perhaps, as they get older.[6]

Recruiter Effects on Offending

The review of patterns of lone and group offending and their relationship to individual rates of offending leads to a number of conclusions that have policy implications.

First, it is apparent that a relatively small number of very high rate youthful offenders can be identified retrospectively at a fairly young age. Their prevalence in a population of offenders will vary by age and place of residence. Were

[5]Sarnecki was well aware that limiting the study to juveniles with police contacts and relying on official reports of delinquency limited the size of the network and its population and may have biased results in other ways (Sarnecki, 1982:235).

[6]Research is needed on the group composition of offenses in offending histories by age of offenders and accomplices.

one able to select these high-rate offenders prospectively and isolate them, one could, in the short run, avert a substantial amount of juvenile crime, both those they commit alone and those attributable to recruiting others. Moreover, to the degree that their incarceration deters or reduces the offending rate of a sizable proportion of their accomplices, considerable additional reductions in crime might be expected since it seems likely that these high-rate offenders seek accomplices who might otherwise not be as active in offending.

Second, although just under two-thirds of all crimes against persons and their property are estimated to have but a single offender (Reiss, 1980:Table 1), an estimated two-thirds of all offenders commit their crimes as members of groups (Reiss, 1980:Table 2). Put another way, although the mean size of offending groups in major crimes against persons and their property is just over two offenders, roughly a third of all offenders offend in groups of four or more persons. Where group offending is involved, one would have to incapacitate a substantial proportion of the offending population since there is on the whole *very little overlap* in accomplices from one offense to the next, especially among older youthful and young adult high-rate offenders.

Third, the most efficient gains in reducing the crime rate might be made by incapacitating high-rate offenders who commit most of their offenses alone. But their number may be trivial even in the population of high-rate offenders. Indeed, since high-rate youthful offenders involve a substantial number of accomplices and since the size of the offending group decreases with the age of offenders, it may be more efficient to incapacitate young high-rate offenders who are also recruiters.

Fourth, the chaining of accomplices in offending provides a means to identify such high-rate individual offenders for intervention strategies. The use of network information may substantially increase the capacity to select high-rate offenders who account for the offending of others. Such identification requires that records be kept that uniquely identify all persons engaging in offenses. The Swedish police information system provides opportunities to trace such offenders as does that of the police in Japan. Typically, U.S. juvenile courts uniquely identify offenders by name, family and personal characteristics, and address. They commonly identify co-offenders by name only, making little systematic effort to link offender records to indicate group-offending careers. Similarly, the adult police arrest record typically lists co-offenders arrested. Yet, no effort is made to select those individuals who may be systematic recruiters of accomplices. Attention needs to be devoted to identifying high-rate offenders who are also recruiters, akin to those in either the Peoria residential burglary study or the Swedish community study. Such recruiters appear logical targets for selective incapacitation or other intervention strategies to reduce their recruitment as well as their offending.

These studies of juvenile offending and recruitment effects suggest that early intervention in the careers of high-rate offenders is possible by selecting those youths who fit the recruiter pattern characterized by a high individual rate of offending with groups involving a large number of different accomplices.

CHANGES IN THE GROUP COMPOSITION OF OFFENDING

One can postulate three kinds of criminal careers characterized by distinct types of offenders and patterns of offending. The first type of offender always offends alone and can be designated as having a solo offending career. The second always offends with others. The third, and by far the most common career, is characterized by both solo and group offending.

The solo offender is relatively rare. For some, such as murderers, their career is very short, usually being limited to a single offense. Others begin their career as a solo offender around a particular offense and never commit any other. This is characteristic of many sex offenders and is especially so for certain kinds of sex offending, such as voyeurism and pedophilia. Just how common a long career of solo offending is cannot be determined from existing investigations. Apart from sex offending, confidence forms of fraud, family assaults, and certain white-collar offending (e.g., embezzlement), most solo offending careers are probably of short duration.

Little also is known about careers characterized exclusively by group offending. Political criminals, such as terrorists, may be exclusively group offenders. A substantial proportion of very young delinquents who have short careers offend only with others. Indeed, their desistance rates are probably greatest at the young ages following a first apprehension (Wolfgang, Figlio, and Sellin, 1972:873–889).

Generally, however, most criminal careers that endure are characterized by a diverse mix of individual and group offending. It has long been known that most adult criminal careers in common crime begin with a juvenile delinquency career. And it is commonly assumed that most careers begin with at least a predominance of group offending and that the rate of solo offending increases with age. This conclusion is based on the following evidence previously cited in this paper:

- Solo offending is relatively uncommon at young ages and does not become the modal form of offending until the late teens or early 20s.
- The mean size of offending groups declines with age; groups of three offenders become relatively uncommon after age 20; groups of four or more become infrequent at an earlier age, perhaps by age 17.
- Solo offending begins to rise sharply at ages 15–16, shortly before the peak age of juvenile offending, and becomes the dominant form of offending at about age 20.

Yet, information from longitudinal studies of criminal careers is lacking to determine whether these aggregate statistics support the contention that offenders move from predominantly group to predominantly solo offending in the course of a criminal career. Before alternative explanations for these aggregate changes are offered, several other facts merit attention because they are consistent with some alternative explanations:

- The peak participation rate in offending occurs around age 17 or 18; the absolute size of the offender population declines rapidly thereafter.
- There is a desistance from offending at every age but especially so in the early teens.
- There are many careers of one or two offenses and these predominate at the very young ages.
- The participation rate declines markedly in the early 20s, suggesting either substantial desistance or declining average individual rates of offending, or both.
- The proportionate increase in solo offending is largely at the expense of a decrease in offending for groups of three or more offenders; the proportion of offenses committed by pairs remains fairly constant from late juvenile years through at least the mid-20s.
- Juvenile offending networks are relatively unstable and few are linked to adult networks.

On the basis of these observations, a number of models of co-offending in criminal careers can be postulated that are consistent with most, if not all, of the observations.

MODELS OF CO-OFFENDING IN CRIMINAL CAREERS

A *stochastic model* might provide a reasonable fit. One would expect that as the size of the offending population decreases, especially in local areas, there would be fewer offending groups of large size and more pair and solo offending. The rather steep rise in solo offending in the mid-teens, however, casts some doubt on how well such a model would fit if appropriate data were available to test it.

A *dynamic population model* assumes offenders have considerable residential mobility, especially as they reach the point of establishing independence from their families. Residential and occupational mobility weaken group ties. Group offending based on prior acquaintance with others in the group should decline as age increases. Those offenders who remain active must either commit offenses alone or search for similar unaffiliated co-offenders. Since groups larger than two persons generally are unnecessary, the search can be truncated when one co-offender is found.

A *functional model* assumes that co-offending is necessary to commit at least some crimes. One can advance several reasons why offending may need more than a single offender. Whenever a division of labor is required to commit a particular offense, co-offending is necessary. The necessity for specialized skills, such as picking a lock, and for collaboration, such as driving an escape vehicle, are examples. Co-offending also may reduce the risk of apprehension, as when an accomplice diverts attention from the crime scene. Not uncommonly, moreover, offenders seem to require social support to plan and commit an offense. Social support appears to be more characteristic of juvenile than adult offending since juvenile offending seems more closely linked to daily routines and activities. Most juvenile groups provide social support for characteristically juvenile crimes, such as vandalism or shoplifting.

This functional model is consistent with the selective attrition of low-offending persons, the decrease in the size of offending groups with the age of offenders, and the increase in solo offending wherein adults seem to commit offenses that usually do not require a division of labor. Yet, it does not seem to account very well for the mix of solo and group offending characteristic of many criminal careers.

A *selective attrition of group offenders* or a *solo survivor* model tries to account for the sharp decline in co-offending with age, especially of large groups, and, correlatively, the marked increase in solo offending. More specifically, the more general explanatory problem can be posed of whether the sharp rise in solo offending is due to a greater survival of solo offending and the selective attrition of group offenders in a population of offenders or to a gradual shift of persisters from group to solo offending. Several explanations seem worth exploring.

First, certain kinds of high-rate career offenders may shift towards solo offending because they require a substantial cash flow. This is characteristic, for example, of drug addicts who must commit a number of crimes each day to support their addiction, especially at the peak of dependence. The necessity to acquire cash and to obtain it quickly to make a buy to satisfy an individual need can lead to solo offending. The addict may consume search time in locating a buy rather than in locating co-offenders or be unwilling to take the time to commit enough crimes to split the income with a co-offender before making a buy. One expects drug dependence to create a substantial rise in solo offending for property crimes that provide cash, especially robbery. Nonaddict offenders, moreover, may shun offending with addicts because they perceive an increased risk of their apprehension because of the higher risk of apprehension an addict in need of a fix may take.

Second, the mix of offenses in an offending career usually changes substantially over time. The offending pattern of very young offenders is to commit in groups such offenses as vandalism and gang fighting. Later careers are characterized largely by offenses that can be committed alone—burglaries, thefts, armed robberies, and assaults.

Third, group offenders may be more likely to desist because their networks and group affiliations change substantially with age. There is considerable evidence that the groups to which juveniles belong are quite unstable and do not persist for long periods of time. There is also evidence (Suttles, 1968) that many youth groups do not persist across the transition from juvenile to young adult years. Indeed, it seems reasonable to assume that the network structure of local communities is age graded so that as offenders age, they move into adult networks, which are less likely to provide informal support for offending.[7] Attrition can be expected in any transitional process. We need to learn more about how such network transitions are made and how they affect offending behavior. It is likely that adult networks on the whole facilitate individual rather than group search behavior. Moreover, it is likely that the adult networks that facilitate individual searches for co-offenders are less cohesive and clique oriented than are those of juveniles. They also are more covert.

Research on criminal careers is needed to determine which of these explanations accounts for the aggregate shift towards solo offending. If it turns out that juveniles who shift early to high-rate, solo offending are most likely to have high-rate careers as adults, they are candidates for early intervention. What may be of special concern for timing incapacitative forms of intervention is identifying such individuals and detecting when the shift to predominantly solo offending occurs.

GROUP OFFENDING AND DESISTANCE FROM CRIMINAL CAREERS

Earlier it was conjectured that the shift towards solo offending with age might be accounted for by the selective attrition of group offenders, i.e., group offenders desist at an early age. More generally, the question arises of whether group processes account for desistance from criminal careers so that the nature of one's affiliation with groups of offenders affects one's desistance probability.

This section begins with a review of several empirical studies of desistance from offending that take into account group characteristics of offending in criminal careers. This is followed by speculation on how group processes may enter into selective attrition from offending.

Empirical Studies of Desistance from Group Offending

There clearly is desistance from offending at every age. The reasons for desisting may well vary with career survival time. Some criminal histories are of very short duration, especially so for those who enter at a very young age;

[7]Excluding formally organized group behavior in which participation increases with age, it can be speculated that the propensity to do almost any activity alone or in pairs increases with age. But just what causes these changes is not well understood; maturation is a description, not an explanation, of what is taking place with age.

others offend over a long period and desist or reduce their rate of offending substantially only at an advanced age (Blumstein, Farrington, and Moitra, 1985). How these points in an offender's history determine the rate and form of desistance is explored below. Since most offenders begin offending by age 16, and since desistance rates appear to be greatest soon after entry, one expects greater aggregate desistance before age 20 than after.

Knight and West (1975) report on temporary and continuing delinquents in a long-term survey of a cohort of 411 boys in a working-class London neighborhood (see also D. J. West, 1969). They selected 83 boys who constituted the most delinquent fifth of their cohort on the basis of prior convictions or admissions of delinquency (Knight and West:43). The 83 delinquents were divided into two groups. One group of 33 was labeled temporary delinquents because each had no official record of delinquency since turning age 17 and denied committing any offenses at age 18–19. The second group of 48 was labeled continuing delinquents because each had one or more criminal convictions since turning 17 or admitted to committing one or more major offenses.[8] Temporary delinquents were conviction-free for a period of at least 3 years; continuing delinquents had a continuing record of convictions or acknowledged offenses.

The largest single difference between the youths in these two groups was their involvement with adolescent peer groups in offending (Knight and West:45). Both official records and self-reports disclose that the continuing delinquents were more likely to commit their offenses alone. None of the official records for the temporary delinquents stated a boy was convicted alone, compared with 14 percent of the convictions for the continuing delinquents, a difference that was significant even when the larger number of convictions for continuing delinquents was taken into account. Although it is clear that the large majority of convictions for continuing offenders involved group offenses, temporary delinquents had been involved only in group offending (Knight and West:45).

Some explanation for this difference may be found in offenders' reported involvement in adolescent peer groups. Knight and West (1975:45), like Scott (1956), found that involvement with peer groups declines with age and can be short-lived. Temporary delinquents reported greater abandonment of their adolescent male peer groups than did continuing delinquents. Although all but one of the temporary delinquents had reported going about in an adolescent peer group of four or more boys between the ages of 15 and 17, somewhat less than half of them said they were doing so at age 17½. The involvement of roughly 80 percent of the continuing delinquents in groups of this size remained unchanged during these years (Knight and West: 45–46). In disengaging from peer groups, the temporary delinquents did not become social isolates. Rather, they generally began to go about with only one or two companions in contrast to their earlier participation with four or more.

It is apparent once again that the more serious and higher rate offending youths who continue in delinquency include some who exhibit solo offending while continuing to associate with the members of rather large groups with which they are

[8]Two youths are not included in the analysis because they were not interviewed at ages 18–19. One was killed in an accident at age 17, and the other was a fugitive from justice and untraceable (Knight and West, 1975:43).

affiliated. In some sense the large group perhaps serves as a reference group and perhaps also as a resource for recruiting accomplices for offending, since persisting offenders maintain a mix of individual and group offending.

From Suttles's (1968) work, it seems that dropping out from the larger participatory group is a function of both mobility to other neighborhoods and a shift to more conventional roles, such as work, marriage, and military service, that bring new forms of association. In addition to the 41 percent of the Addams-area youth who quit their neighborhood group because they moved to another area of Chicago, 26 percent left Chicago for jobs or military service. Another 30 percent either married or went to work in Chicago. Only one left to serve a prison term and only one left because he decided he did not want to belong to the group. Although dropouts were not looked down on for leaving their group "involuntarily," the one who left because he wanted to was reported to have been ostracized for it (Suttles:167). The effect of leaving on offending behavior is unclear in Suttles's study, but the development of conventional bonds (e.g., marriage, regular employment, and getting additional education) and the severing of old ties by moving out of the neighborhood or entering military service could account for a sizable proportion of desistance in the late teens and early 20s. The importance of environmental as well as status transitions on desistance rates is buttressed by a major study of adults paroled directly to the U.S. Army in World War II. Mattick (1960:49–50) found that the 1-year parole violation rate was 5.2 percent for parolees in the army, compared with 22.6 percent for civilian parolees. Moreover, only 10.5 percent of the army parolees had committed an offense within 8 years of discharge from prison, compared with an expected recidivism rate of 66.6 percent (Mattick, 1960:54).

W. G. West (1978) found that just over one-half of 40 high-rate juvenile thieves had retired from active criminality by age 20. Comparing these "reformed" criminals with those who were still "active," West found that 86 percent of the reformed criminals, compared with only 11 percent of those still active, had formed conventional bonds with a woman, a job, and/or schooling (W. G. West, 1978:186). Of course, it is difficult from these behavioral data to determine whether the forming of the bond led to the desistance or whether the bond was formed as a means of extricating oneself from a pattern of offending in a social network. Moreover, one does not know whether those who were still active and had not formed such bonds had tried and failed in doing so. The causal ordering of variables accounting for desistance is not easily resolved either theoretically or empirically.

The effect of leaving on offending behavior also is illuminated by the work of Knight and West (1975). They concluded that the delinquency of temporary delinquents is dominated by group solidarity rather more than by individual motivation to offend. As group offenders mature out of adolescence, many shift towards conventional work and family roles and going about with one or two of "the boys" in sports and bars or pubs. The "true" transient group delinquent in this sense is more likely to be a temporary delinquent whose affiliation is broken by transiency or by maturation into more conventional roles. The continuing delinquent who moves from juvenile into adult offending while maintaining network and large-group affiliations more and more offends alone or offends with one or two accomplices with whom affiliation is transitory. Some confirmation for this pattern of shifting to lone offending with aging was found in a major study by Sveri in Sweden (1965).

Group Processes in Selective Attrition from Criminal Careers

The concern in this section is to account for the selective attrition of group offenders. In doing so, explanations of how group and network processes account for desistance from criminal careers are posited. Three archetypes of desistance are presented. Desistance of group offenders can be attributed to specific deterrence, to status transactions, and to disruption of group affiliations.

Specific Deterrence

This archetype assumes that punishing an offender not only leads the offender to desist but has consequences for other group members as well. It assumes, moreover, that an individual is inducted into offending by others, as a member of a group, and continues to offend with one or more group members until apprehended. The sanction of being caught (particularly if reinforced by parental or other sanctions) leads that individual to desist from offending. The experience of being sanctioned has a specific deterrent effect on the offender. Apprehending and punishing a member of a clique may increase the likelihood that other members, especially accomplices who are not punished, will also desist. The perception of the risk of being caught is increased by apprehension followed by punishment. This is a special kind of specific deterrence whereby the punishment of some specific and significant other leads to desistance. What is critical in this deterrence is that one knows the person who is being punished and consequently has a more direct basis for vicariously experiencing the punishment and calculating one's risk.

This archetype probably accounts for much of the desistance at young ages and early in an offending career. The desistance rate is greatest following the first apprehension (Wolfgang, Figlio, and Sellin, 1972:87).

Status Transitions

Adolescence is characterized by the substitution of peer for parental relationships and control, especially for males, in American society. As boys grow up, peer groups lose some of their influence and control over those affiliated with them. This loss of influence is closely tied to status transitions, particularly those connected with the transition to adult status. But from early adolescence on, individuals make transitions to more conforming affiliations. Such transitions decrease the influence of nonconforming peers.

This archetype can account for the desistance of individuals with low rates of offending. Such offenders usually offend with accomplices. They are recruited by others to participate in offenses others initiate, and they rarely, if ever, initiate offending. They are at most peripheral members in a group and offend as occasional recruits. With marginal affiliation to a group, they desist after one or a few such experiences because they find conforming activities more rewarding and less risky or because they are not selected as accomplices. These low-rate offenders normally desist in the early adolescent years.

This second archetype is especially germane, however, for persons who participate in delinquency as part of diversified peer activity. This is generally characteristic of groups of young males, such as athletic teammates and street-corner gangs. Here one gradually is drawn into the cultural life-style of one's class wherein delinquency is part of that lifestyle. With aging, members turn to courtship, marriage, and having children as well as securing regular employment to fulfill family responsibilities. They may withdraw from their peer group to assume these adult roles. Women and family may play a role in weaning the male delinquent from his gang. Desistance in this archetype is a function of movement to an adult status. This pattern probably explains the desistance of many lower-class ethnics in the United States in their young adult years.

The desistance of group offenders may result not only directly from the declining influence of peers on a member's behavior but also from the indirect effect that has on group cohesiveness and the selection of co-offenders. With declining cohesiveness, groups become vulnerable to dissolution. There appears to be some discontinuity between the individual's maturation and group adaptation to the changing requirements of its members. Since such transitions do not occur at the same rate for all members, the group experiences selective attrition that gradually weakens it. Most cannot recruit replacements since the pool of those eligible also declines with transition to adult status. Failing to recruit enough members to maintain its status quo, the group disintegrates.

Much desistance of group offenders and offending may be tied to the fate of the particular groups to which they belonged. Individuals who depend primarily on co-offending with accomplices affiliated with a particular group or network are particularly vulnerable to its demise. Inasmuch as the demise of delinquent peer groups is most commonly associated with the transition of their members from juvenile to adult status, group demise should account for at least some of the desistance of group offenders in their late teens. Desistance in this second archetype does not depend on apprehension and punishment. The archetype is consistent with explanations of selective attrition of group offenders.

Disruption of Group Affiliation

Individuals are particularly vulnerable to the disruption or dissolution of group ties. Where such ties are primarily responsible for or play a major role in reinforcing one's delinquent or criminal behavior, breaking them may lead to desistance. This is especially likely to occur when the individual is unable to replace those bonds with others that permit continuation of the behavior. The three major ways that group bonds and affiliations that reinforce offending are dissolved are through residential mobility of an offender, affiliation with a total institution, and the dissolution of the reinforcing group itself.

Residential mobility breaks group ties and makes problematic reincorporation into a new group in the area to which one moves. Those who are unlikely to offend without group support drop out if they cannot affiliate with a new offending group or find accomplices. Residential mobility often is combined with other forms of social mobility, such as getting advanced schooling or a job or joining a military organization.

Total institutions also may affect desistance from careers. Two types of total institutions can have important consequences for desistance from criminal careers: prisons and the military. Incarceration affects one's position in a group and, if it still exists on release, one may have difficulty reentering. By disrupting patterns of search for co-offenders, incarceration may also shift offenders from predominantly group to predominantly solo offending. Apart from disrupting co-offending patterns, incarceration also may have specific deterrent effects, especially for young group offenders. If so, incapacitation at young ages may be a viable strategy to bring about desistance from offending.[9]

Another major source of desistance through entry into a conventional total institution is the military. Some criminal careers obviously go on in the military but many appear to be broken. As noted previously, Mattick (1960) found that 87 percent of the Illinois inmates paroled to the army were given honorable discharges and their recidivism rates were far below those of civilian parolees. Research is necessary to examine the effect of military, merchant marine, and other forms of service on interrupting and terminating contemporary criminal careers since Mattick's research was on parole to the World War II army (Mattick, 1958, 1960). Service in conventional total institutions is a potential alternative source of intervention in criminal careers.

This third archetype suggests that breaking group bonds and relationships may be a critical factor in desistance from offending. The breaking of ties is facilitated by forming new relationships or movement to new environments. Such ties are most likely to be broken in the late teens or early adult years. Offenders who continue to offend after these years may be those who usually commit offenses alone or who select different accomplices, often strangers, for each offense. The adult career offender, then, is characterized by transient relationships with other offenders. Relationships with co-offenders are instrumentally contrived rather than by-products of group affiliation.

[9]Imprisonment also introduces one to new offenders and networks. Just how influential such ties are on one's offending after leaving prison is not known. Such ties may not be as important as commonly assumed because inmates with close ties are usually not released at the same time and such ties and prison attitudes become less influential as release nears (Wheeler, 1961).

INTERVENTION ISSUES AND GROUP OFFENDING

Group offending is most characteristic of what we think of as juvenile delinquency and characterizes juvenile careers. Characteristically, the juvenile court deals with a group of co-offenders rather than a solo offender when considering a particular offense for which the juvenile is apprehended. Moreover, the juvenile career is more likely to be characterized by a predominance of group offending when compared with adult careers. Additionally, the juvenile court is better able than is a criminal court to consider co-offenders in dispositions because it is less bound by many of the procedural safeguards attending criminal proceedings and by the obligation to try fact without knowledge of the prior record and current status of the offender and co-offenders. The juvenile court has greater latitude to investigate and dispose of matters involving joint offending and joint careers. When siblings are involved in juvenile offending, there is greater opportunity for family intervention. Given this greater latitude in investigating, examining, and disposing of juvenile cases and the fact that most adult criminal careers are initiated in the juvenile years, serious consideration must be given to identification of and intervention in those juvenile careers most likely to lead to adult careers. A number of issues relating to such interventions are examined below.

Probability of Being Caught in Co-Offending

Earlier, attention was drawn to a possible apprehension selection bias in conjunction with membership in a group

(Erikson, 1971). Specifically, the question is whether there is evidence that group offenders are more likely to be caught than are solo offenders and whether one's risk of apprehension increases with the size of an offending group. Also, the probability of being apprehended as either a juvenile or an adult may well be a function of the prior record of a current co-offender.

It seems reasonable to conclude that one's risk of apprehension is a function both of one's individual rate of offending and that of one's co-offenders. And it is apparent that, at least for juveniles, high-rate offenders with accomplices are more likely to engage in crimes than are those who commit the same acts alone (Hindelang, 1976b:122). One may also expect interaction effects between one's rate of offending, the group mix of one's offenses, and the offending rate of one's co-offenders.

Inasmuch as one of the major ways of estimating an individual's rate of offending is from official records of apprehensions, it is important to know whether the probability of apprehension is substantially greater for group than lone offenders who have the same individual rate of offending. One expects, however, that this could vary by age so that the risk of apprehension is a function of whether one offends alone or with others at older as well as younger ages. It is important also to know whether apprehension is more likely to occur for a co-offending than a solo offense, even for those careers characterized by a substantial proportion of solo offenses. If so, using official records of apprehension will underestimate substantially the individual rate of offending for those who engage predominantly in solo offenses and overestimate the rate for group offenders if the two are not distinguished.

Just how much the individual rate of offending, in comparison with the group status of an offense, increases one's risk of apprehension is most problematic for offenses against the person. A predominantly solo pattern of offending may be disproportionally constituted of nonstranger crimes against the person, since that arrest rate is a function of victim identification at the time of the complaint. In brief, the rate of apprehension for solo offenses against persons who are strangers as well as against property may be substantially lower than that for others at risk. This suggests that it is important to separate solo from group offending rates by type of offense in assessing apprehension risks.

Early Identification of Career Criminals

One of the barriers to early identification of adult criminal careers has been the high apprehension rate of juveniles such that the population of offenders for disposition is large. Moreover, it is commonly presumed that at young ages it is difficult to distinguish high-rate offenders from low-rate offenders. The Wolfgang, Figlio, and Sellin (1972) retrospective cohort study supports this conclusion by reporting probabilities of committing a next offense by offense number and transition probabilities based on number and prior offense type. These probabilities were based on the entire juvenile career without respect to annualized individual rates of offending or of the time between offenses. This may be important information that may help to separate high-rate juvenile offenders from the population of all offenders at a fairly early age.

There is, of course, the possibility that many early high-rate offenders desist from a criminal career well before adulthood. There is no strong evidence that this is the case, however, and there is evidence that high-rate adult offenders can be identified by their juvenile offending rates (Chaiken and Chaiken, 1982).

It has been suggested here that there is an important subset of juvenile offenders that should be identified for special adjudication. These are the high-rate offenders who can have high rates of recruiting co-offenders. They would appear to be easily identified by both their high individual rates of offending and the number of offenses they commit with a large number of different co-offenders. One should be able to distinguish between those high-rate co-offenders whose rate is primarily dependent on affiliation with a small number of co-offenders and those who are continually involved with new associates. Moreover, there is some evidence that these recruiters affect the participation rate of their co-offenders as well as the co-offenders' rates of offending. If that is the case, they are especially opportune targets for early intervention. In any event the evidence presented suggests that the recruiter population for juvenile offenders is a small enough subset to warrant considering early intervention in their careers, perhaps even with strategies of incapacitation, since their incapacitation may have a marked effect not only on the aggregate crime rate but on participation and desistance rates of co-offenders as well. Investigation into these early intervention possibilities and their effects would add appreciably to our understanding of early criminal careers and the possibilities for intervening in them.

Sanctioning Group Offenders

Our adult system of justice is to a substantial degree based on preserving the individual integrity of co-offenders as they are processed in the criminal justice system. This means that not only must their individual history of offending be disregarded when trying a current set of charges but also individuals involved in the same offense can be treated differently based on their role in the charged offenses and that differences in their prior offending or personal histories can be taken into account at sentencing. The particular doctrine of sentencing will determine what will or may be taken into account, but there is a general presumption that the disposition for one offender need not be contingent on that of another so long as equals in all respects under law are treated equally. As noted above, the juvenile court has not been bound as tightly by these considerations and hence may have considerably more latitude to consider alternative strategies for sanctioning accomplices in an offense. Unfortunately, very little evidence about the effects of differences in sanctioning co-offenders is available to guide such choices.

One of the important issues in juvenile sanctioning is the extent to which early sanctioning may be a specific and a general deterrent to offending. It has been suggested here that punishment of one's co-offenders increases the sense of risk. Worth considering is whether early sanctioning of all co-offenders increases the desistance rate. Of special interest also is whether differential sanctioning for offenders in the same offense has different specific deterrent and desistance effects for co-offenders.

Where offenders are linked in the same networks, one expects to find overlap in offending careers. Each of these careers can be treated independently to determine the extent to which sanctioning interventions affect each career. Yet, each may also be regarded as affected by the interventions in the careers of co-offenders. Desistance may be influenced as much by the sanctioning of co-offenders as of the individual offender himself. Similarly, one's pattern of offending with others may be influenced by interventions in their careers or by their desistance. Is one more likely to desist if one's co-offenders have desisted? These seem questions worthy of investigation.

Intervention Strategies and Group Offending

Intervention strategies disrupt the lives of individuals and affect their criminal careers. Although many interventions are individual-change strategies, some aim to change the external conditions believed to cause the behavior of individuals. Klein and Crawford (1967:65–66) concluded that "elimination of external sources of cohesiveness of gangs, in most cases, would be followed by dissolution of a relatively large proportion of gang membership." They reached this position by observing that the internal sources of gang cohesion are weak and that the gang is maintained by strong external pressures (Klein and Crawford:66). From this perspective, juvenile gangs are rather fragile entities. They lack the internal stability of internally generated group goals, have high turnover in membership, generate few unique group norms, and lack a lasting identity with a group name (Klein and Crawford:66). There is also considerable evidence that these internally unstable gangs are kept together by external pressures, such as conflict with other groups (Klein and Crawford:65–66) or political activity (Jacobs, 1976; Short and Moland, 1976).

Disrupting the internal structure of such gangs to diminish their members' delinquency is not likely to be successful. Klein and Crawford (1967) concluded that interventions by group workers in black delinquent gangs in Los Angeles tended to increase the social cohesiveness of the gangs, thereby resulting in increased individual rates of offending. Similarly, Short and Strodtbeck (1965) concluded that disrupting the gang leadership in the black gangs they studied failed to disrupt the gang and may actually have contributed to increased rates of minor delinquent acts.

Although the group workers' intervention strategies that aimed at disrupting group structure and processes may not have achieved their intended result, other strategies of intervention aimed at disrupting networks may nonetheless be consequential for individual careers. Klein and Crawford (1967) suggested that strategies that weaken group cohesion may have that effect.

Incapacitation of offenders similarly does not necessarily disrupt gang structure. Jacobs (1976, 1977, 1983) described the U.S. prison of the 1960s and 1970s in our most urbanized states as organized around an inmate system that was an extension of the gang organization and the conflict relations from which the prison population was drawn. He suggested, moreover, that the prison society tended to increase the cohesion of those gangs and their importance to their members because they performed a wide variety of functions for them. The gangs also recruited members within the prison, especially as the inmate system became politicized (Jacobs, 1976, 1977:145–149). On release a substantial minority of the recruits and many of the former members of the supergangs (which include juvenile and adult divisions in the community and in juvenile and adult correctional institutions) retained ties with at least some former gang members. The prison of this period appeared to extend the network of adult co-offenders through inmate recruitment into the gangs while incarcerated and sustained at least some of them on release.

Group Recruitment and Replacement Processes

When more than one individual is involved in offending, incapacitation of one of the offenders will not necessarily affect the crime rate. Much depends on what happens to the individual rate of offending of his co-offenders. The current practice is to discount the "crimes saved" through incapacitation of an offender by weighting the individual's contribution to the incident, using the mean size of offending groups for that offense. If the mean size of offenders is two, for example, an individual's crime saved is calculated as one-half. Yet, there is no empirical evidence to conclude that individuals reduce their crime rate, on the average, in this way. There is some reason to believe they might not. One would expect that the incapacitation of recruiters, for example, would have a far greater impact on the crime rate than would the incapacitation of followers or many of their co-offenders, even granted equal rates of offending.

What is needed is a comparison of overlapping criminal careers to determine whether incapacitation in the career of any offender has any effect on the individual rate of offending of his co-offenders subsequent to incapacitation. Given the fact that the more organized gangs of career criminals are more adept at recruiting replacements for incarcerated members, incarceration may save only those crimes that are solo offenses. If so, one should not only aim to incapacitate individuals with high solo offending rates but one should expect little impact from incapacitating individuals who have high co-offending rates as accomplices. If this were to be verified empirically, one would also expect to gain less from incapacitating juveniles than adults, since their solo offending rates are on the average lower.

One might also expect to gain more by disrupting processes of recruitment and replacement of co-offenders in juvenile than in adult populations, since juvenile networks that facilitate offending are seemingly based more on solidaristic and personal relationships than on rational choice and impersonal contact. For most juveniles, the selection of co-offenders is far more restricted than it is for adults, being limited to a territorial neighborhood and its environs. We need to know more about how adults recruit their co-offenders and the extent to which their co-offenders are dispersed rather than concentrated in space and time. We clearly need both ethnographic and network studies of adult offending populations to explore these issues of co-offending and their effects.

CONCLUDING NOTES

It should be abundantly clear that research on group offending not only is disproportionally concentrated on juveniles but that it has focused almost exclusively on documenting how pervasive it is and on speculating on its role in the etiology of delinquency. The etiological question therefore remains murky and the consequences of groups for criminal career development remain unexplored. We need, therefore, to devote far more attention to detailed studies of offending careers and to pay special attention to the group composition of offending in those careers, treating each individual's career in terms of its intersections with others. Not only do such investigations provide sociometric information so that such techniques as block-modeling (White, Boorman, and Breiger, 1976) can isolate particular networks, but also they permit us to examine how criminal justice interventions have consequences for the offending of all individuals in the same network. Examination of the consequences of solo and co-offending is but part of a larger need to order over time the life events of offenders with their offending history so that we may determine their consequences. Further study of group offending requires far more information on how juvenile and adult careers are linked. That information must be obtained from prospective longitudinal cohort studies that approximate more closely the design of the Swedish community study undertaken by Sarnecki (1982). That design is based on a social-network approach and expands the study population to include all co-offenders who are not initially part of the cohort. It is well to bear in mind that in a dynamic society there is considerable movement into and out of communities and that individuals are drawn into different networks over time. The artificial divorcement of the cohort from a changing environment and its reduction to a population of individuals unrelated in time and space restrict considerably what can be learned about individual careers.

ACKNOWLEDGMENTS

The persons who have assisted me in different ways in the preparation of this paper number well over 100 scientists in this country and abroad who responded to my requests for information. I am much indebted to them. I owe special thanks also to those who took the time to read and provide help in revising one or more drafts. Numbered among them are some of my colleagues on the Panel on Research on Criminal Careers. Those to whom I owe this special debt include Larry Baron, Alfred Blumstein, Shari Diamond, David Farrington, Malcolm Klein, Richard Lempert, Lloyd Ohlin, James Parker, Elizabeth Piper, Brent Shea, James F. Short, Jr., Marvin Wolfgang, Stuart Wright, and Frank Zimring. I owe a special debt also to Jerzy Sarnecki, who discussed his Swedish study with me, and to Denise Galarraga of the National Criminal Justice Reference Service for a partial translation of that study.

REFERENCES

Blakely, R., Stephenson, P. S., and Nichol, H.
1974 Social factors in a random sample of juvenile delinquents and controls. *International Journal of Social Psychiatry* 20:203–217.

Blumstein, A., Farrington, D., and Moitra, S.
1985 Delinquency careers: innocents, desisters, and persisters. Pp. 187–219 in M. Tonry and N. Morris, eds., *Crime and Justice: An Annual Review of Research*, Vol. 6. Chicago, Ill.: University of Chicago Press.

Bordua, D. J.
1961 Delinquent subcultures: sociological interpretations of gang delinquency. *Annals of the American Academy of Political & Social Science* 338:120–136.
1962 Some comments on theories of group delinquency. *Sociological Inquiry* 32:245–246.

Bottoms, A., and Wyle, P.
1986 Housing tenure and changing crime careers in Britain. In A. J. Reiss, Jr., and M. Tonry, eds., *Communities and Crime*. Chicago, Ill.: University of Chicago Press.

Breckinridge, S. P., and Abbot, E.
1917 *The Delinquent Child and the Home*. New York: Russell Sage Foundation.

Bureau of Justice Statistics
1984 *Criminal Victimization in the United States, 1982*. A National Crime Survey Report. NCJ-92820. Washington, D.C.: U.S. Government Printing Office

Chaiken, J., and Chaiken, M.
1982 *Varieties of Criminal Behavior*. Santa Monica, Calif.: Rand Corporation.

Clinard, R. A., and Ohlin, L. E.
1960 *Delinquency and Opportunity*. Glencoe, N.Y.: Free Press.

Elliott, D. S., Ageton, S. S., Huizinga, D., Knowles, B., and Canter, R. J.
1983 *The Prevalence and Incidence of Delinquent Behavior: 1976–1980*. Boulder, Colo.: Behavioral Research Institute.

Empey, L. T.
1970 Postscript. In A. Manocchio and J. Dunn, *The Time Game*. Beverly Hills, Calif.: Sage Publications.

Erikson, M.
1971 The group context of delinquent behavior. *Social Problems* 19:114–129.

Eynon, T. G., and Reckless, W. C.
1961 Companionship at delinquency onset. *British Journal of Criminology* 2:162–170.

Federal Republic of Germany
1982 *Police Statistics, 1982*. Bonn.
Ferguson, T.
1952 *The Young Delinquent in His Social Setting*. London: Oxford University Press.
Gannon, T. M.
1966 Emergence of the defensive gang. *Federal Probation* 30:44–48.
Glueck, S., and Glueck, E. T.
1930 *Five Hundred Criminal Careers*. New York: Alfred A. Knopf.
1934a *Five Hundred Delinquent Women*. New York: Alfred A. Knopf.
1934b *One Thousand Juvenile Delinquents*. Cambridge, Mass.: Harvard University Press.
1937 *Later Criminal Careers*. New York: Commonwealth Fund.
1940 *Juvenile Delinquents Grown Up*. New York: Commonwealth Fund.
1943 *Criminal Careers in Retrospect*. New York: Commonwealth Fund.
1946 *After Conduct of Discharged Offenders*. London: Macmillan.
1950 *Unraveling Juvenile Delinquency*. New York: Commonwealth Fund.
Gould, L., Bittner, E., Chaneles, S., Messinger, S., Novak, K., and Powledge, F.
1965 *Crime as a Profession: A Report on Professional Criminals in Four American Cities*. President's Commission on Law Enforcement and the Administration of Justice. Washington, D.C.: U.S. Government Printing Office.
Granovetter, M. S.
1973 The strength of weak ties. *American Journal of Sociology* 78:1360–1380.
Hindelang, M. J.
1971 The social versus solitary nature of delinquent involvements. *British Journal of Criminology* 11:167–175.
1976a *Criminal Victimization in Eight American Cities: A Descriptive Analysis of Common Theft and Assault*. Cambridge, Mass.: Ballinger.
1976b With a little help from their friends: group participation in reported delinquency. *British Journal of Criminology* 16:109–125.
Hood, R., and Sparks, R.
1970 *Key Issues in Criminology*. London: World University Library.
Jacobs, J. B.
1976 Stratification and conflict among prison inmates. *Journal of Criminal Law & Criminology* 66:476–482.
1977 *Stateville: The Penitentiary in Mass Society*. Chicago, Ill.: University of Chicago Press.
1983 *New Perspectives on Prisons and Imprisonment*. Ithaca, N.Y.: Cornell University Press.
Jones, M., Offord, D., and Abrams, N.
1980 Brothers, sisters, and antisocial behavior. *British Journal of Psychiatry* 136:139–145.
Kaiser, G.
1982 *Jugendkriminalitat: Rechtsbruche, Rechtsbrecher, und Opfersituationen im Jugendalter*. 3 Aufl., Basel: Weinheim.
Keiser, L.
1969 *The Vice Lords: Warriors of the Streets*. New York: Holt, Rinehart, & Winston.
Klein, W., and Crawford, L. Y.
1967 Groups, gangs and cohesiveness. *Journal of Research in Crime and Delinquency* 4:142–165.
Klockars, C. B.
1974 *The Professional Fence*. New York: Free Press.
Knight, B. J., and West, D. J.
1975 Temporary and continuing delinquency. *British Journal of Criminology* 15:43–50.
Kraeupl, G.
1969 Der Einfluss sozial fehlentwickelter Jugendlicher auf die Enstehung, Entwicklung, Struktur und Funktion krimineller Gruppen 14–25 jahriger. *Staat und Recht* 18:63–75.
Lerman, P.
1967 Gangs, networks, and subcultural delinquency. *American Journal of Sociology* 73:63–72.
Macguire, M., and Bennett, T.
1982 *Burglary in a Dwelling*. London: Heinemann.
Mattick, Hans W.
1958 Parole to the army. Department of Sociology. Unpublished M.A. thesis. University of Chicago.
1960 Parolees in the army during World War II. *Federal Probation* 14:49–55.
Miller, W. B.
1958 Lower class culture as a generating milieu of gang delinquency. *Journal of Social Issues* 14:5–19.
1975 *Violence by Youth Gangs and Youth Groups as a Crime Problem in Major American Cities*. Washington, D.C.: U.S. Government Printing Office.
Morash, M.
1983 Gangs, groups, and delinquency. *British Journal of Criminology* 23:309–331.
Olofsson, B.
1971 *Vad var det vi sa! Om kriminellt och konformt beteende bland skolpojkar*. Stockholm: Utbildningsforlaget.

Olson, M. R.
1977 *A Longitudinal Analysis of Official Criminal Careers*. Ann Arbor, Mich.: University Microfilms.

Peoria Crime Reduction Council
1979 *Criminal Activity of Juvenile Residential Burglars*. Peoria, Ill.: City of Peoria.

Petersilia, J.
1980 Criminal career research; a review of recent evidence. Pp. 321–379 in N. Morris and M. Tonry, eds., *Crime and Justice: An Annual Review*. Vol. 2. Chicago, Ill.: University of Chicago Press.

Polsky, N.
1969 *Hustlers, Beats and Others*. Garden City, N.Y.: Doubleday.

Pyle, G. E., Hanten, E., Williams, P., Pearson, A., Doyle, J., and Kwofie, K.
1974 *The Spatial Dynamics of Crime*. Department of Geography. Chicago, Ill.: University of Chicago.

Reiss, A. J., Jr.
1967 *Studies in Crime and Law Enforcement in Major Metropolitan Areas*. Vol. I: *Measurement of the Nature and Amount of Crime: Field Surveys III*. President's Commission on Law Enforcement and the Administration of Justice. Washington, D.C.: U.S. Government Printing Office.
1980 Understanding changes in crime rates. Pp. 11–17 in S. E. Fienberg and A. J. Reiss, Jr., eds., *Indicators of Crime and Criminal Justice: Quantitative Studies*. Washington, D.C.: Bureau of Justice Statistics.

Sampson, R. J.
1983 The Neighborhood Context of Criminal Victimization. Unpublished Ph.D. thesis. State University of New York, Albany. Ann Arbor, Mich.: University Microfilms.
1985 Neighborhood and crime: the structural determinants of personal victimization. *Journal of Research in Crime and Delinquency* 22:7–40.

Sarnecki, J.
1982 *Brottslighet och Kamratrelationer: Studie av ungbrottsligheten i en svensk kommun*. Rapport 1982:5. Stockholm: Brottsforebyggnderadet (National Council for Crime Prevention). Portions translated in 1984 by Denise Galarraga as *Criminality and Friend Relations: A Study of Juvenile Criminality in a Swedish Community*. National Criminal Justice Reference Service. Washington, D.C.: National Institute of Justice.

Scott, P. D.
1956 Gangs and delinquent groups in London. *British Journal of Delinquency* 7:5–26.

Shannon, L. W.
1978 A longitudinal study of delinquency and crime. In C. Welford, ed., *Quantitative Studies in Criminology*. Beverly Hills, Calif.: Sage Publications.

Shapland, J.
1978 Self-reported delinquency in boys aged 11 to 14. *British Journal of Criminology* 18:255–266.

Shaw, C. R.
1938 *Brothers in Crime*. Chicago, Ill.: University of Chicago Press.

Shaw, C. R. and McKay, H. D.
1931 Male juvenile delinquency as group behavior. In *Report on the Causes of Crime*. No. 13. Washington, D.C.: National Commission on Law Observance and the Administration of Justice.

Shaw, C. R., and Meyer, E. D.
1929 The juvenile delinquent. In *The Illinois Crime Survey*. Peoria, Ill.: Illinois Association for Criminal Justice.

Sherman, L. W.
1970 Youth Workers, Police, and the Gangs: Chicago 1956–1970. Department of Sociology. Unpublished M.A. thesis. University of Chicago

Short, J. F., Jr., and Moland, J., Jr.
1976 Politics and youth gangs: a follow-up study. *Sociological Quarterly* 17:162–179.

Short, J. F., Jr., and Strodtbeck, F. L.
1965 *Group Processes and Delinquency*. Chicago, Ill.: University of Chicago Press.

Shover, N.
1973 The social organization of burglary. *Social Problems* 20:499–514.

Smith, D.
1986 The neighborhood context of police behavior. In A. J. Reiss, Jr., and M. Tonry, eds., *Communities and Crime*. Chicago, Ill.: University of Chicago Press.

Smith, M. W.
1972 An Economic Analysis of the Intracity Dispersion of Criminal Activity. Department of Economics. Unpublished Ph.D. dissertation. North Carolina State University.

Sparks, R. F., Greer, A., and Manning, S. A.
1982 *Crime As Work: Theoretical Studies*. School of Criminal Justice. Final Report to National Institute of Justice, U.S. Department of Justice under Grant # 80-IJ-CX-0060. Newark, N.J.: Rutgers University.

Spergel, I.
1964 *Racketville, Slumtown and Haulburg*. Chicago, Ill.: University of Chicago Press.

Suttles, G. D.
1968 *The Social Order of the Slum*. Chicago, Ill.: University of Chicago Press.

Sveri, K.
1965 Group activity. *Scandinavian Studies in Criminology* 1:173–185.

Thrasher, F.
1927 *The Gang*. Chicago, Ill.: University of Chicago Press.

West, D. J.
1969 *Present Conduct and Future Delinquency*. London: Heinemann.

West, D. J., and Farrington, D. P.
1973 *Who Becomes Delinquent?* London: Heinemann.

West, W. G.
1974 *Serious Thieves, Lower Class Adolescent Males in a Short-Term Deviant Occupation*. Ann Arbor, Mich.: University Microfilms.
1977 Serious thieves: lower class adolescent males in a short-term deviant occupation. In E. Vaz and A. Lodhi, eds., *Crime and Delinquency in Canada*. Toronto: Prentice-Hall.
1978 The short term careers of serious thieves. *Canadian Journal of Criminology* 20:169–190.

Wheeler, Stanton
1961 Socialization in correctional communities. *American Sociological Review* 26:699–712.

White, H., Boorman, S. A., and Breiger, R. L.
1976 Social structure from multiple networks. I: blockmodels of roles and positions. *American Journal of Sociology* 81:730–780.

Whyte, W. F.
1943 *Street Corner Society*. Chicago: University of Chicago Press.

Wolfgang, M.
1978 Overview of Research into Violent Behavior. Testimony to the Subcommittee on Domestic and International Scientific Planning, Analysis, and Cooperation of the House Committee on Science and Technology, 95th Cong., 2d sess.

Wolfgang, M., Figlio, R. M., and Sellin, T.
1972 *Delinquency in a Birth Cohort*. Chicago, Ill.: University of Chicago Press.

Yablonsky, L.
1959 The delinquent gang as a near-group. *Social Problems* 7:108–117.
1962 *The Violent Gang*. New York: Macmillan.

Zimring, F. E.
1984 Youth homicide in New York: a preliminary analysis. *Journal of Legal Studies* 13:81–99.

5

The Rand Inmate Survey: A Reanalysis

Christy A. Visher

In 1982 the Rand Corporation released its findings from a 1978 survey of jail and prison inmates and presented provocative information about the individual offending patterns of criminals. Rand's "second inmate survey," as it is called, involved nearly 2,200 inmates in three states who completed detailed questionnaires about the variety and intensity of their criminal activity.

Analysis of these self-report data revealed that the distribution of the annual number of crimes an offender commits, often referred to as lambda (λ), is highly skewed. Most of the inmates in the Rand survey reported small values of λ, about five crimes per year, for most crime types. Some individuals, however, committed crimes at very high frequencies—more than 100 crimes per year. These results suggest that most criminals, including the majority of those who are incarcerated, actually commit few crimes. High-rate offenders make up only a small proportion of the inmate population, but they may account for most of the crime problem. This finding makes it particularly desirable to identify them.

In one of the Rand reports based on the survey data, *Varieties of Criminal Behavior*, Chaiken and Chaiken (1982a) classified the surveyed inmates into 10 groups according to the combination of crimes in which they engaged. One important result of their research was the identification of a single category of serious criminals, whom they designated as "violent predators." These offenders engaged in assault, robbery, and drug dealing at very

---

Christy A. Visher is research associate at the National Research Council, National Academy of Sciences. She prepared this paper while a National Research Council Fellow at the National Academy of Sciences in 1983.

The data used in this paper were made available by the Inter-university Consortium for Political and Social Research in Ann Arbor, Michigan. The data were originally collected by the Rand Corporation of Santa Monica, California. Neither the original source or collectors of the data nor the consortium bear any responsibility for the analyses or interpretations presented here.

The author would like to thank Alfred Blumstein, Jeffrey Roth, and Douglas Smith for many helpful comments and suggestions in preparing this paper and Allan Abrahamse, Jan Chaiken, Peter Greenwood, and Charles Wellford for providing additional data, documentation, and assistance.

high rates, but they also committed property crimes at high rates. In fact, these "violent predators" committed more burglaries and other thefts than the criminals who specialized in those crimes. Chaiken and Chaiken concluded that these particular offenders are especially troublesome and become entrenched in a deviant life-style in their juvenile years.

The extreme skewness in offending frequencies and the identification of a small group of violent predators have intensified interest in identifying high-rate, serious offenders. If the most serious offenders can be distinguished with information about their patterns of behavior and individual characteristics, the criminal justice system could become more efficient in identifying the most appropriate candidates for long periods of incarceration. The Rand study made an important contribution to this effort by using self-reported information from the inmate survey to identify serious offenders. Chaiken and Chaiken (1982a) showed that personal factors and life-style characteristics, including persistent drug use, certain types of juvenile criminal involvement, and unstable employment, were strongly related to a violent, predatory pattern of offending. Other types of offending groups were similarly distinguished by particular observable behavior patterns and demographic attributes.

The researchers at Rand also went a step further and attempted to translate findings about the characteristics of high-rate offenders into a policy instrument that could be used to guide decisions in the criminal justice system. One suggested approach for addressing simultaneously the problems of prison crowding and high aggregate crime rates is to emphasize incarceration for the particularly serious high-rate offenders and to deemphasize it for the others. Another Rand report (Greenwood, 1982) examined the possibilities and consequences of using this strategy—selective incapacitation—as a specific policy in sentencing convicted offenders. Using a simple scale of seven variables that correlated with high annual offending frequencies, Greenwood estimated that a particular selective incapacitation policy could reduce robbery rates by 20 percent without increasing the prison population in California.

As a crime control strategy, the idea of selective treatment of some offenders is not new. The concept of "predictive sentencing" has a long history (for a review, see Morris and Miller, 1985), and it underlies the common use of risk-factor scales in decisions regarding parole release (see Gottfredson and Gottfredson, this volume). The Rand research has enhanced the potential value of predictive sentencing because of the skewness of the reported distribution of λ. It has also generated considerable controversy.

The criticisms that have been directed at the Greenwood report and at the Rand study in general have both methodological and ethical elements. Some critics argue that the analysis is methodologically flawed and that Rand's sample of prisoners is not representative of the convicted offenders judges have to sentence. Others are skeptical of the truthfulness of inmates' reports concerning the crimes they had committed. Observers are also concerned that most of the variables in the seven-point scale are based on self-report rather than official data and would be much less reliable if based on official records. Still others regard the variables involved as inappropriate as a basis for sentencing in any event. These and other criticisms are reviewed in a later section of this paper.

Criticism of the Rand results has been stimulated by the extensive public attention the seven-point scale has received. Some state legislators introduced bills in 1982 and 1983 to implement selective incapacitation as part of new sentencing policies (see Blackmore and Welsh, 1983). Some police and prosecutors may already be using the scale informally to guide their decisions. An experimental program in Illinois is testing the predictive accuracy of the Rand scale, along with other types of guidelines, in identifying offenders who are likely to recidivate. These actions have raised serious concerns that the results of this single study, which has a number of readily identifiable technical flaws (see Cohen, 1983) and which has not been subjected to internal or external validation, could be implemented widely in making decisions regarding individual liberty.

Thus, an intensive review of the Rand study is necessary. This paper provides a first internal validation based on an extensive reanalysis of the actual inmate responses to validate the findings and test their robustness to variations in the analytic procedures used. An external validation using different settings is also necessary to assess the generalizability of the Rand results to a new sample of inmates and to samples of convicted offenders who are not in prison, but that test is beyond the scope of this effort.

Three interrelated objectives are central to this reanalysis. The first objective is to validate the reported estimates of λ and to assess the sensitivity of those and other findings to the interpretation of ambiguous and incomplete survey responses, arbitrary choices in constructing variables, treatment of missing data, and decisions regarding scale development. The second objective is to examine the predictive accuracy of the seven-point scale in the three states, for specific crime types, and in other subsamples. The third objective is to reevaluate the reported incapacitation effects in light of the reestimation of λ and reconstruction of the prediction tables.

Data for the reanalysis were obtained from a machine-readable, public-use tape of the inmate responses, supplied by the Inter-university Consortium for Political and Social Research, which maintains a data archive for the research community. Data obtained directly from Rand provided additional detail on how the analysts translated the survey responses into the variables used in their analyses. With the generous help of the Rand researchers, every effort was made to determine Rand's analytic procedures. Copies of coding manuals and computer source codes were studied, and persons at Rand who were familiar with the analysis were consulted.

This reanalysis is limited to two key findings in the Rand reports: the estimates of annual individual offending frequencies, λ (Chaiken and Chaiken, 1982a), and the use of the survey data to develop a prediction instrument to identify high-rate offenders (Greenwood, 1982). Robbery and burglary offenses are the exclusive focus because of the prominence they received in the Rand reports and because of their prevalence among the sampled prisoners.

The remainder of this paper is organized into three major sections. First, the purposes and general methods of Rand's second inmate survey and specific findings reported by Chaiken and Chaiken and by Greenwood are summarized. Published critiques of the Rand studies are also reviewed in this section. In the second section the results of the reanalysis are presented and compared with Rand's published findings. In the final section major findings and conclusions are presented.

THE SECOND RAND INMATE SURVEY

The Rand Corporation's 1978 survey of inmates extended previous work at Rand on studies of incarcerated offenders. In an exploratory study Petersilia, Greenwood, and Lavin (1977) conducted extensive interviews with 49 convicted robbers in California prisons. Rand's "first inmate survey" (Peterson and Braiker, 1981) was a self-administered questionnaire given to 642 prison inmates in California. The findings from both studies indicated that most inmates committed few crimes per year and that a small group reported much higher frequencies of offending. The researchers considered their findings preliminary because the information on individual offending frequencies was imprecise, serious offenders were overrepresented in the sample relative to sentenced offenders, and only one state was involved in the studies. Thus, a third, more intensive research project was designed.

Data and Methods

The sample for the second inmate survey, actually the third research project, covered three states, California, Michigan, and Texas. The sample was drawn to represent a typical cohort of incoming inmates for those states; a weighting scheme was used in which "each inmate was given a sampling weight proportional to the inverse of the length of his prison term" (Peterson et al., 1982:54). In addition, to obtain a range of severity among the conviction offenses, inmates from both prisons and jails were sampled. Replacement procedures were used to reduce the usual problems of nonresponse bias. [See Peterson et al. (1982) for other details of the sampling design, site selection, and pretesting procedures.]

The inmates selected for the study were asked to complete a detailed questionnaire that elicited information about their juvenile criminal behavior, adult criminal behavior in the period (up to 2 years) prior to the arrest leading to their current incarceration, past and recent use of illegal drugs and alcohol, as well as information concerning employment history, attitudes, and demographic data. The survey was not anonymous so that official record data, which were collected on all prison inmates, could be matched to the inmates' self-reports. More than 2,500 inmates actually completed the questionnaire, but jail respondents in Texas were excluded from the analysis because, unlike jail inmates in other states, they were predominantly sentenced offenders awaiting transfer to prison. The final sample consisted of 2,190 inmates. The distribution of the 2,190 prison and jail inmates from the three states is shown in Table 1.

Given the focus on robbery and burglary in the reanalysis, of particular interest are the inmates who reported committing robbery or burglary during the 1- to 2-year period before they were arrested for their conviction offense, referred to as

TABLE 1 Distribution of Sample Across States, by Type of Institution and Crime Type

State	Total Survey		Robbers		Burglars	
	Prison	Jail	Prison	Jail	Prison	Jail
California	357	437	168	94	182	163
Michigan	422	373	154	66	174	112
Texas	601	0	145	0	252	0
Total	1,380	810	467	160	608	275

NOTE: Data for robbers and burglars were computed as part of the reanalysis. Offenders in the two groups are defined by their reports of whether they committed any robberies or burglaries during the measurement period. Some individuals are included in both groups.

SOURCE: Chaiken and Chaiken (1982a:6).

the "measurement period." Table 1 shows that Texas had somewhat fewer inmates who reported committing robbery (24 percent) than either California (33 percent) or Michigan (28 percent). Respondents who reported committing burglary were more prevalent and were distributed more evenly among the three states—43 percent, 36 percent, and 42 percent in California, Michigan, and Texas, respectively.

Many potential sources of error exist in a survey of this type. The most readily apparent systematic error arises from members of the sample refusing to participate; those nonrespondents could well be different in their crime patterns from those who were willing to respond. To correct partially for this potential source of bias, a "replacement respondent" was selected for each sampled prison inmate prior to the survey's administration. The replacement was matched with the sampled inmate on several criteria, including age, record, and conviction offense.

The actual response rate varied considerably across states and type of institution. In jails in all three states, the response rate averaged 70 percent. In Michigan and California prisons the rate was 49 percent and in Texas prisons, 82 percent. Replacement respondents in all three states were asked to complete the survey, but the replacement data from Texas were not used because of the low number of refusals among the main sample. After including the replacements, Peterson et al. (1982:viii) concluded that "no statistically significant differences were found between responding and nonresponding inmates in any Michigan or Texas prisons, in terms of age, race, record or conviction offense." In some prisons in California, Chicano inmates were less likely than others to participate. Inmates with reading problems were underrepresented in all three states.

Other major sources of error in surveys eliciting self-reported information are unreliable responses and nonvalid survey instruments. Researchers at Rand carried out extensive analyses of these problems (Marquis, 1981; Chaiken and Chaiken, 1982a; Peterson et al., 1982). Two design strategies were built into the survey for later use in the analysis of reliability: redundant questions were asked within the survey, and 250 respondents were retested 1 week later. Chaiken and Chaiken (1982a:Appendix B) relied on the first approach and developed measures of the internal quality and external reliability of the survey responses. The internal checks included looking for correct skip patterns, consistent answers, minimal confusion, and few omitted questions. The external checks relied on comparisons between each inmate's official record and his responses to 14 self-reported items (e.g., conviction offense, arrest incidents, and prior prison terms). The two measures were strongly correlated in each state.

Chaiken and Chaiken concluded that most individual characteristics and behavior patterns, including age, race, conviction offense, and reports of crimes committed, were unrelated to the quality and reliability of inmates' responses. About 83 percent of the inmates "passed" the internal quality test, whereas only 56 percent achieved a similar level of external reliability.[1] Scattered evidence suggested that respondents who gave consistent and reliable answers were less likely to report very high offending frequencies and less likely to deny committing crimes. Finally, key regression analyses were carried out with and without inconsistent

[1] "Failure" is defined as having more than 20 percent "bad" indicators on the external or internal reliability measures (see Chaiken and Chaiken, 1982a:9, 222–239). Other data reported suggest that the low level of external reliability is partly the result of incomplete official records, especially juvenile records (p. 229). Inmates often reported juvenile convictions or incarcerations that were not found in their records.

or unreliable respondents (42 percent of sample), and no "meaningful differences" were found between the two analyses (Chaiken and Chaiken, 1982a:9), although the actual results were not reported.

Purposes of the Rand Study

The Rand survey was designed to achieve a number of purposes (see Peterson et al., 1982). One major purpose was to gather information on individual patterns of criminal behavior—types of crimes committed, degree of specialization in crime types, and changes in criminal patterns over time. Questions were asked about juvenile criminal activity and criminal behavior during the 6 years prior to incarceration to explore hypotheses about whether offenders progress through stages of increasing crime seriousness.

A large section of the survey was devoted to obtaining offenders' estimates of the number of times they committed each of 10 crime types[2] during the measurement period. Estimates of annual offending frequencies, λ, have been calculated by other researchers using a variety of techniques based primarily on inferences from arrest records (e.g., Greenberg, 1975; Blumstein and Cohen, 1979), but no broad consensus has yet been reached in these estimates (for a review, see Cohen, 1983). The Rand survey was the first to use a self-report technique to obtain annual estimates of λ for a group of known adult offenders.

The use of a self-administered questionnaire also permitted researchers to collect richer data on offenders' personal characteristics than can typically be found in official records. Extensive information was gathered on (1) criminal experiences at young ages; (2) use of illegal drugs as a juvenile and as an adult; (3) adult offender histories, including arrests, convictions, and incarceration; and (4) life-style characteristics, such as marital status, employment record, and geographic mobility. The survey also contained a number of questions about attitudes toward crime. The researchers at Rand believed that the self-report data on personal characteristics and annual offending frequencies might help to distinguish different types of offenders and, particularly, to identify the serious "career criminals." Such information could be helpful to criminal justice agencies in making decisions regarding sentencing, parole, work release, or drug treatment programs.

The Rand Results

The findings from the Rand study appear in several reports (Petersilia and Honig, 1980; Rolph, Chaiken, and Houchens, 1981; Chaiken and Chaiken, 1982a; Greenwood, 1982). Three results are especially relevant to policy decisions in the criminal justice system: (1) estimates of λ and its skewed distribution (Chaiken and Chaiken, 1982a), (2) the development of an offender typology and the use of a multivariate approach to distinguish among types of offenders (Chaiken and Chaiken, 1982a), and (3) the identification of high-rate offenders using self-reported information (Greenwood, 1982).

Rand's summary statistics for the annualized individual offending frequencies are shown in Table 2. The statistics for each crime type are based on only those inmates who reported committing that crime. The distribution of λ, as noted, is highly skewed. More than one-half the

[2]The 10 crimes that were included in the questionnaire were burglary, business robbery, personal robbery, assault during robbery, other assaults, theft, auto theft, forgery/credit card swindles/bad checks, fraud, and drug dealing. The specific wording of the questions is available in Chaiken and Chaiken (1982a:19–20).

TABLE 2 Estimates of λ for Respondents Who Reported Committing the Crime

Crime Type	Median	Value at the 90th Percentile[a]
Burglary	5.45	232
Robbery	5.00	87
Assault	2.40	13
Theft	8.59	425
Forgery and credit cards	4.50	206
Fraud	5.05	258
All except drug dealing	14.77	605

[a]Ten percent of the respondents who commit the crime commit it at or above the rate indicated.

SOURCE: Chaiken and Chaiken (1982a:44).

inmates who committed robbery or burglary in the measurement period did so at rather low rates—about five crimes per year. On the other hand, the worst 10 percent committed robbery and burglary at the rate of two to four crimes per week, or 20 to 40 times as frequently as the median offender. In this highly skewed situation, the mean does not accurately represent the central tendency of such a distribution. Further, the mean is extremely sensitive to the values of the few offenders in the right tail of the distribution and, therefore, the median rate is preferable for estimates of a "typical" offender's crime rate.

The survey also provided the data for Chaiken and Chaiken's development of an offender typology. They found that inmates could be categorized according to the combination of crimes they commit, such as robbery and assault or burglary and drug dealing. In Table 3 the medians and 90th percentile values of λ are compared for offender types that include robbery or burglary as one of the defining crimes. These six types constitute 62 percent of the inmate sample (Chaiken and Chaiken, 1982a:27). As seen from Table 3, violent predators committed robbery and burglary at very high frequencies; however, the median λ was 9. The most active 10 percent in this group reportedly committed at least 516 burglaries per year, whereas the 90th percentile of the "burglar-dealers" (who commit burglary and other property crimes and sell drugs) committed 113 burglaries per year. The violent predators, especially the worst 10 percent, thus appear responsible for the majority of robberies and burglaries committed by the inmates in the Rand survey. Realizing

TABLE 3 Estimate of λ for Robbery and Burglary for Six Offender Types

Offender Type	Percent of Sample	Robbery[a] λ			Burglary λ		
		Median	Mean	90th Pct.	Median	Mean	90th Pct.
Violent predators[b]	15	9	70	154	9	172	516
Robber-assaulters	8	5	50	141	5	69	315
Robber-dealers	9	4	32[c]	87	14	122	377
Low-level robbers	12	2	10	13	4	48	206
Burglar-dealers	10	—	—	—	4	42	113
Low-level burglars	8	—	—	—	2	36	105
Other[d]	38						

[a]Includes both business robbery and personal robbery.
[b]Those who commit robbery, assault, and drug dealing concurrently.
[c]One outlier has been removed.
[d]Includes "mere assaulters," property and drug offenders, low-level property offenders, drug dealers, and about 13 percent who did not report committing any of the crimes studied.

SOURCE: Chaiken and Chaiken (1982a:27, 219).

the impact of these serious offenders on the crime problem, the Rand researchers used several techniques to identify them.

Using a multivariate approach Chaiken and Chaiken found that some self-reported information could distinguish violent predators from other inmates. These offenders were often young people with a history of serious juvenile criminal activity, including initiation of delinquent behavior before age 16, involvement in both violent and property crimes, frequent use of illegal drugs, and multiple commitments to state juvenile institutions. They were generally unmarried, unemployed, and extremely heavy drug users, often at costs exceeding $50 per day for heroin. A regression model using these variables explained 35 percent of the variance in annual offending frequencies. However, many inmates predicted to be high-rate robbers with this model actually reported committing no robberies at all.

Greenwood (1982) independently attempted to identify the high-rate offenders with a simple, seven-point scale. He selected seven variables (six self-report and one official record variable available only for prison inmates—see below) that correlated fairly well with high annual robbery and burglary offending frequencies and whose use might be appropriate for sentencing purposes. The resulting additive scale (variables were scored as 1 or 0 depending on the presence or absence of the attribute) could be used to identify high-rate offenders. Inmates were classified as low-rate (scoring 0 or 1), medium-rate (scoring 2 or 3), or high-rate (scoring 4 or more) offenders. The mean annual offending frequencies were reported to differ sharply across these groups. For inmates in California, the respective mean λs for robbery were 2.0, 10.1, and 30.8. This pattern is consistent for robbery in the other states and for burglary, but the group differentials are widest in California.

Variables Used in Scale to Distinguish Inmates by Individual Crime Rates

Convicted previously for same charge (official criminal record; prison inmates only)
Incarcerated more than 50% of preceding 2 years (self-report)
Convicted before age 16 (self-report)
Served time in state juvenile facility (self-report)
Used drugs in preceding 2 years (self-report)
Used drugs as a juvenile (self-report)
Employed less than 50% of preceding 2 years (self-report)

Using the model of incapacitation developed by Avi-Itzhak and Shinnar (1973), Greenwood estimated the potential crime control effects of increased sentences for the identified high-rate offenders. For California, he reported that a policy of sentencing predicted high-rate robbers to 8-year terms and all other robbers to 1-year jail terms could reduce the robbery rate by a maximum of 20 percent, without increasing the prison population. Such a strategy does not work as well for burglary. (A detailed analysis of the seven-point scale and its use in identifying high-rate offenders is presented in a later section in conjunction with the reanalysis of the Rand data.)

Criticisms of the Rand Study

Because of the provocative policy implications of the Rand results, the inmate study has received a considerable amount of attention, and not all of it has been positive. Some researchers have raised moral objections to the mechanical use of any such scale for determining sentences. Others argue that the findings are flawed and therefore policy proposals should not be based on Rand's results.

Ethical Concerns

Ethical concerns emerged largely in response to the analyses presented in the Greenwood report. The Rand study has also mobilized arguments about selective incapacitation as a sentencing philosophy and, especially, the use of explicit predictions in sentencing. These debates have become quite vigorous. The issues are discussed only briefly here, however.[3]

One of the most frequent objections to the Greenwood report concerns the selection of variables for the seven-point scale. In particular, critics argue that some of the variables in the scale are past behaviors or social characteristics that cannot be changed. Employment status, drug use, and juvenile criminal history account for five of the seven variables. Retributivists and others have pointed out that using these criteria as a basis for sentencing is contrary to the widely accepted "just deserts" philosophy, whereby differences in sentences are based on the seriousness of the conviction offense. Greenwood (1982:Table 4.11) anticipated these criticisms and tested his scale without three of the most "objectionable" predictors (juvenile drug use, recent drug use, and recent employment history). The limited scale, however, was less effective in distinguishing high-rate offenders from medium-rate offenders compared with the full seven-variable scale.

A more fundamental ethical objection has been raised to the concept of sentencing offenders according to a prediction of their future behavior. Because of its explicit relationship to sentencing policy, Greenwood's analysis was the recent target of these critics. Some critics argue that this type of sentencing policy would violate principles of fairness and "just deserts" (von Hirsch, 1976, 1981) and others question whether future high-rate offenders can be accurately identified (Blackmore and Welsh, 1983; von Hirsch and Gottfredson, 1984). Any classification system is likely to misidentify offenders—classifying some low-rate offenders as high-rate ("false positives") and some high-rate offenders as low-rate ("false negatives"). The expected level of error is totally unacceptable to some (von Hirsch and Gottfredson, 1984) but considered reasonable within some definitions by others (Morris and Miller, 1985). Greenwood also raised some of these same issues in his report, but he differs from his critics in believing that these ethical (and some empirical) problems are only limitations on the usefulness of selective incapacitation and not barriers to its potential use.

In summary, the Rand reports have intensified the ethical debate about selective incapacitation and predictive sentencing. Any resolution will involve hard choices about acceptable error rates and appropriate prediction instruments. Empirical information about the predictive capability of different scales may help to inform those choices for some.

Empirical Concerns

Empirical concerns regarding the Rand study cover a wide range of issues, including reliability of the inmates' responses, construction of the seven-point scale, and the robustness of the incapacitation effects to variations in the model. The following discussion reviews published critiques and raises some additional concerns. The examination of potential limitations to Rand's results provides direction for the reanalysis that follows.

First, some observers have questioned the reliability of the inmates' self-reported responses, especially the data used to estimate the annual number of crimes, λ, an inmate committed prior to his incarcer-

[3]For other discussions of these topics, see Dershowitz (1973, 1974), Cohen (1983), von Hirsch (1976, 1981, 1984), Floud and Young (1981), Hinton (1982), Moore et al. (1984), and Morris and Miller (1985).

ation (Blackmore and Welsh, 1983; von Hirsch and Gottfredson, 1984). The many sources of error in self-report methods have been widely discussed (e.g., Gold, 1966; Farrington, 1973; Reiss, 1973). The Rand study presented further problems because of its sample—convicted offenders. Some inmates could have concealed crimes they committed, and others might have exaggerated their criminal activities, and these practices could contribute to the observed skewness in the reporting of offending frequencies. The Rand finding that a small group of inmates reported committing hundreds, or even thousands, of robberies and burglaries a year has led critics to speculate that some respondents inflated their illegal behavior to appear "tough" or important (von Hirsch and Gottfredson, 1984). The opposite type of response error, concealment, is also plausible, especially since between 24 and 36 percent of all convicted robbers in the sample denied committing any robberies in the measurement period (Greenwood, 1982:Table 4.1).

The accuracy of estimates of λ also depends on an assumption of stable offending patterns over time (Cohen, 1983). But criminals may operate erratically, committing many crimes in a short period and then ceasing their illegal activities for a while. If the "crime spurting" phenomenon describes even a minority of Rand's inmate sample, the estimates of annual offending frequencies might well be inflated (Cohen, 1983).

Second, the criticism directed against the Greenwood scale was even more vigorous. The variables in the seven-point scale were mostly self-report measures, and the only scale variable that was constructed from official record information was whether the inmate had a prior conviction for the same offense. Some critics were concerned about the availability of necessary information if predictions regarding future criminal behavior were to be made (Blumstein, 1983; Cohen, 1983). Of course, Greenwood's scale, based on self-reported information, was only suggestive of the kinds of factors that may be predictive of high-rate offending. If the scale was to be used operationally, the needed information would have to come from independent sources, such as official records or other inquiries, like those reflected in presentencing investigations. But the use of official records invariably involves some decay in reliability because of missing records, recording errors, and other mistakes. Data from independent sources are also likely to be incomplete and less helpful because some information, such as drug use, is not gathered consistently.

Third, the treatment of missing data in the scale is another source of concern. Each of the variables in this scale was coded 1 or 0 to indicate the presence or absence of the attribute, and missing information on any scale item was also coded 0. However, for at least one of the scale variables—prior conviction for the same offense—the missing-data problem was systematic: official records were only available for the prison sample, and so all jail inmates were assigned a zero for this variable. In the analysis the past-convictions variable thus becomes a measure that distinguishes jail and prison inmates (Cohen, 1983). Since high-rate offenders are probably already more likely to be sentenced to prison than to jail, this variable is more a "predictor" of who was sent to prison than of any other inmate characteristics. Missing data was a problem for another variable, juvenile drug use; 14 percent of the respondents failed to answer the questions on this topic (Greenwood, 1982:52).

Fourth, the predictive accuracy of the seven-point scale turns out to be no better than that for other prediction instruments developed over the past 10 years. The final sample used in the prediction analysis was prison and jail inmates in the three states who were currently serving a sentence for a robbery or burglary conviction. Among inmates *predicted* to be high-rate offenders, only 45 percent (Cohen, 1983) actually were, according to estimates of their annual offending frequencies. Stated another way, 55 percent of the predicted high-rate group was incorrectly identified. This level of "false positives" is close to the average false-positive rate (60 percent) reported in a review of other prediction studies (Monahan, 1981). The scale does much better among predicted low-rate offenders: the accuracy rate is 76 percent (Cohen, 1983). These differences are due in part to the different base rates of the two groups—arbitrarily specified as the lowest 50 percent for the low-rate group and the highest 25 percent for the high-rate group. However, the data reported by Greenwood and reanalyzed by Cohen focus on overall accuracy rates for the entire analysis sample, and there has been no examination to date of whether the scale's predictive accuracy is consistent across states, crime types, and other important subgroups.

Finally, another area of major concern about the results of the Rand study relates to the validity of the incapacitation effects reported by Greenwood (Blackmore and Welsh, 1983; Cohen, 1983; von Hirsch and Gottfredson, 1984). In her review of research on incapacitation, Cohen (1983) noted that Greenwood's development of a prediction scale is based on retrospective data. The reported incapacitation effects, therefore, do not take into account the possibility that future rates of offending might change (e.g., regress toward a mean) or that there might be a differential likelihood of terminating criminal activity. Thus, the prospective accuracy of the seven-point scale in identifying high-rate offenders can only be judged with an appropriate longitudinal panel design. In fact, the use of retrospective data may lead to an overestimate of the crime-reduction effects.

Another serious validation problem is the lack of any test of the scale on an independent sample. This is particularly important because a selective sentencing policy would be applied to convicted offenders, and predictive information in that population may be different from that in a sample of inmates (Cohen, 1983). Other research has shown that predictive accuracy for the initial sample for which a prediction scale is constructed tends to be greater than for a separate validation sample (Gottfredson and Gottfredson, 1980; Farrington and Tarling, 1985). Thus, reported reductions in aggregate robbery rates that are tied to any particular scale will diminish for new samples. However, Greenwood argues (1982:91) that, since his 0–1 prediction scale was not closely fitted to the inmate sample (as is the case with regression models), the expected shrinkage would be less than with regression weights. This characteristic of Burgess (0–1) scales, compared with closely weighted scales, is discussed by Gottfredson and Gottfredson in Chapter 6.

The state-specific results obtained in the crime control analysis for California and Texas also illustrate the sensitivity of the Rand findings to the population being studied. For California, it is reported that aggregate robbery rates could be reduced by 20 percent and burglary by 12 percent without any increase in prison population by using a selective sentencing strategy (Greenwood, 1982:79). In Texas, however, a similar sentencing policy would actually increase the robbery rate because there are so few high-rate offenders (Greenwood, 1982:Figure 5.3).

In summary, several critical reviews of the Rand inmate study have raised important questions about the sensitivity of the results reported in Chaiken and Chaiken (1982a) and Greenwood (1982) to the interpretation of the survey responses, to variable construction, and to variations in the estimates of the parameters used in the calculation of incapacitation effects. The reanalysis presented in the next section addresses some of these questions.

REANALYSIS

This reanalysis of the Rand inmate data involves many interconnected analyses that must be completed in a particular sequence. As the reader will quickly discover, the complexity of the survey instrument and Rand's novel use of the self-report data also complicated the replication. Moreover, Rand's procedures were not always straightforward. As a result, in some situations the Rand method was known but an alternative approach was chosen, for reasons that are explained as the reanalysis is presented. In other instances Rand's analytic procedures were followed as closely as possible.

The initial task is to replicate Rand's calculations of individual offending frequencies, λ, which are the most important result in the Rand research, and which provide the underpinnnings for all the other major findings. Once λ is recomputed for robbery and burglary, the prediction scale is reconstructed and measures of predictive accuracy for various inmate subgroups (e.g., states, jail inmates) are calculated. Finally, using the recomputed estimates of λ and the prediction scale, the projected incapacitation effects on crime rates and prison populations of selectively incarcerating robbers in California are reestimated. An important part of this reanalysis is to assess the sensitivity of the findings to changes in the model's input variables and to alternative cut points for defining the predicted low-, medium-, and high-rate groups.

Estimating λ from the Rand Data

Ideally, estimates of λ for a group of offenders could be obtained by having a representative sample of "active" criminals keep daily logs of their criminal activities for an entire year. In the expected absence of that level of cooperation, a number of alternative methods for measuring unobservable behaviors have been developed. The Rand researchers chose the "self-report" approach, i.e., they asked inmates to answer a series of detailed questions about the number of crimes they had committed in a defined "measurement period," a period of 1 to 2 years prior to the arrest that led to their current sentence.

Individual offending frequencies can be expressed as a fraction: the number of crimes committed (the numerator) divided by the number of years of "street time" (the denominator), which takes into account any time spent incarcerated during the measurement period. Chaiken and Chaiken (1982a:42) provide an example of how to calculate λ for burglary for a respondent whose measurement period was 14 months, 5 months of which were spent in jail, and who reported committing six burglaries during the 14-month period:

$$\begin{aligned}\lambda &= (6 \text{ burglaries}) \cdot [(12 \text{ months per year}) \div (14 - 5) \text{ months}] \\ &= 6 \cdot (12 \div 9 \text{ months per year}) \\ &= 8.0 \text{ burglaries per year}\end{aligned}$$

"Active" and "Inactive" Offenders

Before turning to the computation of λ, the inmate group that is the focus of the reanalysis must be defined. The relevant group consists of the inmates who reported committing robbery or burglary during the measurement period (see Table 1). In the analyses involving the seven-point scale, the relevant group is somewhat different: all inmates who reported that their current incarceration was the result of a robbery (burglary) conviction, whether or not they reported committing robbery (burglary). Thus, the "convicted" group is not a subset of the

TABLE 4 Percentage of "Active" Offenders: Inmates Convicted of Robbery or Burglary

Type of Involvement	California	Michigan	Texas
Convicted Robbers[a]			
Active	75.2	62.7	71.8
Inactive	21.9	34.7	28.2
Unknown[b]	2.8	2.7	—
Total N	(178)	(150)	(117)
Convicted Burglars[a]			
Active	73.1	68.5	66.0
Inactive	25.6	31.5	34.0
Unknown[b]	1.3	—	—
Total N	(160)	(124)	(203)

NOTE: Active convicted robbers are those who admitted committing robbery during the measurement period, whereas "inactives" denied committing any robberies; the same distinction applies for convicted burglars.

[a]There were 56 inmates in the sample who were convicted of both robbery and burglary. To maintain consistency with Greenwood's (1982) procedure, they are treated in this table and subsequent analyses only as convicted robbers.

[b]Inmates' responses did not permit an unambiguous determination of whether they were active.

SOURCE: Data were calculated by the author from the original survey responses. The total sample size is 932. The number of cases in subsequent tables, when the sample is all convicted robbers and burglars, varies from this number because of the omission of inactive respondents, missing data, and a small weighting factor used for Texas respondents.

"committing" group because some convicted robbers (about one-quarter) denied committing any robberies during the measurement period; the same distinction applies to burglars. The latter group of convicted robbers and burglars are referred to as "inactive" offenders. The distribution of active and inactive offenders among convicted robbers and burglars is shown in Table 4.

The percentage of convicted robbers and burglars who reportedly were inactive in their respective conviction offense types is astonishingly high. About 28 percent of the convicted robbers and 30 percent of the convicted burglars reported that they had not committed any robberies (or burglaries) in the past 1 to 2 years. These figures are similar to those reported by Rand.[4] A group of inactive con-

[4]One of the Rand reports presents comparable data indicating that the percentage of convicted robbers who are defined as active in California, Michigan, and Texas is 76, 64, and 72, respectively (Greenwood, 1982:42). These percentages are very close to those obtained independently in the reanalysis. For convicted *burglars*, however, Rand reports that 94, 91, and 88 percent, respectively, were active in the three states, rates that differ considerably from those reported in Table 4 by this author.

The discrepancy is due to differences between Rand's and this author's definition of "active" and "inactive" burglars. In their Appendix A, Chaiken and Chaiken (1982a:186–189) lay out explicit rules for determining whether a respondent is to be considered active in a particular crime type. But the rules are different for robbery and burglary because "non-burglary robbery" (the definition of robbery used in most of the Rand analyses and adopted by this author) is a summary crime that combines business and personal robbery (see Chaiken and Chaiken:196). Two variables that are used in determining activity for burglary, CK7 and CK14 (see p. 197), have no equivalent for "non-burglary robbery." The robbery category for question CK7 was not considered specific enough to be used as an indicator of activity (J. Chaiken, 1984, personal communication).

Since robbery and burglary offenses are the focus of this reanalysis, the definitions of activity and inactivity for the two crime types were made consistent. As a result of this decision, about 125 burglars (all with annual burglary rates of zero) who were defined as "active" by Rand's definition were defined as inactive in this reanalysis. This accounts for the reduced percentages of reportedly active burglars in Table 4, compared with Rand's figures.

INSTRUCTIONS FOR USING THIS CALENDAR ARE INCLUDED IN THE SURVEY

	Winter			Spring			Summer			Fall		
	January	February	March	April	May	June	July	August	September	October	November	December
YEAR BEFORE ARRESTED												
YEAR ARRESTED	January	February	March	April	May	June	July	August	September	October	November	December

STREET MONTHS ON THE CALENDAR

FIGURE 1 Calendar used by all respondents in calculating street months. Source: Ebener (1983).

victed robbers (N = 42 of the 124 inactives) may have confused robbery with burglary since they did report committing burglary. Of the inactive convicted burglars (N = 149), 11 reported committing robbery. It is also possible that all the "inactives" did not commit those crimes or agreed to plead guilty to that charge. Another interpretation is that these inmates committed only one robbery (or burglary) during the measurement period, were promptly arrested, and did not count that offense in their report.[5] The most plausible explanation, however, is that many of them simply lied, even though they knew that their official records were available to the researchers. Without any additional information, it is difficult to determine the truth in this situation; thus, in this reanalysis the estimate of λ for the "inactive" inmates is zero, as in the Rand analysis.

[5]Respondents may have been confused about whether to include the crimes they committed during their arrest month in their report, especially if they were incarcerated for most of that month (either prior to their arrest or after it). This sequence of questions caused many problems for some respondents. Chaiken and Chaiken (1982a) include a copy of the questionnaire in their report.

Determining Street Months

To estimate λ for the inmate sample, the Rand researchers had to establish a defined measurement period to facilitate the inmates' recall of their criminal activity and other events before their incarceration. It was also important to determine each inmate's "street time," referred to by Rand as "street months," which is the time when they were free to commit crime and the denominator used in calculating λ.

Figure 1 is a copy of the calendar, completed by all respondents, that was used to facilitate recall and determine "street months" for each inmate. Inmates were instructed to mark their arrest month in the year of their arrest with an X and draw a line through the remaining months in that year. (The months prior to and including the arrest month are called the "measurement period" and could range from 13 to 24 months.) Other months in which the respondent had been incarcerated were also marked with an X. An inmate's "street months" is the number of months he was on the street (not in prison or jail) and able to commit crimes, which could be 1 to 24 months.

Questions were then asked about

events during the measurement period. This memory-recall technique was chosen because the amount of time inmates had spent in prison (or jail) since their measurement period varied within the sample. The distribution of inmates' (robbers and burglars) self-reported time served on their current sentence to the time of the survey provides an indication of recall time (see Table 5). Three-quarters of the inmates had served less than 2 years at the time of the survey. Recall may have been more difficult for respondents who served longer, which could result in underestimates of λ for this group. But they were presumably more serious criminals and may have committed more crimes than the others. Thus, the actual effect of recall time on estimates of λ is confounded by the characteristics of the sample, but no attempt is made in this reanalysis to adjust λ for any recall bias.

Despite Rand's procedures for stimulating recall, many inmates had trouble filling out their calendars (see notes about coding decisions, Ebener, 1983:41–43). The estimate of street months could be obtained from four sources—two places in the questionnaire, the calendar, and an estimate by survey editors (left blank if the respondent's answers were consistent and matched his calendar). Although the majority of inmates had no apparent problems with this section of the survey, recalling their activities still appears to have been a complicated cognitive task for many respondents.

TABLE 5 Distribution of Self-Reported Time Served on Current Sentence for Inmates Who Reported Committing Robbery or Burglary

Time Served[a]	Percent	Cumulative Percent
1–6 months	22.3	22.3
7–12 months	23.3	45.6
13–18 months	15.5	61.1
19–24 months	13.2	74.3
25–36 months	12.5	86.8
37–47 months	5.3	92.1
4 or more years	7.9	100.0

[a]Mean = 20.6 months; median = 14.5 months.

SOURCE: Data were calculated by the author from the original survey responses. The N is 1,052, which excludes 48 cases (4.4 percent) because of missing data.

TABLE 6 Cross-Tabulation of Rand's Average Estimate of Street Months for Robbers and Burglars by the Difference Between Rand's Maximum and Minimum Estimates (percentages; N = 1,235)

Maximum-Minimum	Average Estimate of Street Months			
	1–6	7–12	13–18	19–24
0	83.1	63.9	77.9	90.0
1	11.3	11.9	9.0	7.8
2–5	4.2	7.9	5.2	1.9
6–9	0.7	5.1	2.3	0.3
10 or more	0.7	11.1	5.6	0.0
N	142	252	520	321

SOURCE: Data were calculated from data provided by J. Chaiken, Rand Corporation.

Estimating street months was a straightforward task when inmates were consistent in their answers. But, for the inmates who gave incomplete or ambiguous responses, street months had to be estimated differently. Rand analysts relied on editors to examine problematic questionnaires and to generate their own estimates of street months. Then, all possible interpretations of the responses were used to obtain a maximum possible value and a minimum possible value for street months for each inmate (Chaiken and Chaiken, 1982a:185–186). An average estimate was the mean of the two extremes.

As seen in Table 6, for most respondents (78.8 percent) the street months estimate was unambiguous, and so the difference is zero. However, larger discrepancies between the maximum and

TABLE 7 Distributions of Final Estimates of Street Months for Inmates Who Reported Committing Robbery or Burglary: Rand and Reanalysis (percentages)

Street Months	Rand[a]	Reanalysis
Less than 6 months	11.2	11.8
7–12 months	20.0	17.7
13–18 months	41.2	41.7
19–24 months	25.5	28.2
Missing/unknown	2.1	0.6
Total	100.0	100.0
Mean	14.4	14.6

[a]Rand's estimates were calculated from data provided by J. Chaiken, which gave Rand's estimates of maximum and minimum street months for each inmate.

minimum estimates are more common when Rand's average estimate for street months (the mean of the two extremes) is 12 months or less. Such a value could occur only if the respondent had been off the street (most likely imprisoned) for some time in the year before the current incarceration began. That these larger discrepancies appear more often at the lower end of the overall street-month distribution is particularly disturbing because λ may be overestimated if the inmate was actually on the street for less than 12 months. These differences between Rand's minimum and maximum street months suggest that one source of unreliable data for some inmates may be in figuring months "not on the street," which the inmate was supposed to exclude from street months. The Rand editors and some respondents apparently often disagreed on this point.

Review of Rand's procedures raised concerns that the strategy of using minimum and maximum estimates for street months could result in misleading estimates of λ, especially when the minimum was exceptionally low. For the reanalysis, the following set of rules was established for choosing a single estimate of an inmate's street months from the four available sources of information:[6]

1. If the inmate gave consistent answers on the two questions, use the inmate's response.
2. If the inmate gave conflicting answers on the two questions, but the Rand editor provided no corrected estimate, use the response from the second question.[7]
3. If the inmate gave conflicting answers, but the response to the second question was the same as both the editor's estimate and the estimate obtained from the calendar, use the inmate response to the second question.
4. If the inmate's answers, the editor, and the information on the calendar were all in disagreement, use the editor's estimate.
5. If some disagreement existed between the inmate's second response, his calendar, and the editor's estimate, but two of the estimates were in agreement, use the value on which there was some agreement.

In Table 7 the estimates of street months calculated in the reanalysis are compared with the Rand estimates, which are simply the averages of Rand's minimum and maximum estimates. Despite the alternate analytic approach to

[6]A small residual category, which was not encompassed by these rules, included cases in which the Rand editor found the inmate's calendar indecipherable (coded "unknown"), cases in which all four sources were missing (coded "missing"), and four cases that were treated as exceptions to the rules for various reasons.

[7]Of the responses to the two questions, Rand considered the second response (C10) less prone to error than the first response (C9). During routine checks for errors in all questionnaires, the Rand editors were more concerned about correcting errors in C10 than C9 (J. Chaiken, 1984, personal communication). This information was considered in establishing the coding rules for the reanalysis, which focused mainly on C10.

the calculation of street months, the distribution of the recomputed estimates is virtually identical to that generated by the Rand analysts. The average number of street months for inmates who reported committing robbery or burglary according to both estimates was 14 months. About 30 percent of the sample were "on the street" for less than a year, which means that those respondents spent some time in prison or jail during the measurement period.

The ability to replicate Rand's estimates of average street months, however, should not overshadow the conceptual and methodological problems associated with this measure as the denominator of λ. First, the section of the survey involving the calendar was complicated, and respondents had trouble with the questions and the calendar and gave inconsistent answers. Second, it was important to the Rand study design that inmates accurately recall their street months, but the effect of differential recall abilities is unknown. Finally, respondents with few street months may have disproportionately higher estimates of λ, and part of that relationship may be an artifact of the way in which λ is estimated for those inmates.

Determining Crimes Committed

The numerator of λ is the number of crimes of a specific type that the inmate reported committing during the months he was on the street, according to the calendar he filled in. Questions were asked about 10 crime types. Chaiken and Chaiken (1982a:42) describe the general format of these questions:

> After answering "yes" that he had committed a given type of crime, say, burglary, during the measurement period, the respondent was asked to tell how many burglaries he had committed by specifying a range, either "1 to 10" or "11 or more." If the range was "1 to 10," he was asked, "How many?" If the range was "11 or more," he was led through a sequence of questions about the number of months in which he committed burglary and his daily, weekly, or monthly rate of commission.

Figure 2 is a copy of the questions used in the Rand inmate survey to determine the number of business robberies inmates committed during their street months. This series of questions first distinguishes between the inmates who committed 1 to 10 crimes (referred to here as low-frequency offenders) and the group who committed 11 or more crimes (the high-frequency offenders).[8] As the format of Figure 2 shows, the high-frequency offenders had a much more difficult cognitive task. Since the low- and high-frequency offenders answered separate questions, different problems arise in computing their estimates. In the reanalysis Rand's procedures for estimating "crimes did" (Chaiken and Chaiken, 1982a:191–192) were carefully examined, and this information was used as a starting point for recomputing the estimates. Estimates of crimes committed for the 1-to-10 group and the 11-or-more group are discussed separately below.

As shown in Figure 2, offenders who reported committing 1 to 10 business robberies were asked to give a specific number, and most of them did so. However, 17 percent of the inmates who reported committing either robbery or burglary at a low frequency did not answer the follow-up question. For these inmates, Rand analysts assigned 1 as the minimum esti-

[8]For inmates who reported committing business robbery, 72 percent were low-frequency offenders, 24 percent were high-frequency offenders, and 4 percent did not check either box. For personal robbery, the percentages were 76 and 19, respectively, for low- and high-frequency offenders (data were missing for 5 percent). For burglary, 66 percent were low-frequency offenders, 31 percent were high-frequency, and data were missing for 3 percent.

II. 1. During the STREET MONTHS ON THE CALENDAR did you rob any businesses? That is did you hold up a store, gas station, bank, taxi or other business?

YES ☐ 1 NO ☐ 2 ——→ go on to page 20

2. In all, how many businesses did you rob?

☐ 11 OR MORE

☐ 1 TO 10 How many?

↓

▱ Business Robberies

go on to next page ——→

3. Look at the total street months on the calendar. During how many of those *months* did you rob one or more businesses?

_______ Months

4. In the months when you did business robberies, how *often* did you usually do them?

(CHECK ONE BOX)

EVERYDAY OR ALMOST EVERYDAY	☐	How many per day?	▱	How many days a week usually?	▱
SEVERAL TIMES A WEEK	☐	How many per week?	▱		
EVERY WEEK OR ALMOST EVERY WEEK	☐	How many per month?	▱		
LESS THAN EVERY WEEK	☐	How many per month?	▱		

FIGURE 2 Sample page from inmate questionnaire. Source: Greenwood (1982).

mate and 10 as the maximum estimate, which results in an estimate of 5.5 when the minimum and maximum values are averaged.[9]

[9]For these inmates, Rand calculated two estimates of λ using the two numerators (and possibly two denominators if street months had a minimum and a maximum value). For most of the analyses, however, the analysts simply averaged the two λ estimates. The possible distortions introduced by Rand's procedure of using minimum and maximum estimates rather than a single estimate are discussed in a later section.

The "average" or "typical" low-frequency offender, however, did not report committing five or six crimes during his measurement period but more often admitted to only two or three crimes. Thus, the minimum-maximum strategy used by Rand was likely to produce a high estimate of crimes committed for inmates who gave partial answers. To avoid this potential bias in the reanalysis, an alternative approach was taken. For inmates who gave incomplete answers, estimates from 1 to 10 were assigned in a way that

TABLE 8 Average Number of Crimes Reported by Low-Frequency Offenders and Two Estimates for Inmates with Missing Information

Low-Frequency Offenders	Business Robbery		Personal Robbery		Burglary	
	Mean	N	Mean	N	Mean	N
Answered follow-up question[a]	3.3	233	3.5	290	4.0	497
Did not answer follow-up question[b]		55		48		74
Rand estimate	5.5		5.5		5.5	
Alternative estimate	3.2		3.4		4.0	

NOTE: Data are presented only for inmates who were "active" in (i.e., reported committing) the specific crime type.

[a]The follow-up question was posed to all offenders who said they committed "1 to 10" crimes (see Figure 2).

[b]The exact number of low-frequency offenders for whom Rand assigned minimum and maximum values of 1 and 10 could not be determined. The two groups with missing information, however, are essentially identical since missing data were already coded on the public-use tape of the inmates' responses.

simulated the distribution of the responses to the follow-up question for the larger sample.[10]

In Table 8 the mean for inmates who answered the follow-up question is compared with two means for inmates who failed to answer the follow-up question—one obtained using the Rand strategy and the other using the alternative procedure just described. The alternative strategy for handling missing data provides an estimate of crimes committed that more closely approximates the responses of those who did answer the follow-up question than does the Rand procedure. This alternative approach should lower λ estimates, but the overall impact on the distribution may not be significant, since the number of cases involved is small and the offenders are already at the low end of the distribution.

Computing the number of crimes committed by the high-frequency offenders (those who reported "11 or more" crimes) is more complicated. Chaiken and Chaiken (1982a:191–192) give a short description of their general computational strategy, which was also used in the reanalysis. The first task is to determine the number of months during which high-frequency offenders committed crimes. Referring again to Figure 2, in question 3 respondents were asked during how many months (of their total street months) they committed at least one robbery. Then, the respondent was supposed to check one of four categories indicating the frequency with which crimes were committed—every day or almost every-

[10]The distribution-matching procedure was adopted only after other alternatives were considered and rejected. Assigning the mean value (from the group who did answer the follow-up question) for each inmate who left the follow-up question blank would have distorted the true distributions of "crimes-did" and λ by lumping 17 percent of the low-frequency offenders at a particular value. The median was rejected for similar reasons and because it conceals variation in the distribution. (The distribution of crimes committed by low-frequency offenders looked a lot like λ—skewed to the right with few inmates reporting 9 or 10 crimes.)

For burglary, the distribution-matching procedure was used along with another question, CK14D, which was originally intended as a reliability check on the number of burglaries an inmate reported. (This question had ordinal response categories: 0, 1–2, 3–5, 6–10, 10+.) If the inmate failed to answer question CK14D, the estimate of burglaries committed was determined in the same manner as robbery.

day, several times a week, every week or almost every week, or less than every week. A follow-up question elicited a specific number of crimes committed (crimes per day, per week, or per month). Depending on which category was indicated, the total number of crimes committed during an inmate's street months was computed in one of the following ways (see Chaiken and Chaiken, 1982a:191–192):

Crimes = crimes/day · days/week · months did · 4.3 weeks/month, *or*
= crimes/week · months did · 4.3 weeks/month, *or*
= crimes/month · months did.

Incomplete or ambiguous responses in this set of questions were fairly common. Typical problems included checking more than one frequency category, reporting ranges (e.g., 2 to 4 crimes/week), indicating a frequency level (day, week, or month) but not the number of crimes committed, and reporting no information about rate of criminal activity. Chaiken and Chaiken did not provide specific details about their treatment of missing data, but they did report that "reasonable ranges [were] used in the calculations" and that both maximum and minimum estimates were calculated (1982a:191). Examining the detailed materials provided by Rand for the reanalysis clarified how missing data were handled in most cases.[11]

The procedures adopted in the reanalysis for dealing with missing data and other ambiguous responses were conservative. If inmates reported ranges for their answers, the midpoint was taken as the estimate. Multiple responses from high-frequency offenders (answers to more than one of the frequency categories) were averaged. Reasonable estimates were used in place of missing data only if the respondent provided at least a partial answer (i.e., checked "several times a week" but did not specify how many crimes per week). These substituted values were based on responses by similar inmates; the specific value was chosen to match the distribution of others who did provide an answer. However, if questions concerning "months-did" were left blank, the inmate was excluded from any further calculations. Finally, following Rand's procedure, inmates who reported that they committed "11 or more" crimes but left other questions in the sequence blank were also excluded.

Thus, the procedures used in the reanalysis for calculating street months, months-did, and the number of crimes committed (of a specific crime type) differed in important ways from the methods used by the Rand analysts. Most notably, instead of using Rand's strategy of estimating minimum and maximum estimates for the numerator and denominator of λ, an alternative, conservative estimate was developed based on the available data. The next section suggests some im-

[11]In response to a request for additional information about how crimes-did was estimated, especially in ambiguous cases, Jan Chaiken at Rand provided relevant portions of the computer code that was used to transform the raw data into variables. The overall strategy of the Rand analysts was to calculate minimum and maximum estimates if inmates gave incomplete, ambiguous, or conflicting responses. According to Rand's major report (Chaiken and Chaiken, 1982a:184), "minimum and maximum estimates are not intended to be 'worst possible' cases, but rather reasonable conclusions from the data." Information in the computer code indicated that (1) a range of values (e.g., three to five) was substituted for missing answers on questions about rate or number of crimes committed, but those ranges appeared to be arbitrarily chosen by the analysts; (2) if months-did was missing, estimates of minimum and maximum street months were substituted; (3) multiple responses to a single question were treated as minimum and maximum estimates of crimes-did; and (4) if ranges were specified for any response, both the minimum and maximum values were used in the calculations.

plications of Rand's strategy for estimating λ and presents the λ estimates calculated according to the procedures discussed in the last several sections.

Calculation of λ

As discussed earlier, an offender's annual crime rate is simply the number of crimes he committed per year of "street time." Rand's intermediate calculations led to two estimates of λ—a minimum (based on the minimum estimate for crimes-did divided by the maximum estimate of street months) and a maximum (based on the maximum estimate of crimes-did divided by the minimum estimate of street months). However, in the Chaiken and Chaiken report the summary statistics by state and all the analyses are computed using the average of the two estimates of λ. The authors state that the minimum and maximum estimates of λ, and thus the average λ, are reasonable conclusions from the data, but those methods actually produce the smallest possible minimum estimate and the largest possible maximum estimate, which was often double or triple the minimum estimate. The average of these two extremes can be very sensitive to the maximum value, and this could account for some of the skewness in the distribution of λ. In Table 9 the distributions of Rand's minimum and maximum estimates of λ for robbery and burglary are compared with that of the single estimate generated in this reanalysis.

As seen in Table 9, the reanalysis estimates for both robbery and burglary are practically identical to Rand's minimum estimates, but they diverge considerably from Rand's maximum estimates. At some points in the distribution, the values of λ from the reanalysis are actually lower than Rand's lowest estimates. (This is probably the result of using smaller values in substitutions of missing data.) Rand's average estimate of λ, then, will be higher than the reanalysis estimate, as shown in Table 9. But Table 9 confirms one important result of the Rand survey: the distribution of λ computed from reports by the sample of incarcerated offenders is highly skewed, with about 50 percent of the sample reporting fewer than five crimes per year, and the top 10 percent reporting at least 70 crimes per year. (A more detailed cumulative percentage distribution is presented in Appendix Table A.1.)

Important differences emerge when the estimates of λ for incarcerated robbers and burglars are broken down by the three states California, Michigan, and Texas (see Table 10). The annual offending frequencies for the active robbers in the California and Michigan samples are

TABLE 9 Distribution of λ: Rand Minimum and Maximum Estimates and Estimate from the Reanalysis for Inmates Who Reported Committing Robbery or Burglary

	Robbery			Burglary		
Statistic	Rand Minimum	Rand Maximum	Reanalysis (Rand Avg.)	Rand Minimum	Rand Maximum	Reanalysis (Rand Avg.)
25th pct.	1.8	2.3	1.5 (2.0)	2.4	2.8	2.0 (2.2)
50th pct.	3.6	6.0	3.8 (5.0)	4.8	6.0	4.7 (5.5)
75th pct.	12.0	21.5	12.4 (16.0)	23.3	35.0	23.4 (30.0)
90th pct.	68.0	100.5	71.6 (87.0)	196.0	265.0	195.9 (232.0)
Mean	40.6	62.2	43.4	75.8	118.6	79.0

SOURCE: The Rand estimates were calculated from data provided by J. Chaiken.

TABLE 10 Differences in Distributions of λ for Inmates Who Reported Committing Robbery or Burglary, by State

Statistic	California	Michigan	Texas
Robbery			
25th pct.	2.1	1.4	0.9
50th pct.	5.1	3.6	2.5
75th pct.	19.8	13.1	6.2
90th pct.	107.1	86.1	15.2
Mean	42.4	45.4	13.1
Burglary			
25th pct.	2.3	1.9	1.2
50th pct.	6.2	4.8	3.1
75th pct.	49.1	24.0	9.9
90th pct.	199.9	258.0	76.1
Mean	98.8	82.7	34.1

SOURCE: Data were computed as part of the reanalysis.

similar. In contrast, inmates in Texas prisons who admitted committing robbery reported an average of about 13 robberies per year, about one-third the rate of the robbers in the other two states. The estimates of λ for burglary also show a large difference between Texas burglars and those in California and Michigan. Largely the same patterns were observed by Chaiken and Chaiken (1982a:Appendix Tables A.3 and A.6), although the estimates of λ are lower in the reanalysis.

These interstate differences in the distribution of λ for robbery and burglary may reflect actual variation in criminals' offending patterns in the three states. Alternatively, they may be a consequence of different criminal justice processes. In general, the distribution of λ derived from self-reports of incarcerated offenders will not be representative of the distribution for the larger convicted population or for the general criminal population. Biases are introduced because convicted persons are incarcerated selectively rather than randomly, that is, more serious, high-frequency offenders are incarcerated in greater numbers and for longer periods than other offenders. California appears to be especially selective, limiting its available prison space to serious repeat offenders, and Texas appears to operate much less selectively. Once these differences in criminal justice system practices are taken into account, the λ distributions for "street offenders" in California, Michigan, and Texas may be much more similar (see Spelman, 1984).

In any event, the state-specific estimates of λ are consistent with Rand's finding of highly skewed distributions of annual offending. This pattern is weaker for Texas inmates, especially for those convicted of robbery, but the form of the distribution remains unchanged. Despite having replicated the shape of Rand's λ distribution, however, the extent to which ambiguous or missing data used in calculating λ (such as the estimates used in calculating street months or crimes-did) might affect the overall distribution is still a matter of concern. In particular, λ estimates for high-frequency offenders might be less reliable than the estimates for those who commit crimes at a lower level because the questions asked of very active offenders were more complex. Data to address this question are presented in Table 11.

Inmates who reported committing robbery or burglary were divided into five groups for the reanalysis, depending on the types of ambiguity in the responses that were used to calculate λ. The four types of ambiguity were (1) cases with ambiguous numerators (crimes-did), which included low-frequency offenders who did not specify a number between 1 and 10 for crimes committed and high-frequency offenders who gave a range for a number or rate, gave multiple answers for a single question, or gave partial answers; (2) cases with ambiguous denominators, which meant that the respondent had problems answering the questions about street months or completing the

TABLE 11 Distribution of λ for Robbery and Burglary, Adjusting for Types of Response Ambiguity

	Unambiguous Cases (1)	+ Cases with Ambiguous Numerator (2)	+ Cases with Ambiguous Denominator (3)	+ Cases with Street Months Less than 7 (4)	All Inmates Committing Crime[a] (5)	Percent Change from Column 1 to 5 (6)
Robbery						
25th pct.	1.1	1.1	1.3	1.5	1.5	27
50th pct.	2.8	3.0	3.0	3.7	3.8	26
75th pct.	6.9	8.1	8.9	12.5	12.4	44
90th pct.	43.2	36.2	54.8	68.9	71.6	40
Mean	36.5	43.7	39.7	43.2	43.4	16
N	(294)	(362)	(475)	(548)	(594)	
Burglary						
25th pct.	1.8	1.7	1.7	1.9	2.0	10
50th pct.	4.3	4.2	4.3	4.8	4.7	8
75th pct.	17.5	16.7	20.8	23.5	23.4	25
90th pct.	158.4	156.2	180.6	191.7	195.9	19
Mean	55.7	54.7	69.0	77.7	79.0	29
N	(451)	(520)	(682)	(768)	(824)	

[a]The change from Column 4 to Column 5 represents a small group of cases for which *both* numerators and denominators were defined as ambiguous.

calendar; (3) cases with low street months (because of a concern for the validity of λ estimates for this group); and (4) cases with both ambiguous numerators and denominators. Unambiguous cases make up the fifth group.

As seen in Table 11, the estimates are affected by response ambiguity. The percentiles (values) and especially the mean change significantly from the group of unambiguous cases, to cases with varying levels of ambiguity, to all cases (column 5). Moreover, respondents for whom the numerators or denominators are ambiguous and those with short street times do have higher λ estimates than respondents with unambiguous responses. The values of the summary statistics for the unambiguous cases are much lower than the values for all cases, as indicated by the percentage change in column 6. This pattern suggests that λ for higher frequency offenders is particularly susceptible to measurement error and problems of unreliability. Of course, estimates at the high end of any distribution will have a greater variance than those at the low end, but, because λ is a ratio variable, substantial measurement error at the high end may artificially stretch the tail of the distribution. Finally, even with the unambiguous cases, the highly skewed distribution of λ persists, albeit at lower levels.

The High-Frequency Offenders

The extremely high-frequency offenders in the distribution of λ raise a number of serious problems. First, are these few respondents telling the truth about the number of crimes they committed? For 5 percent of the active robbers or burglars in the Rand sample, estimates of λ exceeded 300 (robberies or burglaries). After a thorough review of the data, Chaiken and Chaiken (1982a:245–251) did not find any systematic evidence that overall assessments of validity for respondents were related to their self-reports of crime. However, respondents who exaggerated their criminal activity are probably compensated for by respondents who understated their activity—at least for the median. Indeed, this pattern of response errors (both exaggeration and concealment) emerged in one study of errors in self-reports of arrests (Wyner, 1980). Wyner shows that grouping the data (e.g., into low, medium, and high groups) reduces the impact of these errors, but the group variances may be quite large due to the combination of underreports and overreports. Thus, response errors may inhibit one's ability to predict the actual level of criminal activity of convicted offenders accurately. The issue of prediction is addressed in great detail in the next section.

Second, the small group of high-frequency offenders has a tremendous impact on the overall distribution of λ. Chaiken and Chaiken used a logarithmic transformation of λ in their analysis because of the extreme variation in the data. Otherwise, there is very little association between λ and characteristics of offenders. It is also difficult to describe the distribution of λ using standard measures of central tendency. The arithmetic mean is very sensitive to extreme values; percentile values are presented in the tables in this paper, as in the Chaiken and Chaiken report, for this reason. However, the 90th-percentile value is almost as volatile as the mean because of the wide spread between individual estimates at the high end of the distribution. Thus, the skewness of the distribution poses special problems for data analysis, and the results may be sensitive to the choice of an analytic strategy.

Third, high-frequency offenders may not commit crimes at a stable rate throughout the year, and, therefore, they pose special problems for measuring annual offending frequencies. In a separate Rand report, Rolph, Chaiken, and Houchens (1981:37) analyzed the inmates' self-report crime data and found that some respondents committed crimes in "spurts." However, the questionnaire design and the technique used to estimate λ (especially for high-frequency offenders) in the Rand study assume stable monthly rates of criminal activity. Respondents are supposed to estimate the number of crimes committed during their "street months" by focusing on a typical month. But some offenders appear to alternate between periods of high criminal activity and no activity. Or offenders may be especially active just prior to the arrest month, in which case their reports of offending would reflect this anomalous period. Are these respondents likely to compute an average monthly rate that takes into account these high and low periods? Or might they focus on their most active period and report the number of crimes committed during that month? A similar measurement problem exists for inmates who spent several months in prison or jail just prior to the current arrest, and thus had fewer street months, but were very active during their time on the street. For these types of inmates, self-reports of their crimes in a month probably do not reflect one-twelfth their yearly rate, and, consequently, estimates of their annual offending frequencies may be artificially inflated. Whether active offenders in the Rand sample committed crimes in spurts during the months before their arrest is difficult to determine. However, the estimates of λ for inmates with differing periods of street time can be compared, as is done in Table 12 for the respondents who reported committing robbery or burglary.

The data in Table 12 clearly show a negative relationship between λ and street months. Respondents with short street times (less than 12 months), and especially less than 7 months, have higher estimates of λ (100 or more) than respondents with longer street times. This pattern is stronger for inmates who committed robbery than for those who

TABLE 12 Cross-Tabulation of Street Months By λ for Inmates Who Reported Committing Robbery and Burglary (percentages)

λ	Street Months 1–6	7–12	13–18	12–24	N	Percent
Robbery						
<2	3.6	21.7	36.4	49.4	190	32.8
2–5	14.6	27.4	25.1	22.2	135	23.2
6–30	50.0	33.9	26.4	17.3	166	28.6
31–99	18.3	5.7	4.3	5.5	40	6.9
100+	13.4	11.3	7.4	5.6	49	8.4
N	(82)	(106)	(231)	(162)	580	99.9
Burglary						
<2	3.2	21.3	28.8	36.4	220	26.4
2–5	18.1	20.0	26.5	32.2	215	25.9
6–30	41.4	36.2	20.4	16.4	205	24.7
31–99	10.6	5.6	6.4	7.4	57	6.9
100+	27.6	16.9	17.8	8.2	133	16.0
N	(94)	(160)	(343)	(233)	830	99.9

committed burglary. All inmates with street time of less than 12 months spent some time in jail or prison in the year before their arrest; therefore, those offenders are probably a very active group, although specific estimates of their λs may be inflated. Conversely, low estimates of λ (fewer than two crimes per year) were reported by 49.4 percent of robbers with at least 19 street months, whereas only 3.6 percent of those with less than 7 street months reported such a low rate of criminal activity.

These findings confirm a suspicion that for respondents with very short street times, valid estimates of λ probably cannot be attained using Rand's questionnaire design. Estimates of λ for respondents who commit crimes in "spurts" may also be misleading. As Cohen (1983) predicted, the overall impact of this problem appears to be overestimates of λ for some respondents.

In summary, the distribution of λ for robbery and burglary remains highly skewed even after taking into account unreliable respondents, respondents with few street months (or substantial time "not on the street"), and other problems in the estimation of individual offending frequencies. The precise individual estimates of λ, however, are highly sensitive to analytic choices in computation. Data of this type are probably best grouped into several categories, such as low-, medium-, and high-rate offenders, or transformed with a logarithmic function before analysis. Such procedures preserve the ordering of inmates according to the frequency of their criminal activity but eliminate the need to rely on specific estimates of individual offending frequencies.

Development of a Prediction Scale

The profound skewness in λ for Rand's inmate sample and the existence of a small group of extremely active criminals led the Rand analysts to develop several types of models to identify the high-rate offenders. Of course, a predictive model that prospectively identified likely high-rate offenders would be invaluable to criminal justice decision makers.

Chaiken and Chaiken (1982a:Chapter 3) attempted to develop such a profile using a multivariate approach. As discussed earlier in the review of the Rand results, a variety of self-report measures were predictive of high robbery rates.

However, when inmates were divided into predicted low- and high-rate groups (based on the regression model), 67 percent of the predicted high-rate group reported committing fewer than 10 robberies per year, including 30 percent who committed *no* robberies (Chaiken and Chaiken:88–92). Also, the Rand model that used only official record information (adult prior convictions, recent arrests, juvenile convictions, and recorded drug history) produced a high percentage of false predictions. Chaiken and Chaiken (1982b) concluded that high-rate convicted robbers cannot be adequately distinguished from other convicted robbers because much information that is especially predictive is not in existing official records. In particular, official records are weak predictors because high-rate offenders often have short official records (because they tend to be young), juvenile records are frequently incomplete, and detailed information about drug history is usually unavailable.

In a separate analysis of the inmate data, Greenwood (1982) used an alternate approach in creating a prediction instrument. As discussed, Greenwood selected seven characteristics whose presence or absence was associated with high annual robbery and burglary rates and created a simple, seven-point additive scale. Robbers and burglars were classified into predicted low-, medium-, and high-rate groups based on arbitrary cut points on the seven-point scale. This scale has been the subject of much discussion since the release of Greenwood's report *Selective Incapacitation*, but the report left many questions unanswered. The next several sections of this paper examine the empirical and conceptual relationships of the seven variables to λ and to each other, issues in the development of the seven-point scale, the predictive accuracy of the scale (especially interstate differences), and the scale's utility as an aid in sentencing, crime reduction, and controlling prison populations.

Identifying the Seven Variables

Greenwood initially identified 13 candidate predictors of high-rate offenders on the basis of prior research and possible relevance.[12] Then, focusing only on convicted robbers and burglars, he divided the inmates into low-, medium-, and high-rate groups, depending on their annual offending frequencies (λ) for robbery or burglary. The partitions, used for all offense types and states, were: below the 50th percentile (low), between the 50th and the 75th percentiles (medium), and above the 75th percentile (high). The values for these percentiles differ widely among the states. For example, the 75th percentile cutoff values are 12.0, 6.2, and 3.3 (computed for the reanalysis) for California, Michigan, and Texas, respectively. Thus, "high-rate" offenders have very different estimates of λ in the three states.

Greenwood cross-tabulated each of the 13 candidate predictors against the three frequency groups and chose seven variables based on the strength of their association with the groups (Greenwood: 49–52, 95–107). However, the tabulations were based on the entire sample of con-

[12]The 13 yes-no variables are (1) prior conviction for current offense (robbery or burglary), (2) incarcerated more than 50 percent of 2 years preceding current arrest, (3) convicted before age 16, (4) juvenile commitment to state facility, (5) heroin or barbiturate use in 2 years preceding arrest, (6) heroin or barbiturate use as a juvenile, (7) employed less than 50 percent of preceding 2 years, (8) convicted on multiple counts, (9) prior felony convictions, (10) prior prison term, (11) more than three jobs in the preceding 2 years, (12) less than 23 years old at time of arrest, and (13) prior arrest for current offense type. Greenwood eventually selected the first seven variables for his scale. (The phrase "preceding 2 years" refers to an inmate's measurement period, which could actually range from 13 to 24 months.)

TABLE 13 Means of the Seven Variables for California, Michigan, Texas, and Combined Samples

Variable	All States	California	Michigan	Texas
Prior conviction for current offense[a]	.32	.34	.16	.44
Incarcerated 50% or more of preceding 2 years	.17	.23	.16	.12
Convicted before age 16	.32	.43	.28	.26
Juvenile incarceration	.26	.35	.24	.20
Recent adult drug use	.45	.59	.43	.40
Juvenile drug use	.48	.58	.44	.33
Unemployed 50% or more of preceding 2 years	.54	.60	.62	.42
Sum of the seven variables	2.63	3.12	2.33	2.17
N	(884)	(317)	(255)	(312)

NOTE: All variables are coded 0 or 1; thus, the means represent the proportion of inmates with the attribute. Missing data are also coded 0, following the Rand procedure (Greenwood, 1982:50). The sample is all inmates who were convicted of either robbery or burglary.

[a]These means are slightly distorted because all jail inmates received a zero for this variable, but the Texas sample did not include jail inmates.

victed robbers and burglars from all three states (Greenwood:51–52). This use of the entire sample obscures the possibility that mean values of the predictor variables (i.e., the proportion possessing each attribute) differ across the states, perhaps as a result of criminal behavior, criminal justice system operations, or record-keeping practices. Such state-specific differences will affect the distribution of scale scores, hence the optimal cut points for classification across the states.

State-specific means for the seven variables, shown in Table 13, indicate the magnitude of these interstate differences.[13] The California sample has a higher proportion of inmates who had an early conviction or a juvenile incarceration history in comparison with inmates in the Michigan and Texas samples. California inmates also appear more likely to have a history of serious drug abuse. Finally, inmates seem to have better work records in Texas than in California or Michigan. Thus, the mean of all seven variables is 2.63, based on the entire sample. Because of interstate differences in the individual items, however, the mean ranges from 3.12 in the California sample to only 2.17 in Texas.

Relationships Among Variables

The conceptual and empirical relationships among the seven variables are not discussed in the Rand report. However,

[13]Greenwood provides little information in his report about how the seven variables were constructed (i.e., specific survey questions used), except to say that one was coded from official record data (past conviction for same charge). The variables were independently constructed for this reanalysis and the two procedures compared after Greenwood provided a copy of the computer code he used to create his variables. Very few differences exist between the two procedures. Greenwood's overall means for the seven variables (1982:51–52) are (listed in the order given in Table 13): 0.33, 0.20, 0.33, 0.27, 0.47, 0.50, and 0.56, which are within 0.03 of the means in Table 13. These slight differences are largely due to the change in sample size (781 to 884) because of the redefinition of active burglars. (Two typographical errors exist in Greenwood's table: variable 6 should have frequencies of 509, 255, and 16, and variable 10 should have frequencies of 299, 436, and 45.)

TABLE 14 Inter-Item Correlations of Seven Variables in Greenwood Scale for All Convicted Robbers and Burglars

Variable	(1)	(2)	(3)	(4)	(5)	(6)
(1) Past convictions						
(2) Recent incarceration	.12					
(3) Early conviction	.02	.18				
(4) Juvenile incarceration	.05	.22	.43			
(5) Recent adult drug use	.04	.10	.08	.00		
(6) Juvenile drug use	−.04	.13	.14	.07	.47	
(7) Recent unemployment	−.02	.09	.09	.02	.14	.12

NOTE: Variable descriptions have been abbreviated. See Appendix B for full explanation of each variable.

two pairs of variables seem conceptually dependent: juvenile incarceration and conviction before age 16 and juvenile drug use and recent adult drug use. Also, according to Table 4.4 in the Greenwood report (pp. 51–52), the frequency distributions for these variable pairs are very similar. Thus, one variable in each pair may provide redundant information. To assess the empirical relationships among all seven variables, an inter-item correlation matrix was calculated.

The inter-item correlations, shown in Table 14, are very low, averaging .10, except for the two pairs of variables that overlap conceptually, and their correlations are significantly higher ($r = .43$ and .47, respectively). These two pairs of variables (items 3 and 4 and items 5 and 6) may be the most dominant items in the scale, since drug use and juvenile criminal history are, effectively, being included twice.

A second issue is the bivariate association between each of the seven variables and high-rate offending. Greenwood chose a chi-square test to determine the strength of the relationships between each variable and the three offense groups. In the reanalysis, for which a slightly larger sample was used, the results were similar for the chi-square tests of the seven variables. However, when the chi-square test is adjusted for missing data on the past-conviction variable, it is not significant at the .05 level.[14] Thus, the only official record information in Greenwood's scale is a poor predictor of high rates of robbery and burglary.

Individually the seven variables show moderate to fairly strong associations with λ (statistically significant at least at

[14]Greenwood tested the hypothesis that the percentage of inmates with the attribute in the three groups would be different from the marginal distribution of cases (50 percent—low rate, 25 percent—medium rate, 25 percent—high rate). The appropriate chi-square test is one that assumes a fixed total (the number of inmates responding "yes"), which is a one-tailed test with two degrees of freedom; $\chi^2(p = .01) = 9.2$, $\chi^2(p = .05) = 5.9$. (Greenwood also tested the distribution of the "no" responses, but it is not clear why this is important.) There are some indications that Greenwood did not use the appropriate test, since under these rules and the data in the Rand report, juvenile drug use is definitely significant at the 0.01 level (1982:52). None of the significant variables would change, but some variables reported as nonsignificant may actually be significant.

The problem with the chi-square test is that the null hypothesis of 50, 25, and 25 percent is not the correct comparison for the past-convictions variable (or the juvenile drug-use variable) because of substantial missing data (see Greenwood, 1982:51–57), which affects the marginal distributions. The percentage of cases falling into the three groups, discounting the missing cases, is actually 47.3, 24.3, and 28.4 percent for low-, medium-, and high-rate groups, respectively. This distribution is not significantly different (at the .05 level) from 45, 28, and 30 percent, which is the reported distribution of prior convictions for robbery or burglary across the three groups (p. 51).

TABLE 15 Summary Information from Eight Regressions with Estimates of λ for Robbery or Burglary as the Dependent Variables and the Seven Items in Greenwood's Scale as the Independent Variables

	All States		California		Michigan		Texas	
Independent Variable	λ_R	λ_B	λ_R	λ_B	λ_R	λ_B	λ_R	λ_B
Past conviction		X		X		(X)		X
Recent incarceration	X		X		–X			
Early conviction		X				X		
Juvenile incarceration	X		X		(X)			
Recent adult drug use	X	X	(X)	X	X	X	X	X
Juvenile drug use	X	X	X	X		X		X
Recent unemployment	X	X			X			X
Adjusted R^2	.12	.19	.20	.22	.08	.12	.05	.15
N	(848)		(311)		(245)		(292)	

NOTE: The sample is all convicted robbers or burglars; 36 cases were omitted because of missing data on λ. The dependent variable is $\log_e(\lambda_i + .5)$, calculated separately for robbery and burglary. An "X" indicates that the variable was significant at the .05 level in that equation; a "–X" indicates that the variable was negatively associated with individual crime rates; and (X) indicates that, while the variable was not significant in that particular equation, a differences-between-slopes test revealed that the coefficient was not statistically different from other states' coefficients on that variable.

The variables were all coded 0 or 1, with missing data coded as 0. The variable descriptions are abbreviated; the reader should refer to the text (including Appendix B) for more information.

the .05 level), but how do these factors relate to offending rates when they are combined? To assess both the independent effects of these variables and their collective impact, regression equations were estimated separately for each crime type and within each state, as well as for all data combined (a total of eight regressions). The seven items in the scale are the only independent variables, and the dependent variable is $\log_e(\lambda_i + .05)$, following Chaiken and Chaiken's procedure. (The regression coefficients for these equations are reported in Appendix Table A.2.) The results are summarized in Table 15; an "X" indicates that the variable was significant at the .05 level in that equation.

The pattern of significant variables that is evident from this summary table suggests strong state differences, some effects for offense type, and very different saliency of the seven variables in their associations with λ. The equations based on data from all states mask some important findings. The interstate differences in the percentage of variance explained are especially striking. The equation explains 20, 8, and 5 percent of the variance in self-reported annual robbery rates in California, Michigan, and Texas, respectively. The regression for burglary also fits the data better in California than in the other states. In his report Greenwood focuses primarily on California robbers, but the data in Table 15 suggest the relationships in California are probably much different from the relationships in Michigan and Texas.

The seven variables explain more variance in λ for burglary than for robbery in all three states, but part of this result may be due to the higher variance in the reported burglary frequencies in comparison with the robbery frequencies. Some variables are only significant for a specific offense type (in the state-specific equations). Based on the entire sample, a past conviction for current offense and conviction before age 16 affect only offending frequencies for burglary. In contrast, a juvenile incarceration or incarceration in the 2 years preceding the current arrest is associated only with offending frequencies for robbery. This suggests that separate scales would be appropriate for robbery and burglary.

Finally, at most, only three or four of the seven variables are significant in each state-specific equation. In the combined equations, however, five variables are significant, which is probably due to the larger sample size. Also, these overall equations obscure the different effects of the seven variables. For example, recent incarceration and recent unemployment are significant in only two of the six state-specific regressions. The two juvenile criminal history variables (conviction before age 16 and incarceration in a juvenile facility) do not appear to be strong predictors in these equations, perhaps because of their high intercorrelation. However, at least one of the drug use variables, which are also correlated, is significant in all six state equations.

To summarize, in a multivariate framework the proposed seven-point scale appears weak. The crime-type and state-specific regressions show that, with the exception of drug use, the effects of these variables on individual offending frequencies are not at all robust across states or offense types. The seven variables fit the data best in California, but even there they explain only 20 percent of the respective variances in individual robbery and burglary rates. In contrast, in Texas only one variable is significantly related to λ for robbery, and the R^2 is just 5 percent. Further, several variables in Greenwood's scale appear to be related to λ in only one state, once other factors (such as drug use) are taken into account.

Missing Data

Incomplete data are common in survey research, and the Rand inmate survey was no exception. The questionnaire was long, the skip patterns were complicated, and a few questions probably were confusing to some inmates; hence, respondents left some questions blank. As discussed above, Rand analysts used a variety of ways to deal with missing data for questions about number of crimes committed. Then, in their multivariate analysis, Chaiken and Chaiken (1982a:81) replaced other missing values with the state-specific means.

Missing information is also a problem for some of the seven variables in Greenwood's scale (pp. 51–57). The proportion of cases (convicted robbers and burglars) in which information is missing for any particular variable because of skipped questions or other reasons is generally about 5 percent. However, one variable—past conviction for current offense—is missing for 31 percent of Greenwood's sample. As pointed out by Cohen (1983), this variable was coded from official records, which were only available for inmates surveyed in prisons. Thus, jail inmates account for most of the missing values for the past-convictions variable.

Since missing information for at least one of the seven variables was common among the sample, those cases could not simply be excluded. Instead, Greenwood set missing values for each of the variables in the scale to 0, thus combining the "no's" and the "missing's." He explained that this conservative procedure would "bias [scale] scores downward" (Greenwood:50). However, this solution is not appropriate for the past-convictions variable because all the jail inmates were coded 0 for Greenwood's analysis. The unintended effect is that the variable is transformed into a measure that distinguishes jail and prison inmates in the sample. Such a measure is a priori a predictor of high-rate offending if the prison versus jail decision tends to result in high-rate offenders being sent to prison and others being sent to jail.

TABLE 16 Distribution of the Number of Missing Variables in the Seven-Point Scale

Number Missing	All Cases	Jail Inmates
0	464	—
1	316	133
2	82	51
3	17	9
4	4	2
5	1	1

NOTE: None of the respondents had missing values on more than five variables.

Of course, any attempt to reconstruct the scale faces the same problem. The distribution of the number of missing variables in the seven-point scale for convicted robbers and burglars is shown in Table 16; the distribution for jail inmates is also shown separately. For slightly more than one-half the sample (N = 464), none of the seven variables has missing values; 36 percent of the sample has one variable missing, and another 12 percent is missing two or more variables in the scale. Jail inmates are only 22 percent of the sample but account for 46 percent of cases that have missing values for one or two variables, largely because of the problem with the past-convictions variable.

The seven-point scale is particularly sensitive to missing information because it affects an inmate's maximum scale score. For example, all respondents surveyed in jail (where low-rate offenders are presumably overrepresented) have a possible total score of only six, but are being compared with other respondents whose maximum score can be seven. In this case the missing data would spuriously improve the apparent predictive accuracy of the scale. Other, less prevalent cases of missing data could have other effects.

The problems of missing data that are associated with the seven-point scale are not easily resolved. One "solution" is to omit the major source of error from the scale—the past-convictions variable—and to redefine the prediction scale as one with six predictors. Unfortunately, this variable is also the only official record measure in the scale, but it is not strongly related to high offending frequencies. In some of the following analyses, especially the tests of predictive accuracy, a six-point scale, which excludes the past-convictions variable, is tried and the sensitivity of the results to this change is assessed.[15]

Accuracy of Scale

To simplify his analysis, Greenwood collapsed the seven-point scale into three predicted offense-rate categories: low-rate offenders (scores of 0 or 1), medium-rate offenders (scores of 2 or 3), and high-rate offenders (scores of 4 or greater).[16] One way to measure the effectiveness of this prediction scale is to compare average offense rates among the three predicted groups. In Table 17 both the means reported by Rand and those gen-

[15]Another alternative that would correct for all types of biases introduced by missing data (not just those related to the past-convictions variable) would be to multiply each respondent's score on the seven-point scale by the fraction: 7/(7 − number of missing variables). However, this solution produces noninteger values for respondents' scale scores (e.g., 3.5), which would make comparisons between scales difficult.

[16]In an effort to maintain comparability between this reanalysis of the Rand inmate survey and the Rand results, Greenwood's scale cut points (0–1, 2–3, 4 or more) were used for most of the analyses involving the seven-point scale. But the cut points probably should be based on state-specific distributions of scale scores for each crime type. Later in this reanalysis additional findings for California robbers are presented using cut points that equalize the marginal percentage distributions for the predicted groups with the collapsed categories of reported offense rates (50 percent—low, 25 percent—medium, 25 percent—high).

TABLE 17 Mean Reported Offense Rate and Other Statistics for Predicted Low-, Medium-, and High-Rate Offenders in the Three Sample States: Rand and a Reanalysis

		Reanalysis[a]			Rand[b]
State	Predicted Offense Rate	Percent	λ_{25}–λ_{75}	λ	λ
Robbery					
California	Low	17	0–1.3	0.9	2.2
(N = 166)[c]	Medium	35	0–4.9	8.1	11.0
	High	48	2.5–36.0	20.8	30.9
Michigan	Low	35	0–0.9	2.2	6.1
(N = 142)	Medium	50	0.6–7.4	7.4	11.7
	High	15	0–22.7	9.5	20.6
Texas	Low	40	0–0.9	1.3	1.4
(N = 114)	Medium	41	0–3.9	3.2	5.4
	High	18	1.6–11.8	5.9	7.7
Burglary					
California	Low	25	0–2.2	7.2	12.6
(N = 151)	Medium	41	0–18.2	33.1	87.6
	High	34	5.5–174.6	83.2	156.3
Michigan	Low	24	0–2.8	15.9[d]	71.6
(N = 113)	Medium	50	0–10.6	21.8	34.0
	High	26	0–7.0	42.2	101.4
Texas	Low	34	0–1.6	3.8	6.0
(N = 199)	Medium	48	0–5.0	8.0	20.5
	High	18	1.2–74.1	22.4	51.1

[a]These columns give some information about the three predicted offense-rate groups: the percentage of cases in each group, the range of *reported* offense rates from the 25th to the 75th percentile, and the "truncated means"—all offenders who reported offense rates greater than the 90th percentile have their rate set at the 90th percentile (calculated separately for each state and offense type). See Greenwood (1982:56) for other details.

[b]Truncated means. Source: Greenwood (1982:Table ES.1).

[c]The N's in this table are from the reanalysis and differ from those reported by Greenwood (1982) in Table ES.1 (p. xvii) primarily because his N's include cases for which λ could not be calculated. Thus, the N's in this table are not the ones from which his truncated mean offense rates were calculated.

[d]Two respondents in this category reported an annual crime rate of over 150 burglaries, which inflates the estimate of λ for predicted low-rate burglars.

erated from this reanalysis are presented. A comparison of the last two columns shows that the overall pattern of increasing average λs for the low-rate to the high-rate offender groups, which was reported by Rand, is confirmed in this reanalysis. However, the means in this reanalysis are much lower than the Rand estimates. The large differences in the two estimates of mean offense rates reflect the lower, recomputed estimates of λ and the redefinition of active burglars.[17] These results confirm that estimates of λ, especially the mean, are very sensitive to alternate methods of computation. The

[17]In addition, it was learned that the estimates of λ for all the analyses concerning the seven-point scale were actually Rand's maximum estimates of λ, not the average of the minimum and maximum estimates, which was used by Chaiken and Chaiken. (Greenwood provided the computer source codes that described his estimates of λ.) The estimate of λ computed for this reanalysis is much closer to Rand's minimum estimate (see Table 9). Using the maximum estimate of individual offending frequencies may be a conservative choice for partitioning inmates into low-, medium-, and high-rate offending groups, but it seriously inflates the three average, within-group estimates of λ that are used later in Greenwood's analysis.

lower means may alter the estimated incapacitation effects that Greenwood reports.

Despite the apparent differentiation of predicted groups based on average values of λ, a closer look at the distribution of λ in each group reveals considerable overlap. The λ_{25}–λ_{75} statistic that appears in Table 17 is the range of λs from the 25th to the 75th percentile for inmates predicted to be in a particular group. For example, of the 80 California inmates convicted of robbery who were predicted to be high-rate offenders, 25 percent reported fewer than 2.5 crimes per year, the middle 50 percent reported a crime rate between 2.5 and 36 per year, and the other 25 percent committed more than 36 robberies in the period before their arrest.

The amount of overlap between the 25th and 75th percentiles across the three predicted groups is quite surprising. The values of λ for all the medium- and high-rate groups overlap to some extent with the low- and medium-rate groups, respectively. Moreover, in some instances predicted low-rate and high-rate robbers have similar rates of offending. In Michigan at least 25 percent of both robbers and burglars predicted to be high-rate offenders actually reported not committing any robberies or burglaries at all. Thus, the seven-point scale does not adequately identify which respondents are low-, medium-, or high-rate offenders at the state level when the distributions of λ are compared across the three groups.

Important interstate differences are also evident in Table 17. The scale identifies high-rate robbers much better in California than in Michigan and Texas, perhaps because in California the distribution of λ for robbery is especially skewed. The distinction between predicted high-rate and medium-rate robbers in Michigan and Texas is especially poor. But California's high-rate robbers committed more crimes than similar robbers in Michigan or Texas: the estimates of λ at the 90th percentile for convicted robbers in the three states were 66, 29, and 13, respectively. The three average rates for predicted high-rate robbers—20.8, 9.5, and 5.9—follow this pattern. These state differences raise doubts about the generalizability of the scale as a prediction instrument for convicted robbers outside the state of California.

Finally, in both the robbery and the burglary analyses the predicted *low-rate* offenders are identified surprisingly well. (The exception is low-rate burglars in Michigan, but see footnote d to Table 17). Other data (not presented in tabular form) show that 93 percent of the predicted low-rate robbers and burglars (N = 255) reported committing fewer than six robberies or burglaries per year. These findings may be particularly relevant to the use of the scale in sentencing decisions, and they will be explored more fully below.

A more common method of evaluating a prediction instrument and its cut points is to determine what fraction of respondents are correctly classified. In this case the predicted offense rates are tabulated against actual offense rates, λ, using three predicted groups (based on scale cut points) and three groups based on self-reports of crimes committed. [Recall that actual offense rates are partitioned into low-, medium-, and high-rate categories using the 50th (median) and the 75th percentile values as cut points.] In the Rand report Greenwood presented data of this type that compared respondents' predicted offense rates with self-reported offense rates structured according to these cut points. A replication of this prediction table from the reanalysis is presented in Table 18, and Greenwood's figures appear in a footnote to the table.[18]

[18] In her critical review of Greenwood's analysis, Cohen (1983) pointed out that in Table 4.8 of the Rand report the cut points partitioning offenders on

TABLE 18 Distributions of Offenders by Predicted and Actual Offense Categories (percentages; N = 886)

Predicted Offense Rate (Score Values)	Self-Reported Offense Rate Low	Medium	High	Total
Low (0–1)	22	5	2	29
Medium (2–3)	22	12	10	44
High (4–7)	7	8	12	27
Total	51	25	24	100

NOTE: The cell percentages, based on N = 781, reported by Greenwood and corrected by Cohen (1983) are low: 20, 5, 2; medium: 22, 12, 9; high: 8, 9, 13.

The individual cell percentages for the two tables are very similar and differ by only one or two percentage points.

Based on this reanalysis, the percentage of respondents correctly classified by the seven-point scale is 46 percent (the sum of the diagonal entries), which is slightly higher than Cohen's corrected figure of 45 percent for Greenwood's prediction table (see Cohen, 1983). On the other hand, 54 to 55 percent of the convicted robbers and burglars are misclassified. However, these overall rates mask differences across states and offense types, which were not discussed in the Rand report. Moreover, earlier results of this reanalysis suggest that the scale may be differentially predictive for high- and low-rate offenders.

In Table 19 data are presented that address these questions. The first two columns give accuracy rates for Greenwood's scale among predicted low- and high-rate offenders. For Greenwood's data, Cohen (1983) calculated that 76 percent of the respondents predicted to be low-rate offenders reported low rates of robbery (or burglary), but only 45 percent of the respondents predicted to be high-rate offenders actually reported high offending frequencies. As seen in Table 19, this reanalysis of the Rand data also shows greater accuracy rates among predicted low-rate offenders than high-rate offenders. However, these differences are due in part to the different base rates of the two groups—50 percent of the inmates were defined as low-rate offenders and 25 percent were defined as high-rate offenders.

Accuracy rates also differ substantially within crime types and across states. (The data on which the figures are based are presented in Appendix Table A.3.) Predictions of low offense rates for both robbery and burglary are more accurate in California than in the other states, but predictive accuracy for high-rate offenders is consistently higher in Texas. Moreover, of those classified as high-rate offenders, 60 percent of the robbers in

---

the basis of their reported offending rates resulted in a distribution of 30 percent (low rate), 42 percent (medium rate), and 28 percent (high rate). But earlier in the report Greenwood partitioned the sample into 50 percent (low), 25 percent (medium), and 25 percent (high) to identify variables that were related to high rates of offending. Cohen recalculated Greenwood's prediction table based on the original categories; see Table 18 for a comparison of the replicated prediction table and Cohen's corrected figures.

In his report Greenwood does not explain why the cut points for actual offending categories were changed, but it was learned subsequently that it was done to equalize the marginals for predicted rates and reported rates in the table (Abrahamse, 1983, personal communication), i.e., to equate the base rate to the selection ratio. This redefinition tends to reduce the rate of false-positive errors in classifying high-rate offenders. Therefore, the accuracy of the improvement-over-chance classification implied by Greenwood's Table 4.8 combines the effect of scale accuracy with the artifactual effect of the redefinition.

TABLE 19 Measures of Predictive Accuracy and Percent Relative Improvement Over Chance (RIOC) for Different Respondent Subgroups and Types of Prediction Models (percentage)

Subgroup or Model	Accuracy		RIOC[c]	
	Low-rate[a]	High-rate[b]	Low	High
Greenwood[d]	76	45	48	35
Reanalysis[e]	76	45	50	31
Robbers				
California	93	40	86	57
Michigan	78	41	55	21
Texas	69	52	39	38
Burglars				
California	84	48	67	48
Michigan	74	34	44	19
Texas	68	61	33	48
Six-variable Scale[f]	72	47	48	27
Unambiguous Cases[g]	76	43	43	30

[a]The percentage of respondents predicted to be low-rate offenders (scoring 0 or 1 on scale) who actually reported low rates of robbery or burglary (below the median for their state and offense type).

[b]The percentage of respondents predicted to be high-rate offenders (scoring 4 or more on scale) who actually reported high rates of robbery or burglary (above the 75th percentile for their state and offense type).

[c]These measures adjust for the difference in base rate and are calculated according to the formula provided by Loeber and Dishion (1983). See text and note 20 for details.

[d]The figures in the first two columns are based on Cohen's (1983) correction of Greenwood's data (N = 781).

[e]The sample is all convicted robbers and burglars (N = 886).

[f]Prediction scale without one variable—past conviction for robbery or burglary—and using same cut points.

[g]Includes only respondents for whom λ could be unambiguously calculated, and respondents with only slight ambiguity in responses to questions about number of crimes committed (N = 568).

California and 66 percent of the burglars in Michigan are incorrectly classified, compared with 39 percent of the burglars in Texas. Some of this interstate variation is the result of different distributions of predicted offense groups in the three states (see Table 17). The difference between this selection ratio and the base rate (reported offense rates) affects the accuracy rate in a particular table. However, it is difficult to determine how much of the interstate differences in Table 19 is artifactual.

Another measure of predictive accuracy, the percent relative improvement over chance (RIOC), also indicates sizable interstate differences. Loeber and Dishion (1983) recommend this measure because it relates improvement over chance to maximum possible accuracy, which is an artifact of the difference between actual offending patterns ("base rate") and predicted patterns ("selection ratio").[19] Using RIOC, the accuracy of the

[19]The formula to compute the relative improvement over chance is:

$$\text{RIOC} = \frac{\text{Percent Total Correct} - \text{Percent Random Correct}}{\text{Percent Maximum Correct} - \text{Percent Random Correct}}.$$

The advantage of this measure is that "percent maximum correct," which is the maximum ceiling or accuracy for a given table, adjusts for differences between the base rate and the selection ratio. This measure can be helpful when comparing the efficiency of prediction instruments across different

prediction scale across different subgroups and models is reported in the third and fourth columns in Table 19 in terms of how well the scale predicts low- and high-rate offenders.

The RIOC measures show extreme variability in the predictive power of the scale across states and offense types, even after adjusting for the different distributions of predicted offense groups. In general, the predictions of robbery rates are better than the predictions of burglary rates, and low-rate offenders appear to be predicted better than high-rate offenders. (The one exception is Texas, where the accuracy rate is higher for high-rate burglars.) The scale appears especially strong in California. On the other hand, high-rate robbers and burglars in Michigan are poorly identified; the scale adds only a 20 percent improvement over chance. In part, this variation may reflect differences in the inmate populations. However, the fixed scale cut point of 4 leads to different selection ratios in the different states. The variations in the selection ratios in turn artifactually affect the measures of predictive accuracy. These issues are not explored here but are developed in Volume I (Chapter 6) of the panel's report.

Two modifications to the original scale and sample produced only moderate effects on predictive power using the standard measures of accuracy. (See Appendix Table A.3 for the complete prediction table.) First, a six-variable scale (Greenwood's scale with prior conviction for the same offense removed as a predictor variable) was constructed. This reduced potential biases related to missing data on the seventh variable, but it also removed potentially useful information. This scale appears less accurate in predicting low-rate offenders than the full scale and slightly more accurate in predicting high-rate offenders. However, when the differences in base rate and selection ratio are controlled in the RIOC measure, the scale's predictive capability for high-rate offenders is appreciably lower than the full scale, as would be expected.

The second modification, excluding cases with serious response ambiguity (see Table 11 and related text), did not significantly affect the accuracy of either low- or high-rate predictions. Surprisingly, once the base rate/selection ratio problem is taken into account, removing ambiguous survey responses reduces the ability of the scale to identify low-rate offenders, but it does not affect the accuracy of the high-rate predictions.

Thus, the accuracy of Greenwood's seven-point scale cannot be adequately assessed from data in a "pooled" prediction table. The substantial differences in the measures of predictive accuracy across states and offense type indicate that the scale does not uniformly identify high-rate robbers and burglars. Predictive accuracy for high-rate offenders, according to the RIOC measure, is best for California robbers and worst for Michigan robbers and burglars. Convicted robbers (and burglars, but to a lesser extent) in California prisons and jails appear to be quite different from other respondents in the Rand inmate sample. This reanalysis thus far has shown that robbers and burglars in California, when compared

---

studies or different samples, but it must be interpreted in light of the respective selection ratios and base rates (see Volume I, Chapter 6). For Table 19, the medium- and high-rate offenders are combined to compute RIOC for low-rate predictions, and the low- and medium-rate offenders are combined to compute RIOC for high-rate predictions. The following example illustrates how RIOC was calculated for predicted low-rate California robbers—the uppermost left cell—using the marginals from the collapsed 3 x 3 table (data are presented in Appendix Table A.3):

$$\frac{26 - [(84 \times 28)/166]}{28 - [(84 \times 28)/166]} = 86 \text{ percent}$$

with other subgroups, reported the highest λs (see Table 10), the most extensive juvenile records (see Table 13), and the greatest involvement in multiple drug use both as juveniles and adults (see Table 13). Moreover, in regression analyses the seven-point scale explained more variance in self-reported robbery and burglary frequencies for California inmates than for respondents in other states. Thus, the scale is more sensitive to the attributes of high-rate offenders in California than to the attributes of offenders elsewhere.

Finally, the scale appears to be able to predict low-rate offenders more consistently, and those predictions are more accurate than predictions of high-rate offending. It is possible that Greenwood's scale and other similar prediction instruments could be used to identify the least active criminals since the absence of the seven scale attributes seems to coincide with low rates of criminal activity—under six crimes per year. The data presented here on the predictive accuracy of one proposed prediction instrument suggest that prediction tools in the criminal justice system could play a role in deciding who should be sent to prison and for how long and also who should not be sent to prison. However, these results may be a consequence of particular characteristics of the inmates surveyed from the prisons and jails in California, Michigan, and Texas.

The results of this reanalysis do suggest that any prediction instrument may require some changes for the particular characteristics of the population. The considerable differences in the predictive capability of one prediction instrument reported here indicate that prediction scales developed with one population should be tested extensively before they are applied to different populations. Further, the scale proposed by Greenwood can only diminish in its predictive power when applied prospectively to populations of all convicted offenders, whether incarcerated or not. In view of the potential value of prediction instruments and the sizable error rates presently associated with them, more research in developing prediction instruments appears warranted.

Incapacitative Effects Using a Prediction Scale

The primary objective of the Greenwood report was to identify high-rate offenders in the Rand sample and to determine whether targeted or "selective" incarceration could lead to decreases in crime, decreases in the prison population, or both. In this last phase of the reanalysis, Greenwood's procedures are used to estimate these incapacitation effects for robbers in California, and the sensitivity of his results to alternate estimates of λ and to the reconstruction of his prediction scale are assessed.

The Incapacitative Effect of Incarceration

Incarcerating convicted offenders not only punishes offenders for their criminal behavior but also prevents them from committing crimes in the community. The reduction in crime directly attributable to incarceration is referred to as "incapacitative effect." Calculating this effect requires information about criminal justice system operations and criminal behavior. In particular, one needs to know the expected time spent in prison for a crime and the value of λ for active offenders. The longer the expected incarceration time per crime—which is a function of the probabilities of arrest (q), conviction and incarceration (J), and average sentence length (S)—and the larger the average crime rate (λ), the greater the estimated incapacitative effect. As a first approximation, these relationships can be mathematically expressed as

$$I = \frac{1}{1 + \lambda qJS}.$$

This model was developed by Avi-Itzhak and Shinnar (1973) and expanded in other papers (Shinnar and Shinnar, 1975). Cohen (1978, 1983) provides an excellent discussion of the incapacitation literature, including a comprehensive review of previous research that has estimated the incapacitative effect of incarceration.

Greenwood suggested that the extreme variation in λ that had been observed in the Rand data warranted disaggregating this model to develop estimates for offenders with low, medium, and high values of λ.[20] Greenwood (1982:xiii) reported that with this revised model,

> the amount of crime prevented by any given incarceration level can be increased if we lengthen the terms of those in the high-rate group and shorten the terms of those in the low-rate groups . . . . this type of sentencing policy [is called] "selective incapacitation."

Thus, disaggregation might produce much greater incapacitative effects than those estimated from a model based on an average λ with all offenders treated homogeneously.

Specifically, Greenwood proposed classifying offenders into three groups based on their predicted offending rate, which is determined by their scores on the seven-point scale. To analyze the effects of selective incapacitation, three parameters of the basic model are allowed to vary across the offender groups: individual offending frequencies (λ), probability of incarceration given conviction (J), and the average time served for those incarcerated (S). Then, one can calculate the expected amount of crime contributed (and prison space used) by the low-, medium-, and high-rate groups under the current sentencing policy and contrast that with the expected amount of crime (and prison space) under a selective sentencing policy—for example, one that sends high-rate offenders to prison for long terms and all other offenders to jail for shorter terms.

Several critical assumptions underlie this model and Greenwood's application of it to the Rand inmate data (see Cohen, 1983; Blackmore and Welsh, 1983). Of particular concern here are the accuracy of average estimates of λ, the distribution of inmates and the offender population across the three offense-rate groups, and the stability and continuity of λ over time. This reanalysis explicitly tests the sensitivity of Greenwood's results to variations in estimates of λ and to assumptions about the total offender population. The implications of interstate differences in estimating incapacitative effects are also addressed.

A Selective Incapacitation Model

To estimate the proposed model of incapacitative effects, Greenwood needed information about how offenders in the three states are currently sentenced. He had this information for California only and thus most of his analyses are focused on California robbers and burglars.[21] This reestimation of the inca-

[20] Marsh and Singer (cited in Cohen, 1983) originally demonstrated, with hypothetical data, that larger reductions in crime might be possible if λ was assumed to vary in the criminal population. Cohen (1978) also discussed the statistical underpinnings of such a revised model.

[21] Greenwood also presents some estimates for Texas robbers and burglars using the California values for the probability of arrest, conviction, and incarceration. Since no jail inmates were included in the Texas sample, it is unclear how Greenwood arrived at estimates of the prison and jail populations in Texas. But more importantly, it is inappropriate to use California's sentencing policy as a benchmark for estimating the potential incapacita-

pacitation model used by Greenwood also focuses on the effect of selective sentencing policies on robbery rates and on the prison population in California. In addition, an attempt was made to replicate Greenwood's results for California robbers using his published values for all variables in the model (Greenwood:77, 108–118).

Greenwood tested the model with a highly selective sentencing policy that would double the "expected sentence length" from approximately 4 years to 8 years for predicted high-rate robbers[22] and would send all other robbers to jail for 1-year terms (Greenwood:79). He reports that a large incapacitative effect could be achieved in California: a 20 percent reduction in the robbery rate without any increase in the prison population. But this conclusion is not supported by other data Greenwood presents. The graph that is supposed to depict this relationship is slightly at odds with the text (Greenwood:78, plot 6). More important, there are other difficulties with the data that underlie it. In an earlier attempt to recalculate Greenwood's results, Cohen (1983) was unable to replicate the results precisely using the data Greenwood reports. According to Cohen's calculations, the maximum incapacitative effect (with 8-year expected terms for high-rate offenders) is a 13 percent reduction in crime with an 8 percent decrease in the prison population. The recalculation of Greenwood's findings concerning the potential incapacitative effects of his selective sentencing policy by this author, also using Greenwood's published numbers, produced the same results found by Cohen (see Appendix C).

Thus, this replication and that of Cohen confirm that some reduction in the *California* robbery rate might be possible by selectively imprisoning the predicted high-rate offenders but that the maximum potential using the hypothetical sentencing policy is about 13 percent, not 20 percent as Greenwood reports. Any deviation from the assumptions of the model will probably lower this estimate still further. In fact, Cohen shows that the 13 percent effect is sensitive to some of the input values used in the model, particularly the stability of λ (1983:Figure 3) and the distribution of offenders across crime-rate categories (1983:Figure 4). In previous sections of this paper, lower average estimates of λ were reported for California robbers: 0.9 (low rate), 8.1 (medium rate), and 20.8 (high rate), compared with the 2.0, 10.1, and 30.8 reported by Greenwood. Slightly different values were also computed for several other parameters in the incapacitation model.[23] The alterna-

---

tive effects of a selective sentencing policy in Texas. As shown earlier, California and Texas inmates are very different in their individual offending frequencies and in their values on the predictor variables (especially juvenile criminal history and use of illegal drugs), which suggests that in these two states the sentencing policies or the offender populations are not at all alike. Thus, Greenwood's estimates of incapacitative effects in Texas using the California sentencing parameters are likely to be significantly in error.

[22]The prison term assigned by the judge after conviction is different from the "expected sentence length," which is used in calculating incapacitative effects. Although state policies differ, a convicted offender usually serves only one-half to two-thirds of his sentence because of reductions for "good behavior." Thus, California robbers who are predicted to be high-rate offenders reported an expected sentence length of about 4 years but were probably given prison sentences of 6 to 8 years. (Official information on expected date of release was not available for all California inmates; therefore, the self-report measure was used as a substitute.) Increasing the expected sentence length to 8 years actually means that the prison sentence for robbery for this high-rate group would have to be 12 to 16 years.

[23]In this reanalysis, the distribution by offense-rate group for prison and jail inmates in California was slightly different from that reported by Green-

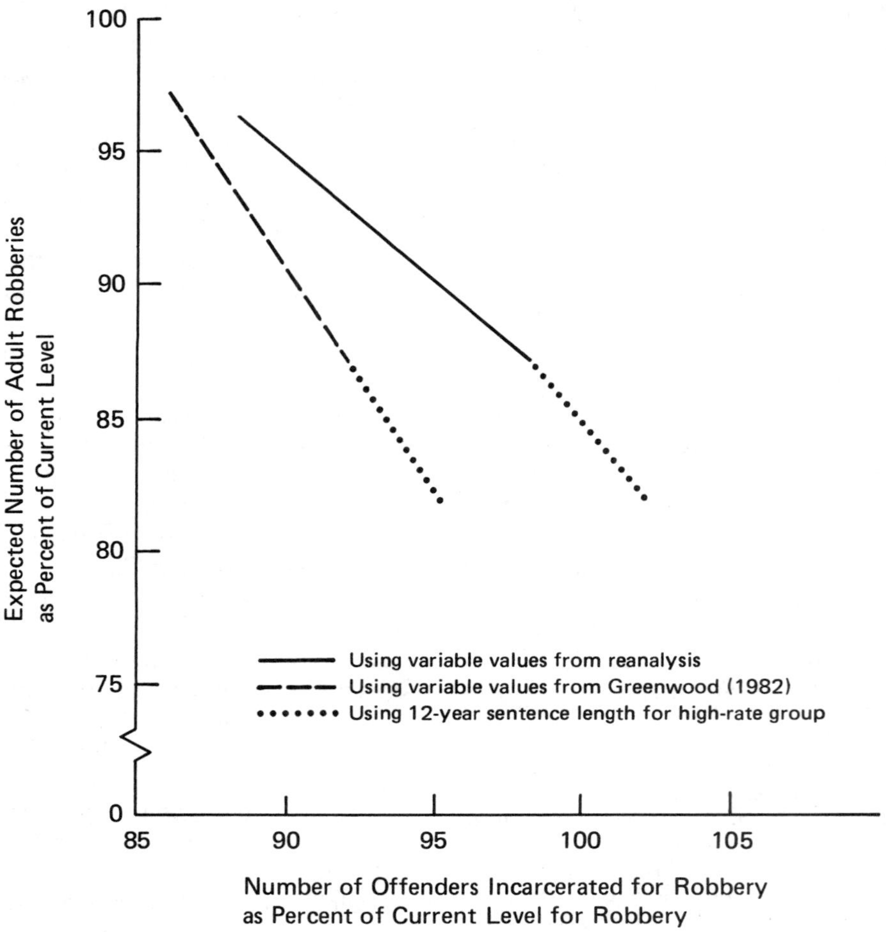

FIGURE 3 Comparison of reanalysis estimates of incapacitative effects for highly selective sentencing policy with effects reported in Greenwood (1982).

wood (in parentheses), which also altered some of the other parameter values:

Predicted Group Rate	Jail Sample	Prison Sample	Estimated Total Incarcerated Population	Estimated Average Sentence Length (months)
Low	20 (24)	14 (17)	2,865 (3,480)	46.7 (49.5)
Medium	19 (14)	45 (43)	4,942 (4,401)	56.3 (53.3)
High	14 (14)	66 (66)	5,942 (6,099)	48.9 (50.6)

The reconstruction of the scale changed the classification of some offenders in the three groups, which probably accounts for the different average expected sentence lengths. The full set of revised parameters for Greenwood's incapacitation model is available in Appendix Table A.4.

tive estimates of these and other parameters for the model were used in the reanalysis of the incapacitative effects of selective sentencing policies in California. The full set of revised parameters for the incapacitation model is given in Appendix Table A.4.

Figure 3 shows two estimates of the potential incapacitative effects of a highly selective sentencing policy for convicted robbers in California; the dashed line represents a corrected interpretation of Greenwood's data and the solid line represents the reanalysis. The reduction in the robbery rate reported by Greenwood is relatively unaffected by using lower estimates of λ. This reanalysis and Cohen's (1983) replication of Greenwood's data both indicate the possibility of about a 13 percent reduction in robbery. But the prison population would remain essentially unchanged using estimates of the input variables obtained from the reanalysis.[24]

Further reductions in the robbery rate beyond 13 percent can only be achieved by increasing the expected sentence length. The end points of the dashed and solid lines in Figure 3 and those in Greenwood's report are based on the hypothetical sentencing policy of 1-year jail terms for low- and medium-rate offenders and about 8-year expected terms for high-rate offenders. Thus, any extension to a lower crime level actually involves a change in the sentencing policy. To see if Greenwood's finding of a possible 20 percent reduction in robbery could be achieved, Greenwood's hypothetical policy was revised and the average time served for high-rate offenders was increased by a factor of 3, to slightly over 12 years. This modification is represented by dotted lines in Figure 3.

These data reveal that with extremely stiff expected sentences for high-rate robbers (actual prison sentences would probably be 16 to 24 years), the robbery rate could be reduced by only 18 percent. Moreover, the prison population might have to be increased (according to the reanalysis estimates) to accommodate the longer sentence lengths. But more important, a sentencing policy that gives 1-year jail terms to most convicted robbers and sentences a small group of predicted high-rate offenders (which includes an error rate of at least 50 percent, according to the prediction tables presented earlier) to about 20 years would represent extreme disparity in sentencing.

Incapacitative effects for Michigan were not estimated in the Greenwood report because the necessary data on current sentencing policies were not available. The data for Michigan robbers were obtained for the reanalysis, and the incapacitative effects that would be expected under Greenwood's model were computed.[25] The results were quite different from those for California. With 8-year sentence lengths for predicted high-rate robbers and 1-year jail terms for all other robbers, the robbery rate in Michigan would increase by 33 percent, but the prison population would decrease by

[24]The model that is used to estimate these incapacitative effects is based on a series of calculations involving a wide range of magnitudes; therefore rounding and truncation error (for example, using 2 decimal places instead of 4 or 5) may slightly alter the estimates of changes in crime rates and prison populations. Details of the model and the intermediate calculations can be found in Cohen (1984a) and Volume I (Chapter 5) of the panel's report. The projections reported here for incapacitative effects are conditional on assumptions stated in those sources, and actual effects are likely to differ from these projections because the assumptions may be violated in ways that are discussed later in the paper.

[25]The data on current sentencing policies in Michigan are taken from the official records of a large sample of Michigan arrestees (Blumstein and Cohen, 1984, personal communication) and state-level summary data supplied by the Michigan State Police. These sources gave nearly identical estimates of the parameters needed for the incapacitation analysis based on Michigan robbers and they were averaged to arrive at the following estimates: conviction rate—.44; number of robbery arrests in 1977—3,281; probability of incarceration given conviction—.86; prison commitment rate—.86; jail commitment rate—.05. These parameters were substituted into Table B.4 (Greenwood, 1982:112) to estimate current numbers of robbers in Michigan prisons and jails. Then, those estimates and data on the 150 convicted robbers in the Michigan subsample were used to generate a table similar to Table B.6 (p. 115) for Michigan. Further details about estimating the potential incapacitative effects of a selective sentencing policy for robbers in Michigan are available from this author.

nearly 50 percent. The hypothetical policy is clearly not satisfactory in Michigan because incarcerated high-rate offenders, as defined by a minimum score of four on the seven-point scale, are apparently a very small group in Michigan prisons and jails, compared with California. Moreover, all convicted robbers in Michigan are already serving long prison terms (an average of 5 years) and few robbers are sentenced to jail. Thus, in Michigan a policy that reserves long prison sentences for only the small group of predicted high-rate offenders actually would increase the crime rate and reduce the prison population. This would occur because most robbers (those defined as low- and medium-rate) would spend a smaller portion of their offending careers in prison or jail under this policy than under Michigan's current policy and would have more "free time" in which to commit more crimes.

The crime rate was also increased when Greenwood applied his incapacitation model and selective sentencing policy to the Texas robbers and burglars (Greenwood:79–81). In Texas predicted high-rate offenders, using the seven-point scale, were also a small group; consequently, Greenwood's selective sentencing policy would reduce the prison population but would not reduce the robbery or burglary rate.

Finally, one important parameter of the original incapacitation model was omitted from the Greenwood version—offender's career length. Other analyses of the Rand data reveal that when career length is included in the model for California, estimates of crime reduction that could be achieved by a selective sentencing policy drop to about 5 to 10 percent (Cohen, 1984a; Spelman, 1984). In a recent report on the duration of criminal careers, Blumstein, Cohen, and Hsieh (1982:55) estimated that the maximum mean residual career length for robbery (the number of years left in a criminal career at any given age) is only 7 years. Therefore, many of the targeted high-rate offenders would likely have ended their careers before the end of their 8-year prison term anyway, in which case the projected reductions in crime would be overstated. Thus, these and other analyses suggest that, under the best assumptions, significant reductions in crime cannot be easily achieved by identifying the high-rate offenders and targeting them for long prison terms.

Selecting Scale Cut Points

One of the fundamental parameters of Greenwood's calculations is the choice of cut points on the seven-point scale that defines the distribution of incarcerated offenders across the three predicted offense-rate groups. The cut points are used to estimate the total offender population in California and the probability of prison (versus jail) for convicted offenders in each group. In Greenwood's incapacitation analysis, the low-, medium-, and high-rate groups are defined by the scores 0–1, 2–3, and 4–7 on the seven-point scale derived from the survey data. The distribution of these scores within the inmate sample is used, along with information about California's current sentencing policy for robbers, to estimate the total annual jail and prison population in California. Using these methods, predicted high-rate offenders turned out to be 43 percent of the incarcerated robber population (Greenwood:77).

Greenwood introduced his scale, however, as a device for identifying a relatively small group of high-rate offenders—specifically, the most active 25 percent of the convicted robbers, according to their self-reports. (Chaiken and Chaiken, 1982a, chose the top 20 percent.) As Loeber and Dishion (1983) noted generally, this excess of selection ratio (43 percent) over base rate (25 percent) guarantees a false-positive rate of at least 18 percent. To maximize predictive efficiency, the selection ratio (the percentage of respondents predicted to be high-rate offenders) should be equivalent to the 25 percent base rate (the percentage of respondents defined as high-rate according to their reported crime rates). Therefore, in the reanalysis the model was reestimated to assess the sensitivity of the results to alternative scale cut points for California robbers.

Adjusting the cut points to equalize approximately the selection ratio and base rate and substituting the lower average estimates of λ for the three groups dramatically altered the potential crime reductions associated with Greenwood's hypothetical selective sentencing policy. The cut points of the prediction scale were changed to 0–2 (low), 3–4 (medium), and 5–7 (high).[26] The values of λ for the newly defined groups indicate less differentiation between the medium- and high-rate groups—2.2 (low), 16.9 (medium), and 20.8 (high), compared with 0.9, 8.1, and 20.8 using the other scale cut points. Surprisingly, changing the cut points did not alter the average *high rate* λ, which highlights the difficulty of distinguishing between medium-rate and high-rate offenders with the prediction scale.

With the alternative scale cut points and resulting changes in the model's parameter values, the California robbery rate would actually increase about 6 percent under Greenwood's selective sentencing policy, although the imprisoned population would decrease about 20 percent. As with the Michigan and Texas estimates discussed earlier, the hypothetical increase in the crime rate and the reduction in prison population would occur because the large majority of robbers would spend a smaller portion of their careers incarcerated, under the assumptions of this revised model, and so would be free to commit crime.

Thus, it appears clear from these analyses that the potential incapacitative effects derived from a model that assumes a selective sentencing structure are sensitive to the choice of scale cut points and

[26]There are actually two closely related issues: one is substantive and the other is technical. The cut point decision is also a policy issue—how much error in prediction is acceptable and how are predicted high-rate offenders to be defined (e.g., having four or five of seven attributes), given the characteristics of a specific offender population. The technical issue relates to the estimated distribution of offenders across the three offense-rate groups. In Greenwood's model (and this reanalysis), this estimate is dependent on the cut points because the distribution of the three groups defined by the cut points in the *sample* is used, in conjunction with other parameters, to estimate the distribution of the three groups in the general offender *population.* These estimates were necessarily based on the small number of convicted robbers in the California inmate sample (N = 178).

Changing the cut points of the prediction scale reduces the high-rate group to 22 percent of the estimated total incarcerated population, which is closer to the 25 percent figure that Greenwood initially thought would be appropriate. Once different proportions of "street time" among the three offender groups (most for the low-rate group and least for the high-rate group) are taken into account, Greenwood's model estimated that about 13 percent of the *total population of robbers* in California are high-rate offenders (see Greenwood:77); the reestimation here of the model with the revised scale cut points makes the explicit assumption that fewer California robbers (i.e., only 6 percent) are high-rate offenders.

Of course, since it is impossible to know how many "active" robbers actually exist in any state or how they are distributed across low-, medium-, and high-rate groups, these numbers must be estimated. But using Greenwood's method could distort the estimated number of offenders in each group if, for example, the incarcerated population contained an unusually large group of predicted high-rate offenders, as was the case in California. An alternate method would be to estimate the total offender population using seven groups (one for each score value on the scale) rather than the three groups arbitrarily defined by the cut points.

the nature of the offender population. The appropriate cut points on the prediction scale may depend on the definition of "high-rate" offender, which could differ across states. The most active 10 percent of the robbers in the Texas sample each reported committing at least 15 crimes per year, but the top 10 percent of the California robbers reported 100 or more crimes a year (see Table 10). Chaiken and Chaiken (1984:223) suggest that the low rates of robbery reported by inmates in Texas compared with inmates in Michigan and California could reflect unmeasured aspects of the environment on patterns of criminality. California officials may be more willing to tolerate some forms of criminal behavior than their counterparts in Texas.

The probable interstate differences in offender populations, criminal justice system practices, and projections of incapacitative effects highlight the need for customizing the development of prediction rules, the selection of cut points, and the implementation of selective sentencing policies within each jurisdiction. Factors specific to the local situation should be considered before any prediction instrument is adopted, even one having some degree of accuracy. Moreover, cut points for decision rules may also be influenced by local values as to the relative costs of the criminal behavior and the sanctions being imposed according to the rule (Blumstein, Farrington, and Moitra, 1985; Morris and Miller, 1985). In any choice of cut points, the lower the cutoff defining the high-rate offenders, the greater the risk of incorrectly classifying some offenders in this group.

SUMMARY AND CONCLUSIONS

The single most important contribution of Rand's second inmate survey is the highlighting of the extreme skewness of the distribution of λ for a sample of known serious criminals. Although the technique used to elicit this information and the Rand sample of incarcerated offenders may have introduced errors into these estimates, the Rand study has significantly advanced our understanding of individual patterns of criminal behavior. Although some minor differences exist in the precise numbers in the distribution, this reanalysis of the Rand data confirms that the distribution of λ is highly skewed—at least for the offenders sampled from the prisons and jails of California, Michigan, and Texas. Half the offenders report committing no more than five crimes a year, while a small but very important group may commit several hundred crimes a year.

The estimates of λ for robbery and burglary, however, are sensitive to choices in computation, such as the interpretation of ambiguous survey responses, the treatment of missing data, and the computation of the length of respondents' "street time." Moreover, the veracity of some respondents, particularly the large group of convicted robbers and burglars who denied committing any robberies or burglaries and the few respondents whose reports implied annual rates of 1,000 or more robberies or burglaries, may be affecting the observed distribution of λ. Another problem is obtaining accurate annualized rates for those respondents who are incarcerated for long portions of the observation period and who have intensive, but short, street time, or for those who commit crime sporadically. Changes in the design of the Rand questionnaire or some analytic adjustments to the estimates of annual offending rates may be necessary to provide more valid estimates of crime rates for such respondents. Finally, λ varies considerably across the three state samples and further research is needed to determine whether this variation is due to differences in the states' offender populations or is a consequence of different selectivity arising from the criminal justice processes in these states.

The Rand finding that has received the greatest public attention is also the one about which the most questions are raised in this reanalysis: the Greenwood formulation of a particular scale for identifying high-rate offenders. A fundamental problem relates to how well this identification can be accomplished in an operational setting and how well the Rand report demonstrates the feasibility of doing so.

Although the scale certainly does better than chance in all the jurisdictions examined, one would expect improvement from any scale that invoked the predictors it did and that was fitted to the sample data. There is no indication that Greenwood's scale would perform any better, even in California, than any other scale that has been used operationally. The relative improvement over chance varied considerably across the three states; the best performance was observed for California (57 percent for robbery and 48 percent for burglary) and the worst for Michigan (21 percent for robbery and 19 percent for burglary). The prediction scale also seems to work somewhat better in identifying low-rate offenders than the high-rate offenders at whom it was targeted, even adjusting for the higher prevalence of low-rate offenders in the population. These results emphasize the importance of each jurisdiction's developing and validating its own scale rather than simply applying the seven-point prediction instrument developed by Greenwood or any other instrument.

If one could identify the high-rate offenders prospectively, the extreme skewness in the distribution of λ should certainly make it possible to reduce crime by selectively incarcerating those high-rate offenders. This reanalysis of the Rand data found that Greenwood overestimated the anticipated reduction in the California robbery rate. Using a seven-item scale and a sentencing policy that would double sentence lengths for high-rate offenders, the most favorable effect achieved in the reanalysis was a reduction of about 13 percent. However, the scale used to identify high-rate offenders is more sensitive to the attributes of those offenders in California than to the attributes of high-rate offenders elsewhere. If the same sentencing policy and prediction scale were applied in Michigan and Texas, the crime rate would probably *increase* because of differences in current criminal justice practices and offender populations in the three states.

More importantly, even in California, the assumptions necessary to make the calculation inflate the estimate of incapacitation effects. The estimate of a 13 percent reduction in crime with a selective sentencing policy, which has been demonstrated only with California data, will decline further if any of the following obtain:

1. Predictive power decreases as the model is applied to any new population ("shrinkage") and especially to a population of all convicted offenders rather than prisoners;
2. The comprehensive self-report data used in the Rand analyses are replaced by less complete official records of the predictor variables;
3. The reports of λ gathered retrospectively in the Rand survey fail to persist into the future, especially after the longer periods of incarceration implied by the selective incapacitation policy;
4. The criminal justice system limits the proposed policy through judicial dis-

cretion or other adaptive responses in ways that reduce the disparity that arises from a sentence of 8 years for predicted high-rate offenders compared with 1 year for other convicted persons.

Thus, future research is needed to identify characteristics of high-rate offenders and how those characteristics vary across offender populations. Research is also needed to develop and test locally appropriate, prediction-based selection rules to distinguish high-rate offenders from other offenders using operationally available data. On the basis of this reanalysis, much more realistic estimates of the true operational effectiveness of a prediction instrument are needed before the current enthusiasm about the estimated reduction in crime through selective incapacitation is warranted.

APPENDIX A: SUPPLEMENTAL TABLES

TABLE A.1 Comparison of the Cumulative Percentage Distribution of Rand Estimates of λ with Estimates Produced from a Reanalysis of the Rand Data

	Robbery		Burglary	
λ	Rand	Reanalysis	Rand	Reanalysis
λ < 1	13.1	16.8	9.4	12.1
< 2	24.9	33.0	20.8	26.5
< 3	35.3	41.8	32.7	35.8
< 4	43.8	52.9	40.1	46.0
< 5	49.4	56.1	48.2	52.2
< 10	65.8	71.9	62.1	65.7
< 20	77.5	81.2	70.3	73.1
< 30	82.7	85.4	75.0	77.0
< 40	85.1	87.4	77.3	79.1
< 50	86.6	87.7	78.8	80.4
< 100	90.9	92.1	82.4	83.9
≥ 100	99.9	99.9	100.0	99.9

SOURCE: Chaiken and Chaiken (1982a:206, robbery; 203, burglary).

TABLE A.2 Regressions of Estimates of λ on the Seven Variables in Greenwood's Scale: Inmates Convicted of Robbery or Burglary

	Unstandardized Coefficients	
Variable	Robbery	Burglary
I. Three States (N = 848)		
Past conviction	−.01	.46[a]
Recent incarceration	.43[a]	.28
Early conviction	.11	.44[a]
Juvenile incarceration	.40[a]	.18
Recent drug use	.46[a]	.99[a]
Juvenile drug use	.48[a]	.71[a]
Recent unemployment	.33[a]	.47[a]
Constant	−.39	−.37
Adjusted R^2	.12	.12
II. California (N = 311)		
Past conviction	−.01	.58[a]
Recent incarceration	1.18[a]	.16
Early conviction	.12	.32
Juvenile incarceration	.50[a]	.35
Recent drug use	.31	1.50[a]
Juvenile drug use	.62[a]	.68[a]
Recent unemployment	.22	.27
Constant	−.41	−.54
Adjusted R^2	.20	.22
III. Michigan (N = 245)		
Past conviction	.15	.44
Recent incarceration	−.71[a]	.41
Early conviction	−.01	.64[a]
Juvenile incarceration	.46	.16
Recent drug use	.57[a]	.78[a]
Juvenile drug use	.39	.80[a]
Recent unemployment	.61[a]	.40
Constant	−.30	−.34
Adjusted R^2	.08	.12
IV. Texas (N = 292)		
Past conviction	−.14	.40[a]
Recent incarceration	.14	.19
Early conviction	.19	.39
Juvenile incarceration	−.11	−.005
Recent drug use	.39[a]	.65[a]
Juvenile drug use	.29	.70[a]
Recent unemployment	.10	.62
Constant	−.27	−.22
Adjusted R^2	.05	.15

NOTE: Missing data for the independent variables were coded as 0. In the regression including all three states, 36 cases were excluded because of missing data for the dependent variable. For similar reasons, 6 cases were excluded in California, 10 cases were excluded in Michigan, and 20 cases were excluded in Texas.

[a] $p < .05$.

TABLE A.3 Frequency Distribution of Offenders by Predicted and Self-Reported Offense Rates for Specific Subgroups

Predicted Offense Rate	Self-Reported Offense Rate		
	Low	Medium	High
Reanalysis with All Cases (N = 886)			
Low	193	41	22
Medium	193	109	88
High	65	67	108
California Robbers (N = 166)			
Low	26	2	0
Medium	35	13	9
High	23	26	32
Michigan Robbers (N = 142)			
Low	38	6	5
Medium	25	24	22
High	8	5	9
Texas Robbers (N = 114)			
Low	32	11	3
Medium	22	11	14
High	3	7	11
California Burglars (N = 151)			
Low	31	4	2
Medium	35	16	11
High	10	17	25
Michigan Burglars (N = 113)			
Low	20	3	4
Medium	29	17	11
High	12	7	10
Texas Burglars (N = 200)			
Low	46	15	7
Medium	47	28	21
High	9	5	22
Only Cases with Unambiguous Responses (N = 568)			
Low	149	34	14
Medium	126	72	59
High	29	36	49
Six-Variable Scale (N = 886)			
Low	231	60	30
Medium	178	103	102
High	43	54	87

TABLE A.4 Parameters for the Incapacitation Model According to Estimates from the Reanalysis

Parameter	Symbol	Predicted Offense Rate			Total
		Low	Medium	High	
Number of offenders	N	95,500	16,473	10,611	—
Average annual offense rate	λ	.9	8.1	20.8	—
Probability of arrest and conviction	q	.03	.03	.03	—
Probability of incarceration given conviction	J	.86	.86	.86	—
Probability of prison given incarceration	p	.12	.27	.46	—
Average jail term in years	s	1.0	1.0	1.0	—
Average prison term in years	S	3.892	4.692	4.075	—
Average time served in years	$\bar{S}$	1.347	1.997	2.415	—
Incarcerated population	R	2,865	4,942	5,942	13,749
Fraction of time free	η	.97	.70	.44	—
Total crime	C	83,372	93,402	97,112	273,886

APPENDIX B: DESCRIPTION OF QUESTIONS USED TO CONSTRUCT THE SEVEN VARIABLES

The following information provides an overview of how the seven variables selected for the scale used in the Greenwood report were constructed. All variables are coded either 1 (yes) or 0 (no or missing). Short variable labels are used in the following descriptions.

1. *Prior Conviction*

Official records for most prison inmates contained information on the number of past convictions for several crime types. This variable was coded 0 if a convicted robber (or burglar) had no prior convictions in his record for robbery (or burglary) and 1 if one or more of the defining convictions were in his record.

2. *Incarcerated Before Arrest*

A question on the survey asked inmates to indicate the months that they were in jail or in prison on their calendars. The percentage of possible "street time" spent imprisoned was calculated, and inmates with more than 50 percent were coded 1. (Greenwood used Rand's minimum estimate of street months for his calculations; thus, more inmates were coded 1 for this variable in his analysis than in the reanalysis.)

3. *Convicted Before Age 16*

The survey asked, "How old were you when you were first convicted of a criminal offense (an adult or juvenile conviction, other than a traffic violation)?" Inmates who reported a first conviction at age 15 or younger were coded 1.

4. *Juvenile Incarceration*

The survey asked, "Were you ever sent to a *statewide* or *federal* juvenile institution?" Inmates who responded "yes" were coded 1.

5. *Recent Drug Use*

The survey asked, "During the months when you were using drugs, how often would you say you usually used each of the drugs listed below?" The drug types were: heroin/methadone, barbiturates/downers/"reds," and amphetamines/uppers/"whites"; the response categories were: did not use at all, few times a month, few times a week, every day, or more than once a day. This variable was coded 1 if inmates responded that they used heroin or barbiturates at all.

6. *Juvenile Drug Use*

The survey asked about drug use of the following types before age 18: marijuana, LSD/psychedelics/cocaine, uppers/downers, heroin; frequency levels were: often, sometimes, just once or twice, never. According to Greenwood's definition only the uppers/downers and heroin responses are relevant, but Rand's computer code indicates that the LSD/psychedelics/cocaine category was also included. In the reanalysis this variable was coded as "yes" if inmates used heroin or uppers/downers either sometimes or often as juveniles, and "no" otherwise.

7. *Unemployed Before Arrest*

The survey asked, "During how many of the street months on the calendar did you work?" The percentage of street months spent working was calculated, and inmates who worked *less* than 50 percent of the time were coded 1.

APPENDIX C: CALCULATION OF POTENTIAL INCAPACITATIVE EFFECTS USING DATA REPORTED BY GREENWOOD

Greenwood (1982:74) found the maximum incapacitative effects using the following hypothetical policy: "low- and medium-rate offenders are sentenced to jail and high-rate offenders are sentenced to prison for terms of increasing length." He also states that "none of . . . the sentence lengths for high-rate offenders [is] increased by more than a factor of 2" (p. 79). This means that the end point in his graph (Figure 5.1) represents an expected sentence length of 8.43 years (twice the 50.6 months reported in Table 5.1, p. 77).

Using this information and the data in Table 5.1, the maximum incapacitative effect for a sentencing policy that assumes 1-year jail terms for low- and medium-rate offenders and 8.43 years in prison for high-rate robbers can be calculated as follows:

	Low	Medium	High	Total
Number of Offenders[a]	49,714	11,895	9,028	
"Time Free"[b] (η)	.95	.79	.13	—
Incarcerated Population[c] (R)	2,486	2,498	7,854	12,838
Total Crime[d] (C)	94,457	94,910	36,148	225,515

[a]These estimates are reported in Greenwood (p. 77) with the exception of the low-rate offender estimate, which was corrected by Cohen and confirmed by Abrahamse (1984, personal communication).

[b]Using equation for η reported in Greenwood (p. 75):

$$\eta_L = 1/[1 + (2.0)(0.03)(0.86)(1)] = 0.95$$
$$\eta_M = 1/[1 + (10.1)(0.03)(0.86)(1)] = 0.79$$
$$\eta_H = 1/[1 + (30.8)(0.03)(0.86)(8.43)] = 0.13$$

[c]Using equation for R_i reported in Greenwood (p. 75):

$$R_L = 49{,}714(1 - 0.95)$$
$$R_M = 11{,}895(1 - 0.79)$$
$$R_H = 9{,}028(1 - 0.13)$$

[d]Using equation for C_i reported in Greenwood (p. 75):

$$C_L = 49{,}714(0.95)(2.0)$$
$$C_M = 11{,}895(0.79)(10.1)$$
$$C_H = 9{,}028(0.13)(30.8)$$

Under the current sentencing policy, the estimated incarcerated population is 13,930 (Table 5.1, p. 77) and the estimated number of robberies is 259,917 (corrected figure; Abrahamse, 1984, personal communication).

Percent decrease in incarceration:
$1 - (12{,}838/13{,}930) = 8$ percent
Percent decrease in robbery:
$1 - (225{,}515/259{,}917) = 13$ percent

REFERENCES

Avi-Itzhak, B., and Shinnar, J.
1973 Quantitative models in crime control. *Journal of Criminal Justice* 1:185–217.

Blackmore, J., and Welsh, J.
1983 Selective incapacitation: sentencing accord-

ing to risk. *Crime and Delinquency* 29(October):504–528.

Blumstein, A.

1983 Selective incapacitation as a means of crime control. *American Behavioral Scientist* 27(1):87–108.

Blumstein, A., and Cohen, J.

1979 Estimation of individual crime rates from arrest records. *Journal of Criminal Law and Criminology* 70(4):561–585.

Blumstein, A., Cohen, J., and Hsieh, P.

1982 The Duration of Adult Criminal Careers. Unpublished final report for the National Institute of Justice. Grant No. 79 NI-AX-0099. Urban Systems Institute, Carnegie-Mellon University.

Blumstein, A., Farrington, D., and Moitra, S.

1985 Delinquency careers: innocents, desisters, and persisters. Pp. 187–200 in M. Tonry and N. Morris, eds., *Crime and Justice: An Annual Review of Research, Volume 6*. Chicago, Ill.: University of Chicago Press.

Chaiken, J., and Chaiken, M.

1982a *Varieties of Criminal Behavior*. Prepared for the National Institute of Justice, U.S. Department of Justice. Report R-2814-NIJ. Santa Monica, Calif.: Rand Corporation.

Chaiken, J., and Chaiken, M., with Peterson, J.

1982b *Varieties of Criminal Behavior: Summary and Policy Implications*. Prepared for the National Institute of Justice, U.S. Department of Justice. Report R-2814/1-1015. Santa Monica, Calif.: Rand Corporation.

Chaiken, M., and Chaiken, J.

1984 Offender types and public policy. *Crime and Delinquency* 30(2):195–226.

Cohen, J.

1978 The incapacitative effect of imprisonment: a critical review of the literature. Pp. 187–243 in A. Blumstein, J. Cohen, and D. Nagin, eds., *Deterrence and Incapacitation: Estimating the Effects of Criminal Sanctions on Crime Rates*. National Research Council. Washington, D.C.: National Academy Press.

1983 Incapacitation as a strategy for crime control: possibilities and pitfalls. Pp. 1–84 in M. Tonry and N. Morris, eds., *Crime and Justice: An Annual Review of Research, Volume 5*. Chicago, Ill.: University of Chicago Press.

1984a Career Length and the Selective Incapacitation Model. Paper presented at the 1984 annual meeting of the American Society of Criminology, November, Cincinnati, Ohio.

1984b Selective incapacitation: an assessment. *Illinois Law Review* 1984(2):253–290.

Dershowitz, A.

1973 Preventive confinement: a suggested framework for constitutional analysis. *Texas Law Review* 51:1277–1324.

1974 The origins of preventive confinement in Anglo-American law. Part I: the English experience. *University of Cincinnati Law Review* 43:1–60.

Ebener, P.

1983 *Codebook for Self-Report Data from the 1978 Rand Survey of Prison and Jail Inmates*. Prepared for the National Institute of Justice, U.S. Department of Justice. Report N-2016-NIJ. Santa Monica, Calif.: Rand Corporation.

Farrington, D.

1973 Self-reports of deviant behavior: predictive and stable? *Journal of Criminal Law and Criminology* 64:99–110.

Farrington, D., and Tarling, R., eds.

1985 *Prediction in Criminology*. Albany, N.Y.: SUNY Press.

Floud, J., and Young, W.

1981 *Dangerousness and Criminal Justice*. London: Heinemann Educational Books.

Gold, M.

1966 Undetected delinquent behavior. *Journal of Research in Crime and Delinquency* 13:27–46.

Gottfredson, M., and Gottfredson, D.

1980 *Decisionmaking in Criminal Justice: Toward the Rational Exercise of Discretion*. Cambridge, Mass.: Ballinger.

Greenberg, D.

1975 The incapacitative effect of imprisonment: some estimates. *Law and Society Review* 9:541–580.

Greenwood, P., with Abrahamse, A.

1982 *Selective Incapacitation*. Report prepared for the National Institute of Justice, U.S. Department of Justice. Report R-2815-NIJ. Santa Monica, Calif.: Rand Corporation.

Hinton, J., ed.

1982 *Dangerousness: Problems of Assessment and Prediction*. London: Allen and Unwin.

Loeber, R., and Dishion, T.

1983 Early predictors of male delinquency: a review. *Psychological Bulletin* 94:68–99.

Marquis, K., with Ebener, P.

1981 *Quality of Prisoner Self-reports: Arrest and Conviction Response Errors*. Prepared for the National Institute of Justice, U.S. Department of Justice. Report R-2637-DOJ. Santa Monica, Calif.: Rand Corporation.

Monahan, J.

1981 *Predicting Violent Behavior: An Assessment of Clinical Techniques*. Beverly Hills, Calif.: Sage Publications.

Moore, M., Estrich, S., McGillis, D., and Spelman, W.

1984 *Dangerous Offenders: The Elusive Target of*

Justice. Cambridge, Mass.: Harvard University Press.

Morris, N., and Miller, M.
1985 *Predictions of Dangerousness*. Pp. 1–50 in M. Tonry and N. Morris, eds., *Crime and Justice: An Annual Review of Research, Volume 6*. Chicago, Ill.: University of Chicago Press.

Petersilia, J., and Honig, P., with Hubay, C.
1980 *The Prison Experience of Career Criminals*. Prepared for the National Institute of Justice, U.S. Department of Justice. Report R-2511-DOJ. Santa Monica, Calif.: Rand Corporation.

Petersilia, J., Greenwood, P., and Lavin, M.
1977 *Criminal Careers of Habitual Felons*. Report R-2144-DOJ. Santa Monica, Calif.: Rand Corporation.

Peterson, M., and Braiker, H., with Polich, S.
1981 *Who Commits Crime?* Cambridge, Mass.: Oelgeschlager, Gunn and Hain Publishers.

Peterson, M., Chaiken, J., Ebener, P., and Honig, P.
1982 *Survey of Prison and Jail Inmates: Background and Method*. Prepared for the National Institute of Justice, U.S. Department of Justice. Report N-1635-NIJ. Santa Monica, Calif.: Rand Corporation.

Reiss, A.
1973 Surveys of Self-Reported Delicts. Unpublished paper. Yale University, New Haven, Conn.

Rolph, J., Chaiken, J., and Houchens, R.
1981 *Methods for Estimating Crime Rates of Individuals*. Prepared for the National Institute of Justice, U.S. Department of Justice. Report R-2730-NIJ. Santa Monica, Calif.: Rand Corporation.

Shinnar, R., and Shinnar, S.
1975 The effect of the criminal justice system on the control of crime: a quantitative approach. *Law and Society Review* 9:581–611.

Spelman, B.
1984 A Sensitivity Analysis of the Rand Inmate Surveys. Paper presented at the 1984 annual meeting of the American Society of Criminology, November, Cincinnati, Ohio.

von Hirsch, A.
1976 *Doing Justice: The Choice of Punishments*. New York: Hill and Wang.
1981 Desert and previous convictions in sentencing. *Minnesota Law Review* 65(4):591–634.
1984 The ethics of selective incapacitation: observations on the contemporary debate. *Crime and Delinquency* 30(2):175–194.

von Hirsch, A., and Gottfredson, D.
1984 Selective incapacitation: some queries on research design and equity. *New York University Review of Law and Social Change* 12(1):11–51.

Wyner, G.
1980 Response errors in self-reported number of arrests. *Sociological Methods and Research* 9(3):161–177.

6

Accuracy of Prediction Models

Stephen D. Gottfredson and Don M. Gottfredson

Any decision made under uncertainty with respect to future events, behaviors, activities, resources, trends, demands, or outcomes is a predictive one. If the goal of the decision being made is utilitarian, prediction certainly is critical to the decision-making process. Accordingly, the concept of prediction is central to traditional crime-reduction or crime-preventive concerns of the criminal justice system, such as deterrence, incapacitation, and rehabilitation (S. D. Gottfredson and D. M. Gottfredson, 1985). Prediction is implicit in the decisions made but rarely is that explicitly recognized. It is quite possible, however, to characterize the American criminal justice system as a network of interrelated decision points (M. R. Gottfredson and D. M. Gottfredson, 1980b); when this is done, the ubiquity of prediction to most of the decisions encountered is made clear.

This paper concerns the *accuracy* of prediction in criminal justice settings and the utility of statistically developed decision-making tools intended for practical implementation. We have been forced to limit our review in several ways. First, our principal focus is the prediction of criminal or delinquent behavior. Thus, we do not address a variety of important criminal justice prediction problems involving resource allocation, criminal population projections, estimation of rates of offending and the length of criminal careers, and many others, except as they are relevant to assessing the impacts of some proposed decision-making devices (e.g., those proposed for selective incapacitation strategies).

Second, we omit detailed discussion of work concerning the psychological or psychiatric assessment of offenders, even though much of this clearly is of a predictive nature. We also give less attention to predicting the behavior of criminal justice system functionaries (e.g., judges, prosecutors, parole board members) than to predicting the behavior of offenders. Since the accuracy of prediction models cannot responsibly be assessed in a vac-

Stephen D. Gottfredson is executive director, Maryland Criminal Justice Coordinating Council, Baltimore, Md., and Don M. Gottfredson is professor, School of Criminal Justice, Rutgers University.

uum, however, some attention to the behavior of functionaries is necessary.

Detailed critical reviews concerning several distinct and important issues have been published recently. Given the ready availability of this information, we do not give detailed attention to the prediction of violence (reviewed by Monahan, 1978, 1981; Monahan and Klassen, 1982), to longitudinal studies bearing on prediction issues (reviewed by Farrington, 1979, 1982), or to the prediction of sentencing decisions (reviews are available in Hagan, 1974; L. Cohen and Kluegel, 1978; Garber, Klepper, and Nagin, 1983; Hagan and Bumiller, 1983; Klepper, Nagin, and Tierney, 1983).

Because insufficient information is available to allow reliable generalizations, we ignore the areas of policing and corrections, although the nature of decisions made in these settings often clearly is predictive. Our focus is on bail and pretrial release decision studies and on decisions involving prosecution, sentencing (although as noted above, we do not provide a detailed review of these), and parole. We give attention to efforts designed to provide advice, based on scientific principles of assessment and prediction, to those confronted daily with the variety of decision-making tasks considered.

In the first section of this paper we discuss the nature of decisions generally, and in criminal justice settings in particular. Because the accuracy of predictive decision making is of concern, we discuss some of the issues involved in such assessments. In the next section we discuss both descriptive and (where appropriate) normative prediction studies for each of the decision arenas under consideration. Special attention is given to items of information commonly observed to be predictive, the general level of accuracy of these (both in the bivariate case and when considered in conjunction with other predictors), and the general level of predictive accuracy achieved in equations or models of the decisions under consideration. Then, we summarize the preceding discussion by focusing on predictors commonly observed across the decision arenas studied. We provide a summary of those variables found to predict the decisions of functionaries and those found to predict the behavior of offenders and show how they differ. Next, for each of the decision arenas considered, we examine the efficacy of statistically developed decision-making tools that are in use, or have been proposed for use, in a number of jurisdictions. Finally, we discuss ways to improve the accuracy—and hence the utility—of prediction tools designed for application in criminal justice settings.

PREDICTIVE DECISION MAKING

The Logic of Prediction

Any decision has three components: a goal, the existence of alternatives, and information upon which the decision may be based (M. R. Gottfredson and D. M. Gottfredson, 1980b). Decisions cannot rationally be made (or studied) if decision-making goals are unstated or unclear. Unfortunately, goals for criminal justice decisions rarely are explicitly stated, and often they are complex. Rarely is a single goal for a decision given.[1] Without alternatives, there can be no decision problem; and without information on which to base the decision, the "problem" reduces to reliance on chance. As we shall see, decision makers often are not sufficiently attentive to the relation of information used to the goal desired, which results in decisions being made that would have been better left to chance.

---

[1]See D. M. Gottfredson and Stecher (1979) for an example within the context of sentencing.

It is in the relation of information used to the goal desired that prediction studies are of most value to the criminal justice decision maker. If decision makers desire to minimize errors in the decision process, prediction studies also are to be desired, for it is this that they are designed to accomplish. In brief, prediction simply refers to the utilization of informational items, singly or in combination, to estimate the probable future occurrence of some event or behavior (known as the criterion). Methods of using the informational items (known as independent or predictor variables) may be intuitive, clinical, or subjective, or they may be statistical or "actuarial." If of the latter type, any of a wide variety of approaches may be used. The specification of these is beyond the scope of this paper, but we assume the reader has some familiarity with the more common methods.[2]

The Nature of Decisions

Decisions involve choice, because of the requirement that alternatives be available. Much of psychology, economics, and philosophy concerns the study of choices that people make. What determines the amount of money one will pay this fall for a house? What is responsible for the selection of a Labrador retriever over a Chihuahua as a family pet? Why does one (generally) obey the law? What is the role of unconscious motivation, of altruism, of superstition, of morality, or of value in the choices made? Clearly, detailed discussion of the nature of human choice behavior is beyond the scope of this paper. We do, however, briefly consider decision-making study that has as a premise the notion that human decision makers value rationality (for a delightful discussion of rationality in decision making, see Lee, 1971). Following Lee, decision theory considers the rational person to be one who, when confronted with choice, makes the decision that is "best"; this decision is the optimal or rational one. This decision (1) must be one of those available, (2) will depend on the decision principles under study (thus, different studies, proceeding from different bases, may identify different optimal choices), (3) may differ among persons (e.g., due to differing utilities assigned to alternatives, differing subjective probability estimates), but (4) must depend on the information available to the decision maker.

Behavioral decision theory (Edwards, 1954, 1961; Becker and McClintock, 1967; Rapoport and Wallsten, 1972; Slovic, Fischoff, and Lichtenstein, 1977; R. M. Hogarth, 1980; Einhorn and Hogarth, 1981; Pitz and Sachs, 1984), "cognitive algebra" (Anderson, 1968, 1974, 1979), utility theories (Lee, 1971:Chapter 5), and "game theories" and their assessments of strategies (e.g., minimax and maximin principles) (von Neumann and Morgenstern, 1947; Luce and Raiffa, 1957; Lee, 1971) are examples of general considerations of ways in which one may model the choice or decision behavior of the rational person (Lee, 1971, and R. M. Hogarth, 1980, review much of this vast literature).

We note this literature to make two points. First, there is a distinction to be drawn between normative and descriptive decision studies (Lee, 1971). Normative studies concern the decisions that people should make in a choice situation, regardless of the decisions that they actually make. Descriptive studies concern the decisions actually made, regardless of those that should be made. This distinction, although clear, may become blurred in practice, particularly when the goal is to improve rational decision making. We

[2]For general discussions of the logic of prediction, see Sarbin (1943), Gough (1962), and D. M. Gottfredson (1967).

believe that studies of both sorts may be of considerable value and, accordingly, we report on both in the sections that follow.

The second point to be raised is that very often human decision makers do not appear to behave optimally, regardless of the particular strategies under study. We elaborate on this point later; here, we simply suggest that for this reason we believe the provision of decision-making tools for criminal justice applications is necessary and desirable.[3]

Francis Bacon observed: "We do ill to exalt the powers of the human mind, when we should seek out its proper helps" (quoted in R. M. Hogarth, 1980). Indeed, in most decision-making situations, it has been found that actuarially developed predictions outperform human judgments. This is true with respect to psychiatric judgments (e.g., Meehl, 1954; Gough, 1962; Ennis and Litwack, 1974); graduate school admissions (e.g., Dawes and Corrigan, 1974; Dawes, 1979); and in other areas (Goldberg, 1970). Later, we review results of these and other studies and suggest how human judgments and actuarial predictions can profitably be used together; here, suffice it to say that normative decision studies appear to have the potential to improve decisions made in criminal justice settings significantly. Although we do "exalt the powers of the human mind," we also believe in attempts to provide it with "proper helps."

Problems of Measuring "Accuracy"

An obvious question to be asked when considering predictive information is "how good is it?" The answer is "it depends." The predictive accuracy of information is a function of many things: among the more salient are the reliabilities of the items of information used, the method(s) used to combine items of information, the reliability of the criterion variable chosen, the kinds of measurements used, the base rate, the selection ratio used, and the representativeness of samples employed. Two questions should be addressed: one considers the accuracy of individual items of information; the other refers to the accuracy of items in combination with one another. Our discussion requires that we first outline the nature of the issues already raised.

Reliability

Reliability refers essentially to the stability with which measurements may be made, and statistical validity—here imprecisely considered as "accuracy"—is constrained by the reliability with which both criterion and predictor measurements are made. No prediction device can be better than the data from which it is constructed. Often, attention is given to the reliabilities of the predictor items but the reliability of the criterion is neglected.[4]

Methods of Combining Information

Many statistical methods have been used in criminological prediction studies, including the simple inspection of cross-classification tables (e.g., Warner, 1923), multiple regression (e.g., D. M. Gottfredson and Bonds, 1961; D. M. Gottfredson, Wilkins, and Hoffman, 1978), multiple discriminant-function analysis (e.g., Brown,

---

[3]There are other reasons also, such as the desirability of making the decision process explicit. See M. R. Gottfredson and D. M. Gottfredson (1980b) for discussion of these.

[4]One would be wise to view measurements of a table with skepticism if the yardstick used is made of rubber elastic. The careful investigator would want to ensure as well that the table is not elastic.

1978),[5] multidimensional contingency-table analysis (e.g., Solomon, 1976; van Alstyne and Gottfredson, 1978), tobit analysis (e.g., Palmer and Carlson, 1976), and a variety of clustering approaches (e.g., Ballard and Gottfredson, 1963; D. M. Gottfredson, Ballard, and Lane, 1963; Fildes and Gottfredson, 1968).[6] For a variety of statistical and practical reasons, one or another approach may be preferred, and the technique used theoretically could have dramatic consequences for the accuracy of resultant prediction devices. In criminal justice applications this potential unfortunately remains largely theoretical. Several researchers have attempted to demonstrate the relative utility of different statistical approaches to criminal justice prediction problems (e.g., D. M. Gottfredson and Ballard, 1964a; Babst, Gottfredson, and Ballard, 1968; Simon, 1971, 1972; Wilbanks and Hindelang, 1972; Farrington, 1978), and the potential advantages of different approaches have been discussed by Wilkins and MacNaughton-Smith (1964; see also Simon, 1971; S. D. Gottfredson and D. M. Gottfredson, 1979, 1980). S. D. Gottfredson and D. M. Gottfredson (1979, 1980) compared the relative utility of six of the more commonly used or promising methods, concluding (as did the other studies cited) that "no clear-cut empirical advantage in prediction is provided by one or another method" (1979:63). Reasons for this disappointing observation have been suggested by Farrington (1978), S. D. Gottfredson and D. M. Gottfredson (1979), and Loeber and Dishion (1983). In addition to serious problems of criterion measurement, problems of the reliability of predictor information and the consequences of this for certain of the methods (particularly least-squares methods; see Wainer, 1976) especially are deserving of mention.

Meehl (1954) and Gough (1962) provide good reviews of specific actuarial methods that have been used widely in the behavioral sciences generally, often with reference to problems and application in criminal justice system settings. Mannheim and Wilkins (1955), Simon (1971, 1972), and S. D. Gottfredson and D. M. Gottfredson (1979) have provided reviews of methods typically used in criminology.

The Base Rate

The base rate for any given event is defined as the relative frequency of occurrence of that event in the population of interest.[7] Typically, base rates are expressed as proportions or percentages. In many criminal justice applications, which traditionally have treated criterion measures as dichotomous, the base rate is found simply through inspection of the appropriate marginal distribution of the expectancy table.

The difficulty of predicting events of interest increases as the base rate differs from .50 (Meehl and Rosen, 1955). Thus, the more frequent or infrequent an event, the greater the likelihood of inaccurate prediction. (While this seems intuitively true for rare events, it must be remembered that the occurrence of very frequent events requires the simultaneous occurrence of very rare events—unless the probability of an event is precisely 0 or 1.) As an example of the difficulty of such prediction, suppose that the base rate for failure on parole is .20. Given this information alone, one would make cor-

[5]It should be noted, however, that when the criterion measure is dichotomous, as in the example cited, Fisher's discriminant function is equivalent (within a transformation) to the multiple regression approach; see Porebski (1966).

[6]For discussions of clinical methods of combining items of information, see Gough (1962) or Monahan (1981).

[7]This discussion is adapted from S. D. Gottfredson and D. M. Gottfredson (1979).

rect predictions 80 percent of the time if one simply predicted that no one will fail on parole. One would also, of course, be wrong 20 percent of the time. (Note that given only the base rate as a guide, there is no way of estimating which 20 percent will fail.)

Now assume that a predictive device has been developed that allows one to predict parole outcomes with 78 percent accuracy. Even given this apparently powerful device, one would still be better off in expecting that no one will fail on parole—that is, in "predicting" performance on the basis of the base rate alone. Although the predictive device does beat a naive chance rate (50 percent), the true chance rate is considerably higher, and in fact is greater than the power of the predictive device.

Those concerned with the development of predictive tools for use in criminal justice applications (and in other areas) often have failed to consider base rates in the development process and, consequently, have made classifications or predictions based on criteria that produce larger errors than would the simple use of the base rate. In 1955 Meehl and Rosen summarized the consequences of failure to consider base rates and concluded that then-contemporary research reporting neglected the base rate, making evaluation of utility difficult, if not impossible. Although Reiss (1951c) clearly and dramatically illustrated this point more than 30 years ago in a classic review of Glueck and Glueck's *Unraveling Juvenile Delinquency* (1950; see also Hirschi and Selvin, 1967), failure to consider base rates remains an unfortunately common practice (but such studies are now found rarely in the published literature).

Selection Ratios

The selection ratio is simply the proportion of individuals or events studied and identified by the prediction method as belonging to the criterion classification of interest. In delinquency studies, for example, the selection ratio is the proportion of persons studied and selected as expected delinquents by means of some prediction instrument (see Loeber and Dishion, 1983, for a discussion). Thus, the base rate provides one marginal distribution for an expectancy table, and the selection ratio (essentially) provides the other; together, the marginal distributions determine the chance expectancies for the table. Selection ratios may be altered through manipulation of the cutting score, which has obvious but sometimes unrecognized consequences for prediction (Cronbach, 1960). These may be particularly dramatic if the bivariate distribution is heteroskedastic (J. Fisher, 1959).

Representativeness of Samples

If accuracy of prediction is desired, samples used in constructing selection devices must be representative of the population on which the device is intended to be used.[8] This ensures that the appropriate base rate is considered and minimizes subsequent shrinkage of power from the construction to the operational samples.

The adage that no two people are exactly alike properly is extended to groups: no two groups of people are identical.[9] If, however, the groups have been selected by some appropriate mechanism (such as random sampling), they can be expected to have a great deal in common in terms of both their overall characteristics and the interrelations of various individual characteristics. It is this similarity of relations within different groups of people on

---

[8]Note that this is not the same as saying that the sample must be representative of the population as a whole.

[9]Portions of this discussion are adapted from S. D. Gottfredson and D. M. Gottfredson (1979).

which all statistical predictions ultimately rely. If in one group of subjects the young do better in relation to some outcome, it can be assumed that in a similar group of subjects the young again will do better. Prediction methods are intended to estimate, on the basis of some group of people available for study, how members of other similar groups will behave. There is a danger, however, of overestimating the extent to which relations found in one sample can be used to explain relations in a similar sample. Within the original sample alone, there is no adequate way to distinguish how much of the observed relation is due to characteristics and underlying associations that will be shared by new samples and how much is due to unique characteristics of the first sample. This is because the apparent power of a prediction device developed on a sample of observations derives from two sources: the detection and estimation of underlying relations likely to be observed in any similar sample of subjects and the peculiar or individual properties of the specific sample on which the device has been created. Cross-validation is important in estimating the relative importance of these two sources of predictive power. This is particularly advisable when the prediction study is intended for practical application in new samples. If not done, the utility of the instrument as a predictor in new samples is likely to be overestimated.

Cross-Validation

Cross-validation is simply an empirical approach to the problem of obtaining an unbiased estimate of the accuracy of prediction (whether based on a single item of information or on some combination of items). Typically, this is accomplished by dividing the sample at hand in two, constructing the device on one, and using the other to estimate predictive accuracy. Horst (1966) refers to this general procedure as the "sample fractionation" approach and argues, quite correctly, that there are serious disadvantages to it. First, the stability of estimates is dependent on the number of cases on which they are made. Thus, dividing the sample reduces the reliability of the device constructed, which, as already noted, may reduce validity. Second, the approach gives only one estimate (from a potentially large universe of estimates). In effect, one regards coefficients that result from cross-validation as an estimate of the average expected validity in independent samples and expects those validities to be normally distributed. Accordingly, one is as likely to underestimate as overestimate true validity, but a single sample offers weak empirical evidence of shrinkage (Horst, 1966).

There appears to be no "best" answer to the cross-validation problem; rather, a trade-off of concerns is raised. Sample fractionation procedures do constrain validity (unless the sample obtained is very large, which is unusual in criminal justice research). A single estimate of shrinkage is not optimal, is unlikely to represent the actual mean validity, and is as likely to underestimate as overestimate that value. As noted by Horst, one can obtain two estimates by examining expected validities from each sample on the other (in the traditional fractionation approach), but one is then left with deciding which of the devices actually to use. Similarly, one could further fractionate the sample and develop several empirical estimates. Again, however, one encounters problems of reliability as the sample size decreases. To meliorate this, one could recombine the subsamples and create a device on the full sample, relying on the subsample estimators to provide an index of shrinkage (see Horst, 1966:380). It seems likely, however, that the validity of the device developed in this fashion will be underestimated (perhaps seriously) given that the samples from which validity is estimated are much smaller than is the sample on which the final device is constructed.

Some argue for a "longitudinal" validation approach (e.g., Horst, 1963, 1966) in which one develops a device on the largest sample available and applies the device in operational use. Validity is assessed over time, and research is integrated into the administrative process. It seems to us that the central issue has to do with (1) the types of decisions to be made on the basis of a predictive device and (2) the expected validities of the devices used. For certain relatively benign applications, when expected validities may be relatively high, we would not object to such a procedure. When the decisions to be made involve consequences of liberty, however, and when expected validities are low (as commonly is the case in criminal justice applications), we would object. Wright, Clear, and Dickson (1984) recently illustrated that the consequences (in terms of reduced validities) of the wholesale adoption in several jurisdictions of devices developed in one locale can be dramatic.

Measures of Predictive Accuracy

The issues considered so far can affect the accuracy of a predictive device, but we have not yet considered how best to assess that accuracy. This section focuses on such a consideration.

In selection applications, predictive devices reduce to a dichotomy resulting in a decision situation, with actual outcomes considered, that can be represented by a 2 × 2 contingency table (Figure 1). The cutting score decided on determines the selection ratio and the marginal distribution of the columns in Figure 1. The base rate determines the marginal distribution of the rows. Together, these determine the distribution of cases within the table, subject to one degree of freedom. They also determine the distribution of cases within the table to be expected by chance. Although statistics such as χ^2 are useful in assessing independence in tables such as this, the value of χ^2 is a function of the dimensionality of the table and the number of cases considered, as well as of the relation beyond that expected by chance. Further, χ^2 is used to assess statistical significance; directly, it tells the investigator nothing about the magnitude of the effect discovered. It gives an assessment of "accuracy" to the extent that the investigator may be confident of the reliability of the effect

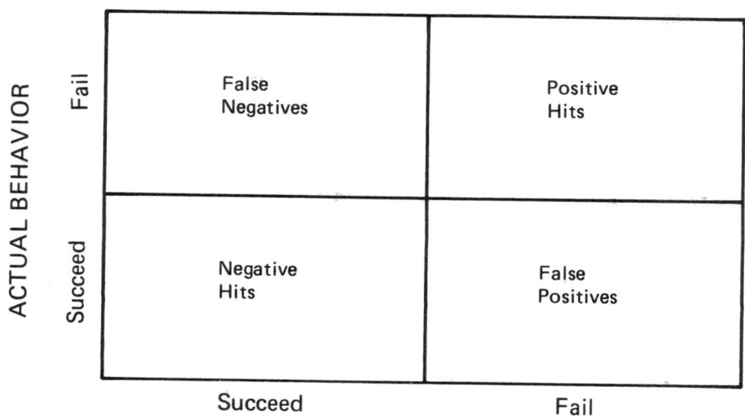

FIGURE 1 The selection decision problem.

discovered, but it does not depict the degree of relation associated with that effect. A variety of statistics are available to help in this assessment (e.g., the contingency coefficient or Cramer's V; see Hays, 1963:604–606), but none completely overcomes the dimensionality problem.

The use of ϕ (phi coefficient) (Hays, 1963:604) is meliorative when used for tables with one degree of freedom. Since the practical application of predictive tools for selection purposes often reduces to such a table, ϕ (which is simply $\sqrt{\chi^2/N}$) would appear to be an attractive choice for an index of predictive efficiency. The marginal distributions of a table with only one degree of freedom, however, constrain ϕ by imposing an upper limit on the possible relation observed in the table (Guilford, 1965).[10] Moreover, ϕ is subject to a limitation common to correlational measures: it is sensitive to the base rate.

As noted by Richardson (1950), the standard error of prediction provides an immediate, but incomplete and potentially misleading, answer to the question of the predictive value of a selection device. This statistic is given by:

$$\sigma_y \sqrt{1 - r^2},$$

where σ_y is the standard deviation of the criterion measure. As we have noted, most selection applications of predictive devices use some cutting score, essentially reducing the predictor scale to a dichotomy. As commonly used, however, the standard error of prediction assesses the predictive device and the criterion measured continuously and may, in fact, result in an underestimation of the power of the selection device, since the device as used simply is predictive of success or failure. The standard error of prediction, however, is a function also of degrees of success or failure; that is, it requires an assessment of just how good a success, or how bad a failure, an individual is (Richardson, 1950). Further, the standard error of prediction also is sensitive to variations in the base rate and, hence, may be of little value in assessing the relative merits of devices used on different populations.

A number of indices are intended to provide an estimate of the "proportionate reduction in error" resulting from use of some selection or predictive device. In general, these indices are designed to offer an evaluation of predictive power above that afforded by simple use of the chance rate. Ohlin and Duncan (1949), among the first to give practical attention to the problem in the criminal justice field, suggested an "index of predictive efficiency" (see also Horst, 1941; Reiss, 1951a; Goodman, 1953a, b; McCord, 1980; Loeber and Dishion, 1983), which is defined simply as the percentage reduction in error gained by use of a predictive device over that achieved by knowledge of the base rate alone.

The index of predictive efficiency also has the limitation of sensitivity to the base rate. Thus, it has little utility for the examination of accuracy across different situations.

Considering specifically cases such as that diagrammed in Figure 1 (in which one essentially wishes to predict membership in one or the other of two mutually exclusive categories), Berkson (1947) noted that there are utilities, defined as true positives and negatives, as well as costs, defined as false positives and negatives, associated with the decision made. Arguing that predictive devices should be evaluated with respect to a comparison of costs and utilities, he developed an index of effectiveness (which may be used at any utility) called "mean cost" and defined the "mean cost rating" (MCR) to allow the index to vary from 0 to 1. The MCR is less sensitive to the base

[10] This does not appear to be true for the point-biserial, as commonly applied to 2 × k tables (B. F. Green, Jr., personal communication, 1979).

rate than is ϕ or the point-biserial coefficients. The index was introduced to criminologists by Duncan et al. (1952), and it has seen widespread use since as a measure of the predictive efficiency of a selection device. It recently was shown that the MCR is related to Kendall's tau, providing a method of testing the statistical significance of the index (Lancucki and Tarling, 1978); and Fergusson, Fifield, and Slater (1977) have shown the relation between the MCR and the familiar proportion of area under a receiver operating characteristic (ROC) curve, which provides a grounding for the index in the framework of signal detection theory (Green and Swets, 1966).

For the two-by-two decision case (which represents the "fairest" test of a predictive device as used in selection decisions), Loeber and Dishion (1983) developed an index called the RIOC (relative improvement over chance), which considers chance occurrence within the table as well as the maximum correct value that prediction could achieve given applicable selection-ratio and base-rate conditions. Since this statistic is more recent than others described and less common in the criminal justice literature, we describe it further.

The RIOC is defined as

$$\text{RIOC} = \frac{\%\text{IOC}}{\%\text{MC} - \%\text{RC}} \cdot 100,$$

where the numerator represents the percentage improvement over chance (IOC) and the denominator is the difference between the maximum percentage correct (MC) that could be achieved and the percentage required by chance (RC), both given the joint marginals observed. Although not independent of either the base rate or the selection ratio, the RIOC correlates much less highly with either than does the simple index of predictive efficiency (Loeber and Dishion, 1983).

None of the indices yet developed, however, can answer completely the question of how accurate a predictive device is. Correlational indices and indices such as the RIOC and the index of predictive efficiency suffer because they are affected by variations in the base rate. Thus, they do not readily allow a comparison of devices (or items) across base-rate conditions. The MCR does allow this, but it is not often that one wishes to evaluate a specific predictive device regardless of base-rate conditions, although this is the most common application of this index (S. D. Gottfredson and D. M. Gottfredson, 1979; Hoffman, 1983).

Measures that are sensitive to base rates and those that are not can lead to dramatically different conclusions concerning the value of predictive devices (Fergusson, Fifield, and Slater, 1977). The former (e.g., correlation measures) describe the performance of the instrument in application with given populations and decision rules; the latter (such as the MCR) essentially give an indication of the general power of the device without respect to constraints of base rates and selection ratios.

Which to use depends on the question at hand. If one seeks to evaluate the relative power of different devices developed on different populations (for which the base rates may well be different), indices that are less sensitive to base rates would seem preferable. If, however, one wishes to estimate the power of a particular device, administered with particular decision rules on a particular population, base-rate-dependent indices will be more informative.

Other Problems Concerning "Accuracy"

The practical application of predictive tools in criminal justice raises other problems related to the "accuracy" question. One almost always is attempting to construct, validate, and assess the accuracy of devices under circumstances that already have required some selection: thus, true base rates often cannot be known, nor "accuracy" assessed relative to them. One cannot, for example, know the true base rate for parole violation for all offenders considered for parole. Since not all are in fact paroled, one can at best identify the base rate for known violations by paroled inmates.

Problems exist also in the area of assessing the relative contributions of specific predictor variables to the overall accuracy of a predictive or selection device. Items that may be highly predictive under some base-rate conditions may be much less so under other base-rate conditions (this is most likely to be the case when the distribution of the predictor variable itself is skewed). Items that may prove predictive for some defined populations may be less (or more) predictive when the composition of the population is different (e.g., the item "race" may be predictive of criminal convictions in some large urban populations and not at all predictive in suburban or rural populations). Items that are predictive during some age ranges may not be predictive if other age ranges are considered. As we have pointed out elsewhere (S. D. Gottfredson and D. M. Gottfredson, 1979), such issues are meliorated if one remembers that the greatest limitation of prediction methods [is] that the devices

> . . . are developed and validated with respect to specific criteria, using available data, in a specific jurisdiction, during a specific time period. Thus, any generalizations to other outcomes of interest, or after modifications of the item definitions used, or to other jurisdictions or populations, or to other time periods, are to be questioned.

Still, the question of the "best" predictors is an important one, both for providing guidance for those who wish to construct predictive devices and for theoretical development. Several criteria of "best" could be considered: (1) most powerful (in unique contribution to prediction), (2) most stable (e.g., from population to population), (3) most readily available (e.g., age, sex), or (4) most ethically or legally defensible. In the discussion that follows, each of these will be considered. The "most powerful" criterion, however, is difficult to apply for several reasons. First, few authors have provided sufficient information to allow a comparison of the predictive efficiency of items across an adequate variety of situations. Ideally, one would like to calculate RIOCs or MCRs to assist in this evaluation; the data provided usually are insufficient for this. Second, devices constructed following a simple unweighted linear model (and there are many of these) provide no assessment of the relative value of individual items of information. Third, although devices constructed using multiple regression methods do provide information for such an assessment, studies on which these are based almost always have used a dichotomous criterion. Under such circumstances, beta weights are quite unstable (Palmer and Carlson, 1976) and cannot be relied on to provide unbiased estimates of the unique contributions of the variables considered. Other regression methods that would be meliorative (e.g., the logistic model) are not used often.

Two kinds of errors will be made in any predictive decision-making situation: some persons predicted to belong to criterion classification A in fact will not (false positives), and some persons predicted to belong to criterion classification B in fact will not (false negatives) (Figure 1). Each of the various indices discussed above considers that the two types of errors are equivalent. In practice, of course, they may not be, whether measured in monetary, social, or ethical terms. In most practical decision-making situations, and particularly those in criminal justice settings, the social, ethical, or programmatic consequences of one type of error may be dramatically different from the other. Although one typically evaluates devices without respect to this "weighting" of errors in a statistical fashion, political, ethical, and policy arguments tend not to ignore the differential consequences of the types of errors made (von Hirsch and Gottfredson, 1984). Loeber and Dishion (1983) have demonstrated that the relative evaluation of predictions made can change dramatically depending on the consequences assigned to one or the other type of error. Often recommended in personnel selection situations (Cronbach and Gleser, 1957; Rorer, Hoffman, and Hsieh, 1965; Wiggins, 1973), determining the expected utility of predictive devices based on a differential weighting of errors is common, although not in justice system settings.

RESEARCH EVIDENCE: THE POWER OF PREDICTION

Bail and Pretrial Release Decision/Prediction Studies

A number of prediction studies concerning bail and pretrial release/detention have been conducted. Given the enormous consequences of decisions made at this stage of the criminal justice process, however (see President's Commission, 1967; Goldkamp, 1979; M. R. Gottfredson and D. M. Gottfredson, 1980a,b, for discussion of these), it is somewhat surprising that more attention has not been focused on the area. Goldkamp (1979), M. R. Gottfredson and D. M. Gottfredson (1980a,b:Chapter 4), and Goldkamp and Gottfredson (1980, 1981a,b) have provided detailed reviews of most of this literature, and we draw heavily on these reviews in the discussion that follows.

Descriptive Studies

The early "bail reform" movement and subsequent legislation (e.g., as outlined by Freed and Wald, 1964; American Bar Association, 1968; Angel et al., 1971; National Advisory Commission, 1973; see also Goldkamp, 1979; M. R. Gottfredson and D. M. Gottfredson, 1980b; Goldkamp and Gottfredson, 1981a,b) focused attention on factors deemed legitimate or appropriate for consideration in bail and pretrial detention decisions. The identification and specification of these factors prompted several investigators to attempt a determination of the extent to which they actually were considered by judges making these decisions.

Bock and Frazier (1977) studied the setting of bond[11] in a six-court district in Florida. Five types of informational variables related to the defendant, recommended for consideration by the American Bar Association (ABA) and the National Advisory Commission on Criminal Justice Standards and Goals, were studied; these included the length and character of residence in the community; employment status and history and financial condition; family ties; reputation, character, and mental condition; and prior criminal record. Bock and Frazier operationally defined these rather nonspecific recommendations in several ways. In all, 18 variables reflective of the five recommendations were studied, and each recommendation was represented by at least 2 variables. Five of the variables examined (currently on probation, presence of a juvenile record, the seriousness of the first charge, defendant's appearance, and defendant's demeanor) were related significantly to the bond

[11]Operationally defined as release on personal recognizance, with bond set at less than \$500, \$500–\$4,999, and \$5,000 or more.

decision made;[12] only one of these—the seriousness of the charge—approached a magnitude suggesting that it may be of practical significance (τ_c = .37; τ_c for the remainder ranged from .12 to .21). The multivariate procedures used were not described in the report, and no overall assessment of the utility of these items of information was given. Neither race, sex, age, adult criminal record, the total number of charges, whether the defendant currently was on parole, any of seven indices of the defendant's financial and employment status or condition, nor any of four indices of the nature and quality of the defendant's ties to the local community were related statistically to the bond decision outcome. Assessments of defendants' demeanor and appearance, however, were related statistically to the disposition (τ_c = .18 and .12, respectively).

Goldkamp (1979) examined release and bail-setting practices in Philadelphia using a sequential model. More than 50 variables were available for analysis, and many of these had statistically significant zero-order relations with a release-on-recognizance criterion (see Goldkamp's Table 7–2, pp. 146–147, for examples). Only five variables, however, added at least 1 percent to the overall R^2 observed when multiple regression techniques were used. (The best equation developed, using 51 variables, resulted in an R^2 of .43; only 2 added more than 1 percent: the seriousness of the charge and the seriousness value of the most serious prior arrest.) Goldkamp demonstrated that a probable best estimate of the unique contribution of the seriousness of the charge is about 14 percent of the variance in the decision made—and that this single variable is about seven times as powerful as its nearest competitor (which has to do with the seriousness of the defendant's prior record).

The same 51 variables were used to "predict" the amount of cash bail set for those defendants for whom such a determination was made. Here, only two variables added at least one percentage point to the explanation of the amount of variation in bail required beyond that explained by the "best" predictor—whether there were weapons charges (accounting alone for 23 percent of the variance in bail amount).[13] Goldkamp was able to demonstrate that, although first-order effects were not powerful (for example, using all 51 variables only about 26 percent of the variance could be explained), the inclusion of interaction terms, particularly those involving offense characteristics, improved prediction substantially.

In a small but carefully designed and analyzed questionnaire/simulation study, Ebbesen and Konecni (1975) did observe a sizable effect for community ties on the setting of bail (respondents were 18 members of the judiciary; stimuli were contrived "robbery" cases with a variety of independent variables that were manipulated systematically), and lesser, but statistically significant, effects for prior record and for the bail recommendation made by the district attorney. No effect was observed for the defense attorney's recommendation, nor were any of the interaction terms significant. Ebbesen and Konecni followed this simulation study with a passive observational study of 106 cases actually judged by five of the subjects of the simulation study; they observed significant effects (on bail amount) for (in order of magnitude) the district attorney's recommendation, the defense attorney's recommendation, the interac-

[12] The last two measures were based on observations made by passive observers. Information concerning the reliability of the assessments is not given.

[13] These were number of transcripts (indicating extent of criminal processing) and number of prior arrests.

tion of these, the interaction of the defense attorney's recommendation and the seriousness of the charge, and the seriousness of the charge itself. By far, the district attorney's recommendation had the greatest effect. Local ties (measured on two levels) were not significantly associated with the amount of bail set. In a clever post-hoc analysis, these investigators demonstrated that the seriousness of the crime and local ties were important to the judges' decisions, but that these also were important to the district attorneys' recommendations. They posit that the judges are aware of this, and that these factors therefore indirectly (through the district attorneys' recommendations) do influence the decisions made.

In a sample limited to persons eligible for release to one of three "release programs," Bynum (1976) found that only prior record consistently related significantly to the probability that the defendants would actually be released to the programs; demographic variables and community ties were found to have little impact. Similarly, Roth and Wice's (1978) large study of some 11,000 pretrial releasees in Washington, D.C., demonstrated that charge seriousness and prior record were significantly related to judges' pretrial release decisions, but that race, sex, age, employment status, and residence were not. In multivariate analyses (with a criterion of release without financial conditions versus financial conditions), the charge and prior record remained consistently related to the decisions made, as did the judge and the capacity of the District of Columbia jail.

Goldkamp and Gottfredson (1981a,b, 1985) used a large sample (approximately 4,800 defendants appearing before the Philadelphia courts between 1977 and 1979) stratified by decision maker (20 judges) and the seriousness of the charge (six levels, ranging from misdemeanors to felonies). Following Goldkamp (1979), they developed a sequential model of the decision-making process. In essence the model treats the bail decision as a contingent, two-part process, in which "the judge first weighs whether a defendant merits outright release pending trial (ROR); if a defendant does not meet the judge's criteria for ROR, the second decision task becomes the selection of a particular amount of cash-bail" (1981b:192). Thus, the ROR decision may be treated as binary, and the cash-bail decision may be treated as a continuous variable. Logit analysis was used to study the former; multiple regression (on a logarithmic transformation of bail amount) was used to investigate the latter.

Forty-three variables that either had been shown to be related to the ROR decision in prior work or had been purported to play a role in those decisions were examined at the bivariate level and in combination (via the logit procedure). Variables considered included victim and offense characteristics, community ties, prior criminal history, and offender demographic characteristics. On the bivariate level, information concerning victim characteristics appeared largely unrelated to the ROR decision, regardless of the charge category considered (the charge category, in this case, largely reflects seriousness level). Within charge categories, other offense characteristics also appeared largely unrelated to the decision. Evidence (again, at the bivariate level) concerning community ties was mixed; some variables examined (e.g., employment, on welfare or not) appeared promising, others did not (e.g., marital status, length of present residence). Offender demographic characteristics were significantly related to the decision for some charge categories but not for others. Only sex appeared rather consistently to be related to the ROR decision regardless of the charge category considered. Finally, variables reflective of criminal history did appear to be related to the decision, and typically, this was the case regardless of the charge category considered (Goldkamp and Gottfredson, 1981b:194–195). The charge category itself, which largely reflects a seriousness weighting, strongly influenced the ROR decision. Based on examination of these bivariate relations, eight dichotomous variables and the charge classification were selected for further examination using the logit procedure.[14] These reflected race, sex, attachment, employment, arrests, pending charges, prior failures to appear, felony convictions, and charge (six categories). The final reduced model decided on considered only males[15] and heavily weighted the charge. Variables reflective of prior record were also represented in the model. Attachment and employment, although represented, were given little weight (see Goldkamp and Gottfredson:206). Apparently, the ROR decision is "based primarily on charge, secondarily on prior record, and tertiarily on community ties" (p. 205).

The model developed was found to be a significant predictor of the amount of bail set: a regression equation including (essentially) only the model of the ROR decision and a judge dummy vector accounted for about 32 percent of the variance in bail amount set. The regression equation decided on as "best" included the charge seriousness, the number of charges, the seriousness of injury, whether there was a personal victim of the crime, two criminal history variables, age, and a dummy vector for judge; it accounted for 48 percent of the criterion variance.

[14]One practical difficulty is that the dimensionality of the multidimensional cross-classification table quickly can become unmanageable and the procedure unstable as the number of empty cells increases.

[15]Other things equal, females were more likely to be granted ROR.

Normative Studies

Normative prediction studies concerning bail have been constrained by a substantial base-rate problem. As examples, failure to appear (FTA) based on officially reported rates ranged only from 4 to 24 percent in the 72 cities surveyed by Wice (1973), and almost 90 percent of the jurisdictions sampled reported FTA rates of less than 10 percent. In a survey of 20 cities that covered a several-year period, Thomas (1976) reported FTA rates of from 1 to 15 percent in 1962 (median = 6) and 3 to 17 percent for 1971 (median = 11). With respect to a recidivism criterion, Locke et al. (1970) found that 17 percent of those released pretrial in Washington, D.C., were rearrested later, and M. R. Gottfredson (1974) found that only 5 percent of those released in Los Angeles were rearrested for crimes against the person.

Besting a chance rate under these conditions has proven difficult indeed. For example, Locke et al. (1970) could not discriminate, among felony and misdemeanor offenders, those likely to fail on release based on a variety of background characteristics. Similar results were observed by Feeley and McNaughton (1974) with respect to failure to appear for trial and for rearrest while on release. Angel et al. (1971) also had little success in studying the predictive validity of the District of Columbia's preventive detention codes (in Boston). Not only was this study constrained by a low base rate, but many of the potential predictors also showed remarkably low variance (see Angel et al.:306–309). The act under study specified a number of criteria that should be taken into account in detention decisions, and Angel and colleagues operationalized them with 26 variables thought reflective of the criteria. No variable considered correlated higher than .23 with crime committed while on bail (see p.

392), and more than half (54 percent) correlated at .10 or less. Variables that correlated greater than this with bail recidivism included age at first incarceration (.23), number of prior defaults (.22), number of charges (.13), "dangerous" crimes in past 10 years[16] (.22), years of education (.12), number of misdemeanor convictions (.15), release status at time of initial arrest (.16), amount of prior incarceration (.21), number of arrests for drunkenness (.11), age at first court appearance (.16), juvenile record (.15), and "violent" crimes in the past 10 years (.14). None of the community-ties variables considered correlated better than .10 with the criterion (indeed, most of these were approximately zero). Multivariate analyses suggested that all 26 variables considered together accounted for only 13 percent of the outcome variance.[17] Although the equation results in prediction that is modestly above the base rate (indeed, as Cureton, 1957, has demonstrated, any valid continuous predictor, properly used, must provide advantage over the base rate), it is far from desirable: under assumptions of the equation, one would have to detain about 10 persons for every pretrial release crime to be prevented.

In the Los Angeles study mentioned above, M. R. Gottfredson (1974) was able to explain 16 percent of the variation in FTA rates and 21 percent of the variance in arrests on release. The study used a relatively short "release period" (90 days), however, because time on release and failure were substantially correlated (.53) (see also Clarke, Freeman, and Koch, 1976). The bulk of the power of the FTA equations derived from variables concerning the present offense or offense history; little weight was given other factors, although some "community ties" variables were predictive (e.g., employment, living arrangements, and relatives in the area). The same is true for the equation developed to predict arrest on release. When examined on a validation sample, however, the most powerful model explained only about 3 percent of the variance in outcome considered.

Clarke, Freeman, and Koch (1976) studied 756 defendants released on bail in Charlotte, N.C., in 1973, and found that

> court disposition time, defined ... as the amount of time elapsing from the defendant's release until the disposition of his case by the court (or until he fails to appear or is rearrested, if either of these occurs before disposition) must be considered the variable of greatest importance. Among the defendants studied, the likelihood of "survival"—avoidance of nonappearance or rearrest—dropped an average of five percentage points for each two weeks their cases remained open (p. 34).

Criminal history (measured in terms of prior arrests) and the form of release (e.g., cash bail, bondsman) also were significantly associated with risk on bail (considered as either failure to appear or rearrest). Offense type, seriousness (felony or misdemeanor), sex, age, race, and income were not observed to be related to the outcome. In light of the finding that form of release is associated with outcome, it would be of interest to know what determined that, but the issue was not studied by Clarke and colleagues.

Roth and Wice (1978) included a study of the predictors of failure to appear and arrests while on pretrial release in their report concerning Washington, D.C., and found information concerning offense type, employment, and drug use to be associated with the former. Those same variables (with different offense catego-

[16]These are defined with reference to the District of Columbia act and are somewhat odd. Definition of "crimes of violence" is even more peculiar; for example, burglary is included, while assault and battery is not.

[17]It is not clear whether the approach used was a discriminant function or multiple regression. Probably, it was the latter; in any event the two are functionally equivalent in this case.

ries being predictive), along with information about the use of weapons and offense history, were also associated with arrest while on release.

In the Philadelphia study described earlier, Goldkamp and Gottfredson (1981a,b) also sought to predict failure to appear and rearrests on pretrial release. Again, logit analyses were used, since the dependent variables considered were dichotomous. Examination of bivariate relations showed that, generally, those variables associated with rearrest also were related to failure to appear, but that the relations usually were not as strong for the latter. Variables related to criminal history were markedly better than those of other types in relation to the rearrest criterion; this did not appear to be as true for the FTA criterion. Community-ties variables also were related to both criterion measures, and the relations appeared somewhat stronger for the FTA criterion than for rearrests. Of the personal characteristics considered, only drug use and age appeared likely to prove useful.

As already noted, other investigators (e.g., Roth and Wice, 1978) have observed that the type of instant offense, rather than its seriousness, seems to be related to bail outcomes. This also was found in the Goldkamp and Gottfredson studies; the relations of offense seriousness to the criteria examined were inconsistent and weak, while those for type were more consistent and powerful. Multivariate analyses were carried out on four criteria: FTA, rearrest, rearrest for "serious offenses" (homicide, rape, arson, robbery, burglary, aggravated assault, and the manufacture-delivery and sale of drugs), and a combined rearrest and FTA index. As would be expected from examination of the bivariate relations (and from range attenuation in the case of the "serious offense" criterion), the final logit models developed were to some extent similar, and to some extent different. Type of offense, age, prior FTAs, pending charges, recent arrests, and the interactions of some of these (e.g., over age 44 x prior FTAs) were important in terms of impact on expected log odds of the combined index. Summarizing differences between the models descriptive of the rearrest and FTA criteria, Goldkamp and Gottfredson (1981b:311–312) reported that

> the two criteria of flight and rearrest did share common correlates; most of the defendant attributes and the prior criminal history variables that were associated with failure to appear at trial were also associated with rearrest. There were, however, some significant exceptions . . . charge seemed to play a different role in the two phenomena. Gambling charges were indicative of a low FTA probability, but a high rearrest probability. And prostitution charges appeared to be associated with rearrest probabilities, but failed to reach significance in the FTA model. Employment correlated with rearrest but not with FTA. However, age, pending charges, prior FTAs, recent arrests, and the charge of serious personal offense were all associated both with the probability of FTA and rearrest.

When the serious arrest criterion was considered, only four items (age, employment, pending charges, and recent arrests) were significant.

Prosecution Decision Studies

Despite the enormity and importance of prosecutorial decision making, empirical studies of the charging decision are not common (M. R. Gottfredson and D. M. Gottfredson, 1980b; Adams, 1983). Observational studies (e.g., Miller, 1970), self-report or introspective studies (e.g., Kaplan, 1965), reports based on structured and unstructured interviews (e.g., Cole, 1970; Jacoby, Ratledge, and Turner, 1979), and simulation studies (e.g., Lagoy, Senna, and Siegel, 1976) have given a number of solid clues about the manner in which prosecutors appear to use information in their decision making. As noted by M. R. Gottfredson and D. M. Gottfredson (1980b:153), however, "if systems are to be designed to enhance rationality . . . it is important also to know what factors are the primary influences in most cases. This requires systematic empirical study based upon representative samples and quantifiable data."

Descriptive Studies

In a study of more than 1,200 males arraigned for felonies during a 5-month period in New York City, Bernstein, Kelly, and Doyle (1977) attempted to identify factors that influenced decisions to prosecute or to terminate cases by dismissal. Forty percent of the cases were dismissed (cf. Forst, Lucianovic, and Cox, 1977). Most important to the dismissal decision was a charge-reduction variable: the likelihood of dismissal increased substantially if a defendant's felony charge was reduced to a misdemeanor at the latest possible opportunity (at or after the preliminary hearing). Unfortunately, charge reductions themselves were not the subject of study in this investigation. Also significantly related to the dismissal decision was the nature of the offense charged (the likelihood of dismissal increased if the most serious arrest charges were burglary or assault), the total number of arrest charges (those with fewer were more likely to be dismissed), and pretrial detention status (those detained prior to final disposition were more likely to be dismissed). None of the demographic variables studied was related significantly to the decision (these included age, race-ethnicity, time employed, education, and marital status), nor were a variety of criminal history variables (e.g., a weighted index of prior convictions, the time elapsed since the most recent prior arrest). Bernstein and colleagues interpreted these findings as suggestive that evidentiary issues primarily were considered (i.e., witnesses are rare in burglary cases, and a large number of charges may indicate that a strong case can be made).

In a separate study involving both male and female defendants, Bernstein and colleagues (Bernstein, Kicks, et al., 1977) did study the issue of charge reductions. More than 1,400 cases involving burglary, assault, larceny, and robbery charges were studied. The dependent variable, charge reduction, was defined relative to the absolute reduction possible. Separate analyses are reported for cases disposed at first presentation and those not so disposed. In neither case was prediction powerful (R^2 = .19 for the former and .13 for the latter). Considering only cases disposed at first presentation, seriousness of the first charge, offense type (burglary, assault), weapon charge, age, and criminal record were significant predictors; no demographic variable other than age appeared related to the criterion. For cases not disposed at the first presentation, the seriousness of the first presentation charge, resisting arrest, race, and criminal record were significant predictors. In both equations the greater the criminal record, the greater the reduction in charges.

These studies raise two intriguing issues. These concern the influence of evidentiary issues on the charging decision and prosecutorial treatment of recidivistic offenders. Using data available through the PROMIS system,[18] Forst, Lucianovic, and Cox (1977) found that 21 percent of the more than 17,000 arrests studied were rejected by prosecutors at initial screening and that witness and evidentiary reasons were given by the prosecutors for about 59 percent of those rejections (cf. Brosi, 1979). For cases dismissed later,

[18]See Hamilton and Work (1973) for a general description of this management information system.

witness problems remained important to the decision (about 13 percent), but evidentiary issues infrequently were cited as important to the decision. Also using the PROMIS system, Adams (1983) studied the relation between evidentiary factors and charge reductions. Significant, but very modest, effects were observed for the recovery of property or physical evidence (ϕ = .05),[19] arrest made at the scene of the offense (ϕ = .08), the relation between the victim and the offender (ϕ = .10), and the number of witnesses (low or high; ϕ = .06). When considered by offense category, relations differed both in terms of significance and magnitude.

Jacoby (1977) also has observed that victim-offender relations, evidentiary factors, and offenders' prior records are important to charging decisions. Williams (1978), using PROMIS data, has not only shown the importance of victim-offender relations to the charging decision but also that the effect varies with type of offense considered.

Forst and Brosi (1977:190–191) examined both evidentiary and recidivistic issues in relation to the charging decision and concluded that the study

> provides strong support for the hypothesis that the prosecutor attaches importance to the strength of evidence in a case. More prosecutive attention was also given to cases involving more serious offenses, although the prosecutor's decision to carry a case forward appears to have been about an order of magnitude more sensitive to strength of evidence than to crime seriousness. . . . The findings, on the other hand, provide no empirical support to the hypothesis that the prosecutor attempts to give more attention to cases involving defendants with extensive arrest records.

This conclusion may be questioned, however, because prior record was included in the "strength of evidence" variable.

Normative Studies

Normative prediction studies of prosecutorial decisions are very rare. Given the absence of offender behavioral outcomes to study, the first question to be addressed is "what is it that should be predicted?" If, in general, prosecutors wish to "win" cases, perhaps a criterion of "conviction obtained" is a reasonable one. This issue received attention in a study by Rhodes (1978), who used probit analysis to estimate the probability of conviction given that cases were accepted for prosecution. Once cases were accepted for prosecution, Rhodes found it difficult to predict whether they would lead to a conviction at trial. R^2 for equations developed for assault, robbery, larceny, and burglary cases ranged from .10 (for larceny) to .37 (for robbery). Although differences were observed across offense types (see Rhodes: 80), the following variables were found to be significantly associated with the probability of conviction: age, whether the defendant was arrested the same day that the offense occurred, whether physical evidence was available, the number of charges, whether the defendant was arrested at the scene of the crime (although not necessarily at the time of the offense), the number of lay witnesses, whether the defendant was released on recognizance pretrial, whether the defendant was granted a third-party release, if there was corroboration that a crime was committed, and whether exculpatory evidence was present.

Sentencing Decisions

It is in the sentencing of convicted offenders that discretionary decision making in the criminal justice system is most

[19]These are approximate values, calculated by us form summary tables reported in the article.

publicly apparent, and it also is in this area that the relation of desired goals to decisions made can most readily be explicated (M. R. Gottfredson and D. M. Gottfredson, 1980b). There is a large and controversial literature on the goals and proper purposes for the sentencing of criminal offenders (cf. H. L. A. Hart, 1968; Kleinig, 1973; Morris, 1974; Dershowitz, 1976; von Hirsch, 1976; Mueller, 1977; Grossman, 1980). Four traditional goals have been central to this debate: rehabilitation or treatment, desert or retributive punishment, deterrence (general or specific), and incapacitation. Each has a long history in practice, in moral philosopy, and in legal discussion and debate. Philosophical and legal debate concerning sentencing purposes and practices, however, is far more extensive than research on those purposes and practices. Although considerable research has been focused on the correlates of sentencing decisions (e.g., Galton, 1895; Gaudet, Harris, and St. John, 1933; J. Hogarth, 1971; Pope, 1976, 1978; Sutton, 1978; see reviews in Hagan, 1974; L. Cohen and Kluegel, 1978; Garber, Klepper, and Nagin, 1983; Hagan and Bumiller, 1983; Klepper, Nagin, and Tierney, 1983), rather less has been focused on the purposes and consequences of those decisions.

Of the goals cited, only one does not require prediction. The goal of deterrence involves the prediction that punishment of known offenders will discourage others from crime, or, in the case of specific deterrence, that the offender punished will be deterred from future criminal involvement. The goal of treatment or rehabilitation involves the prediction that offenders may be changed to reduce the likelihood of repeated offending; and that of incapacitation requires the prediction of new offenses if offenders are not restrained from committing them. Only the goal of desert (the application of punishment in proportion to the gravity of the harm done and the culpability of the offender) seems to require no prediction (S. D. Gottfredson and D. M. Gottfredson, 1985).[20]

As noted earlier, this paper is concerned primarily with the prediction of offender's individual-level behavioral outcomes. It is possible, we believe, to treat sentencing decisions within a selection framework, but this is not often done. For selection to be effective, the goal of the selection decision must be explicit. Ideally, decision makers would agree not only on the goal for the selection decision, but also on the criteria on which the decision will be based. One has but to review the literature cited above to realize quickly that no such agreement exists. We do not find it surprising, therefore, that evidence concerning the effectiveness of rehabilitation or treatment efforts has proven discouraging (Lipton, Martinson, and Wilks, 1975; Sechrest, White, and Brown, 1979; cf. M. R. Gottfredson, 1979b) or that the efficacy of deterrence and incapacitation has proven difficult to estimate (Blumstein, Cohen, and Nagin, 1978).

Rarely are the intents of a sentencing decision unitary. Not only do judges apparently seek to deter some offenders, punish others, incapacitate some, and rehabilitate still others, but also these "simple" intents may in fact be melded in a sanctioning decision even with respect to a single offender. These need not be—and probably are not—independent concerns on either the aggregate or the individual level. D. M. Gottfredson and Stecher (1979) studied the purposes

[20]Other less commonly cited goals, such as retribution or retaliation, also do not appear to us to require prediction (O'Leary, Gottfredson, and Gelman, 1975).

given by 18 judges in imposing criminal sanctions on almost 1,000 adult offenders. The judges usually did not assign any single goal as the purpose for the sentence imposed; rather, they generally distributed the sanction among several purposes.[21] Rehabilitation was the purpose given the principal weight in the largest proportion of cases (36 percent), followed closely by "other purpose, including general deterrence" (34 percent). Retribution was assigned the principal weight in 17 percent of the cases; special deterrence, in only 9 percent.[22] Surprisingly, only 4 percent of the cases reportedly had incapacitation as a primary intent (although imprisonment was not, of course, the only sanction applied). Based on multivariate analyses, however, the authors (D. M. Gottfredson and Stecher, 1979:179) report:

> The one item that appeared from the discriminant analysis to have the strongest association with the choice of primary aim (in the context of all the items included) was the judge's prediction of recidivism by an offense against persons. This suggests that the relatively infrequent selection of incapacitation as a principal goal may be misleading and that judges may employ this concept without necessarily labeling it as such. Alternatively, it may suggest that, for those judges, utilitarian purposes may provide a partial justification for retributive aims.
>
> In any case, these data support the contention that all the main purposes of sentencing play a role in the choice of alternative sanctions. The specific purposes related to judgments are rarely specified explicitly, however, and such identification is required if it is desired to learn how the rationality of such decisions can be improved.

[21]The judges were asked to distribute 100 points among several commonly cited purposes—or to assign this value to any single purpose. The only constraint imposed was that the total points assigned sum to 100.

[22]The judges had decided on the purposes to be studied.

Regardless of the actual proportion of cases for which an incapacitative intent is primary, it is clear that judges can rather easily apportion a sanction in terms of its compound intents. Further, it is clear that at some level at least, judges make an intuitive or clinical judgment of the risk—particularly risk associated with recidivistic harm to persons—associated with the offender.

S. D. Gottfredson and Taylor (1983) recently demonstrated that in a sample of 86 criminal court judges, half (51.4 percent) reported that rehabilitation should be the principal purpose for sanctions imposed; the remaining half, however, were as likely to avow any one of the remaining goals studied (incapacitation, retributive punishment, or general deterrence) as any other. Hale (1984) subsequently demonstrated that these "goal preferences" are related to the lengths of terms imposed on offenders even after controlling for offense and offender characteristics.[23] Not surprisingly, interactions of goal preferences and offender and offense characteristics also were identified as determinants of the term imposed.

Descriptive Studies

Given the recent and extensive reviews of the correlates of judicial decisions (Blumstein et al., 1983; Garber, Klepper, and Nagin, 1983; Hagan and Bumiller, 1983; Klepper, Nagin, and Tierney, 1983), we do not consider descriptive studies in detail here. Our own reading of the literature, however, leads to agreement with Garber, Klepper, and Nagin (1983:133–134):

> The conclusions of the various studies of final case outcome can be summarized as follows. First, virtually all the studies that include a variable measuring the charge found that the

[23]Information concerning sanctions other than imprisonment was not available.

> seriousness of the offense is the most important factor affecting case outcome. This is most evident for studies that analyze only convictions. Second, all the studies conclude that the prior record of the defendant is important. Third, all the studies that include a variable denoting whether the defendant makes bail infer that it is an important factor in case outcome. Fourth, most of the studies that include legal representation found that it affects case outcome, but the nature of this effect varies considerably among the studies. . . . Fifth, type of conviction generally seems to be important: Defendants who plead guilty fare worse on average than those who plead not guilty . . . but fare better than defendants who are convicted at trial. . . . The inferences concerning the role of extralegal characteristics [e.g., race, socioeconomic status] differ considerably across studies. One point of agreement is that if extralegal characteristics affect outcome, their quantitative significance is small compared with other factors discussed above.

Despite the consistency of observed effects, particularly for offense seriousness and prior record, the bulk of the variation in sentencing decisions remains unexplained; studies in which R^2 exceeds .30 to .35 are uncommon.

Normative Studies

Given the lack of clarity of goals that was discussed above, it is difficult to conceive of the optimal normative sentencing-decision study. With respect to the goal of rehabilitation, one could attempt to assess offenders with respect to amenability for treatment,[24] and selection devices then could be developed and their accuracy and operational efficacy assessed. With respect to the goal of specific deterrence, which may be considered a subproblem within the rehabilitation orientation, the operational definition of an adequate criterion measure is exceedingly complex (Manski, 1978). In practice, it likely would reduce to an unsatisfactory recidivism measure of some sort. How one would set about assessing offenders' differential amenability to a specific-deterrence effect is not clear to us. But it should be noted that the general selection problem is the same whether persons are to be selected, on the basis of amenability, for the treatments of confinement, education, therapy, or some other procedure intended to modify the criminal behavior of the offender.

It is with respect to the goal of incapacitation that normative prediction studies may be of most value. (Or at least, most immediate value—we continue to cling to a concern for the goal of rehabilitation, for which such tools can be important.) Judges do appear to include a risk consideration in the setting of sanctions, and we do know something (unfortunately not enough) about the assessment of risk. Indeed, recent proposals for "selective incapacitation" (Greenwood and Abrahamse, 1982; Forst, 1983; cf. also Greenberg, 1975; von Hirsch and Gottfredson, 1984) rely heavily on statistical assessments of the risk of recidivism. Accordingly, these (and other) studies may properly be treated within our normative decision-study framework. Examination of the efficacy of the proposals, however, depends heavily on critical estimates of rates of offending (Blumstein and Cohen, 1979; Blumstein and Graddy, 1982; J. Cohen, 1983b). In other portions of this paper, we summarize what is known about the accuracy and validity of normative recidivism-prediction studies, and we also consider proposals for selective incapacitation in detail in a later section.

Parole Prediction-Decision Studies

As we have noted, prediction studies involving criminal populations or relating in some way to concerns of the criminal

[24]This, of course, quickly could become complex given the wide variety of rehabilitative treatments that have been proposed.

justice system are voluminous. This is especially true of normative studies concerning paroling decisions.[25] Schuessler (1954) outlines the historical development of such studies from the early 1920s (beginning with the work of H. Hart, 1923) through the mid-1950s (e.g., Glaser, 1954; Kirby, 1954). Mannheim and Wilkins (1955) review research efforts to about 1953, and Rose (1966) and D. M. Gottfredson (1967) summarize research in parole prediction through the mid-1960s. Simon (1971) offers a very careful and detailed review of more than 40 of the more prominent studies (e.g., Vold, 1931; Glueck and Glueck, 1950; Ohlin, 1951; Mannheim and Wilkins, 1955; D. M. Gottfredson and Beverly, 1962; Glaser, 1964). Mannheim and Wilkins (1955) and D. M. Gottfredson, Wilkins, and Hoffman (1978) provide brief historical reviews that show the parallel development of such efforts in the English-speaking and European literatures (e.g., Shiedt, 1936; Trunck, 1937; Kohnle, 1938; Meywerk, 1938; Gerecke, 1939; Frey, 1951); the 1978 review includes some detail concerning developments during the 1970s.

Descriptive Studies

Descriptive studies of parole decision makers are rare and have tended to be primarily ethnographic (e.g., Dawson, 1969). The earliest such effort was that of Warner (1923), in which tables summarized the relations of 67 items of information (then available to decision makers at the Massachusetts Reformatory) to the parole decision and parole outcome. Warner did not test the significance of any of these relations, yet concluded that the decision makers attended well to salient information and that "poor as the criteria now used by the Board are, the Board would not improve matters by considering any of the sixty-odd pieces of information placed at its disposal, which it now ignores" (Warner: 196). In a quick rebuttal, H. Hart (1923:405) suggested "that the percentage of violations of paroles among men paroled from the Massachusetts Reformatory could be reduced one-half through scientific utilization of data . . . is the conclusion which should have been reached by the analysis of statistical data presented by Professor Warner." In fact, it is quite likely that neither Warner nor H. Hart was correct: Warner had systematically sampled equal numbers of successes and failures and examined "only 80 cases of prisoners not paroled . . . because a larger number of cases with complete records could not be found" (p. 176, footnote 3). Although one might be able to reweight cases from other information presented by Warner, the relatively small sample sizes, particularly of persons not paroled, probably would make this risky. In any event neither Warner, in his analyses by inspection, nor H. Hart, who made use of very recently developed statistical methods, attended to the base rate and other sampling concerns. Still, H. Hart is usually, and appropriately, credited with first introducing the concept of the experience table for parole prediction (Schuessler, 1954). Warner was, we believe, the first to attempt to compare the practices of parole decision makers with the potential power of "statistics."

Although he did not specifically address the question of factors apparently used by decision makers, Glaser (1955, 1962) demonstrated the relative superiority of an actuarially derived predictive device to decisions made by sociologists and psychiatrists. The prognostic judgments were of likely parole outcome; actual parole outcome was the criterion. Predictions made by the sociologists

[25]Savitz (1965) compiled a bibliography of such studies that contains more than 600 entries.

studied were marginally more accurate than those made by the psychiatrists (MCRs were .19 and .14, respectively); and the decision makers' overall assessments were more accurate than was a classification based on ratings of a number of personality factors. Still, a simple statistical combination of items was most accurate (MCR = .35). Similarly, D. M. Gottfredson (1961, D. M. Gottfredson and Beverly, 1962) demonstrated that, although both subjective prognostic parole judgments and a simple actuarial device correlated significantly with actual outcomes, the device was the more powerful predictor (r = .48 versus .20). Further, when the subjective judgments and the statistical information were combined, "the subjective ratings added nothing to the predictive accuracy of the simple checklist" (1962:58).

There is evidence to suggest that, when differences in cases judged are controlled, parole decision makers tend to make very similar decisions (D. M. Gottfredson and Ballard, 1966). Whether this results from the similar subjective treatment of similar items of information was not investigated. Parker (1972, cited in Kastenmeier and Eglit, 1973) surveyed parole board members for opinions of "the general worth" of a variety of prisoner characteristics for "predicting the success of a man on parole," and compared those opinions with the ranges of actual success rates of parolees showing these characteristics (relative to the base rate). Characteristics thought to be prognostic of parole outcome included a history of frequent intoxication, age (but only in one direction; the decision makers correctly believed that older inmates tend to succeed, but failed to report that younger inmates tend to fail—as they do), juvenile record, whether the inmate left home at an early age, whether the inmate's family showed active interest in the inmate during his imprisonment, narcotic addiction, employment history, constructive use of prison time, whether the inmate was a "leader" in the commitment of the crime for which he was imprisoned, probation violations, and offense type (they were wrong more often than right, with respect to the latter). How these judgments related to actual decisions made is not known.

Scott (1974) studied parole decisions in a "midwestern state" during 1968, a period in which indefinite or indeterminate sentencing was in effect. Thus "not only [did] the parole board have the responsibility of determining the proper length of incarceration for each offender [given] an indefinite sentence, but . . . they [had] the prerogative to overrule legislatively enacted minimum sentences, or judicially imposed minimum or definite sentences, and release inmates when they [felt] the inmates should be released" (p. 215). By studying the factors associated with time served, Scott was in effect studying paroling decisions, with the advantage that a continuous outcome criterion could be used. Six of the variables studied had significant zero-order correlations with time served: the seriousness of the crime (defined as the legal minimum sentence, in months, imposed by the court; .84), disciplinary reports (the number received while incarcerated; .24), age (.59), education (−.27), IQ (as measured by the revised beta; −.16), and sex (females served less time; −.16). Practice in this jurisdiction was such that only inmates' files were reviewed in making a paroling decision; inmates did not appear before the board until after the decision had been made. Of the factors available in the files and studied by Scott, only those listed were significantly related to the decisions made. When they (and others) were studied in a multiple regression framework, the zero-order effects for education and IQ did not hold up, and effects (in order of relative magnitude) for socioeconomic status, marital status, and prior record were observed. The remaining zero-order effects remained significant in the multiple regression equation (R^2 = .79). By far, the measure of offense seriousness used had the greatest effect on time served (beta = .64), followed by age (.31), disciplinary reports (.18), sex (−.17), socioeconomic status (−.10), marital status (.08), and prior record (−.06). The negative effect observed for prior record reportedly was due to a policy of paroling inmates against whom detainers had been filed; these inmates also typically had longer records.

Evidence that parole decision makers are influenced by institutional variables (e.g., punishment received for infractions while incarcerated, escapes) also is available. Using data from a series of studies concerning federal parolees (D. M. Gottfredson, Hoffman, et al., 1975), M. R. Gottfredson (1979a) assessed the effects of these variables on the length of time served, after this had been residualized with respect to the original sentence length; both the number of "prison punishments" received and escape history explained significant proportions of the variation in time served, once this had been residualized for the term set. Using both items, 28 percent of the remaining variance in time served was explained.

Elion and Megargee (1979) studied parole decisions made relative to 958 black and white men incarcerated at the Federal Correctional Institution in Tallahassee over a 4-year period (1970–1974). Using multiple discriminant function analysis, they found that the maximum term imposed by the court (Wilk's λ = .84), a scale reflecting adult maladjustment and deviance (.79), a rating of the violence of the instant offense (.75), the rate of disciplinary reports (.72), and juvenile conviction record (.71) significantly predicted the parole decisions made. Complete data were available for only 310 offenders, but the function correctly identified 79 percent of them.

Adapting Wilkins' "information board" method (Wilkins and Chandler, 1965), D. M. Gottfredson, Cosgrove, et al. (1978) sought to understand parole decision makers' use of case-file information. Only three items of information were always requested by decision makers: offense, age, and alcohol history; the first two typically were requested early in the decision process, the third typically was used later. In general, decision makers "paroling" and those "not paroling" sought different informational items. Further, "the same decision often was made on entirely different bases; that is, different information was used by different people to arrive at the same conclusion" (p. 182).

In a separate analysis, D. M. Gottfredson, Cosgrove, et al. (1978) used multiple regression methods to examine the influence of decision makers' subjective judgments of the seriousness of the instant offense, institutional program participation, the offender's institutional disciplinary record, and risk of parole violation on two decision criteria: continuance (in months, with "parole" treated as zero) and a recommendation of time to be served prior to the next review. Neither the judgments of disciplinary record nor program participation (which were highly correlated) were significant predictors of each decision. The subjective assessment of the seriousness of the commitment offense and the risk prognosis together explained about half the variance in each decision studied; but offense seriousness alone accounted for a vastly disproportionate amount of that variation. Similarly, Daiger et al. (1978) found a measure of offense seriousness and predictions of future behavior to be related to parole decisions.

Carroll and colleagues (Carroll, 1977, 1978a,b; Carroll and Payne, 1976, 1977a, b; Carroll et al., 1982) have studied parole decisions from the framework of attribution theory. One study (Carroll and Payne, 1977a) involved tape-recording parole decision makers as they "thought out loud" about the cases being reviewed. Attributional statements represented the single largest category of statements made (beyond the factual information read). Often, these were causal attributions concerning the "instant" criminal event or the offenders' criminal histories (see Carroll, 1978a). These causal attributions were found to be significantly associated with decision-making outcomes: offenders whose crimes were attributed to stable, enduring causes (e.g., serious drug abuse) were considered worse parole risks than other offenders and received less favorable parole consideration (Carroll, 1978b). Carroll et al. (1982) found that for the Pennsylvania Parole Board, institutional behavior and "predictions" of future risk and rehabilitation, in addition to causal attributions, were important to paroling decisions. On follow-up, however, these predictions were found to be virtually unrelated to actual post-release outcomes.

A descriptive study of parole board decisions in California, a setting characterized at the time of the study by wide indeterminacy in sentencing and broad authority of the board to set terms and to grant or withhold parole, was completed by D. M. Gottfredson and Ballard (1964b). Various decision outcomes were modeled for male and female offenders (who had separate parole boards) in terms of attributes of the offenders. The decision outcomes used as criteria included: total terms set, months to be served in prison, months to be served on parole, and months to be served in prison after the minimum parole eligibility date. The minimum parole eligibility date was a legal constraint, varying among offenders and determined by the law, on the time the offender would be required (by the parole board) to remain in prison. Thus, the last criterion listed above is of most interest in terms of the discretion of the board.

For males, an R^2 of .45 was found, in a validation sample, for prediction (by multiple regression) of prison sentences beyond the legal constraint. Items most closely associated with that criterion were classification of the legal offense of conviction, an offense seriousness rating, the number of prior prison confinements, and a history of opiate drug use. Based on a clustering method that suggested a marked decrease in heterogeneity of the sample when offenders were classed as with and without prior prison terms, separate equations were developed for those two groups. This improved prediction overall.

For men who had been in prison before, the legal offense class and the number of prior prison confinements were most closely associated with the criterion (prison time beyond minimum). For men not in prison before, the best predictors were the offense seriousness rating and the history of opiate drug use (although the record of prior incarcerations also was found to be a useful predictor).

For offenders generally, when the length of time required on parole (for those who were paroled) was the criterion, the best predictors were the number of months required before the minimum eligible parole date (the legal constraint on time to be served in prison but not on parole) and the history of opiate use.

For female offenders, separate analyses were done with data for three groups of women. These groups were defined by a clustering method (intended to reduce the heterogeneity of the total sample) that resulted in three subgroups (D. M. Gottfredson and Ballard, 1965a). These were called: "conventional offenders" (women with no prior incarceration in either jails or prisons); "persistent offenders" (women with prior incarceration but no history of heroin use); and "persistent offender-users" (women with prior incarceration and a history of heroin use). When prediction models were developed for the total group and for the three groups separately, the offender characteristics studied accounted for about one-third of the variation in terms beyond the legal constraints on the board's decisions. The three groupings by themselves were good discriminators of both the parole board's decisions as to time required to be served and a recidivism criterion.

Also studied were decisions as to the granting of parole. If parole was not granted, consideration was usually postponed, although the person could, in most cases, be discharged. (Of 14,682 men who appeared before the board in the fiscal year 1962–1963, parole was granted to 39 percent, consideration was postponed for 57 percent, and 4 percent were discharged.) Differences among the groups paroled and not paroled included, for example: the type of commitment (original, parole violator), the legal offense, prior board appearances, assaultive history, use of weapons, opiate use history, custody classification, disciplinary infractions, work assignments, participation in various institutional programs, and aspects of the person's parole plans.

Analyses aimed at modeling the parole board's decisions in North Carolina, Virginia, Louisiana, Missouri, California (Youth Authority), Washington, and New Jersey had somewhat similar results, although these varied by jurisdiction (D. M. Gottfredson, Cosgrove, et al., 1978). Case evaluation forms were completed by the decision makers at the time of the hearings, and a number of items reflected their subjective judgments (e.g., "parole prognosis," an estimate of the risk of parole violation if paroled).

In North Carolina the following correlates (point biserial coefficients) of decision-maker ratings with the decision to parole or not were observed: parole prognosis (.60, N = 2,968), institutional discipline (.49, N = 2,968), program participation (.53, N = 2,520), social stability (.39, N = 2,974), prior record (.32, N = 2,980), assaultive potential (.27, N = 2,963), and prior criminal record (.32, N = 2,980). The rated seriousness of the offense, the maximum sentence, the number of prior hearings, and the time already served were not related to the decision to grant or deny parole (p. 42).

Similar results were observed in Virginia. Decision-maker ratings were correlated with the decision to grant or deny parole as follows: parole prognosis (.77, N = 1,685), institutional discipline (.39, N = 1,641), program participation (.38, N = 1,532), social stability (.37, N = 1,663), prior criminal record (.33, N = 1,680), and assaultive potential (.28, N = 1,670). Ratings of the offense seriousness were correlated with the decision outcome also, but slightly (.08, N = 1,688). The time served, the maximum sentence, and the number of prior hearings were not correlated with the decision (D. M. Gottfredson et al.:75). Findings from Louisiana and Missouri were similar to those just noted (Gottfredson et al.:107–108, 135–136).

In Washington state, for reasons associated with the legal structure at the time of the study, which resulted in wide discretion for the parole board, the analyses focused on the setting of the minimum sentenced and the time required to be served in prison. A multiple regression equation to predict the minimum sentence set, including classifications of the offense and maximum sentences, together with ratings of the seriousness of the offense, resulted in a study sample R^2 of .63 (N = 502). An equation to predict the time served by offenders paroled, which included four items, resulted in an

R^2 of .43 (N = 530). The four items were drug sales offense with a maximum sentence of 20 years or more, nonviolent offense with maximum sentences of more than 10 but less than 20 years, and decision-maker ratings of the seriousness of the offense and the prior criminal record (D. M. Gottfredson et al.:223–224).

In New Jersey, multiple regression equations were calculated for the dependent variables "months served in prison by offenders paroled" and "parole grant/deny." In the case of the first, five items provided an R^2 of .88 (N = 233) in the study sample. These were maximum sentence, rated offense seriousness program participation, prior criminal record, and parole plan. With the second criterion (parole or not) an R^2 of .48 (N = 504) was found when these items were used: maximum sentence, rated offense seriousness, parole prognosis, program participation, and quality of the parole plan (D. M. Gottfredson et al.:248–249).

Although the correlates of parole board decisions vary among jurisdictions (as do legal structures and paroling authority goals), common correlates include decision makers' judgments about the offenders' prior criminal records and institutional adjustment, whether the latter is assessed in terms of disciplinary infractions or participation in programs or both, and about the likelihood of new offenses if paroled (particularly the estimated probability of violent crimes). Often, and differing by jursidiction, ratings of the seriousness of the offense of conviction are correlated with decision outcomes, as is the time that already has been served when the decision is made.

Normative Studies

Given the ready availability of several detailed reviews of this voluminous literature (e.g., Mannheim and Wilkins, 1955; Rose, 1966; D. M. Gottfredson, 1967; Simon, 1971; D. M. Gottfredson, Wilkins, and Hoffman, 1978), we will not repeat that effort. Rather, we focus in this section on two issues: the identification of specific variables that have been found to have predictive utility across a range of samples and studies and a consideration of the general degree of accuracy obtained in such studies. We therefore do not give detailed attention to individual studies (as in previous sections). We were greatly assisted in this effort by the reviews cited, particularly those of Simon (1971) and D. M. Gottfredson (1967), and by a comparative summary prepared by Glaser and O'Leary (1966).

Our focus here is on behavioral and demographic correlates; thus, we largely ignore several extensive research traditions, which also largely have been ignored in previous reviews. In particular, we do not treat research relating to psychological or psychiatric prognostications, tests, or other personality assessments. Nor do we treat research concerning the impacts of large-scale social and economic forces (e.g., Ehrlich, 1973, 1974; Forst, 1976; Vandaele, 1978). Finally, we do not review research concerning the areal or ecological correlates of crime and recidivism, despite growing evidence that inclusion of these factors may do much to improve the prediction of recidivism (S. D. Gottfredson and Taylor, 1986). For reviews, see Baldwin (1979) and S. D. Gottfredson and Taylor (1986); for suggestions of the likely importance of situational factors, see Monahan (1978, 1981) and Monahan and Klassen (1982).

Past Criminal Behavior. It is a psychological truism that the best predictor of future behavior is past behavior. Not surprisingly, one of the best predictors of future criminal conduct is past criminal conduct, and the parole-prediction literature amply supports this fact. From the earliest studies (e.g., Burgess, 1928; Vold,

1931) to the latest (e.g., Palmer and Carlson, 1976; D. M. Gottfredson, Cosgrove, et al., 1978; Schmidt and Witte, 1979; Carroll et al., 1982; S. D. Gottfredson and Taylor, 1986), indices of prior criminal conduct consistently are found to be among the most powerful predictors of parole violations, arrest for the commitment of new offenses, and conviction and reincarceration for these.

This generalization tends to hold regardless of the measure of prior criminal conduct used or of specific operational definitions of that conduct. For example, the previous arrest history, the prior conviction history, the record of commitments to jail or to prison, the length of "gaps" in the arrest or conviction history (e.g., time free without arrests), the history of prior probation or parole violations, the age at first arrest, the number of commitments to correctional institutions, the number of prior court dispositions of any type, and the types of prior offenses all provide examples of variates often found predictive of future arrests or convictions. The apparent strength of associations with the criteria of interest vary among samples and criteria, but it is nevertheless commonly found that such items are among the best predictors identified. Some are more reliable than others, some are more readily extracted from the records, and some—depending on the intended application—present legal or ethical objections. All these factors would, of course, be important to consider in the selection of predictor candidates.

Although the means of assessing prior criminal involvement have varied widely, we know of no prediction study in which a measure of criminal history, if available for assessment, did not emerge as significantly associated with the outcome criterion (which also has varied widely). In most studies, prior record appears to be the most powerful of the variables examined—although this leaves much to be desired. Because few studies have used common criteria or definitions, it is difficult to provide an adequate summary of the relation between past and future criminal behavior; this difficulty is exacerbated by the fact that samples also have varied. Finally, a wide variety of methods have been used to examine these relations, and they often are not readily comparable. As examples: Mannheim and Wilkins (1955) used a contingency coefficient adjusted for restriction and observed values of from .31 to .24; Vold (1931) used unadjusted contingency coefficients and observed a value of .28 for the relation of prior record and parole outcome. This index may be readily calculated from data given by D. M. Gottfredson, Wilkins, and Hoffman (1978) and results in coefficients of .23 to .21, depending on the item assessed. Tibbets (1931) and Borden (1928) reported values of Pearson's r of between .15 and .20, depending on the definition of prior criminal conduct used. Several authors report values of MCR for items [e.g., Glaser, 1955 (.21 to .20); Babst, Inciardi, and Jaman, 1971 (.22)]; others report univariate F-ratios, discriminant weights, or asymptotic *t*-ratios (e.g., Kirby, 1954; Palmer and Carlson, 1976; Brown, 1978; Schmidt and Witte, 1979); some report no indices at all (e.g., Hakeem, 1948).

In general, considering adult samples, the relation between prior record and future criminal activity, both measured variously, appears to be on the order of .2, whether assessed by the correlation coefficient, by a related contingency coefficient, or via the MCR. The relation changes little whether only men are studied (e.g., Borden, 1928; Tibbets, 1931; Kirby, 1954; Glaser, 1955; Babst, Inciardi, and Jaman, 1971) or if women are included in the sample (e.g., Brown, 1978; D. M. Gottfredson, Wilkins, and Hoffman, 1978; Carroll et al., 1982). Restricting the sample to certain types of offenders, however, appears to reduce the effect. For example, Babst, Koval, and

Neithercutt (1972) studied a large national sample of paroled burglars and observed MCRs relating prior record and parole outcome of from .08 to .14 (depending on the definition of prior record used). In a study of institutionalized narcotics addicts, Inciardi (1971) did not find prior criminal record to be among the salient predictors of parole outcome. In further support of the truism noted earlier, however, the variable "number of previous treatments for narcotics use" was found predictive.

Prior record is similarly predictive of probation outcomes (e.g., Monachesi, 1932; Caldwell, 1951; Simon, 1971). For both probation and parole, such variables are found predictive in American, British, and European (e.g., Shiedt, 1936; Trunck, 1937) samples and for youths (e.g., Mannheim and Wilkins, 1955) as well as for adults.

Age. Information concerning offender age appears consistently to be related to parole outcomes, although there are contrary examples. Age alone, usually measured at or shortly before release, has variously been found positively related to outcome (studies finding that older releasees more often are successful include, as examples, Burgess, 1928; Kirby, 1954; Palmer and Carlson, 1976; Brown, 1978; Schmidt and Witte, 1979); unrelated to outcome (studies finding no, or very little, relation include Borden, 1928; Vold, 1931; Babst, Inciardi, and Jaman, 1971; Simon, 1971; Babst, Koval, and Neithercutt, 1972; S. D. Gottfredson and D. M. Gottfredson, 1979); and even negatively related to outcome (e.g., Tibbets, 1931). When found to be positively related with release outcome, the effect of age usually is small, although statistically significant in the studies cited. The zero-order correlation reported by Kirby is 0.08; the mean difference of about 25 months reported by Brown is associated with an F-ratio of 70.5 on 1, 638 degrees of freedom (half that of the most powerful zero-order predictor, which was offense type); in the multivariate model, however, it emerged as the most salient predictor. Age at release had by far the smallest coefficient in Schmidt and Witte's (1979) truncated log normal analysis, and one of the smallest in Palmer and Carlson's (1976) study, which used the same method. Studies that we have classified as showing no relation actually do show small, nonsignificant, but positive coefficients (.004 to about .06 to .08); the significance of the single negative relation noted was not assessed, and inspection of the distribution shows it to be slight and inconsistent (Tibbets, 1931:37).

To summarize, the evidence available seems to suggest that age, usually measured at time of release, is positively associated with outcomes, but that the relation is slight, particularly when considered in multivariate contexts. In the literature reviewed, its statistical significance often appears largely to be a function of sample size. Babst, Koval, and Neithercutt (1972) found no zero-order effect for age, but did find that the interaction of age with other variables (drug or alcohol abuse and criminal record) was highly significant (although still only marginally predictive).

Many studies have examined the age variable in relation to the onset of noticed (or official) criminal behavior, and here, the evidence is compelling: the earlier the onset of criminal activity, the poorer the prognosis.[26] Kirby (1954) reports a correlation of .21 between age at first arrest and failure on parole; we calculate a contingency coefficient of .14 between age at first commitment and failure from data presented by D. M. Gottfredson, Cosgrove, et al. (1978); Mannheim and

[26]Unofficial delinquency proxies also have been used. For example, Glaser (1954) reports an MCR of .22 for the relation between the age at which the offender first left home for a period of at least 6 months and failure on release.

Wilkins (1955) report an adjusted contingency coefficient of .19 between age at first finding of guilt and failure; Simon (1971) reports a ϕ of .13; S. D. Gottfredson and D. M. Gottfredson (1979) report point-biserial correlations of .18 for age at first arrest, .17 for age at first conviction, and .18 for age at first commitment. Although not large, the effect is at least consistent (and is not remarkably smaller than zero-order effects cited above for criminal history variables). When examined in multivariate contexts, the relation usually remains significant, although the unique contribution is small (S. D. Gottfredson and D. M. Gottfredson, 1979).

Marital Status. Marital status occasionally has been found predictive of parole outcomes; single offenders do more poorly on follow-up (Burgess, 1928; Vold, 1931; Kirby, 1954; S. D. Gottfredson and D. M. Gottfredson, 1979). The zero-order relations are slight (the correlations are about .15, varying, of course, with the study), and usually, but not always, disappear in multivariate analyses (S. D. Gottfredson and D. M. Gottfredson, 1979; cf. Kirby, 1954; Palmer and Carlson, 1976). Marital status is colinear with age variables (which are rather more powerful) and with variables that assess release plans (e.g., planned living arrangement). Simon (1971) found no effect for marital status, but her sample was very young. In general, the unique contribution of marital status appears modest in relation to the assessment of parole outcomes.

Sex. Most studies reported in the literature have been restricted to samples of males. Those that included both men and women (e.g., D. M. Gottfredson, Wilkins, and Hoffman, 1978; S. D. Gottfredson and D. M. Gottfredson, 1979; Schmidt and Witte, 1979; Carroll et al., 1982) either find or report no significant effect for sex. An exception is Brown (1978), who found that sex remained statistically significant in a multiple discriminant function analysis. The variable's unique contribution, however, is very slight (see p. 98). S. D. Gottfredson and D. M. Gottfredson (1979) systematically studied the effect of sex and found it to be negligible. In part, this likely is due to the small number of women available for study, even when overall sample sizes are large.

Race–Ethnicity. Although some of the earliest studies paid detailed attention to race or ethnicity (e.g., Tibbets, 1931, studied the zero-order relations between 20 racial and ethnic classifications and parole outcome), few later studies specifically report on or appear to have examined these variables. Either the variables were not available for study (e.g., Brown, 1978), or investigators appear to have ignored them. It also may be that investigators simply have not reported finding no effect. Some (e.g., S. D. Gottfredson and D. M. Gottfredson, 1979) had an expressed goal of developing operationally useful prediction tools and, hence, excluded the variable from consideration. (We consider the ill-advised wisdom of this in a later section.) In one multivariate study (Schmidt and Witte, 1979), a zero-order race effect failed to reach significance when considered in combination with other factors; in others (Kassebaum, Ward, and Wilner, 1971; Palmer and Carlson, 1976) the effect (substantially diminished) remained significant. Perhaps the best that may be said at this point is that race and ethnicity effects appear to have been understudied in relation to parole outcomes.[27]

[27]In a descriptive parole-prediction study, Elion and Megargee (1979) found little evidence for the effect of race on parole decisions made, but more evidence for racial differences in the severity of sentences imposed.

Employment History. Employment history consistently is found predictive of parole outcomes (although there are exceptions, e.g., Tibbets, 1931). The zero-order relations are modest (correlation coefficients of .21, .12, .17 to .14, .17, and .13 to .16 have been reported by Borden, 1928; Vold, 1931; Kirby, 1954; Simon, 1971; and S. D. Gottfredson and D. M. Gottfredson, 1979, respectively; contingency coefficients of .25 to .22 and .12 were observed by Mannheim and Wilkins (1955) and by D. M. Gottfredson, Cosgrove, et al. (1978), respectively; and an MCR of .17 was reported by Glaser, 1954). In general, variables that measure the stability of employment appear to be modestly more predictive than do other means of assessing employment history (Simon, 1971; S. D. Gottfredson and D. M. Gottfredson, 1979). Employment history variables generally retain a unique contribution in multivariate analyses, but the effect is small. Occupational classifications may be somewhat more powerful (Palmer and Carlson, 1976).

Offense. The nature of the commitment offense and, in some studies, the nature of the offender's offense history consistently are predictive of parole outcomes: those who offend against property are poorer risks than are those who have offended against persons (Vold, 1931; Kirby, 1954; Mannheim and Wilkins, 1955; Babst, Inciardi, and Jaman, 1971; Palmer and Carlson, 1976; Brown, 1978; D. M. Gottfredson, Wilkins, and Hoffman, 1978; S. D. Gottfredson and D. M. Gottfredson, 1979; Schmidt and Witte, 1979; Carroll et al., 1982; cf., however, Simon, 1971). Brown (1978) systematically studied a number of offense classification schemes, finding that a simple "person/property" dichotomy was about as efficient as any other. Such a measure is most commonly used, although some (e.g., D. M. Gottfredson, Cosgrove, et al., 1978; S. D. Gottfredson and D. M. Gottfredson, 1979) have found specific combinations of property-type offenses to be predictive of parole outcomes. Zero-order relations typically observed are in the .15 to .25 range (cf., Mannheim and Wilkins, 1955; D. M. Gottfredson, Cosgrove, et al., 1978; S. D. Gottfredson and D. M. Gottfredson, 1979). When considered in multivariate models, offense type typically does make a unique, but small, contribution to explained variation in outcome (cf. Kirby, 1954; Brown, 1978; S. D. Gottfredson and D. M. Gottfredson, 1979; Schmidt and Witte, 1979; Carroll et al., 1982).

Alcohol and Drugs. A history of problematic alcohol use is correlated with parole outcomes (Vold, 1931; Hakeem, 1948; Ohlin, 1951; Mannheim and Wilkins, 1955; Glaser, 1964; D. M. Gottfredson and Ballard, 1965b; D. M. Gottfredson, 1967; Babst, Koval, and Neithercutt, 1972; Palmer and Carlson, 1976; Brown, 1978; S. D. Gottfredson and D. M. Gottfredson, 1979; Schmidt and Witte, 1979), but the relation is slight. In multivariate models, variables indicative of alcohol use occasionally make small unique contributions (e.g., D. M. Gottfredson, 1961; Palmer and Carlson, 1976; Brown, 1978); just as often, however, they appear to share sufficient variance with other (more highly predictive) variables that no multivariate effect is observed (Schmidt and Witte, 1979; S. D. Gottfredson and D. M. Gottfredson, 1979).

The evidence about drug abuse, particularly of natural or synthetic opiates, is less mixed. Most studies investigating the issue observe statistically significant, although modest, zero-order effects (e.g., Vold, 1931; D. M. Gottfredson and Bonds, 1961; Babst, Inciardi, and Jaman, 1971). In large samples of federal offenders (e.g., D. M. Gottfredson, Cosgrove, et al., 1978; S. D. Gottfredson and D. M. Gottfredson, 1979), in extremely large samples based on the Uniform Parole Reports data base (e.g., Babst, Inciardi, and Jaman, 1971; Brown, 1978), and in a sizable Michigan sample (Palmer and Carlson, 1976) variables reflective of drug usage do make a modest unique contribution; in one sample, however, drug usage did not remain significant when tested in a multivariate model (Schmidt and Witte, 1979).

Education. Education (variously defined and studied, but most typically measured in terms of attainment) seems to be associated with parole outcomes in the bivariate case (e.g., Vold, 1931; Kirby, 1954; Glaser, 1955; Babst, Inciardi, and Jaman, 1971; D. M. Gottfredson, Wilkins, and Hoffman, 1978; S. D. Gottfredson and D. M. Gottfredson, 1979).[28] Multivariate models suggest that the contribution to explained variance made by education is negligible (e.g., Kirby, 1954; S. D. Gottfredson and D. M. Gottfredson, 1979).

Other Predictors. Dozens of other variables have been examined for association with parole outcome, and they usually provide support for the null hypothesis. For listings of many of these, see Mannheim and Wilkins (1955), Simon (1971), or S. D. Gottfredson and D. M. Gottfredson (1979). A few have shown sufficient promise to mention here, although they often are supported by few studies. A record of punishments (reprimands, reports, misconduct citations, et cetera) received while incarcerated has proven prognostic on occasion (e.g., Borden, 1928; Tibbets, 1931; Vold, 1931; Kirby, 1954; Mannheim and Wilkins, 1955; S. D. Gottfredson and D. M. Gottfredson, 1979; Carroll et al., 1982). Zero-order relations are low to moderate (.03 to .23 range), but multivariate analyses suggest that the small contribution made is relatively unique. Whether the offender acted alone in the commitment offense or acted with accomplices has been found modestly predictive in some studies (e.g., Tibbets, 1931; Kirby, 1954); association with criminal gangs appears moderately more predictive (Simon, 1971), and the latter remains predictive in a multiple regression framework. A variety of "assessment scales" have proven predictive in some studies [e.g., Burgess's "social types"; see Burgess, 1928; Hakeem, 1948; Ohlin, 1951; or Glaser's (1955, 1964) "social development pattern"] but have proven difficult for others to score reliably.

COMMON CORRELATES

Our review of descriptive and normative decision studies across a variety of criminal justice system settings suggests that decision makers tend to rely with some regularity on a few common items of information regardless of the decision being made. Likewise, there is considerable commonality among items found useful in normative prediction studies—again, regardless of the decision for which the prediction is made. Finally, it appears that the descriptive and normative studies seem to recommend different items of information as predictive.

Table 1 provides a general summary of those variables found to predict the decisions of functionaries and those found to predict the behavior of offenders for a variety of criteria and across the decision arenas studied.

Some caveats with respect to this summary are in order. As discussed earlier, few of the studies we reviewed provided

[28]However, Simon (1971) observed no zero-order relation between education and outcome. A measure of school conduct, however, was modestly correlated with recidivism.

TABLE 1 Common Correlates of Criminal Justice Decision Making

Decision Stage	Criterion	Salient Predictors: Descriptive Studies	Salient Predictors: Normative Studies
Bail; pretrial release	Failure to appear (FTA) for trial	Seriousness of charge, seriousness of prior charges, prior record, "community ties"	Offense type, prior record, "community ties," drug use, prior FTAs, pending charges
	Cash bail	Seriousness of charge, weapons charge, juvenile record, age, personal victim of crime?, "community ties,"[a] D.A. recommendation,[a] defense attorney recommendation[a]	N.A.
	Recidivism on pretrial release	N.A.	Offense type, prior record, employment, age, "community ties," weapons use, pending charges, prior FTAs
	Failure to appear or recidivism	N.A.	Type of release,[b] court disposition time,[b] offense type, age, pending charges, recent offense history, prior FTAs
Prosecution	Charge	Witness and evidentiary factors, victim-offender relation, seriousness of charge	N.A.
	Charge reduction	Seriousness of offense, type of offense, age, prior record	N.A.
	Prosecute fully or dismiss	Charge reductions, offense type, number of charges, pretrial detention status	N.A.
	Conviction obtained	N.A.	Offense type, evidentiary and witness factors, pretrial status, age
Sentencing	Various[c]	Seriousness of offense, prior record, pretrial status, counsel and representation, type of conviction, various extralegal factors	N.A.
Parole	Time served	Seriousness of offense, maximum term set, subjective risk assessment, institutional behavior, prior record, age, sex, socioeconomic status, marital status, juvenile record	N.A.
	Parole/no parole	Seriousness of offense, subjective risk assessment, prior record, attributions regarding offender and offense, institutional behavior, alcohol history, age	Prior record, offense type, age, particularly "age at onset," employment, marital status, alcohol-drug use, education, institutional behavior, criminal associates

NOTE: The first two or three entries in each cell represent, in order, the most powerful predictors. Subsequent factors vary sufficiently from study to study to prohibit conclusions with respect to relative accuracy.

[a]Based on a simulation study.

[b]Not deemed useful for most practical applications of prediction tools.

[c]The most powerful predictors appear to be seriousness and prior record, regardless of the particular criterion used (e.g., sentence type, sentence length, measures of sentence "severity"). Accordingly, we have not differentiated criteria for purposes of this summary table.

sufficient detail to allow us the degree of specificity desired. Some studies provided detailed information concerning bivariate relations, but no (or little) information concerning those relations in a multivariate context. When the latter was provided, often the former was not. Comparable statistics are not reported for many studies, whether bivariate or multivariate in nature.

We are not the first reviewers to make this lament (see Hagan and Bumiller, 1983, for a discussion of the difficulties of cumulating information from a variety of studies) nor, we are certain, will we be the last. With Hagan and Bumiller, we note that we intend no criticism of the authors whose reports we have reviewed—indeed, on occasion we found ourselves among the worst culprits. We do believe that there remains promise in meta-analytic methods (Glass, 1976; Glass, McGaw, and Smith, 1981), despite well-recognized difficulties (e.g., B. F. Green and Hall, 1984), and had hoped to provide a "quantitative literature review." Unfortunately, we cannot.

Entries in Table 1 are intended to represent constructs, and it should be remembered that these have been operationally defined in many ways in the literature reviewed. This is true both for entries under the heading "Salient Predictors" and for those listed under "Criterion."

The first two or three entries in each cell of the table represent, in order, the most powerful predictors of the relevant criterion. The power of variables represented by subsequent entries varies sufficiently from study to study to prohibit conclusions with respect to relative accuracy. We already have noted difficulties encountered in attempting to assess the predictive accuracy of items of information across (and often within) studies. Accordingly, with the exception of the first two or three entries in each cell, we do not have confidence in the relative ordering of predictive factors listed.

These caveats made, the table rather clearly shows our original impression to have been more or less correct. Reading down columns in the table, items of predictive information are remarkably consistent across decision settings (with the possible exception of the prosecutorial stage, at which evidentiary factors become important both to decisions made and to trial outcomes). This is true for both descriptive and normative studies. Reading across rows, however, the descriptive and normative studies regularly tend to recommend that attention be paid to different items of information. This is particularly true with respect to information concerning the offense: decision makers tend to focus on seriousness (which generally is not predictive of behavioral outcomes), while normative studies focus on offense type, which *is* predictive of behavioral outcomes.

HOW SUCCESSFUL ARE PREDICTION-BASED SELECTION RULES?

The evidence just summarized suggests that with respect to the criteria investigated, at any rate, criminal justice functionaries likely do not make optimal decisions. We have noted that the normative studies also hardly may be said to be optimal, in that by far the largest proportion of criterion variance remains unexplained. Still, we have identified a number of factors that appear to have some predictive utility across a variety of settings, and it appears that decision makers do not pay heed to those factors. Rather, they appear to focus on items of information that demonstrably are not statistically related to the behavioral outcomes of interest. Despite substantial base-rate problems, most investigators have achieved normative prediction that exceeds the chance rate and that, if implemented, should improve criminal justice decision making.[29]

In virtually every decision-making situation for which the issue has been studied, it has been found that statistically developed predictive devices outperform human judgments (reviews are available in Meehl, 1954, 1965; Gough, 1962; Goldberg, 1965, 1968, 1970; Sawyer, 1966; Dawes and Corrigan, 1974; Dawes, 1979). This is one of the best-established facts in the decision-making literature, and to find otherwise in criminal justice settings would be surprising (at best) and suspicious or very likely wrong (at worst). Meehl (1954) originally established the "rules" for making comparisons of clinical and statistical predictions, which really are minimal. One rule is that both the clinical predictions and those of the statistical model are to be made on the basis of the same information (for obviously, the statistical model is disadvantaged if information is not to be made available to it). In fact, this "rule" may not even be necessary, since even when it is disregarded, the models almost always are more valid than clinical predictions. Even "bootstrapping" studies, in which a statistical model of clinical assessments is constructed, show that the models developed—even though they are of the decision makers' judgments—outperform the original judgments often by substantial amounts.

The limited information available concerning criminal justice settings would not, we think, disappoint those on the "statistical" side of this continuing (but unproductive) argument. Already noted were the studies by Glaser (1955, 1962), in which an actuarially derived device was shown superior to prognostic judgments made by sociologists and psychiatrists relative to a parole-violation criterion, and those of D. M. Gottfredson (1961; D. M. Gottfredson and Beverly, 1962), in which a statistical combination of items proved substantially more accurate than judgments made by parole board members. Recently, Holland et al. (1983) found that a statistical composite consistently outperformed mental health professionals and correctional case workers in the prediction of recidivism.[30] Carroll et al. (1982) found that parole board members' judgments of risk to be virtually uncorrelated with offender behavioral outcomes and that a simple statistical model, although not powerful, outperformed the decision makers.

The relative superiority of statistical to intuitive methods of prediction is due to many factors. For example, human decision makers often do not use information reliably (e.g., Ennis and Litwack, 1974), they often do not consider base rates (Meehl and Rosen, 1955), and this has been specifically illustrated in criminal justice decision making (Carroll, 1977); they may inappropriately weight items of information that are predictive, or they may assign weight to items that in fact are not predictive (as our review shows; see also Ebbesen and Konecni, 1981); and they may be overly influenced by causal attributions (e.g., Carroll, 1978a) or spurious correlations (Monahan, 1981). In fairness, it should be pointed out that there

[29]It is important to remember the cautions of previous sections: implementation of prediction instruments may conflict, wholly or in part, with other objectives of the decisions being discussed. Those objectives are multiple, often conflicting, and usually poorly articulated. It is because prediction of "risk" (of failure to appear for trial, or of new offenses, or of parole or probation violations) is only one of the apparent objectives of decisions that the question of "improvement" of criminal justice decision making is problematic in relation to prediction alone.

[30]However, after a correction for range restriction was applied, the human judges did better than the instrument in identifying indices of violent recidivism.

may be advantages to intuitive judgments as well. For example, human decision makers can make use of information that cannot be made available to a statistical device (at least readily). Demeanor during an interview may be one such example. Other factors in favor of intuitive judgments are reviewed in Dawes (1975).[31]

Due in part to the demonstrable superiority of statistical prediction methods, a great deal of effort has been expended in attempts to provide criminal justice functionaries with tools to aid them in the decision-making process. We review several of these in the next section.

APPLICATIONS OF PREDICTION IN STRUCTURING DISCRETION

This section focuses on recent attempts to provide structure for a variety of discretionary criminal justice decisions. Our charge from the Panel on Research on Criminal Careers was to "review research findings on existing prediction-based rules for structuring criminal justice decisions, with special attention to their adequacy in terms of predictive accuracy, efficiency, and validity, and to the relative contribution of individual predictor variables to adequacy." Since the most commonly used devices have been based on studies very similar (or identical) to those reviewed earlier in this paper, we can provide a simple response: (1) they are of low-to-moderate predictive accuracy; (2) they usually therefore are not very efficient (in a predictive sense), and they are at best modestly valid; (3) it commonly is observed that only a few variables, notably those concerning offense type and offense history, make a substantial contribution to the prediction attained; and (4) this appears to be true regardless of the decision arena investigated.

This "simple" response is unsatisfactory, however. The panel also asked us to assess "the success of prediction-based rules in affecting the behaviors they are intended to affect (e.g., have prediction rules used in structuring parole decisions reduced the prevalence of failure on parole?)." This is not a simple question, although it is an obvious and important one. Had the parenthetical example not been included, our response simply would be: when properly implemented, apparently they can be successful.

We will review the evidence for our assertion later; here, we wish to point out that in evaluating the efficacy of attempts to structure discretionary decision making in criminal justice settings, it is first necessary to examine the purposes underlying the innovations. Criminal justice system functionaries typically make decisions relative to compound (and complex) goals. In the context of sentencing, for example, we noted that judges may seek to apply a criminal sanction for rehabilitative, deterrent, incapacitative, or desert purposes; often, they report seeking to satisfy more than one of those concerns at once (D. M. Gottfredson and Stecher, 1979). Decision-making goals of paroling authorities also are complex, and vary widely among decision makers and across the country (O'Leary and Hall, no date). Although it is commonly perceived that paroling authorities have the minimization of recidivism risk as a principal goal, that simply is not the case. For example, the Maryland parole board has the stated purpose of ensuring just deserts (A. Hopkins, personal communication, 1983); and the U.S. Parole Commission asserts three goals (related to accountability for the crime, institutional behavior, and risk of parole violation) (D. M. Gottfredson, Cosgrove, et al., 1978). Thus, prediction is not a stated concern for the Maryland

[31]See also Cronbach and Gleser's (1957) discussion of the relative advantages and disadvantages of "narrow band" and "broad band" assessment procedures.

board; and prediction is only one of several concerns for the federal board.

Still, the concept of prediction generally is central to the decisions made in most of these settings. Accordingly, many of the attempts to provide structure for those decisions do have a predictive component. However, we are aware of no attempt to structure the decisions discussed that involves only a predictive component. In practical application, decision makers invariably seek not only to structure decisions with respect to prediction, but with respect to other goals as well (e.g., the satisfaction of just deserts). As we shall see, such a choice invariably constrains—often very seriously—the predictive component of the tools developed.

Second, evaluating the "success" of any innovation requires that comparisons be made. James Thurber, when once asked how his wife was, reportedly answered "Compared to what?" (Einhorn and Schact, 1975). The needed comparisons may be made essentially in three ways: with respect to past practice; with respect to other innovations (including, desirably, a "no innovation" condition); and with respect to some ideal standard. Obviously, the criteria on which the comparisons would be made must be stated, and, if the exercise is to have other than academic utility, those criteria must be related to the goals identified for the innovation(s) studied.

In justice system settings, comparisons relative to an ideal standard are doomed to failure and thus are trivial. Debates concerning differing "ideal" standards and purposes for sentencing decisions (for example) are accelerating, as we have noted in a previous section. The ideal standard of one who advocates a just deserts perspective is radically different from that advocated by proponents of "selective incapacitation"; succinct reviews and summaries of these differences can be found in a recent "debate" between Greenwood and von Hirsch (NIJ Reports, 1984). Similar arguments could be made for ideal standards based on other philosophies. Comparisons made relative to ideal standards of the type mentioned are not scientifically interesting; indeed, they essentially are not matters of science. Although science may inform the ethical and philosophical debate and although this debate is of obvious interest and importance, scientific comparisons of an innovation relative to an ideal will become important only when society eventually comes to consensus on what that shall be. We do not think this likely for some time to come.

Comparisons made with past practice are of value, but that value is constrained by well-known limitations of simple pre- and post-test research designs (Campbell and Stanley, 1963; Cook and Campbell, 1979). In brief, a finding that the effects anticipated for the innovation are observed does not, of course, mean that the innovation produced the effects. Without controls for many potential threats to validity, one cannot rule out the possibility that the effects result from something else—even something completely exogenous to the innovation and the research setting. For the same reasons, a finding that the effects anticipated for the innovation are not observed does not mean that the innovation produced no effect. Although one is used to thinking about alternative hypotheses (usually with a view toward discrediting them) when observing a presumed effect, one is not used to thinking about them when an effect is not observed. This, of course, is critical when the research design is a simple pre-post comparison.

With the exception of the case study, the simple pre-post test is the weakest of all commonly used experimental designs. And with one exception, it is the only kind of comparison made to date concerning the utility of devices designed to structure discretionary decision making in criminal justice settings.

The very first question that must be asked concerns whether the innovation in fact has been implemented. An influential report recently concluded that in several jurisdictions studied, an attempt to provide decision makers with devices to assist in the structuring of sentencing decisions was unsuccessful, in that the devices were not, in fact, implemented (Rich et al., 1982). Unfortunately, the authors exceeded the bounds of common sense by reporting also that the innovation had no effect. An unimplemented innovation cannot be expected to have an effect; to observe otherwise would obviously be spurious.

Bail and Pretrial Release Prediction-Based Tools

Beginning in the early 1960s, numerous federal and state jurisdictions engaged in attempts to provide bail and pretrial-release decision makers systematically with information relevant to the decisions to be made (Freed and Wald, 1964, describe several of these). The pioneering and most widely known (and emulated) of these programs was the Vera Institute of Justice's *Manhattan Bail Project*, begun in the fall of 1961 and subsequently modeled by several other jurisdictions (Freed and Wald, 1964; M. R. Gottfredson, 1974; D. M. Gottfredson, 1975). In this project a scale—clearly designed to be predictive of risk of failure to appear, but not empirically derived—was applied to defendants to determine release recommendations. The risk evaluation was based on information concerning residential stability, family ties and contacts, employment history, and prior criminal record. An arbitrary weighting scheme was used, which resulted in a total "risk" score, according to which recommendations were made concerning release.

Considerable success was claimed for this and related projects. For example, Freed and Wald (1964:62) report that "the Manhattan Bail Project and its progeny have demonstrated that a defendant with roots in the community is not likely to flee, irrespective of his lack of prominence or ability to pay a bondsman. To date, these projects have produced remarkable results, with vast numbers of releases, few defaulters and scarcely any commissions of crime by parolees in the interim between release and trial." Of course, the predictive utility of the scale is an empirical, rather than an experiential, question, and, when finally empirically studied (over a decade after the implementation and widespread transfer of the innovation), it was demonstrated that, in all likelihood, the validity of the Vera scale had little, if anything, to do with the success claimed (M. R. Gottfredson, 1974). As already discussed, the base rate alone (when failure to appear is the criterion) could well provide the results and claims such as those made by Freed and Wald. In the M. R. Gottfredson study (described in a preceding section), Vera scale scores were found to account (at best) for 2 percent of the variance in either failure to appear or arrest rates. Further, considerable colinearity of individual Vera scale items was observed (e.g., between points assigned for family ties and for residence), which suggests that the weighting scheme intuitively developed was highly inappropriate (on empirical grounds). The plan worked in the sense of starting a social movement; the scale, however, did not work in predicting failure to appear.

As described earlier, in his Los Angeles study, M. R. Gottfredson (1974) attempted to construct normative predictive devices for both failure to appear and arrest criteria, with fair success. On validation, however, the power of the devices constructed reduced approximately to the low level observed for the Vera scale.

Goldkamp and Gottfredson (1985) recently completed a study of guidelines for pretrial release and bail decisions that are based, in part, on an empirical assessment of risk. The general approach to guidelines development that they followed was patterned after D. M. Gottfredson, Wilkins, and Hoffman (1978), and the empirical work on which the experimental project was based is described in Goldkamp and Gottfredson (1981a,b).

The study was essentially a policy experiment; it was not intended to provide an empirical test of the relative power of empirically derived prediction instruments and unguided or intuitive predictions. Three guideline models were developed: a purely descriptive model, a purely normative (actuarial) model, and a model that attempted to combine the descriptive and normative approaches to guidelines development. Depending on the goals of the experiment, any of these could be compared with unguided practice; all such comparisons would be of considerable interest, but different results, of course, would be expected. The descriptive model essentially provides judges with normed information concerning past practices and summarizes experience concerning those factors thought most influential to past decisions. Because it does not explicitly address risk of future behavior, the model is not designed to be predictive (in the sense we have been using this term). One might anticipate, however, that the provision of this information would serve to constrain variability in subsequent decisions made, relative to those made in unguided practice. A comparison of the normative models with unguided practice would directly address the question of relative accuracy; but that was not attempted in this experiment. Rather, it was the third guidelines model—that which combined experiential and predictive concerns—that was implemented and experimentally studied.

The judges of the Philadelphia Municipal Court very directly were "partners" in the development, modification, and experimental study of the guidelines selected for implementation (for discussions of the importance of such "partnerships," see D. M. Gottfredson, Wilkins, and Hoffman, 1978; Galegher and Carroll, 1983). Without this partnership, it is highly unlikely that any guidelines models could have been developed, and it is a virtual certainty that the experimental study of these could not have been achieved. After reviewing the models, the judges chose the combined approach but also required modifications based on a series of policy-development meetings. The judges chose a guidelines model that simultaneously considered the seriousness of the charge (which, as described above, is not associated with subsequent risk, either of failure to appear or of pretrial arrests, but is predictive of judges' decisions) and statistical risk. With respect to the latter, however, the judges chose a prediction model developed with respect to a combined criterion measure. That is, rather than separately considering risk of failure to appear and risk of new offenses, they chose an outcome measure that combined both. As described earlier, different independent variables are associated with the two criteria, and the models developed concerning the combined outcome measure were less powerful than those predictive of a single criterion. In at least these two ways, the judges' choice of models constrained the likely predictive accuracy of the guidelines implemented: seriousness of charge was to receive approximately equal weight as considerations of risk, and the prediction model chosen, based on an outcome measure that reflects two quite distinct prediction goals, was not optimal.

Sixteen Municipal Court judges participated in the experiment; they were randomly assigned to treatment (use of the guidelines model) and control (no training, no use of guidelines) groups. Cases, stratified by six charge-seriousness categories, were screened and assigned to judges (20 per stratification level). Follow-up for all cases was achieved for a 90-day period. The random assignment and stratification plan sought to ensure, and subsequent analyses demonstrated, that the treatment and control group cases were similar.

Goldkamp and Gottfredson (1985; see also D. M. Gottfredson, Cosgrove, et al., 1978; M. R. Gottfredson and D. M. Gottfredson, 1980a) suggest that four general concepts are of central importance in the implementation and evaluation of decision-making guidelines: visibility, rationality, equity, and effectiveness. These are related but may be treated separately for purposes of discussion and for construction of testable hypotheses. Decision tools seek, among other things, to make explicit the goals, nature, and outcome of the decision-making process (see especially D. M. Gottfredson, Hoffman, et al., 1975). As we described in the introduction to this paper, this is of great importance in criminal justice settings, where many of the decisions made are clearly predictive in nature, although this fact is not commonly recognized. Further, it is the "hidden" nature of decisions made, lack of explicit goals and policies, and a lack of information concerning the effectiveness of the decision process that result (in part) in claims of unwarranted disparity and ineffectiveness and in appeals for reform (Kastenmeir and Eglit, 1973; Harris, 1975).

The concept of rationality suggests that guidelines should assist in relating decisions made to the goals specified. These may be predictive in nature (e.g., associated with desired offender outcomes), but they may be of another nature (e.g., of ensuring just deserts or of increasing equity). In neither of these examples is prediction (in the sense that we have been using the term) an issue.

The concept of equity does suggest that guidelines should reduce the disparate treatment of similarly situated individuals, both within and across decision makers. To the extent that reductions in unwarranted disparity are achieved, equity may be said to be increased.

Finally, the questions posed by the panel stressed that guidelines should increase the effectiveness of the decisions made. It must be remembered, however, that the question of effectiveness must be addressed relative to the goals sought by the designers of the innovation. Clearly, any of the three concepts briefly discussed above—visibility, rationality, and equity—may be evaluated relative to some effectiveness criterion. Goldkamp and Gottfredson (1985) primarily address the rationality and equity concerns.

An important but often overlooked issue that must be addressed in any study purporting to evaluate the impact of guidelines (whether or not they use prediction methods) is whether the innovation was in fact used. The availability of coding sheets and a scoring grid does not ensure that decision makers understand or make use of the tools. Neither, of course, will simple debriefing sessions prove of much help in finding out if the tools are used. It is well known that experimental subjects typically attempt to provide the investigator with the information sought. The question of compliance, particularly with a voluntary program, is a complex one. The problem of complexity is exacerbated in most guidelines applications by the provision that decision makers may, at their discretion, apply a sanction or make a decision other than that recommended by the device (that is, a decision "outside the guidelines" may reflect compliance with the general model). Thus, simple monitoring is not very effective in addressing the compliance issue. Goldkamp and Gottfredson address the compliance issue in a straightforward way: in addition to training sessions, monitoring, and debriefing, it is assumed that, if the guidelines are found to be effective, compliance, at least to some degree, must have been achieved. This does not assume, of course, that compliance was complete, or that greater compliance might not have resulted in increased effectiveness, but the logic is straightforward. If the innovation is used, and if it "works," effectiveness may be demonstrated. If it is not used, it cannot be found effective; if it does not "work," it cannot be found effective even if used. The point is a simple one, but we stress it because prior attempts to evaluate other guidelines systems appear not to have paid attention to the issue (e.g., Rich et al., 1982).

Experimental group judges in the Philadelphia study do appear to have used the guidelines: 76 percent of the decisions made fell within the range suggested by the innovation; this varied from a "compliance" rate of 91 to 64 percent when individual judges were considered.[32] Exceptions to the guidelines do not appear to have been random; they were less frequent in ROR and ROR/low-cash-bail zones, and more frequent in higher cash-bail zones, than would be required by chance. Given that the guidelines studied were purposefully in large part descriptive, however, one would not expect, necessarily, that decisions made under the innovation would depart markedly from those made in the unguided condition. When considered in the aggregate, this was found to be the case. Approximately equal proportions of the samples were treated in similar manners by judges in the experimental and control groups. However, when cases judged by the control group were assigned, post hoc, to a "guidelines recommendation," only 57 percent of the decisions actually made fell within the recommendation (as compared with 76 percent for the experimental group). Further, only 13 percent of the experimental group's decisions resulted in more severe detention consequences; 29 percent of the unguided decisions resulted in a consequence more severe than that that would have been recommended by the innovation. Deviations in the opposite direction were about equally likely to be made by either group (11 percent for the experimental group, 14 percent for the control group).

The Philadelphia judges specifically sought the goal of increased equity in their decisions. This was addressed through two classifications of decisions; based on charge (the six stratification levels) and the 75-cell guidelines matrix (codetermined by charge seriousness and risk and intended, by the judges, as an operational definition of "similarly situated"). If equity is increased through application of the innovation, the variability of decisions made should be reduced, for appropriate classifications of offenders, relative to decisions made in an unguided fashion. This was observed to be the case for both classifications considered (i.e., based on offense seriousness and on the guideline matrix). With respect to the former, variability in the amount of cash bail required was similar for treatment

[32]Analyses and subsequent debriefing demonstrated that one experimental group judge completely misconstrued the experiment and purposefully did not consult the guidelines until after his decision was made. Accordingly, these data were not considered further in the analyses reported. However, Goldkamp and Gottfredson (1985) report that analyses that include these data are little different from those presented, and they offer to provide tables documenting this on request.

and control groups at lower levels of seriousness but was greatly different for higher ranges of offense seriousness. This difference (in interquartile ranges) was almost twofold for the penultimate seriousness category, and almost threefold for the most serious category. Similarly, it was in the cash-bail zone that reductions in interquartile ranges were observed when the guidelines matrix provided the offender classification. When variances (rather than interquartile ranges) were studied (for matrix cells having sufficient cases to permit the analysis), significant reductions in the expected direction were observed for 80 percent of the cells; the overall (across cells) effect for variance reduction also was significant. Goldkamp and Gottfredson (1985:174) conclude that "in short, we can safely say that variability appears to have been systematically reduced under the guidelines or experimental bail format."

A second goal of the Philadelphia judges directly involved prediction: they sought to increase the effectiveness of decision making relative both to failure to appear and pretrial arrests. If the guidelines "work" relative to these goals, "the bail decisions of the experimental judges should be more effective in result (FTAs, rearrests) than those of the control judges who decided bail in the normal fashion" (Goldkamp and Gottfredson:176). We are less optimistic. Given the modifications noted earlier, concerning a choice of less-than-optimal prediction tools and the inclusion, with equal weight, of the seriousness dimension, we would be somewhat surprised to find effectiveness with respect to identification of FTAs and pretrial arrests demonstrated. (As will be described shortly, the seriousness dimension actually received greater weight than did the risk dimension.)

Despite the demonstration that guideline-structured decision making differed in important respects from unguided decision making, Goldkamp and Gottfredson found little differential effect (on the amount of bail set) for the influence of charge seriousness and the risk dimension. Zero-order relations were similar for both groups, and resulting R^2s differed little (but in the expected direction; that is, the influence of these factors was slightly greater for the experimental group's decisions).

With respect to failure to appear and to arrests while on pretrial release, decisions made under either condition appear equally effective. No advantage, with respect to either criterion, could be demonstrated for guidelines-based versus unguided decisions.

Did the guidelines "work"? With respect to an effectiveness criterion involving equity, the answer appears to be yes. With respect to the predictive criterion, apparently the answer is no. Again, however, we stress the design issues discussed earlier and point out also that although the risk and seriousness dimensions that constitute the innovative matrix were intended to receive equal weight, they did not; the variance of the latter is considerably (three times) that of the former. Thus, in addition to problems associated with the prediction model chosen by the judges (developed nonoptimally, with respect to two goals at once), and partial reliance on a dimension known not to be associated with risk, seriousness received disproportionate weight in the guidelines grid. It therefore is appropriate to note that, despite these limitations, and in addition to achieving the goal of increased equity, the guidelines-based decisions were no worse than unguided decisions relative to the risk considerations.

Sentencing Decision Tools

In an earlier section we noted that although descriptive studies of judicial decision making are common, normative studies are not. Indeed, since normative prediction studies require the availability of a measurable criterion variable and since these are problematic in the sentencing area, it is not surprising that normative studies of judicial decisions are not available. As we have argued, normative studies concerning the goals of incapacitation and rehabilitation would appear most likely to be potentially fruitful, but the undertaking and completion of such studies would be difficult indeed. We are not aware of any normative prediction study concerning judicial decisions, although we think that these should be conducted.

There are, however, studies that have made claims for the potential utility of prediction devices for sentencing decisions (e.g., Greenwood, 1982) and studies that attempt to provide some structure for sentencing decisions based in part on an assessment of risk (e.g., the various "guidelines" studies recently reviewed by Rich et al., 1982; Sparks, 1983; J. Cohen and Tonry, 1983). In this section we comment on these.

Proposals for "Selective Incapacitation"

The concept of selective incapacitation (Greenberg, 1975; Greenwood, 1982) has received wide attention in the public press (*Newsweek*, 1982; *New York Times*, 1982a,b; *U.S. News and World Report*, 1982) and in criminal justice policy debates (J. Cohen, 1983a,b; NIJ Reports, 1984; von Hirsch and Gottfredson, 1984). The concept provides a clear illustration of the relevance of the prediction of offenders' future criminality to policy choices.[33]

It is useful to make a distinction between collective and selective incapacitation strategies: the former would assign the same (or a very similar) sanction to all persons convicted of common offenses; the latter involves sentences based on predictions of future rates of offending (J. Cohen, 1983a,b). Studies of collective incapacitation effects are rare, and they report widely varying effects (ranging in estimated crime-reduction effects of from 1 to 25 percent, depending on crime-rate assumptions and the crime types considered) (J. Cohen, 1983a:12). When mandatory terms are considered, crime-reduction estimates are somewhat larger, but impacts on prison populations appear unacceptable given the modest impact on crime (J. Cohen, 1983a:23, 30).

Studies of selective incapacitation also are rare, and they also report varying impacts on crime (and on prison populations) (Blumstein and J. Cohen, 1979; J. Cohen, 1983a; Greenwood, 1982). In general, these strategies are of two types: those that make use only of information concerning criminal history and current offense based on aggregate estimates (e.g., the J. Cohen and Blumstein approach), and those that make use of a wider variety of predictive information measured at the individual level (e.g., the Greenwood approach). The latter has been criticized on both ethical and empirical grounds (see, for example, J. Cohen, 1983a; von Hirsch and Gottfredson, 1984); the former requires estimates of average individual arrest and crime rates, as well as estimates of the average length of criminal careers. Although we do not address the ethical arguments in this paper, it should be noted that although the J. Cohen and Blumstein approach meliorates some ethical concerns, it still is incompatible with a strict just deserts position (since offender history is used). Either approach depends heavily on (1) predictive power and (2) the accuracy of the other estimates made. Our concern is with the former. Since our focus has been on individual-level pre-

[33]Although as we stressed in the introduction to this paper, prediction is central to any crime control strategy. Prediction of events is a requisite to their control.

diction, we will concentrate on that approach. It must be noted, however, that although the nature of the prediction problem is somewhat different in the Cohen approach, it involves prediction nonetheless (cf. J. Cohen, 1983a:73 ff.).

Detailed critical reviews of the report by Greenwood (1982) are available in J. Cohen (1983a), in von Hirsch and Gottfredson (1984), and in Visher (this volume). Since these reviews contain extended discussion of both empirical and ethical issues concerning that study, we focus specifically on the issue of accuracy.

The analyses reported in Greenwood (1982) are retrospective only: no prospective analyses were conducted. Thus, even if the instrument could be shown to have substantial retrospective predictive accuracy, its utility for prospective application also would have to be shown before the scheme could be applied responsibly in practice. Moreover, the report essentially contains no consideration even of retrospective accuracy. J. Cohen (1983b) and von Hirsch and Gottfredson (1984) do provide such a consideration, with results on the accuracy issue that are disappointing. Although the scale is fairly accurate with respect to low-rate offenders (76 percent correct prediction for predicted low-rate offenders), J. Cohen adds (1983b:48–49):

> The scale's performance is more uniformly poor for high-rate offenders. Among those predicted to be high-rate offenders, only 45 percent actually were high-rate offenders. This involves a false-positive rate of 55%. For purposes of selective incapacitation, where predicted high-rate offenders will be subject to longer prison terms than all other offenders, much better discrimination of the high-rate offenders would seem to be required.

J. Cohen also compared the "accuracy" of the scale relative to current practice, as implied by sentence lengths given, and found that "the seven-point scale does only marginally better overall and results in slightly more false-positives than existing subjective judgments in distinguishing offenders by their crime commission rates" (p. 50).

Predictive accuracy as just considered involves the construction sample alone. Another criticism of the Greenwood study is that no validation was attempted. If this ever is done and if the typical result is observed, predictive accuracy in new samples will be even lower. Thus, in addition to the concerns already raised about prospective prediction and the lack of validation with respect to this issue, even retrospective validation on a separate sample was not attempted.

Other criticisms could be made. For example, colinearity among predictor items was not investigated, nor was the weighting scheme designed in an optimal fashion. It must be noted, however, that in practice, this has seemed to make little difference (S. D. Gottfredson and D. M. Gottfredson, 1979), and the items used are of the type generally observed to be predictive of future criminal behavior. In the retrospective construction sample, the device does appear of similar predictive power as commonly is observed. As noted, however, its accuracy in prospective or cross-validation samples is not known.

Sentencing Guidelines

Sentencing guidelines recently were considered in some detail by Rich et al. (1982), by Galegher and Carroll (1983), and by the National Research Council (Blumstein et al., 1983). Methodological limitations concerning the development of sentencing guidelines (Rich et al., 1982; F. M. Fisher and Kadane, 1983; Sparks, 1983), ethical concerns (F. M. Fisher and Kadane, 1983), issues of implementation (Martin, 1983), and of efficacy (J. Cohen and Tonry, 1983) have been discussed. Elsewhere (M. R.

Gottfredson and D. M. Gottfredson, 1984), we have provided a "partisan review" of these critiques, and we invite attention to the issues we raise there. Here, we concentrate on the adequacy, in terms of predictive accuracy, of "prescriptive" sentencing guidelines.

Distinctions have been made between sentencing guidelines that are intended to be "descriptive" and those intended to "prescribe" sentencing practices (D. M. Gottfredson, Cosgrove, et al., 1978; J. Cohen and Tonry, 1983). This differentiation parallels an important organizing principle of this paper. Previously, we made a distinction between predictive decision studies that are descriptive and those that are normative. The parallel, we believe, would equate the descriptive prediction studies and the descriptive guidelines approaches on the one hand, and the normative prediction studies and prescriptive guidelines approaches on the other.

In practice, the distinction between descriptive and normative prediction studies often becomes blurred, especially when the goal is to improve rational decision making. Thus, for example, D. M. Gottfredson, Wilkins, and Hoffman (1978:10) stressed that "the research that undergirds the guidelines developed and the guidelines themselves are essentially descriptive, not prescriptive; yet the very term [guidelines] implies prescription." (The referent is parole guidelines, but the statement applies equally to sentencing guidelines.) Although the distinction may become blurred, it nonetheless is an important one to bear in mind, for the consequences of emphasis on one or the other of the two approaches for issues such as that addressed by the Panel on Research on Criminal Careers will be very different.

Some (e.g., F. M. Fisher and Kadane, 1983) have criticized descriptive sentencing guidelines precisely because they are intended to be descriptive of past practice; others have criticized them because they are insufficiently descriptive of past practice (e.g., Rich et al., 1982; Sparks, 1983); and some have criticized them because they are insufficiently prescriptive [see discussion by Sparks (1983: 238–239) concerning the widths of "prescribed normal ranges"].

The first criticism suggests that descriptive sentencing guidelines are "unthoughtfully conservative" and reduce to "a species of computer-driven conservatism" (F. M. Fisher and Kadane, 1983:192). Preferable, it is suggested, is a deduction of guidelines from ethical principles. Finally, it is suggested that the empirical approach avoids hard ethical questions but that the approach advocated would not.

As F. M. Fisher and Kadane correctly point out, the empirical approach can attempt to tackle hard ethical questions, but this has not, to our knowledge, been done. Rather, guidelines developers have taken a much less sophisticated approach to the elimination of ethically questionable predictors; as nicely illustrated by F. M. Fisher and Kadane, this may lead to misspecification of the descriptive prediction models developed, which leads to further ethical difficulties. Even following the approach recommended, it is clear that ethical decisions must be made in the specification problem.

Descriptive guidelines are conservative, in the sense that dramatic changes in the nature of past practice are not expected—rather, the attempt is to improve on past practice by providing structure for future decisions. That structure, however, is based on models of past practice. J. Cohen and Tonry (1983:415) asserted that "descriptive/voluntary guidelines are likely to involve the smallest impact on sentencing. Since descriptive guidelines recommend essentially no departure from current practice for the court as a whole, only those judges who deviate widely from current practice are expected to change their sentences." If the guidelines are voluntary, the extent of expected compliance from this deviant group may be questioned. As originally envisioned, however, the descriptive guidelines model proposes a routine feedback mechanism that is intended specifically to allow decision makers to change (probably incrementally, and it is to be hoped, for the better) the guidelines themselves and, hence, the nature of the decisions made. Persons certainly may differ with respect to a preference for gradual improvement or radical change; guidelines developers appear to have preferred the more thoughtfully conservative approach or at least to have believed the approach taken to be preferable on pragmatic grounds. Radical proposals for change often are rejected by those in authority.

The suggestion by F. M. Fisher and Kadane (1983) that a better model involves a deduction of guidelines purely from ethical considerations is debatable. Requisite to such development would be some demonstrable societal consensus with respect to the variety of ethical concerns that invariably must arise in the exercise. Absent that consensus, the empirical approach holds considerable further promise.

The second general line of criticism of descriptive sentencing guidelines is that such guidelines are insufficiently and (more damaging) imprecisely descriptive of past practice (Rich et al., 1982; Galegher and Carroll, 1983; Sparks, 1983). Although these reviews vary considerably in detail, common themes arise in each. These have to do with sampling issues, statistical modeling issues, and implementation issues. Also apparent is some misunderstanding of the distinction made here and elsewhere concerning the descriptive and prescriptive nature of decision studies. Each of the three general issues raised can have important consequences for the potential accuracy of prediction models.

The sampling issue, as raised in the reviews cited, is most important with respect to the appropriate unit(s) of analysis concerning which decisions should be modeled. It has been demonstrated that systematic variation due to (unknown differences in) judges may be observed in sentencing (e.g., Rich et al., 1982) and in bail-setting (e.g., Goldkamp and Gottfredson, 1981a,b) decision situations. The evidence in other areas is not clear: for example, D. M. Gottfredson and Ballard (1966) found no differences associated with parole decision makers after controlling for differences in cases seen. For some decision-study purposes, the individual decision maker may be the appropriate unit of analysis; for other purposes, it may not be. If one seeks to describe court behavior, rather than the behavior of individual judges, decisions aggregated across judges would seem to be preferable. It is the case, however, that, if substantial between-judge variability is discovered, perhaps the analysis properly should be conducted on the individual case data, residualized with respect to judge effects. To our knowledge, this has not been done. Whether substantially different models would result remains an empirical question. It seems clear, however, that models of individual decision makers, if they are very different from one another, would do little to constrain the disparity associated with court discretion now so widely criticized.

Statistical models used in the descriptive modeling of sentencing practices also have been criticized. Important issues concerning potential misspecification resulting from insufficient attention to ethical concerns already have been mentioned. The other principal criticism has to do with the use of standard multiple regression methods for decisions that are dichotomous. The criticism, which is correct, is that reliance on the simple regression model may lead to an inappropriate model of past practice: regression weights and the overall measure of fit (R^2) are unstable (the latter may even exceed a value of 1.0). Other regression models (e.g., probit or tobit) are to be preferred but have not often been used.

Two observations may be made. First, the models as applied in practice will be imprecise anyway, since (1) the weights usually are smoothed to simplify practical application and (2) the decision makers to whom a device may be recommended often rather arbitrarily change the weights in an attempt to reflect some policy concern. Second, the recommended regression procedures have been used in a number of studies (e.g., Palmer and Carlson, 1976; Solomon, 1976; Forst and Brosi, 1977; Rhodes, 1978; van Alstyne and Gottfredson, 1978; S. D. Gottfredson and D. M. Gottfredson, 1979, 1980; Schmidt and Witte, 1979; Goldkamp and Gottfredson, 1981a,b, 1985), all but one of which predate the criticisms made (Rich et al., 1982; Galegher and Carroll, 1983; Sparks, 1983). The net result of these several studies is a demonstration that the results of the models are little different. The best available methods should, of course, be used, and the proper specification of past practice is to be desired. Given the poor quality of presently available data, however, it appears that the power inherent in the models of choice often is not realized. Indeed, if the data are sufficiently poor, it may be observed that less sophisticated methods can be preferable (Wainer, 1976; D. M. Gottfredson, Cosgrove, et al., 1978; S. D. Gottfredson and D. M. Gottfredson, 1979).

In short, descriptive guidelines often have not been developed using the best and most recent methods available. As a practical matter, however, it probably has not made much difference, either to the specification of the models or to their accuracy.

The third general criticism of descriptive guidelines is that they are insufficiently prescriptive. In general, attention has focused on the widths of ranges offered in the guidance schemes. Although we think it odd that the tools would be criticized for this reason, it is quite possible, and potentially quite desirable, that the criticism be extended. If prescription with respect to predictive accuracy is desired, it is through normative decision study that practice should be altered. We can envision considerable advantage to a purely normatively based guidelines approach, and we think that resulting accuracy would be much improved.

It must be remembered that in the descriptive case the issue of accuracy has to do with the accuracy with which past practice is modeled. If prescriptive accuracy is desired, normative decision study is desired. To our knowledge, no guidelines have been developed in this fashion.

J. Cohen and Tonry (1983) suggest that prescriptive guidelines are exemplified by those developed and implemented in Minnesota. Neither dimension of the grid used, however, was intended to be predictive; such an intent was explicitly excluded by the Minnesota Sentencing Guidelines Commission (1982). It is the case that one of the axes (the "criminal history score") bears a remarkable resemblance to many instruments that are designed with a predictive intent; and items repeatedly found to be predictive, such as prior felony sentence, a prior felony-type juvenile record, and prior nontraffic misdemeanor or gross misdemeanor sentences, are used to construct this scale. One could, of course, assess the predictive utility of the criminal-history score; but this hardly could be viewed as germane to an evaluation of the Commission in achieving its goals.[34] So far as we know, no such analysis has been done.

It is notable (and, we believe, laudable) that the commission sought to ensure that its sentencing guidelines "be neutral with respect to the race, gender, social, or economic status of convicted felons" (Minnesota Sentencing Guidelines Commission, 1982:1). This admirable objective, which may be shared by those who would include an explicit predictive intent, is difficult to achieve—especially in view of correlations among offense or criminal-history (or other) items thought legitimate for inclusion and measures of race, gender, or socioeconomic status not desired to be bases for decisions. This point must be discussed further, along with the contribution of F. M. Fisher and Kadane (1983) already noted; suffice it to say here that this problem may remain whether or not there is a predictive intent.

In summary, our charge was not to assess the impact of sentencing guidelines per se, be they descriptive, prescriptive, or some combination of these. As noted by Martin (1983), complex implementation issues must be addressed if sentencing guidelines are to survive in evaluatable form. J. Cohen and Tonry (1983) did attempt such an evaulation, and others (Rich, Sutton, et al., 1982) also make evaluative statements (although without first ensuring that some innovation had been seriously implemented). Currently, Abt Associates is engaged in an evaluation of voluntary guidelines in several states; but preliminary reports of this evaluation study could not be made available to us in time to be included in this review (D. Carrow, personal communication, 1984). In general, these evaluations likely will focus on issues of compliance and of disparity reduction; little in the way of achievement relative to a predictive component is likely to be assessed because, as we have suggested, little in the way of a predictive component is provided by these guidelines attempts.

Tools to Structure Parole Decision Making

The "guidelines" approaches described in the two preceding sections were first developed in parole decision-making settings. The model used in the early studies is more similar to that used in the Philadelphia bail experiment than to those discussed relative to sentencing decisions. Unlike the latter, the parole and bail guidelines do make use of an empirical assessment of risk.

It is not our intent here to discuss in detail the development and implementation of parole guidelines, nor to provide an assessment of their utility for the purposes originally intended for them. Rather, our focus is on one component of the guidelines of the U.S. Parole Commission, the Salient Factor Score, since it is in regard to that score that an assessment of predictive accuracy can be made. Because we were specifically requested to assess a parole-risk screening instrument recently developed in Iowa, that too is provided. A complete description of the proposals for parole guidelines and their original development can be found in D. M. Gottfredson, Wilkins, and Hoffman

[34]The relation between items of information acceptable under a just desert orientation and those found predictive of future criminal behavior was discussed in D. M. Gottfredson, Cosgrove, et al., 1978:149: "So far as the major dimension of the proposed just-desert sentencing procedure is concerned, the prescription is very similar indeed to that of the United States Parole Commission. The Goodell Committee (von Hirsch, 1976) specifically rejected any predictive basis for their sentencing determination; but, of course, the fact that they wished to take into account the prior record of the offender, in fact, provided a predictive dimension."

(1978) and in D. M. Gottfredson, Cosgrove, et al. (1978).

The Salient Factor Score

Parole guidelines were developed in the early 1970s for consideration by the U.S. Board of Parole (now the U.S. Parole Commission) and were first implemented by that body in 1972. They were formally adopted for national use in 1973. The guidelines are in part descriptively based and in part based on a normative prediction study. One axis of the decision-making tool reflects the seriousness of the commitment offense; this was developed in an iterative process of judgments by the responsible parole board members, which resulted in ordinal classifications on this dimension.

The other axis is based on an empirically derived assessment of recidivism risk. The instrument on which this axis is based is called the Salient Factor Score (Hoffman and Beck, 1974). This device was developed, as were the guidelines themselves, in collaboration with members of the parole board. Although other models of constructing normative predictive tools were presented to the commission (e.g., the regression-based "base expectancy" scales developed in California; see D. M. Gottfredson and Beverly, 1962), the board preferred a simple, unweighted, additive model (similar to the approach originally advocated by Burgess and used for years by the Illinois parole board; this subsequently was modified and evaluated by Ohlin, 1951). Accordingly, this model was followed in the development of the Salient Factor Score.

The original Salient Factor Score was developed on a 25 percent sample (N = 902) of all persons released from federal prisons by parole, mandatory release, or expiration of sentence during the first 6 months of 1970. Two validation samples were used: a different 25 percent sample of persons released during the same time period (N = 919), and a 20 percent sample of persons released during the latter half of 1970 (N = 662). Sampling was conducted in a manner that allowed a reasonable assumption that randomness was approximated. More than 60 items of data concerning the offenders' criminal and social histories, demographic characteristics, living arrangements (past and anticipated), and prison conduct were coded from case records for each individual; follow-up data (based on a 2-year period) were based on parole board records and on "rap sheets" made available by the Federal Bureau of Investigation. A criterion measure was developed that could be used regardless of an offender's type of release and that was acceptable to the parole board collaborators. An unfavorable outcome, for example, was considered to have occurred if any of the following were observed: a new conviction that resulted in a sentence of 60 days or more; a return to prison for a technical violation of release conditions; or an outstanding warrant for absconding from supervision. Otherwise, the outcome was classified as favorable.

Variables were selected for inclusion in the additive model based simply on the inspection of bivariate relations with the criterion measure described. The selection criteria used were: that the measure be significantly associated with the outcome (based on chi-squared tests with $\alpha = .05$); that the variable not pose ethical problems; and that it appear frequently enough to be useful for most cases, but not appear to overlap substantially with other variables to be included (D. M. Gottfredson, Cosgrove, et al., 1978:48–49). Using these criteria (some of which clearly involved subjective judgment on the part of the investigators), nine variables were selected for inclusion in the model initially used. Each of these was dichotomized to reflect presence or absence of the attribute represented, except for two, which were trichotomized (these were prior convictions and prior incarcerations).

The items used in the original Salient Factor Score model, and their relations with the criterion described (in the construction sample) are (1) prior convictions as an adult or a juvenile (.21); (2) prior incarcerations as an adult or juvenile (.23); age at first adult or juvenile conviction (.14); commitment for auto theft (.20); parole revocation or commitment for a new offense while on parole (.21); history of heroin, cocaine, or barbiturate dependence (.13); completion of twelfth grade or receipt of general equivalency diploma (GED) (.08); verified employment (or full-time school attendance) for a total of at least 6 months during the last 2 years in the community (.12); and release plan to live with spouse or children (.16).[35] Thus, it may be seen both that the types of items considered are similar to those found predictive in most settings and that the general level of predictive accuracy of these is on a par with that commonly observed.

Two of the items referenced above were not originally examined in the form described (i.e., parole revocations and drug usage); these were modified, based on consideration by the parole board, into the format we have described here.

In the construction sample, the Salient Factor Score was observed to correlate significantly with the outcome criterion (point-biserial correlation = .32; MCR = .36); some shrinkage was noted when the device was applied to the two validation samples (on the first sample, the point-biserial was .28 and MCR = .33; on the second, these values were .27 and .32, respectively).

In operational use the device is collapsed from a 0 to 11 scale to a 4-category scale. This, when combined with a 6-category seriousness of offense ranking, gives the guidelines matrix actually used.

Since the adoption of the guidelines, the Salient Factor Score has been validated on new samples a number of times (cf. Hoffman and Beck, 1976; Hoffman, Stone-Meirhoefer, and Beck, 1978) and recently has been revised in light of further ethical concerns (Hoffman, 1983). Each validation effort has provided results substantially equivalent to the first such efforts; the device has held up well in prospective validation samples. The reconstruction effort and its validation (Hoffman, 1983) show little change in performance.

The level of predictive accuracy of the scale thus may be considered to be rather firmly established. But what of the additional question raised by the Panel on Research on Criminal Careers: Has use of the instrument as a component of the decision guidelines led to a reduction in recidivism? We know of no study that has sought to test this hypothesis.[36] And it seems clear such a study would be fraught with methodological difficulties that could only be overcome at best by a careful quasi-experimental or experimental design of some sort.

But it also may be asked why such a result would be expected. It is not known to us that the parole board claimed this as an objective. Nearly all inmates of all prisons eventually are released, and, most commonly, they are released on parole. Unless time served in prison reduces the probability of reoffending, a proposition not supported by the literature (see M. R. Gottfredson and D. M. Gottfredson, 1980b, for a review), an effect on recidi-

[35]These are contingency coefficients calculated by us from data presented in D. M. Gottfredson, Cosgrove, et al. (1978:50–51).

[36]There is one report (Janus, 1984) that appears to show the potential for this, but it is not clear whether the sample used is of paroled persons or the general federal prison population.

vism rates would not be expected. It is plausible, however, that one could expect (and speculate that it has been the intent of the parole board to achieve) a selective incapacitation effect. Assessments of such an effect, so far not published to our knowledge, must address the myriad problems noted in the recent National Research Council report on the topic (Blumstein et al., 1983).

Finally, we would note that here, as with the bail guidelines study described earlier, decision-maker preferences for the inclusion of competing goals in the guidelines device adopted may well constrain the potential predictive utility of the model. In the parole guidelines adopted by the federal board, as in the bail guidelines adopted by the Philadelphia judges, a competitive tension exists between seriousness of the offense—included probably to satisfy a just desert motivation—and the empirically derived risk assessment. The extent to which these effects constrain one another has not been adequately investigated to date.

The Iowa Instrument

In light of claims made for dramatic improvements in the accuracy with which offender risk assessments may be made (Chi, 1983; Fischer, 1983, 1984), we were asked to pay special attention to the instrument developed and used in Iowa. Since the Bureau of Justice Statistics has indicated interest in exploring the transferability of the device (Fischer, 1984) and some jurisdictions (e.g., Washington, D.C.) are engaged in this process, a critical review of the development and accuracy of the system was seen to be desirable.

To our knowledge, no information concerning the development, validity, or use of the instrument is available in the published literature; accordingly, in the review that follows we rely on unpublished planning and research documents made available by the Panel on Research on Criminal Careers. No document available to us contained sufficient information concerning the development of the device to allow comment on the statistical models used.[37] Similarly, we cannot comment on the predictive value of specific items of information used. (We will, however, comment on the appropriateness of some of the items in a later section.) We first discuss the original scheme developed and then the more recent versions of this scheme.

The risk-assessment system developed in Iowa appears to be based on an excellent, and relatively untried, concept. It long has been stressed that sample heterogeneity may constrain validities of predictive devices. Correlation matrices for various subsamples often do not provide accurate estimates of the parameters for the larger sample; thus, the correlations providing the basis for the equations are inadequate for estimates made for the subsamples (D. M. Gottfredson and Ballard, 1966; D. M. Gottfredson, 1967). This is particularly problematic given use of regression-based prediction methods that do not include interaction terms and is only partly meliorated by use of configural approaches or log linear models. It appears that those who developed the system in Iowa approached the problem rather directly, in that the assignment to risk categories seems actually to be based on the application of several risk-assessment instruments. Cases first are classified with respect to age (18, 19, 20, 21–24, 25–29, 30+); within age classifications, other criteria are applied (e.g., prior arrests) to further subdivide the sample. In

[37]One report (Statistical Analysis Center, 1983: 106) notes only that "new methods, such as configural analysis, were incorporated with well-established techniques to maximize predictive efficiency."

all, 12 subsamples are developed (Statistical Analysis Center, 1980:96). Depending on subgroup membership, different combinations of one of seven "general" risk-assessment instruments and one of four "violence" risk-assessment instruments are applied to a given case. All cases are subject to a "supplementary" risk assessment (Statistical Analysis Center:109); in combination, these devices determine a "risk" category. An undefined and unexplained "smoothing function" then is applied, which results in a final assignment to one of eight risk categories.[38] Finally, classification with respect to "violence" may be further refined (through classification with respect to current offense type), which results in classification to one of nine "violence" risk categories (Statistical Analysis Center:113).

The statistical adequacy of any of these several devices is not discussed in the available reports. If, as we may speculate, the devices have about the same validity as other such devices, in combination they may well be expected to demonstrate considerably more power—indeed, it is probably use of this bootstrapping technique that accounts for the improved validity noted for the final classification. To summarize, it appears that the final classification is based on a very good idea: devices are constructed for several more-homogeneous subgroups and the resulting classifications are combined in a final "expectancy table." It is important to note that persons may be classified into a given category based on very different combinations of predictor variables. We are, of course, concerned that the classification relies, in part, on certain items of information that many find objectionable (both on ethical and legal grounds; see Underwood, 1979; von Hirsch and Gottfredson, 1984) for use in applications such as those proposed for this classification (Chi, 1983; Statistical Analysis Center, 1983; Fischer, no date). This concern is exacerbated when we are told that these "are among the best predictors" (Statistical Analysis Center, 1983:16).

Exaggerated Claims, Improved Accuracy, or Both? Several reports (e.g., Chi, 1983; Fischer, 1983; Fowler, 1983) aimed at the practitioner audience have hailed the "unprecedented accuracy" of the Iowa classification scheme. Chi (1983:8) reports that "values of the Mean Cost Rating (MCR = .637) and the Coefficient of Predictive Efficiency (CPE = .807) demonstrated in Iowa are much higher than for risk assessment devices elsewhere." In addition to some probable increase in accuracy, a number of other factors combine to provide the basis for this remarkable claim. As we discuss below, both of the figures cited above are at best misleading; at worst, they are meaningless for the purposes intended. The source of the figures cited by Chi (1983) is Statistical Analysis Center (1980), which forms the basis for much of the discussion to follow.

The classification scheme described above was developed on a construction sample of 4,704 adult offenders released from probation and parole in Iowa during the 3-year period 1974–1976. Time at risk varied (and averaged 11.7 months) but does not appear to have been controlled for in the analyses. Follow-up data included (1) information concerning up to three new criminal charges (if any), (2) type of release (discharge, revocation, escape/abscond), and (3) jail time prior to release. The classification was validated on a sample of 7,813 offenders released during 1977–1979 (time at risk is not specified for this sample).

[38]Reports do suggest that the "smoothing function" compensates for low-frequency cells; it may also adjust small reversals (the latter is our supposition only).

An outcome measure designed to reflect rearrest and the number and seriousness of charges was developed (called a weighted outcome measure). The development of this measure is not detailed in reports available; we do not know if the scaling is arbitrary, but it appears to be (see Statistical Analysis Center, 1980:2). The index heavily weights felony offenses against persons and gives little weight to technical violations. The maximum achievable score is 17 (15 points for three felonies against persons, plus 2 points for a revocation of probation or parole); the minimum is zero (for a discharge without new charges or jail time for technical violations). The mean value of this index for the construction sample is 1.18; it is 1.22 for the validation sample.

It is with respect to this index that the classification scheme was developed (Statistical Analysis Center, 1980:3). Twenty-five variables were reported to have significant associations with the index: type of current offense(s), age, age at first arrest, prior arrests, juvenile convictions, juvenile commitments, prior adult convictions, prior adult jail terms, prior adult prison commitments, prior probations (juvenile or adult), prior convictions (juvenile or adult), prior adult incarcerations, prior incarcerations, prior jail terms/juvenile commitments, prior jail/prison/probation, known aliases, history of drug or alcohol problem, narcotics use, employment status (most recent in community), possession of employable skills, possession of high school diploma/GED, years of school, legal marital status, pretrial services or detention, and probation time in jail/residence. These items must be highly colinear, but the extent of this as a problem in the development of the classification scheme cannot be determined since the nature of that development is not specified. (However, the scheme does not appear to use weighted variables, and so the issue probably is not terribly important.)

The ordinal (perhaps interval) criterion measure should provide advantage in terms of predictive power (cf. S. D. Gottfredson and Taylor, 1986); however, the criterion measure is not used directly in evaluating the accuracy of the classification scheme. The rank-order (or other) correlation between levels of classification and the criterion (for both the construction and the validation samples) would be of considerable interest, but it is not provided. In fact, the potential power of the index is not used. Cases in each classification level are assigned the mean criterion value for that level, thus discarding all within-group (or level) variance; only between-group variance remains to be assessed. Clearly, this provides substantial advantage in demonstrating the "accuracy" of the device (indeed, since there are no reversals, the rank-order correlation will be 1). From here, the developers define a new "outcome index" for each classification level as the mean index value for that level, divided by the mean value for the highest risk-classification level. The resulting proportion is changed to a percentage. This has the effect, of course, of making the transformed mean for the highest risk group equal to 100 percent;[39] means for the other risk levels are a percentage of this "base group" mean. The authors correctly noted that "this change of scale in no way alters the relative degree of success or failure of any of the risk categories" (Statistical Analysis Center, 1980:5), but they apparently failed to recognize that the original problem remains; they

[39]This manipulation was made based on the construction sample, and the mean "weighted outcome" score for the highest risk group is used in transformations for the validation sample as well. Although this meliorates the variance reduction problem, it does not obviate it.

have discarded within-cell variability. In a traditional assessment strategy, the simple correlation would be examined, or, if the dependent measure is a dichotomy (as it usually is), the proportion of success or failure is examined directly. In either case, within-cell variability remains. Here, all cases in the highest risk group are treated (in essence) as "failures" (whether they were or not), and the percentages examined simply reflect cell means as a percentage of that of the base group. The authors acknowledged some of the difference between these two types of "percentages" in a brief and rather confused discussion (Statistical Analysis Center, 1980:8) involving "units" of success and failure and concluded that "with the preceding convention we can now talk about the predictive efficiency of the general risk assessment—and the extent to which we fall short of perfect prediction—in terms of the distribution of our units of success and failure among the eight risk levels." Values of the MCR are calculated, on the percentages described above, to be .65 for the construction sample, .639 for the validation sample, and .637 for the combined construction and validation samples. The authors also calculated MCRs for a variety of hypothetical base-rate conditions; here, a slight embarrassment occurs when the percentage for the high-risk group rises above 100; however, a quick "down-scaling" (Statistical Analysis Center, 1980:14) handles this. The MCRs for the construction, validation, and combined samples reported by Hoffman and Adelberg (1980) using the Salient Factor Score on federal samples are offered for comparison (these are, respectively, .33, .37, and .35). Thus it is asserted, that even under varying base-rate conditions, the advantage of the Iowa classification is demonstrated.

However, by providing the Salient Factor Score (in the examples used) the "logical" advantage provided the Iowa classification scheme, we calculate an MCR of .711 (for the construction sample). This is achieved simply by "rescaling" in the same manner as used in the Iowa studies; that is, each of the levels is considered simply as a proportion of the failures observed in the highest risk group. To use the terminology of the authors of the Iowa report, this is a "lofty value" indeed. It also is essentially meaningless.

The authors also developed and used a "coefficient of predictive efficiency," defined as "the variance of the outcome indices (or rates of failure) of the risk levels divided by 2500, where the base (overall) index for the study group has been adjusted to 50%" (Statistical Analysis Center, 1980:15; see also Statistical Analysis Center, 1984). This coefficient is used to describe the "accuracy" of the Iowa model in several reports; in some of the most recent reports available, only this coefficient is used (e.g., Statistical Analysis Center, 1984). Accordingly, a brief exploration of its properties is required.

In essence, this description and equations given in Statistical Analysis Center (1984) provide a shorthand method for calculating the variance of the means of expectancy cell observations, when the distribution of means has been transformed such that the grand mean is equal to 50. Once the variance has been found, its value is "unencoded" by dividing the coded-score variance by 2,500 (the square of the transformed base rate). The result, of course, is not the variance of the cell means. To obtain the true variance, one would divide the coded-score variance by the square of the weighting factor used to create the transformation; very rarely would this be 50. Using the data provided in Statistical Analysis Center (1980:7), we calculated the variance of the distribution of cell means to be 566.18. When we encoded the distribution so that the grand mean was 50, we observed a coded-score variance of 2,016.41. To obtain the unencoded variance, we divided this by the square of the factor used to transform the distribution (50/26.5) (since we are told that the "variance" is of interest), which, within hand-calculator rounding error, of course gives the variance of the original scores (566.41).

The Iowa investigators do not do this; they unencode the coded-score variance by dividing by the square of the transformed base rate and obtain the value reported (.807). Under the same conditions, the federal parole prediction method achieves a value of only .198. It is suggested that "for 'perfect' prediction in the Iowa sample, using a 50 percent outcome index, we would have [a value of CPE] = 1.00. Thus, using CPE as a measure of predictive efficiency, we can think of the Iowa system as roughly 81% of perfect, remembering—of course—that 'perfect' in this sense does not necessarily mean the ideal 0% – 100% prediction" (Statistical Analysis Center, 1980:16). In a footnote, readers are advised that the "CPE can theoretically be greater than 1 if the net effect of prediction is greater than the ideal 0 – 100% result" (Statistical Analysis Center, 1980:15). In fact, all that is necessary for the index to exceed 1 is that the variance of the coded scores exceed 2,500; this can occur for many reasons that only tangentially are related to the prediction problem.

We see nothing of value in the coefficient used to assess the "accuracy" of the Iowa model, but we see many reasons why it should not be used. First, it is a least-squares measure (of a peculiar sort); accordingly, it gives disproportionate weight to extreme scores. Although the developers appear to desire this,[40] the use of a least-squares measure of variability when the distribution is markedly skewed is not advised (Guilford, 1965; Minium, 1970). Simple inspection shows that skew is marked for this and others of the Iowa samples. Second, we fail to understand why a squared index term is useful. Usually, when one wishes to interpret an index of variability, one relies on the standard deviation (which, of course, may be interpreted in the original metric). Third, and related to the two concerns already raised, the index is not independent of scale value. In general, the larger the scores, the larger the value of the index. In comparing the Iowa and the federal models, for example, markedly different scale values are observed. The highest encoded score for the federal sample is 75.7; for the Iowa model it is 179.8. Sums of squares must be larger (all else equal) for the latter distribution. Thus, depending on the outcome metric used, values of the CPE will vary.

In general the index appears roughly to be nonsense for the purpose intended; in any event it is very different from the usual index of predictive efficiency as described earlier in this paper. Although as noted, that index is not problem free, it does at least have a clear, specific, and useful meaning; for the Iowa data we calculated it (in a manner to be described below) to be about 13 to 19 percent (depending on the criterion measure considered). The value for the Salient Factor Score (as described in Hoffman and Adelberg, 1980) is about 11 percent.

To summarize, the accuracy of the Iowa classification system as considered in Statistical Analysis Center (1980) and touted by Chi (1983) and others is wrong and exaggerated. Not only are the values of the MCR and the "coefficient of predictive efficiency" reported based on the combined construction and validation samples, but the former is calculated relative to an absurd criterion, and the latter, despite its familiar-sounding name, is es-

[40]They report that "one difficulty in using MCR to measure predictive efficiency [is that] it doesn't reward the researcher for isolating extremely high risk groups—that is, groups with performance at least twice as unfavorable as the overall sample performance" (Statistical Analysis Center, 1980:15).

sentially meaningless for the purpose intended.[41]

How Accurate Is the Classification Scheme? Unfortunately, we cannot answer this question well, but we can provide some clues. Statistical Analysis Center (1980:vii; see also Chi, 1983:5) provides a table that gives outcome distributions relative to a revocation/absconder criterion and to a rearrest criterion. Also given in the table is a "threat to public safety" criterion, which is the unfortunate criterion described above and the index of choice of the authors. We make the assumption in the discussion that follows that the rates (percentages) reported in the first two columns of the table have not been "adjusted" in the same or a similar manner as has the third column. If this assumption is warranted, MCRs can readily be calculated for these data. We have done this, and obtained values of .55 (for the absconder criterion) and .58 (for the rearrest criterion).[42] These values are impressive and suggest that the classification scheme developed in Iowa does have substantial potential power. Unfortunately, however, the data are presented only for the combined construction and validation samples, and hence the values cited above likely are overestimates. In addition, there remains the problem of varying time at risk, which we do not believe the researchers addressed.

The values shrink only a bit (to .51 and .54) when a collapsed (three-category) version of the classification is considered. Considered as a selection device (in our use of this term), the classifications result in an index of predictive efficiency of 12.5 and 19.3 percent for the revocation/absconder criterion and the rearrest criterion, respectively. Values of the RIOC index are 46.7 and 48.8 percent. For comparison, the index of predictive efficiency of the Salient Factor Score (using the data provided by Hoffman and Adelberg, 1980) is 11 percent, and the value of the RIOC index is 40.5 percent.

Later Iterations: the 1983 and 1984 Models. Again, insufficient information concerning issues of sampling, measurement, and device construction is contained in available reports to allow us to provide detailed comment. In general, it appears that modification to the scheme resulted from criticisms of the choice of predictor items (as raised above). Objectionable items of information appear not to be included in the newer devices, and, as found by many others, predictive accuracy does not appear to have suffered dramatically (S. D. Gottfredson and D. M. Gottfredson, 1985). Rather than essentially repeat earlier discussion, let us raise some reservations that have not been resolved (and in some cases are exacerbated) by information concerning the newer models.

First, we are concerned about potential Type I error problems in the development of the devices used. It is clear that a great many statistical tests have been used and a great many devices constructed on the same samples of cases. Since we do not know how many tests have been used or devices developed, we cannot provide an assessment of the Type I error problem, but we can note that one ought to be sensitive to it. Consequences of this problem will, of course, be observed on validation; but we are not convinced that this has been achieved properly.

We are also concerned about scaling and measurement issues, particularly with respect to the outcome criteria used.

---

[41] For a description of an index that is conceptually similar but that is not subject to these limitations, see John (1963).

[42] In a later report (Fischer, 1981), we find these coefficients reported for a rearrest and a program-failure criterion, based on the sample of 12,517.

As noted above, the original outcome measure was weighted in an apparently arbitrary manner with respect to the seriousness of offenses alleged. Although time at risk was not considered in the early version of the scheme, it does appear to have been included in development of the outcome measure used to develop and assess the later versions (Statistical Analysis Center, 1984). The seriousness issue also appears to be addressed in a manner different from that originally developed. Neither the treatment of time at risk (Stollmack and Harris, 1974; Maltz and McCleary, 1977; Levy, 1978; Lloyd and Joe, 1979; Maltz, McCleary, and Pollock, 1979; S. D. Gottfredson and Taylor, 1986) nor the measurement of offense seriousness (Thurstone, 1927; Sellin and Wolfgang, 1964; Rossi et al., 1974; S. D. Gottfredson and Goodman, 1983) is a trivial or easy matter. Each is fraught with considerable methodological and practical difficulties, not one of which appears to have been considered. For example, the seriousness measure used in the later reports appears highly arbitrary (indeed, simple multiples of an initial "weight" are applied based on statutory maximum penalties; see Statistical Analysis Center, 1984); this results in some rather peculiar possibilities (e.g., an alcohol offense may receive the same score as a homicide). (In fairness it should be noted that this is not likely to occur.) Given that the scheme remains heavily weighted toward felonies, distribution of the outcome measure is highly skewed. Not surprisingly, when the "CPE" is calculated on such measures, it is large. The MCRs, as calculated by us, are much lower (but still are larger than typically observed).

We do not believe that the comparisons of the utility of the Iowa model and several others (e.g., INSLAW, Rand, Salient Factor Score, Michigan) offered in one report (Statistical Analysis Center, 1984) are of value. First, they appear to compare the efficiency of all models using the Iowa data, which provides an advantage to the model developed on those data. Second, the outcome index used appears to be that also developed in Iowa. Again, since the other devices were not constructed relative to that peculiar criterion, they are disadvantaged. Third, the "CPE" is the only index made available for comparative purposes; as described earlier, it is not meaningful for the purpose intended. In short, the comparisons provided are inappropriate.

We are concerned that the validation efforts described give insufficient information regarding sampling methods used. One report on recent validation of the model suggests that "the data collection was limited to offenders for whom quality presentence investigations giving comprehensive criminal histories were available in inmate files" (Fischer, 1983: 18). We cannot determine if this is part of the sample reported later (indeed, one problem is that the "sample," with the exception of the large, early samples reported on in 1980, seems to keep changing), nor do we know what other selection may have occurred. If the selection described above indeed occurred, it could well be expected to have serious biasing effects. At a minimum, if one is to have confidence in the model and in the validations reported on, a great deal more information concerning the samples and their selection must be available.

Finally, for all these reasons (and others; see S. D. Gottfredson and D. M. Gottfredson, 1979, for a discussion), we would urge that, prior to applications in other jurisdictions, the methods be defined more explicitly, the sampling issues be clarified, the validation evidence be presented in conventional terms and with commonly used measures, and tests of validity in the jurisdictions of interest be performed.

Summary

This section has considered a number of models designed for application in criminal justice decision making in the areas of bail and pretrial release, sentencing, and parole. In the sentencing area, guidelines models have included a predictive component, but these have been descriptive, rather than normative. The guidelines model as implemented in Minnesota explicitly was intended not to be predictive per se, but the offender-history dimension undoubtedly is predictive to some extent given the nature of the items used and their demonstrable relation to recidivism in other jurisdictions. The extent of this relation in the Minnesota application is not known.

The Rand report (Greenwood, 1982) discussed in this section did involve normative prediction study and is purported to have implications for sentencing policy and practice. Predictive accuracy in retrospective construction samples is modest at best; no information concerning accuracy in cross-validation or prospective validation samples is available. Since to our knowledge no application of the model proposed has been achieved, it is not known whether the device would "work" in practice.

In the area of parole, we considered the federal guidelines model, particularly the predictive component of the model, the Salient Factor Score. The device was constructed in a very simple manner, makes use of few items, and has rather low predictive power: it does have about the same level of accuracy as is commonly observed for instruments of this type. Like the Rand instrument, it is constructed of items of the nature most often found to be predictive of recidivism. Although predictive power is low, the same level of power is observed in several validation samples; the relation observed apparently is stable. In application, the device is simplified further by collapsing it into four categories of risk. These are combined, in a matrix format, with an offense-seriousness measure. We know of no evidence concerning the extent to which inclusion of the empirically derived risk dimension in the guidelines model has led to a reduction in recidivism.

The device developed in Iowa seems based on a sound principle: it appears that normative prediction models for homogeneous subgroups are combined to provide an overall expectancy table. Claims made for the power of the various versions of the model appear to be wrong and exaggerated, but it does appear that the model may be a bit more powerful than others. Still, predictive accuracy can only be described as modest, at best. Again, items used are similar to those discussed earlier in this paper. Although claims have been made for the utility of the model for decreasing recidivism among paroled populations, reports available to us do not provide sufficient information to enable us to assess the adequacy of those claims. Certainly, caution is to be advised in considering the application of the Iowa model in other jurisdictions.

In the area of bail and pretrial release, the Philadelphia experiment described does provide sound advice concerning the utility of an empirically derived, risk-assessment device applied in practice. The risk-assessment device was developed using sound methodological and statistical procedures, included commonly used variables, and had modest predictive validity. In the guidelines application, it is simplified and combined in a matrix format with an assessment of the seriousness of the offense. No effect for the guidelines model was observed with respect either to a failure-to-appear or a recidivism criterion.

DISCUSSION

Summaries are rather like statistical averages: rarely do they adequately describe the nature of the original data, and variability is of course ignored. The analogy could be carried forward cynically by noting that arithmetic averages often in fact take values (on the underlying distributions) that cannot naturally occur. Still, statistical averages are useful for many purposes, and so, we hope, may be this summary. To highlight, the evidence reviewed in this paper suggests the following:

- At present, researchers' ability to predict the decisions of criminal justice system functionaries or the behavior of offenders can most politely be called "modest." Generally, descriptive decision studies are more powerful than are normative decision studies; that is, we are better at predicting decisions made in practice than we are at predicting offender (or other) outcomes of interest. When normative prediction studies are considered, the proportion of criterion variance explained rarely exceeds .15 to .20; it often is lower. Considerable room for improvement clearly remains.
- Criminal justice decision makers appear to rely with regularity on a few common items of information regardless of the decisions being made. Likewise, there is considerable commonality among items found useful in normative prediction studies—again, regardless of the decision-making arena and criterion variables studied. An exception may be in the area of prosecution, where evidentiary factors appear important.
- The descriptive and normative decision studies reviewed recommend rather different items of information as predictive. In particular, it may be noted that decision makers tend to focus heavily on offense seriousness, which generally is not found to be predictive of behavioral outcomes, while the normative studies focus on offense type, which generally is found to be predictive of offender behavioral outcomes.
- The best predictors of future criminal behavior appear to be measures of prior criminal behavior. Both the length of offenders' records and the age at which involvement with the criminal justice system began appear to be consistent and important indices.
- When decision-making aids that incorporate an empirically based predictive component are implemented in practice, there is little evidence that they reduce the prevalence of the criterion offender behaviors. It must be noted, however, that little empirical evidence concerning this important question is available.
- It does appear that when properly implemented, decision-making tools that incorporate a predictive component can provide advances relative to an equity criterion. With respect to the goal of changing the behavior of functionaries, the devices appear more successful.

Do Prediction Models Improve Criminal Justice Decisions?

As Cureton (1957) has shown, any valid continuous predictor can improve on the base rate, and, as we have observed, there appear to be several of these relative to the criteria considered in this paper. Validities are low, but equations and devices discussed do provide advantage over base-rate prediction. As we also have shown, statistical prediction devices typically outperform human judgments; what is true for other decision-making situations appears also to be true for criminal justice settings. Why, then, does no predictive advantage appear to accrue from use of these devices?

First, we stress again that advantages relative to offender behavioral outcomes are only one sort of advantage that may be sought through use of the device. There is growing evidence that when properly implemented and evaluated, attempts to provide structure for criminal justice decisions do result in increased equity. Often, this has been a principal goal for the introduction of the innovation.

Second, it must be noted that some of the models proposed for use do not attempt to provide an empirically derived normative risk assessment, even though they appear to.

Third, we know of no device in operational use that has not been constrained, perhaps severely, by policy considerations. Decision makers often change the coding of predictor or criterion information based on policy concerns. For example, the federal parole board chose to alter some predictor items, chose the criterion to be used based on policy concerns, and decided on weights to be applied to some items (D. M. Gottfredson, Cosgrove, et al., 1978). Each of these considerations may constrain the utility of the device constructed. In the Philadelphia experiment, the judges chose a criterion variable known not to be optimal for purposes of risk classification (Goldkamp and Gottfredson, 1981a,b). In both these examples the decision makers decided to give more weight to a concern for offense seriousness than to a concern for risk. Since offense seriousness is at best inconsistently related to risk of recidivism, this may have had important constraining consequences. Thus, the statistical risk assessment invariably is only part of the "guidance" provided by the decision-making models, and often, it is the lesser part.

It is appropriate that concerns other than risk be considered in criminal justice decision making. It must be recognized, however, that consideration of these may work at cross-purposes relative to the risk dimension.

Can Predictive Accuracy Be Improved?

If statistical prediction tools can provide benefits to decision making in criminal justice system settings, we clearly must work to improve the accuracy of those tools. In this brief section we mention a variety of issues that, if addressed, may help to increase the validity of predictions in criminal justice.

Improved Reliabilities

The first effort, we believe, should be devoted to a consideration of improving both the predictor and criterion variables used. The reliability of many criminal justice data sources is notoriously poor (see M. R. Gottfredson and D. M. Gottfredson, 1980a, for an extended discussion of this issue). This often is recognized with respect to predictor variables, but forgotten with respect to the criterion variables used; greater attention also must be paid to the reliability of criterion information. Hindelang, Hirschi, and Weis (1981) consider the accuracy of a variety of means of obtaining outcome data.

Case-specific data often are needed, and these typically are found only in case files available through parole and probation or correctional agencies. Although it has been observed that trained persons can code the data available in those files with respectable reliabilities (e.g., S. D. Gottfredson and D. M. Gottfredson, 1979), little is known about the reliability of those data in the first place. Commenting on Ohlin and Duncan's (1949) comparison of a number of prediction schemes, Vold (1949:452) lamented:

> The most discouraging thing about the whole field of prediction in criminology is the con-

tinued unreliability and general worthlessness of much of the so-called "information" in the original records. Opinions, hearsay, and haphazardly recorded judgments still constitute the bulk of any parole file. Statistics made of this can be no better than the original data.

From our experience, we can report that little appears to have changed in the past 35 years: these data must be regarded with considerable skepticism. (Actually, one thing has changed: apparently unreliable information is readily available in computerized form in many jurisdictions. In point of fact, this may be undesirable, since investigators not familiar with the nature of this information may accept it uncritically.) Sparks (1983:244) has suggested that we seek to increase the reliability of information by collecting it prospectively, rather than by relying on case records. This is attractive but would prove very expensive.

Improved Measurement

Improved measurement of both predictor and criterion variables is needed. Variously considered, prior record consistently proves of predictive value. Generally, however, this has been operationally defined in crude fashion. Improved scaling of this construct potentially could improve the accuracy of predictions based on it. Offense-seriousness scales have been developed but are not often used. We have experimented with seriousness scales considered as a criterion measure with demonstrable success (S. D. Gottfredson and Taylor, 1986). Similarly, perhaps we should seek to predict criteria of interest other than recidivism, considered as a dichotomy. For some purposes, the prediction of "time to failure" may prove advantageous (for illustration, see Schmidt and Witte, 1979; S. D. Gottfredson and Taylor, 1986). Finally, multiple criteria of failure should be explored.

Use of the Most Appropriate Analytic Methods

As we have noted, many prediction studies have not capitalized on the potential power of sophisticated analytic methods, and some studies may in fact be subject to specification error resulting from inappropriate use of simple regression methods. When more appropriate methods are available, they should be used. However, little advantage is likely to result unless the measurement and reliability issues just raised are resolved; several studies cited earlier attest to this fact. If the measurement and reliabilities of both predictor and criterion variables are improved, the power of more sophisticated methods could well be realized.

Statistical Bootstrapping

As described earlier, models such as that apparently developed in Iowa potentially could do much to increase the utility of prediction in criminal justice settings. The basic procedure simply would require the identification of relatively homogeneous subgroups of offenders, the construction of statistical prediction equations for each, and the combination of these into an "expectancy table" for the full sample. Although not a new idea, it is a good one, and one that potentially holds considerable promise.

Theory-Driven Approaches to the Prediction Problem

Sparks (1983) correctly noted that theoretical considerations could be of substantial benefit to those working in the area of prediction but offered little in the way of advice concerning directions such theories might take. Generally, it appears that criminal justice prediction research has been rather atheoretical, although it seems to have been of some value in theory construction. Recently, Monahan (1981; Monahan and Klassen, 1982) has proposed ways in which situational approaches may aid in the prediction problem. This clearly represents a theory-driven approach to increasing predictive accuracy (and understanding of the phenomena investigated). S. D. Gottfredson and Taylor (1986), following the person-environment integrity model of Olweus (1977), recently have demonstrated that recidivism predictions can be improved if person-environment interactions are included in the models developed. Further, the magnitude and nature of the effects observed varied depending on the criterion variable used and on the nature of the offender and environmental variables considered.

Statistical-Subjective Bootstrapping

We would argue that, just as decision makers may learn from statistically based information, the actuary may learn from the human decision maker. We already have noted that models of subjective decisions can have more predictive accuracy than the subjective decisions alone (e.g., Goldberg, 1970), and recent evidence suggests that subjective judgments may be more accurate than actuarial devices for some limited but important purposes (Holland et al., 1983). In general, this has become known as the "clinical versus statistical" problem, and debate concerning the relative value of the two general approaches continues. We believe this debate to be counterproductive. Although we tend to come down on the "statistical" side of the argument, we also agree with Horst (1941), DeGroot (1960), D. M. Gottfredson (1967), Underwood (1979), and Monahan (1981) that prediction may be improved through a combined use of methods. An iterative bootstrapping process in which successive normative and descriptive devices are used to inform and modify each other may well prove productive.

Attention to Ethical Concerns

Finally, it is clear that investigators must pay more sophisticated attention to ethical considerations involved in the construction of prediction devices intended for operational use (F. M. Fisher and Kadane, 1983). Ethical concerns can be addressed within complex statistical models (although ethical choices always must be made), but this has not often been done adequately. Comparisons of models constructed via an approach that attempts to suppress unwarranted effects and models constructed in a simpler fashion would be of interest.

Is Prediction Currently Accurate Enough to Be Useful?

The prediction literature that we have reviewed leads inescapably to the conclusion noted above: predictive accuracy is rather low. Devices used to structure criminal justice decisions appear to have little impact on offender behavioral outcomes, even when an empirically derived prediction instrument is part of the device used. (We already have noted several reasons why this may be so and have attempted to identify some ways in which weaknesses of currently available prediction studies may be improved and validities increased.)

Yet, prediction tools are being used in criminal justice settings, and calls for their use are increasing. There is no escaping the question, then, of whether prediction currently is accurate enough to justify its use in practice. (This section concentrates on the selection issue only. Prediction methods clearly are accurate enough to be useful for purposes of conducting quasi experiments and program evaluations and for other applications.)

There are those who argue against the use of prediction, whether statistically or subjectively based, on ethical grounds alone. A strict just desert argument, for example, would suggest that prediction properly is irrelevant to decisions made concerning criminal offenders—the ensuring of deserved punishment and resulting demonstrable equity are the desired ideals. (These too will be difficult to achieve, even if desired. Many complex issues of measurement remain before the goal of ensuring desert adequately could be met.) No statistical or pragmatic argument is likely to sway these critics, for those arguments would be seen as fundamentally irrelevant. Philosophical or ethical arguments may be persuasive, but it is not our intent to attempt them here. Only the strict desert orientation, however, rejects the concept of prediction as important to decisions made concerning offenders. Discussion here is directed to those who will, at least, allow the argument.

Other arguments against the use of statistically based prediction tools all reduce to considerations of their accuracy. The technically sophisticated arguments focus directly on the accuracy issue and cite low proportions of variance explained and resulting high error rates (focusing usually on false positives; false negatives may be equally, or even more, undesirable depending on the application). Others cite potential, or even demonstrable, misspecification of prediction models. Less technically sophisticated critics continue to complain of "reducing people to numbers" and observe that human behavior is too complex to allow judgmental decisions to be made on the basis of an "equation." This, too, essentially is a complaint concerning accuracy.

In an earlier section concerning the evaluation of innovations, we noted the need for comparative study. The point must be made here as well: accuracy must be assessed relative to something. The most obvious comparison is with an ideal standard. Whatever that standard might be, it clearly is desirable that as few errors as possible be made in decision making. Unless prediction is perfect, however, errors will be made. Whether statistical or subjective, prediction falls short of an ideal standard.

Decisions will be made in criminal justice settings with or without the aid of statistical prediction tools. Those who make the decisions—the parole board members, the judges, the prosecutors, and others—typically receive no training with respect to the difficult decision problems confronting them. We have mentioned a variety of factors that combine to decrease the validity of subjective predictive judgments, and Monahan (1981) reviews several more. The literature very strongly suggests that in comparison even with trained decision makers, statistical tools are more accurate. On simply an accuracy consideration, their use would seem to be preferred. Einhorn and Schact (1975) have shown that the correlation between clinical judgments and any criterion is likely to be low to moderate under a wide variety of conditions, and that the only way to better the selection problem without trading off among false positives and false negatives is to increase that correlation. As we have argued, statistical methods can help do this.

Part of the answer to the question of whether statistical prediction tools are accurate enough to justify their use depends, we think, on the use to which it is proposed the tool be put. Summarizing a recent review of "career criminal" research, which to date is meager, Petersilia (1980:322) noted that "the data accumulated to date on criminal careers do not permit us, with acceptable confidence, to identify career criminals prospectively or to predict the crime reduction effects of alternative sentencing proposals." Similarly, J. Cohen (1983b:49) noted with respect to the Rand study that "for purposes of selective incapacitation, where predicted high-rate offenders will be subject to longer prison terms than all other offenders, much better discrimination of the high-rate offenders would seem to be required." We agree: proposals for dramatic change in sentencing and incarceration policies based on individual-level prediction studies are at best premature. Prediction of such low validity as demonstrated here cannot, we think, justify the policy changes proposed.

We do, however, think that prediction tools of comparable validity can be used appropriately for other purposes, and we will try to explicate this position below. We have attempted in this paper to concentrate on the question of accuracy. In so doing we intentionally have not addressed ethical questions in detail. There is no avoiding those questions entirely, however, and some will be raised in the following discussion. We describe concerns about the two types of errors to be made in any selection or prediction problem, and we focus on ethical considerations involved in the type of policy changes to be made by the proposed use of prediction tools.

Figure 2 summarizes an imaginary selection-decision problem that is based on prediction. For purposes of explication, we assume that both the criterion (Y) and the measurements on which selection will be based (X) are measured continuously. In the figure they are represented in standardized form. The correlation implied by the elipse drawn is moderate (but any positive correlation, save unity, would suffice). Let X_c represent the cutting score, and Y_c the criterion cutoff, that is, that point on the criterion distribution at or above which we assume the case a "failure" and below which we assume it a "success." At or above X_c, we predict failure and select accordingly; below X_c we predict success.

In Figure 2, X_c and Y_c are set at the means of the distributions. For any value of r, positive and negative hits are equal, as are false positives and negatives (assuming a normal bivariate surface). In fact, of course, rarely does the practical situation seem to be as depicted in this figure. Usually one does not select based on the mean score, nor does one observe

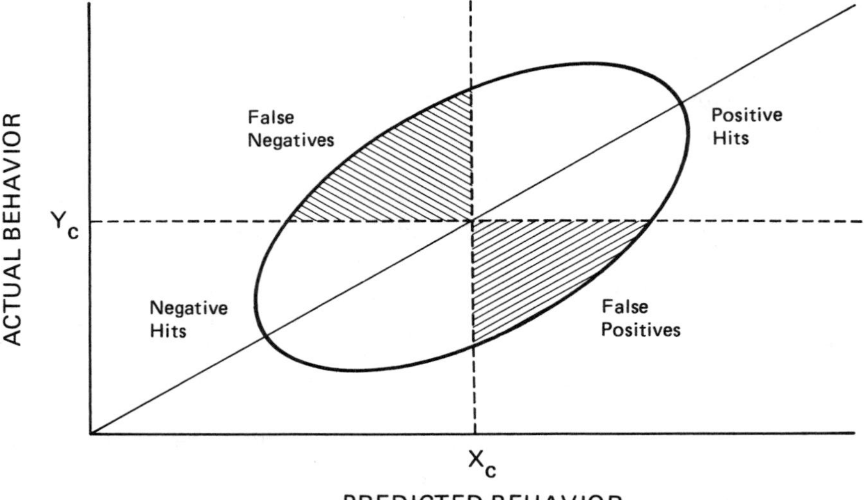

FIGURE 2 Hypothetical prediction-based selection decision problem.

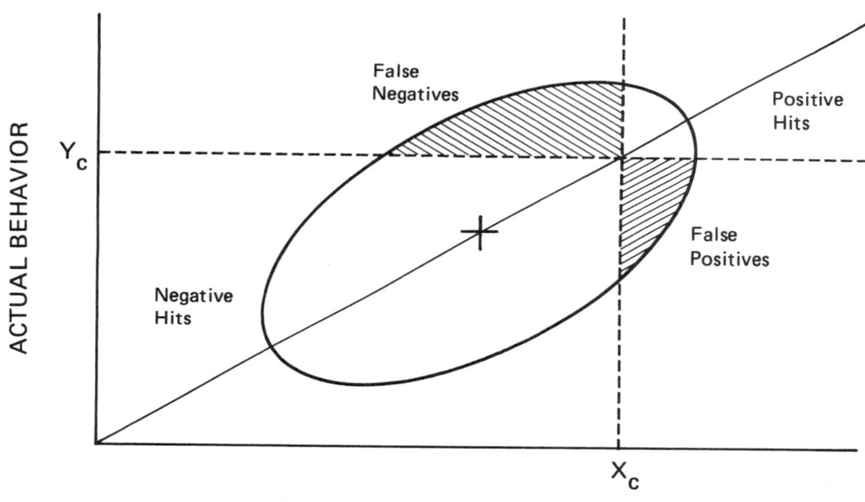

FIGURE 3 Hypothetical selective incapacitation scheme.

base rates equal to .50 (as represented on the ordinate). The symmetry observed in Figure 2 would not hold if one increased or decreased X_c from the mean (imagine X_c moving to either the right or the left along the abscissa). Neither would it hold if one increased or decreased Y_c.

Consider Figure 3 in light of a "selective incapacitation" proposal. The distribution shown is assumed to be of offenders to be sentenced either to incarceration or to longer than usual terms of incarceration, based on predicted future criminality. The proposal argues for a change in sentencing policies: persons are to be incarcerated (or incarcerated for longer terms) based on the predicted risk of repeated (high-rate) offending. Accordingly, it would seem that the cutting score probably would lie above the mean of the "risk" distribution (or else one is not selecting the high-risk cases) and that the criterion "cutting score" would lie above the mean of the distribution representing subsequent criminal behavior (or else one would be "selectively incapacitating" average or below-average offenders).

Figure 3 is based on these assumptions: as shown, false positives are reduced at the expense of false negatives. Either may be decreased, but always at the expense of the other; one has only to change the selection ratio. (We assume that the cutting score represents a "standard." The standard could, of course, be changed; this too could have consequences for the ratio of false positives and negatives.)

Neither error is desirable. False positives are not to be desired on ethical grounds (that is, persons are falsely imprisoned or falsely imprisoned for a longer term because of inaccuracy of prediction). False negatives also are not desired (because of inaccurate prediction, persons who pose a risk to society are not incarcerated or not incarcerated for longer terms). Which error is more important is a question that society has neither sufficiently addressed nor answered, and it may well be that the costs of the two types of error are not equal. Moreover, concern about each type of error may be expressed on different ethical grounds.

Consider next Figure 4. Here, the pop-

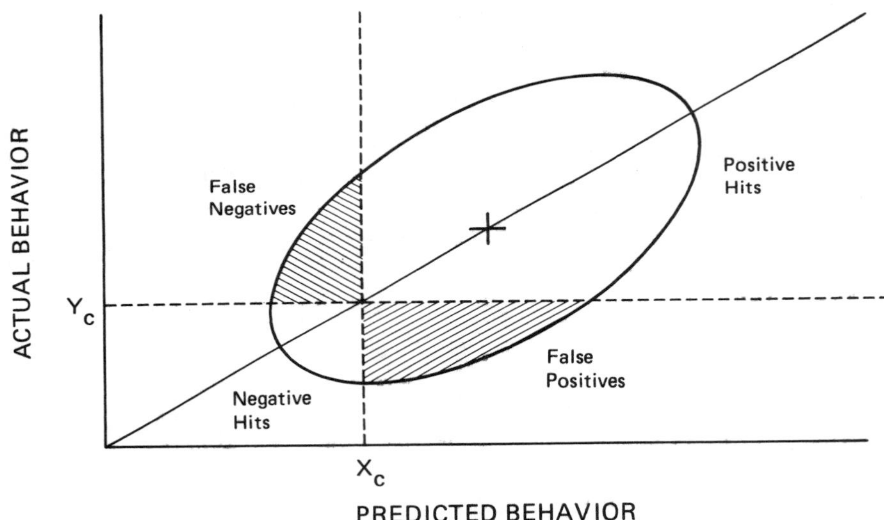

FIGURE 4 Hypothetical "emergency release" scheme.

ulation of interest has changed. In Figure 3 the distribution shown was of persons about whom an incarceration decision is to be made. In Figure 4 the distribution is of persons already incarcerated under present sentencing policy (whatever that is). We assume that in incarcerating these persons the sentencing judges held a variety of goals for the decisions made.

Suppose that one is forced to decrease that population for some reason. Perhaps one wing of the prison burned down or the courts have ordered population reductions due to prison crowding or perhaps it simply has been decided that it costs too much money to imprison this many people. Selection criteria that might be considered in decisions about whom to release could be risk of recidivism or of high rates of offending. (Other criteria could of course be used. For example, one might choose to release those "least deserving" of punishment.)

Here, the selection criterion lies below the mean of X (X_c less than mean X); that is, one wishes to select those inmates who appear to present the least risk of repeat (or repeated) offending. Since one seeks to identify the best risks, the cutting score for the criterion variable also likely would lie below the mean. Just as before, one can manipulate the trade-off of false positives and false negatives by moving X_c to the left or the right. For a given Y_c, the value of X_c chosen will determine whether more false positive or false negative errors will be made.

The ethical consequences of errors made in the two scenarios are different. In the selective incapacitation scenario, the effect of a false positive is to deny liberty (or to deny it for a longer time) based on faulty prediction at the sentencing stage. Although some (e.g., Gordon, 1977) have argued that this is acceptable, the argument requires justification based on a desert, rather than an incapacitative, principle. That is, it is argued that false positives, although perhaps not deserving of additional punishment based on actual risk, typically are so deserving based on desert principles. Since the predictions and resulting errors are based largely on past criminal conduct, the argument is that the false positive legitimately may be treated more harshly because of that past conduct. Extended confinement of false positives cannot, however, be justified on prediction-based utilitarian grounds. On these premises, it must be seen as undesirable. Note also that the selective incapacitation concept apparently seeks to minimize false negatives (that is, failure to select those who in fact pose a substantial risk of continued criminal behavior). Unless predictive accuracy can be increased, this can only be done at the expense of increasing false positives.

In the second scenario false positives will also be punished more harshly than will those selected for release based on the selection device. *But they will not be punished more harshly than they would have been had the device (and prediction) not been used.* This is a critical distinction. Rather than falsely treating some persons more harshly than "necessary," the proposal treats some persons less harshly than "necessary," treats some persons no more harshly than "necessary," and is agnostic with respect to the harshness of punishment received by others. The scheme implicitly assumes that punishment is imposed for a variety of reasons; thus, although release may be granted or denied based on risk considerations, those denied release—including those "falsely" denied the privilege—appropriately are confined for whatever purpose originally intended. (We do not claim that all original purposes necessarily are appropriate. We simply point out that the scheme appears to be atheoretical with respect to them.)

It must be remembered that the actual consequences of the two types of prediction errors probably are not equal. This likely will prove true whether one considers costs in social, economic, or ethical terms. Earlier, we provided a simple model whereby one could assign relative weights to the consequences of one or the other type of error, but so far as we know, this has not yet been attempted. We would urge that such modeling be considered.

The two scenarios also differ substantially with respect to policy changes proposed and the consequences of those changes. Selective incapacitation suggests clearly that there is a proper purpose for the sentencing of criminal offenders: removing them from normal society, thereby preventing them from engaging in normal criminal activity. An extreme position would suggest that this is the only proper purpose for the sentencing decision.[43] The suggestion, then, is for a radical change in sentencing and imprisonment policy, and this proposal is based in large part on claims made for the accuracy of prediction.

The second scenario, which we have elsewhere called "selective deinstitutionalization" (S. D. Gottfredson, 1984) makes no such presumption. Indeed, sentencing decision policy is not directly affected through adoption of the scheme. Consequences relative to decisions made, of course, would result. Fundamentally, however, the scheme presumes that all purposes for sentencing currently practiced are equally valid. The scheme does propose that risk (and accordingly, an incapacitative purpose) should be a primary consideration in early-release decisions.

Thus, it may be noted that the selective incapacitation notion argues, based in part on considerations of the accuracy of prediction, that sentencing policies and practice should be changed. The selective deinstitutionalization concept makes no such argument. Indeed, in our example we were *forced* to make selections due to other considerations (e.g., prison crowding).

There is a fundamental difference between the two situations, and this difference requires some clarification of our original question: Is prediction currently accurate enough to be useful? When the

---

[43]We do not argue that this position necessarily has been advanced by the proponents of the strategy.

question is stated this way, the answer can only be "yes and no." Prediction in criminal justice settings clearly is not sufficiently accurate to form the basis of social policy. Proposals for dramatic changes in policy and practice that rely on the accuracy of prediction are premature at best. Once social policy has been set, however, prediction clearly is sufficiently accurate to be useful, and decisions made will be made more accurately if statistically based prediction tools are used. Even when validity is very low, it has been demonstrated that selection devices provide significant improvements in accuracy (Dunnette, 1966).

We freely admit the judgmental nature of our preference for the selective deinstitutionalization proposal over the selective incapacitation proposal and note that the choice largely is an ethical one. It does appear, however, that consequences of the proposal we advocate are more benign than are consequences arising from a selective incapacitation proposal. And we believe that predictive accuracy, while in need of much improvement, is sufficient for the former but insufficient for the latter. If society should decide that selective incapacitation is the appropriate strategy for sentencing criminal offenders, it is clear that prediction tools should be used in the decision-making process. To decide the policy question on the basis of current predictive accuracy, however, would be foolish.

REFERENCES

Adams, K.
1983 The effect of evidentiary factors on charge reduction. *Journal of Criminal Justice* 11:525–537.

American Bar Association
1968 *Standards Relating to Pretrial Release*. New York: Institute for Judicial Administration.

Anderson, N.
1968 A simple model for information integration. Pp. 731–743 in R. P. Abelson, Elliot Aronson, William J. McGuire, Theodore M. Newcomb, Milton J. Rosenberg, Percy H. Tannenbaum, eds., *Theories of Cognitive Consistency: A Sourcebook*. Chicago, Ill.: Rand McNally.
1974 Cognitive algebra: integration theory applied to social attribution. Pp. 1–101 in L. Berkowitz, ed., *Advances in Experimental Social Psychology*. New York: Academic Press.
1979 Algebraic rules in psychological measurement. *American Scientist* 67:555–563.

Angel, A., Green, E., Kaufman, H., and Van Loon, E.
1971 Preventive detention: an empirical analysis. *Harvard Civil Rights—Civil Liberties Law Review* 6:301–396.

Babst, D. V., Gottfredson, D. M., and Ballard, K. B.
1968 Comparison of multiple regression and configural analysis techniques for developing base expectancy tables. *Journal of Research in Crime and Delinquency* 5(1):72–80.

Babst, D. V., Inciardi, J. A., and Jaman, D. R.
1971 The uses of configural analysis in parole prediction research. *Canadian Journal of Criminology and Corrections* 13(3):200–208.

Babst, D. V., Koval, M., and Neithercutt, M.G.
1972 Relationship of time served to parole outcome for different classifications of burglars based on males paroled in fifty jurisdictions in 1968 and 1969. *Journal of Research in Crime and Delinquency* 9:99–116.

Baldwin, J.
1979 Ecological and areal studies in Great Britain and the United States. Pp. 29–66 in N. Morris and M. Tonry, eds., *Crime and Justice: An Annual Review of Research*. Chicago, Ill.: University of Chicago Press.

Ballard, K. B., Jr., and Gottfredson, D. M.
1963 Predictive Attribute Analysis in a Prison Sample and Prediction of Parole Performance. Institute for the Study of Crime and Delinquency. Vacaville, Calif.

Becker, G., and McClintock, C.
1967 Value: behavioral decision theory. *Annual Review of Psychology* 18:239–286.

Berkson, J.
1947 Cost utility as a measure of efficiency of a test. *Journal of the American Statistical Association* 42:246–255.

Bernstein, I., Kelly, W., and Doyle, P.
1977 Societal reaction to deviants: the case of criminal defendants. *American Sociological Review* 42(October):743–755.

Bernstein, I., Kick, E., Leung, J., and Schulz, B.
1977 Charge reduction: an intermediary stage in the process of labelling criminal defendants. *Social Forces* 56(2):362–384.

Blumstein, A., and Cohen, J.
1979 Estimation of individual crime rates from arrest records. *Journal of Criminal Law and Criminology* 70:561–585.

Blumstein, A., and Graddy, E.
1982 Prevalence and recidivism in index arrests: a feedback model. *Law and Society Review* 16:265–290.

Blumstein, A., Cohen, J., and Nagin, D., eds.
1978 *Deterrence and Incapacitation: Estimating the Effects of Criminal Sanctions on Crime Rates*. Washington, D.C.: National Academy of Sciences.

Blumstein, A., Cohen, J., Martin, S., and Tonry, M., eds.
1983 *Research on Sentencing: The Search for Reform*. Washington, D.C.: National Academy Press.

Bock, E. W., and Frazier, C. E.
1977 Official standards versus actual criteria in bond dispositions. *Journal of Criminal Justice* 5:321–328.

Borden, H. G.
1928 Factors for predicting parole success. *American Institute of Criminal Law and Criminology* 19(3):328–336.

Brosi, K.
1979 *A Cross-City Comparison of Felony Case Processing*. Washington, D.C.: INSLAW.

Brown, L. D.
1978 The development of a parolee classification system using discriminant analysis. *Journal of Research in Crime and Delinquency* 15:92–108.

Burgess, E. W.
1928 Factors determining success or failure on parole. In A. A. Bruce, E. W. Burgess, and A. J. Harno, eds., *The Workings of the Indeterminate Sentence Law and the Parole System in Illinois*. Springfield, Ill.: Illinois State Board of Parole.

Bynum, T.
1976 An Empirical Exploration of the Factors Influencing Release on Recognizance. Unpublished doctoral dissertation, Department of Criminology, Florida State University, Tallahassee.

Caldwell, M. G.
1951 Preview of a new type of probation study made in Alabama. *Federal Probation* 15 (June):3–15.

Campbell, D. T., and Stanley, J. C.
1963 *Experimental and Quasi-experimental Designs for Research*. New York: Prentice-Hall.

Carroll, J. S.
1977 Judgments of recidivism risk: conflicts between clinical strategies and base-rate information. *Law and Human Behavior* 1(2): 191–198.
1978a Causal attributions in expert parole decisions. *Journal of Personality and Social Psychology* 36:1501–1511.
1978b Causal theories of crime and their effect upon expert parole decisions. *Law and Human Behavior* 2(4):377–388.

Carroll, J. S., and Payne, J. W.
1976 The psychology of the parole decision process: a joint application of attribution theory and information processing. In J. Carroll and J. Payne, eds., *Cognition and Social Behavior*. Hillsdale, N.J.: Erlbaum.
1977a Crime seriousness, recidivism risk, and causal attribution in judgments of prison terms by students and experts. *Journal of Applied Psychology* 62:592–602.
1977b Judgments about crime and the criminal: a model and a method for investigating parole decisions. In B. Sales, ed., *Perspectives in Law and Psychology*, Vol. I: *Criminal Justice System*. New York: Plenum.

Carroll, J. S., Wiener, R. L., Coates, D., Galegher, J., and Alibrio, J. J.
1982 Evaluation, diagnosis, and prediction in parole decision making. *Law and Society Review* 17(1):199–228.

Chi, K. S.
1983 Offender risk assessment: the Iowa model. *Innovations* 1–12. Lexington, Ky.: Council of State Governments.

Clarke, S. H., Freeman, J. L., and Koch, G. G.
1976 The Effectiveness of Bail Systems: An Analysis of Failure to Appear in Court and Rearrest While on Bail. Institute of Government, University of North Carolina, Chapel Hill, N.C.

Cohen, J.
1983a Incapacitating criminals: recent research findings. *NIJ Research in Brief*. Washington, D.C.: National Institute of Justice (December).
1983b Incapacitation as a strategy for crime control: possibilities and pitfalls. Pp. 1–84 in M. Tonry and N. Morris, eds., *Crime and Justice: An Annual Review of Research*. Vol. V. Chicago, Ill.: University of Chicago Press.

Cohen, J., and Tonry, M.
1983 Sentencing reforms and their impacts. Pp. 305–459 in A. Blumstein, J. Cohen, S. Martin, and M. Tonry, eds., *Research on Sentencing: The Search for Reform*, Vol. II. Washington, D.C.: National Academy Press.

Cohen, L., and Kluegel, J.
1978 Determinants of juvenile court dispositions: ascriptive and achieved factors in two metro-

politan courts. *American Sociological Review* 43(April):162–176.

Cole, G.
1970 The decision to prosecute. *Law and Society Review* 4:331–343.

Cook, T. D., and Campbell, D. T.
1979 *Quasi-experimentation: Design and Analysis Issues for Field Settings.* Chicago, Ill.: Rand McNally.

Cronbach, L. J.
1960 *Essentials of Psychological Testing.* New York: Harper.

Cronbach, L. J., and Gleser, G. C.
1957 *Psychological Tests and Personnel Decisions.* Urbana: University of Illinois Press.

Cureton, E. E.
1957 Recipe for a cookbook. *Psychological Bulletin* 54(6):494–497.

Daiger, D. C., Gottfredson, G. D., Stebbins, B., and Lipstein, D. J.
1978 Explorations of Parole Policy. Center for Social Organization of Schools, Johns Hopkins University, Baltimore, Md.

Dawes, R. M.
1975 Case by case versus rule-generated procedures for the allocation of scarce resources. Pp. 83–94 in M. Kaplan and S. Schwartz, eds., *Human Judgment and Decision Processes in Applied Settings.* New York: Academic Press.
1979 The robust beauty of improper linear models in decision making. *American Psychologist* 34(7):571–582.

Dawes, R. M., and Corrigan, B.
1974 Linear models in decision making. *Psychological Bulletin* 81(2):95–106.

Dawson, R.
1969 *Sentencing: The Decision as to Type, Length, and Conditions of Sentencing.* Chicago, Ill.: Little, Brown.

DeGroot, A. D.
1960 Via Clinical to Statistical Prediction. Invited address, presented at the meetings of the Western Psychological Association, San Jose, California (April).

Dershowitz, A.
1976 *Fair and Certain Punishment.* Report of the Twentieth Century Fund Task Force on Criminal Sentencing. New York: McGraw-Hill.

Duncan, O. D., Ohlin, L. E., Reiss, A. J., and Stanton, H. R.
1952 Formal devices for making selection decisions. *American Journal of Sociology* 58:573–584.

Dunnette, M. D.
1966 *Personnel Selection and Placement.* Belmont, Calif.: Brooks/Cole.

Ebbesen, E., and Konecni, K.
1975 Decision making and information integration in the courts: the setting of bail. *Journal of Personality and Social Psychology* 32(5):805–821.
1981 On the external validity of decision-making research: what do we know about decisions in the real world? Pp. 21–43 in T. Wallsten, ed., *Cognitive Processes in Choice and Decision Behavior.* Hillsdale, N.J.: Erlbaum.

Edwards, W.
1954 The theory of decision making. *Psychological Bulletin* 51(4):380–417.
1961 Behavioral decision theory. *Annual Review of Psychology* 12:473–498.

Ehrlich, I.
1973 Participation in illegitimate activities: a theoretical and empirical investigation. *Journal of Political Economy* 81(3):521–565.
1974 Participation in illegitimate activities: an economic analysis. Pp. 69–134 in G. S. Becker and W. M. Landes, eds., *Essays in Economics of Crime and Punishment* New York: Columbia University Press.

Einhorn, H., and Hogarth, R. M.
1981 Behavioral decision theory: processes of judgment and choice. *Annual Review of Psychology* 32:53–88.

Einhorn, H., and Schacht, S.
1975 Decisions based on fallible clinical judgment. Pp. 126–144 in M. Kaplan and S. Schwartz, eds., *Human Judgment and Decision Processes in Applied Settings.* New York: Academic Press.

Elion, V., and Megargee, E. I.
1979 Racial identity, length of incarceration, and parole decision making. *Journal of Research in Crime and Delinquency* 16:232–245.

Ennis, B. J., and Litwack, T. R.
1974 Psychiatry and the presumption of expertise: flipping coins in the courtroom. *California Law Review* 62:693–752.

Farrington, D. P.
1978 The family background of aggressive youths. In L. Hersov, M. Berger, and D. Shaffer, eds., *Aggression and Antisocial Behavior in Childhood and Adolescence.* Oxford, England: Pergamon.
1979 Longitudinal research on crime and delinquency. Pp. 289–348 in N. Morris and M. Tonry, eds., *Crime and Justice: An Annual Review of Research,* Vol. 1. Chicago, Ill.: University of Chicago Press.
1982 Longitudinal analyses of criminal violence. Pp. 171–200 in M. E. Wolfgang and N. A. Weiner, eds., *Criminal Violence.* Beverly Hills, Calif.: Sage.

Feeley, M., and McNaughton, J.
1974 The Pretrial Process in the Sixth Circuit. Unpublished manuscript, University of California, School of Law, Berkeley.
Fergusson, D. M., Fifield, J. K., and Slater, S. W.
1977 Signal detectability theory and the evaluation of prediction tables. *Journal of Research in Crime and Delinquency* 14(2):237–246.
Fildes, R., and Gottfredson, D. M.
1968 Cluster analysis in a parolee sample. *Journal of Research in Crime and Delinquency* 5(1):2–11.
Fischer, D. R.
1981 Offender Risk Assessment: Implications for Sentencing and Parole Policy. Statistical Analysis Center, Iowa Office for Planning and Programming. 523 E. 12th St., Des oines, Iowa.
1983 Better public protection with fewer inmates? *Corrections Today* (December):16–20.
1984 Risk Assessment: Sentencing Based on Probabilities. Statistical Analysis Center, Iowa Office for Planning and Programming, 523 E. 12th St., Des Moines, Iowa.
No date Selective Incapacitation of Potentially Violent Adult Offenders. Statistical Analysis Center, Iowa Office for Planning and Programming, 523 E. 12th St., Des Moines, Iowa.
Fisher, F. M., and Kadane, J. B.
1983 Empirically based sentencing guidelines and ethical considerations. Pp. 184–193 in A. Blumstein, J. Cohen, S. Martin, and M. Tonry, eds., *Research on Sentencing: The Search for Reform*, Vol. II. Washington, D. C.: National Academy of Sciences.
Fisher, J.
1959 The twisted pear and the prediction of behavior. *Journal of Consulting Psychology* 23:400–405.
Forst, B.
1976 Participation in illegitimate activities: further empirical findings. *Policy Analysis* 2(3):477–492.
1983 Selective incapacitation: an idea whose time has come? *Federal Probation* 46:19–23.
Forst, B., and Brosi, K.
1977 A theoretical and empirical analysis of the prosecutor. *Journal of Legal Studies* 6: 177–191.
Forst, B., Lucianovic, J., and Cox, S.
1977 *What Happens After Arrest?* Washington, D.C.: INSLAW.
Fowler, L.
1983 Classification and prediction: improving on chance. *Corrections Today* (December): 44–47.
Freed, D., and Wald, P.
1964 *Bail in the United States: 1964*. Washington, D.C.: U.S. Department of Justice and the Vera Institute of Justice.
Frey, E.
1951 *Der fruhkriminelle Ruckfallsverbrecher. Criminalite precoce et recividisme, Schweizerische Criminalistische Stud., 4.* Basel: Berlag fur Recht und Gesellschaft.
Galegher, J., and Carroll, J. S.
1983 Voluntary sentencing guidelines: prescription for justice or patent medicine? *Law and Human Behavior* 7(4):361–400.
Galton, F.
1895 (*Nature*, June). Cited in E. Banks, 1964, Reconviction of young offenders. *Current Legal Problems* 17:61–79.
Garber, S., Klepper, S., and Nagin, D.
1983 The role of extralegal factors in determining criminal case dispositions. Pp. 129–183 in A. Blumstein, J. Cohen, S. Martin, and M. Tonry, eds., *Research on Sentencing: The Search for Reform*, Vol. II. Washington, D.C.: National Academy Press.
Gaudet, F., Harris, G., and St. John, C.
1933 Individual differences in the sentencing of judges. *Journal of Criminal Law and Criminology* 23:811.
Gerecke
1939 Zur Frage der Ruckfallsprognose. *Monatsschrift fur Kriminalbiologie und Strafrechtsreform* 30:35–38.
Glaser, D.
1954 A reconsideration of some parole prediction factors. *American Sociological Review* 19: 335–341.
1955 The efficacy of alternative approaches to parole prediction. *American Sociological Review* 20:283–287.
1962 Prediction tables as accounting devices for judges and parole boards. *Crime and Delinquency* 8(3):239–258.
1964 *The Effectivenes of a Prison and Parole System*. New York: Bobbs-Merrill.
Glaser, D., and O'Leary, V.
1966 *Personal Characteristics and Parole Outcome*. National Parole Institutes. Office of Juvenile Delinquency and Youth Development, Washington, D.C.: U.S. Department of Health, Education, and Welfare.
Glass, G. V.
1976 Primary, secondary, and meta-analysis of research. *Educational Research* 5:3–8.
Glass, G. V., McGaw, B., and Smith, M.
1981 *Meta-analysis in Social Research*. Beverly Hills, Calif.: Sage.
Glueck, S., and Glueck, E.
1950 *Unraveling Juvenile Delinquency*. New York: Commonwealth Fund.

Goldberg, L. R.
1965 Diagnosticians vs. diagnostic signs: the diagnosis of psychosis vs. neurosis from the MMPI. *Psychological Monographs* 79(9).
1968 Seer over sign: the first "good" example? *Journal of Experimental Research in Personality* 3:168–171.
1970 Man versus model of man: a rationale, plus some evidence for a method of improving on clinical inference. *Psychological Bulletin* 73:422–432.

Goldkamp, J.
1979 *Two Classes of Accused: A Study of Bail and Detention in American Justice*. Cambridge, Mass.: Ballinger.

Goldkamp, J., and Gottfredson, M. R.
1980 Bail decision making and pretrial detention: surfacing judicial policy. *Law and Human Behavior* 3(4):227–249.
1981a *Bail Decisionmaking: A Study of Policy Guidelines*. Washington, D.C.: National Institute of Corrections.
1981b *Bail Decisionmaking: Appendices*. Washington, D.C.: National Institute of Corrections.
1985 *Policy Guidelines for Bail: An Experiment in Court Reform*. Philadelphia, Pa.: Temple University Press.

Goodman, L. A.
1953a The use and validity of a prediction instrument. I. A reformulation of the use of a prediction instrument. *American Journal of Sociology* 58(5):503–510.
1953b The use and validity of a prediction instrument. II. The validation of prediction. *American Journal of Sociology* 58(5):510–512.

Gordon, R. A.
1977 A critique of the evaluation of the Patuxent Institution, with particular attention to the issues of dangerousness and recidivism. *Bulletin of the American Academy of Psychiatry and the Law* 5(2):210–255.

Gottfredson, D. M.
1961 Comparing and combining subjective and objective parole predictors. *Research Newsletter* 3(Sept.–Dec.). Vacaville: California Medical Facility.
1967 Assessment and prediction methods in crime and delinquency. Pp. 171–187 in *Task Force Report: Juvenile Delinquency and Youth Crime*. Task Force on Juvenile Delinquency, President's Commission on Law Enforcement and the Administration of Justice. Washington, D.C.: U.S. Government Printing Office.
1975 *Decision-making in the Criminal Justice System: Reviews and Essays*, ed. Center for studies of Crime and Delinquency. Rockville, Md.: National Institute of Mental Health.

Gottfredson, D. M., and Ballard, K. B.
1964a Association Analysis, Predictive Attribute Analysis, and parole behavior. Paper presented at the Western Psychological Association meetings, Portland, Oregon (April).
1964b *Estimating Sentences Under an Indeterminate Sentencing Law*. Institute for the Study of Crime and Delinquency, Vacaville, Calif.
1965a *Prison and Parole Decisions: A Strategy for Study*. Final Report to the National Institute of Mental Health. Institute for the Study of Crime and Delinquency, Vacaville, Calif.
1965b The Validity of Two Parole Prediction Scales: An Eight Year Follow-up Study. Institute for the Study of Crime and Delinquency, Vacaville, Calif.
1966 Differences in parole decisions associated with decision-makers. *Journal of Research in Crime and Delinquency* 3:112–119.

Gottfredson, D. M., and Beverly, R. F.
1962 Development and operational use of prediction methods in correctional work. *Proceedings of the Social Statistics Section*. Washington, D.C.: American Statistical Association.

Gottfredson, D. M., and Bonds, J. A.
1961 *A Manual for Intake Base Expectancy Scoring (Form CDC-BE 61A)*. Research Division. Sacramento, Calif.: California Department of Corrections.

Gottfredson, D. M., and Stecher, B.
1979 Sentencing Policy Models: An Action Research Program. Paper presented at the meetings of the American Psychological Association, Toronto, Ontario, Canada.

Gottfredson, D. M., Ballard, K. B., and Lane, L.
1963 Association Analysis in a Prison Sample and Prediction of Parole Performance. Institute for the Study of Crime and Delinquency, Vacaville, Calif.

Gottfredson, D. M., Wilkins, L. T., and Hoffman, P. B.
1978 *Guidelines for Parole and Sentencing: A Policy Control Method*. Lexington, Mass.: D. C. Heath.

Gottfredson, D. M., Hoffman, P. B., Sigler, M. H., and Wilkins, L. T.
1975 Making paroling policy explicit. *Crime and Delinquency* 21(1):34–44.

Gottfredson, D. M., Cosgrove, C. A., Wilkins, L. T., Wallenstein, J., and Rauh, C.
1978 *Classification for Parole Decision Policy*. Washington, D.C.: U.S. Government Printing Office.

Gottfredson, G. D., and Gottfredson, D. C.
1984 *Victimization in Six Hundred Schools: An*

Analysis of the Roots of Disorder. New York: Plenum.

Gottfredson, M. R.

1974 An empirical analysis of pre-trial release decisions. *Journal of Criminal Justice* 2:287–304.

1979a Parole board decision making: a study of disparity reduction and the impact of institutional behavior. *Journal of Criminal Law and Criminology* 70(1):77–88.

1979b Treatment destruction techniques. *Journal of Research in Crime and Delinquency* 16:39.

Gottfredson, M. R., and Gottfredson, D. M.

1980a Data for criminal justice evaluation: some resources and pitfalls. Pp. 97–118 in M. Klein and K. Teilman, eds., *Handbook of Criminal Justice Evaluation*. Beverly Hills, Calif.: Sage.

1980b *Decisionmaking in Criminal Justice: Toward the Rational Exercise of Discretion*. Cambridge, Mass.: Ballinger.

1984 Guidelines for incarceration decisions: a partisan review. *University of Illinois Law Review* 2:291–317.

Gottfredson, S. D.

1984 Institutional responses to prison crowding. *New York University Review of Law and Social Change* 12(1):259–273.

Gottfredson, S. D., and Goodman, A. C.

1983 *The Dimensions of Judged Offense Seriousness*. Center for Metropolitan Planning and Research. Baltimore, Md.: Johns Hopkins University.

Gottfredson, S. D., and Gottfredson, D. M.

1979 *Screening for Risk: A Comparison of Methods*. Washington, D.C.: National Institute of Corrections.

1980 Screening for risk: a comparison of methods. *Criminal Justice and Behavior* 7(3):315–330.

1985 Screening for risk among parolees: policy, practice, and method. Pp. 54–77 in D. Farrington and R. Tarling, eds., *Prediction in Criminology*. Albany, N.Y.: SUNY Albany Press.

Gottfredson, S. D., and Taylor, R. B.

1983 *The Crisis in Corrections: Prison Populations and Public Policy*. Washington, D.C.: National Institute of Justice.

1986 Person-environment interactions in the prediction of recidivism. In J. Byrne and R. Sampson, eds., *The Social Ecology of Crime*. New York: Springer Verlag.

Gough, H. G.

1962 Clinical versus statistical prediction in psychology. Pp. 526–584 in L. Postman, ed., *Psychology in the Making*. New York: Knopf.

Green, B. F., Jr., and Hall, J. A.

1984 Quantitative methods for literature reviews. *Annual Review of Psychology* 33:37–53.

Green, D. M., and Swets, J. A.

1966 *Signal Detection Theory and Psychophysics*. New York: John Wiley & Sons.

Greenberg, D. F.

1975 The incapacitative effect of imprisonment: some estimates. *Law and Society Review* 9:541–580.

Greenwood, P. W., with Abrahamse, A.

1982 *Selective Incapacitation*. Report to the National Institute of Justice. Santa Monica, Calif.: Rand Corp.

Grossman, B. A., ed.

1980 *New Directions in Sentencing*. Toronto: Butterworth.

Guilford, J. P.

1965 *Statistics for Psychology and Education*. New York: Prentice-Hall

Hagan, J.

1974 Extra-legal attributes and criminal sentencing: an assessment of a sociological viewpoint. *Law and Society Review* 8(Spring): 357–383.

Hagan, J., and Bumiller, K.

1983 Making sense of sentencing: a review and critique of sentencing research. Pp. 1–54 in A. Blumstein, J. Cohen, S. Martin, and M. Tonry, eds., *Research on Sentencing: The Search for Reform*, Vol. II. Washington, D.C.: National Academy Press.

Hakeem, M.

1948 The validity of the Burgess method of parole prediction. *American Journal of Sociology* 53(5):376–386.

Hale, M. M.

1984 The Influence of Sentencing Goals on Judicial Decision-Making. Unpublished doctoral dissertation, Department of Psychology, Johns Hopkins University, Baltimore, Md.

Hamilton, W. A., and Work, C. R.

1973 The prosecutor's role in the urban court system: the case for management consciousness. *Journal of Criminal Law and Criminology* 64(2):183–189.

Harris, M. K.

1975 Disquisition on the need for a new criminal justice sanctioning system. *West Virginia Law Review* 77:263.

Hart, H.

1923 Predicting parole success. *Journal of Criminal Law and Criminology* 14:405–413.

Hart, H. L. A.

1968 *Punishment and Responsibility: Essays in the Philosophy of Law*. New York: Oxford University Press.

Hays, W. L.

1963 *Statistics for Psychologists*. New York: Holt, Rinehart, & Winston.

Hindelang, M., Hischi, T., and Weis, J.
1981 *Measuring Delinquency.* Beverly Hills, Calif.: Sage.

Hirschi, T., and Selvin, H.
1967 *Delinquency Research: An Appraisal of Analytic Methods.* New York: Free Press.

Hoffman, P. B.
1983 Screening for risk: a revised Salient Factor Score (SFS 81). *Journal of Criminal Justice* 11(6):539–547.

Hoffman, P. B., and Adelberg, S.
1980 The Salient Factor Score: a non-technical overview. *Federal Probation* 44(1):44–57.

Hoffman, P. B., and Beck, J. L.
1974 Parole decision-making: a Salient Factor Score. *Journal of Criminal Justice* 2:195–206.
1976 Salient Factor Score validations: a 1972 release cohort. *Journal of Criminal Justice* 4:69–76.

Hoffman, P. B., Stone-Meirhoefer, B., and Beck,J. L.
1978 Salient Factor Score and release behavior: three validation samples. *Law and Human Behavior* 1:47–62.

Hogarth, J.
1971 *Sentencing as a Human Process.* Toronto, Ontario: University of Toronto Press.

Hogarth, R. M.
1980 *Judgement and Choice: The Psychology of Decision.* Chichester, England: John Wiley & Sons.

Holland, T. R., Holt, N., Levi, M., and Beckett, G. E.
1983 Comparison and combination of clinical and statistical predictions of recidivism among adult offenders. *Journal of Applied Psychology* 68(2):203–211.

Horst, P.
1941 The prediction of personal adjustment. *Social Science Research Council Bulletin No. 48.* New York: Social Science Research Council.
1963 The statewide testing program. *Personnel and Guidance Journal* XLI: 394–402.
1966 *Psychological Measurement and Prediction.* Belmont, Calif.: Wadsworth.

Inciardi, J. A.
1971 The use of parole prediction with institutionalized narcotic addicts. *Journal of Research in Crime and Delinquency* 8(1):65–73.

Jacoby, J. E.
1977 *The Prosecutor's Charging Decision: A Policy Perspective.* Washington, D.C.: U.S. Government Printing Office.

Jacoby, J. E., Ratledge, E. C., and Turner, S. H.
1979 *Research on Prosecutorial Decisionmaking: Phase I Final Report.* Washington, D.C.: Bureau of Social Science Research.

Janus, M. G.
1984 *Selective Incapacitation: Have We Tried It? Does it Work?* Federal Prison System. Washington, D.C.: U.S. Department of Justice.

John, H.
1963 Prediction Improvement Using the Split-Sample Technique and Criterion-Scaled Independent Variables. Unpublished master's thesis, University of Illinois.

Kaplan, J.
1965 The prosecutorial discretion: a comment. *Northwestern University Law Review* 60:174.

Kassenbaum, G., Ward, D., and Wilner, D.
1971 *Prison Treatment and Parole Survival.* New York: John Wiley & Sons.

Kastenmeier, R. W., and Eglit, H. C.
1973 Parole release decision-making: rehabilitation, expertise, and the demise of mythology. *American University Law Review* 22(3): 477–525.

Kirby, B. C.
1954 Parole prediction using multiple correlation. *American Journal of Sociology* 59(6): 539–550.

Klepper, S., Nagin, D., and Tierney, L.
1983 Discrimination in the criminal justice system: a critical appraisal of the literature. Pp. 55–128 in A. Blumstein, J. Cohen, S. Martin, and M. Tonry, eds., *Research on Sentencing: The Search for Reform,* Vol. II. Washington, D.C.: National Academy Press.

Klienig, J.
1973 *Punishment and Desert.* The Hague, Netherlands: Martinus-Nijhoff.

Kohnle, E. F.
1938 *Die Kriminalitat entlassener Fursorgezoglinge un die Moglichkeit einer Erfolgsprognose.* Leipzig, East Germany: Kriminalistische Abahandlungen, No. 33.

Lagoy, S. P., Senna, J. J., and Siegel, L. J.
1976 An empirical study on information usage for prosecutorial decision making in plea negotiations. *American Criminal Law Review* 13:435–471.

Lancucki, L., and Tarling, R.
1978 The relationship between mean cost rating and Kendall's rank correlation coefficient tau. *Social Science Research* 7(1):81–87.

Lee, W.
1971 *Decision Theory and Human Behavior.* New York: John Wiley & Sons.

Levy, K. J.
1978 Predicting the time at which a specified number of subjects will achieve "success." *Educational and Psychological Measurement* 38:939–942.

Lipton, D., Martinson, R., and Wilks, J.
1975 *The Effectiveness of Correctional Treatment.* New York: Praeger.

Lloyd, M. R., and Joe, G. W.
1979 Recidivism comparisons across groups: methods of estimation and tests of significance for recidivism rates and asymptotes. *Evaluation Quarterly* 3(1):105–117.

Locke, J., Penn, R., Rock, R., Bunten, E., and Hare, G.
1970 *Compilation and Use of Criminal Court Data in Relation to Pretrial Release of Defendants: A Pilot Study.* Washington, D.C.: U.S. Government Printing Office.

Loeber, R., and Dishion, T.
1985 Early predictors of male delinquency: a review. *Psychological Bulletin* 94(1):68–99.

Luce, R. D., and Raiffa, H.
1957 *Games and Decisions.* New York: John Wiley & Sons.

Maltz, M. D., and McCleary, R.
1977 The mathematics of behavioral change: recidivism and construct validity. *Evaluation Quarterly* 1(3):421–438.

Maltz, M. D., McCleary, R., and Pollock, S. P.
1979 Recidivism and likelihood functions: a reply to Stollmack. *Evaluation Quarterly* 3(1): 124–131.

Mannheim, H., and Wilkins, L. T.
1955 *Prediction Methods in Relation to Borstal Training.* London, England: Her Majesty's Stationery Office.

Manski, C. F.
1978 Prospects for inference on deterrence through empirical analysis of individual criminal behavior. Pp. 400–424 in A. Blumstein, J. Cohen, and D. Nagin, eds., *Deterrence and Incapacitation: Estimating the Effects of Criminal Sanctions on Crime Rates.* Washington, D.C.: National Academy of Sciences.

Martin, S. E.
1983 The politics of sentencing reform: sentencing guidelines in Pennsylvania and Minnesota. Pp. 265–304 in A. Blumstein, J. Cohen, S. Martin, and M. Tonry, eds., *Research on Sentencing: The Search for Reform,* Vol. II. Washington, D.C.: National Academy Press.

McCord, J.
1980 Patterns of deviance. In S. Sells, R. Crandell, M. Roff, J. Strauss, and W. Pollin, eds., *Human Functioning in Longitudinal Perspective.* Baltimore, Md.: Williams and Wilkins.

Meehl, P. E.
1954 *Clinical versus Statistical Prediction.* Minneapolis: University of Minnesota Press.
1965 Seer over sign: the first good example. *Journal of Experimental Research in Personality* 1:27–32.

Meehl, P. E., and Rosen, A.
1955 Antecedent probability and the efficiency of psychometric signs, patterns, or cutting scores. *Psychological Bulletin* 52(3):194–216.

Meywerk, W.
1938 Beitrag zur Bestimmung der sozialen Prognose an Ruckfallsverbrechern. *Monatsschrift* 29.

Miller, F.
1970 *Prosecution: The Decision to Charge a Suspect with a Crime.* Boston: Little, Brown.

Minium, E. W.
1970 *Statistical Reasoning in Psychology and Education.* New York: John Wiley & Sons.

Minnesota Sentencing Guidelines Commission
1982 Preliminary Report on the Development and Impact of the Minnesota Sentencing Guidelines. Report prepared by the Minnesota Sentencing Guidelines Commission, Suite 284 Metro Sq. Bldg., 7th and Robert Sts., St. Paul, Minn.

Monachesi, E. D.
1932 *Prediction Factors in Probation.* Hanover, N.H.: Sociological Press.

Monahan, J.
1978 The prediction of violent criminal behavior: a methodological critique and prospectus. Pp. 244–269 in A. Blumstein, J. Cohen, and D. Nagin, eds., *Deterrence and Incapacitation: Estimating the Effects of Criminal Sanctions on Crime Rates.* Washington, D.C.: National Academy of Sciences.
1981 *Predicting Violent Behavior: An Assessment of Clinical Techniques.* Beverly Hills, Calif.: Sage.

Monahan, J., and Klassen, D.
1982 Situational approaches to understanding and predicting individual violent behavior. Pp. 292–319 in M. E. Wolfgang and N. A. Weiner, eds., *Criminal Violence.* Beverly Hills, Calif.: Sage.

Morris, N.
1974 *The Future of Imprisonment.* Chicago, Ill.: University of Chicago Press.

Mueller, G.
1977 *Sentencing: Process and Purpose.* Springfield, Ill.: Charles C Thomas.

National Advisory Commission on Criminal Justice Standards and Goals
1973 *Corrections.* Washington, D.C.: U.S. Government Printing Office.

New York Times
1982a Cutting crime tied to jailing of busiest criminals. October 6.
1982b Making punishment fit future crimes. November 14:E-9.

Newsweek
1982 To catch a career criminal. November 15:77.

NIJ Reports
1984 Selective incapacitation: two views of a compelling concept. January 4–8. Washington, D.C.: National Institute of Justice.

Ohlin, L. E.
1951 *Selection for Parole*. New York: Russell Sage.

Ohlin, L. E., and Duncan, O. D.
1949 The efficiency of prediction in criminology. *American Journal of Sociology* 54:441–451.

O'Leary, V., and Hall, J.
No date *Frames of Reference in Parole*. National Parole Institutes training document. Hackensack, N.J.: National Council on Crime and Delinquency Training Center. Ca. 1976.

O'Leary, V., Gottfredson, M. R., and Gelman, A.
1975 Contemporary sentencing proposals. *Criminal Law Bulletin* 11:55.

Olweus, D.
1977 A critical analysis of the "modern" interactionist position. Pp. 221–234 in D. Magnusson and N. Endler, eds., *Personality at the Crossroads: Current Issues in Interactional Psychology*. Hillsdale, N.J.: Erlbaum.

Palmer, J., and Carlson, P.
1976 Problems with the use of regression analysis in prediction studies. *Journal of Research in Crime and Delinquency* 13(1):64–81.

Petersilia, J.
1980 Criminal career research: a review of recent evidence. Pp. 321–379 in N. Morris and M. Tonry, eds., *Crime and Justice: An Annual Review of Research*. Vol. 2. Chicago, Ill.: University of Chicago Press.

Pitz, G. F., and Sachs, N. J.
1984 Judgment and decision: theory and application. *Annual Review of Psychology* 35: 139–164.

Pope, C.
1976 The influence of social and legal factors on sentence dispositions: a preliminary analysis of offender-based transaction statistics. *Journal of Criminal Justice* 4(3):203–221.
1978 Sentence dispositions accorded assault and burglary offenders. *Journal of Criminal Justice* 6:151.

Porebski, O. R.
1966 On the interrelated nature of the multivariate statistics used in discriminatory analysis. *British Journal of Mathematical and Statistical Psychology* 19(2):197–214.

President's Commission on Law Enforcement and the Administration of Justice
1967 *The Challenge of Crime in a Free Society*. Washington, D.C.: U.S. Government Printing Office.

Rapoport, A., and Wallsten, T.
1972 Individualized decision behavior. *Annual Review of Psychology* 23:131–175.

Reiss, A. J.
1951a The accuracy, efficiency, and validity of a prediction instrument. *American Journal of Sociology* 61:552–561.
1951b Delinquency as the failure of personal and social controls. *American Sociological Review* 16(2):196–207.
1951c Unraveling juvenile delinquency. II: An appraisal of the research methods. *American Journal of Sociology* 57:115–120.

Rhodes, W. M.
1978 *Plea Bargaining: Who Gains? Who Loses?* PROMIS Research Publication No. 14. Washington, D.C.: INSLAW.

Rich, W. D., Sutton, L. P., Clear, T. R., and Saks, M.
1982 *Sentencing by Mathematics: An Evaluation of the Early Attempts to Develop and Implement Sentencing Guidelines*. Williamsburg, Va.: National Center for State Courts.

Richardson, M. W.
1950 Effectiveness of selection devices. In D. H. Fryer and E. R. Henry, eds., *Handbook of Applied Psychology*. Vol. I. New York: Rhinehard.

Rorer, L. G., Hoffman, P., and Hsieh, K.
1965 Utilities as base rate multipliers in the determination of optimum cutting scores for the discrimination of groups of unequal size and variance. *Journal of Applied Psychology* 50:364–368.

Rose, G.
1966 Trends in the use of prediction. *Howard Journal of Penology and Crime Prevention* 12(1):26–33.

Rossi, P., Waite, E., Bose, C., and Berk, R.
1974 The seriousness of crime: normative structure and individual differences. *American Sociological Review* 39:224–237.

Roth, J., and Wice, P.
1978 Pretrial Release and Misconduct in the District of Columbia. PROMIS Research Project Publication No. 16. Washington, D.C.: INSLAW.

Sarbin, T.
1943 Contributions to the study of actuarial and individual methods of prediction. *American Journal of Sociology* 48:593:602.

Savitz, L. D.
1965 Prediction studies in criminology. *International Bibliography on Crime and Delinquency*. National Clearinghouse for Mental Health Information. Chevy Chase, Md.: National Institute of Mental Health.

Sawyer, J.
1966 Measurement *and* prediction, clinical *and* statistical. *Psychological Bulletin* 66:178–200.

Schmidt, P., and White, A. D.
1979 Models of criminal recidivism and an illustration of their use in evaluating correctional programs. Pp. 210–224 in L. Sechrest, S. White, and E. Brown, eds., *The Rehabilitation of Criminal Offenders: Problems and Prospects*. Washington, D.C.: National Academy of Sciences.

Schuessler, K. F.
1954 Parole prediction: its history and status. *Journal of Criminal Law and Criminology* 45(November):425–431.

Scott, J. E.
1974 The use of discretion in determining the severity of punishment for incarcerated offenders. *Journal of Criminal Law and Criminology* 65(2):214–224.

Sechrest, L., White, S., and Brown, E., eds.
1979 *The Rehabilitation of Criminal Offenders: Problems and Prospects*. Washington, D.C.: National Academy of Sciences.

Sellin, T., and Wolfgang, M.
1964 *The Measurement of Delinquency*. New York: John Wiley & Sons.

Shiedt, R.
1936 *Ein Beitrag zum Problem der Rukfalls-prognose*. Munich.

Simon, F. H.
1971 *Prediction Methods in Criminology, Including a Prediction Study of Young Men on Probation*. London, England: Her Majesty's Stationery Office.
1972 Statistical methods of making prediction instruments. *Journal of research in Crime and Delinquency* 9(1):46–53.

Slovic, P., Fischoff, B., and Lichtenstein, S.
1977 Behavioral decision therapy. *Annual Review of Psychology* 28:1–39.

Solomon, H.
1976 Parole outcome: a multidimensional contingency table analysis. *Journal of Research in Crime and Delinquency* 13:107–126.

Sparks, R. F.
1983 The construction of sentencing guidelines: a methodological critique. Pp. 194–264 in A. Blumstein, J. Cohen, S. Martin, and M. Tonry, eds., *Research on Sentencing: The Search for Reform*, Vol. II. Washington, D.C.: National Academy Press.

Statistical Analysis Center
1980 The Iowa Offender Risk Assessment Scoring System: Volume I: System Overview and Coding Procedures. Iowa Office for Planning and Programming, 523 E. 12th St., Des Moines, Iowa.
1983 The Impact of Objective Parole Criteria on Parole Release Rates and Public Protection. Final Report to the General Assembly of Iowa. Iowa Office for Planning and Programming, 523 E. 12th St., Des Moines, Iowa.
1984 Offender Risk Assessment: The Iowa Model—Validation Results First Draft. Iowa Office for Planning and Programming. 523 E. 12th St., Des Moines, Iowa.

Stollmack, S., and Harris, C. M.
1974 Failure-rate analysis applied to recidivism data. *Journal of the Operations Research Society of America*. 22:1192–1205.

Sutton, L.
1978 *Federal Sentencing Patterns*. Washington, D.C.: National Criminal Justice Information and Statistics Service.

Thomas, W. H., Jr.
1976 *Bail Reform in America*. Berkeley: University of California Press.

Thurstone, L. L.
1927 The method of paired comparisons for socialvalues. *Journal of Abnormal and Social Psychology* 21(4):384–400.

Tibbets, C.
1931 Success and failure in parole can be predicted. *Journal of Criminal Law, Criminology, and Police Science* 22:11–50.

Trunck, H.
1937 *Soziale Prognosen an Strafgefangenen*. 28 Monatsschrift fur Kriminalbiologie und Strafeschtsreform.

Underwood, B. D.
1979 Law and the crystal ball: predicting behavior with statistical inference and individualized judgment. *Yale Law Journal* 88(6):1408–1448.

U.S. News and World Report
1982 Key to criminals' futures: their pasts. October. van Alstyne, D. J., and Gottfredson, M. R.
1978 A multidimensional contingency table analysis of parole outcome: new methods and old problems in criminological prediction. *Journal of Research in Crime and Delinquency* 15:172–193.

Vandaele, W.
1978 Participation in illegitimate activities: Ehrlich revisited. Pp. 270–335 in A. Blumstein, J. Cohen, and D. Nagin, eds., *Deterrence and Incapacitation: Estimating the Effects of Criminal Sanctions on Crime Rates*. Washington, D.C.: National Academy of Sciences.

Vold, G. B.
1931 *Prediction Methods and Parole: A Study of Factors Involved in the Violation or Non-violation of Parole in a Group of Minnesota Adult Males.* Minneapolis, Minn.: Sociological Press.
1949 Comment on "The efficiency of prediction in criminology." *American Journal of Sociology* 54:451–452.

von Hirsch, A.
1976 *Doing Justice: The Choice of Punishments.* New York: Hill-Wang.

von Hirsch, A., and Gottfredson, D. M.
1984 Selective incapacitation: some queries about research design and equity. *New York University Review of Law and Social Change* 12(1):11–51.

von Neumann, J., and Morgenstern, O.
1947 *Theory of Games and Economic Behavior.* Princeton, N.J.: Princeton University Press.

Wainer, H.
1976 Estimating coefficients in linear models: it don't make no nevermind. *Psychological Bulletin* 83(2):213–217.

Warner, F. B.
1923 Factors determining parole from the Massachusetts Reformatory. *Journal of Criminal Law and Criminology* 14:172–207.

Wice, P.
1973 *Bail and Its Reform: A National Survey.* Washington, D.C.: U.S. Government Print ing Office.

Wiggins, J.
1973 *Personality and Prediction: Principles of Personality Assessment.* Reading, Mass.: Addison-Wesley.

Wilbanks, W., and Hindelang, M.
1972 The comparative efficiency of three prediction methods. Appendix B in D. Gottfredson, L. Wilkins, and P. Hoffman, *Summarizing Experience for Parole Decision-Making.* Davis, Calif.: National Council on Crime and Delinquency Research Center.

Wilkins, L. T., and Chandler, A.
1965 Confidence and competence in decision-making. *British Journal of Criminology* 5 (January):1.

Wilkins, L. T., and MacNaughton-Smith, P.
1964 New prediction and classification methods in criminology. *Journal of Research in Crime and Delinquency* 1(1):19–32.

Williams, K.
1978 *The Role of the Victim in the Prosecution of Violent Crimes.* PROMIS Research Publication No. 12, Washington, D.C.: INSLAW.

Wolfgang, M. E., Figlio, R. M., and Sellin, T.
1972 *Delinquency in a Birth Cohort.* Chicago, Ill.: University of Chicago Press.

Wright, K., Clear, T., and Dickson, P.
1984 Universal applicability of probation risk-assessment instruments: a critique. *Criminology* 22(1):113–134.

7

Some Methodological Issues in Making Predictions

John B. Copas and Roger Tarling

Methodological considerations are central to all quantitative or actuarial predictions, although each particular prediction study invariably presents its own special issues. At its most general level, a prediction study investigates the extent to which criterion measures (the dependent variables) can be predicted by one or more measures of other factors (the predictor or independent variables).

It is outside the scope of this paper to discuss all the important methodological steps in the process: the selection and measurement of appropriate information; the choice of statistical method; the practical application of a prediction instrument and its utility. Instead, we concentrate on four aspects. First, we examine in detail the Burgess and Glueck point-scoring methods, which have been used extensively in criminological prediction. Second, we consider the important topic of validating and calibrating the prediction instrument. Third, we review the various measures that have been proposed to assess an instrument's predictive power. Fourth, we describe methods for reusing samples to carry out a prospective validation. At each stage we attempt to synthesize some of the previous work in the area and present the results of our more recent statistical and methodological research.

POINT-SCORING METHODS

A variety of statistical methods have been used to construct prediction instruments. Chief among them are the Burgess and Glueck point-scoring methods, multiple regression, log-linear methods, and logistic regression. In addition, various clustering, classification, and segmentation techniques have been used. (The latter group of techniques are not discussed here; see Fielding, 1979; Tarling and Perry, 1985.[1]) For examples of the

John B. Copas is professor of statistics, University of Birmingham, England; Roger Tarling is deputy head, Home Office Research and Planning Unit, England.

[1]The statistical methods listed above have severe limitations for much criminal career research, especially when the dependent variable is not binary

application of all these methods in criminological research, see the studies included in Farrington and Tarling (1985).

Invariably, these methods have been used in studies in which the dependent variable is binary (e.g., reconvicted/not reconvicted). Many criminologists have found that simple point-scoring methods are more efficient or robust than more sophisticated methods and shrink less when applied to a validation sample. This seems especially so when the data contain measurement errors or "noise" (S. D. Gottfredson and Gottfredson, 1985; Wilbanks, 1985). This finding, plus the fact that point-scoring methods are simple in conception and administratively easy to use, has led to their being adopted in practice, particularly in studies of parole and sentencing decision making (D. M. Gottfredson, Wilkins, and Hoffman, 1978; Nuttall et al., 1977). However, some commentators have said that point-scoring methods are intolerably crude, have no statistical foundations, and do not result in any direct probabilistic interpretation.

In this section we explore point-scoring methods to see if we can resolve some of these tensions and anomalies. In addition, we show how point-scoring methods, reconceptualized in the way we recommend, can be extended.

There are two basic point-scoring methods, one ascribed to Burgess (1928) and the other to Glueck and Glueck (1950). In the Burgess method each subject is given a score of either 0 or 1 on each of a number of predictors, depending on whether the subject falls into a category with a below- or above-average success rate. The Glueck method is more sophisticated in that, instead of contributing a score of 0 or 1, each category of each predictor is weighted according to the percentage of subjects in that category who are successes. The Glueck method can be applied to polychotomous independent variables, but in practice it has only been used for binary predictors. We keep to this simpler situation in our discussion.

Both the Burgess and the Glueck methods have their parallels in standard statistical theory—the "independence Bayes method." First, consider the Burgess method.

Let x_i be a series of binary predictive factors, let q be the overall success rate, and suppose that within the success (S) and failure (F) groups separately, the factors x_i are statistically independent of each other. Let

$$h_i = P(x_i = 1|S),\ g_i = P(x_i = 1|F).$$

Assume the x_i's are coded such that $h_i > g_i$. Then, by Bayes theorem,

$$P(S|x_i = 1) = h_i\, q/P_i$$

and

$$P(S|x_i = 0) = (1 - h_i)\, q/(1 - P_i)$$

where

$$P_i = P(x_i = 1) = h_i\, q + g_i(1 - q).$$

By independence and Bayes theorem again,

$$\frac{P(S|x)}{P(F|x)} = \frac{q}{1-q} \cdot \frac{\Pi P(x_i|S)}{\Pi P(x_i|F)}$$

and so log odds for S after observing x is

$$= \log \frac{q}{1-q} + \sum \log \frac{P(x_i|S)}{P(x_i|F)}.$$

This can be written as

$$k + \Sigma W_i x_i$$

where

and the focus of interest is on the time interval to some event, for example, the next offense. We would suggest that alternative statistical methods, stochastic point-process models, and failure-rate regression models are more appropriate in these situations and should receive more attention from criminologists.

$$W_i = \log \frac{h_i(1 - g_i)}{(1 - h_i)g_i},$$

which is just the log odds ratio for the 2 × 2 table classifying $x_i = 1$ or 0 against S and F. Given independence, these are therefore the optimum weights. By the Neyman-Pearson Lemma in statistical theory, any other set of weights must be less efficient (i.e., they do not use all the information available in the x_i's).

The Burgess method has $W_i = 1$, or, since a scale factor in the score is irrelevant, $W_i =$ constant. Thus, the Burgess method is only optimum if the cross-product ratio is the same for each factor (i.e., each x_i gives the same amount of information about S or F).

The Glueck method is equivalent to

$$W_i = P(S|x_i = 1) - P(S|x_i = 0),$$

which, from above, simplifies to

$$W_i = \frac{q(1 - q)(h_i - g_i)}{P_i(1 - P_i)}$$

Again, a constant multiple is irrelevant, so essentially

$$W_i = \frac{(h_i - g_i)}{P_i(1 - P_i)} \neq \text{log odds ratio for } x_i.$$

However, if x_i has only modest predictive power, we can write

$$h_i = g_i + \varepsilon_i$$

where ε_i is small. We can then show that

$$\log \frac{h_i(1 - g_i)}{g_i(1 - h_i)} = \frac{h_i - g_i}{P_i(1 - P_i)} + \text{terms involving } \varepsilon_i^2.$$

Hence the Glueck method is approximately optimum if ε_i is small, that is, if each individual x_i contributes only a modest amount of information. In many practical cases the score may involve a relatively large number of x_i's, none of which by itself is spectacular, but together they may be useful. This, we suggest, accounts for the apparent success of the Glueck method.

As set out above, Burgess and Glueck are not separate and distinct models but are, in fact, simple log-linear models in which all the predictor variables are treated as independent, i.e., they are not correlated. We would advocate the use of the formal independence Bayes method in preference to the more ad hoc Burgess and Glueck approaches because it has several important advantages:

1. It is equally simple yet is based on a coherent theory and is optimum within the framework of that theory.
2. It provides a direct estimate $P(S|x)$, whereas the scoring methods of Burgess and Glueck have to be separately calibrated on the data, that is, the probability of success given a certain score is estimated by calculating the proportion of all subjects with that score who succeeded.
3. Similarly, the value of the score is seen to be a log odds ratio. Hence if the score is s, the probability of success must be of the form

$$\frac{e^s}{1 + e^s}.$$

There are two further advantages of the Bayes method that make it extendable in ways not possible for the Burgess and Glueck methods. (Extensions of this kind have been considered in the medical literature under the name of "computer-aided diagnosis models.") First, it can more readily accommodate x_i's that are not binary. The formula is then

$$\text{log odds for } S \text{ given } x = \log \frac{q}{1 - q} + \sum \log \frac{f_i(x_i)}{g_i(x_i)},$$

where

$$f_i(x_i) = P(x_i|S) \text{ and } g_i(x_i) = P(x_i|F).$$

Of course, all these probabilities are estimated from the data. Note that we need the proportions of the various values of x_i within the F and S groups separately and not the proportions of S and F within the groups defined by various values of x_i (a crucial distinction). The above formula is not necessarily linear in each x_i (but there is no reason to expect it to be). Thus we avoid the need arbitrarily to dichotomize each predictor variable, the full information in each value of x_i being retained in an optimum way. Of course, if the x_i's are divided into too many categories, each term, such as $P(x_i|S)$, is estimated less accurately, and so, if there are too many categories (e.g., age measured in years), it is better to treat x_i as a continuous variable and use a regression technique. Thus if some x_i's are continuous, the term

$$\log \frac{f_i(x_i)}{g_i(x_i)}$$

can be estimated directly as a regression on x_i. Hence the method can accommodate mixed data in which some x_i's are continuous, e.g., age, and some x_i's are binary, e.g., sex (cf. analysis of covariance methods).

Second, the Bayes method can be generalized to take account of particular circumstances concerning the distribution of the x_i's. For example, if the x_i's are not independent but correlated to a roughly equal extent (e.g., they are all positively correlated), a modification simply involves multiplying W_i by a constant, and so the relative weights remain essentially the same. Thus, if the Bayes formula is recalibrated on the data (which allows an appropriate linear transformation of the score to be estimated), it works well even when the x_i's are moderately correlated with each other. If the x_i's are correlated, but not all to the same degree, the so-called "Lancaster models" can be used, which are based on a second-order approximation to the joint distribution of the x_i's. These models have been found useful in medical diagnosis applications; see review in Titterington et al. (1981).

Apart from the obvious simplicity, an important advantage of all these methods is the relative precision with which the weights (or coefficients, if viewed as a log-linear model) are estimated. This is because the assumption of independence allows each weight to be estimated separately, and any sampling effects in the intercorrelations of the x's have no effect. If the sample size is relatively small, and the correlations between the x's are, at most, modest, point-scoring methods do well. Larger correlations between the x's, but with a similar sample size, can be dealt with in an approximate way by one of the modifications mentioned above. For somewhat larger sample sizes, however (say several hundred), a prediction equation should make proper allowance for the dependence between the x's, and a logistic model or log-linear model (in the usual sense for categorical data) is the preferred alternative. In such models, each weight or coefficient is, of course, not just a function of the relevant x_i but depends in a much more complicated way on the joint distribution of all the x_i's. The complexity of the model affects the degree of shrinkage, which will be discussed later in the paper. If our suggestions for correcting for shrinkage are used, the increased shrinkage of these complicated models should not present a problem.

PREDICTIVE POWER, CALIBRATION, AND SHRINKAGE OF PREDICTION EQUATIONS

Much statistical work in criminology has been concerned with the construction and use of prediction equations. For each individual, some response y (a binary yes-no variable, a time to arrest, et cetera) is measured, along with values of explanatory variables $x_1, x_2, \ldots$, and on the basis of these x's a predicted value of y, say $\hat{y}$, is formulated. How good is $\hat{y}$ as a predictor of y? Issues related to this general question are to be discussed in this section. We are concerned here with the underlying methodology of the assessment of prediction equations, rather than with details of prediction equations in specific applications.

There are two contrasting, and yet complementary, approaches to the discussion of this question, corresponding roughly to the two philosophies of statistical inference and decision theory as understood in the statistical literature. The inference approach is taken up in the next section, where we ask: Given that an individual is described by $x = x_1, x_2, \ldots$, what information does that give us about y? A prediction equation, with value $\hat{y}$, is seen as an estimate of the expectation of y in some sense. The properties and behavior of a prediction instrument are studied in terms of the accuracy of $\hat{y}$ over the totality of all different values of y and x. We argue that a particular advantage of the inference approach is that a clear discussion of shrinkage is possible. Our discussion leads to a correction for shrinkage or to "preshrunk" prediction equations as we will call them.

The other approach is more pragmatic; it views a prediction equation as a means to an end, that of a decision instrument. All the issues are illustrated by a binary classification, conventionally labeled positive-negative. Each individual falls into one or other group (e.g., success-failure), the decision as to which is the true group being made on the basis of x. The discussion focuses entirely on the frequencies of correct and incorrect decisions. A confusing array of measures of predictive power has appeared in the criminological literature (and in the parallel literature on computer-aided diagnosis in medicine). We show that the more important of these are in fact very closely related to each other.

There is an obvious link between the two approaches. If y is an observed response, a binary classification could be: success if $y \geqslant k_1$ and failure if $y < k_1$. The classification from the prediction equation would by analogy be: success if $\hat{y} \geqslant k_2$ and failure if $\hat{y} < k_2$ (there is no reason to insist that $k_1 = k_2$). We would argue in favor of formulating $\hat{y}$ to optimize such properties as calibration and validation (discussed in the next section) and then choosing k_2 to secure desirable aspects of error rates and/or utility (discussed later).

It is worth noting, however, that prediction equations are sometimes useful as a research tool in their own right, not just as a means of implementing the positive-negative decision. For instance, to control for differences between cases in a study, the value of an appropriate prediction $\hat{y}$ could sensibly be used either as a covariate in statistical analysis using covariance adjustments or as a criterion for matching cases and controls in a matched-pairs design. An example of the former approach is in Bottoms and McClintock (1973:Chapter 11).

Validation and Shrinkage

It is almost universal experience that, when a prediction equation is fitted to data and then applied to some new cases or a new cohort, the usefulness and accuracy of the prediction are much more disappointing than expected. The term "shrinkage" has been used to describe this deterioration in predictive power. Although the effect is real enough, and noted in many studies, the term has never been given a precise definition. Quite independently of the experience of criminologists in using prediction equations, there has been the remarkable development in the statistical literature of so-called "shrinkage estimation," a technique whereby a set of related parameters can be estimated more accurately (on average) than by conventional techniques, such as least squares. The use of the same term in these different contexts has appeared at best coincidental and at worst grotesquely misleading. However, there are known to be close connections between them, as discussed in Copas (1983b). Using the theory described in that paper it is possible to (a) clarify the manifestations of shrinkage, (b) highlight the reasons for them, (c) derive alternative methods of fitting prediction equations that will eliminate some of the adverse effects of shrinkage, and (d) enable the extent of shrinkage in any given application to be estimated in advance from the original data. These points are discussed in this section, and a brief outline of Copas's theory is illustrated by a criminological example.

In fitting a prediction equation to data, we will have, as before, observations on some response y (e.g., the number of convictions in a long-term follow-up, or a binary factor describing whether some event, such as rearrest, has occurred) together with information on a number of predictive factors x (number of previous convictions, age, et cetera). The aim is to formulate a predictor $\hat{y} = f(x)$ for some function f [e.g., multiple regression, in which case $f(x) = \alpha + \beta' x$]. The fit of the equation relates to the proximity of $\hat{y}$ to the actual observed values of y. Two aspects of the prediction equation are distinguished:

1. *Calibration.* Here we group cases with the same or similar values of $\hat{y}$ and ask whether the average of the associated y's is equal to the predicted value $\hat{y}$. The greater the difference, the worse the calibration.

2. *Efficacy.* Here we ask whether values of $\hat{y}$ discriminate clearly between cases with different x's. A simple measure of this is the correlation between y and $\hat{y}$. (In the case of multiple regression this is just the multiple correlation coefficient or the coefficient of determination, R.) A large R shows that $\hat{y}$ changes substantially as x changes, while a small R means that $\hat{y}$ is almost the same for all x (and so is useless as a predictor).

The ideal predictor, never realized in practice, is one in which $y = \hat{y}$ for all x, which calibrates perfectly and has maximal efficacy (R = 1). In practice, if the model behind the prediction equation is correct, when judged by values of y and $\hat{y}$ in the data, $\hat{y}$ will calibrate well but have R somewhat less than 1 (this is essentially the Gauss-Markov theorem of least squares).

A second crucial distinction is between retrospective fit and validation fit. Retrospective fit concerns the comparison between values of y and $\hat{y}$ in the data on which the prediction equation is fitted. Validation fit envisages the prediction equation being applied to a new set of cases or subjects and compares the actual values of y in the new data with the predictions $f(x)$, calculated using the original prediction equation f but using the new values of x. The difference between the sets of data is emphasized by the terms "construction data" and "validation data." Shrinkage implies that validation fit is worse than retrospective fit. In practice, the predictions $\hat{y}$ calibrate well in the construction data but less well, and sometimes very badly, in the validation data. Efficacy is nearly always worse in the validation data than in the construction data. Copas's theory quantifies both these aspects of the deterioration of fit.

There are (at least) three possible causes of the deterioration in both these aspects of fit: (a) a purely statistical effect that is the inevitable result of unexplained (random) variation in the data; (b) changes in the population of x's from construction data to validation data (e.g., there might be some intermediate change of policy or other intervention that alters the range of subjects available for study); and (c) the underlying associations between y and x might change (e.g., a change in some latent factor that is not observed in x). Each of these causes of shrinkage is discussed below.

Shrinkage as a Statistical Effect—Cause (a)

Cause (a) will be illustrated in the case of multiple regression, in which the statistical model is

$$y = \alpha + \beta' x + \varepsilon,$$

ε being the usual random error. Without loss of generality, we can assume the x's are standardized to have mean zero, so that α merely reflects the overall average value of y. Suppose causes (b) and (c) do not operate, so that we have a stable population of x's and constant true values of α and β as we go from construction to validation data. This, therefore, represents the ideal situation as far as fitting and validating a prediction equation is concerned.

If $\hat{\alpha}$ and $\hat{\beta}$ are least squares estimates in the construction data, the prediction equation is

$$\hat{y} = \hat{\alpha} + \hat{\beta}' x.$$

Suppose we test this out on a very large validation sample, so that we compare $y = \alpha + \beta' x + \varepsilon$ with $\hat{\alpha} + \hat{\beta}' x$ over a population of new cases (y, x). To study calibration, we calculate the average y (i.e., $\alpha + \beta' x$) over those cases x that relate to a specific prediction $\hat{y}$. This is done by fitting a linear regression of y on $\hat{y}$, which can be shown to have slope

$$K = \frac{\beta' V \hat{\beta}}{\hat{\beta}' V \hat{\beta}},$$

where V is the variance-covariance matrix of the x's. The average of K, over statistical errors in $\hat{\beta}$, which is evaluated in Copas (1983b), is always less than 1. Hence large values of y tend to be overestimated and small values of y tend to be underestimated. This is because

$$E(\hat{\beta}' V \hat{\beta}) = \beta' V \beta + \frac{m\sigma^2}{n} > \beta' V \beta = E(\beta' V \hat{\beta}),$$

where n is the sample size in the construction data and m is the number of variables measured in x. By the same reasoning, $\beta' V \hat{\beta}$ can be estimated by $\hat{\beta}' V \hat{\beta} - m\sigma^2/n$, where σ^2 is the usual residual mean square, and so K itself can be estimated by

$$\frac{\hat{\beta}' V \hat{\beta} - m\sigma^2/n}{\hat{\beta}' V \hat{\beta}} = 1 - \frac{1}{F},$$

where F is the usual F-ratio of multiple regression. A more thorough analysis, valid if $m \geqslant 3$, shows that the slightly modified estimate

$$\hat{K} = 1 - \frac{m - 2}{mF}$$

is unbiased in the sense that $E(\hat{K}) = E(K)$. Thus K measures the deterioration in calibration; in a set of validation data, the average value of y to be expected for a given $\hat{y}$ is not $\hat{y}$, as might be anticipated from the construction data, but

$$\tilde{y} = \bar{y} + \hat{K}(\hat{y} - \bar{y}),$$

where $\bar{y}$ is the overall observed average of y. The smaller $\hat{K}$ is, the greater the distortion in calibration. Of course, this is itself a prediction in the sense that $\tilde{y}$ is calculated from the construction data and cannot be expected to be invariably correct when applied to practical validation data. However, on average, and to an approximation examined in detail in Copas (1983b),

$$E(y|\tilde{y}) = \tilde{y}$$

for a typical validation case (y, x). Thus $\tilde{y}$ can be said to be preshrunk in the sense that it is expected to calibrate well (show no calibration shrinkage) on validation data. Of course $\tilde{y}$ will not calibrate well on the construction data (because it is $\hat{y}$

that does), but, from a pragmatic point of view, retrospective performance of a predictor is irrelevant.

The pedigree of $\tilde{y}$ is confirmed in Copas (1983b), in that $\tilde{y}$ corresponds exactly to a "shrinkage estimator" in the sense of the term used in the statistical literature. It is proved that, within the assumptions outlined above, $\tilde{y}$ is uniformly better than $\hat{y}$ in the mean squared error sense, i.e.,

$$E(\tilde{y} - y)^2 < E(\hat{y} - y)^2$$

over validation data (y, x), provided $m \geqslant 3$, where m is the number of x variables. If $m = 2$, $\hat{K} = 1$ and so preshrinkage has no effect. If $m = 1$, the whole theory breaks down, since the expectations of quantities such as K cease to exist (the relevant infinite integrals diverge). In fact, it is shown that for $m = 1$ and $m = 2$ no uniform improvement on least squares is possible. The theory of preshrinking is therefore useful only if there are three or more predictive variables in x.

Turning to efficacy, but still in the multiple regression case, the deterioration in correlation is inevitable and cannot be removed by preshrinking. In fact

$$\text{Corr}(\tilde{y}, y) = \text{Corr}(\hat{y}, y),$$

and so the discrimination afforded by $\tilde{y}$ is identical to that of $\hat{y}$. The inevitable decline in correlation is simply due to the fact that in the construction data $\hat{y}$ has knowledge of the actual y's, whereas in validation data it does not. The above theory is immediately extended to predict the validation correlation of y and $\hat{y}$ (or $\tilde{y}$): it is

$$\tilde{R} = \frac{(n - 1)R^2 - m}{(n - m - 1)R},$$

where R is the multiple correlation coefficient in the construction data. Always we have $\tilde{R} < R$. For prediction, the retrospective R is irrelevant; efficacy should be measured by $\tilde{R}$, which on average will be (approximately) the correlation obtained if the predictor ($\hat{y}$ or $\tilde{y}$) were to be validated.

A minor point to mention is that $\hat{K}$ can be negative, in which case $\hat{y}$ inverts the predictions made by $\hat{y}$. However, in the worst case, in which x has no effect ($\beta = 0$), $E(F) > 1$ and so $E(\hat{K}) > 0$. Thus, if $\hat{K}$ is negative, the correlations between y and x are even worse than one would expect from pure random numbers, and it would be apparent that any prediction equation based on x is doomed to failure. The same comment applies to the circumstance that $\tilde{R} < 0$.

The multiple regression model being discussed implicitly assumes that y is a continuous variable. Models for discrete and categorical data are mentioned elsewhere in this paper, including the important case of binary data. Suppose that y is defined to be 1 if an event occurs (success) and 0 if it does not (failure), with the predictive factors x as before. A multiple regression of y on x can still be fitted, with $E(y)$ being interpreted as the probability of success. All the above quantities in shrinkage theory can be calculated in the same way, although their mathematical validity can only be taken as an approximation (but often a reasonable one if n is large and the correlations between y and each x are not too close to 1). The more informative model is logistic regression, for which

$$f(x) = \frac{e^{\hat{\alpha}+\hat{\beta}'x}}{1 + e^{\hat{\alpha}+\hat{\beta}'x}}.$$

The overall significance of a fitted model of this kind is measured by a value of χ^2 ("deviance" in computer output from the statistical package GLIM), and it can be shown that in many practical cases $\chi^2 \doteq mF$, where F is the F-ratio in an ordinary multiple regression of y on x. Thus $\hat{K}$ becomes

$$\hat{K} = 1 - \frac{m-2}{\chi^2}.$$

Calibration relates to the probability of success rather than to the average value of y. A binary predictor is well calibrated if, over all cases in which $f(x) = \hat{p}$, say, the proportion of successful cases is in fact $\hat{p}$. In a large validation sample, this proportion will be expected to be

$$\tilde{p} = \frac{e^{\hat{\alpha}+\hat{K}\hat{\beta}'x}}{1 + e^{\hat{\alpha}+\hat{K}\hat{\beta}'x}},$$

for the same reasons as in the multiple regression case. Thus $\tilde{p}$ is the preshrunk form of the predictor, by analogy with $\tilde{y}$ above.

This is illustrated in a particular application to the problem of predicting the probability of absconding from open borstals, taking into account known social and criminological indicators (using data kindly made available by the Prison Department's Young Offender Psychology Unit, Home Office, England). Here $y = 1$ if the trainee absconded during sentence, $y = 0$ otherwise, and $m = 22$ predictive factors were studied. A logistic regression on $n = 500$ cases gives $\chi^2 = 50.2$ on 22 degrees of freedom, which is highly significant; $\hat{K}$ is 0.602. Calibration was examined by using a nonparametric smoothing method to plot the actual proportion of absconding cases, say p, against the predicted proportions $\hat{p}[=f(x)]$; the method is from Copas (1983a). This is shown in Figure 1, in which both axes are on logistic scales. The calibration is satisfactory in the construction data, in that the plotted curve (labeled "construction data") is tolerably close to the diagonal line $p = \hat{p}$. A further set of 1,500 cases was then used as validation data and the plotting process repeated. The shrinkage is very marked (Figure 1); the plotted curve is much shallower than the diagonal (large p's are overestimated by $\hat{p}$, small p's underestimated). The use of $\tilde{p}$ instead of $\hat{p}$ is equivalent to retaining the graph with $\hat{p}$ as the horizontal coordinate, but replacing the diagonal line with a line of slope $\hat{K} = 0.602$, shown as the dashed line. The reasonable fit of the validation curve to the dashed line confirms that the validation calibration of $\tilde{p}$ is satisfactory.

The ordinary multiple correlation coefficient between y and x for these data is $R = 0.322$, whereas the validation correlation discussed above is $\tilde{R} = 0.194$. The substantial shrinkage has almost halved the correlation, the efficacy of the predictor on validation being extremely modest. This magnitude of the drop in correlation is not at all unusual in practice (e.g., Simon, 1971).

The multiple and logistic regression models discussed above are fixed models in the sense that the variables in x are fixed in advance. In practice, prediction equations are often simplified by using stepwise regression or some other procedure for subset selection; the variables in x are then selected using the data, and only those x's showing reasonably strong correlation with y are retained. The usual theory of least squares is, of course, completely upset by such selection. A recent discussion in the *Journal of the Royal Statistical Society* (A. J. Miller, 1984) has highlighted the complex issues involved. Shrinkage theory has been extended to stepwise regression, but the details in Copas (1983b) will not be repeated here. The main result is that shrinkage for regression on a subset of x is greater, usually much greater, than would be anticipated if the subset were fixed in advance. Given certain assumptions, the value of K corresponding to validation calibration is the value as calculated from the full regression on all x's and not as calculated using the above formula based on the subset actually used. These assumptions are often reasonable in practice, and in cases of doubt a rather elaborate significance test proposed in Copas (1983b) can be used. The formula for shrinkage of the correlation coefficient is modified to

$$\tilde{R} = \frac{(n - 1)R^2 - m}{(n - 1 - m)R^2} R^* ,$$

where R^* is the multiple correlation between y and the selected x's, and as before, R is the corresponding correlation for all the x's.

Since many x's in the absconding study appeared to be of low predictive value, a subset of just four x's was chosen for the logistic regression, with $\chi^2 = 29.0$ on four degrees of freedom. If selection is ignored, this would give $\hat{K} = 0.931$ (indicating very little shrinkage). For the full logistic regression $\hat{K} = 0.602$, as before. The validation fit of the reduced regression is shown in Figure 2, which was constructed in the same way as Figure 1. As can be seen the shrinkage is consistent with $\hat{K} = 0.602$ and much greater than that implied by the value $\hat{K} = 0.931$.

Shrinkage in the Light of Changes in the Population—Cause (b)

The theory expounded so far accommodates cause (a)—the purely statistical effect—but assumes that there are no changes in the distribution of x [cf. (b)] or the response function [cf. (c)]. Neither assumption will be exactly true, although each will often hold to a reasonable approximation. In this section we discuss the effect of changes in the population (i.e., in the distribution of x) on the validation performance of predictors. We suppose that x has mean m_1 in the construction sample and mean m_2 in the validation sample, with the variance-covariance matrices V_1 and V_2 defined in an analogous way. We therefore wish to

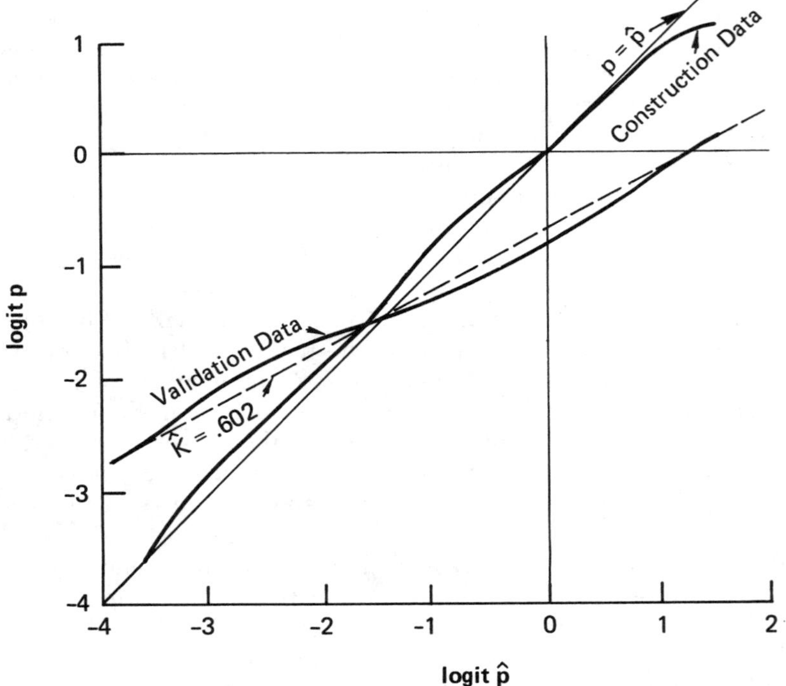

FIGURE 1 Shrinkage for absconding study (full regression). Source: Derived from data provided by Prison Department's Young Offender Psychology Unit, Home Office, England.

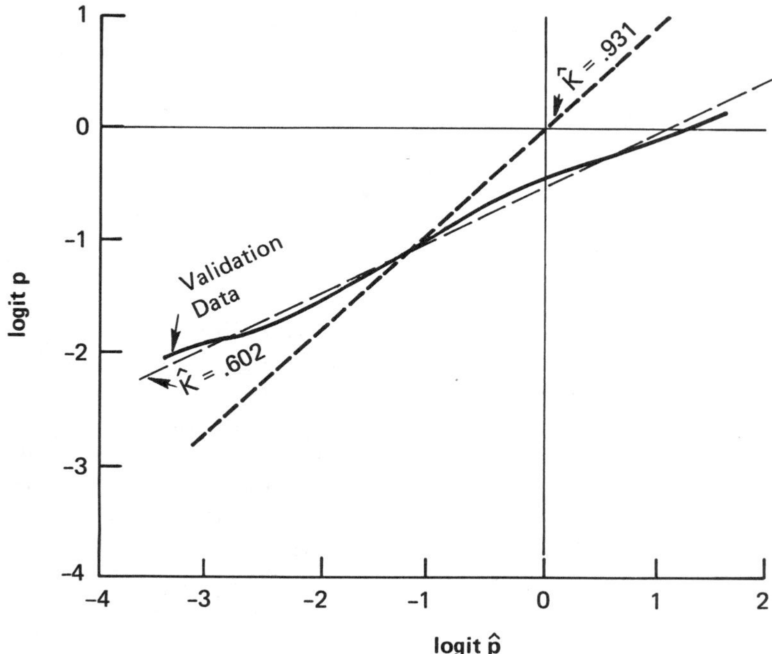

FIGURE 2 Shrinkage for absconding study (stepwise regression). Source: Derived from data provided by Prison Department's Young Offender Psychology Unit, Home Office, England.

study the case in which $m_1 \neq m_2$ and/or $V_1 \neq V_2$.

A number of approaches are discussed in turn, corresponding to various ways in which changes in distribution can occur, and to different ways in which the performance of predictors can be assessed. Some of these correspond to well-established results in the statistical literature, others to work in progress.

Wishart Variation. Perhaps the simplest case is to assume that the construction and validation samples are both sampled randomly from the same underlying population. The matrices V_1 and V_2 will then be independent samples from the same Wishart distribution indexed by the (unknown) true variance-covariance matrix. Similarly, m_1 and m_2 will be independent with identical multivariate normal distributions. It can be shown that the uniform improvement of the shrinkage predictor over least squares continues to hold in this more general setting, i.e.

$$E(\tilde{y} - y)^2 < E(\hat{y} - y)^2,$$

where the expectation is over (y, x) in the validation sample, over the distribution of regression parameters, as well as over sampling variation in the m's and V's. The only requirement is, as before, that $m \geqslant 3$. Again, the improvement holds over all possible true regression parameters, no matter what are the underlying parameters of the population. Thus differences in samples caused by sampling variation only do not affect the shrinkage arguments put forward in the last section.

Mathematical Conditions for Uniform Improvement. The Wishart variation case suggests that if $m_1 - m_2$ and $V_1 - V_2$ are small, shrinkage theory is unaffected. To investigate what happens when these differences are larger, define the matrix

$$W = V_1^{-1/2}[V_2 + (m_2 - m_1)(m_2 - m_1)']V_1^{-1/2},$$

and let $\lambda_1 \geqslant \lambda_2 \geqslant \ldots \geqslant \lambda_m$ be the m ordered eigenvalues of W. Then it is shown in Brown and Zidek (1980) that the prediction mean squared error of $\tilde{y}$ is better than that of $\hat{y}$ for all possible regression parameters if

$$\lambda_1 \leq 2(m + 2)^{-1}\Sigma\lambda_i$$

Roughly speaking, the largest eigenvalue of W should not exceed about twice the average of all the eigenvalues. (If $V_1 = V_2$ and $m_1 = m_2$, W is the identity matrix and so all the λ_i's are unity). This puts an upper bound on the differences between construction and validation samples that can be allowed if $\tilde{y}$ is to remain uniformly superior to $\hat{y}$.

Robustness Region for Superiority of $\tilde{y}$. When the matrix W leads to failure of the above inequality, the question of whether $\tilde{y}$ has a lower prediction mean squared error than $\hat{y}$ depends on the true (and unknown) vector of regression parameters β. Typically, when the inequality fails, shrinkage will be better if the coefficients of β are sufficiently small, but worse if the coefficients are large. Extremely large regression coefficients do not usually characterize empirical relationships in the social sciences, and so in practice differences between construction and validation samples can often be considerably larger than implied by the Brown-Zidek inequality. Explicitly, it is possible to define a "robustness region," $RR(m_1,m_2,V_1,V_2)$, such that the preshrunk predictor is superior to least squares if, and only if,

$$\beta \,\varepsilon\, RR(m_1, m_2,V_1,V_2).$$

Jones and Copas (in press) have formulated a precise specification of RR and, further, have developed a significance test by which the hypothesis $\beta \,\varepsilon\,$ RR can be assessed in the light of the estimated regression coefficient vector. Thus, when constructing a prediction equation, m_1 and V_1 are taken directly from the construction sample; the likely superiority of the shrinkage correction can then be checked using the robustness region test against a variety of changes in population that might be contemplated.

The Effect of Screening Based on One or More Explanatory Variables. A common way in which populations can change is represented by screening on one or more of the explanatory variables. Suppose, for example, that the values of x_i in the construction sample are representative of the underlying population of subjects, but that future use of the prediction equation will be restricted to subjects with $x_i > c$, where c is some screening threshold. This may happen, for instance, if some intervention or change of policy occurs following a preliminary prediction study. Given m_1 and V_1 from the construction sample and the value of any screening threshold, it is possible to estimate m_2 and V_2 corresponding to the appropriately truncated distribution of the validation sample and, hence, tc estimate W. If the Brown-Zidek inequality fails, the robustness region test can be carried out for the observed vector of regression parameter estimates. By this procedure the value of the shrinkage correction can be assessed. A number of case studies along these lines have been investigated in Jones and Copas (1985). In general, quite a heavy truncation can be tolerated while retaining the superiority of the shrinkage predictor; at least one-half and as much as two-thirds of a population can be screened out in this way.

Sample-Reuse Studies of Screening. Sample-reuse methods provide a rich source of techniques for studying the properties of a prediction equation in the context of a particular study, as will be discussed in a later section of this paper. Two particular applications lend themselves to the monitoring of screening. First, a simulation study can be undertaken in which the prediction equation is fitted to a random subset of the data, and the remaining cases are screened in the appropriate way to form the validation sample. The random sampling of the construction data is repeated a large number of times to obtain expected values of prediction mean squared error to other measures of predictive performance. The second method involves the bootstrap: both construction and validation data are artificially sampled with replacement from the complete set of available data. The method of screening under study is applied to the validation cases before the prediction equation is evaluated. Again, some detailed results are given in Jones and Copas (1985); the general conclusion is similar to that made earlier, namely, that a moderate degree of screening does not usually affect the advantages of the shrinkage correction.

Shrinkage Correction Adapted for a Change in Population. Comments so far in this section have concerned robustness, i.e., the study of how the preshrunk predictor $\tilde{y}$ performs in the light of changes in the distribution of x. If some particular change in population is envisaged, can the shrinkage correction be designed to take account of it? A reworking of the theory leading to the correction $\hat{K}$, explained above, leads to

$$K^* = 1 - \frac{(m - 2)\sigma^2 \mathrm{tr}(V_1^{-1}V_2)}{n\hat{\beta}'V_2\hat{\beta}}.$$

Note that $K^* = \hat{K}$ if $V_1 = V_2$. The corresponding form of the preshrunk predictor is

$$y^* = (\hat{\alpha} + \hat{\beta}'(m_2 - m_1))(1 - K^*) + K^*\hat{y}.$$

Unfortunately, the sampling theory of K^* and y^* is very much more complicated than that of $\hat{K}$ and $\tilde{y}$, and optimum mean squared error properties have yet to be proved. Presumably, if $m_2 - m_1$ and $V_2 - V_1$ are both fairly small, the favorable properties of $\tilde{y}$ will continue to hold, but the situation for large population changes is less clear.

An Adaptive Formulation of Shrinkage Based on Cross-validation. A very different approach is reported in Copas (1984). Here none of the usual assumptions of linear regression is made (e.g., constant variance of residuals), but instead a shrinkage correction K^{**} is estimated directly from the available construction data. Following the sample-reuse approach mentioned above, the sampling distribution of the empirical slope of y on $\hat{y}$ for randomly chosen subsets of the data is studied mathematically, and an asymptotic approximation to the expected shrinkage is thereby obtained. The form of this approximation is applied to the whole set of data, given the nonparametric shrinkage correction K^{**}. It is shown in Copas (1984) that, as expected, K^{**} is equal to $\hat{K}$ if and only if the usual assumptions of the underlying model hold. The correction K^{**} is most sensitive to heteroskedasticity of the residuals; K^{**} can shrink more or less than $\hat{K}$ according to the particular observed pattern of model residuals. Case studies carried out using this new approach suggest that only exceptionally will K^{**} differ markedly from $\hat{K}$, and the validation properties of the corresponding nonparametric shrinkage predictor will often be rather similar to those of $\tilde{y}$.

Changes in the Regression Relationship—Cause (c)

It is obvious that if the relationship between y and the x's changes dramatically between construction and validation data, the shrinkage will be equally dramatic and nothing in the way of useful prediction will be possible. Conversely, minor changes in the coefficients α and $\beta_1, \beta_2, \ldots$ will result in only small changes in predictive performance, and $\tilde{y}$ can still be regarded as an adequate approximation. Little work has been done in studying the effects of changes of intermediate size. As in the discussion of cause (b) in the previous section, if something is known in advance about the likely changes, corresponding modifications to the prediction equation can be made (e.g., a 10 percent rise or fall in values of y is anticipated). However, such circumstances will occur rarely, if ever, and so this remains an open research problem.

Some Concluding Remarks

We conclude this discussion of validation and shrinkage with a few comments that may help in formulating guidelines on the choice of prediction equation in any given application.

First, a simple method shrinks less than a complex one. (This can be seen in the above algebra by noting that the denominator of K exceeds the numerator by $m\sigma^2/n$ on average—this quantity increases as m, the number of variables in the equation, increases.) However, this is not so when a preshrinking correction is applied; provided the model and assumptions hold true, a preshrunk predictor is always approximately well calibrated. Thus the argument that a simple model (e.g., point scoring) is preferable to a more complicated one (e.g., multiple regression) because of shrinkage effects alone cannot be sustained. Proper statistical principles should be used in assessing the fit between a given model and the data; any shrinkage problems that arise are allowed for by preshrinking rather than by distorting the model being fitted.

Second, in selecting from among several x variables using a stepwise procedure, it is often supposed that a small subset is better than a large one because the smaller number of coefficients causes less shrinkage. In general this argument is false. As explained above, the empirical selection effect itself leads to an increase in shrinkage. Again, a larger subset, with appropriate preshrinking correction, is better than an artificially small set with its own shrinkage correction. Usually, however, very little is gained by the later variables entering a stepwise regression procedure and so on the grounds of simplicity, with little loss of efficacy, a sensible subset (with preshrinking) will nearly always be used in the final prediction equation. For example, in the absconding study mentioned above, there is little basis for choosing on statistical grounds between the fits with the total of 22 x's and with a subset of just 4 x's (Figures 1 and 2).

Third, caution is needed if a prediction equation is to be applied outside the range of the construction data. The new theory of robustness to changes in the distribution of the x's, outlined above, suggests that modest changes can be tolerated within the framework of the same preshrinking method. However, if very marked changes are anticipated, or if erratic changes in the model are likely to occur, no prediction equation can be expected to work well. These circumstances are perhaps the only ones in which oversimplified methods (e.g., Glueck) can be justified on the grounds of robustness, but a clear formulation of such properties would be difficult.

Fourth, a prediction equation is essentially a statement of conditional expectation: *if* the x's are such and such, *then* the expectation of y is estimated to be such and such. In reality no particular model is exactly correct, and so an argument that one set of x's is "right" and another is "wrong" has no logical basis. One can imagine values of the response variable (y) and the explanatory variables (x's) being distributed jointly in some space—each subset of x's, and each particular model, providing a separate form of conditional expectation of y. Choosing a prediction equation involves choosing which conditional expectation is closest to the actual values of y (has least conditional variance), such a choice being made over whatever set of candidates is available. It may be that y is most closely correlated with an x that cannot actually be used in routine prediction, and so no subset containing such an x can be entertained. Typically, the best subsets or models will be ones that act as the best proxies to the prohibited x. Such equations may do less well than others involving the sensitive variable, but they cannot be discredited on statistical grounds alone.

Practical Utility

Predictive Power

Our starting point in this section is the familiar "risk classification," which compares predicted and actual outcomes. This approach to assessing the utility of different prediction instruments is completely different from (yet complementary to) that discussed in the previous section.

Risk classes can be defined as the range of the predicted probability of some event (e.g., $k_1 = 0 < 0.1$, $k_2 = 0.1 < 0.2$, et cetera); as a score, such as the Salient Factor Score calculated in parole prediction research (D. M. Gottfredson, Wilkins, and Hoffman, 1978); or by some other classification, such as low-, medium-, and high-rate offenders, as in Greenwood's (1982) study of criminal careers. The example adopted here to illustrate and develop the discussion of predictive power is taken from Copas and Whiteley (1976) as it was subsequently used by Tarling (1982) to show the relationship between various measures. Copas and Whiteley's aim was to construct a prediction instrument to evaluate the effects of therapeutic treatment at the Henderson Hospital. The criterion of success was taken to be no further admission to a psychiatric hospital or no further conviction for a criminal offense during the 2 to 3 years following release. Table 1 sets out the results for their construction and validation samples.

Several summary statistics have been proposed to measure the predictive power of this and similar risk classifications, in particular mean cost rating (MCR) (Duncan et al., 1953) and P(A)—the area under the receiver operating characteristic curve in signal detection theory (Fergusson, Fifield, and Slater, 1977). However, as the risk classification in Table 1 can be regarded as an ordered

TABLE 1 Predicted Success and Observed Outcome, Construction and Validation Samples

Risk Class (k_i)	Probability of Success (P)	Construction Sample Success (s_i)	Construction Sample Failure (f_i)	Construction Sample Total (t_i)	Validation Sample Success (t_i)	Validation Sample Failure (f_i)	Validation Sample Total (t_i)
k_1	0 to .3	5	33	38	7	18	25
k_2	.3 to .5	7	12	19	14	15	29
k_3	.5 to .7	21	12	33	12	9	21
k_4	.7 to 1.0	11	3	14	8	4	12
Total		$N_s = 44$	$N_f = 60$	$T = 104$	$N_s = 41$	$N_f = 46$	$T = 87$
		MCR = .57			MCR = .28		
		P(A) = .78			P(A) = .64		
		$\tau_c = -.55$			$\tau_c = -.28$		
		$\gamma = -.71$			$\gamma = -.40$		

SOURCE: Copas and Whiteley (1976) data as used by Tarling (1982).

contingency table, Kendall's rank correlation coefficient tau, τ_c (Kendall, 1970), and Goodman and Kruskal's gamma, γ (Goodman and Kruskal, 1963), can also be used to measure the degree of association. There is as yet no consensus about the measure to be adopted, but Tarling (1982) has in fact shown that all four measures are related because all are functions of the statistic S (where $S = P - Q$, where P is the number of "concordant pairs" and Q is the number of "discordant pairs").

Expressing each as a function of S and using the notation of Table 1, the four measures can be defined as:

$$\text{MCR} = \frac{-S}{N_s N_f}$$

$$\text{P(A)} = \frac{-S + N_s N_f}{2N_s N_f}$$

$$\tau_c = \frac{4S}{T^2}$$

$$\gamma = \frac{S}{P + Q}.$$

Two advantages follow from knowing that all four measures are a function of S. First, by calculating S the calculation of all four measures is greatly simplified. Second, as the distribution of S has long been known, a test of the null hypothesis, $E(S) = 0$, is a test that prediction is no better than chance.

The measures τ_c and γ have a further advantage over MCR and P(A) in that the variance of both can be estimated, thu permitting tests of alternative hypotheses and facilitating comparison of alternative prediction instruments or their respective power in the construction and validation samples. For τ_c, however, only an upper bound to the variance is available, so only a conservative test for the difference of two observed values is possible. On the other hand, the exact value of the variance of γ is available (Goodman and Kruskal, 1963), which permits a more powerful test. For this reason Tarling (1982) recommended that γ should generally be preferred.

Prediction Errors

The four measures discussed above are still only indicators of overall fit and just give an indirect assessment of how a prediction instrument will perform in practice. It is essential, therefore, to calculate the number or proportion of correct and incorrect predictions that would result from the application of any rule.

Given the discussion of overfitting and shrinkage in the previous section, estimates should be derived from a validation sample. Before applying the Copas and Whiteley instrument to identify likely successes, a cutoff point must be chosen. From the risk classification, as it is presented above, there are three possible cutoff points: all subjects with a predicted probability of success of .7 or above; all those with a predicted probability of .5 or above; and all those with a predicted probability of .3 or above.

Figure 3 shows, for each cutoff point in the validation sample, the following:

1. the number of true positives (TP), that is, the number of subjects predicted to succeed who did in fact succeed;
2. the number of false positives (FP), that is, the number of subjects predicted to succeed who in fact failed;
3. the number of false negatives (FN), that is, the number of subjects predicted to fail who in fact succeeded; and
4. the number of true negatives (TN), that is, the number of subjects predicted to fail who did in fact fail.

The two marginal distributions of these tables are usually defined as the base rate and the selection ratio. The base rate (or

A: Cutoff point .7 and above

		Actual Outcome: Success	Actual Outcome: Failure	
Predicted Outcome	Success	TP 8	FP 4	$NP_s = 12$
	Failure	FN 33	TN 42	$NP_f = 75$
		$N_s = 41$	$N_f = 46$	

Selection ratio = .138

Base rate = .471

B: Cutoff point .5 and above

		Actual Outcome: Success	Actual Outcome: Failure	
Predicted Outcome	Success	TP 20	FP 13	$NP_s = 33$
	Failure	FN 21	TN 33	$NP_f = 54$
		$N_s = 41$	$N_f = 46$	

Selection ratio = .379

Base rate = .471

C: Cutoff point .3 and above

		Actual Outcome: Success	Actual Outcome: Failure	
Predicted Outcome	Success	TP 34	FP 28	$NP_s = 62$
	Failure	FN 7	TN 18	$NP_f = 25$
		$N_s = 41$	$N_f = 46$	

Selection ratio = .713

Base rate = .471

FIGURE 3 Correct predictions and errors for each cutoff point.

the prevalence or the incidence) is the proportion of the sample that actually succeeded. It can be seen that this is the same for all three cutoff points (i.e., 47.1 percent). The second marginal distribution, the selection ratio, is the proportion of the sample predicted to succeed. It can be seen that the selected ratio changes depending on the cutoff point: it is 13.8 percent when the cutoff point is set at .7 and above, 37.9 percent when the cutoff point is set at .5 and above, and 71.3 percent when the cutoff point is set at .3 and above.

Defining the base rate and the selection ratio in terms of the four outcomes:

$$\text{Base rate, BR} = \frac{\text{TP} + \text{FN}}{\text{T}}$$

$$\text{and } (1 - \text{BR}) = \frac{\text{FP} + \text{TN}}{\text{T}},$$

$$\text{Selection ratio, SR} = \frac{\text{TP} + \text{FP}}{\text{T}}$$

$$\text{and } (1 - \text{SR}) = \frac{\text{FN} + \text{TN}}{\text{T}},$$

where

$$\begin{aligned} T &= \text{total sample} \\ &= \text{TP} + \text{FP} + \text{FN} + \text{TN}. \end{aligned}$$

Considering the relationship between the base rate and the selection ratio reveals several interesting properties. When the selection ratio is larger than the base rate, false positives exceed false negatives; conversely, when the base rate is larger than the selection ratio, false negatives exceed false positives. When the base rate equals the selection ratio, the number of false positives and false negatives is the same. Furthermore, when both the base rate and the selection ratio equal .5, prediction becomes most accurate and results in fewest total errors (FP + FN). However, when the base rate (which is fixed) is not .5, as is often the case in practice, total errors are minimized when the selection ratio is set to equal the base rate. These phenomena are revealed in Figure 3 and can be used to guide the choice of the appropriate cutoff point.

Dunn (1981) sets out the various measures that can be derived from the kind of information presented in Figure 3, for example, sensitivity and specificity, but they are not discussed in any detail here. Loeber and Dishion (1982, 1983) also discuss the significance of the base rate and the selection ratio. They point out that the base rate and the selection ratio determine the maximum number of correct predictions that could be achieved by the prediction instrument but, further, that a certain number of correct predictions could be expected by chance alone. Loeber and Dishion therefore propose a measure, relative improvement over chance (RIOC), which attempts to assess how an instrument performs relative to its expected performance and its best possible performance given the base rate and the selection ratio.

They define RIOC as:

$$\text{RIOC} = \frac{\text{AC} - \text{RC}}{\text{MC} - \text{RC}},$$

where AC = actual number of correct predictions, RC = randomly expected number of correct predictions, and MC = maximum possible number of correct predictions. In the notation of Figure 3 it can be seen that

$$\text{AC} = \text{TP} + \text{TN}$$

$$\text{RC} = \frac{(\text{TP} + \text{FN})(\text{TP} + \text{FP})}{\text{T}} + \frac{(\text{FP} + \text{TN})(\text{FN} + \text{TN})}{\text{T}}$$

$$\text{MC} = \text{TN} + \text{TP} + 2\min(\text{FN},\text{FP}).$$

Substituting for AC, RC, and MC in the above equation, RIOC reduces to:

$$\text{RIOC} = \frac{\text{TP.TN} - \text{FP.FN}}{[\text{TP} + \min(\text{FN,FP})][\text{TN} + \min(\text{FN,FP})]}.$$

From the relationships presented earlier, RIOC can also be expressed in terms of the base rate and the selection ratio. Substituting in the denominator, RIOC reduces to:

$$\text{RIOC} = \frac{\text{TP.TN} - \text{FP.FN}}{\text{T}^2[\min(\text{BR,SR}) - \text{BR.SR}]}.$$

A commonly used measure of association for 2 × 2 classifications such as Figure 3 is ϕ, which is the product moment correlation coefficient for dichotomous variables.

In the notation of Figure 3,

$$\phi = \frac{\text{TP.TN} - \text{FP.FN}}{[(\text{TP} + \text{FP})(\text{TP} + \text{FN})(\text{FP} + \text{TN})(\text{FN} + \text{TN})]^{1/2}}.$$

Expressing the denominator in terms of BR and SR, ϕ reduces to:

$$\phi = \frac{\text{TP.TN} - \text{FP.FN}}{\text{T}^2(\text{BR.SR} - \text{BR.SR}^2 - \text{BR}^2\text{.SR} + \text{BR}^2\text{.SR}^2)^{1/2}}.$$

The relationship between RIOC and ϕ is therefore:

$$\text{RIOC} = \phi \left[\frac{(\text{BR.SR} - \text{BR.SR}^2 - \text{BR}^2\text{.SR} + \text{BR}^2\text{.SR}^2)^{1/2}}{\min(\text{BR,SR}) - \text{BR.SR}} \right]$$

However, if the base rate BR equals the selection ratio SR, an important result follows. Substituting BR for SR:

$$\text{RIOC} = \phi \left\{ \frac{[(\text{BR} - \text{BR}^2)^2]^{1/2}}{(\text{BR} - \text{BR}^2)} \right\}$$

i.e., RIOC = ϕ. By using any of the above formulae, it can be calculated that for Figure 3A, RIOC = .3696 (or 37.0 percent) and ϕ = .157; Figure 3B, RIOC = .2549 (or 25.5 percent) and ϕ = .211; Figure 3C, RIOC = .4056 (or 40.6 percent) and ϕ = .243.

The above set of results suggests that care should be exercised when using RIOC or ϕ. The measure RIOC is less (25.5 percent) for cutoff point .5 and above, as depicted in Figure 3B, than for the other two cutoff points: .7 and above, Figure 3A, and .3 and above, Figure 3C; ϕ, too, is lower than for Figure 3C, although it is greater than for Figure 3A. However, the total number of errors in Figure 3B is 34, 1 less than for Figure 3C and 3 less than for Figure 3A.

It should also be emphasized perhaps that the measures discussed are merely point estimates. Another study that found, for instance, 340 errors in a sample of 870 subjects would give the same total error rate, although it would be considered as more accurate since it is derived from a larger sample. This suggests the construction of confidence intervals around these estimates to get a range of plausible values. Invariably criminologists have not presented confidence intervals for their estimates although they are relatively straightforward to calculate. Tables exist for binomial confidence intervals, but for large samples the normal approximation may be used. The standard deviation is given by:

$$\text{S.D.} = \left[\frac{n(N - n)}{N^3} \right]^{1/2},$$

where n is the numerator and N the denominator of the rate. In this example the 95 percent confidence limits for the total error rate are .289 and .493.

Before leaving this section there is just one final point that we would like to make. A criticism of the measures so far discussed is that they do not reflect the relative seriousness of the different types of outcome but assign equal value to true and false positives and true and false negatives. In practice, and dependent on the issues under consideration, it is usually the case that the consequence of one type of outcome is more important than another. Had our interest in the previous section been to minimize false positives, say, rather than to minimize total errors, we could have used the approach outlined there to guide our choice of cutoff point. However, decision theory provides a more direct framework for taking into account the weights to be attached to different types of outcome. Although the decision-theory approach has been widely advocated in criminological applications (e.g., Loeber and Dishion, 1983), it has not been used to any great extent, except by Blumstein, Farrington, and Moitra (1985). While it is outside the scope of this paper to discuss decision theory in any detail, we would recommend that more attention be paid to it in prediction research, especially when the results are to be applied in practice.

SAMPLE-REUSE METHODS

Previous sections of the paper have stressed the distinction between retrospective fit and prospective (or validation) fit of a prediction instrument. A simple way of carrying out a prospective validation, and the one most commonly used in criminology, is the split-half method, which divides the data into two halves (at random). The equation is fitted to the first half (the construction sample) and tested on the second (the validation sample). Although unbiased estimates of shrinkage and error rates result from this method, there are two obvious disadvantages: (a) construction of the prediction instrument does not use all available information, but only half the sample, and (b) the comparability of the two subsamples will always be open to doubt; for example, there is a 1-in-20 chance that the two subsamples will be significantly different at the 5 percent level. Various techniques have been developed in the statistical literature to overcome these two problems. The principle underlying them is to generate many subsamples rather than merely two.

The first, simple extension of the principle is cross-validation, of which the split-half method is merely a special case. To construct and validate the prediction instrument, the sample need not be split in half but could, instead, be split in many different ways; for example, 80 percent of the sample could be used for the construction sample and the remaining 20 percent could form the validation sample. Moreover, any number of construction and validation subsamples could be drawn. The jackknife and the bootstrap techniques are more formal developments of this latter idea. The jackknife (see, for example, R. G. Miller, 1974), or "hold-one-out," proceeds as follows. Suppose the sample has N members; delete one member and develop the prediction instrument on the remaining $N - 1$ and use it to predict $\hat{y}$ for the missing member. The procedure is repeated N times, a different member being omitted each time. By this means a set of *independent* values of y and $\hat{y}$ are obtained, and shrinkage and error rates can be calculated using the methods presented earlier as if these values related to a completely new sample of N cases.[2]

The bootstrap technique (Efron, 1982) proceeds slightly differently. If sampling with replacement is permitted, a large number of samples of size N can be drawn, 2^N as opposed to only N by the jackknife procedure. The bootstrap replications can be used to assess the prediction instrument. The method is illustrated by an example given in Efron and Gong (1981, 1983) that is analogous to many criminological prediction studies. Efron and Gong were concerned to construct an instrument to predict whether patients

[2]These ideas can be extended to other problems relevant to the construction of prediction instruments; Mabbett, Stone, and Washbrook (1980), for instance, consider the stepwise choice of variables in forming a binary predictor.

suffering from acute hepatitis would survive or die. There were 155 patients in the sample, 33 of whom died. There were 19 independent variables available for analysis. A prediction instrument was developed in the usual way. First only x variables associated at the 5 percent level were retained; this left 13 variables. Second, a kind of forward, stepwise, multiple-logistic-regression program was used, stopping when no additional variable achieved the 5 percent significance level. Four of the 13 variables were included in the final prediction instrument. The cutoff point c was set at $c = \log 33/122$. Full information was available for 133 of the original 155 patients. When the prediction instrument was applied to the 133 patients, 21 were misclassified, giving an error rate of 21/133 = .158. The bootstrap technique was then used to assess how overoptimistic this error rate was or how much it could be expected to shrink. Five hundred bootstrap samples were drawn and the same procedure was used to construct a prediction instrument. On each occasion the "overoptimism random variable," R', was calculated, which is merely "the error rate for the bootstrap replication minus .158." The 500 values of R' were plotted and the mean of R' was found to be .045, which suggests that the expected overoptimism is about one-third as large as the apparent error rate .158. This gives the bias-corrected estimated error rate .158 + .045 = .203. In addition, the standard deviation of R' was .036. Another advantage of the bootstrap technique is illustrated by this example. At each replication a check was made of the variables included in the prediction instrument and this revealed, for example, that one variable was selected 37 percent of the time, another 59 percent of the time, and so on, giving an intuitive, if not theoretically rigorous, indication of the importance of the various predictor variables.

Technical details of sample-reuse methods are given in Efron (1982), and simplified descriptions appear in Diaconis and Efron (1983) and Efron and Gong (1983). Comparing and contrasting the various methods, split-half or cross-validation methods are the simplest to perform but have certain limitations. The advent of computer power and the increasing availability of appropriate algorithms make the jackknife and the bootstrap methods more attractive and relatively easy to use. The jackknife and the bootstrap are in fact theoretically closely related: the jackknife is almost a bootstrap itself. The bootstrap is entirely nonparametric and is, therefore, more flexible. Efron (1982) suggests that the jackknife performs less well than the bootstrap in situations that he has investigated but it requires less computation. The close relation between sample-reuse methods and Copas's theory of shrinkage and validation was discussed earlier.

CONCLUSIONS

At the beginning of this paper we showed how simple point-scoring methods could be incorporated within the framework of general linear models, along with regression, logistic regression, and log-linear models. In addition, we noted that point-scoring methods, reconceptualized in the way we suggest, permit certain extensions that have been found useful in medical diagnosis.

It has long been recognized and empirically demonstrated that a prediction instrument developed on one sample will perform less well when applied to a subsequent sample. The phenomenon of shrinkage has recently been subjected to rigorous theoretical investigation, which we outlined. The findings stemming from this work enable the researcher to understand and anticipate the degree of shrinkage that can be expected in any study and, where necessary, to make any adjustments to (or preshrink) the prediction equation.

To examine shrinkage in practice, researchers have tended to use split-half subsamples. We pointed out the range of other and superior "sample-reuse" methods, including the jackknife and the bootstrap.

The usefulness of a prediction instrument can also be gauged by the number of errors and correct decisions that result from its application. We pointed out the similarity between many of the indices that have been proposed to assess the utility of a risk classification. In addition, we showed the importance of the base rate and the selection ratio in determining false-positive and false-negative errors and how the selection ratio can be set to alter the balance between the two.

When predicting rare events it may be the case that any prediction instrument will not improve significantly over the base rate. For example, a prediction instrument developed to identify "dangerous" offenders may result in more errors than occur by merely classifying all offenders as not dangerous. This has led some commentators to eschew attempts to predict these kinds of events. An analogous situation occurs in medical science, where mass-screening programs are costly and may result in large false-positive errors, causing considerable stress, but where they are nevertheless considered to be worthwhile to detect the small number of true positives who actually have the rare disease. Therefore, the worth of any prediction instrument depends on the values to be attached to the various outcomes emanating from its application, not simply on the total number of errors that may accrue. Decision theory provides a framework for making these assessments and could be used more widely in prediction in criminology.

REFERENCES

Blumstein, A., Farrington, D. P., and Moitra, S.
1985 Delinquent careers: innocents, desisters and persisters. Pp. 187–219 in M. Tonry and N. Morris, eds., *Crime and Justice*. Vol. 6. Chicago, Ill.: University of Chicago Press.

Bottoms, A. E., and McClintock, F. H.
1973 *Criminals Coming of Age*. London, England: Heinmann.

Brown, P. J., and Zidek, J. V.
1980 Adaptive multivariate ridge regression. *Annals of Statistics* 8:64–74.

Burgess, E. W.
1928 Factors determining success or failure on parole. In A. A. Bruce, A. J. Harno, E. W. Burgess, and J. Landesco, eds., *The Workings of the Indeterminate-Sentence Law and the Parole System in Illinois*. Springfield, Ill.: Illinois State Board of Parole.

Copas, J. B.
1983a Plotting p against x. *Applied Statistics* 32:25–31.
1983b Regression, prediction and shrinkage (with discussion). *Journal of the Royal Statistical Society, Series B* 45:311–354.
1984 *Cross-validation Shrinkage of Regression Predictors*. Research Report, Department of Statistics. Birmingham, England: University of Birmingham.

Copas, J. B., and Whiteley, J. S.
1976 Predicting success in the treatment of psychopaths. *British Journal of Psychiatry* 129:388–392.

Diaconis, P., and Efron, B.
1983 Computer-intensive methods in statistics. *Scientific American* 248(5):96–108.

Duncan, O. D., Ohlin, L. E., Reiss, A. J., and Stanton, H. R.
1953 Formal devices for making selection decisions. *American Journal of Sociology* 58:573–584.

Dunn, C. S.
1981 Prediction problems and decision logic in longitudinal studies of delinquency. *Criminal Justice and Behavior* 8:439–476.

Efron, B.
1982 *The Jackknife, the Bootstrap and Other Resampling Plans*. Philadelphia, Pa.: Society for Industrial and Applied Mathematics.

Efron, B., and Gong, G.
1981 Statistical Theory and the Computer. Unpublished manuscript. Department of Statistics, Stanford University, Calif.
1983 A leisurely look at the bootstrap, the jackknife, and cross-validation. *American Statistician* 37(1):36–48.

Farrington, D. P., and Tarling, R., eds.
1985 *Prediction in Criminology.* Albany, N.Y.: SUNY Press.

Fergusson, D. M., Fifield, J. K., and Slater, S. W.
1977 Signal detectability theory and the evaluation of prediction tables. *Journal of Research in Crime and Delinquency* 14:237–246.

Fielding, A.
1979 Binary segmentation. In C. A. O'Muircheartaigh and C. Payne, eds., *Exploring Data Structure.* Vol. 1 of *The Analysis of Survey Data.* London, England: John Wiley.

Glueck, S., and Glueck, E. T.
1950 *Unraveling Juvenile Delinquency.* Cambridge, Mass.: Harvard University Press.

Goodman, L. A., and Kruskal, W. H.
1963 Measures of association for cross classifications III. *Journal of the American Statistical Association* 58:310–364.

Gottfredson, D. M., Wilkins, L. T., and Hoffman, P. B.
1978 *Guidelines for Parole and Sentencing.* Lexington, Mass.: Lexington Books.

Gottfredson, S. D., and Gottfredson, D. M.
1985 Screening for risk among parolees. Pp. 54–77 in D. P. Farrington and R. Tarling, eds., *Prediction in Criminology.* Albany, N.Y.: SUNY Press.

Greenwood, P. W.
1982 *Selective Incapacitation.* Santa Monica, Calif.: Rand Corporation.

Jones, M. C., and Copas, J. B.
1985 On the Robustness of Shrinkage Predictors in Regression: Exemplifying and Using the Theory. Research report. Department of Statistics, University of Birmingham, England.
In press On the Robustness of Shrinkage Predictors in Regression: Some Theoretical Considerations. *Journal of the Royal Statistical Society, Series B* 48.

Kendall, M. G.
1970 *Rank Correlation Methods.* London: Griffin.

Loeber, R., and Dishion, T. J.
1982 Strategies for Identifying At-Risk Youths. Unpublished report. Oregon Social Learning Center, Eugene.
1983 Early predictors of male delinquency: a review. *Psychological Bulletin* 94:68–99.

Mabbett, A., Stone, M., and Washbrook, J.
1980 Cross-validatory selection of binary variables in differential diagnosis. *Applied Statistics* 29:198–204.

Miller, A. J.
1984 Selection of subsets of regression variables (with discussion). *Journal of the Royal Statistical Society, Series A* 147:389–425.

Miller, R. G.
1974 The jackknife—a review. *Biometrika* 61(1): 1–15.

Nuttal, C. P., et al.
1977 *Parole in England and Wales.* Home Office Research Study No. 38. London, England: Her Majesty's Stationery Office.

Simon, F. H.
1971 *Prediction Methods in Criminology.* Home Office Research Study No. 7. London, England: Her Majesty's Stationery Office.

Tarling, R.
1982 Comparison of measures of predictive power. *Educational and Psychological Measurement* 42:479–487.

Tarling, R., and Perry, J. A.
1985 Statistical methods in criminological prediction. Pp. 210–231 in D. P. Farrington and R. Tarling, eds., *Prediction in Criminology.* Albany, N.Y.: SUNY Press.

Titterington, D. M., Murray, G. D., Murray, L. S., Spiegelhalter, D. J., Skene, A. M., Habbema, J. D. F., and Gelpke, G. J.
1981 Comparison of discrimination techniques applied to a complex data set of head injured patients. *Journal of the Royal Statistical Society, Series A* 144:145–175.

Wilbanks, W. L.
1985 Predicting failures on parole. Pp. 78–94 in D. P. Farrington and R. Tarling, eds., *Prediction in Criminology.* Albany, N.Y.: SUNY Press.

8

Purblind Justice: Normative Issues in the Use of Prediction in the Criminal Justice System

Mark H. Moore

In the workaday world of criminal justice, predictions are commonplace (Dershowitz, 1974:1–60, 781–846; Wilson, 1983a:157, 1983b:279). Moreover, they are consequential for defendants: they affect the magnitude of the criminal liabilities that defendants confront. Judges consider the risk that a defendant will flee (or commit additional crimes) in setting bail (Dawson, 1969:80; N. Morris, 1974: 28–57; Roth and Wice, 1980; Gaynes, 1982; Blumstein et al., 1983a,b; N. Morris and Miller, 1985:12) and the prospects for rehabilitation in imposing sentences. Prosecutors weigh the gravity of the threat posed by accused offenders in deciding how much effort to put into preparing their cases and in setting the minimum acceptable plea bargains (Kaplan, 1965:174; Forst and Brosi, 1977:177–191). Police study the modus operandi of offenders to thwart future crimes and to help them identify likely suspects in current cases (Moore et al., 1983a,b).

The widespread, consequential use of predictions in the criminal justice system prompts normative questions. If the justice of the system rests on the notion that punishment should be for past acts, not guesses about future behavior, it is wrong to impose criminal liabilities on the basis of predictions. It would be wrong even if the predictions were perfectly accurate. If they are inaccurate, however (as they inevitably will be), additional objections

Mark Moore, Guggenheim Professor of Criminal Justice Policy and Management, Harvard University, notes: "In producing this paper, I am principally indebted to Susan Estrich, Daniel McGillis, and William Spelman, my collaborators on the Harvard Project on Dangerous Offenders and coauthors with me of *Dangerous Offenders: The Elusive Target of Justice* (Cambridge, Mass.: Harvard University Press, 1984). Indeed, some material on the use of predictions in sentencing and bail is reproduced here exactly as it appears in *Dangerous Offenders*, and a great deal else is borrowed less directly from that analysis. I am also indebted to those on the Panel on Research on Criminal Careers who read and commented on this work, specifically, John Kaplan, Norval Morris, and James Q. Wilson. I am also greatly indebted to Andrew von Hirsch and Michael Tonry, whose sharp disagreements may have improved the quality of my arguments and whose patience in instructing me has been extraordinary. With such great assistance, it is hard to believe errors could be made. But no doubt there are many, and they are mine alone."

come to the fore. Offenders incorrectly predicted to commit crimes in the future would be exposed to criminal liabilities that are doubly undeserved: once because they were based on predictions rather than past deeds, and twice because the predictions were inaccurate. And, to the extent that the predictions were based on characteristics of offenders that lie outside the ordinary purview of the criminal justice system or are imperfectly measured, defendants would be exposed to more intrusive investigations and greater risk of errors than would be the case if the focus of the system remained on past crimes. In short, predictions undermine the rigorous discipline essential to criminal justice in a free society.

On the other hand, criminal justice officials now rely on predictions because they seem to add to the overall justice and performance of the criminal justice system. The most obvious virtue of predictions is that, by focusing the attention of the system on those offenders who are most likely to commit crimes in the future, they allow the community to maintain tolerable levels of crime with less extensive use of imprisonment than would be possible without them. Given that it is desirable to reduce criminal victimization and to be economical in the use of the state's moral and financial resources in doing so, it seems desirable to exploit the focus on dangerous offenders that predictions make possible.

Many view this apparent virtue as a dangerous temptation—one that will lure the community into increasing its overall demands for security at the expense of the rights and liberty interests of alleged criminal offenders and, therefore, at the risk of the overall quality of justice. But even viewed from the special perspective of protecting the rights and interests of accused offenders from the community's demands for order, the use of predictions has virtues, for predictions can justify more lenient treatment for some offenders than their acts alone would justify. If an offender's crimes seem uncharacteristic (and therefore unlikely to be repeated in the future), the current system (which is tolerant of predictions) can be lenient. This opportunity would be denied if predictions of future conduct were excluded from criminal justice decision making.

Finally, if interests in individual justice and aggregate efficiency continue to motivate and sanction the widespread use of predictions in the criminal justice system, it would be valuable to recognize the practice explicitly. That way, the society could guarantee that the predictions were made consistently, accurately, and usefully rather than on an *ad hoc* basis.

So, the question of whether consequential predictions are tolerable in our criminal justice system might not have a general answer. Some moral intuitions and ethical standards might exclude them entirely, while others would countenance them. For the ethical systems that tolerate predictions, the particular form of the prediction may matter a great deal: some predictions may be more just than others.

The central purpose of this paper is to develop moral intuitions about whether consequential predictions are tolerable in the criminal justice system, and, if they are, to establish what sorts and for what purposes. This requires an examination from several vantage points: from the perspective of moral intuitions about the fundamental values that animate the criminal justice system and their connections to different systems of ethical theory; from an analysis of the tension between ideal standards and the implicit sanction granted to current practices by virtue of their traditional acceptability; from a detailed consideration of aspects of predictions that seem to have normative significance; and from an inquiry into how the moral issues involving predictions differ at different stages of the criminal justice system.

THE ANATOMY OF PREDICTION IN THE CRIMINAL JUSTICE SYSTEM

To fix conceptions, it is useful to delineate the basic elements of prediction in the criminal justice system. Essentially, there are four: an offense, an associated offender, a predictive rule that links characteristics of the offender to predictions of future conduct, and a discretionary decision to be made by a criminal justice official that could be influenced by predictions of future criminal activity and that affects the criminal liability of the offender.

The Offense

A criminal offense is central because it is the thing that occasions the interest of the criminal justice system. Without a crime, there are no decisions to be made. Not even the most enthusiastic advocates of predictions in the criminal justice system would advocate the imposition of criminal sanctions without a criminal offense.

The crime is also important because it constrains the decisions that will be made. A minor offense cannot be used to justify a major intrusion into the offender's life even if the predictions are very ominous. Exactly how tightly the characteristics of the crime should bind the decisions of criminal justice officials is one of the major controversies surrounding the use of predictions. Those who think that the justice of the system rests entirely on proportional and consistent responses to criminal acts seek to bind the decisions very closely to the act and to leave little room for consideration of the offender's characteristics and predictions of his or her future conduct (von Hirsch, 1985). Those who think that the overall justice of the system requires some consideration of the character and future conduct of the offender will leave more room for these aspects to be considered in criminal justice decision making (Monahan, 1982). But no one thinks that the nature of the offense is irrelevant to the decisions of criminal justice officials.

Obviously, the offenses can vary along many dimensions. One is the gravity of the offense. It can be murder or petit larceny. It can involve serious injury to victims, threats of serious injury, or only minor property losses. A second is the certainty with which the criminal justice system has established that an offense has occurred and that a particular offender did it. This connection may have been definitively established through a criminal conviction or persuasively alleged in a criminal indictment or simply suspected as a guide to investigative activity. In general, the more serious the offense and the stronger the established connection to an offender, the greater the license criminal justice officials have to impose liabilities on offenders. Whether this includes a greater right to make and use predictions about future criminal conduct, however, remains unclear.

The Offender

The offender is also central to predictions in the criminal justice system. Without him, there is little of consequence for criminal justice officials to decide. It is most natural to think of the offender as someone who has just been convicted and is awaiting sentencing. But the offender could be at earlier stages of criminal justice system processing. He could be someone who has been indicted and is waiting to have bail set. He could be someone who has a strong evidentiary case against him and is awaiting a formal charge and indictment. Or, he could be a leading suspect who is the focus of a police investigation.

From the point of view of the criminal justice system, the most important attribute of the offender is the connection to a current offense. That is what makes him the subject of criminal justice action. But the offender has other characteristics as well. One of the most important is a criminal record. The criminal record may be nonexistent, or it may be quite extensive; it may involve only minor offenses or may include serious offenses; it may be a record of nothing more than arrests, or it may include convictions; it may be an adult record, or it may include crimes committed as a juvenile. In addition to a criminal record, the offender has such other characteristics as levels of alcohol and drug use, neighborhood ties, employment status and experience, age, race, religion, political beliefs, favorite foods, and tastes in music. These characteristics differ from one another in several ways. One concerns their moral and legal status. Some characteristics, such as prior criminal conduct and current illegal drug use, are themselves crimes and therefore of direct interest to the criminal justice system. Others, such as race, religion, and political beliefs, are the opposite: they are specially protected against being used by criminal justice officials in making decisions. Some characteristics, such as prior crimes, drug use, and perhaps employment, are thought to be under the control of the offenders and therefore expressions of their inclinations and values. Other characteristics, such as age or race, are not under the control of the offenders and consequently are of little moral significance: they cannot be expressions of a person's character although they might be good predictors of future conduct.

These offender characteristics also differ from one another in terms of how accurately they can be determined for individuals and how conveniently they can be observed. Some characteristics, such as employment history, are relatively objective and can be established and verified for individuals through intuitively obvious, if laborious, methods. Others, such as psychopathic tendencies, may be relatively objective, but the methods used to validate them are special and arcane. Still others, such as community ties, are quite subjective and hard to establish, although one can develop operational measures of an intangible characteristic that can be objectively determined. Similarly, some of the characteristics of offenders are already known and recorded in files available to criminal justice agencies. Some can be inexpensively learned because they are recorded elsewhere or because the information is not carefully guarded by the defendant. But some characteristics can only be discovered through expensive and intrusive investigative efforts.

A Predictive Rule

The characteristics of offenders are important for they form the basis for all predictions. All predictive tests have the same structural form: if an offender has a certain specified set of characteristics, that offender is predicted to be more (or less) likely to engage in future criminal activity than offenders with different characteristics. Any particular predictive rule has certain properties that are normatively significant.

One important feature of the predictive rule is exactly which characteristics of offenders are selected to serve as predictors. As noted above, the characteristics included in the test may be acts over which the individual has a great deal of control and are themselves criminal, or they can be characteristics over which the individual has no control and, far from being criminal, are given special protection. The characteristics included in the test may be more or less convenient and accurate to observe for individual offenders. Somewhat less obviously significant is the fact that the test can include many or few characteristics. The more characteristics included, the greater the opportunity to accommodate important individual differences among offenders. But the more characteristics, the more complicated the rule, and the greater the chance of errors.

Beyond the properties of the set of characteristics incorporated in the test, the test has other features that are normatively significant. It is more or less accurate in terms of its capacity to identify all those offenders who will, in fact, commit crimes in the future and to exclude those who will, in fact, not commit crimes in the future. The test may be designed to identify small (and therefore more unusual) segments of the offending population, or it may be less discriminating. The validity of the test may be based on common sense, elaborate statistical investigations, or clinical theories and judgments. The test can be explicitly promulgated or implicitly used. It can be authorized by a legislature, established through administrative guidelines, or sanctioned by common professional practice.

A Consequential Decision

In addition to an offense, an offender, and a predictive rule, the consequential use of prediction in the criminal justice system requires that an action be taken by a criminal justice official with respect to the offender. A sentence must be imposed; bail must be set; a plea bargain offered; or an allegation pursued with more or less zeal by prosecutors and police. The consequences of these decisions register in three quite different domains through different causal and evaluative systems. The decisions obviously affect the rights and liberty interests of the individuals who are affected. These may be either enhanced or diminished by the effects of predictions. The decisions also affect overall levels of crime in the community through the mechanisms of deterrence (both specific and general), incapacitation, and rehabilitation. And, finally, the decisions affect the community's overall perception that justice is being done in terms of striking the right balance between the community's interests in security and the offender's interests in freedom, and between the desire to treat cases with consistency and at the same time acknowledge important particular differences.

The Central Ethical Issues

The central ethical question raised by the use of predictive rules in the criminal justice system is whether an offender may be exposed to additional criminal liabilities in the form of a longer sentence, higher bail, more determined prosecution, or closer police scrutiny because of characteristics indicating that he is more likely than others to commit crimes in the future. A less fundamental but equally important question given the widespread current use of predictions is what kinds of predictions are better than others. These questions can be answered directly. But it seems that views about these questions are linked to much broader and more general notions of justice and of what constitutes a worthwhile improvement in the performance of the criminal justice system. It is as though the subject of prediction in the criminal justice system raises general moral connotations as well as specific normative issues. It is worth addressing these general ideas before examining closely the specific ethical issues raised by prediction lest the influence of the moral connotations be decisive but unexamined.

GENERAL NOTIONS OF JUSTICE AND STANDARDS OF CRIMINAL JUSTICE SYSTEM PERFORMANCE

Most normative discussions of the criminal law and the operations of the criminal justice system proceed on the basis of shared intuitions about the virtues of these social enterprises. The shared intuitions are captured in a few words that stand for whole clusters of more particular ideas.

Moral Intuitions of Criminal Justice

One key virtue of criminal justice is its "fairness." At the center of the concept of fairness are notions such as the following: that citizens should know in advance what actions will be punished and how alleged offenses will be investigated (Packer, 1968:80); that the system should be consistent, i.e., treat like cases alike (Hart, 1968a:36–37, 1968b:24–25; Packer, 1968:139–145; Winston, 1974:1–39; von Hirsch, 1976:77–83; N. Morris, 1982:179–209); that criminal liability for conduct should be distributed across possible acts according to the seriousness of the offense, not the social status or power of potential offenders (von Hirsch, 1976: 77–83); that people should be held responsible for things they can control and not for things they cannot control (Hart, 1968a:158–185, esp. 174, 1968b:24–25); and that the actual operations of the system in imposing criminal liability should be unbiased with respect to race, social class, and other social variables (McNeely and Pope, 1981; Blumstein et al., 1983a: 8, 13–21; Klepper et al., 1983:55–128; Petersilia, 1983).

At the edges, the concept of fairness shades into the concept of justice. Indeed, the concept of justice seems to incorporate all the particular ideas associated with fairness. However, while the concept of fairness seems to emphasize the distribution of criminal liability through the society, the concept of justice seems equally concerned about the amount of criminal liability and the intrusiveness of the means used to impose it. In a free society the concept of justice implies restraint—a sense of proportion and frugality in using the coercive power and moral indignation associated with criminal sanctions (Packer, 1968:249–260). Thus, particular ideas central to the notion of justice are those that give citizens significant rights against the state and against those who accuse them: for example, the right of citizens to be free from unwarranted searches and seizures (McNamara, 1982:26–54); to confront their accusers in open trial (McNamara, 1982:169–177); and to have adequate time to prepare a defense (McNamara, 1982:214–230). By establishing such rights for individuals, society constrains the amount and nature of state power that can be exercised against individuals on behalf of the community.

To some, the notion of justice is not restricted to concern for the rights of defendants. Arguably, justice is equally concerned with protecting the moral standing of the law and with guaranteeing that those who deserve punishment receive it (van den Haag, 1975:24–50; Weinreb, 1979:5; Carrington, 1983:15–19). Sometimes this position is described as one that protects "victims' rights" as well as "offenders' rights" (Bedau, 1977; Reiff, 1979; Carrington, 1983:10–12). Insofar as the victim is interested in righting the wrong done through retribution, this is an appropriate characterization. The criminal justice system has many practical as well as moral reasons to accommodate the victim's interests in its proceedings (Greenwood, Chaiken, and Petersilia, 1977; Blumstein et al., 1983a:41). In our system of justice, however, it seems much more accurate to describe the obligation to administer just punishment as belonging to the state rather than the victim. As Aeschylus portrays in *The Eumenides*, a great moment in Western history is the moment when the concept of justice changed from private vengeance to public retribution. In that moment the state took from victims the right to punish those who had offended against them in the interests of ensuring an accurate determination of guilt or innocence and fairness and moderation in the imposition of penalties.

In a free society the desire to mete out deserved punishment must be tempered. Punishments should fit crimes, not be excessive. The process of deciding whether a person is guilty or innocent should be sufficiently deliberate to prevent passions from overwhelming evidence. And the standard of proof should be set very high to ensure that those judged to be guilty are in fact guilty, even if that means that many guilty people are found innocent. It is all of these features that distinguish public justice in a democratic state from either private vengeance in primitive societies or totalitarianism. Still, it is important to keep in mind that like private vengeance, public justice has passion and moral indignation as key ingredients. Indeed, without these features, it is almost impossible to distinguish criminal sanctions from civil sanctions (von Hirsch, 1976:48; von Hirsch and Gottfredson, 1983–1984:34).

Standing somewhat apart from these traditional notions of fairness and justice is the notion that the system should be useful and effective as well as fair and just (Blumstein, Cohen, and Nagin, 1978). To most people, this means that the system should succeed in reducing crime and should do so at the lowest possible cost (Nagel and Neef, 1977; Blumstein, Cohen, and Nagin, 1978; Silberman, 1978; Andreano and Siegfried, 1980:411–426; Wilson, 1983b). Some would add reducing fear to the utilitarian purposes of the criminal justice system (Moore et al., 1984:9–22, esp. 15–19). Most would also probably recognize the interests in fairness and justice as important constraints on the practical pursuit of reduced victimization and fear (Blumstein, Cohen, and Nagin, 1978; Sherman and Hawkins, 1981:106). And perhaps everyone would quickly agree that, to be effective, a criminal justice system must command the active support of the community, and that that, in turn, might depend on how fair and just it seemed (Weinreb, 1979:6–12; Andreano and Siegfried, 1980:85–92).

At the edges, an interest in an effective criminal justice system thus leads one back toward a system that imposes criminal sanctions with fairness and restraint. Nonetheless, most people still see an important distinction between a criminal justice system that is animated by a concern for justice and fairness and one that is preoccupied with effectiveness. Specifically, it seems that the interest in effectiveness elevates the community interest in security over the interest in protecting the rights of the accused, allows estimates of aggregate social consequences to guide decisions that profoundly affect individuals, and leaves more room for social science and technology to be used to enhance the efficiency or effectiveness of the system's operations, even at the cost of procedures honored by long tradition. All this makes the general idea of an effective criminal justice system quite different from one animated by justice and fairness.

Ethical Theory and Moral Intuitions About Criminal Justice

The different intuitions about the virtues of a criminal justice system in a free society correspond to important differences in modern systems of moral reasoning. Modern ethical theory establishes a sharp distinction between "deontological" and "utilitarian" philosophies (Frankena, 1973:12–60). The difference between them is that deontological theories assert that an act is right or wrong in itself, regardless of its consequences. Utilitarian theories, on the other hand, assert that acts can be judged to be good or bad only in terms of their consequences.

The moral intuitions that lie behind the concepts of fairness and justice seem closer to the spirit of deontological than to utilitarian reasoning. These intuitions see virtue in the criminal justice system insofar as it acts properly with respect to accused citizens and ignores the practical consequences of its actions both for the defendant and the broader community. The intuitions that prompt a commitment to effectiveness seem much more utilitarian in spirit. The concern for effectiveness finds the virtue of acts by the criminal justice system in terms of their consequences for the future of the offender and the future security of the community.

The link between moral intuitions about criminal justice and the different modes of ethical reasoning means that the normative standing of the different moral intuitions about criminal justice is inextricably linked to the general standing of these different modes of reasoning in ethical discourse. In general, it seems that the deontological systems have greater standing. Why this should be true remains unclear since philosophers have not as yet reached a decisive conclusion in favor of deontological systems. The dominance of deontological moral systems seems to reflect a general expectation, rooted in tradition, that ethical pronouncements should take the form of rules prescribing conduct rather than ends that must be pursued. This, in turn, may be based on the notion that rules honor God or human traditions more reliably than particular calculations, which depend so heavily on the qualities of the individual calculator; or on a prudential judgment that reliance on rules would avoid many temptations and errors that would otherwise corrupt the particular calculations; or simply on the intellectual appeal of reasoning from principles rather than concrete instances. Whatever the reasons, the general preference for deontological systems makes it hard for utilitarian arguments to be taken seriously in ethical arguments. Particularly in the criminal justice system, where the stakes for individuals seem so high and where so much of the work involves the application of substantive rules to individual cases, utilitarian arguments seem a bit shabby.

The sharp distinction between deontological and utilitarian systems of reasoning is unfortunate, for the challenge facing those who guide the operations of the criminal justice system is to integrate the values and concerns of each system of thought. In principle, this should not be difficult since our moral intuitions about the criminal justice system commingle deontological and utilitarian principles. As we have seen, fairness and justice are often defended not simply as virtues in themselves, but also as qualities that enhance the overall effectiveness of the system by drawing broad support from the community. Similarly, one can argue that the notion that the criminal justice system should be effective and economical in the use of state power and money is not simply a shabby interest of the society, but a fundamental duty of those who guide, and operate within, criminal justice institutions. It might be possible, then, to have a criminal justice system that successfully integrates the particular values that are contained within and shared among our general moral intuitions.

The difficulty is that the schism between deontological and utilitarian systems may make it difficult for us to see when a successful integration has been achieved. The integration will always look a little too unprincipled to a deontologist and a little too ineffective to a utilitarian. And each will feel free to complain about the apparent corruption of the system viewed from his or her vantage point. There may be no strong philosophical voice to step forward and say that the successful integration represents a coherent view, because the successful integration will not fit wholly within either of the two systems of thought that have become familiar.

Standards of Criminal Justice System Performance

The general notions of fairness and justice, on the one hand, and economy and effectiveness, on the other, offer alternative conceptions of the directions in which improvements in criminal justice system performance might lie: i.e., toward more consistent treatment of offenders, toward a more refined balance of community and individual interests, or toward less use of the state's limited financial and moral authority to achieve the same amount of community security. They do not in themselves define tolerable levels of criminal justice performance in the pursuit of one or the other ideals. And yet the extent to which the current system realizes any of these idealized notions may be as important in judging the overall quality of the system as which ideal it is approximating.

The most demanding standard for the criminal justice system is that it be an exact expression of an ideal system: that it be perfectly fair, perfectly just, or perfectly economical. Although no one would really hold any human institution to these exalted standards, when one is talking about the criminal justice system, one is tempted to set the minimal standards of performance very high and to be impatient with mere improvements in a basically corrupt system. The reason is that the decisions of the criminal justice system are so consequential for individuals (and for the overall character of the community) that the obligation to express the community's highest ideals is very strong. This is particularly true when one is talking about fairness and justice, for these qualities do not seem to exist in degrees. In common parlance, people conclude that the system is tolerably fair and just, or it is not. And any system of criminal justice that is unfair or unjust is intolerable. So, our moral intuitions push us toward idealism in setting standards for criminal justice, and particularly so in the areas of fairness and justice.

A different standard of justice would be whether the operations of the criminal justice system meet constitutional requirements. Often, this standard is confused with the first standard because many observers of the criminal justice system would like to believe that their idealized notions of justice are not only sanctioned by the Constitution but also required by it. Moreover, the room to make this claim often exists because the Supreme Court decisions that establish constitutional principles are rarer and less definitive than is necessary to banish ambiguity about constitutional issues. Nonetheless, one can distinguish what is clearly unconstitutional from something that is conceivably acceptable, and this provides a second standard of criminal justice performance.

A third standard is simply whether a proposed policy or program constitutes an improvement in one or another dimension of performance compared with current operations. Inevitably, all real systems of justice fall short of idealized notions. They may also sometimes fall short of constitutional standards. Consequently, it may be important to know whether proposed changes in criminal justice system operations are moving us toward or away from an idealized concept of the criminal justice system. If a proposal promises to smooth the rough justice that is actually meted out in the system even a little bit, it may be worth adopting even though the proposal fails to usher in a heretofore unattainable ideal.

To a degree, these standards form a hierarchy for evaluating proposed changes in criminal justice policy. The most demanding is whether the proposed change is the final step in establishing an ideal system of justice. Much less demanding is that the proposed change further the aims expressed in the Constitution. Less demanding still is that the proposed change be an improvement over current practices.

These different standards of what constitutes a valuable or worthwhile improvement in criminal justice operations are as important to keep in mind as the different intuitions about the substantive values that should guide the criminal justice system, for they, too, become part of our discussions about whether predictions are tolerable in the criminal justice system. There are many proposals that might enhance the justice, fairness, and efficiency of the criminal justice system but that could be rejected because they fail to establish perfect justice. The crucial question is whether such proposals would be worth adopting.

Once again, this important issue is affected by the difference between deontological and utilitarian systems of reasoning. In principle, both schools have their "idealists" and their "realists." But the spirit of deontological systems is more given to idealism and exacting standards. The spirit of utilitarianism, on the other hand, is quite tolerant of practical realities and keenly interested in marginal improvements wherever they can be made. This means that those who want to hold the moral high ground by sticking to the spirit of deontological systems will tend to establish very high standards across the board. Those who are interested in encouraging small improvements in current operations might well be tarred with the brush of utilitarianism, even if the improvements they seek are in the areas of fairness and justice.

My own position is that we all have a fundamental duty to encourage improvements in criminal justice system operations in the directions of justice, fairness, and efficiency and to do so regardless of how large or small the changes. That may seem far too utilitarian, or realistic, or pragmatic to have much standing in moral discourse. And it is certainly true that this position would not only countenance but also enthusiastically embrace many proposals that seem shabby against the backdrop of an idealized system. But the weight of the duty to make improvements where they can be found can be measured by asking what we would think of a criminal justice official who knowingly abandoned some opportunity to improve the fairness, justice, or efficiency of the system without significant loss to society.

ETHICAL ISSUES IN PREDICTION IN THE CRIMINAL JUSTICE SYSTEM

The most fundamental objection to the use of prediction in the criminal justice system is that it is unjust and that any explicit or implicit use of prediction disgraces our system of justice (Dershowitz, 1973:1277–1324; N. Morris, 1974:62–73; N. Morris and Miller, 1985:65). This position is held by those who think that the most fundamental quality of the criminal justice system is justice (rather than effectiveness) and that a just system is one that holds people accountable only for acts committed in the past. This position has come to be called the "retributivist" or "just deserts" position (von Hirsch, 1976: 124–127; von Hirsch and Gottfredson, 1983–1984:34–37; von Hirsch, 1984b: 175–194, esp. 179).

Retributivist Attacks on Prediction

A second objection to predictions of criminal activity is that they are inaccurate and that inaccuracy results in injustice to those offenders who are mistakenly predicted to commit crimes in the future and are thereby exposed to unwarranted penalties and liabilities within the criminal justice system (N. Morris, 1974:62–73; von Hirsch, 1976:21–36; N. Morris and Miller, 1985:24–36; von Hirsch and Gottfredson, 1983–1984:177). This view is often embraced also by retributivists, since it reflects their general suspicion of the reliability of social science technology, is consistent with their strong concern for individual justice for criminal offenders, and, in any case, offers an additional line of attack on proposals to use predictive methods more extensively. Nonetheless, this objection can be sharply distinguished from the first objection. The difference is that this second view does not say that it would be wrong to impose additional liabilities on those predicted to commit offenses—only that it would be wrong to do this inaccurately. "False positives" are the problem—not liability being placed on individuals for acts in the future.

The first and second objections would effectively rule out the current use of prediction in the criminal justice system: the first because prediction is ruled out absolutely; the second because current predictive techniques cannot measure up to required levels of accuracy. Consequently, unless these objections can be overcome, the discussion of prediction is at an end.

A third objection is less fundamental because it focuses on the characteristics included in the predictive rule rather than the appropriateness of prediction in general or the requirement that the predictive rule meet a high standard of accuracy to prevent injustice to individuals. By this standard, only certain characteristics of offenses and offenders may be included in the predictive test. Appropriate characteristics are those that the individual controls and that themselves reflect criminal conduct (such as prior offending and drug abuse). These are appropriate because they establish "morally relevant differences" among offenders (von Hirsch, 1976:212–213, 1981b). Inappropriate characteristics are those over which the individual has only limited or no control, that are not in themselves criminal conduct, and that are correlated with deprived social status, such as employment status, race, or poverty. Also inappropriate are such variables as religion or political views. Indeed, it may be so important that the criminal justice system avoid any taint of bias with respect to race, income, religion, or political views that it not only resist using these variables explicitly but also avoid variables that are correlated with these especially sensitive variables (N. Morris and Miller, 1985).

At the extremes, concern about the characteristics incorporated in the predictive tests may make it impossible to construct any useful and decent test. This is particularly true if the tests must meet a high standard of accuracy and be neutral with respect to sensitive variables on a *de facto* as well as a *de jure* basis. So, scruples about the characteristics used in predictive tests may not only reduce the practical value of the tests but also rule them out completely on normative grounds (Moore et al., 1984:70–79).

Thus, from a retributivist position, the whole notion of predictions and particularly predictions that establish differences among individuals on the basis of morally irrelevant characteristics is fundamentally objectionable. Moreover, the objections work together. Restrictions on the characteristics to be used in tests render the tests less accurate. Less accurate tests exacerbate the problem of false positives. Both together create more injustice and reduce the practical value of the proposals. And besides, it is always wrong to have any criminal liability attached to predictions of future conduct.

Justifications from the "Modified Just Deserts" Position

The common attack on the "retributivist" position objects to its exclusive concern for a particular vision of justice and its idealism (Walker, 1982:276–289). Essentially, the argument is that the retributivist position is fine in theory, but wrong in practice (N. Morris and Miller, 1985:2). Although it is commonsensical to base a system of justice on past acts, it also makes sense to exploit opportunities to control crime more effectively when they come along. Moreover, since the community expects the system to be effective, and since criminal justice officials will respond to this demand by making predictions, it is in the interests of justice to make sure that the predictions are made as accurately and decently as possible. In effect, while it might be wrong in theory to use predictions in the criminal justice system, the system can be made to perform more effectively and more fairly than it does by explicitly introducing and managing predictive techniques (N. Morris and Miller, 1985). Although this hardly sounds like an ethical argument for the use of prediction, one can reasonably argue that we have an obligation to make improvements in current performance even if the improvements do not usher in the ideal.

This position—which has been called "modified just deserts"—honors retributive principles and keeps them in the dominant position in its conception of the virtues of criminal justice policies, but it also leaves some room for utilitarian concerns and practical opportunities. And this, in turn, allows room for some kinds of prediction as part of criminal justice system operations. But the problem of inaccuracy in predictions and the inevitable injustice to individuals wrongly predicted to commit offenses in the future remain.

To this difficulty, those who take a "modified just deserts" position seem to have two answers. One is that predictions of future criminality should be the basis for leniency and mercy but not for enhanced punishment (N. Morris, 1974:75, 1982:179–209, esp. 203). Benign predictions can mitigate, but adverse predictions should not aggravate, criminal penalties. Thus, no offender's liability would be increased by the use of prediction. This position not only alleviates concerns that offenders might be unjustly punished but also ensures the aggregate consequence that the scope of social control would not be widened by the broader use of predictions.

Unfortunately, this answer creates other problems. To the extent that justice establishes an affirmative obligation to punish criminal acts, being merciful to those who are predicted to be safe seems no more just than being harsh to those predicted to be dangerous. Obviously, the frailties of human institutions and judgments always counsel one to err on the side of leniency when moral judgments are being made and penalties exacted, and this is what generally makes mercy a virtue (N. Morris, 1974:52). The point, however, is not that leniency and mercy are not virtues, but that they must be justified in individual cases, and there is no guarantee that the characteristics of the offense or offender that might incline one toward mercy are those that distinguish those who will be safe in the future (Moore et al., 1984:101).

Similarly, granting mercy in individual cases on the basis of predictions of future criminal activity can create problems of equity and fairness. In principle, there is no problem if our notion of just penalties remains precise and fixed, and if the bases for granting mercy are well established. But if (a) our idea of just penalties is based on current average practices, (b) we think of penalties above the average practice as being unfair, and (c) there are many people in the system who seem to deserve mercy, many offenders who receive penalties that are just when compared with the initial standard of justice will appear to be unjustly treated because they received penalties that were above the average. We may try to explain why they did not qualify for mercy but many others did and, in any case, why their punishment was deserved. But this argument still leaves them with the question of "Why me?"—a question that has some force given the apparent inequity. So, the idea of using predictive techniques to lessen but not enhance punishments may alleviate the concern that individual offenders will be excessively punished, but it increases concerns that some of those who deserve punishment will not receive it and that defendants who have committed similar offenses might be treated differently.

The second answer to the problem of false positives offered by those who hold a "modified just deserts" position is that most people have misconstrued the nature of prediction. In this view, predicting that a person is dangerous does not necessarily imply that a person will commit a criminal act; it implies only that a criminal act is more likely (Floud and Young, 1981:48–49; N. Morris and Miller, 1985:24–28). Therefore, if an offender predicted to be dangerous does not, in fact, commit an offense, the prediction was not necessarily wrong. In this view: "a prediction of dangerousness . . . is the *statement of a condition* (membership in a defined group with . . . certain attributes) and *not the prediction of a result* (of future violent acts in each individual case)" (N. Morris and Miller, 1985:24). Thus, the crucial factual question in making predictions is not whether a person will commit offenses but whether that person does or does not have the attributes that qualify for membership in a particularly high-risk or particularly low-risk group. Since that factual question can typically be answered with great accuracy, there are very few errors in "prediction."

This explanation does away with worries about mistaken predictions but raises a new question: namely, why people who unambiguously have the attributes that make them members of a group predicted to be active offenders in the future should be exposed to additional penalties and liabilities from the criminal justice system. The answer to that is sometimes cast in the language of "just deserts." As Floud and Young (1981:48) observe: "the fact that if we were to set (those offenders predicted to be dangerous) at liberty, only half of those we are at any time detaining as dangerous would do further serious harm, does not mean that the other half are all in this sense *innocent* [emphasis added]." They have the qualities that make them risky and dangerous in the same sense that all unexploded bombs are dangerous even though most never explode (N. Morris and Miller, 1985:25; von Hirsch, 1985:280). And it is those qualities that justify different treatment in both moral and pragmatic terms. While this, at first, seems appealing, and while it is not hard to imagine the practical interests we have in treating such offenders differently, it is difficult to answer the question of exactly why they are not innocent. To put the matter differently, it is hard to say of exactly what offense such offenders are guilty.

To avoid this problem, the argument for treating differently offenders who have qualities that place them in high-risk groups quickly shifts to practical interests. Such offenders are risks that the society must bear. The crucial question is who will bear the costs of that risk: the offenders who must give up their freedom to protect the society or the society that must live with the risk of having dangerous people at liberty (N. Morris and Miller, 1985:24–36, esp. 28). This is considered a policy problem to be resolved by legislatures balancing social interests rather than either a constitutional question or a matter of individual justice to be decided by judges, prosecutors, or police (N. Morris and Miller, 1985:35). Once the legislature strikes the balance and defines the groups, the system can implement the policies in good conscience.

While this argument has some aspects that make it seem a principled position, the fact of the matter is that this argument pushes the justification of prediction far from the retributive perspective and puts it at the center of utilitarian concerns. In essence, the argument is the following: There is a social problem to be managed that consists of people who are inclined, or at least willing, to hurt or threaten other citizens or to take their property. This makes social life unpleasant. The society has a right to take action to protect itself from the risks. Because the risks come from other citizens, however, efforts to manage the risks must take account of their rights and interests as well. One way to accomplish that goal is to limit social control to those who have qualities that indicate they are much greater risks than others. To protect the rights and interests of those who represent greater risks, it is crucial that there be an evidentiary hearing on whether the offenders do or do not have the requisite qualities and that the scope of the state's penalties and controls be commensurate with the magnitude of the risks such offenders represent. Ideally, legislatures rather than individual administrative officials should balance these competing interests. Obviously, this position simply drapes the utilitarian argument for prediction in the clothing of legislatively balanced risks and due process protections for those who are about to be exposed to enhanced criminal liabilities on largely utilitarian grounds.

Justifications from a Utilitarian Perspective

The most direct counterargument to retributive objections is simply to assert not only the relevance but also the dominance of utilitarian concerns in the design of the criminal justice system. In this conception the criminal justice system has not only an interest but also an affirmative obligation to use whatever is available to reduce crime and promote security (Blumstein, Cohen, and Nagin, 1978:3–14). Because it is important to enlist the support of the community, and the community is as worried about excessive state power as about criminal offenders, it is prudent for the criminal justice system to be restrained, to protect rights to due process, and to operate consistently with the community's moral interests in a just and decent criminal justice system. But the touchstone for all innovations in the criminal justice system is to enhance effectiveness in reducing crime and promoting security.

In this utilitarian conception the concern about punishing people for predicted future offenses disappears entirely—unless the means seem so grossly unjust and so bizarre as to be repugnant to the community. Similarly, the concern for "false positives" fades, but does not entirely disappear. It stays partly because even the most pragmatic utilitarian might see some moral virtue in punishing only those who deserve it. Besides, economy in the use of both the moral and financial resources of the government would be considered a virtue by utilitarians, and there is no reason to waste those resources on people who are unlikely to commit offenses in any case. So, if one were to adopt a predominantly utilitarian position, the most fundamental objection to making criminal justice system actions contingent on predictions of future criminal conduct would be overcome. Some scruples might remain about the characteristics used in making predictions. For example, race, religion, and political views might be excluded to enhance other social purposes. But much greater room would be created for the use of predictions.

VIRTUES OF PREDICTIVE METHODS AND RULES

So far, the basic objections to the use of predictive rules in the criminal justice system have been examined from the vantage points of retributive, modified just deserts, and utilitarian ethical positions. As one moves through these different positions, more scope for prediction is created largely because concerns for "effectiveness" and some aspects of "fairness" gain in relative importance to concern for "justice." This suggests that one way of deciding whether prediction is ethically acceptable is to decide first on one's general ethical position and then see whether it allows prediction.

A slightly different way of thinking about the ethical issues raised by prediction is simply to imagine what the virtues of predictive methods might be. Obviously, if one is a strict retributivist, this exercise holds little interest since even the most virtuous system of prediction would be ruled out as unjust. Similarly, if one is a basic utilitarian, the exercise holds little interest since the best system must be the one that produces the greatest reduction in crime for the smallest use of the moral authority and financial resources of the state. But if one is a practically minded retributivist or a principled utilitarian, identifying the virtues of a system of prediction has some appeal because it not only identifies the qualities that would make the system acceptable but also indicates where and how improvements might be made.

Attractive Qualities of Predictive Rules

In thinking about the qualities that make systems of prediction more or less acceptable or virtuous, it is worth distinguishing features of the predictive rule itself and the circumstances under which the rule is applied. At least five important qualities of the predictive test or rule can be examined.

Focus of the Predictive Test

The first important question focuses on the behavior that the rule is trying to predict and the distinctiveness of the population that is being singled out by the rule when it works well. In general the more important the behavior that is being predicted and the smaller and more distinctive the population that is being singled out, the more appropriate seems the use of the predictive rule.

This principle applies in both retributive and utilitarian ethical systems. In the retributive conception a tolerable idea might be to single out the most wicked offenders (those who are most callous and show the fewest signs of remorse) and expose them to special punishments. Moreover, this seems much more appropriate if the rule singles out only a few who are outliers in the distribution of all offenders, rather than a substantial minority of offenders who are much closer to the center of the distribution in terms of "wickedness." Similarly, in a utilitarian framework the value of a predictive rule goes up if it isolates the worst kinds of criminal offenses and if it identifies the worst 5 to 10 percent of offenders, rather than more ordinary offenses and offenders.

The narrow focus is desirable in both systems partly as a matter of economy in the utilization of the state's limited moral and financial capacity to punish and partly because the more serious the conduct and the smaller the population that is identified, the more plausible the argument that the offenders are at least quantitatively and perhaps qualitatively different from ordinary offenders and therefore deserving of special treatment. Thus, a narrow, discriminating focus is to be preferred on both retributive and utilitarian grounds to predictive rules that place more offenders in special categories.

Accuracy of the Predictive Test

A second important feature of the predictive rule is its accuracy. As noted earlier, two quite different notions of accuracy exist. One is the idea that the rule does in fact predict who will commit serious offenses in the future: the actual conduct of the offenders determines the truth or falsity of the prediction. The second is that an accurate assessment is made of whether an offender does or does not have the characteristics that qualify for membership in a group predicted to engage in unusually high levels of criminal activity. In this conception the actual conduct of the offenders is not considered relevant: they are "dangerous" if they have the proper characteristics. The first conception of accuracy is central to some notions of "justice" and to all utilitarian concerns. The second is fundamental to notions of justice as fairness.

This discussion of accuracy is limited to the first notion: that the rule predicts accurately who will commit serious offenses at high rates. Obviously, accuracy in a predictive rule is a virtue in retributive systems because it minimizes the problem of exposing people who are not in fact dangerous to whatever special liabilities attach to this designation. It is a virtue in utilitarian systems because it economizes on the use of the state's resources in producing crime-reduction benefits.

The difficulties with this concept arise because a predictive rule can be inaccurate in two ways: it can incorrectly identify as dangerous offenders who are not dangerous (so-called "false positives"), and it can incorrectly identify offenders who are in fact dangerous as not dangerous (so-called "false negatives"). Liberal democratic societies, acutely aware of the frailties of human institutions, have typically treated "false positives" as much worse than "false negatives." So, a test that is attractive is not only one that makes few errors of both types but also one that distributes the errors in an appropriate way—i.e., makes many fewer errors of inclusion in the category of dangerous offenders than of exclusion. People's views differ about the proper tradeoffs between reducing errors of all types and reducing errors of one type at the expense of increasing the total number of errors of both types. So do their views about the rates at which they will trade one kind of error for the other in a world in which the total number of errors of both kinds remains constant. But everyone agrees on the directions in which improvements lie: fewer errors are better than more; errors of inclusion are worse than errors of exclusion when the offender is to be given special penalties or control by virtue of inclusion in a group predicted to be dangerous.

Basis of the Predictive Rule

A third important quality of the predictive rule is the basis on which it is established. The standard distinctions in this area are made between rules established on the basis of "statistical" or "actuarial" methods and those established on the basis of "clinical" methods (Monahan, 1981:45–93). Norval Morris and Marc Miller (1985:18–19) have added a third kind of prediction, which they call "anamnestic," that is, a predictive rule is developed for an individual on the notion that individual behavior is repetitive and thus becomes predictable to those who know the individual very well without necessarily being generalizable to others.

At first it might seem odd that the basis of a predictive rule would hold much ethical or normative interest. Of course, we might assume some connection between the basis of the rule and its accuracy. And, to the extent that we thought accuracy was important and had views about which basis produced the most accurate rules, the basis of the rule would assume normative significance. But the significance would be exhausted by an examination of the rule's accuracy regardless of its basis. Yet many commentators seem to attach significance to the basis of the rule *beyond its implications for the accuracy of prediction* (Monahan, 1981: 95–101).

On reflection, this concern seems to be tied to three features of the predictive rule that are linked to moral intuitions about the just construction of such rules. One notion is that, if predictions are to be made, they should emerge from a unique consideration and understanding of the individual (N. Morris and Miller, 1985: 20). This honors the principle of individualized justice (but it sometimes jeopardizes, or at least complicates, the principle of like cases being treated alike). By this standard, "anamnestic" and "clinical" predictions, both of which are based on detailed case information, might be preferred to "statistical" methods, which concern aggregates and abstract from individual circumstance.

A second notion is that it should be possible to state the predictive rule simply and to have it conform with ordinary common sense. This is consistent with aspirations for "fairness" in the system and for mobilizing community support for the operations of the criminal justice system. By this standard, "anamnestic" rules are once again dominant, "actuarial" rules are close behind (depending on how commonsensical they appear), and "clinical" rules appear the least attractive.

The third notion—closely related to the second—is that the development and interpretation of the rules should minimize the use of specialized professionals. This is primarily to protect the connection of the criminal justice system to the community and to tradition but also perhaps to maintain the professional dominance of lawyers over other professionals in the criminal justice system. By this standard, anamnestic predictions once again seem the best; actuarial and clinical predictions are far behind because both involve arcane methods and different kinds of professionals.

So, the basis of predictive rules seems to be important, independent of their prospects for accuracy. When all characteristics associated with the basis of rules are considered, most commentators seem to prefer statistical methods (Meehl, 1954; Floud and Young, 1981:26; Monahan, 1981:97–98; N. Morris and Miller, 1985:20). Rules established by such methods have the virtues of calibrated accuracy, simplicity of form, and consistency of application. They have the liabilities of being indifferent to most individual characteristics (which is the opposite side of the coin to simplicity), of being rooted in aggregate rather than individual experience, and of engaging unfamiliar techniques. Anamnestic rules, on the other hand, have the virtues of being rooted in individual experience, responsive to individual circumstances, and commonsensical. They have the liabilities of unproven accuracy and uneven application. Clinical rules have the virtue of being responsive to individual circumstance and the liabilities of being inaccurate, of being complicated to state and to apply, and of surrendering some of the powers of the criminal justice system to a (suspect) group of professionals (Stone, 1975).

Characteristics Used to Make Predictions

A fourth quality of predictive rules that bears on their fairness, justice, or efficacy is the character of the variables that are used to assign people to groups and to make predictions. This point has already been discussed. From a retributive perspective, the only appropriate variables are those that an individual can control and are themselves reflective of criminal conduct—although not necessarily the most serious forms of criminal conduct. From a utilitarian perspective, variables are appropriate to include if they are successful in predicting criminal conduct. From a mixed perspective, the challenge is to balance interests in having the characteristics used in the test be just and in predicting reliably.

There is some consensus about what variables may properly be included. Everyone agrees that the seriousness of the current offense is proper to consider in sentencing (N. Morris, 1974:73; von Hirsch, 1976:Chapters 8 and 9; Blumstein et al., 1983a:11–12, 83–84). The main reason is that since it is the offense that justifies the punishment, the seriousness of the offense must determine the seriousness of the punishment. The seriousness of the offense is often judged not only on the objective harm done by the offender, however, but also on the state of mind of the offender (Hart, 1968b:113–135; von Hirsch, 1976:80). If the violence was particularly wanton or if the offender behaved very recklessly with respect to life and property, the penalty (and perhaps future suspicion) will be greater than if the offense was more moderate (Vera Institute of Justice, 1977). In short, the offense itself may indicate the dangerousness of the offender as well as produce the objective harm to victims that justifies intervention by the state.

Nearly everyone also agrees that the adult record of the offender may properly be included (von Hirsch, 1976:84–94, 1981a). The only people who disagree with this position are the most strict retributivists, who think the right (and the obligation) to punish is tied strictly to acts and that punishment is meted out to balance the wrongs done. In their view each act deserves a discrete penalty and to enhance the penalty for a third or fourth offense is to be unjust (von Hirsch, 1976:172; Fletcher, 1978:463–466; Singer, 1979:67–74). Other retributivists think that it might be just to enhance penalties for those with criminal records not because criminal records necessarily predict well but because they reveal the offender as unusually persistent and therefore unusually deserving of punishment (von Hirsch, 1976:84–94). Thus, while these reasons for considering criminal record are different from those held by the "modified retributivists" and the "utilitarians," many retributivists would allow criminal record to influence the extent of punishment and control asserted by the system. The utilitarians approve of the use of criminal record because it is correlated with future criminal offending (Monahan, 1981:104–105). And the "modified retributivists" accept the idea because this variable fits within the principle that the variables used to predict should be under the control of the offender and consist of conduct that is itself criminal (Monahan, 1981:104–105; N. Morris and Miller, 1985).

Virtually everyone but the hardest-core utilitarians also agree that there are some variables that should clearly be excluded from any predictive test. Such variables would be those that define groups that have special protection under the Constitution, such as religious groups, political organizations, and groups that have historically been the object of discrimination (e.g., racial groups and, perhaps, age groups). It is quite clear that the *de jure* use of characteristics such as religion, political beliefs, and race are ruled out (Wilson, 1983b:158). It is more controversial whether to countenance the use of variables that might themselves be proper but are sufficiently correlated with other characteristics to result in *de facto* discrimination if utilized (Moore et al., 1984:73). At any rate, everyone agrees that the characteristics used in predictive tests should be as far removed from any taint of political, cultural, or racial bias as possible.

These points mark out areas of agreement. The field of contention is wider, however. Some of the disagreement focuses on the degree of certainty one must have about whether an offender actually has a certain attribute to be able to use it in making predictions. This arises most sharply and obviously in the use of criminal record; the issue is whether the predictive test should be restricted to convictions or whether it might also include indictments and arrests. There is a strong argument for relying only on convictions: since they are the only criminal acts that have been confidently attributed to an offender, they are the only acts that could justify any additional penalty or control. The argument for allowing indictments and convictions is weaker and relies much more heavily on a utilitarian justification: since indictments and arrests can only be made on the basis of enough evidence to establish "probable cause" to believe that an offense occurred and that the particular suspect committed the offense, since inclusion of information on indictments and arrests seems to improve the accuracy of predictions of future criminal activity, and since this information is already widely used in the criminal justice system, it is tolerably just to use this information. Indeed, it may be much better to rely on indictments and arrests, which have the virtues of having some relationship to criminal conduct and of being recorded relatively accurately, than to rely on characteristics (e.g., drug use or employment status) that do not necessarily reflect serious criminal conduct, are unreliably measured, and may be only imperfectly under the control of the offender.

This raises the second main area of disagreement: how close to criminal conduct must the behavior be and how confident must one be that the behavior was under the control of the individual (Hart, 1968b:174; Underwood, 1979:1432–1447). These issues arise most directly when we consider the appropriateness of incorporating variables such as drug use and employment status. Drug use seems closer to acceptability than employment status because it is closer to criminal conduct and much more under the control of the individual than employment status. But one can reasonably argue that drug use in itself is only criminal by virtue of laws that make it so; that many drug users have lost control over their use; and that, in any case, it is hard to measure accurately for individuals (Wish et al., 1981). Hence, it would be unjust to make levels of punishment and supervision conditional on drug use. And, if this argument is accepted for drug use, it would also exclude use of employment status—for there is nothing remotely criminal about being unemployed (although it is certainly a virtue to be employed) and people may have relatively little control over this status (although there may be opportunities for them to work or to make investments in themselves so that they will be qualified for employment).

Perhaps the most interesting area of disagreement involves the use of juvenile records. On one hand, from a retributive perspective, a juvenile record of criminal offenses seems appropriate to use because it is part of a criminal record indicating persistent criminal activity. On the other hand, we tend to view juvenile offenses as less under the control of the offenders—and therefore less indicative of intent and character—than adult offenses (Institute for Judicial Administration, 1977:1). Moreover, we have institutionalized this conception of diminished criminal responsibility by establishing juvenile courts, which do not find juveniles "guilty" of specific offenses, but instead find them "delinquent" or "nondelinquent," and do so through relatively informal systems in which records are deliberately kept spare to avoid future stigmatization and labeling (Institute for Judicial Administration, 1977:250–252; Zimring, 1978:46–49, 66–69). Since juvenile offenses are conceived to be less under the control of individuals and since they are measured imperfectly, it would be unjust and unfair to use them in predictive tests.

But there is an additional part of this issue that is emphasized by utilitarian interests and concerns. Much criminological research indicates that rates of offending peak for individuals between the ages of 18 and 25 (Collins, 1978; Moore et al., 1983b). Moreover, those who are very active and violent offenders in this period tend to have accumulated serious juvenile records (Moore et al., 1983b). Hence, if juvenile records were used as part of the predictive tests, the tests would identify the most dangerous offenders not only more accurately but also *earlier* than they otherwise would be. In fact, they could be identified during their peak years of offending. If, on the other hand, juvenile records are excluded from the predictive tests, the system will identify people as dangerous offenders less accurately and later in the individual careers of the offenders. This means that some important crime-control potential is lost (Boland and Wilson, 1978:22–35).

As in other areas of normative debate, the question of which variables are proper to use in predictive tests comes down to the balance between retributive and utilitarian principles. It seems clear that current offense and prior adult convictions can be used. It also seems clear that race, political views, and religious beliefs may not properly be used. After that, a great deal is contested. The Harvard Project on Dangerous Offenders concluded that indictments for adult offenses could properly be included since they did represent evidence of criminal conduct and were routinely used in sentencing anyway but that employment status and history should not be included (Moore et al., 1983a:132, 1984:74–75).

The Harvard project also concluded that juvenile records of serious criminal offenses could be included if the offender committed an additional serious offense shortly after graduating from the juvenile system (Moore et al., 1983b:324–327, 1984:173–176). This position was justified with both a retributive and a utilitarian argument. The retributive argument was that, while there was a presumption that juvenile offenders were not responsible for their offenses in the same way that adults were because they did not will them, this presumption was vitiated by those few juveniles who persisted in criminal offending as adults, because their persistence gave a different meaning to their juvenile offenses. Viewed in retrospect, the youthful offenses were not indiscretions occasioned by the confluence of circumstances, peer pressure, and transient recklessness but, instead, were early signs of determined criminality. The utilitarian argument is the following: since the main reason to seal juvenile records is to relieve youthful offenders of the stigmatizing burden of past offenses and make it easier for them to stop offending, and since those youthful offenders who continue committing serious crimes have already failed to take advantage of that opportunity, no practical purpose is served by continuing to protect their juvenile records and some practical purpose is lost by not exposing their records of serious offending as juveniles. So, both retributive and utilitarian arguments line up in favor of including records of serious offenses committed as juveniles for those offenders who continue to commit crimes as adults.

The basic logic that leads to these conclusions on particular characteristics is the desire to keep the predictive rules close to retributive principles, and perhaps even to improve the justice and fairness of current operations, while at the same time exploiting some of the crime-control benefits that might come from improved predictions. Thus, characteristics involving criminal conduct were treated as more acceptable than variables describing noncriminal conduct or statuses, and concessions to utilitarian interests in crime control were made on the basis of the accuracy with which such variables were measured rather than in terms of the nature of the variables themselves. This position undoubtedly goes too far for retributivists and not far enough for utilitarians, but those features may be the virtues rather than the vices of the position.

Auspices of the Prediction Rule

The fifth quality of a predictive rule that affects its acceptability is the auspices that establish it as a guide for criminal justice decision making: i.e., whether the rule is promulgated by a legislative body, a court, or an administrative agency. The rule has different kinds and degrees of legitimacy depending on the source that established it and the process that lay behind its establishment.

In general, we think of legislative bodies as having the broadest kinds of responsibility and legitimacy. As representatives of the people, they are competent to assess current problems, weigh alternative solutions, and balance competing social values at stake in alternative policy responses. Moreover, in reaching conclusions, they are free to consult widely—including specialists in legal reasoning, in statistical methods, and in psychiatry. Thus, in principle, when they reach a decision about a proper predictive rule, that decision should carry great weight. It can be changed only by a successful argument that an important constitutional principle was violated—a judgment that is fairly rare. In practice, though, we often worry that legislatures are too responsive to transient passions of the majority; that important traditions or rights of minorities and individuals might be overwhelmed; and that important scientific and technical issues might not be well enough understood. In effect, legislatures might have the undeniable virtue of reflecting the people's will but might fail to take advantage of institutions that embody other virtues.

Courts might be a better author of predictive rules. They typically lack the close connections to the political community that legislatures have and might well be as incompetent as legislatures in addressing the technical issues of statistics and psychiatry that could arise in formulating a predictive rule. But they have the virtue of representing tradition and a deep concern for the rights of minorities and individuals. And since these are importantly at stake in the design and use of predictive rules, perhaps the courts are the most legitimate authors.

Alternatively, administrative agencies—either correctional systems, criminal justice planning agencies, or specially established commissions—might be the proper authors of predictive rules. While they lack the close connection that courts have to tradition and individual rights and the close connection that legislatures have to the popular will, they are assumed to have the virtue of being able to command technical expertise. And since there are a great many technical issues to be discussed and resolved in formulating a predictive rule, and since neither courts nor legislatures provide an appropriate forum for this debate, perhaps the rules should be formulated by administrative agencies.

The ideal would be a legislatively established rule, formulated through a legislative process that effectively synthesized the perspectives and expertise of professional criminal justice administrators, judges, lawyers, statisticians, and psychiatrists. Anything short of this would be distinctly inferior. But probably the worst situation is one in which either courts or administrative agencies formulate their own predictive rules without the benefit of connections to the political community or to the knowledge of technical experts. And that seems to be the most common contemporary source of predictive rules.

Attractive Qualities in Applying Predictive Rules

Obviously, predictive rules are vulnerable to a great many vices: they can be too indiscriminate, too inaccurate, built from inappropriate methods, based on unjust characteristics, and promulgated by the wrong agencies. Perhaps some of these vices can be overcome by virtues in application.

Some commentators have suggested, for example, that some degree of inaccuracy or some flawed characteristics or some informality in the construction and promulgation of the rule might be acceptable if the action to be taken by criminal justice officials was relatively insignificant (N. Morris and Miller, 1985:20, 30–33). In effect, it is appropriate to think of a balance to be struck among the importance of the social objective being pursued through the application of the predictive test, the size of the sanction to be applied by criminal justice officials, and the requirements placed on the test itself. The more important the objective and the smaller the infringement on the interests of offenders, the less demanding the standards for the predictive test. If, for example, it was plausible that the use of predictive tests might substantially reduce the likelihood of a presidential assassination, and if the predictive test resulted in nothing more than refusing admission to a public speech by the president, a quite imperfect test could be used (N. Morris and Miller, 1985:31). If, on the other hand, the society sought to eliminate "joyriding" and wanted to do so by placing those teenagers predicted to be active joyriders under close, continuing supervision, even predictive tests that met the strictest possible standards might be unacceptable. Virtue in application comes in balancing competing interests, and the standard of what sorts of test are acceptable is somewhat elastic. A great deal depends on the size of the harm to be avoided and the magnitude of the penalties or controls exerted over those who are the subjects of predictions.

It also seems clear that predictions are more acceptable if they are made after an offender has been convicted of a crime. The predictions of dangerousness associated with civil commitments have always been suspect (Dershowitz, 1974). The obvious deficiencies of the predictive rules in use have been justified by the assertion that civil commitment was therapeutic and in the interests of the person who was committed. As it has become apparent that the "treatment" available to those who were civilly committed was virtually indistinguishable from the "punishment" meted out to those judged guilty of crimes, however, this justification has worn thin, and the entire idea of prediction has been tainted with the hypocrisy and overreaching of civil commitment procedures (Dershowitz, 1974; Stone, 1975). On the other hand, predictions have long been tolerated—even enthusiastically endorsed—in making sentencing decisions once an offender is convicted of a crime (*Williams* v. *New York*, 337 U.S. 241, 247, 1949). No doubt some of this enthusiasm for prediction comes from the expectations that predictions will mitigate rather than aggravate sentences and that explicit predictions might introduce some consistency into haphazard patterns of sentencing. But the wider scope given to the use of prediction in sentencing also has a great deal to do with the fact that the liberty interests of an offender are taken less seriously by the society once he has been convicted of a criminal offense. Our laws and moral intuitions establish a fairly broad zone of discretion in limiting the freedoms of those who have been convicted of criminal offenses, and there is less objection to using prediction to fill out this zone of discretion than there is to using predictions as the sole basis for restricting a citizen's liberty—even if the purpose is terribly important.

These two principles of application—that the quality of the predictive tests or rules should be commensurate with the significance of the harm to be reduced and the sanction to be imposed on individuals predicted to be dangerous and that prediction is more justified when it involves people who have been convicted of criminal offenses—have important and subtle implications for the appropriateness of using predictive methods at different stages of the criminal justice system. These will be discussed in detail in the next section, but it is worth beginning the discussion here.

The principle that predictive tests are more (or only) appropriate when they involve convicted offenders seems to imply that predictions are appropriate at the sentencing stage and inappropriate at any stage prior to sentencing (e.g., investigation, prosecution, or bail). After all, to use predictions before that stage is to violate the presumption of innocence and to expose innocent people to heightened state interest and control—including the loss of liberty in pretrial detention. Such actions lack even the thin justification of "treatment" available within civil commitment procedures.

To a degree, one can argue against this view by insisting that the "presumption of innocence" is an important principle to be used in criminal trials but certainly not as a guide for the agencies that investigate crimes, prosecute offenders, or seek to ensure appearance at trial. In fact, their task is generally the opposite: to develop evidence that constitutes a case showing that a given person is very likely to have committed an offense. In allocating resources and pursuing their objectives, it might be proper for them to make predictions of whether an offender is likely to be an active offender.

While this argument has some merit, it sounds a bit tendentious even to those who support proposals to use predictions of dangerousness at the stages of investigation, prosecution, and pretrial decision making. What gives the argument added weight, however, is the observation that predictive methods would most commonly be used at these stages for people who had been convicted for serious offenses *at some time in their careers*—and generally quite recently (at least in terms of "street time"). This raises the question of whether convictions for offenses in the past could justify exposing offenders to the use of predictive methods to vary levels of investigative and prosecutorial effort even though the current offenses of which they are suspected are so far unproven. Strict retributivists, who view the offender's liabilities as exhausted when they complete their punishment for previous acts, might object to this idea. So would some utilitarians who are interested in maximizing offenders' chances for rehabilitation and who would regard the heightened police and prosecutorial interest as antitherapeutic. But to many, the idea that a person convicted of previous crimes and plausibly accused of more recent crimes should receive greater attention from investigators and prosecutors, might even face higher bail, seems both just and commonsensical. In effect, the society reserves the right to be a little more suspicious of those who have been convicted of previous offenses and seem to be persisting in committing offenses.

So, it is by no means clear that the broader scope granted to prediction once a person has been convicted of an offense rules out predictions at earlier stages of criminal justice processing. If a person has been convicted of previous offenses recently, and the current case is serious and well supported by evidence, there may be scope in our moral intuitions, law, and current practice to increase levels of investigation, prosecution, and bail guarantees.

The principle that the quality of predictive tests should be commensurate with the significance of the social harm to be avoided and the sanctions to be imposed on offenders also affects judgments about the appropriateness of using predictions at different stages of the criminal justice system. What the implications are depends on how one regards the significance of the actions taken at different stages of the criminal justice system for the offender. If one regards the sentencing decision as relatively insignificant—an anticlimax to the drama of the trial and its crucial judgment of guilt or innocence—one would grant relatively wide discretion to the use of predictions in sentencing and much less discretion to those parts of the system that affect the judgment of guilt or innocence at trial. On the other hand, if one regards the sentencing decision as very significant because it directly affects the length of time an offender will be imprisoned and considers decisions regarding levels of investigation and prosecutorial effort as much less significant because they have, at most, only a minor effect on the possibility of a guilty judgment at trial, one would grant much more latitude for predictions to police and prosecutors than to sentencing judges.

It is not clear which position is correct. Observers may make much of the importance of guilt or innocence, but I suspect offenders are much more concerned about sentence length than the level of police scrutiny and prosecutorial zeal they must endure. Moreover, I suspect this is particularly true for those who are most likely to be exposed to prediction methods, namely, those who have been convicted of prior offenses.

In sum, the application of predictive rules may itself have qualities that enhance or detract from the overall fairness, justice, or efficacy of the predictive rules. In fact, judiciousness in application might compensate to some degree for defects in the construction, promulgation, or character of the rule itself. In general, predictive rules are more acceptable if they are used to manage important social problems, if the liabilities contingent on predictive rules are relatively minor, and if the predictions are made with respect to people who have already been convicted of recent criminal offenses. The implications of these principles for use at different stages of the criminal justice system are a little subtle since they turn on judgments about whether convictions for past offenses sanction enhanced investigative and prosecutorial attention, and about the relative significance of sentencing decisions versus investigative, prosecutorial, and bail decisions for the interests of accused offenders. These questions deserve further treatment, but at the outset it should be clear that predictions are not clearly excluded at investigative, prosecutorial, or pretrial stages.

PREDICTION AT DIFFERENT STAGES OF THE CRIMINAL JUSTICE PROCESS

Discussions of prediction in the criminal justice system have a certain sameness about them. As discussed, from a retributive perspective, prediction of any sort seems unethical and illicit. Yet, there are often practical reasons to make predictions—particularly if they can be made with decency and reasonable accuracy. And the explicit use of well-developed prediction methods might well enhance the quality of justice if the practical alternative is to have biased and impressionistic predictions bootlegged into the system by the thousands of criminal justice officials who are doing jobs that seem to require predictions. Besides, it is by no means clear that the best criminal justice system would be one that honored retributive principles to the exclusion of utilitarian interests in overall crime control effectiveness and in making incremental improvements in criminal justice system operations.

In discussing issues of prediction at different stages of criminal justice system processing, we cannot escape from the general shape of this argument. But the use of prediction at different stages does raise different normative issues—partly because the relevant constitutional and statutory laws are different and partly because current operational practices have accommodated the interest in prediction in different ways. The approach here will be to examine the justice of making predictions of dangerousness at the sentencing stage, in setting bail, and in developing prosecutorial strategies, and to do so from the vantage point of current practices, constitutional law, and moral intuitions.

Sentencing

For the past 30 to 40 years, the dominant philosophy and practice of sentencing has been "rehabilitative sentencing" (Blumstein et al., 1983a:60–61). The aim has been to use the process of sentencing to encourage the rehabilitation of criminal offenders. The legal authority to pursue this goal lay in "indeterminate sentencing" laws. The principal agents who operated this system were judges (aided by probation officers), who set the initial sentence, and parole and corrections officials, who decided whether a person could be released earlier than the maximum limit on his sentence and, if so, exactly when.

Although by no means widely advertised, this system was built around a core of prediction. When judges sentenced defendants under indeterminate sentencing laws and when parole boards chose to grant or deny inmates' requests for parole or early release, they were implicitly or explicitly making predictions about future offenses (N. Morris and Miller, 1985:10–12). As an operational matter, that is what it meant to gauge the rehabilitative achievements and potential of a given offender. Moreover, they made these predictions not on the basis of the offenses committed by the offender (as would be recommended by retributivists) or on the basis of well-developed prediction methods (as would be recommended by utilitarians), but instead on the basis of a detailed but essentially discretionary examination of the offender's background, characteristics, and behavior while in prison.

Professional opinion among judges and correctional officials supported this form of sentencing. So did legislatures. And so did the Supreme Court. As summarized in Moore et al. (1984:107–108):

> In deciding the case of *Williams* v. *New York* (1949), for example, the Supreme Court found that criminal sentences should be based "on the fullest information possible concerning the defendant's life and characteristics." Similarly, in *Pennsylvania* v. *Ashe* [302 U.S. 51, 55, 1937], the Court decided that "for the determination of sentences, justice generally requires consideration of more than the particular acts by which the crime was committed and that there be taken into account the circumstances of the offense together with the character and propensities of the offender."
>
> [In understanding the Court's view of sentencing,] the *Williams* case is particularly instructive. The trial judge overruled a jury recommendation of life imprisonment and imposed the death penalty on the basis not only of the shocking details of the crime, which had been revealed, of course, to the jury, but also on the information in the presentence investigation. According to the Supreme Court's account, the trial judge "referred to the experience appellant 'had had on thirty other burglaries in and about the same vicinity' where the murder had been committed. The appellant had not been convicted of these burglaries although the judge had information that he had confessed to some and had been identified as the perpetrator of some of the others. The judge also referred to certain activities of appellant as shown by the probation report that indicated the appellant possessed a 'morbid sexuality' and classified him as a 'menace to society'." The Supreme Court upheld the imposition of the death penalty on this basis against a due process challenge. Noting that the "New York statutes emphasize prevalent modern philosophy of penology that the punishment should fit the offender and not merely the crime," the Court reasoned that strict adherence to evidentiary rules limiting the basis for sentencing to testimony given in open court by witnesses subject to cross-examination would undermine the ability of judges to individualize sentences on the basis of the best available information [*United States* v. *Grayson*, 438 U.S. 41, 1978].

This sentencing philosophy also tapped an important moral current: the notion that justice must recognize that crimes emerged not simply from evil intentions of offenders but also from social circumstances; that there must, therefore, be mitigating facts behind many criminal offenses; and that the best form of justice would be one that tailored social responses to the guilt of the offender and gave the offender the best chance for rehabilitation. This idea drew on both retributive and utilitarian ideas. The idea that guilt might be mitigated by social circumstances is essentially an idea of justice, since it finds the agency of a crime somewhere outside the mind or conscious will of the defendant. The idea that we might do better to control crimes by rehabilitating offenders rather than simply imprisoning them is essentially a utilitarian idea. For a generation, individualized, rehabilitative sentencing was sanctioned by practice, law, and moral aspirations. It had prediction at its core.

The dominance of this philosophy was eroded by attacks by both the retributivists and the utilitarians. The retributivists attacking from the left focused on the broad discretion granted to sentencing judges and parole boards, the resulting disparities in sentences for similar offenses, and the room left for racial discrimination and other forms of unfairness

(American Friends Service Committee, 1971; Frankel, 1973). The retributivists attacking from the right focused on the degradation of both the criminal law and the broad presumption of individual responsibility (van den Haag, 1975; Szasz, 1977). The utilitarians, attacking from both left and right, focused on the apparent ineffectiveness of rehabilitative programs for offenders (Martinson, 1974:22–54). Together, these attacks weakened the popular and professional support for the concept of rehabilitative sentencing.

The current debate on criminal sentencing seeks an elusive balance of retributive and utilitarian principles. The crucial questions are not about the features of pure systems but on what terms the integration of the systems will proceed. And it is here that retributivists, utilitarians, and "mixed-system" advocates do battle.

The strongest retributive position has been advanced by von Hirsch (1976:77–88; 1981a:591–634; von Hirsch and Gottfredson, 1983–1984:34). In his conception, three crucial principles must guide criminal justice sentencing. The first is that the reprehensibility of the criminal offense for which the offender has been convicted is the essential factor that must be recognized in setting criminal penalties—not the likelihood of committing future acts or the general deterrent value of punishing the offender (von Hirsch, 1976:66–94; 1981a:592).

The second is that, while exactly how much punishment is deserved by a given criminal offense is somewhat indeterminate, it is possible to establish a rank ordering of the reprehensibility of criminal acts and that rank ordering must be rigorously preserved in the ordering of punishments meted out (von Hirsch, 1983:213–214, 221–230, 1984a:1097). Thus, someone convicted of a burglary should never receive a sentence longer than that given to someone else convicted of a robbery, and a second-degree burglar should never receive a punishment more severe than a first-degree burglar. While this principle does not necessarily determine the size of the bands of punishment surrounding a given offense, the requirement to preserve ordinal relationships across a great many offenses within the constraints established by the ordinary lengths of human life may, in fact, require that the bands around the offenses be quite narrow.

The third principle is that people convicted of the same act should receive the same punishment unless some "morally relevant difference can be established between the offenders" (von Hirsch, 1983: 212–213, 226–227). The likelihood of committing future crimes would not be considered morally relevant, although the fact of past crimes might be (von Hirsch, 1976:84–88; 1981a:591–634).

Taken together, these principles leave little room for utilitarian interests in general deterrence or incapacitation or rehabilitation to come into play. These interests and objectives gain a purchase only within the bands established around offenses (which are narrowed by the requirement that ordinal relationships be preserved in a limited space of possible punishments), and only insofar as the differences among offenders may be made "morally relevant" to our judgment of them. A general social interest in reducing crime through deterrence or rehabilitation or incapacitation is not sufficient for treating an offender differently.

A weaker position in retributive terms, but stronger in utilitarian terms, has been advocated by such scholars as John Monahan (1982:103–113) and Norval Morris (1974:73–77, 1982:179–209; N. Morris and Miller, 1985). Monahan (1982) has called this position a "modified just deserts" position. In this conception the outer limits of punishment for given offenses are once again established by retributive concerns. On the question of how broad the range of punishments surrounding a given offense could be without doing injustice to the offender, the authors are silent. Moreover, there is no strict principle requiring the preservation of ordinal relationships to establish a sense that the bands must be tight. So, it seems that a "just punishment" in this conception may be broader than in the von Hirsch conception. Similarly, there is no rigorous statement that similar cases (defined in terms of offenses) must be treated alike. So, there is a great deal of room for utilitarian concerns to come into play.

Obviously, if the bands around offenses are sufficiently wide, and if there is no rigorous principle requiring that similar offenses be treated similarly, utilitarian concerns could determine everything within the hollow shell of retributive principles. And it is this that focuses von Hirsch's criticisms (1981b:772–789, esp. 784–785). On the other hand, the "modified just deserts" position has the virtue of allowing the criminal justice system to fit criminal liability to the varied forms of human conduct and misery that appear in the system and to the limited capacities of the system to punish (N. Morris, 1982: 190), and to do so in a way that preserves some of the society's interest in a valuable and useful criminal justice system, as well as a just one.

The strongest utilitarian position has been adopted by Peter Greenwood (1982). His argument is that the society has an interest in both minimizing crime and reducing its reliance on prisons. In a world in which rehabilitation seems to have failed, the efficacy of general deterrence remains uncertain, and general incapacitation costs too much in terms of liberty and money per unit of crime reduction achieved, it is valuable to focus scarce prison capacity on those who are likely to commit the most crimes. This is particularly true when it seems that the differences among offenders in terms of the seriousness and rate of offending are quite substantial, and when some capacity exists to distinguish the high-rate, serious offenders from the lower-rate, less serious offenders. If the opportunity created by this situation was exploited, the society could have both less crime and fewer people in prison than it now has (N. Morris, 1974:63; N. Morris and Miller, 1985:6; Wilson, 1983b:155–156; von Hirsch and Gottfredson, 1983–1984: 22–31, 44–45; Moore et al., 1984:79–89).

Obviously, these different positions balance retributive and utilitarian concerns in quite different ways. In particular, they come to radically different conclusions about how great a role the society should grant to predictions of individual conduct in imposing criminal sentences and about how just distinctions among people convicted of similar offenses might be made. But this brief account of the history of sentencing policy indicates that there must be room for predictions in our normative conception of sentencing. It has been, and is now, sanctioned by current practice and by statutory and constitutional law. Moreover, all but the most stringent retributivists would accept predictions based on some characteristics of offenders as part of sentencing policies. There may well be limits on the use of predictions with respect to the magnitudes of the sentence increases that could be meted out and the sorts of variables that could be included. It might also be important to establish procedural devices to ensure that the characteristics of offenders relevant to sentencing were accurately assessed. But it seems strange to insist that there is no room for predictions of future criminality in sentencing.

Bail and Pretrial Decisions*

To many, the notion of jailing someone not yet convicted of a crime on the basis of uncertain judgments about the danger he presents to the community seems antithetical to our most fundamental legal traditions. And although pretrial detention is not the explicit goal of guidelines that increase bail for offenders estimated to be dangerous, that is the frequent and unlamented result.

Two objections to both preventive detention and risk-adjusted bail are commonly voiced. It is wrong to jail—and therefore punish—people who have not been convicted of crimes. And it is particularly unjust to detain them on the basis of predictions about future crimes. Stated affirmatively rather than negatively, the argument is that the state's only proper interest is to guarantee that accused individuals appear for trial. The amount of bail should be determined with this purpose in mind, and bail can hardly ever be denied on that basis. It is especially inappropriate to detain people solely to promote community security.

While compelling in principle, this position is undercut by three observations. First, the actual operations of the existing system reveal the bankruptcy of the guiding principles. The defendants who are detained are not those whose appearance at trial is of greatest concern to the state, but instead those whose financial resources are most limited. Some critics urge the release of more defendants on their own recognizance; others propose substitution of community sureties for money bail on the grounds that these would be more equally available to all defendants (Freed, 1982). Such reforms might well lead to less pretrial detention without harming the state's interest in guaranteeing appearance at trial. But the most important implication of the present system is that we are apparently willing to detain people without a finding of guilt simply to guarantee their appearance at trial. If the right to be free before trial can be overwhelmed by the state's limited interest in guaranteeing future appearance, then the right cannot be so fundamental, and it occasionally might be overwhelmed by the state's interest in reducing crime as well.

Second, many deny that the state's interest is limited to guaranteeing appearance at trial. Some legal scholars have argued that bail and sureties were also designed to promote community security (Goldkamp, 1979:15–31; Freed, 1982). And as a practical matter, both citizens and judges clearly think it is not only appropriate but crucially important that the citizens' interests in security be reflected in pretrial detention decisions.

Finally, the Supreme Court has so far refused to establish an unlimited right to bail, nor has it been willing to limit the state's interest to guaranteeing the defendant's appearance at trial. True, the Court has not yet heard a case on the constitutionality of preventive detention because all such cases have become moot before the Court could take them up (*Pretrial Reporter* 6 (March 1982):13). And in the leading bail case, *Stack* v. *Boyle*, the Supreme Court did indicate that guaranteeing appearance should be the most important factor (*Stack* v. *Boyle*, 342 U.S. 1 (1951):5). But the constitutional right of an individual to be set free on bail based solely or primarily on the need to guarantee appearance at trial has not been established.

To many, the Court's reluctance in this area seems inexplicable, for the constitutional language seems clear and straight-

*This section, in its entirety, originally appeared in Mark H. Moore, Susan R. Estrich, Daniel McGillis, and William Spelman, 1984, *Dangerous Offenders: The Elusive Target of Justice*, pp. 122–125.

forward. The Eighth Amendment to the U.S. Constitution asserts flatly that "excessive bail shall not be required." Unfortunately, this simple assertion can be given at least three interpretations (Goldkamp, 1979:16–17). One is that defendants have a right to reasonable bail, and the Supreme Court will determine what is reasonable. That interpretation, which would establish a right to be released on reasonable bail, has been supported by a historical analysis of bail in England (Foote, 1965:959–999; Fabricant, 1968:303–315). A second interpretation restricts the amount of bail to reasonable levels but leaves it to the states to pass laws indicating what is reasonable. No conception of a constitutional right is envisioned in this interpretation. Indeed, the states could decide that it was reasonable in some cases to deny bail. A third interpretation is that "in the absence of constitutional or statutory discretion . . . judicial discretion determines the appropriateness of bail within the bounds that it should not be excessive" (Goldkamp, 1979). This also rejects the notion of any right to bail, but it allows judges to set bail when statutes do not explicitly authorize it.

The District of Columbia enacted a preventive detention statute in 1970 that explicitly allowed offenders who were predicted to be dangerous to be detained. The constitutionality of the statute was tested in *United States* v. *Edwards* (No. 80–294 (D.C. App. May 8, 1981), cert. denied, 22 March 1982). The District of Columbia Court of Appeals held that the statute was constitutional, narrowly rejecting the interpretation that the Eighth Amendment guarantees a right to bail. The court reviewed the origins of the excessive bail clause and the case law pertaining to it and concluded that the aim of the Eighth Amendment was not to limit the power of Congress to deny pretrial release for specified classes of offenders or offenses, but rather to limit the discretion of the judiciary in bail setting. The court also ruled that the Fifth Amendment's due process clause was not violated by the preventive detention statute. Opponents of the statute objected on grounds that it permitted punishment of the defendant prior to full adjudication of the case. The court concluded that pretrial detention is not a form of punishment but rather a regulatory action and hence permissible.

The case was appealed to the Supreme Court, but the Court declined to consider it, perhaps for reasons similar to those justifying its reluctance to consider a previous Nebraska case, *Murphy* v. *Hunt* (No. 80–2165, 30 Cr L 3075, 1982; *Parker* v. *Roth*, 278 NW 2d 106, 1979). That case involved the constitutionality of Nebraska's constitutional amendment requiring "the denial of bail to defendants charged with forcible sex offenses when the proof is evident or the presumption great" (*Murphy* v. *Hunt*). The U.S. Court of Appeals for the Eighth Circuit found the amendment to be an unconstitutional restriction on the right to bail and asserted that "the constitutional protections involved in the grant of pretrial release by bail are too fundamental to foreclose by arbitrary state decree" (*Hunt* v. *Roth*, 648 F. 2d 1148, 1981). The Supreme Court vacated the Eighth Circuit's decision and found that the case was moot because the defendant had already been convicted for rape and sentenced to prison (*Murphy* v. *Hunt*). The *Edwards* case might also have been viewed by the court as not presenting a "live" issue because Edwards entered guilty pleas in both cases in which preventive detention was sought. Such a ruling poses an interesting dilemma since "pretrial detention orders will almost surely not outlive the appellate process" (*Pretrial Reporter* 6 (March 1982):13). The Court could choose to treat a future case as an exception embodying the principle of being "capable of repetition, yet evading review," and this rule was employed by the District of Columbia Court of Appeals in its review of the case (*United States* v. *Edwards*).

As in the case of sentencing, current practice and constitutional law both seem to sanction bail decisions (including a decision to deny bail altogether) based on predictions of dangerousness. This does not necessarily establish any affirmative reason for doing this, however, and it does seem contrary to our most important legal traditions. One justification for prediction is the community interest in controlling crimes committed by people on bail. But by most estimates, the practical effect will be small, and there are other ways of controlling crime on bail, such as special penalties or going to trial sooner (Lazar Institute, 1981:48).

Perhaps the most important reason to use prediction in making pretrial decisions is not to reduce crime on bail but to limit and rationalize the current system (Moore et al., 1984:125). Just as judicious use of prediction in sentencing convicted offenders could lead to fewer people being imprisoned, pretrial detention of dangerous offenders might lead to fewer people being detained and to the use of explicit criteria that would be fairer. A system that detained only those few who represented great risks of flight or new crimes, regardless of their financial resources, would be a welcomed relief, even if it required making explicit decisions about who was to be detained and who released. Compared with the current system, the only loss to justice would be in the explicit recognition of a community interest in controlling crime committed on bail, a principle that already seems to have some political and legal vitality despite the controversy over whether it is constitutionally recognized.

Prosecution

To some, the prosecutor seems the most powerful criminal justice official—partly because his or her decisions are consequential for defendants but even more importantly because the prosecutor has broad discretion to make the choices (Vorenberg, 1981:1521–1573). The prosecutor can quash charges, make a deal to trade information for a forgone prosecution, threaten a defendant with serious charges, and determine when a case will go to trial. Moreover, these choices are neither guided by explicit policies nor commonly reviewed.

Despite the wide discretion, professional norms and community pressures lend some consistency to prosecutorial decision making. Generally, prosecutors decide how much effort to apply to individual cases according to the seriousness of the current offense and the strength of the evidence: serious cases with strong evidence attract a great deal of prosecutorial attention; minor cases with weak evidence are screened out early or dispatched to overworked sections of the office that cannot give them anything but negligible attention (Institute for Law and Social Research, 1976a,b, 1977).

The focus on offenses and the strength of the evidence in the case can be understood from both retributive and utilitarian perspectives. It makes sense to retributivists because it ensures that prosecutorial attention will be focused on those who are likely to have committed serious criminal acts and because it imposes less liability on those whose acts are less serious or whose guilt is less likely. It makes sense to utilitarians since it seems to ensure that scarce resources will be spent where they will do the most good: in punishing those who seem to cause the worst part of the crime problem.

Although the offense-based focus of prosecutors remains the dominant principle in guiding prosecutorial discretion, in the last decade prosecutors have experimented with a new principle that would give priority attention to "career criminals" or "major offenders" (Harper and McGillis, 1977; Moore et al., 1984:137). In effect, in deciding how determinedly to pursue a case, prosecutors have decided to consider characteristics of the offender as well as the offenses and the strength of the evidence. The characteristics that qualify an offender for special treatment include a history of serious, repetitive, and persistent criminal conduct—although there are important differences among prosecutors' offices with respect to the relative weights given to the different characteristics or criminal history (Harper and McGillis, 1977; Withcomb, 1980; Rhodes et al., 1982). Some officials think a few serious crimes—even if widely separated in time—would qualify an offender for special attention; others pay much closer attention to the rate and persistence of criminality and worry less about the seriousness of the offense. The special treatment to which offenders are exposed includes special efforts to gather, preserve, and protect evidence in the case; charges filed at the highest possible level sustainable at trial; restrictions on plea bargaining; and prompt trials. The aim is to increase the likelihood that those with a serious record will be convicted and to extend sentences for those who are convicted.

This change in prosecutorial procedures can also be understood in both retributive and utilitarian terms. The retributive justification is the same as that for habitual offender sentencing laws: that offenders with long records have shown themselves to be unusually unrepentent and careless of society's values and, therefore, unusually deserving of punishment. The utilitarian justification is that offenders who have committed crimes repeatedly in the past are particularly likely to commit crimes in the future, and, therefore, it is particularly valuable to focus scarce prosecutorial time on ensuring that these unusually dangerous offenders will be punished and incapacitated.

Obviously, this focus on criminal record and characteristics of the offenders is related to the question of prediction. To the extent that a utilitarian logic motivates the shift from the focus on current offenses to past offenses and to the extent that past offenses predict future conduct well, one can argue that prediction has crept into prosecutorial decision making and is therefore sanctioned by current practice. Nonetheless, it would probably be more accurate to say that predictions of dangerousness have not yet been as systematically or as explicitly introduced into prosecutorial decision making as they have into sentencing decisions or even bail decisions. So, explicit use of predictions of dangerousness is not yet sanctioned by current prosecutorial practice. The important ethical questions are whether such methods would be constitutional and consistent with moral intuitions about the criminal justice system.

At the outset, the idea of selective prosecutions focused on those predicted to be dangerous seems to threaten the principles of equal protection and due process. Indeed, it seems even more threatening if dangerous offenders are prosecuted more determinedly for relatively minor offenses or for charges in which the evidence is relatively weak (Moore et al., 1984:141–142). As noted above, if prosecutors organized an overwhelming onslaught against a dangerous offender charged with a serious crime, or if they kept prosecuting dangerous offenders for vagrancy or disorderly conduct, or if they kept bringing robbery cases on the basis of trumped-up evidence, they would have crossed an important line that makes our system of justice fair and restrained.

The interesting question, however, is not at the extremes but in the middle range. Should prosecutors give a slightly more vigorous and determined prosecution to cases involving dangerous offenders? A vigorous prosecution could mean enhanced effort in cases of serious crime in which the evidence was very strong—refusing to accept plea bargains, conducting extensive collateral investigations, or moving very quickly in a case in which there were strong physical evidence and eyewitnesses. It could also mean a greater willingness to prosecute less serious offenses where the evidence was strong—for example, holding out for a felony conviction in a case of gun possession when the testimony of two police officers is corroborated by a witness. Or, it could mean being willing to risk failure in prosecuting a serious crime in which the evidence was well above the constitutional standard but much less than the usual prosecutorial standard of 90 percent certainty to win at trial—for example, a robbery case in which there is no physical evidence and the eyewitness testimony is shaky. It is in these areas that a selective focus among prosecutors would operate, and it is the justice of these actions that must be considered.

As a constitutional matter, it seems fairly clear that prosecutors do have the leeway to establish principles for adjusting levels of prosecutorial effort among offenders as long as the principle serves some legitimate social purpose, and as long as the policies are not based on an unjustifiable standard (such as race, religion, or social class), the motives of the prosecutor are not vindictive, and the policies are not designed to frustrate defendants in their exercise of constitutional rights, such as freedom of speech, assembly, and religion (Cardinale and Feldman, 1978:659–692; Vorenberg, 1981). While there have been a few cases in which the mere exercise of discretion was found objectionable on equal protection grounds (*Village of Fairlawn* v. *Fuller*, 8 Ohio Misc. 266, 221 N.E. 2d 851), the dominant court opinion has been that it was not sufficient for a defendant to show that offenders escaped punishment [*Oyler* v. *Boyles*, 368 U.S. (1962); *Washington* v. *United States*, 401 F.2d 915, 925 (D.C. Cir. 1968)]. On the other hand, where prosecutors seem to have been motivated by arbitrary, racially tainted standards, or where they seem to have been guided by vindictiveness, the courts have found constitutional violations [*Yick Wo* v. *Hopkins*, 118 U.S. 356 (1886); *People* v. *Utica Daw's Drug Co.*, 16 A.D.2d 12, 225 N.Y.S.2d 128 (1962); *United States* v. *Berrios*, 501 F.2d 1207 (2d Cir. 1974)]. But in showing discriminatory enforcements the courts have generally placed the burden on defendants (*People* v. *Utica Daw's Drug Co.*). Such cases do not affirmatively establish a license for prosecutors to vary levels of effort according to predictions of future criminality. But to the extent that such predictions were accepted by the courts as a legitimate law enforcement purpose and they were formulated in a way that avoided any taint of arbitrariness or racial bias, the courts would probably accept the policies as within the range of prosecutorial discretion. Indeed, what makes the conclusion seem particularly justifiable is not so much that the court countenances predictions as that the court has been extremely reluctant to exercise any control over prosecutorial discretion at all. As Judge (now Chief Justice) Burger wrote in *Newman* v. *United States*, 382 F.2d 429, 480 (D.C. Cir. 1967): "Few subjects are less adapted to judicial review than the exercise by the Executor of his discretion in deciding when and whether to institute criminal proceedings. . . ."

If established legal principles are not a bar, what about moral intuitions? Here, one is once again plunged into the general discussion of deontological objections to and utilitarian justifications for prediction. The only difference is that here we are talking about "special" prosecutorial efforts, and much turns on what is meant by "special." If what is meant is nothing more than special efforts to collect and preserve evidence and to proceed quickly to trial, surely there is little objection. Although an interest in "fairness" among defenders might be violated, one can reasonably argue that offenders do not have a constitutional or even moral right to the ordinary, sloppy prosecution they receive in today's overburdened criminal justice system. And, since no due process issue is raised, this kind of "special treatment" seems acceptable.

Somewhat more worrisome are those concerns related to due process: that defendants might be overawed by zealous prosecutors, that the trial process might be contaminated if it was known that a defendant was one of those predicted to be dangerous, and that the balance between the resources available to defense and prosecution might be upset. All of these are important because they affect the substantive findings of guilt or innocence and do so in a way that violates the defendant's rights to due process and the community's interest in being sure that justice is being done.

There are answers to these concerns. Special procedures could be developed to make sure that judges and juries were unaware of the special status of the offenders to avoid the informal introduction of prejudicial information at trial. Special resources could be made available to the defense as well as the prosecutor in cases involving those predicted to be dangerous. And by developing prediction criteria based on an extensive criminal record, we could guarantee that the defendants who were vulnerable to the special prosecution were relatively experienced offenders who would not easily be frightened by a prosecutor's bluffs and threats. But none of these answers is wholly satisfactory.

As is generally the case, the decision comes down to a balance among the community's interest in security, the defendant's interest in avoiding criminal liability, and a broad social interest in guaranteeing certain standards of justice. In striking the balance, many see special prosecutions as particularly threatening to standards of justice since they may have a decisive effect on the question of guilt or innocence. Hence, they judge the defendant's rights and interests to weigh more heavily in this regard than in sentencing decisions. And this would clearly be true if a defendant was being prosecuted for the first time. But the more interesting question is whether special prosecution would be inappropriate when a defendant has already been convicted of several offenses *and* when he is predicted to be dangerous. Arguably, this is more acceptable because it makes it less likely that the defendant will be overawed and may, in any event, diminish the defendant's rights in the same way that they seem to be diminished in determining sentences.

PREDICTION AND BLAMEWORTHINESS

After one has been through the intellectual contortions of evaluating prediction-based criminal justice decisions from retributive and utilitarian perspectives, and, as a general idea and in particular applications, one longs for a simpler view. The very complexity of the analysis weakens its credibility.

In my view this complexity is unnecessary. It is forced on us by a recently found sophistication in reasoning about this issue. Indeed, the sharp distinction drawn between retributive and utilitarian positions that is the cornerstone of much contemporary analysis obscures a far simpler and more coherent view. This simpler view depends on seeing what is common to retributive and utilitarian views rather than what is different. The idea that emerges is unfamiliar and unconventional in today's debates, but I think it might be treated as commonplace and obvious in a world in which the current distinctions were less firmly and sharply drawn.

The contemporary view of retributive theories is that they properly focus the attention of the criminal justice system on current acts rather than the character of offenders. It is the criminal act that provides the justification for punishment. The more serious the act, the more serious the punishment.

There is much to commend this position. It connects to more primitive ideas of justice as vengeance without being hostage to the excessive passions and penalties that might characterize private vengeance. The offense is against the community and the state—not a private individual. The response is regulated by concerns for equal protection and due process—not the strength of the victim's comrades. It also turns out to be a position that limits the state's interest and surveillance to narrow areas marked by actual criminal offenses (Moore, 1983:17–42). This not only protects much of social life from government scrutiny but also guarantees that, when the state's interest is engaged, it is focused on an area in which it can do some good rather than mischief. And the focus on acts prevents the society from developing any permanent view of the character and status of criminal offenders (von Hirsch, 1981a:599). All this seems to strike a nice balance between the community's interests in simultaneously engaging state power to protect a limited number of community values and preventing the state itself from becoming too powerful and intrusive.

Attractive as the focus on acts seems to be, however, it produces some curious anomalies when used to explain our current criminal laws. The most glaring is the importance that the criminal law attaches to the mental state of the offender at the time he committed the offense. If the act itself is so important to criminal punishment, one might expect many criminal statutes to establish strict liability for criminal offenses. In fact, however, strict liability is very rare in criminal statutes (Packer, 1968:121–131). It is generally important that some demonstration be made that the offender willed an act as well as that the act occurred. Similarly, there are many diminished-competence defenses and statuses (including mental illness, compulsion, and youth) that mitigate blameworthiness by casting doubt on whether the offender was in fact the author of the act in the sense that the outcome of the act was a complete expression of what the offender wanted. Finally, under some circumstances (defined in the law of "entrapment"), government complicity in a crime can absolve an offender. Thus, anything that drives a wedge between a criminal act and the intention of the offender tends to mitigate guilt because it confuses our capacity to infer criminal intentions from criminal acts. So, the act alone is not sufficient for criminal responsibility. The intention to do the crime—to deny the values of the society—must be shown, as well as the act.

What is even more surprising is that a harmful act is not even necessary for criminal responsibility. Laws that make attempts or conspiracies to commit crimes vulnerable to criminal prosecution essentially make a durable, visible intention to do a crime worthy of punishment even if the substantive offense never occurs (Packer, 1968:100–101). True, these laws typically carry less severe penalties than the completed offenses would justify. And true, some overt acts are necessary to trigger the investigation and provide proof of a durable criminal intention. But the point is that the acts are important not in themselves but only as they afford insight into the intentions of offenders, and it is the intentions alone that justify punishment.

So, even though we are accustomed to thinking of acts as the most essential focus of the criminal justice system, a harmful act is neither sufficient nor even necessary for findings of "blameworthiness." Intention, on the other hand, which seems less essential, is not only necessary for criminal responsibility, but sufficient itself! One possible implication of these observations is that it is criminal intention—the willing rejection of society's values, including that obligation to respect the life, liberty, and property of others—that justifies the punishment. The act is important not only in itself but also and most fundamentally as an objective piece of evidence about the intentions, values, and character of citizens.

If this interpretation were accepted, it would also help to explain why most people—including many retributivists—believe that it is appropriate to adjust the severity of criminal justice sanctions in response to prior criminal acts as well as to the seriousness of current criminal offenses. This is true regardless of whether the criminal justice sanction in question involves sentencing and is established through statutes (as in habitual offender statutes) or involves prosecution and is established by administrative fiat (as in the establishment of "career criminal units"). This position is problematic, however, to a strict retributive position that ties criminal liability only to acts.

The inconsistency can be resolved in three ways. One is to point out that the series of offenses indicates that an offender is unusually resistant to learning from punishment and therefore more punishment is called for. This may make sense, but it is a utilitarian rather than a retributive argument. A second argument is that the fourth robbery is somehow worse than the first and therefore is more deserving of punishment. But that is simply an assertion. The obvious question that is unanswered is exactly what makes the fourth robbery worse.

A third argument, which seems more satisfactory, is that the criminal law adjusts penalties for offenses on the basis of what can be discerned about intention and character and that a series of offenses reveals an offender as clearly more willing to commit crimes than others and, therefore, as more deserving of punishment. We all understand that criminal offenses can be caused by circumstance and transient passion as well as by clear intention. When we look at first offenders, it is quite possible that their values and character—their commitment to the society's values—are much like everybody else's and that they were simply unlucky enough to stumble into a situation that produced an uncharacteristic offense. When we look at someone who has committed many offenses, however, the hypothesis that the offender is much like everyone else in terms of his values must yield to the alternative hypothesis that the values are different: the offender is less solicitous of and more willing to attack the lives, liberty, and property of fellow citizens. It is this increased certainty about the offender's values that justifies enhanced punishment.

So, there is a certain coherence in thinking of retributive conceptions of justice as being concerned about the intentions, values, and character of offenders as well as their acts. This is important, for if intentions and character are durable (i.e., if people have guiding values that last for at least a little while), past actions of offenders might well predict future actions. Consequently, a policy that sanctioned extra punishment for past repeated criminal acts would produce about the same results as a policy that adjusted penalties on the basis of predictions of future criminal acts. Thus, retributive and utilitarian justifications coalesce in a focus on those who have revealed their intentions and capacity to commit criminal acts through a pattern of past offenses. What ties these principles together is the argument that character—relatively durable values and intentions—is fundamental to both retributive and utilitarian justifications for punishment.

Note that to accept the idea that character is durable and fundamental to both retributive and utilitarian justifications for punishment is not to accept the idea that it is permanent. People's values and intentions can change. Even the most cynical might excuse offenders who had aged and matured before their just penalties were served and be reluctant to exact the maximum penalties from those 20-year-olds who committed many offenses, on the grounds that such offenders might change. So, we need not decide that character is permanent to decide that it is somewhat durable and relevant to criminal justice decisions.

If this interest in character provides the basis for a synthesis of retributive and utilitarian principles, why is it an unfamiliar idea? My answer is that this idea runs counter to a dominant ideology guiding criminal justice policy. Central to that ideology is the idea that moralism must be kept out of the criminal law because the passions that would be released if it were invited in are uncontrollable (Gillers, 1983:402). The focus on the intentions and values of offenders—indeed the argument that it is *wrong* values as revealed by acts that justify punishment—puts values at the center of the criminal justice system and thus runs directly counter to the dominant ideology. Perhaps equally important, we have been guided by a hopeful view of human nature: human character is transient, changeable, and influenceable; guilt for current offenses is therefore always mitigated; and bright hopes for rehabilitation are reasonable. The focus on durable character treats the role of outside influence as morally irrelevant and is less optimistic about the rate at which important changes in values can occur. So, the focus on character flies in the face of ideologies that have been central to our contemporary jurisprudence.

Obviously, no one is interested in unleashing a new age of moral oppression. We value our freedom, our mobility, our ability to experiment with different values far too highly for this. But it does seem valuable to remind ourselves of some simple principles we seem to have forgotten: that the criminal law is a moral statement about the values that bind our society together by imposing minimal obligations on one another; that the society insists that people honor those laws and the values that lie behind them; and that, when a person clearly shows an indifference to those obligations through his or her actions, the society has a right to respond with indignation moderated by concerns for due process and equal protection. This set of principles sanctions an interest in character—in those who have committed offenses in the past and will do so in the future. At the same time, it limits the reach of the system to those who have committed offenses in the past. It does not try to reach for extra state control through improved techniques of prediction that provide less satisfactory ways of exploring character than prior criminal conduct.

SUMMARY AND CONCLUSIONS

Our shared vision of the world of criminal offenses and criminal justice policy has become a great deal more complicated than it once was. We now think of criminal offenses as the result of accidents and transient passions as well as considered intentions. We think of criminal justice decision making as discretionary and relying on professional knowledge and expertise rather than automatic application of well-established principles. Simple notions of justice that combined concern for justice with ordinary prudence have become elaborate, sharply differentiated ethical theories emphasizing retributive or utilitarian aims of criminal justice policy. So, it is hard to find the thread of decency and justice in proposing criminal justice policies.

Into this tangled and overburdened world come proposals to make wider use of improved prediction techniques in targeting offenders for investigation and prosecution, in setting bail, and in imposing sentences. The appeal of such techniques comes from their apparent potential to produce greater community security from the financially (and morally) limited capacities of the state to punish, and to impose some rational order on what is otherwise a crazy-quilt pattern of discretionary decision making that leaves great room for injustice.

But there are problems with the idea of relying on predictive tests. To retributivists, it seems wrong to impose criminal liabilities on the basis of predictions of further criminal acts. To many others, it seems wrong to impose liabilities on people who are falsely predicted to commit crimes in the future. Still others worry about the characteristics that will be used in the predictive tests, thinking that it would be wrong to use characteristics that were not under the control of the offender and were not themselves criminal in nature. And there are always the questions of exactly at what point in the criminal justice process the tests would be applied and what consequences the use of the tests would have for criminal offenders.

One can wrestle with these questions at many levels. It seems to me, however, that the easiest way through this tangle is to be guided by two principles: First, the best guide to both blameworthiness and future criminal conduct is prior criminal offenses. Second, it is a virtue to be economical in the use of the state's moral and financial capacity to punish and control.

If accepted, these principles would have the following implications:

- That predictive or discriminating tests should be designed to identify a small and distinctive element of the offending population.
- That the tests should be based predominantly on prior criminal conduct.
- That no one should be identified as, or predicted to be, dangerous who does not have repeated adult criminal convictions on his or her record.
- That juvenile records of serious offenses could be used for purposes of discerning dangerousness or predicting future crimes if a person committed serious offenses soon after graduating from the juvenile justice system.
- That the use of information on indictments and arrests *in addition to convictions* can be used in the tests and is probably to be preferred to the use of employment or marital data.
- That the required accuracy of the tests should be consistent with the size of the practical benefits of the test and with the size of the burdens imposed on defendants.
- That the tests could be used not only

for sentencing, but also for targeting investigations and prosecutions.

- That the additional liability at sentencing should be limited by the seriousness of the offense for which the person was convicted.
- That the additional liability at investigation and prosecution stages be exposure to more vigorous investigation and prosecution but within due process protections.
- That the principal justification for using improved prediction techniques at the bail stage would be to reduce the use of pretrial detention, guarantee that detention is focused on the most dangerous offenders, and rationalize the current chaotic system.
- That the tests be thought of less as prediction techniques and more as a way of focusing attention on those offenders who have revealed tendencies to be unusually dangerous through their past acts.

These proposals may have the effect of dampening some of the technocratic enthusiasm for prediction. But in my view that is their virtue rather than their vice.

REFERENCES AND BIBLIOGRAPHY

American Friends Service Committee
1971 *Struggle for Justice: A Report on Crime and Punishment in America.* New York: Hill and Wang.

Andreano, Ralph, and Siegfried, John J., eds.
1980 *The Economics of Crime.* New York: John Wiley & Sons.

Attorney General's Task Force on Violent Crime
1981 *Final Report.* Washington, D.C.: U.S. Department of Justice.

Bedau, H.
1977 Concessions to retribution in punishment. In J. Cederblom and W. Blizek, eds., *Justice and Punishment.* Cambridge, Mass.: Ballinger.

Blumstein, Alfred, Cohen, Jacqueline, and Nagin, Daniel, eds.
1978 *Deterrence and Incapacitation: Estimating the Effects of Criminal Sanctions on Crime Rates.* Washington, D.C.: National Academy of Sciences.

Blumstein, Alfred, Cohen, Jacqueline, Martin, Susan E., and Tonry, Michael, eds.
1983a *Research on Sentencing: The Search for Reform.* Vol. I. Washington, D.C.: National Academy Press.
1983b *Research on Sentencing: The Search for Reform.* Vol. II. Washington, D.C.: National Academy Press.

Boland, Barbara
1983 Identifying serious offenders. In Mark H. Moore, Susan Estrich, Daniel McGillis, and William Spelman, eds. *Dealing With Dangerous Offenders, Vol. II: Selected Papers.* John F. Kennedy School of Government. Cambridge, Mass.: Harvard University.

Boland, Barbara, and Wilson, James Q.
1978 Age, crime and punishment. *Public Interest* 51:22–35.

Brown, Peter
1981 Assessing officials. In Joel L. Fleischman, *Public Duties.* Cambridge, Mass.: Harvard University Press.

Caplan, Gerald M., ed.
1983 *ABSCAM Ethics: Moral Issues and Deception in Law Enforcement.* Washington, D.C.: The Police Foundation.

Cardinale, Philip J., and Feldman, Steven
1978 The federal courts and the right of nondiscriminatory administration of the criminal law: a critical view. *Syracuse Law Review* 29:659–692.

Carrington, Frank
1983 *Crime and Justice: A Conservative Strategy.* Washington, D.C.: The Heritage Foundation.

Cederblom, J., and Blizek, W., eds.
1977 *Justice and Punishment.* Cambridge, Mass.: Ballinger.

Chelimsky, Eleanor, and Dahmann, Judith
1981 *Career Criminal Program: National Evaluation: Final Report.* Washington, D.C.: U.S. Government Printing Office.

Collins, James, J.
1978 *Offender Career and Restraints: Probabilities and Policy Implications.* Philadelphia, Pa.: University of Philadelphia Press.

Curtis, Lynn A., ed.
1985 *American Violence and Public Policy.* New Haven, Conn.: Yale University Press.

Dawson, Robert O.
1969 *Sentencing.* Boston, Mass.: Little, Brown.

Dershowitz, Alan
1973 Preventive confinement: a suggested framework for constitutional analysis. *Texas Law Review* 51:1277–1324.
1974 The origins of preventive confinement in Anglo American law. *University of Cincinnati Law Review* 43:1–60, 781–846.

1976 Background paper. In Twentieth Century Fund Task Force on Criminal Sentencing. *Fair and Certain Punishment*. New York: McGraw-Hill.

Eck, John E.
1983 Investigative strategies for identifying dangerous repeat offenders. In Mark H. Moore, Susan Estrich, Daniel McGillis, and William Spelman, eds. *Dealing with Dangerous Offenders, Vol. II: Selected Papers*. John F. Kennedy School of Government. Cambridge, Mass.: Harvard University.

Fabricant, Neil
1968 Bail as preferred freedom and the failures of New York's revision. *Buffalo Law Review* 18:303–315.

Fleischman, Joel L., ed.
1981 *Public Duties*. Cambridge, Mass.: Harvard University Press.

Fletcher, George
1978 *Rethinking Criminal Law*. Boston, Mass.: Little, Brown.

Floud, Jean, and Young, Warren
1981 *Dangerousness and Criminal Justice*. London, England: Heinemann.

Foote, Caleb
1965 The coming constitutional crisis in bail: I. *University of Pennsylvania Law Review* 113:959–999.

Forst, Brian, and Brosi, Kathleen B.
1977 A theoretical and empirical analysis of the prosecutor. *Journal of Legal Studies* 6:177–191.

Frankel, Marvin E.
1973 *Criminal Sentences: Law Without Order*. New York: Hill and Wang.

Frankena, William K.
1973 *Ethics*. 2nd ed. Englewood Cliffs, N.J.: Prentice Hall.

Freed, Daniel
1982 Dangerous Offenders and the Bail Process: Protecting Public Safety Without Preventive Detention. Unpublished paper. Yale University, New Haven, Conn.

Gaynes, Elizabeth
1982 *Typology of State Laws Which Permit the Consideration of Danger in the Pretrial Release Decision*. Washington, D.C.: Pretrial Services Resources Center.

Gillers, Stephen
1983 Selective incapacitation: does it offer more or less? *Record of the Association of the Bar of the City of New York* 38 (4).

Golding, Martin P., ed.
1966 *The Nature of Law*. New York: Random House.

Goldkamp, John
1979 *Two Classes of Accused: A Study of Bail and Detention in American Justice*. Cambridge, Mass.: Ballinger.

Greenwood, Peter, with Abrahamse, Allan
1982 *Selective Incapacitation*. Santa Monica, Calif.: Rand.

Greenwood, Peter, Chaiken, Jan, and Petersilia, Joan
1977 *The Criminal Investigation Process*. Lexington, Mass.: Heath.

Harper, Andrew, and McGillis, Daniel
1977 *The Major Offense Bureau: An Exemplary Project*. Washington, D.C.: U.S. Government Printing Office.

Hart, H. L. A.
1968a *Law, Liberty and Morality*. Stanford, Calif.: Stanford University Press.
1968b *Punishment and Responsibility*. New York: Oxford University Press.

Institute for Judicial Administration and American Bar Association
1977 *Standards for Juvenile Justice*. Cambridge, Mass.: Ballinger.

Institute for Law and Social Research
1976a *Case Screening*. Briefing Paper No. 2. Washington, D.C.: Institute for Law and Social Research.
1976b *Uniform Case Evaluation and Rating*. Briefing Paper No. 3. Washington, D.C.: Institute for Law and Social Research.
1977 *Curbing the Repeat Offender: A Strategy for Prosecutors*.Washington, D.C.: U.S. Government Printing Office.

Kaplan, John
1965 The prosecutorial discretion. *Northwestern Law Review* 60:174–193.

Klepper, Steven, Nagin, Daniel, and Tierney, Luke-Jon
1983 Discrimination in the criminal justice system. Pp. 55–128 in Alfred Blumstein, Jacqueline Cohen, Susan E. Martin, and Michael Tonry, eds., *Research on Sentencing: The Search for Reform*. Vol. II. Washington, D.C.: National Academy Press.

Lazar Institute
1981 *Pretrial Release: A National Evaluation of Practices and Outcomes*. Washington, D.C.: Lazar Institute.

Lindsey, Edward
1925 Historical sketch of the indeterminate sentence and parole system. *Journal of Criminal Law and Criminology* 16.

Martinson, Robert
1974 What works: questions and answers about prison reform. *Public Interest* 35:22–54.

McNamara, Richard B.
1982 *Constitutional Limitations on Criminal Procedure.* New York: McGraw-Hill.

McNeely, R. L., and Pope, Carl E., eds.
1981 *Race, Crime and Criminal Justice.* Beverly Hills, Calif.: Sage Publications.

Meehl, Paul E.
1954 *Clinical Versus Statistical Prediction: A Theoretical Analysis and a Review of the Evidence.* Minneapolis: University of Minnesota Press.

Mitford, J.
1973 *Kind and Usual Punishment: The Prisoner's Business.* New York: Knopf.

Monahan, John
1981 *Predicting Violent Behavior.* Beverly Hills, Calif.: Sage Publications.
1982 The case for prediction in the modified desert model of criminal sentencing. *International Journal of Law and Psychiatry* 5:103–113.

Monahan, John, and Steadman, Henry
1983 Crime and mental disorder: an epidemiological approach. Pp. 145–189 in Michael Tonry and Norval Morris, eds., *Crime and Justice: An Annual Review of Research.* Vol. 4. Chicago, Ill.: University of Chicago Press.

Moore, Mark H.
1983 Invisible offenses: a challenge to minimally intrusive law enforcement. Pp. 17–42 in Gerald M. Caplan, ed., *ABSCAM Ethics: Moral Issues and Deception in Law Enforcement.* Washington, D.C.: The Police Foundation.

Moore, Mark H., Estrich, Susan R., McGillis, Daniel, and Spelman, William
1983a *Dealing With Dangerous Offenders, Vol. I: Final Report.* John F. Kennedy School of Government. Cambridge, Mass.: Harvard University.
1983b *Dealing With Dangerous Offenders, Vol. II: Selected Papers.* John F. Kennedy School of Government. Cambridge, Mass.: Harvard University.
1984 *Dangerous Offenders: The Elusive Target of Justice.* Cambridge, Mass.: Harvard University Press.

Morris, Herbert
1976 Persons and Punishment. Pp. 31–63 in Herbert Morris, ed., *On Guilt and Innocence: Essays in Legal Philosophy and Moral Psychology.* Berkeley: University of California Press.

Morris, Norval
1974 *The Future of Imprisonment.* Chicago, Ill.: University of Chicago Press.
1982 *Madness and the Criminal Law.* Chicago, Ill.: University of Chicago Press.

Morris, Norval, and Miller, Marc
1985 Predictions of Dangerousness. Pp. 1–50 in Michael Tonry and Norval Morris, eds., *Crime and Justice: An Annual Review of Research,* Vol. 6. Chicago, Ill.: University of Chicago Press.

Morris, Norval, and Tonry, Michael, eds.
1983 *Crime and Justice: An Annual Review of Research.* Vol. 3. Chicago, Ill.: University of Chicago Press.

Nagel, Stuart, and Neef, Marian G.
1977 *The Legal Process.* Beverly Hills, Calif: Sage Publications.

National Institute of Justice
1981 *Pretrial Release: A National Evaluation of Practices and Outcomes.* Washington, D.C.: U.S. Department of Justice.

Packer, Herbert
1968 *The Limits of the Criminal Sanction.* Stanford, Calif.: Stanford University Press.

Petersilia, Joan
1983 *Racial Disparities in the Criminal Justice System.* Santa Monica, Calif.: Rand.

President's Commission on Law Enforcement and the Administration of Justice
1967a *The Challenge of Crime in a Free Society.* Washington, D.C.: U.S. Government Printing Office.
1967b *Task Force Report: Juvenile Delinquency.* Washington, D.C.: U.S. Government Printing Office.

Rawls, John
1972 *A Theory of Justice.* Cambridge, Mass.: Harvard University Press.

Reiff, Robert
1979 *The Invisible Victim.* New York: Basic Books.

Rhodes, William, Tyson, Herbert, Weekly, James, Conly, Catherine, and Powell, Gustave
1982 Developing Criteria for Identifying Career Criminals. Unpublished paper. Institute for Law and Social Research, Washington, D.C.

Roth, Jeffery A., and Wice, Paul B.
1980 *Pretrial Release and Misconduct in the District of Columbia.* Washington, D.C.: Institute for Law and Social Research.

Sellin, Thorsten, and Wolfgang, Marvin E.
1964 *The Measurement of Delinquency.* New York: John Wiley & Sons.

Sherman, Michael, and Hawkins, Gordon
1981 *Imprisonment in America.* Chicago, Ill.: University of Chicago Press.

Silberman, Charles E.
1978 *Criminal Justice, Criminal Violence.* New York: Random House.

Singer, Richard G.
1979 *Just Deserts: Sentencing Based on Equality and Desert.* Cambridge, Mass.: Ballinger.

Steffel, Linda
1977 *The Law and the Dangerous Criminal.* Lexington, Mass.: Lexington Books.

Stone, Alan
1975 *Mental Health and the Law: A System in Transition.* Washington, D.C.: U.S. Government Printing Office.

Szasz, Thomas
1977 *Psychiatric Slavery.* New York: Free Press.

Twentieth Century Fund
1978 *Confronting Youth Crime.* New York: Holmes and Meier.

Twentieth Century Fund Task Force on Criminal Sentencing
1976 *Fair and Certain Punishment.* New York: McGraw-Hill.

Underwood, Barbara
1979 Law and the crystal ball: predicting behavior with statistical inference and individualized justice. *Yale Law Journal* 88:1432–1447.

van den Haag, Ernest
1975 *Punishing Criminals: Concerning a Very Old and Painful Question.* New York: Basic Books.

Vera Institute of Justice
1976 *Impact Evaluation of the Victim/Witness Assistance Project's Appearance Management Activities.* New York: Vera Institute of Justice.
1977 *Felony Arrests: Their Prosecution and Disposition in New York City Courts.* New York: Vera Institute of Justice.

von Hirsch, Andrew
1976 *Doing Justice: The Choice of Punishments.* New York: Hill and Wang.
1981a Desert and previous convictions in sentencing. *Minnesota Law Review* 65:591–634.
1981b Utilitarian sentencing suscitated: the American Bar Association's second report on criminal sentencing. *Rutgers Law Review* 33:772–789.
1983 Commensurability and crime prevention. *Journal of Criminal Law and Criminology* 74:209–248.
1984a "Equality," "anisonomy," and justice: a review of "Madness and the Criminal Law." *Michigan Law Review* 82:1093–1112.
1984b The eithics of selective incapacitation: observations on the contemporary debate. *Crime and Delinquency* 30:175–194.
1985 *Past and Future Crimes.* New Brunswick, N.J.: Rutgers University Press.

von Hirsch, Andrew, and Gottfredson, Don M.
1983–1984 Selective incapacitation: some queries about research design and equity. *New York University Review of Law and Social Change* VII:11–45.

Vorenberg, James
1981 Decent restraint of prosecutorial power. *Harvard Law Review* 94:1521–1573.

Walker, Nigel
1982 Unscientific, unwise, unprofitable or unjust? *British Journal of Criminology* 22:276–289.

Weinreb, Lloyd L.
1979 *Denial of Justice.* New York: Macmillan.

Wilson, James Q.
1983a *Crime and Public Policy.* Cambridge, Mass.: Harvard University Press.
1983b *Thinking About Crime.* 2nd rev. ed. New York: Basic Books.

Winston, Kenneth
1974 On treating like cases alike. *California Law Review* 62:1–39.

Wish, Eric D., Klumpp, Kandace, Moorer, Amy, Brady, Elizabeth, and Williams, Kristen
1981 *An Analysis of Drugs and Crime Among Arrestees in the District of Columbia.* Washington, D.C.: U.S. Department of Justice.

Withcomb, Debra
1980 *Major Violator Unit, San Diego California: An Exemplary Project.* Washington, D.C.: U.S. Government Printing Office.

Wolfgang, Marvin E., and Tracy, Paul E.
1983 The 1945 and 1958 birth cohorts: a comparison of the prevalence, incidence and severity of delinquent behavior. In Mark H. Moore, Susan R. Estrich, Daniel McGillis, and William Spelman, eds., *Dealing With Dangerous Offenders, Vol. II: Selected Papers.* John F. Kennedy School of Government. Cambridge, Mass.: Harvard University.

Zimring, Franklin L.
1977 Making the punishment fit the crime: a consumer's guide to sentencing reform. *University of Chicago Law School Occasional Papers* No. 12.
1978 Background paper. In Twentieth Century Fund, *Confronting Youth Crime.* New York: Holmes and Meier.

9

Dynamic Models of Criminal Careers

Christopher Flinn

BEHAVIORAL MODELS IN CRIMINAL CAREER RESEARCH

Economists have long been interested in the determinants of criminal activity (e.g., Bentham, 1780), but only in the past few decades have economic applications in this field of inquiry become something of a growth industry (see, for example, Schmidt and Witte, 1984, and references therein). A number of models of individual decision making have been applied to the problem of criminal activity, and those models share several common features. First, they all posit rational behavior on the part of individuals, in that, subject to a set of constraints facing the individual, a function characterizing the individual's preferences is maximized. Second, all models recognize that risk is an essential component of the decision to engage in criminal activity. In contrast to the purchase of a can of soup, which has a virtually certain level of ultimate satisfaction associated with consumption of the product, the eventual level of satisfaction associated with the decision to undertake criminal activity can only be described probabilistically. All models of criminal activity, then, must include some method by which the potential outcomes of risky activities can be evaluated. Third, attention is typically restricted to monetary or monetarized yields from criminal activity. In particular, the "psychic" rewards (whether positive or negative) obtained from criminal activity are not explicitly modeled. The aversion that many neoclassical economists have to explaining differentials in behavior through differences in preferences is reflected in the strong and controversial assumption that individuals have identical preferences;[1] all differences

[1]Christopher Flinn is associate professor, Department of Economics, University of Wisconsin-Madison. The author is indebted to his colleagues Arthur Goldberger and Charles Manski for many valuable discussions and comments. Detailed discussions with Alfred Blumstein, Jacqueline Cohen, and John Lehoczky were extremely helpful in preparing this revision. Glen Cain and Ariel Pakes also provided helpful comments. This research was partially supported by a grant from the Sloan Foundation to the Institute for Research on Poverty at the University of Wisconsin-Madison.

[1]Alternatively, it is assumed that differences may be captured in some simple, parametric manner.

in behavior arise through differences in the choice sets individuals face. Finally, the theoretical models that have been formulated are essentially static in nature; they do not take account of how the criminal and legitimate opportunities expected to prevail in the future affect current decisions about criminal activity. Owing to the neglect of these intertemporal considerations, it might be claimed, no theory of rational criminal choice has as yet been rigorously formulated.

The report of the Panel on Deterrence and Incapacitation (Blumstein, Cohen, and Nagin, 1978) cited a need for increased behavioral and statistical modeling at the individual level of analysis. In the second part of this paper an econometric model of the criminal career is presented that is designed for use with individual-level data. While this econometric model is not explicitly derived from a behavioral model, it does provide a relatively general statistical representation of criminal careers, and the parameters of the model may be interpreted in the context of standard behavioral theories of criminal activity choice.

In the first part of this paper, behavioral models of criminal activity are developed to begin to address the issue of what type of criminal careers these models might generate. To this end, analytic results are presented when possible; alternatively, some limited simulation experiments are presented when analytic results are not available. These behavioral models are also used as a baseline against which some of the statistical models used in this field of inquiry can be evaluated. (Some discussion along these lines is contained in the second part of this paper.) Many behavioral assumptions are implicit in the statistical descriptions of criminal careers, and it may be of some interest to assess the value of various statistical models not only in terms of their ability to predict behavior (which is typically quite low, see Chaiken and Chaiken, 1981, for example), but also in terms of the degree of correspondence between characteristics of the statistical model and characteristics of a consistent, dynamic model of decision making and criminal activity. The converse is also obviously true; current empirical knowledge regarding the dynamics of criminal careers must be used as a guide in the construction and evaluation of any theoretical model that purports to describe the criminal activity decision over time.

Structural models of decision making also serve a related purpose. They are often required for an assessment of the effects of changes in the distributions of rewards and punishments associated with criminal activity on the amount of time spent on those activities. The practical need for structural models was insightfully presented by Marschak (1953). To paraphrase Marschak's argument, say we are interested in the development of a model to explain some measure of the degree or intensity of criminal activity, denoted by x. Generally speaking, individual differences in x may arise from differences in earnings potentials in legitimate activities (e), background characteristics (b), the distributions of rewards associated with criminal activities (R), and distributions of penalties if apprehended (P). Then we assume there exists a functional relationship among these characteristics $x = x(e, b, R, P; \mathbf{\Omega})$, where $\mathbf{\Omega}$ is the vector of parameters that, in conjunction with the functional form $x(\cdot)$, completely characterizes the relationship between x and the characteristics e, b, R, P. In this case a decision-theoretic model may be of use in guiding our choice of a functional specification of $x(\cdot)$; but once the function is selected the determination of the effects of the exogenous variables on x is simply an empirical matter. The qualitative and quantitative effects of all exogenous variables are contained in the parameter estimates $\hat{\mathbf{\Omega}}$.

Such an empirically based strategy has at least one advantage over a highly structured approach to the problem. By specifying a flexible functional form for $x(\cdot)$, we are likely to be able to capture the observed relationships among the variables well—that is, we will be able to fit the data. We would then be able to assess the effects of changes in the distributions of punishments on the level of criminal activity, for example, comparing $\tilde{x} = x(e, b, R, \tilde{P}; \hat{\mathbf{\Omega}})$ with $\hat{x} = x(e, b, R, P; \hat{\mathbf{\Omega}})$, where $\tilde{P}$ denotes the "new" punishment distribution. This evaluation is straightforward even if x is a highly nonlinear function.

This approach runs into one major problem in practice, however. If we are to estimate the parameters associated with the exogenous variables, those attributes must exhibit a sufficient degree of sample variability. If we want to assess the effects of the distribution of punishments on criminal activity, the sample members cannot all be subject to the same set of punishment distributions. If all individuals are subject to the same P, at least one element of the parameter vector $\mathbf{\Omega}$ will not be estimable. Even if a few different values of P are present in the sample, thus making it possible to estimate all elements in $\mathbf{\Omega}$, sample variability in P may be so low as to preclude precise estimation of $\mathbf{\Omega}$. The choice the analyst has is to ignore the effects of characteristics that vary little or not at all across sample members or to formulate a behavioral model in which those characteristics appear as parameters. For example, assume R and P vary little or not at all in the sample. Following the first option, we would estimate a function of the form $x = x_a(e, b; \mathbf{\Theta})$, where x_a is the new functional form and $\mathbf{\Theta}$ is the new parameter vector. It is impossible to say anything concerning the effect of changes in R and P on x. Following the second option, we would estimate a function of the form $x = x_b(e, b; R, P, \mathbf{\Delta})$, where we treat R and P as parametric to the problem, and $\mathbf{\Delta}$ is a vector of other parameters. The functional form of x_b will be derived from an explicit behavioral model. Using this approach it will be possible to perform conceptual experiments in which the effects of changes in R and P on x are analyzed. Thus, this "structural" approach to modeling behavior is not pursued for reasons of aesthetics; it enables the analyst to perform conceptual experiments that are not possible with models less closely linked with behavioral theory.

Dynamic Models of Criminal Behavior

In this section three models of the proportion of time allocated to criminal activity are developed to analyze how this allocation of time changes as a function of the individual's age and as a function of criminal career. All models are definitionally simplifications of and abstractions from the "real" world. It may be disquieting to some to view criminal behavior simply as the outcome of a rational calculus. However, if behavior is a manifestation of conscious choice, it seems necessary to posit that individuals make decisions in a way that is consistent with some underlying set of preferences or view of the alternatives facing them. In the models discussed below, individuals are assumed to act rationally.[2] Their pref-

[2]In our legal system, individuals charged with crimes are "punished" when found guilty at least partially because the commission of the crime is held to have been an outcome of conscious choice. Only when individuals are adjudicated to have been noncompetent at the time of the crime are they not held legally responsible for the crime they are found guilty of committing. Thus, rationality only requires that individuals make consistent choices with respect to some objective and given the choice sets they face. It is a large leap from the assumption of rationality, *per se*, to the simple utility-maximization

erences and choices are specified in a deliberately limited way. In terms of areas of potential application, these models may be useful in the analysis of the rates at which various types of property crimes are committed. (The symbols used in this section are listed below for easy reference.)

θ_t	Proportion of time devoted to criminal activity in period t ($0 \le \theta_t \le 1$).
w_t	Legitimate work wage rate in period t.
H_t	The individual's criminal record as of time t (e.g., arrests, time in prison).
c^*	Consumption flow from incarceration.
$P(\theta_t)$	Probability of arrest in period t.
Y_{it}	Total monetarized returns from criminal activity in period t for individual i.
$F_i(Y_{it} \vert \theta)$	The conditional distribution function of criminal rewards.
$U(c)$	The utility of consumption level c.
δ_i	The parameter describing the conditional expectation of rewards in criminal activity for individual $i[E_i(Y \vert \theta) = \delta_i \theta]$.
$G(\delta)$	The distribution function of δ in the population.
τ	Sentence length if arrested.
β	Discount factor ($0 \le \beta < 1$).
η	The parameter describing the probability of incarceration function [$P(\theta) = \eta\theta$].
V	Value of being free at the beginning of any period in the constant-wage model.
α	The increment to wage rates for each period of nonincarceration.
$V(w_t)$	Value of being free for individual with current wage w_t in changing-wage model.
S_t	Previous number of arrests as of period t.
$\tau(S_t)$	Sentence length function.
$V(S_t)$	Value of being free for individual with arrest record S_t in variable-sentence-length model.

models developed below. Unfortunately, it is often the case that discussions of the manner in which criminal behavior should be modeled conclude with the claim that rational-choice models are too simplistic to be useful. The point is not whether rationality is a reasonable assumption; no social science investigation can be attempted without it. The correct point is that current attempts at behavioral modeling of criminal behavior using the expected-utility-maximization principle are unquestionably overly simplistic. Realistically, to capture the dynamics of criminal behavior adequately, structural models will have to evolve substantially.

All three models have a number of common features. Individuals are assumed to be infinitely lived, or, equivalently, to have an unknown length of life (T) which is distributed as an exponential random variable. Since the vast majority of individuals seriously engaged in criminal activity are inactive after age 40, the assumption of infinitely lived individuals is not artificial for purposes of analysis.[3] Within the context of these dynamic behavorial models, the individual's time-allocation decision will be investigated. The proportion of time spent in crime in period t is denoted θ_t. The total amount of time in each period of life is normalized

[3]Explicitly incorporating finiteness of life would considerably complicate the analysis, and the substantive results would be unchanged.

to 1. The remainder of time in each period $(1 - \theta_t)$ is spent in "legitimate" market work, which is compensated at a rate w_t. Leisure is ignored in what follows, or, equivalently, the leisure decision is assumed to be exogenous to the criminal activity decision, and the time to be allocated between market work and criminal activity is the residual (total time in period minus leisure).

It is also assumed that no capital markets exist so that individuals cannot borrow or lend money in any period. Total consumption in any given period, then, is purchased solely with contemporaneous income if the individual is not incarcerated at any time during the period. This lack of the existence of capital markets is a limitation of the model; however, for purposes of studying behavior in the criminally active subpopulation, it may not be entirely unrealistic.

Unlike legitimate activity, criminal behavior is "risky" in a particular sense. If an individual is caught engaging in criminal activity, he or she is incarcerated for a total of $\tau(H_{t-1})$ periods beginning with the period in which apprehension occurs, where H_{t-1} denotes the individual's criminal record through period $t - 1$. Thus, if apprehension occurs in period t, the individual will be incarcerated for periods $t, t + 1, t + \tau(H_{t-1}) - 1$. Note that sentence length is a deterministic function of the individual's criminal history, which at the beginning of period t is summarized by H_{t-1}. In general, it is reasonable to assume that the sentence length is an increasing function of the number of previous arrests, past time served in prison, or other observable characteristics of previous criminal activity. While incarcerated, the individual has a consumption level c^* each period.

The probability of being apprehended for criminal action in a period is a function of the amount of criminal activity engaged in over the period. This functional relationship is expressed as $P_t = P(\theta_t)$, where $P(\cdot)$ is monotonically increasing in θ_t and $P(0) = 0$, that is, if the individual is not criminally active in the period, there is a zero probability of apprehension. It is not necessarily the case that $P(1) = 1$; that is, "full-time" criminals are not necessarily certain to be apprehended. In general, $P(1) \leq 1$. Note that individual apprehension probabilities are a function of current period activities only, not of criminal activities in previous periods.

To complete the specification of the choice set individuals face, we next consider the potential rewards from criminal activity. Let the total monetary and psychic rewards from criminal activity in period t for individual i be denoted Y_{it}. When the time-allocation decision is made in period t, the final outcome or realization of Y_{it} is unknown. Each individual does know the distribution of rewards he or she faces conditional on the time devoted to criminal activity. The conditional distribution function for individual i is given by $F_i(Y_{it}|\theta)$. Unlike the other parameters of the problem, these conditional distribution functions differ across population members. This variation is meant to capture, in an admittedly limited way, the notion that individuals differ in their valuation of rewards from criminal activity. For all individuals, we assume that increases in θ, criminal activity, will increase the expected value of criminal rewards in the period. By the assumptions below, we do not need to consider the effect of θ on higher-order moments of the distribution.

Finally, we must consider the total valuation of rewards from legitimate activities. Conditional on not being apprehended in period t, the expected utility of individual i in period t is given by

$$E\, U_{it}(\theta_{it}, S) = \int U[(1 - \theta_{it})w + Y]\, dF_i(Y|\theta_{it}), \quad (1)$$

where it is assumed that $E_i(Y|\theta_{it})$ is bounded for θ_{it} in the unit interval, and where S (success) indicates that the individual was not apprehended in the period.

In what follows we will assume that individuals are risk neutral, so that $U(x) = x$. This is done for reasons of tractability and because there seems to be no compelling reason to make differences in attitudes toward risk the basis of a model of differential criminal activity. Then Equation 1 becomes

$$E\ U_{it}(\theta_{it}, S) = (1 - \theta_{it})w_t + \int Y\, dF_i(Y|\theta_{it}). \quad (2)$$

The last term on the right-hand side of Equation 2 is the expectation of criminal rewards in period t conditional on an activity level θ_{it}. We will consider the case in which conditional expectation is linear, $E_i(Y|\theta_{it}) = \delta_i\theta_{it}$. This would be true, for example, if the distribution of rewards was normal. The heterogeneity in individual valuations of criminal rewards is reflected in the fact that δ_i in the conditional expectation function varies across individuals in the population. The population distribution of δ is given by $G(\delta)$, defined over the interval $[\underline{\delta}, \bar{\delta}]$.

Now we can state for the current period the expected utility associated with a level of criminal activity θ_{it}. First, note that, given success, the expected utility from action θ_{it} is given by $(1 - \theta_{it})w_t + \delta_i\theta_{it}$ and the probability of not being apprehended is $1 - P(\theta_{it})$. If the individual is apprehended and incarcerated, the utility yield is a certain c^*, and the probability of this occurring is $P(\theta_{it})$. Then expected utility in period t is

$$E\ U_{it}(\theta_{it}) = [1 - P(\theta_{it})]\,[(1 - \theta_{it})w_t + \delta_i\theta_{it}] + P(\theta_{it})\,c^*. \quad (3)$$

Before proceeding to the three dynamic models, a few obvious restrictions on the parameters in this model should be noted. First, if $c^* > w_t$, there is no incentive not to engage in criminal behavior, for even if incarcerated, the individual would have a higher consumption value that when engaged in any level of market work. Second, assuming $c^* < w_t$, it must be the case that $\delta_i > w_t$ for at least some individuals in the population or no criminal activity would be undertaken. These restrictions are

$$w_t > c^* \quad (4a)$$

$$\bar{\delta} > w_t. \quad (4b)$$

Note that for any individual with a value of δ that satisfies the inequality $\delta \leq w_t$, no criminal activity will be undertaken in period t.[4] The analyses below pertain only to individuals with $\delta > w_t$; all others will optimally choose not to engage in criminal activity. Let us turn to the consideration of dynamic behavior under three specifications of constraints on criminal choices.

The Constant-Wage Model

To begin, we consider the case in which the wage of each individual in the population is fixed over time: $w_t = w$, $t = 0, 1, \ldots$. We will also begin by assuming that conditional on apprehension, sentence length is the same for all individuals, regardless of criminal history, so $\tau(H_{t-1}) = \tau$, $t = 1, 2, \ldots$. Since we assume individuals are infinitely lived and that the choices individuals face are constant over time (but may differ across individuals), each individual will devote the same amount of time to criminal activity in each period in which not initially incarcerated. For an individual, the constant rate of criminal activity, θ^*, will be a function of the parameters characterizing preferences and constraints. In this first

[4]This condition is strictly correct only if the wage sequence $w_1, w_2, \ldots$ is increasing, which is the case in all models considered here.

simple model, $\theta^* = \theta^*(c^*, \delta, P(\cdot), w, \tau)$. (The individual subscript i has been dropped for notational simplicity.) We now turn to an investigation of the function θ^*.

Denote the value of being free (not incarcerated) at the beginning of any period by V. Conditional on choice of θ in the period, an individual's expected utility given that he is not incarcerated is $(1 - \theta)w + \delta\theta + \beta V$. The term βV is interpreted as follows. If the individual is not incarcerated in this period, he will be free to make a time-allocation decision next period. By the structure of this problem, the value of the decision is given by V. But rewards in the future are not perceived by individuals to be as valuable as rewards today. The rate at which individuals discount future rewards is given by the discount factor β $(0 \leq \beta < 1)$. (If $\beta = 0$, individuals completely ignore the effect of their current actions on future choices. As β approaches 1, individuals consider current and future rewards as virtually perfect substitutes.) Thus the value of being free next period, evaluated as of this period, is βV. The probability of not becoming incarcerated is $1 - P(\theta)$.

The "value" of becoming incarcerated during the period is determined in the following way. If incarcerated, the individual will serve τ periods in prison, beginning today. The value of being in prison in the current period is c^*; as of today, the value of being in jail next period is βc^*; and for m periods from now, it is $\beta^m c^*$. Then the utility yield during the period of incarceration is $\sum_{i=0}^{\tau-1} \beta^i c^*$. In addition, the individual will be free to allocate time optimally in τ periods—the value of this is $\beta^\tau V$. Then the total value of incarceration is $\sum_{i=0}^{\tau-1} \beta^i c^* + \beta^\tau V$. The probability of incarceration is $P(\theta)$.

When we combine all the elements discussed above, the maximum value of the individual's time allocation problem in all periods when he is not incarcerated as of the beginning of the period is given by

$$V = \max_{0 \leq \theta \leq 1} \left\{ [1 - P(\theta)][(1 - \theta)w + \delta\theta + \beta V] + P(\theta) \left(\sum_{i=0}^{\tau-1} \beta^i c^* + \beta^\tau V \right) \right\}. \quad (5)$$

To simplify discussion, we make a further assumption about functional form. Let the conditional probability of apprehension $[P(\theta)]$ be given by $P(\theta) = \eta\theta$, $0 < \eta \leq 1$. Then we have

$$V = \max_{0 \leq \theta \leq 1} \left\{ (1 - \eta\theta)[(1 - \theta)w + \delta\theta + \beta V] + \eta\theta \left[c^* \sum_{i=0}^{\tau-1} \beta^i + \beta^\tau V \right] \right\}. \quad (5')$$

Denote by $\tilde{\theta}^*$ the amount of time devoted to criminal activity not taking into account the restriction that this is a proportion lying in the unit interval. Then $\tilde{\theta}^*$ is given by

$$\tilde{\theta}^* = [2\eta(\delta - w)]^{-1} \left[\delta - w(1 + \eta) - \eta\beta V + \eta c^* \sum_{i=0}^{\tau-1} \beta^i + \eta\beta^\tau V \right]. \quad (6)$$

The solution to Equation 5′ is denoted θ^*. Then

$$\theta^* = \begin{cases} 0 \text{ if } \tilde{\theta}^* \leq 0 \\ \tilde{\theta}^* \text{ if } 0 < \tilde{\theta}^* < 1 \\ 1 \text{ if } \tilde{\theta}^* \geq 1. \end{cases} \quad (7)$$

If $\theta^* = 0$ or $\theta^* = 1$, we say that the individual's time-allocation problem yields a corner solution. If $\theta^* = 0$, the individual is always engaging in legitimate activity; if $\theta^* = 1$, he is a "full-time" criminal. An interior solution exists if $0 < \theta^* < 1$; in this case the individual devotes some time to criminal activity and some time to legitimate activity.

For this model it is possible to find a closed-form solution in the following manner. Note that V is defined by

$$V = (1 - \eta\theta^*)[(1 - \theta^*)w + \delta\theta^* + \beta V] + \eta\theta^*\left(c^* \sum_{i=0}^{\tau-1} \beta^i + \beta^\tau V\right). \quad (8)$$

Solving for V, we obtain

$$V = [1 - \beta(1 - \eta\theta^*) - \eta\theta^*\beta^\tau]^{-1} \cdot \left[(1 - \eta\theta^*)[(1 - \theta^*)w + \delta\theta^*] + \eta\theta^* c^* \sum_{i=0}^{\tau-1} \beta^i\right]. \quad (9)$$

This can be written as

$$V = \frac{a_0 + a_1\theta^* + a_2(\theta^*)^2}{b_0 + b_1\theta^*} \quad (9')$$

where $a_0 = w$, $a_1 = \delta - w(1 + \eta) + \eta c^* \sum_{i=0}^{\tau-1} \beta^i$, $a_2 = \eta(w - \delta)$, $b_0 = 1 - \beta$, and $b_1 = \eta(\beta - \beta^\tau)$. From Equation 6, write

$$\theta^* = c + dV, \quad (6')$$

where $c = [2\eta(\delta - w)]^{-1}[\delta - w(1 + \eta) + \eta c \sum_{i=0}^{\tau-1} \beta^i]$ and $d = [2(\delta - w)]^{-1}(\beta^\tau - \beta)$.

Substituting Equation 9′ into 6′,

$$(\theta^*)^2 + e\theta^* + q = 0,$$

where $e = 2b_0/b_1$ and $q = (b_1 a_2)^{-1}(a_1 b_0 - b_1 a_0)$.

Thus the solution for θ^* is given by

$$\theta^* = -b_0/b_1 + \left[\frac{b_0^2 a_2 - a_1 b_0 b_1 + b_1^2 a_0}{b_1^2 a_2}\right]^{1/2}. \quad (10)$$

Since a closed-form solution is available for the proportion of time spent in criminal activity, determining the qualitative effect of changes in the parameters (η, β, w, δ, c^*, τ) on behavior is straightforward. Qualitatively, the following results hold:

$$\frac{\partial\tilde{\theta}^*}{\partial\delta} \geq 0; \frac{\partial\tilde{\theta}^*}{\partial c^*} \geq 0; \frac{\partial\tilde{\theta}^*}{\partial\tau} \leq 0; \frac{\partial\tilde{\theta}}{\partial\eta} \leq 0; \frac{\partial\tilde{\theta}^*}{\partial w} \leq 0. \quad (11)$$

That is, an increase in the expected marginal rate of return to criminal activity δ results in an increase in the rate of criminal activity. The rate of criminal activity also is increasing in the utility associated with "failure" (incarceration), which is given by parameter c^*. As punishments increase in length (τ), criminal activity declines. Increases in the marginal arrest rate (η) result in decreases in crime rates. An increase in the direct opportunity cost of crime, the wage rate in legitimate work (w), causes decreases in the rate of crime.

Results of this type have been obtained previously in a number of static rational-choice models of criminal behavior. In fact, if sentence length τ is equal to 1, this model reduces to a series of static optimization problems. By allowing $\tau \geq 2$, individuals face one of two choice problems at the beginning of each period. If they are not incarcerated at the beginning of the period, they choose the amount of time to engage in criminal activity θ and as noted above, in this model, they will always set θ to the same value. If they begin the period incarcerated, their utility for the current period is predetermined at the value c^*.

The only parameter that reflects the dynamics of the problem, aside from the sentence length τ, is the discount factor β. In this model the sign of $\partial\theta^*/\partial\beta$ is ambiguous. This partial derivative can be computed in a straightforward manner, but the result is not particularly enlightening. The intuition is basically the following. In any period in which individuals are free initially, their expected current period utility is given by Equation 3 and by the assumptions of the model, $E\ U(\theta^*) > c^*$ for each individual in the population. If the sentence length is τ periods, the difference in expected utility of freedom versus incarceration is $(1 + \beta + \beta^2 + \ldots + \beta^{\tau-1})\ [E\ U(\theta^*) - c^*]$. Holding constant θ^*, an increase in β increases this cost. However, for any finite-length sentence τ, an infinitely lived individual (or an individual with a sufficiently long but finite life) will eventually be released. The value of being free at the time of the release is $\beta^\tau V$. As β approaches 1, $\beta^\tau \rightarrow \beta$ so the value of being free at the beginning of the period τ periods from the present ($\beta^\tau V$) approaches the value of being free next period (βV). At the same time, as $\beta \rightarrow 1$, the value of the optimization problem goes to infinity. Thus, the penalty $(1 + \beta + \ldots + \beta^{\tau-1})\ [E\ U(\theta^*) - c^*]$ becomes insignificant, and this results in increases in criminal activity. Which effect will dominate depends on the values of all the parameters in the model.

By the assumptions of this model, individuals commit a constant rate of crime over their lifetime, which is contradictory to the empirical evidence that exists. In the model in the next section, criminal activity decreases, on average, as individuals age.

Accumulation of Human Capital in Legitimate Activity

Using the constant-wage model, the proportion of time nonincarcerated individuals devote to criminal activity remains constant as they age. This simple model can be modified in several ways so as to produce the result that the crime is a decreasing function of age. One obvious modification is to allow the returns from legal and illegal activity to be age dependent. Intuitively, if the difference between returns from legitimate work and expected returns from criminal activity diminishes over time, other things equal, the crime rate will decrease with age, (Recall that it was necessary to assume that the expected returns from crime were strictly greater than the legitimate wage if we were to observe any criminal activity. As the legitimate wage approaches the expected returns from crime, we will observe a continuous decline in the crime rate of an individual.)

The approach taken in this section is to hold the expected returns from criminal activity constant but to allow the legitimate wage to change systematically over the life cycle as a result of individual behavior and random events. While it would be desirable to allow the expected returns from criminal activity to vary systematically over the life cycle also, such an extension would add greatly to the complexity of the model. Furthermore, what is really of interest is the difference between expected rewards from criminal activity and legitimate work. Thus, it is somewhat inconsequential whether we model the change in this difference as resulting from shifts in the legitimate wage, the expected returns from crime, or both.

There exists a voluminous literature on the subject of human capital accumulation. For a statement of the general theory, see Becker (1975). We will assume here that there is no accumulation of crime-specific human capital—that is, individuals do not become more proficient criminals as they acquire criminal experience. Market wage rates do increase as individuals acquire market experience, however. We will characterize this dependency in the following way. In period t, when the amount of criminal activity is given by θ_t, we will say that the individual accumulates a total of $(1 - \theta_t)$ units of experience if not incarcerated during the period. If incarcerated during the period, he accumulates no market experience. Similarly, if incarcerated at the beginning of the period—he is not free—he accumulates no market experience. The amount of market-related human capital the individual has at the beginning of period t will be denoted by h_t. The wage rate an individual faces in the period will be assumed equal to $h_t(w_t = h_t)$. The amount of human capital the individual possesses at the beginning of period t is defined in the following way. First, define a variable: $\hat{\theta}_k = \theta_k^*$ if the individual was not incarcerated during period k; $\hat{\theta}_k = 1$ if incarcerated during period k. Then, the total amount of market experience the individual has at the beginning of period t is

$$\sum_{k=1}^{t-1} (1 - \hat{\theta}_k) .$$

Market-related human capital is assumed to be a simple transformation of market experience,

$$h_t = g\left[\sum_{k=1}^{t-1} (1 - \hat{\theta}_k)\right], \qquad (12)$$

where g is a monotonically increasing function; human capital is increasing in labor market experience.

The choices an individual can make at any time t depend on his past allocation of time, $\{\theta_k^*\}_{k=1}^{t-1}$, in all periods when free, and on luck—that is, how often he was incarcerated in the past. These are the sources of variation in the sequence $\{\hat{\theta}_k\}_{k=1}^{t-1}$, which determine beginning of period t human capital, and hence the period t wage rate.

At any age, $t = 1, 2, \cdots$, individuals will in general be differentiated according to their stock of human capital. Consider an individual making a time-allocation decision in period t. His choice of a rate of criminal activity will depend on wage rate for the current period h_t. This wage rate changes over time and is a state variable. An individual in state h_t faces the optimization problem

$$V(w_t) = \max_{0 \le \theta_t \le 1} \Bigg\{(1 - \eta\theta_t)\{(1 - \theta_t)w_t + \delta\theta_t + \beta V[w_{t+1}(\theta_t, w_t)]\} + \eta\theta_t\left[c^* \sum_{i=0}^{\tau-1} \beta^i + \beta^\tau V(w_t)\right]\Bigg\}, \qquad (13)$$

where $w_{t+1}(\theta_t, w_t)$ denotes the fact that given the wage rate in period t (w_t), the time allocated to criminal activity (θ_t), and the fact that the individual was not incarcerated during the period, the period $t + 1$ wage is known with certainty. The function $w_{t+1}(\theta_t, w_t)$ is decreasing in the amount of time spent in criminal activity and increasing in the previous wage rate. Note that, if an individual is incarcerated in period t, when he is released in period $t + \tau$ he will be able to work at the same wage as in period t. Thus we have assumed an absence of stigma—the effect of jail on wages is simply an absence of growth, not a decline.

In the changing-wage model there exist a number of additional costs of criminal activity. To review the structure of the model, the costs are as follows:

1. In the current period t, if the individual is not incarcerated, the opportunity cost of crime is simply forgone market work, which is remunerated at rate w_t.
2. In period t, increased criminal activity increases the probability of incarceration. The difference between the level of expected utility as a free individual and that obtained as a prisoner, multiplied by the increase in the probability of being incarcerated, is an additional cost of increased criminal activity.
3. Conditional on the current wage rate w_t, increases in criminal activity de-

crease next period's wage w_{t+1} (given no incarceration in period t) owing to forgone human capital accumulation. Since the expected utility of all individuals is an increasing function of the market wage in all periods, the lower future wage rate must lower expected utility levels in future periods.

4. Increased criminal activity leads to an increased probability of incarceration, and, while incarcerated for τ periods, the individual does not accumulate any market capital. This represents a permanent wage reduction in future periods, or a persistent effect of incarceration.

Solving Equation 13 turns out to be quite difficult in practice, even for simple forms of the human capital accumulation function g. Therefore, for the remainder of this section the discussion is confined to the following special case. We will assume that as long as an individual is not incarcerated during period t, his wage will increase by α in period $t + 1$. Then, $w_{t+1} = w_t + \alpha$ (given no incarceration in period t). Given that the individual is not incarcerated in period t, the period $t + 1$ wage is independent of $\theta_t[w_{t+1}(\theta_t, w_t) = w_{t+1}(w_t)]$. The cost referred to in Point 3 above is absent. However, Point 4 is still operative—increased crime increases the probability of incarceration, which is associated with forgone human capital accumulation.

With this simplification, Equation 13 can be rewritten

$$V(w_t) = \max_{0 \leq \theta_t \leq 1} \Big\{ (1 - \eta\theta_t)[(1 - \theta_t)w_t + \delta\theta_t + \beta V(w_t + \alpha)] + \eta\theta_t \Big[c^* \sum_{i=0}^{\tau-1} \beta^i + \beta^\tau V(w_t) \Big] \Big\}. \qquad (13')$$

Now the individual's time-allocation problem depends on the set of parameters in the constant-wage model, plus the wage-growth parameter α. Unlike the constant-wage model, it is not possible to find closed-form solutions for $\tilde{\theta}^*(w_t)$ or $V(w_t)$, so numerical methods must be used to investigate quantitative properties of these functions. However, all the comparative static results in Equation 11 hold for the changing-wage model, and, in addition, $\partial\tilde{\theta}_t^*/\partial\alpha < 0$—the larger the wage increment, the lower the crime rate, for the larger is the opportunity cost of incarceration.

Finally, some numerical examples will illustrate the individual-level and aggregative characteristics of this model. These computations do not constitute an exhaustive study of the Function 13′; rather they demonstrate the types of criminal careers that can be generated by this simple model. The parameter values selected for this illustration were not chosen after an exhaustive search. It appears that this model can generate "interesting" career patterns (i.e., not all corner solutions) without extensive search over the parameter space.

The actual parameter values chosen are arbitrary. The initial wage level (w_1) is set to .5. Then Condition 4a is imposed by setting $w_1 > c^*$ and, in particular, setting $c^* = 0$. The wage increment (α) is set to .05. The discount factor (β) is equal to .8, the arrest parameter (η) is set to .5, and the sentence length (τ) is set to three periods. All individuals face these same parameters; however, two distinct values of δ are assumed to exist in the population. The conditional expectation parameter is given the value 3 for 50 percent of the population, and the value 2 for the other 50 percent. The $\delta = 3$ individuals are "high crime" types and the $\delta = 2$ individuals are "low crime" types.

In Table 1 the amount of time devoted to criminal activity is shown as a function of the beginning-of-period wage level for both population groups. Note that both types devote substantial amounts of time to crime at initial wage level .5. Criminal activity quickly drops off for the low-crime types—no criminal activity occurs at a wage of .8. This is not the case for the high-crime types—criminal activity only ceases at a wage of 1.25. In particular, at wage .8, when low-crime types cease criminal activity, the high-crime types still devote 43 percent of their time to criminal activity.

Using the decision rule given in Table 1, we can investigate patterns of individual offending in the population. The procedure used is straightforward. Consider low-crime individuals. In period 1, their wage is .5 and consequently they spend 43 percent of their time in criminal activity. Since η = .5 and the probability of incarceration is $\eta\theta$, in the first period the probability of arrest is .215. A random number generator is used to determine the outcome of this chance event. If arrested, they are sent to jail in period 1 and not released until period $\tau + 1$ (period 4 in the case $\tau = 3$). If not arrested, they are free at the beginning of period 2 with a wage of .55. The process is repeated in this manner for 50 periods of life for each of 1,000 "individuals" in the low- and in the high-crime groups.

In Table 2 the total amount of crime committed by the cohort, the total number of arrests, and the beginning-of-period jail population are displayed. Note that, initially, high-crime individuals are responsible for a bit less than 60 percent of total crime. By period 10, they are responsible for 90 percent of total crime, and by period 20, they are responsible for virtually all crime. This obviously has implications for identification of high- and low-crime offenders. Classification of individuals arrested in period 1 into low- and high-crime types involves a substantial amount of error. An individual arrested in period 20, however, may be classified with virtual certainty as a high-crime type. An even more accurate classification can be made if the wage rate of the arrested individual is available. From Table 1 we know that, if an individual with a wage greater than or equal to .8 is arrested, he must be a high-crime type. At wages less than .8 the relative likelihoods are given by the ratio of column three and column two.

TABLE 1 Time Allocation to Criminal Activity Given Wage Growth with Constant Sentence Length

Wage Level	Low-Crime Types	High-Crime Types
0.5	.4305	.6007
0.55	.3726	.5774
0.6	.3082	.5524
0.65	.2370	.5258
0.7	.1590	.4972
0.75	.0747	.4663
0.8	0.0	.4330
0.85		.3969
0.9		.3579
0.95		.3156
1.0		.2698
1.05		.2205
1.1		.1675
1.15		.1111
1.2		.0515
1.25		0.0

Note that while these results indicate the potential for identifying members of population subgroups, no individual is incorrigible. By altering the wage rates of high-crime types or lowering their expected return from criminal activity, these individuals, once identified, can be induced to spend the same or less time in crime than the other group in the population.

Increasing Penalties for Criminal Activity

In the last section it was demonstrated that as the benefits of legitimate market work increase, on average, over the life

TABLE 2 Aggregate Crime Statistics in Simulated Population Given Wage Growth with Constant Sentence Length; 1,000 Individuals in Each of High- and Low-Crime Groups

	Total Crime		Arrests		Jail Population	
Period	Low	High	Low	High	Low	High
1	430.4	600.7	214	301	0	0
2	292.9	403.6	143	201	214	301
3	198.2	275.1	92	144	357	502
4	222.7	366.9	112	188	235	345
5	192.6	365.8	92	200	204	332
6	138.6	322.2	67	161	204	388
7	105.7	328.6	54	158	159	361
8	92.1	343.2	48	151	121	319
9	64.3	334.5	30	172	102	309
10	40.3	314.9	22	158	78	323
11	35.4	300.8	17	150	52	330
12	24.6	298.3	14	164	39	308
13	13.5	278.6	8	115	31	314
14	11.4	277.5	11	153	22	279
15	7.4	264.5	1	126	19	268
16	4.0	235.6	3	100	12	279
17	4.4	237.6	0	114	4	226
18	2.6	217.8	1	112	3	214
19	1.4	186.3	2	92	1	226
20	0.6	172.3	1	86	3	204
25	0.0	89.2	0	48	0	121
30	0.0	42.4	0	20	0	47
35	0.0	10.2	0	7	0	17
40	0.0	1.5	0	0	0	8
45	0.0	0.4	0	1	0	1
50	0.0	0.2	0	0	0	0

cycle, the rate of criminal activity decreases with age. In this section the manner in which differential sentencing would produce the same relationship between age and the rate of criminal activity is examined.

As with the constant-wage model, we assume that legitimate market wages w are constant over time so that we can isolate the sentencing effect. Previously, we assumed that sentence lengths τ were constant, which is obviously not the case in practice. Not only do sentence lengths differ by type of crime, the length of a sentence typically depends on the number of times the individual has previously been convicted of criminal activity. We will continue to confine our attention to one crime type. We will be concerned only with modeling the dependence of sentence length on the number of past convictions for this one type of crime.

In this model we define a new state variable, S_t, which denotes the number of previous convictions as of the beginning of period t. Sentence length is no longer a constant, but is a function $\tau(S_t)$, where it is reasonable to assume $\tau(0) \leq \tau(1) \leq \ldots$. The rewards for legitimate work are the same in all periods, as are rewards for criminal activity if successful. Only the punishments change as a consequence of changes in the state variable S_t. The individual's time-allocation problem is

$$V(S_t) = \max_{0 \leq \theta_t \leq 1} \Bigg\{ (1 - \eta\theta_t)[(1 - \theta_t)w + \delta\theta_t + \beta V] + \eta\theta_t \Bigg[c^* \sum_{i=0}^{\tau(S_t)-1} \beta^i + \beta^{\tau(S_t)} V(S_t + 1) \Bigg] \Bigg\}. \quad (14)$$

Corresponding to this problem there exists a solution $\theta^*(S_t)$. The ordering of the solutions is $\theta^*(0) \geq \theta^*(1) \geq \theta^*(2) \geq \ldots$. The larger are the differences in the sentence length function $\tau(k) - \tau(k - 1)$, $k = 1, 2, \ldots$, the larger are the differences $\theta^*(k) - \theta^*(k - 1)$. (Note that large changes in τ as a function of sentence length may result in individuals who originally devote a substantial amount of time to criminal activity eventually switching out of crime completely.)

An example similar to the one used above illustrates the characteristics of criminal careers generated by this model. All parameter values are exactly the same with the exception of the sentence length τ. In this model, τ is set to 1 if the individual has no prior convictions and is set to 5 if the individual has any prior convictions.

The decision rules are presented in Table 3. The amount of criminal activity for the low- and high-crime types is greater than was the case in Table 1, conditional on no previous arrests. This increased activity results in increased arrest probabilities, however, and, after one arrest, individuals devote less time to criminal activity than was the case in Table 1. After one arrest, a low-crime type receiving a wage of .5 will spend only about one-third as much time in criminal activity as was previously the case. High-crime types also substantially reduce criminal activity after one arrest but not to the same degree as low-crime types.

TABLE 3 Time Allocation to Criminal Activity Given Wage Growth with Varying Sentence Length

	Low-Crime Types		High-Crime Types	
Wage Level	No Arrests	Some Arrests	No Arrests	Some Arrests
0.5	.5711	.2176	.6693	.4786
0.55	.5525	.1326	.6513	.4466
0.6	.5374	.0406	.6330	.4117
0.65	.5242	0.0	.6145	.3734
0.7	.5098		.5962	.3313
0.75	.4937		.5786	.2851
0.8	.4755		.5621	.2345
0.85	.4544		.5472	.1796
0.9	.4297		.5343	.1204
0.95	.4004		.5233	.0574
1.0	.3652		.5137	0.0
1.05	.3222		.5042	
1.1	.2697		.4941	
1.15	.2058		.4832	
1.2	.1291		.4714	
1.25	.0392		.4587	
1.3	0.0		.4449	
1.35			.4298	
1.4			.4131	
1.45			.3945	
1.5			.3736	
1.55			.3499	
1.6			.3228	
1.65			.2915	
1.7			.2553	
1.75			.2132	
1.8			.1646	
1.85			.1089	
1.9			.0463	
1.95			0.0	

Aggregate statistics are presented in Table 4. Compared with Table 2, we see that a greater amount of crime occurs in the first few periods given varying sentence lengths, but eventually total crime is reduced as more individuals are subject to the stiffer sentence $\tau = 5$. The jail population is substantially smaller over the life of the cohort in this model.

Identification of Structural Models

The models proposed above were primarily designed to illustrate how various empirical regularities, such as the decline of crime rates with age, can be generated from dynamic behavioral models. As discussed earlier, such structural models may be preferable to less behaviorally motivated statistical models in that all parameters have relatively clear interpretations. Structural models are probably not useful when their structure precludes them, a priori, from reproducing salient empirical regularities.

If these structural models are to prove useful empirically, we must of course be able to obtain consistent estimates of all or most of the parameters in the decision rules. The first consideration is one of identification. What types of data are required to estimate one of these models? Let us consider the variable-sentence-length model presented above as an example.

The model with increasing sentence lengths is described by the following set of parameters: η, w, δ, β, c^*, $\pi(\cdot)$. Identification may proceed in the following way. First, recognize that the consumption value of being in prison (c^*) is arbitrary. Setting it to a given value essentially fixes the location of the utility index. It seems most natural to set $c^* = 0$. The rates of arrest, conviction, and incarceration may be computed from victimization surveys, which give an estimate of the total number of crimes committed (of a particular type). These, combined with the number of individuals incarcerated for the crime, will yield an estimate of η. Computing the sentencing function $\pi(\cdot)$

TABLE 4 Aggregate Crime Statistics in Simulated Population Given Wage Growth with Varying Sentence Length, 1,000 Individuals in Each of High- and Low-Crime Groups

	Total Crime		Arrests		Jail Population	
Period	Low	High	Low	High	Low	High
1	571.1	669.3	265	368	0	0
2	463.7	587.8	213	292	0	0
3	351.3	488.9	190	264	27	81
4	228.2	386.8	103	195	61	193
5	152.4	302.3	72	158	70	296
6	112.1	229.3	55	122	70	399
7	87.7	209.4	43	91	43	410
8	67.7	207.8	38	103	12	364
9	45.1	189.6	24	111	8	346
10	31.2	164.6	22	74	11	337
11	20.5	139.2	12	79	11	311
12	14.8	105.4	8	52	8	315
13	10.8	103.9	4	45	3	278
14	7.0	102.4	3	52	0	226
15	3.7	87.4	1	44	0	210
16	1.1	72.3	0	30	0	183
17	0.0	54.6	0	23	0	164
18	0.0	52.0	0	35	0	145
19	0.0	48.1	0	31	0	128
20	0.0	40.9	0	18	0	116
25	0.0	19.2	0	10	0	61
30	0.0	9.2	0	3	0	30
35	0.0	4.1	0	2	0	9
40	0.0	1.2	0	1	0	2
45	0.0	0.4	0	1	0	0
50	0.0	0.1	0	0	0	0

is also relatively straightforward. Either actual sentencing records may be used or official guidelines, when available.

The parameters β, w, and δ present more of a challenge. Often the value β is not estimated in analyses of this sort—it is merely set to a "reasonable" value, typically .9 or .95. Since criminally active individuals are often thought to discount the future rather heavily (that is, they have low values of β), in an analysis such as this it may be of interest to estimate β. This parameter is in principle identified in this model, at least if we are able to observe θ_t^*—the proportion of criminal activity in period t. The other individual-level data needed for purposes of identification are wage rates. Wage rates are obviously not identical over time and individuals—nor are they identical over time for the same individual. We can incorporate this observation by assuming $w_{it} \sim N(\mathbf{X}'_{it}\,\gamma, \sigma^2)$, for example, where $\mathbf{X}'_{it}$ is a vector of individual characteristics at time t and γ and σ^2 can be estimated. In periods when individuals are full-time criminals no wage will be observed, but by making a distribution assumption regarding w_{it}, data from such periods will still be informative for γ, σ^2.

Estimation of the parameter δ or its distribution in the population is the most difficult. It is not necessary to measure the returns from criminal activity to estimate this parameter, however. One could proceed in the following fashion. First, assume a form for the population distribution of δ, say $M(\delta, \xi)$, where ξ is a parameter vector that characterizes M. The likelihood of observing w_{it} and θ_{it}^* in a period can be constructed conditional on a value of δ. By taking the expected value of this conditional likelihood with respect to the distribution of δ, we can form an unconditional likelihood that depends on the parameters (γ, σ^2, β, ξ). By conjecture, for identification of ξ, β must be fixed. But note that in this analysis it is possible to estimate a rather abstract but interesting distribution $M(\delta, \xi)$, even if we assume that criminal rewards are not measurable or even operationally definable.

ECONOMETRIC MODELS OF CRIMINAL CAREERS

The dynamic models of the criminal career developed above are based on optimizing behavior. As discussed, there are advantages and disadvantages to the estimation of such highly structured models. In short, the principal advantage is unambiguous interpretation of parameter estimates and statistical tests. The principal disadvantages are the complicated computational algorithms that are required for estimation and the typically poor "explanatory" power of such models. Given the current level of understanding of the simple statistical properties of the criminal career process, perhaps it is beneficial to work with econometric models that are less closely linked with a specific behavioral model, but that allow for statistical associations precluded in any tractable decision-theoretic model. Actually, the choice is not between one approach or the other. Both can and should be used in any systematic study of the criminal career.

In this section the relevant theory is outlined and a relatively general framework is presented in which parameters of continuous time behavioral models may be estimated. The focus of the discussion is the econometric and statistical properties of continuous time models.

To fix ideas, consider a continuous time, discrete state space stochastic process X, where the state space consists of the nonnegative integers $S = Z^+$ and where the parameter set $T = (0, \infty)$. The state of the process at time t (s_t) indicates the number of times some event has occurred from the origin of the process, normalized at 0 without loss of generality, through time t. For example, say life began at time 0, and there is only one type of crime individuals can commit. Then s_t indicates the number of times an individual has committed this crime as of age t. Let the times at which crimes occur be given by $\tau_1, \tau_2, \ldots$. The number of crimes previously committed as of time t (s_t) is equal to s^* if and only if $\tau_{s^*} \leq t < \tau_{(s^* + 1)}$. Also, define the duration until the first crime as $w_1 = \tau_1 - 0 = \tau_1$. The duration of the kth spell, i.e., the elapsed time between crimes k and $k - 1$, is $w_k = \tau_k - \tau_{k-1}$.

The stochastic process can be characterized in a number of alternative ways. For the most part in this section the discussion is focused on the interval specification of the process. Starting from time 0, the process is characterized by the joint distribution of intervals between events, $F_n(w_1, w_2, \ldots, w_n)$, for $n = 1, 2, \ldots$.

In terms of a specific application to the analysis of criminal careers, the formalism above reduces to the following. Say an individual is born at time 0 and lives to age T ($T \leq \infty$). At each instant of life t ($0 \leq t \leq T$) the individual either commits a crime or does not. The length of time between successive criminal acts is, in general, not constant. Loosely speaking, the individual's propensity to commit a crime at some particular time $\tilde{t}$ depends not only on his or her "normal" rate of crime commission and the elapsed time since the last crime was committed but also on the opportunities for crime commission that exist at that particular moment. Thus, even if an individual would "normally" be highly likely to commit a crime at $\tilde{t}$, the fact that a police officer happened to be in close proximity would probably induce a postponement to a later date. Or the fact that an attractive "mark" appears may induce a crime before we would normally expect one. Unanticipated or anticipated changes in the choice sets of individuals will cause variations in criminal behavior over the life cycle, as the preceding section demonstrated. To the extent that those changes are not anticipated by the individual or observable to the analyst, the process of crime commission must be considered to be random. Then, the length of time from the beginning of life to the time the first crime is committed is w_1, which is a random variable. The distribution of w_1 is given by $F_1(w_1)$. Analogously, the length of time between the first and second commission (w_2) has distribution $F_2(w_2)$, and in general the duration of time between crime $(i - 1)$ and i is $F_i(w_i)$. The joint distribution over the first n crimes is given by $F_n(w_1, w_2, \ldots, w_n)$, as stated above.

To be useful for purposes of statistical (or theoretical) analysis of the criminal career, some structure must be imposed on the general joint distribution $F_n(w_1, w_2, \ldots, w_n)$. A natural starting point is to assume that, for a given individual, all spell lengths are independently distributed, i.e., the joint distribution of durations $w_1, w_2, \ldots, w_n$ can be written as

$$F(w_1, w_2, \ldots, w_n) = \prod_{i=1}^{n} F_i(w_i), \qquad \text{for } n = 1, 2, \ldots.$$

Simply stated for the case $n = 2$, this implies that the length of interval 1 does not alter our assessment of the likelihood of observing any particular value for the duration of the second spell.

By adding another assumption concerning the joint distribution of the spell lengths, we can produce a class of models often used in engineering and increasingly in the social sciences. If we assume that the distribution functions have the same (identical) form,

$$F_1(s) = F_2(s) = \ldots = F_n(s); \quad s \geq 0, n = 1, 2, \ldots,$$

then we can write the joint distribution of the first n spells as

$$F_n(w_1, w_2, \ldots, w_n) = \prod_{i=1}^{n} F(w_i).$$

A point process in which the spell lengths are independently and identically distributed (i.i.d.) is a *renewal process*.

If the common (to all spells) duration distribution is everywhere differentiable (as is assumed throughout this paper), there exists an associated probability density function $f(W)$. A renewal process can be completely characterized by $F(w)$ or $f(w)$, if it exists. Alternatively, it can be characterized by its hazard function $h(w)$, which is defined as

$$h(w) = \frac{f(w)}{1 - F(w)}, \qquad w \geq 0.$$

The hazard function is the conditional density of duration times given the individual has not committed a crime for a period of length w. The hazard function h is used in the econometric model formulated below.

One of the most important characteristics of a duration density from both a behavioral and statistical perspective is the degree and type of duration dependence exhibited. Duration dependence is most easily investigated through the hazard function. Simply differentiate $h(w)$ with respect to w, dh/dw. If

$$\left.\frac{dh(w)}{dw}\right|_s \gtreqless 0,$$

we say that the hazard function (or density) exhibits positive, no, or negative duration dependence when evaluated at duration s. If the sign of the derivative is the same for all $s \subset (0, \infty)$, we say that the hazard or density exhibits monotonic duration dependence. If the signs switch at least once, duration dependence is nonmonotonic. The only duration density that exhibits no duration dependence over the entire interval $(0, \infty)$ is the exponential $f(w) = \phi \exp(-\phi w)$, $\phi > 0$.

Parameterizing the hazard directly has many econometric advantages, which are discussed below. One of these is that information from incomplete spells, those which began during the sample period but had not been completed when the sample period ended, can be incorporated into the estimation procedure in a straightforward way. In actuality, individuals are only observed over some portion of their lifetime. Let the sampling period be the interval $(0, l)$ and assume that over this interval the individual is observed to commit m crimes. For the pure renewal process described above, we know that the mth event occurred at time τ_m; however, we did not observe the time at which the $(m + 1)^{st}$ event occurred. We do know that this event had not occurred by the end of the sample l. This occurs with probability $1 - F(l - \tau_m)$. It is easy to show that this quantity, referred to as the survivor function, is equal to exp $[-\int_0^s h(u)du]$, where $s = l - \tau_m$.

Environments are, of course, highly nonstationary, and at a single point in time there exist substantial amounts of heterogeneity with respect to budget sets and preferences. Renewal processes can still provide a useful framework for analyzing dynamic behavior if we generalize them so as to incorporate some forms of nonstationary and heterogeneity. We may retain the i.i.d. assumptions regarding the density of duration times, but make the parameters describing the duration density functions of observable and unobservable individual characteristics. These characteristics may change over time. For example, we may write the conditional hazard function as $h[w_{ik} \mid \mathbf{Z}_{ik}(\tau_{ik} + w_{ik}); \theta]$, where k indexes the serial order of the spell, w_{ik} is the duration of the kth spell for individual i, $\mathbf{Z}_i(\cdot)$ is an individual-specific vector of observable and unobservable sources of heterogeneity that can be time-varying, and θ is a conformable parameter vector.

In the case of the pure, unconditional renewal process first described, the density of duration times $f(t)$ could be estimated by parametric or nonparametric methods simply from a sufficiently large number of completed spells for one individual. Once we allow for conditioning on a set of individual characteristics $\mathbf{Z}_i$, some of which may be time invariant, it is clear that to estimate all elements of θ we will need observations for many individuals. The econometric model developed below is designed for use with event-history data (dates of criminal actions for large numbers of individuals).

Most dynamic models of behavior imply restrictions as to the form of the conditional hazard function. This is also true for models of criminal behavior. For example, a popular model of the criminal career assumes that individuals commit crimes at some constant rate λ over the course of a criminal career $(0, T^*)$, where T^* is random. This implies that the duration times between successive criminal acts over the period $(0, T^*)$ are distributed exponentially with parameter λ. As already discussed, the exponential distribution exhibits no duration dependence. An individual is equally likely to commit a crime in the next small interval of time no matter how long it has been since the last criminal action. Alternative models of criminal activity would not be consistent with an exponential distribution of times between successive crimes. For example, if the opportunity costs associated with committing a crime increased in the length of time since the last crime was committed, while the distribution of potential rewards from criminal actions was constant, the duration distribution of intervals between crimes would exhibit negative duration dependence—the greater the duration since the last crime, the lower the instantaneous rate of committing a crime.

The flexible econometric model presented in Flinn and Heckman (1982a) controls for observed and unobserved heterogeneity in the population by parameterizing the hazard function in a general way. If we assume that spell lengths for an individual are i.i.d. conditional on observed and unobserved heterogeneity and that only one spell is observed for each individual (for notational simplicity), we can write the hazard function as

$$h_i(w) = \exp\,[\mathbf{Z}_i(w)\beta + \mathbf{A}(w)\gamma + V_i(w)], \qquad (15)$$

where we have assumed for notational simplicity that the start of the observational period corresponds to calendar time 0. The vector of observable, exogenous individual characteristics at time w is denoted $\mathbf{Z}_i(w)$, and β is a conformable parameter vector. The vector $\mathbf{A}(w)$ consists of polynomial terms in duration, that is, $\mathbf{A}(w) = (w, w^2, \ldots, w^k)$, and γ is a k-dimensional parameter vector. An unobservable variable $V_i(w)$ is permitted to be a function of duration. Exponentiation of the term in brackets ensures that $h_i(w)$ is nonnegative, as is required, since $h_i(w)$ is a conditional density function.

Many stochastic models of the duration between crimes can be nested within this model as special cases. In many models the role of individual-specific, unobserved heterogeneity is stressed—the $V_i(w)$ in Equation 15. Conditional on $V_i(w)$, these models typically restrict γ to be a zero vector; thus they posit no duration dependence. Where duration dependence is allowed, functional forms are estimated that restrict the hazard function to be monotonically increasing or decreasing in time since the last criminal event. By using a polynomial "approximation," $\exp[\mathbf{A}(w)\gamma]$, we allow for nonmonotonic patterns of duration dependence. In the absence of a behavioral model that gives the analyst a strong reason to restrict his or her attention to special cases, it can be argued that as general a form of estimating the equation as is feasible should be used. Computationally it is straightforward to introduce the term $\exp[\mathbf{A}(w)\gamma]$, as is done in what follows.

The one-state renewal model can be generalized in several ways that may prove useful in the study of criminal careers. The assumption that the criminal career is a conditional renewal process (i.e., conditional on other exogenous stochastic processes) can be dropped. Flinn and Heckman (1982b) discuss several forms of departure from the basic renewal process that may be relevant for the analysis of dynamic behavior.

First, consider a case in which criminals acquire crime-specific human capital in the course of engaging in criminal behavior. Experienced criminals may be better at avoiding detection or identifying profitable targets than nonexperienced criminals. Then, if the rewards from legitimate market activity remain approximately constant over the life cycle, we would expect both the frequency with which crimes are committed and the yield from criminal activity to change over the career. We should unambiguously expect the yields from crime to increase; the frequency with which crimes are committed may increase or decrease as criminal experience is acquired. Even if it were possible to measure criminal human capital or yields from crime sufficiently precisely, by conditioning on those characteristics the criminal career could still not be considered a renewal process, since the level of those characteristics depends on the past history of the process.

We can model this departure in a relatively straightforward way. Consider the intervals between crimes for an individual who has committed n crimes. Conditional on all observable exogenous characteristics, we can consider the durations $w_1, w_2, \ldots, w_n$ to be independently but not identically distributed. Then,

$$F(w_1, w_2, \ldots, w_n) = \prod_{i=1}^{n} F_i(w_i),$$

but it is not the case that $F_1 = F_2 = \ldots = F_n$. Consider a multiple spell version of Equation 15. Let j index the serial order of the spell ($j = 1$ corresponds to the spell beginning at time 0 and ending with the first crime, $j = 2$ is the spell between the first and second crimes, and so on). Then we can write the hazard function for interval j for individual i as

$$h_{ij}(w) = \exp[\mathbf{Z}_i(\tau_{ij} + w)\beta_j + \mathbf{A}(w)\gamma_j + V_{ij}(\tau_{ij} + w)], \quad (16)$$

where τ_{ij} is the calendar time at which individual i committed his jth crime, β_j and γ_j are parameters associated with the hazard function for the jth spell, and V_{ij} is the unobserved heterogeneity component associated with the jth spell for individual i. By analogy with the variance components model often used in the analysis of discrete time panel data, we write

$$V_{ij}(\tau_{ij} + w) = \phi_i + \eta_{ij} + \varepsilon(\tau_{ij} + w),$$

where ϕ_i is an individual-specific, spell- and time-invariant heterogeneity component; η_{ij} is a spell-specific, time-invariant heterogeneity component; and $\varepsilon(t)$ is white noise [that is, $\varepsilon(t) - \varepsilon(s)$ is normally distributed with mean 0 and variance $(t - s)$ for $t > s$].

In what follows, we neglect continuously varying components of unobserved heterogeneity. While it would be highly desirable to model such components explicitly, their inclusion in the econometric model does not seem computationally feasible. We assume that unobserved heterogeneity components are constant within spells, i.e., $V_{ij}(\tau_{ij} + w) = V_{ij}$. To simplify calculations further, we adopt a one-factor specification of unobserved heterogeneity

$$V_{ij} = C_j\, \phi_i, \qquad j = 1, \ldots, J,$$

where the C_j are parameters of the model and J is the maximum number of spells observed in the sample. Thus, individual heterogeneity is constant over time and spells, although the relationship between ϕ_i and the rate of exit from the spell depends on the serial order of the spell through the parameter C_j.

The rate of criminal activity will, in general, depend not only on the length of time since the previous crime was committed, but also on the individual's age, and, more important, his previous record of crime commission. Consider spell j. The previous history of individual i's criminal career consists of $[w_{i1}, w_{i2}, \ldots, w_{i,j-1}; \mathbf{Z}(t), 0 \leq t \leq \tau_{i,j-1}]$. Suppose certain characteristics of this history are of interest to us, for example, the mean, variance, or some other moments of the sample distribution of $(w_{i1}, w_{i2}, \ldots, w_{i,j-1})$. These characteristics are simply functions of the history, $S[H_i(\tau_{i,j-1})]$, where $H_i(\tau_{i,j-1})$ is individual i's history up to time $\tau_{i,j-1}$. Then we can estimate the conditional hazard function for the jth interval as

$$h_{ij}(w) = \exp\{\mathbf{Z}_i(\tau_{ij} + w)\beta_j + \mathbf{A}(w)\gamma_j + S[H_i(\tau_{i,j-1})]\,\xi_j + V_{ij}\},$$

where ξ_j is the parameter vector associated with characteristics of the history up through crime $j - 1$. In this version of the model, spells between crimes are neither identically nor independently distributed; thus, the criminal career is modeled as a point process rather than as a strict renewal process. Because the process evolves unidirectionally in time, the time dependence is recursive. Presumably, a model along these lines is required to assess the degree of state dependence in criminal careers—that is, the extent to which the current commission rate depends on the criminal history after conditioning on both observed and unobserved exogenous processes.

Up to this point we have assumed that only one type of crime is committed in the population or, at the least, that each individual commits only one type of crime, although different individuals may specialize in different crimes. It is relatively straightforward to generalize the econometric model presented above to cover the possibility of crime switching when each individual may commit any one of a number of types of crimes. Say there are K types of crime, $K > 1$. We will initially restrict our attention to (conditional) renewal processes. Imagine that an individual commits a crime of type k at time τ. Then, we are interested in estimating the parameters of the length of time between the commission of a type k crime and the commission of all other crimes, for $k = 1, 2, \ldots, K$. For simplicity, assume $K = 2$. At time τ a type 1 crime is committed. The "latent" time to commission of another type 1 crime will be denoted t^*_{11}. The density of these latent times is assumed to exist and to be given by $g_{11}(t^*_{11})$. If type 2 crimes did not exist, this density could be directly estimated using observed durations between successive type 1 crimes. Denote the "latent" duration between type 1 crimes and type 2 crimes by t^*_{12} and its associated density by $g_{12}(t^*_{12})$. It is necessary to assume that the random variables t^*_{11} and t^*_{12} are independent. In terms of the observed outcome of the criminal process, a type 1 crime will be the next type observed if $t^*_{11} = \min(t^*_{11}, t^*_{12})$, and a type 2 crime will be observed if $t^*_{12} = \min(t^*_{11}, t^*_{12})$. Then if $t^*_{1j} = \min(t^*_{11}, t^*_{12})$, we will observe a type j crime at time $\tau + t^*_{1j}$. Similarly conditional on a type 2 crime at time τ, there will exist latent duration densities $g_{21}(t^*_{21})$ and $g_{22}(t^*_{22})$ generating times until the next crime, so $t^*_{2j} = \min(t^*_{21}, t^*_{22})$. Then, in this two-crime world, we would be interested in estimating the parameters of the four latent densities g_{11}, g_{12}, g_{21}, and g_{22}. These densities constitute a complete description of the criminal history.

For the general K state case, we will need a total of K^2 latent density functions to describe the crime process g_{ij}, $i, j = 1, \ldots, K$. (In addition, we will have to estimate densities g_{0j}, $j = 1, \ldots, K$, which correspond to the latent duration densities from initial entry into the population at risk of committing a crime, which we will denote by state 0, until a crime of type j is committed.) For each latent density g_{ij}, $i = 0, 1, \ldots, K; j = 1, \ldots, K$, there is a corresponding hazard function h_{ij}. The joint density of the k latent durations is given by

$$\prod_{j=1}^{K} h_{ij}(t_{ij}^*) \exp\left\{-\int_0^{t_{ij}^*} h_{ij}(u)\, du\right\}, \qquad i = 1, \ldots, K.$$

An individual is observed to commit a type j' crime after the type i crime if the latent time $t_{ij'}^*$ is the smallest of the K possible latent times, $t_{i1}^*, \ldots, t_{iK}^*$. Let the probability that an individual commits a type j' crime after a type i crime be denoted $P_{ij'}$. Then,

$$\begin{aligned} P_{ij'} &= \int_0^\infty \left[\int_{t_{ij'}^*}^\infty \cdots \int_{t_{ij'}^*}^\infty \left\{\prod_{j \neq j'}^{K} h_{ij}(t_{ij}) \cdot \exp\left[-\int_0^{t_{ij}^*} h_{ij}(u) du\right] dt_{ij}^*\right\} \right. \\ &\quad \left. \times \left\{h_{ij'}(t_{ij'}^*) \exp\left[-\int_0^{t_{ij'}^*} h_{ij'}(u) du\right]\right\}\right] dt_{ij'}^* \\ &= \int_0^\infty h_{ij'}(t_{ij'}^*) \cdot \exp\left\{-\int_0^{t_{ij'}^*} \left[\sum_{k=1}^{K} h_{ik}(u)\right] du\right\} dt_{ij'}^*. \end{aligned}$$

The conditional density of exit times from state i into state j' given that $t_{ij'}^* < t_{ij}^* (\forall j: j \neq j')$ is

$$g(t_{ij'}^* | t_{ij'}^* < t_{ij}^*)\ \forall j: j \neq j' = \frac{h_{ij'}(t_{ij'}^*) \exp\left\{-\int_0^{t_{ij'}^*} \left[\sum_{k=1}^{K} h_{ik}(u)\right] du\right\}}{P_{ij'}}.$$

It follows that the marginal density of exit times from state i can be written

$$g_{i\cdot}(t_{i\cdot}^*) = \sum_{j'=1}^{K} P_{ij'} g(t_{ij'}^* | t_{ij'}^* < t_{ij}^*;\ \forall j: j \neq j') = \left[\sum_{k=1}^{K} h_{ik}(t_{i\cdot}^*)\right] \cdot \exp\left\{-\int_0^{t_{i\cdot}^*} \left[\sum_{k=1}^{K} h_{ik}(u)\right] du\right\}.$$

The probability that the spell is not complete by some time T, where T is the end of the observation period, is prob $(t_{i\cdot}^* > T) \equiv 1 - G_{i\cdot}(T)$, where $G_{i\cdot}$ is the cumulative distribution function associated with $g_{i\cdot}$. This expression is

$$\text{Prob}(t_{i\cdot}^* > T) = \int_T^\infty g_{i\cdot}(t_{i\cdot}^*) dt_i^* = \exp\left\{-\int_0^T \left[\sum_{k=1}^{K} h_{ik}(u)\right] du\right\}.$$

This term enters the likelihood function for incomplete spells at least T in length.

Say we have access to event-history data for I individuals. For a given individual i, we observe his or her criminal career from time of entry into the criminal process $[\tau_0(i)]$ until some termination time $T(i)$, which corresponds to the end of the sample period or the time of death (both events are assumed unrelated to criminal activity). In general we observed a total of $m(i)$ crimes over the sample period. Denote the calendar time of each criminal event by $\tau_l(i)$, $l = 1, 2, \ldots, m(i)$. Now, define a function of

$s[\tau_l(i)] \equiv s_l(i)$, which gives the type of crime committed at calendar time $\tau_l(i)$.[5] Then, conditional on a set of unknown parameters, $\mathbf{\Omega}$ and unobserved person-specific heterogeneity component V_i, the likelihood of observing the recorded criminal history for individual i is

$$\pi_i(\mathbf{\Omega}|V_i) = \left\{ \prod_{l=0}^{m(i)-1} g_{s_l(i)s_{l+1}(i)}[t^*_{s_l(i)s_{l+1}(i)}| \right.$$

$$t^*_{s_l(i)s_{l+1}(i)} < t^*_{s_l(i)j};\ j = 1, \ldots,$$

$$s_{l+1}(i) - 1,\ s_{l+1}(i) + 1, \ldots, K;\ V_i]$$

$$\left. \times P_{s_l(i)s_{l+1}(i)}(V_i) \right\} G_{s_m(i)} \cdot [T(i) - \tau_m(i)|V_i],$$

where $t^*_{s_l(i)\ s_{l+1}(i)} = \tau_{l+1}(i) - \tau_l(i)$. By substitution,

$$\pi_i(\mathbf{\Omega}|V_i = \left\{ \prod_{l=0}^{m(i)-1} h_{s_l(i)s_{l+1}(i)}(t^*_{s_l(i)s_{l+1}(i)}{}^*|V_i) \right.$$

$$\cdot \exp\left[-\int_0^{t^*_{s_l(i)s_{l+1}(i)}} \left(\sum_{j=1}^{k} h_{s_l(i)j}\,(u|V_i) \right) du \right]\Bigg\}$$

$$\cdot \exp\left[-\int_0^{T(i)-\tau_{s_m(i)}} \left(\sum_{j=1}^{k} h_{s_m(i)j}\,(u|V_i) \right) du \right]\Bigg\}.$$

This is the conditional likelihood for an individual observation given a value of the unobserved heterogeneity component V_i—which, recall, has the substantive interpretation of an individual's inherent propensity to commit crimes. Individual propensities to commit crimes are assumed to be distributed according to $B(V; \mathbf{\Phi})$ in the population, where $\mathbf{\Phi}$ is a vector of parameters that describes the distribution. Note that we assume that V_i is distributed independently of other observable characteristics $\mathbf{Z}$. The unconditional likelihood, or integrated likelihood, for an individual observation is

$$\pi_i(\mathbf{\Omega}, \mathbf{\Phi}) = \int \pi_i(\mathbf{\Omega} \mid V_i) dB(V_i; \mathbf{\Phi}).$$

The log likelihood for the entire sample is

$$L(\mathbf{\Omega}, \mathbf{\Phi}) = ln \prod_{i=1}^{I} \pi_i(\mathbf{\Omega}, \mathbf{\Phi})$$

$$= \sum_{i=1}^{I} ln\ \pi_i(\mathbf{\Omega}, \mathbf{\Phi}).$$

Then, the maximum likelihood estimates of $\mathbf{\Omega}$ and $\mathbf{\Phi}$ can be obtained under standard regularity conditions as the solution to

$$\max_{\Omega,\Phi} L(\mathbf{\Omega}, \mathbf{\Phi}). \qquad (17)$$

Given that the distributional assumptions regarding h and B are correct, the maximum likelihood estimator defined by Equation 17 has optimal statistical properties asymptotically (as the number of individuals grows large).

This model is relatively general and has been used to estimate the stochastic structure of labor market attachments. The generality of the model, however, seems to preclude treatment of complicated initial-conditions problems or common forms of sample selection. The solutions to those problems seem only to be tractable when sufficient stationarity is imposed—as when the underlying crime process is exponential—see for example Rolph, Chaiken, and Houchens (1981). The difficult choice for the analyst appears to be either to use relatively general econometric models, which require a type and quality of data rarely available to students of criminal behavior, or to tailor the econometric models to the data currently available. This latter option results in stationarity assumptions that are not consistent with the spirit of the dynamic behavioral models presented above and, more importantly, are not testable. It is essential, first, to estimate general models for stochastic processes on some "ideal" data set (no doubt yet to be collected) so that we can determine what types of stationary assumptions are reasonable. Until that time, we should remain cautious in interpreting the results from the empirical analyses of criminal careers.

[5]For example, say that robbery is defined as type 2. If the first and third crimes the individual committed were robberies, $s_1(i) = s_3(i) = 2$.

CONCLUSION

In this paper various approaches to the modeling of criminal careers were presented. A number of dynamic behavioral models of criminal activity were developed, and characteristics of the solutions were discussed. Although closed-form solutions are not typically available for dynamic optimization models, numerical methods may be used in a relatively straightforward way.

The behavioral models were designed to illustrate the fact that the effect of current choices on future options has potentially important deterrence effects. Thus, the fact that an individual facing a 1-year sentence if caught committing a crime will face stiffer sentences in the future if caught committing additional crimes will, in general, affect criminal behavior at all points over the life cycle. The static models usually employed in empirical research are not capable of capturing these dynamic deterrence effects. It was also shown that personal characteristics, such as race, age, or drug usage, may not be simple indicators of an individual's "inherent" propensity to commit criminal acts but instead may merely reflect the relative rewards to criminal versus noncriminal actions that the individual faces. Thus these characteristics may be better thought of as indicators of differences in choice sets than of differences in preferences. While these interpretations may seem indistinguishable for purposes of conducting empirical analysis, they imply very different policy actions in dealing with criminal behavior.

Econometric models of the duration of time between criminal activities (differentiated by type) were also presented. These models are capable of capturing the dynamics of the criminal career more adequately than the behavioral models from a strictly empirical perspective. One is left with the difficulty of substantive interpretation of parameter estimates, however, since no explicit behavioral model is used to generate the function estimated. It should be possible to learn something interesting, even if descriptive, about the dynamics of criminal careers from the estimation of such models.

REFERENCES

Becker, G.
1975 *Human Capital.* 2nd ed. New York: Columbia University Press.

Bentham, J.
1780 *An Introduction to the Principles of Morals and Legislation*, J. Burns and H. Hart, eds. London, England: Athlone Press (1970).

Blumstein, A., Cohen, J., and Nagin, D., eds.
1978 *Deterrence and Incapacitation: Estimating the Effects of Criminal Sanctions on Crime Rates.* Report of the Panel on Deterrence and Incapacitation. Washington, D.C.: National Academy Press.

Chaiken, J., and Chaiken, M.
1981 *Varieties of Criminal Behavior.* Santa Monica, Calif.: Rand Corporation.

Flinn, C., and Heckman, J.
1982a Models for the analysis of labor force dynamics. Pp. 35–95 in R. Basmann and G. Rhodes, eds., *Advances in Econometrics I.* Greenwich, Conn.: JAI Press.

1982b New methods for analyzing individual event histories. Pp. 99–140 in S. Leinhardt, ed., *Sociological Methodology 1982.* San Francisco, Calif.: Jossey-Bass.

Marschak, J.
1953 Economic measurements for policy and prediction. Chapter 1 in W. C. Hood and T. C. Koopmans, eds., *Studies in Econometric Method.* Cowles Commission Monograph 14. New York: John Wiley & Sons.

Rolph, J., Chaiken, J., and Houchens, R.
1981 *Methods for Estimating Crime Rates of Individuals.* Santa Monica, Calif.: Rand Corporation.

Schmidt, P., and Witte, A.
1984 *An Economic Analysis of Crime and Justice.* Orlando, Fla.: Academic Press.

10

Random Parameter Stochastic-Process Models of Criminal Careers

John P. Lehoczky

INTRODUCTION

Background

In the past decade there has been great growth in the development of quantitative methodologies to deal with criminal justice problems. This has included extensive data gathering and analysis and some modeling of offender behavior. As this data analysis proceeds, one can gain clearer insights into the nature of offender behavior and these should be incorporated into increasingly detailed models. As the models increase in accuracy, one can begin to use them as policy tools to analyze the impact of various approaches to crime control, such as selective incapacitation.

Unfortunately, it seems that the quantitative models of offender behavior that have been developed to date do not capture the recent insights about offender behavior found in major data analysis projects, such as the Rand prisoner self-report study. Indeed, the stochastic modeling approach began in 1973 with the work of Avi-Itzhak and Shinnar. This work, described below, treats individual-offender recidivism as a Poisson process. A great deal of subsequent modeling has been done, but most of the models are simple extensions of the Poisson-process model, namely renewal-process models. This class of models assumes that recidivism times are independent and have the same distribution. Such models may fit data better than a Poisson-process model, but they do not incorporate the current improved understanding of offender behavior. This paper represents an attempt to develop a stochastic model that is in better accord with this understanding.

John P. Lehoczky is professor and head, Department of Statistics, Carnegie-Mellon University. I wish to express my thanks to Alfred Blumstein and Jacqueline Cohen for their major contributions to the paper. The approaches developed in this paper are the outgrowth of a long series of discussions concerning appropriate models for criminal behavior and the empirical evidence supporting those models. In addition, I wish to thank Donald Gaver for his many discussions concerning hierarchical models and corrections to biases in criminal justice data sets. My thanks also to Arthur Goldberger, Jan Chaiken, Chul Woo Ahn, and Mark Schervish for their many comments on earlier drafts of this paper.

Three major aspects of offender behavior have been observed with sufficient frequency to merit incorporation into analytic models:

- Crime-commission propensities change as a function of age.
- Offender populations are markedly heterogeneous.
- Offenders often are thought to commit crimes in spurts and then to have periods with little or no activity.

The age effect is very pronounced. It is widely recognized that offender behavior is at its peak during the late teens and early 20s and then drops significantly during the 30s. Any stochastic model must address this age effect. Standard renewal-process models do not incorporate such effects, because they assume that the times between arrests are independent and identically distributed (i.i.d.) and hence stationary. There is need to develop models that account for age effects but that simultaneously offer analytic tractability. Such models will be presented in this paper.

It is evident from recidivism data as well as self-report data that there is great heterogeneity in the offender population. This heterogeneity refers to differences between offenders, including markedly differing offense rates, career lengths, and types of crimes engaged in. This variation goes beyond differences that can reasonably be observed from independent replications of a single stochastic process. Most models do not take this heterogeneity into account. The few exceptions arose from work at the Rand Corporation, including Chaiken and Rolph (1980) and Rolph, Chaiken, and Houchens (1981). In this paper, I argue for the use of hierarchical models to represent heterogeneity. In such models each individual's criminal career is regarded as a stochastic process governed by parameters. Those parameters are themselves treated as random variables drawn from a parent distribution (superpopulation). The parent distribution captures the heterogeneity of the population of offenders or the variation between individuals. One wishes to estimate the parameters of the parent distribution to gain insight into the population of offenders. In addition, one wishes to estimate the rate-influencing parameters of individuals to understand the behavior of each of the offenders. Hierarchical models form the basis of the analysis in this paper. They are formally described, applied, and estimated in the discussions that follow.

There is another aspect to criminal careers that has generally not been incorporated into stochastic models. This is the occurrence of quiescent periods in the course of the career. Self-report data reveal that criminal behavior often occurs in spurts and is followed by lulls in activity. This is not surprising if, for example, the offender was attempting to gain sufficient money through a series of crimes and then, having reached that goal, stopped for a period. The typical renewal-process models do not incorporate such behavior. A new class of models that includes this behavior is developed below.

Several other aspects of stochastic modeling of criminal careers are dealt with in this paper. One of the most interesting is the use of the hierarchical modeling approach to correct for natural biases in data sets. Generally, criminal justice data sets do not provide random samples from the offender population. Rather, individuals are part of a sample because they meet a specific criterion that may be directly or indirectly related to their parameter values. For example, one might gather data on prisoners. This group of offenders is, however, not representative of the offender population because it typically consists of individuals with high offense rates, more serious offenses, or longer careers. Similarly, if one took a sample of arrestees in some time period, such a sample would overrepresent high-rate offenders, since they have a greater probability of falling into such a sample. As illustrated below, the hierarchical modeling approach can help to overcome this problem. It offers the opportunity to develop a correction for nonrandom sampling, so that one can make more nearly correct inferences about the offender population from inherently biased data sets.

Overview

This paper introduces a hierarchical (superpopulation) model for criminal careers within a population of offenders or potential offenders. There are two levels to the hierarchy. The top level is used to explain variation between individuals in the population, that is, to explain the heterogeneity of the population. At the low level of the hierarchy, individuals engage in criminal careers that are treated as independently evolving stochastic processes governed by certain distributions. These distributions contain parameters with values at the top level. The low level thus uses a stochastic-process model to help explain differences within careers governed by the same parameter values.

Covariates can be introduced at both levels of the hierarchical model. Covariates are of two types: "historical" covariates, which are fixed at the start of the career, and "dynamic" covariates, which can change during the evolution of the career. For an analysis of adult offending careers, historical covariates could include juvenile record or the age at the time of the first juvenile arrest. Relevant dynamic covariates might include employment status or drug use. The historical covariates can influence the choice of parameters for each individual at the highest level of the hierarchy. Since these parameters are selected and fixed at the beginning of the career, dynamic covariates cannot be used. All covariates are allowed to influence the evolution of the career of any particular offender, the lowest level of the hierarchy.

A new family of stochastic models is introduced in the paper. The models are characterized by two states, one of which corresponds to a high rate of crime commission and the other of which represents a low rate of activity (which is taken to be zero). Parameters are included for the time spent in each state, state-switching probabilities, arrest probabilities, crime-type termination probabilities, and the times between crimes. For multiple crime types, a competing-risks formulation is used. The models offer tractability, can include covariates, provide periods of high and low activity, and introduce some behavorial parameters.

Methods are also developed to assess and correct the biases that occur in many criminal justice data sets. Three specific issues are addressed:

1. If a data set is gathered by taking individuals who were arrested during a certain window of time, the data set will overrepresent individuals with high crime rates among those at liberty and underrepresent those who are in prison for part of the window period.
2. If a data set comes from self-reports of prisoners, it is not representative of the population in general, since prisoners tend to be high-rate offenders and to commit more violent crimes.
3. Even at the level of the individual parameters, the individual crime or arrest rates that are estimated from among arrestees or prisoners will be biased upward. This is because individuals are more likely to be caught in a period of high activity (even if their parameter values may be low) and hence empirically show a high arrest rate.

The hierarchical model developed in this paper can help to assess and correct these biases.

Finally, a class of "phase distributions" is introduced. This class is very versatile in that it can approximate arbitrarily closely the distribution of any nonnegative random variable. In addition, the class is closed under a number of operations that are useful for the models presented in this paper. The closure properties include convolution and mixtures, as well as maxima and minima of random variables drawn from this class.

HIERARCHICAL MODELS

This section describes the use of hierarchical stochastic models for studying criminal careers. There are several reasons why this class of models is especially useful and of great conceptual value. First, it has frequently been observed that criminal behavior varies widely between individuals. This is especially true for crime rates, as measured by self-report data; some individuals report committing crimes at a very high rate, while others report they commit crimes rarely. Even allowing for biases in these data and deliberate falsification, it is clear that there is great variation between individuals. It is, therefore, appropriate to use a model that can represent this great variation.

A second benefit of using a hierarchical model is that it can help to improve parameter estimates for each individual. Suppose one treated each individual in isolation and attempted to estimate parameter values for each individual using only his data (for example, arrest record and the values of covariates). One would find that these estimators have a large variance. With a hierarchical model, however, the data for other individuals can be used to help estimate parameter values for a single individual. This follows because the parameter values for all individuals are related, since they are modeled as coming from a common parent distribution. This situation has been observed and exploited with increasing frequency in statistical studies. This statistical formulation leads to "shrinkage" estimators. This type of estimator was first introduced by James and Stein (1961). This topic has been receiving substantial recent attention in the statistics literature (see the review by Morris, 1983). Methods based on maximum likelihood, empirical Bayes, and Bayes procedures have been developed. These approaches will be discussed in the section on parameter estimation; however, a recent example provided by Dempster, Rubin, and Tsutakawa (1981) may help to explain the benefits of the methodology. These authors present several examples, along with a theoretical treatment of likelihood methods. One example deals with estimating the first-year performance of law school students using several explanatory variables. For a single law school, the estimates of regression coefficients are highly variable. It is possible to improve the estimates for a single law school markedly by simultaneously carrying out the analysis for many (82 in this case) law schools. One believes there is a reasonable similarity among law schools, and so the data for other schools are pertinent for any individual school. The estimates for one school gain precision by considering many similar schools simultaneously. Other examples of this type are cited in Morris (1983).

The situation is analogous to Model II analysis of variance or random-effects models. One can distinguish the variation within a particular career and the variation between careers. Criminal careers are modeled using stochastic models. This is appropriate because any career has many random elements that control its evolution. If two individuals have the same stochastic mechanism (i.e., the same parameter values), the two resulting careers may nevertheless be quite different. The offenders have possibly different criminal opportunities, possibly different arrest realizations, possibly different sentences, and so on. If an individual were allowed a second realization of his career, it would differ from the first. This is variation within a career. Variation between careers arises when individuals have different stochastic mechanisms (parameter values) governing their careers. Once the individuals have been linked through a superpopulation or hierarchical model, the data for all individuals can be used in addition to the data for a single individual. The individual parameter estimates will be drawn toward the average of the population. This is known as shrinkage. The amount of shrinkage will depend on the size of the variation within careers versus the variation between careers. If there is relatively small variation between individuals, the shrinkage can be great. The formal idea of the hierarchical model (presented in more detail in the next section) is that one has a family of parameters, θ, that controls the evolution of an individual career, which is denoted $\{\mathbf{X}_\theta, t \geq 0\}$. The parameters θ are treated as random variables with some distribution $\pi(\theta)$, which itself may contain some unknown parameters. One then wishes to use a data set to estimate individual θ values and π or the unknown parameters of π.

Given the above formulation, there is a third advantage to using hierarchical models. This is the possibility of assessing and correcting for sampling biases in a data set. Generally, criminal justice data sets are not randomly sampled from the population of offenders. More typically, one generates a data set by selecting from individuals having a particular attribute, such as an arrest in a certain time period, or who are in prison at a particular time. Each of these sampling mechanisms yields a sample that is not random from π. If one is, therefore, to make inferences concerning the offender population, one must assess and correct those biases. The hierarchical formulation is useful in carrying out this process, as will be illustrated below. (Cohort samples can overcome the biasing problem; however, they generally yield too small a sample of criminal activity to be of great utility.)

A NEW STOCHASTIC MODEL

This section introduces a new family of stochastic models of the crime process and arrest process associated with a single criminal career. These new models are intended to encompass more of the salient aspects of criminal behavior than has been possible with previous models. The basic model presented is itself still oversimplified but should serve as an introduction to a set of ideas and tools that future researchers will find useful. Only the most tractable versions of this family of models are presented in detail. This section is organized in a sequential manner. First, some of the most familiar, early stochastic models of criminal careers are summarized, including their good and bad points. Next, a model is presented that overcomes some of the objections to previous models. Finally, a class of flexible models is presented that seems to improve previous efforts considerably. Of course, further changes are to be anticipated as understanding of the underlying processes increases.

Poisson Crime Processes

A frequently used model for the process of crimes committed by a single individual is that crimes form a Poisson process (see Karlin and Taylor, 1975) during the times the individual is not in prison (see, for example, Avi-Itzhak and Shinnar, 1973; Rolph, Chaiken, and Houchens,

1981). The times between crimes (after removing time in prison) are independent random variables with an exponential distribution having some mean, say $1/\lambda$. Associated with a crime process is an arrest process. This arrest process is a thinned version of the crime process in that only a subset of the crimes results in arrest[1] (and only a subset of the arrests results in imprisonment). A common assumption in all work is that an arrest is determined at random for each crime. This means that there is an arrest probability q and that a crime event yields an arrest event with probability q independent of anything else. With this type of thinning to construct the arrest process, if the crime process is Poisson (λ), the arrest process is Poisson (λq).

This simple model of the crime process has several attractive features:

1. The Poisson process is well understood and very tractable. In addition, given the assumption of random thinning, both the crime and arrest processes are Poisson. If the crime process is a renewal process and one thins it at random, the arrest process will be approximately Poisson even if the crime process is not.
2. The Poisson process has a single parameter, and the statistical inference for it is well understood.

On the other hand, several drawbacks to the model must be addressed:

1. The Poisson model, as such, does not account for population heterogeneity.
2. The Poisson model for the arrest process may not fit recidivism data (see Holden, 1983, for a discussion). That is, the times between arrests (after eliminating time in prison) are not exponentially distributed.
3. It has been observed, especially from prisoner self-report data, that arrests and crimes appear to be more clustered than would be suggested by a Poisson model. Moreover, this model does not allow for any sort of aging effects. It has been widely noted that the frequency of arrests varies with time and at some point drops to essentially zero, suggesting an effective end to the career.[2]
4. A major drawback of the simple Poisson model is that the individual exerts no control over the career other than picking λ. There are no decision points built into such models at which, for example, the individual could decide to stop, or change, λ. The events of the past career do not influence the future. Clearly, one would suspect that past events can have an important effect on the future and so one would like to broaden the class of models to allow for this.

Some of the previous issues can be overcome in a straightforward way. For example, one could introduce a random lifetime. Each individual has a career length (often assumed to be exponentially distributed, to enhance tractability). When the length is exceeded, the individual no longer engages in crime (and so presumably is no longer arrested). One problem with this approach is that the career length, if determined at the start of

[1]It is assumed there is no problem of "false arrest."

[2]The concept of a finite career length is somewhat controversial (see, for example, Holden, 1983: 26). It is argued that there can be no logical point at which a criminal career can end, except death. Any former criminal could be presented with an opportunity such that he would again commit a crime. While one may respect this point of view, it should be realized that no single stochastic model can be expected to represent an exact truth. Rather, one strives to construct models that are approximately true, that account for important effects, and that offer a tractable analysis. It may be that some criminals whose careers are said to have "ended" may, in fact, commit a few additional crimes. In such a case, one would expect the frequency of those crimes to be very low. When coupled with the fact that the arrest probability is generally very small, one expects that the arrest processes may be no different.

the career, is not influenced by any factors in the career. (Overcoming the poor fit offered by the exponential distribution is discussed in the next section.)

One can introduce population heterogeneity in two ways:

1. One can allow λ to depend on covariates, such as juvenile record or age at first juvenile arrest.[3]
2. One can allow λ to be random (see, for example, Rolph, Chaiken, and Houchens, 1981). In this way, λ can represent the heterogeneity of a population of offenders.

Renewal-Process Models

Some improvement in fit can be achieved by replacing the Poisson-process model for crimes with the more general renewal-process model. Recall that a renewal process is a point process in which the times between points (crimes) are independent, identically distributed random variables having a cumulative distribution function F, which is not necessarily exponential. Arrests are then commonly considered to be a randomly thinned version of crimes. Arrests will also form a renewal process with distribution G. One can determine G in terms of F and q; however, the relation is most easily expressed in terms of the Laplace-Stieltjes transform (Neuts, 1981), $\Psi_F(s) = E[\exp(-sT)]$, where T represents a generic random time between crimes. We find

$$\Psi_G(s) = \frac{\Psi_F(s)*q}{1 - (1 - q)*\Psi_F(s)},$$

where G is the distribution of times between arrests.

Many authors have used renewal-process models for the crime process (see, for example, Holden, 1983). Many distributions have been used for F. These include the exponential, Weibull, lognormal, gamma, mixtures of various distributions, and defective distributions. In addition, logistic regression methods have also been used. In each case a particular distribution was used to fit a particular data set. One can readily see that no universally appropriate family seems to fit recidivism data. However, a family of continuous distributions, called phase distributions (Ph-distributions), seems particularly useful for several reasons:

1. The family is dense in the set of all positive distributions, that is, any positive distribution can be approximated arbitrarily closely by a phase distribution.
2. Commonly used distributions, such as the exponential, some gamma, and their mixtures, are phase distributions (lognormal and Weibull are not but they can be closely approximated).
3. These distributions have a Markovian structure (see Neuts, 1981) and so are useful in stochastic model building, because of their tractability.
4. The distributions are closed under such operations as mixing and convolution.

The renewal-process approach to modeling the crime process helps in that recidivism data can be better fit; however, the other difficulties cited earlier remain. The principal problems are the following:

1. The general renewal-process model still assumes independent, identically distributed arrest times and does not offer the clustering of crimes or arrests usually reported or observed.
2. The model does not allow the individual to make decisions concerning behavior.

[3]See, for example, Stollmack and Harris (1974), Barton and Turnbull (1981), and Holden (1983).

3. The model does not account for the great amount of population variability that has been observed in criminal justice data sets.

4. The model does not build in interactions between individuals and the criminal justice system.

A New Class of Models

In this section, I present a new model designed to overcome some of the difficulties with earlier models. The new model makes use of a pair of states between which the individual moves.[4] When the individual is in one of the states (the "high" state), he commits crimes at a high intensity. When in the other state (the "low" state), crimes are committed at a low intensity (which is taken to be zero). In addition, switching between states allows the individual some decision-making latitude. I begin with a single crime type, generalize to multiple crime types, and then develop a hierarchical formulation.

The following parameters are used in the model:

T: number of distinct crime types.

$\mathbf{A}$: initial crime types for an individual, $\mathbf{A} \subset \{1, 2, \ldots, T\}$.

F_t: the cdf of the time between crimes of type t, $1 \le t \le T$.

q_t: the arrest probability for crime type t, $1 \le t \le T$.

β_t: the probability of terminating crime type t, $1 \le t \le T$.

α: the probability of switching from the high-rate state to the low-rate state.

G: the cdf of the time in the low-rate state.

Let us define—

- a crime process that is a renewal process with the time between crimes being a phase distribution F with mean $1/\lambda$;
- an arrest probability q;
- a state-switching probability α;
- a phase-type distribution G governing the amount of time the individual spends in the low state, during which no crimes are committed; and
- a probability β giving the probability that the career ends with the start of the current low period.

We can describe the process intuitively, as follows. A cycle begins with the individual in the high state. Crimes are committed according to a renewal process with distribution F. After each crime, two issues must be resolved:

1. with probability q, the individual is arrested, and
2. with probability α, the individual switches to the low state.

If the individual switches to the low state, he may terminate his career with probability β. With the complementary probability, he stays in this state for a period determined by the cumulative distribution function G. While the individual is in the low state, no crimes are committed.

The arrest, state-switching, and termination probabilities are applied at random, that is, without any dependence on the realization of the process to that point. Indeed, it is interesting to consider a generalized model in which the process up to that time can influence these transitions. For example, one can introduce a reinforcement effect. If any individual commits a crime and is not arrested, that might provide reinforcement to stay ac-

[4]A two-state model of this sort was studied by Maltz and Pollack (1980). It is also mentioned in Rolph, Chaiken, and Houchens (1981:37).

tive. Two unarrested crimes provide further reinforcement, and so on. One could simply introduce a sequence $\{\alpha_n\}$ in which α_n represents the probability the individual offender moves to the low state after n consecutive unarrested crimes. The sequence could be chosen so that it strictly decreases to a positive limit.

Any arrest may result in a conviction and a prison sentence. We are only interested in the behavior during free time; consequently, the model is applicable only while the person is not in prison. This brings up the issue of how the processes should be initiated at time 0 (which we take to be age 18 for adult offending) and how they should be restarted after release from prison, if applicable. It is mathematically convenient to keep the process in equilibrium as much as possible. (The advantage of this will be seen below in the discussion of corrections for sampling biases.) This suggests that we should take the initial time to the first crime to be given by the equilibrium forward recurrence time distribution. Once the first crime occurs, the renewal-process model begins.

Under the assumptions presented earlier, the crime process is a renewal process (if prison time is deleted). After each crime, a coin is flipped, and depending on the result, the next crime comes according to F with probability $(1 - \alpha)$ or according to $F*G$ with probability $\alpha(1 - \beta)$, or no further crimes occur with probability $\alpha\beta$. (Here $*$ denotes convolution, since the time to the next crime is the sum of the length of the low period and the times to the first crime in the next high period.) This gives us a mixture of two-phase distributions, which will also be a phase distribution, and the resulting distribution is defective in that it allows a positive probability of the value ∞. Let us refer to this distribution of times between crimes by H, and let its Laplace-Stieltjes transform be given by Ψ_H. The arrest process is also a terminating renewal process. This is easily seen, since each crime has an independent arrest probability. The time between arrests is thus a random sum of independent random variables having distribution H. If we let the distribution be K, then

$$\Psi_K(s) = \frac{q*\Psi_H(s)}{1 - (1 - q)*\Psi_H(s)}.$$

It should be noted that

$$\Psi_H(0) = P(\text{time between crimes} < \infty) = 1 - \alpha\beta$$

and

$$\Psi_K(0) = P(\text{time between arrests} < \infty) = \frac{q*(1 - \alpha\beta)}{1 - (1 - q)(1 - \alpha\beta)}.$$

This model has several attractive features:

1. The model is, in reality, a terminating renewal process for both crimes and arrests. In this instance though, the model explicitly builds in parameters to represent ways in which the individual can control activities and does so in a realistic way. After each crime, the individual controls whether to continue or change states and, if he or she continues, whether to terminate the crime type or not. Rather than merely fitting K, the arrest-process distribution, the model shows how it is composed of more fundamental behavioral parameters. Thus, the model overcomes the objection to the lack of individual control over the career while retaining the simplicity of a renewal process.
2. The model introduces important behavioral effects in a tractable way and allows for the generality provided by phase distributions.

It should be noted that the model can be further generalized in several ways. As mentioned before, the single α parameter can be replaced by a sequence of parameters to represent a reinforcement effect. In addition, one can increase the number of states (from "high" and "low"). This allows for more complex behavior. Despite this added generality, I have retained the two-state model with no crimes in the low state. This reduces the number of parameters in the model. Currently available data sets lack the size or detail needed to estimate a more complex model successfully. As better data sets become available, they can be used to extend the model. In fact, if the duration of the low state is sufficiently short, the two-state model is little different from a one-state model. The two-state model is beneficial when low periods are of at least moderate duration.

Multiple Crime Types

The previous model can be generalized to allow for multiple crime types. Such a generalization can be carried out in several ways. In this section I explore several possibilities and arrive at a final version of the model. Throughout this discussion, T denotes the total number of crime types, which in turn are indexed by t.

Crime-switch Models

The simplest approach is to consider crime types as having no influence on the stochastic structure described above. The distributions F and G, as well as the parameters q, α, and β, are unchanged. Rather, crime type serves only to label the crimes. This can be done by assuming T distinct types and introducing a $T \times T$ Markov crime-switch-transition matrix $\mathbf{C} = (c_{ij})$, where c_{ij} is the probability that the offender, having last committed a crime of type i, will next commit a crime of type j.

The Markov crime-switch approach is much used in stochastic models of the crime process. Moreover, it can be made more general by allowing arrest probabilities to depend on crime type. I do not pursue this approach any further in this paper, however, for two reasons. First, one adds $T(T - 1)$ parameters to the model through $\mathbf{C}$ while gaining only a little more explanatory power. Second, I prefer to pursue an alternate approach that enables one to deal better with the age effects, which are clear in crime data but are not yet incorporated in the model.

Competing Risk Model

An alternate approach to constructing a multiple-crime-type model is to introduce a set of distributions of phase type F_t, $1 \leq t \leq T$, where T is the number of crime types. Suppose that the individual commits a crime and stays in the high state or that the individual leaves the low state and enters the high state. We need to define the time until the next crime occurs. This can be done using a "competing risks" formulation. In this formulation we imagine random variables $\mathbf{X}_t$ being drawn independently with distribution F_t, $1 \leq t \leq T$. The time until the next crime is given by $\mathbf{X} = \min_{1 \leq t \leq T} \mathbf{X}_t$, the crime with the shortest time to its occurrence. The type of crime is given by the index t, which gives $\mathbf{X}$. The family of phase distributions is well suited to this approach, since if each of the $\mathbf{X}_t$ has phase distributions, then $\mathbf{X}$ will also have a phase distribution (see below). This version of the multiple-crime-type model is therefore essentially equivalent to the single-crime-type model with the exception that the distribution F belongs to a special subset of the phase distributions, those that arise as minimums of other phase distributions.

The Final Version of the Model

The competing-risk version of the multiple-crime-type model leaves one issue unaddressed. In many criminal justice data sets pertaining to individual offending, there is a pronounced age effect. Individuals seem to have high crime-commission rates as older juveniles or young adults, and those rates sharply diminish at older ages. None of the models presented thus far addresses this issue. Indeed, a renewal-process model of crimes or arrests would not allow for such an age effect. Fortunately, there appears to be a straightforward way to introduce such effects, and this approach is supported somewhat by empirical evidence. Studies by Peterson and Braiker (1981) indicate that for a single crime type, there is no age effect. Rather, an individual commits a particular crime type in a time-stationary way (although in a clustered fashion, like that given by the two-state model), then at some time point in the career the individual essentially stops committing that crime type altogether. This process goes on independently for the T crime types (although some offenders specialize in a subset of these types). The individual has a set of active crime types. The time until the next crime (when the individual is in the high state) is taken to be the minimum of the times for the active crime types. As time progresses, the portion of the offender's career involving crime type t will end, and so the set of active crime types decreases in size. As more crime types are eliminated, the time between crimes will naturally increase. This will, in turn, result in an age effect.

The multiple crime type can be summarized. It consists of the following:

- a set of phase-type distributions, F_t, $1 \leq t \leq T$,
- an initial set of active crime types $\mathbf{A} \subset \{1, \ldots, T\}$,
- an arrest probability for crime type t, q_t, $1 \leq t \leq T$,
- a state-switching probability α,
- a crime type t termination probability, β_t, $1 \leq t \leq T$, and
- a phase-type distribution G, denoting the length of the low period.

Note that α and G could be allowed to be crime-type dependent, as well.

An intuitive description of the criminal career is as follows. The individual begins his or her career with a set of active crime types $\mathbf{A}$. Each crime type has a distribution associated with it. Let X_t, $1 \leq t \leq T$ represent random variables, where X_t has distribution F_t. The time until the next crime is given by $\min_{t \in A} \mathbf{X}_t$, and the type of that crime is given by the index associated with the minimum. When a crime of type t is committed, with probability β_t, that crime type is removed from the active set $\mathbf{A}$. With probability $1 - \beta_t$, this crime type is kept in $\mathbf{A}$. With probability q_t the individual is arrested, and with probability α the individual switches to the low state. After a period having distribution G, he moves back to the high state. The process continues in the same fashion, except that over time the active set $\mathbf{A}$ will be reduced in size. When $\mathbf{A}$ becomes empty, the career is ended. As $\mathbf{A}$ becomes smaller, the times between crimes (and hence arrests) will increase. This will produce an age effect. (One could allow $\mathbf{A}$ to increase in size, i.e., new crime types to be added. I do not consider such a possibility in this paper.)

In the next section, I discuss the hierarchical version of the model and the addition of covariates. It is clear that, at any point in time, the decision to terminate a crime type, to drop the low state, to adjust the arrest probability, and so on will be influenced by covariates, such as drug use or employment status. The basic model described above can be enhanced to allow such considerations.

Hierarchical Versions of the New Model

The model developed above does not build in any population heterogeneity. It is important to include this, and it can be done in two ways:

1. by allowing the model to depend on covariates and
2. by using a hierarchical model that assumes that the distributions governing the individual crime and arrest processes contain random parameters.

Both approaches will be used here. It will be assumed that each of the parameters is random and that they are jointly sampled from a joint distribution. Moreover, this joint distribution can depend on covariates.

A large number of parameters have been introduced into this model of the criminal career. These include F_t, q_t, β_t, $1 \leq t \leq T$, α, G, and **A**. The distributions F_t and G are of phase type and so have parametric representations (γ_t, R_t) and (δ, S). One can consider drawing (γ_t, R_t), $(\delta, \mathbf{S})$, q_t, β_t, α, and **A** jointly from some superpopulation. This would allow for an arbitrarily large amount of dependency among the parameters. For example, the distributions associated with the times between burglary and robbery might be highly positively correlated. Nevertheless, given the data sets currently available, it seems most reasonable to simplify the model as much as possible; it can be expanded when more detailed data sets are available. One simplification would be to consider F and G to have generalized gamma distributions. This would replace (γ_t, R_t) by T sets of parameters $(n_t, r_{1t}, \ldots, r_{n_t t})$ corresponding to the parameters of the exponentials that will be convolved to form the generalized gamma distribution. A similar reduction could be made for G. Indeed, it seems reasonable to reduce even further to a gamma distribution. One could consider F_t to be a gamma (γ_t, λ_t) and G to be gamma (δ, σ). The number of parameters would be dramatically reduced. If this family does not fit sufficiently, the models could be easily expanded to enhance the fit.

One will still want to model some dependencies among the parameters. One will expect the random vectors (γ_1, λ_1), $\ldots$, (γ_T, λ_T) to be correlated. Indeed, the parameter set **A** (which is a set denoting the initial crime types) offers many intriguing possibilities. One can create specialist offenders or generalists or both. Such offenders may have in their initial set **A** only property crimes, only violent crimes, or some offense mixture. Moreover, the initial active set may well be correlated with the parameters that govern F_t. The hierarchical approach thus offers a natural way to build in dependencies among the fundamental parameters while still retaining a relatively simplified individual career structure. As more data are gathered, these dependencies can be explored more fully.

It is useful to include covariates in the superpopulation distribution. Two broad classes of covariates should be distinguished. First are the historical covariates, i.e., those that are fixed at the start of the career and remain unchanged throughout the career. For adult offenders, these might include variables such as sex, race, juvenile record, and age of first juvenile offense. A second class of covariates are "dynamic," i.e., variables that can change with time. These might include employment status, drug use, and arrest record. It is very desirable to include both classes of covariates in the model; however, some care is required. Under the current formulation, the random parameters are selected independently by each individual once at the start of the career and are then fixed forever. Consequently, the group of historical covariates could influence the choice of those parameters. The group of dynamic covariates, however, cannot be used in this fashion. This second group can be entered only by modifying the stochastic structure of the model.

It seems that F_t, G, $\mathbf{A}$, α, and β_t are the most important parameters to allow to have a dependence on covariates. Furthermore, $\mathbf{A}$ is chosen at the start of the career and can be influenced only by historical covariates. There are surely factors in an individual's past that influence whether he will ever engage in a particular crime type. It follows that any distribution for $\mathbf{A}$ should involve some historical covariates. Marginally, $\mathbf{A}$ will be chosen from a probability distribution over the subsets of $\{1, \ldots, T\}$ that depends on $\mathbf{X}$, a vector of covariates.

The times between crimes of any particular type, the length of time in the low period, and the probability of eliminating a particular crime type are much more likely to depend on dynamic covariates than historical ones. For example, if the individual is currently "on drugs," one would expect frequent crimes and shorter low periods. If, on the other hand, the individual is employed, one should expect longer times between crimes. Other covariates may well also be influential.

Let us consider a very simple example of how covariates might be included in the dynamic model. Suppose $\mathbf{Z}(a)$ is a vector of covariates that includes both historical and dynamic covariates for an individual of age a. We assume that F_t has a gamma $(\gamma_t, \lambda_t, e^{Z(a)b_1})$, $1 \leq t \leq T$ distribution, where $\mathbf{Z}$ and b_1 conform, and a is the age at which the current crime was committed. In this model the unknown coefficients b_1 are the same for each crime type. We assume that a crime of type t, committed by a person of age a, leads to an arrest with probability $q_t e^{Z(a)b_2}$. The probability that an individual who commits a crime of type t at age a will drop this crime from his active set is given by $\beta_t e^{Z(a)b_3}$. The probability that such an individual switches to a low period is given by $\alpha\, e^{Z(a)b_4}$. The low-period duration has a gamma $(\delta, \sigma e^{Z(a)b_5})$ distribution. The parameters γ_t, λ_t, q_t, β_t, α, δ, and σ are random and are drawn jointly from a superpopulation. The vectors $b_1, \ldots, b_5$ are unknown and must be estimated from data.

It should be noted that the model is appropriate when crimes (as opposed to arrests) are observable. In this case the likelihood function can be written and the parameters estimated. Prisoner self-report data are an approximation to such a data set. If, however, one has access only to arrest data for individuals, one cannot construct the likelihood function. In this instance one should start with a different, reduced model. Recall that the times between arrests will still be of phase type; however, rather than computing this in terms of the various parameters, it is simplest to model it directly as being of phase type with its own set of parameters. This will eliminate α and G from the model and cause F_t to be redefined as a time to arrest for crime type t rather than a time to the next crime of a given type.[5]

The approach to modeling criminal careers in this paper is somewhat related to the work of Flinn and Heckman (1982a, b, 1983). In the context of a criminal career as opposed to a more traditional labor career, this approach would define the time between crimes (or perhaps arrests) in terms of the hazard function. Suppose, for example, that the last crime occurred at time τ, and we want to construct the distribution of the time until the next crime. Let X represent this inter-event random variable. The hazard function is defined to be

[5]With only arrest data, the parameters in the full model are not fully identified. This reduction helps to identify the model. The notion of an active crime set and dropout probability is still present.

$$h(t) = \lim_{\Delta \to 0} \frac{P(t \le X \le t + \Delta | X \ge t)}{\Delta}.$$

Knowledge of the hazard function is equivalent to knowledge of the distribution. Flinn and Heckman allow the hazard function to have a general parametric form that depends on covariates and random quantities. This form is

$$h(t) = \exp[\mathbf{Z}(t + \tau)\beta + \gamma_1 t^{k_1} + \gamma_2 t^{k_2} + V(t + \tau)],$$

where $k_2 > k_1 \ge 0$, $\mathbf{Z}(t + \tau)$ is a vector of covariates corresponding to time $\tau + t$, β is a vector of coefficients, and $V(t + \tau)$ is restricted to being stationary, i.e., $V(t + \tau) = V$. This formulation can allow for the ith individual to have a hazard function $h_i(t)$ with associated covariates $\mathbf{Z}_i$ and unobserved variables V_i. In addition, the form can be generalized to a multistate, multispell formulation.

There may be some advantage to parameterizing the hazard function rather than the distribution if the covariates are rapidly changing. In the case of criminal careers, the time between crimes is relatively small compared with the change in covariates and so there is little gain in modeling the hazard function. Moreover, the class of phase distributions used in this paper is very versatile and capable of modeling any positive distribution. Nevertheless, the two approaches naturally complement each other and perhaps can be successfully combined.

PARAMETER ESTIMATION

This section addresses the problem of parameter estimation for the hierarchical models developed in this paper. The statistical literature on the estimation of hierarchical models and the empirical Bayes approach is quite large and rapidly growing. For reviews of this literature, see Deely and Lindley (1981), Dempster, Rubin, and Tsutakawa (1981), Copas (1983), and Morris (1983). Only the basic approach is described here.

The Formulation

Suppose there are n individual offenders. Each individual selects a vector of parameters θ from a distribution parameterized by an unknown parameter ϕ, $g(\theta|\phi)$. Conditional on the value of θ, the ith individual undertakes a criminal career, $\{\mathbf{X}^i_{\theta_i}, s \ge 0\}$. We assume that $\mathbf{X}^i$ is defined in such a way that it is observable. We can therefore observe $\{\mathbf{X}^i_{\theta_i}, 1 \le i \le n\}$, and we seek to estimate θ_i, $1 \le i \le n$, and ϕ, the parameter of the superpopulation distribution. The parameter ϕ is important, because it characterizes the offender population. The individual θ_i parameters characterize the behavior of the ith individual and can be used to help predict future behavior of that individual. If ϕ were known, only $\mathbf{X}^i_{\theta_i}$ would be useful in estimating θ_i. This leads to the shrinkage estimators mentioned above.

The problem as stated fits comfortably in the empirical Bayes framework. There are a number of approaches to the estimation problem. The focus here is on only likelihood-based methods, although other approaches, such as methods of moments, could well be used. Three basic approaches are considered:

1. a full Bayesian approach,
2. an empirical Bayes approach, and
3. a simultaneous-likelihood approach.

The Full Bayesian Approach

The full Bayesian program is straightforward. One treats ϕ as an unknown and hence as having a probability distribution, prior distribution, $f(\phi)$. The prior joint distribution of ϕ and θ_i, $1 \le i \le n$ is given by $f(\phi)\Pi_{i=1}^{n}[g(\theta_i|\phi)]$, since $\theta_1, \ldots, \theta_n$ are conditionally independent given ϕ.

One must calculate the posterior joint distribution of ϕ and θ_i, $1 \leq i \leq n$ given $\mathbf{X}^i$, $1 \leq i \leq n$. This calculation may involve significant numerical integration. Once the posterior distribution has been calculated, it can be used to estimate any of the parameters or to predict future values of $\mathbf{X}^i$, $1 \leq i \leq n$. The reader should consult Deely and Lindley (1981) for details and examples.

It seems generally difficult to determine $f(\phi)$ accurately, say by elicitation. Fortunately, for many criminal justice data sets, n can be very large. If this is the case, the prior distribution of ϕ, $f(\phi)$, will have very little influence on the estimates. It will be dominated by the data. One can, therefore, select a prior distribution that maximizes computational convenience, say by picking a conjugate prior distribution if one exists. Far more care is required if n is small.

The Empirical Bayes Approach

Morris (1983) discusses the empirical Bayes approach and includes many citations for the use of this methodology. The general approach in this instance is to proceed in two steps. First, one integrates out the conditional distribution of θ given ϕ to find the conditional distribution of each $\mathbf{X}^i$ given ϕ. The data $\mathbf{X}^i$, $1 \leq i \leq n$, are then used to estimate ϕ. This is typically done using maximum-likelihood estimation, although one could follow Deely and Lindley (1981) in using Bayesian estimation. In addition, the method of moments is often very convenient; however, its small sample behavior is unclear. Notice that all the data are used to estimate ϕ, and this will result in an estimate $\hat{\phi}$. It remains to estimate the individual θ_i parameters. This is done using likelihood methods by assuming θ_i has distribution $g(\theta|\hat{\phi})$ and using $\mathbf{X}^i$ as data. Again a choice of methods is possible, but the Bayes approach using the posterior distribution of θ given $\hat{\phi}$ and $\mathbf{X}^i$ is preferable.

The Simultaneous-Likelihood Approach

A third approach is the simultaneous-likelihood approach. This approach is very unreliable and should be ignored because it can produce inconsistent estimators. It entails writing the joint likelihood of θ_i and $\mathbf{X}^i{}_{\theta_i}$. This function is then simultaneously maximized over ϕ and θ_i, $1 \leq i \leq n$. The method is unreliable, in part because the number of parameters grows with the number of observations. This situation is one in which the maximum-likelihood method may perform in an undesirable fashion. Such behavior is shown in the examples below.

Some Simple Examples

The following example is designed to illustrate the ideas developed in the previous three sections. The example is based on the simplest model of a criminal career, given in the discussion of the Poisson process above.

Assume that each of n individual offenders is arrested according to a Poisson process with parameter θ. In addition, the n values of θ are drawn independently from a gamma (α, β) distribution. The shape parameter α is known, but the scale parameter β is unknown. The individual Poisson processes are observed over an interval of length L. By sufficiency and the memoryless property, we merely need to consider the total number of arrests over this time interval. We denote this quantity by $\mathbf{X}_i$. Conditional on θ_i, $\mathbf{X}_i$ has a Poisson distribution with mean $\theta_i L$.

We can calculate the conditional distribution of $\mathbf{X}_i$ given β by integrating out the parameter θ_i. This results in

$$P(\mathbf{X}_i = x_i|\beta) = \frac{\Gamma(\alpha + x_i)}{\Gamma(\alpha)\Gamma(x_i + 1)}\left(\frac{\beta}{\beta + L}\right)^{\alpha}\left(\frac{L}{\beta + L}\right)^{x_i},\ x_i = 0, 1, 2, \ldots,$$

a negative binomial distribution. Again α and L are known.

The Full Bayesian Approach

In this approach a prior distribution for β is introduced. The most convenient choice is to introduce the conjugate prior distribution for the negative binomial distribution, the beta distribution. We let $\beta/(\beta + L)$ have a beta (a, b) prior distribution. The full hierarchical model then becomes:

- $\beta/(\beta + L)$ has a beta (a, b) distribution,
- $(\theta_1, \ldots, \theta_n)|\beta$ are independent with gamma (α, β) distribution,
- $\mathbf{X}_1, \ldots, \mathbf{X}_n|\theta, \beta$ are independent and $\mathbf{X}_i$ has a Poisson $(\theta_i L)$ distribution.

One now wishes to find the posterior joint distribution of β and $\theta_1, \ldots, \theta_n$ given $\mathbf{X}_1, \ldots, \mathbf{X}_n$. This can be easily carried out, and we find

- $\beta/(\beta + L)|\mathbf{X}_1, \ldots, \mathbf{X}_n$ has a beta $(a + n\alpha, b + \sum_{i=1}^{n} x_i)$, and
- $\theta_1, \ldots, \theta_n|\beta, \mathbf{X}_1, \ldots, \mathbf{X}_n$ are conditionally independent with gamma $(\alpha + \mathbf{X}_i, \beta + L)$ distribution.

One can now construct Bayes estimates of the parameters. This requires the introduction of a loss function. For simplicity, consider nonsimultaneous estimation of the parameters based on the conditional mean. This would result in

$$\hat{\beta} = \frac{L(a + n\alpha)}{b + \sum_{i=1}^{n} x_i - 1},$$

$$\hat{\theta}_i = \frac{\alpha + \mathbf{X}_i}{L}\cdot\left(\frac{b + \sum_{i=1}^{n} x_i}{a + n\alpha + b + \sum_{i=1}^{n} x_i}\right).$$

For large n, these estimates are given approximately by

$$\hat{\beta} = L\alpha/\bar{x},$$

$$\hat{\theta}_i = \frac{(\alpha + x_i)(\bar{x})}{L(\alpha + \bar{x})}.$$

Note that the estimate of θ_i involves all the data. In addition, for large n, the choice of prior parameters (a, b) becomes immaterial.

Empirical Bayes Approach

The first step of this approach is to estimate β after integrating out θ. We treat $\mathbf{X}_1, \ldots, \mathbf{X}_n|\beta$ as being i.i.d. with negative binomial distribution. The maximum likelihood estimate is $\hat{\beta} = \alpha L/\bar{x}$, the same as the limiting version of the Bayes estimate of β.

To find the estimate of each θ_i, we treat the following problem:

- θ_i has gamma $(\alpha, \alpha L/\bar{x})$ distribution, and
- $\mathbf{X}_i|\theta_i$ has Poisson $(\theta_i L)$ distribution.

One can then find the posterior distribution of $\theta_i|\mathbf{X}_i$ to be a gamma $(\alpha + \mathbf{X}_i, L + \alpha L/\bar{\mathbf{X}})$ distribution. The Bayes estimator would then be given by

$$\hat{\theta}_i = \frac{(\alpha + x_i)\bar{x}}{L(\alpha + \bar{x})},$$

which is again identical to the limiting form of the Bayes estimate.

The Simultaneous-Likelihood Approach

This method involves writing a simultaneous likelihood, including that of the θ_i and $\mathbf{X}_i$, $1 \leq i \leq n$. One then maximizes over θ_i and β. The log-likelihood is given by

$$\text{constant} + n\alpha\log\beta + \sum (\alpha + \mathbf{X}_i - 1) \log\theta_i - (\beta + L)\sum \theta_i .$$

The likelihood equations are

$$\theta_i = \frac{\alpha + \mathbf{X}_i - 1}{\beta + L},$$

and

$$\sum \theta_i = n\alpha/\beta.$$

These can be simultaneously solved to give

$$\hat{\beta} = \frac{aL}{\bar{x} - 1},$$

and

$$\hat{\theta}_i = \frac{\alpha + x_i - 1}{\hat{\beta} + L}.$$

This estimate of β can be negative and even if positive is inconsistent. The point of this example is to give a simple illustration of a situation in which the method gives an unreasonable estimate. In other cases the method of maximum likelihood may not even provide an answer because infinite likelihood can be generated at some boundary of the parameter space.

In summary, either the full Bayes or empirical Bayes method should be used, if possible. The simultaneous-likelihood method should be avoided.

PHASE DISTRIBUTIONS

This section is intended to introduce the class of *phase distributions* and to list several properties of this class. These distributions have recently been rediscovered and extensively developed by Neuts (1981). The reader should consult this text for a complete treatment.

Only continuous time phase distributions are considered here. These distributions arise naturally in the context of continuous time Markov chains. A phase distribution arises as the amount of time it takes such a Markov chain to first reach a designated state in its state space. Consider a continuous time Markov chain with state space $\{1, 2, \ldots, m + 1\}$ and infinitesimal generator:

$$\mathbf{Q} = (q_{ij}) \text{ with } q_{ii} < 0,\ q_{ij} \geq 0 \text{ if } i \neq j,\ \sum_j q_{ij} = 0,$$

and

$$q_{m+1,i} = 0,\ i \leq m + 1.$$

For the given assumptions about the q_{ij}s, it follows that state $m + 1$ is an absorbing state. For any other state i, the chain is held in the state for an exponential period of time with mean $1/(-q_{ii})$. One must also introduce an initial distribution, $p = (p_1, \ldots, p_{m+1})$. The chain is started in a state selected at random from the distribution p. Once the initial state is selected, the chain evolves according to $\mathbf{Q}$. Eventually, the chain will reach state $m + 1$, and this is called the hitting time of state $m + 1$. This hitting time has a phase distribution with representation $(p, \mathbf{Q}_0)$. Given this description, one can see that the $(m + 1) \times (m + 1)$ matrix $\mathbf{Q}$ has a block form given by

$$\mathbf{Q} = \begin{pmatrix} \mathbf{Q}_0 & \mathbf{Q}_1 \\ 0 & 0 \end{pmatrix},$$

where $\mathbf{Q}_0$ is $m \times m$.

One problem with any particular phase distribution may be that the $(p, \mathbf{Q}_0)$ representation is not unique. This point is addressed in Neuts (1981).

The following facts about phase distributions are useful.

1. A phase distribution puts mass p_{m+1} on 0 and has density $p_0 \exp(x\mathbf{Q}_0)\mathbf{Q}_1$ on $(0,\infty)$, where $p = (p_0, p_{m+1})$.

2. The Laplace-Stieltjes transform of the distribution is given by

$$\Psi(s) = p_{m+1} + p(sI - \mathbf{Q}_0)^{-1}\mathbf{Q}_1 \quad \text{for } \mathrm{Re}(s) \geq 0.$$

3. The nth moment of the distribution is given by

$$\mu_n = (-1)^n n!\, (p\mathbf{Q}_0{}^{-n} e_m),$$

where $e_m = (1, \ldots, 1)$ and is $1 \times m$.

4. Suppose F and G are phase distributions with orders m and n and representations $(p, \mathbf{Q}_0)$ and $(r, \mathbf{S})$, respectively. The convolution $F*G$ is also a phase distribution with representation

$$\left\{(p, p_{m+1}r)\begin{pmatrix}\mathbf{Q}_0 & \mathbf{Q}_1\mathbf{R}_1\\ 0 & \mathbf{S}_0\end{pmatrix}\right\}$$

where $\mathbf{Q}_1\mathbf{R}_1$ is the $m \times n$ matrix with elements $\mathbf{Q}_{ij}r_j$, for $1 \leq i \leq m$ and $1 \leq j \leq n$.

5. If one considers a renewal process with phase distribution F governing the times between events, the equilibrium forward and backward recurrence time distributions are also phase distributions with modified initial vector.[6] This property is useful for correcting biases in data sets in which sampling is not random but rather is length biased (see next section).

6. The family of phase distributions is also closed under the operations of "maximum" and "minimum." Suppose X and Y are independent random variables with phase distributions given by F and G. Then the distribution $H_1(t) = F(t)G(t)$ corresponding to max (X, Y) and $H_2(t) = 1 - [1 - F(t)][1 - G(t)]$ corresponding to min (X, Y) are both of phase type (see Neuts, 1981:60). This property is useful for constructing a competing-risk model of the times between crimes for multiple crime types, as was used above.

The class of phase distributions is very large and explicitly contains a number of important parametric families. In particular, the exponential, gamma, and generalized gamma distributions are of phase type. They can be obtained by setting $\mu_{i,i+1} = -\mu_{ii}$ and $p_1 = 1$. The distribution is then a sum of m exponential random variables with possibly different parameter values. The hyperexponential can be obtained by setting $\mu_{i,m+1} = -\mu_{ii}$, and more complex mixtures can be obtained similarly. The class of phase distributions can be used to approximate any nonnegative continuous distribution. A construction is given by Kelly (1979). Indeed the class of generalized gamma densities alone is dense in the family of nonnegative continuous distributions. This result is useful, since the class is smaller and easier to handle than others.

Finally, note that the class of phase distributions is ideal for stochastic modeling. If one models some time (such as a recidivism time) as having a phase distribution, by augmenting the state space with a single variable (which denotes the current phase) the model will retain a Markov structure, if it had one originally. This allows one to stay within a tractable family of models, while introducing the flexibility of being able to approximate any nonnegative probability distribution.

CORRECTING BIASES IN SAMPLES

This section addresses the problem of biases in data sets that arise from

[6] See Neuts (1981:52) for the exact representations and p. 63 for a discussion of special properties of renewal processes governed by phase distributions.

nonrandom sampling from the offender population.[7] The hierarchical-model approach can be used to understand quantitatively the nature of the bias and therefore to correct for it. Several specific situations are considered in this section:

1. biases arising from restricting attention to offenders with at least one offense in a "window period,"
2. biases that arise in self-report data in which the sample is restricted to a prison population, and
3. biases that arise from estimating an individual crime rate from an individual record of a person who is caught in the midst of a period of high activity, so the estimates are biased upward.

Window Arrest Data Sets

Consider a general, delayed-renewal process with initial distribution G and general distribution F. Consequently, starting at time 0, the first event in the process occurs according to the distribution G, while all subsequent interevent distributions occur according to F. In the setting of a hierarchical model, we allow F and G to depend on parameters, and these parameters have some distribution given by cdf H and density h.

Suppose we select an individual at random from among the population of individuals who have an arrest in $[t,t + \delta]$. That is, we restrict our sampling to individuals having this "window arrest" property. An offender satisfying this window-arrest criterion will typically have more arrests than an individual randomly selected from the general offender population. The sampling plan thus is biased in favor of offenders with higher crime and arrest rates. If no adjustment is made, we will generate overestimates of crime rates, arrest rates, and the parameters of the superpopulation. It is, however, straightforward to correct the likelihood function to account for the bias in the window-arrest sampling procedure. We begin by calculating the likelihood of a criterion arrest in $[t,t + \delta]$.

Let us take, first, the standard renewal theoretic case, where $F = G$. Define

$$p(t) = P\,[\text{renewal event occurs in } (t,t + \delta)],\ t \geq 0.$$

The function $p(t)$ gives the probability an offender has a criterion arrest in the specified window $[t,t + \delta]$.

By conditioning on the time of the first event, we can write an integral equation for $p(t)$,[8]

$$p(t) = F(t + \delta) - F(t) + \int_0^t p(t - x)\mathrm{d}F(x).$$

This equation can be solved (see Karlin and Taylor, 1975:184) to find

$$p(t) = F(t + \delta) - F(t) + \int_0^t [F(s + \delta) - F(s)]\mathrm{d}M(s),$$

where $M(t) = \Sigma F^{(*n)}(t)$ is the renewal function. The quantity $p(t)$ is thus determined completely by the cdf F.

The expression is somewhat difficult to interpret, because there are two variables, t and δ, in addition to F. Some insight can be gained by considering the behavior of $p(t)$ for large t. As $t \rightarrow \infty$, one can apply the key renewal theorem to find $p(t) \rightarrow p$, where

[7]Professor A. Goldberger has pointed out to me that there is an extensive literature on correcting biases in samples in the educational psychology, economics, and evaluation research literature. This is treated under the rubric of selectivity bias, nonequivalent groups, and quasi-experiments. None of these, however, addresses the stochastic-process aspects dealt with in this paper.

[8]Note that $p(t)$ is also a function of δ but that it is ignored in the notation.

$$p = \int_0^\infty \frac{[F(t + \delta) - F(t)]dt}{m}$$

and

$$m = \int_0^\infty x dF(x) = \int_0^\infty [1 - F(x)]dx$$

is the mean time between events.

Some simple algebra allows us to compute

$$p = \int_0^\delta \frac{[1 - F(t)]}{m} dt.$$

The integrand is itself a density function. It represents the equilibrium backward or forward recurrence time distributions associated with F. The factor p, when treated as a function of δ, is a cdf. It begins at 0 and increases monotonically to 1 as δ increases to ∞. For very small values of δ, p is approximately given by δ/m, while for large values it is nearly 1. This is quite reasonable, since as the window size δ is increased, more and more individuals in the population can be included, and the window effect is reduced.

We are interested in the behavior of $p(t)$ for all values of t, not just the asymptotic behavior. The reason that $p(t)$ varies with t is that we have an initial condition, namely, that an event occurs at time 0. It takes some time for the effect of this condition to wear off and for equilibrium to be approached. If we begin with the renewal process in equilibrium, then $p(t)$ will no longer depend on t.

We can also achieve equilibrium by using a delayed renewal process formulation with $G'(t) = \dfrac{1 - F(t)}{m}$. There are two relevant integral equations. Let $p_D(t)$ be the probability of a criterion arrest in the window $[t,t + \delta]$ for the (F,G) delayed formulation, while $p(t)$ is the same quantity for the standard (F,F) formulation. Conditioning on the time of the first event (if any) gives

$$p_D(t) = G(t + \delta) - G(t) + \int_0^t p(t - x)dG(x),$$

$$p(t) = F(t + \delta) - F(t) + \int_0^t p(t - x)dF(x).$$

The second equation was solved earlier, and the resulting $p(t)$ can be substituted into the first to find $p_D(t)$. We take $G'(t) = [1 - F(t)]/m$ and do extensive algebra to find

$$p_D(t) = \frac{\int_0^\delta [1 - F(u)]du}{m} \qquad t > 0,$$

which is independent of t.

The expression for $p_D(t)$ can be used as a correction factor for the likelihood function. A given individual will have a criminal record that provides an enumeration of arrests that occurred prior to the window $[t,t + \delta]$, as well as those that occurred within the window. There will, of course, be at least one arrest within the window. The likelihood function will be constructed by multiplying the densities for the observed inter-event times; however, it must be modified to account for the presence of at least one event in $[t,t + \delta]$. This entails a division of the likelihood by $p_D(t)$.

We can consider the effect of this factor $p_D(t)$ on the posterior distribution of the parameters of the superpopulation. The posterior distribution will be proportioned to $h(\theta)L/p_D(t)$, where $h(\theta)$ is the prior density of the superpopulation and L represents the likelihood function.

An informative special case occurs when δ is small so that $p_D(t)$ is approximately δ/m. The posterior distribution of θ is proportional to $h(\theta)mL/\delta$ or $h(\theta)mL$. The extra factor m accounts for the sampling bias and weights the distribution more in favor of larger values of θ.

An example will help to illustrate the utility of this calculation. Suppose the arrest process is Poisson with parameter λ, and λ is treated as a random variable with distribution h. If we restrict attention to individuals with an arrest in $[t,t + \delta]$ for small δ, the posterior distribution of λ when corrected for this sampling plan will contain an extra factor of $1/\lambda$ (since $m = 1/\lambda$). This will tend to reduce the weight on large λ and counteracts the artificially inflated likelihood. For example, suppose the prior were to have a gamma (α,β) distribution. The posterior would be corrected to a gamma $(\alpha - 1,\beta)$ distribution and then used with the likelihood function, which has been inflated by the required window arrests. This correction is closely related to the length-biased sampling phenomenon of renewal theory. This posterior representation allows one to correct for the biases introduced by using only individuals with an arrest in the particular time window.

As δ increases, the size of the biasing effect is reduced, and, assuming an equilibrium formulation is measured by $\{\int_0^\delta [1 - F(x)]dx\}/m$ for any δ. For large δ, this factor is near 1.

Biases in Samples of Prisoners

Two other biases can arise in sampling and analyzing criminal justice data sets involving prisoners. First, individuals are generally sentenced to prison as a result of a high frequency of offenses. Individuals with a high observed offense rate are much more likely to be imprisoned than comparable individuals with a lesser observed offense rate. Since individuals with high propensities to commit crimes will in general have high empirical offense rates, this group can be expected to be overrepresented in prison populations. Data drawn from prisoners are, therefore, not representative of the offender population. A hierarchical model can, however, help to understand and correct for this bias.

A second issue concerns the stochastic nature of the crime process. Imagine two individuals with the same crime-committing propensity but different sample paths. The individual with the higher empirical frequency of offenses is more likely to be caught and sentenced. One may infer a higher crime rate for this individual than is actually appropriate, since individuals tend to be caught after a spurt of activity.

This second type of bias has been the subject of a recent lively debate. The controversy has been fueled by a paper of Maltz and Pollack (1980), which challenges the results of Murray and Cox (1979). The controversy centers on the evaluation of certain treatment programs for juveniles. It was noted empirically that juveniles selected for certain treatment programs exhibited a steep rise in the rate of police contact per unit time before admission. Surprisingly, these juveniles then exhibited a substantially diminished contact rate after admission to the program. The strong drop in contact rate after admission to the program has been called a "suppression effect" and was attributed by Murray and Cox solely to the success of the program.

This positive interpretation has been challenged by Maltz and Pollack (1980). They argue that the results could have been an artifact of a decision rule used by judges. Specifically, Maltz and Pollack assume that all individuals have the same value of λ. They posit a selection rule whereby an individual is placed in a treatment program at a time t—provided he experiences a contact at t and has at least k other contacts in the last τ time units. At the time an individual is placed in a program, he will exhibit a contact-rate significantly higher than λ (of course, this depends on λ and k). If τ is taken to be random with some appropriate distribution, the theoretical contact-rate curve matches the data very well. This is done under the assumption of a common λ. The judicial decision rule produces the effect, not the treatment program. Once individuals are placed in the program, the rate returns to its normal, lower value.

The impact of the work of Maltz and Pollack was reduced by Tierney (1983), who pointed out an error in their analysis. They had, in fact, not correctly calculated the theoretical contact rate prior to assignment to the program. No firm conclusions have been reached by any of the authors. A recent paper by Pollack and Farrell (1984) added some limited insight into the analysis but did not help to interpret these data.

It is very reasonable to assume in both a juvenile and an adult context that sentencing is based on the type of crime committed, the number of crimes committed, and the recent crime-committing behavior. If an individual has committed three crimes, he might or might not be sentenced to prison. If the three crimes were bunched near each other, commitment to prison is much more likely than if the previous crimes were committed over a long period. The decision rule articulated by Maltz and Pollack (1980) is quite reasonable. However, Maltz and Pollack and Tierney should have paid much closer attention than they did to the time at which the crimes were committed. Suppose we assume an individual begins the crime process at age 12 and is sentenced according to the Maltz and Pollack rule for some values of τ and k. For a given value of λ, we can compute the distribution of the time (age) T at which the individual will first be sentenced. Clearly a large value of λ tends to result in small T, since the offender commits crimes at a high rate. Conversely, if we observe T and attempt to infer λ, a large T tends to be associated with a small λ. There is information about λ in T; however, Maltz and Pollack and Tierney ignore this information by putting all individuals on a common time scale with time 0 representing the time of admission to the treatment program regardless of the actual age of the individual.

The inclusion of the time random variable can help to correct biases. Let us assume an individual begins a contact process at time 0. This might be age 12 for juveniles or age 18 for adults. Assume that contacts occur according to a Poisson process. We imagine that sentencing occurs at the time of the first contact having the property that there are also k other contacts within τ units of time. We now compute the density function associated with the time of the sentencing event.

We assume the Poisson process has parameter c. This refers to the contact process in the juvenile context or the parameter of the exponential times between convictions in an adult case. We wish to make inferences about c.

For clarity, we adopt a simple assumption concerning the sentencing rule. We assume that sentencing—

- never occurs on the first contact,
- occurs on the second contact only if the first was within the prior τ time units, and
- always occurs on the third contact, if not before.

This rule is reasonable, is in the spirit of Maltz and Pollack, and can be extended to more complex versions. Unlike the problems encountered in Pollack and Farrell (1984), calculations can be carried out for more complicated versions of this rule. First, we assume that individuals have drawn their rate parameter c at random from a parent distribution $h(c)$. We focus on the group of individuals (in either the juvenile or adult context) who receive a first sentence and note the value of T for each. Notice that our data set is restricted to those who receive a sentence. This means that we will have a much greater likelihood of selecting a high c individual than a low c individual. Interestingly, the presence of the value of T will have a modifying influence. If T is small, the value of c is even more likely to be large, since the offender was sentenced at the beginning of the career. If T is moderate to large, we should find that c is only slightly elevated. The individual was sentenced, but it took a long time to meet the criteria. If T is large, c should be small, since only low-rate offenders can avoid sentencing for a prolonged time period under this sentencing rule. We can quantify these heuristic comments by computing the density of T given c, $f_T(t)$. There are two cases to consider.

In the first case $t \le \tau$, sentencing would occur on the second offense in $(0,\tau)$. The time to the second offense has a gamma $(2,c)$ density, so the density has the form c^2te^{-ct}, $0 < t < \tau$.

After τ, sentencing can occur in two ways. First, if T_1 is the time of the first arrest and T_2 is the time of the second arrest, incarceration will occur if $T_2 - T_1 \le \tau$, i.e., if the individual falls into the window. Here $T_2 = t$. Second, if $T_2 - T_1 > \tau$, the individual does not fall in the window, and sentencing will occur on the third arrest.

Suppose that arrests form a renewal process with interevent density f [in this example, we assume f is exponential (c)]. For $t > \tau$, the density of the time T at which the contact or conviction leading to sentencing occurs has density

$$f_T(t) = \int_{t-\tau}^{t} f(s)f(t-s)ds + \int_{0}^{t-\tau} f(s) \cdot \int_{s+\tau}^{t} f(u-s)\, f(t-u)du\, ds.$$

For $f(s) = ce^{-cs}$, we find

$$f_T(t) = \begin{cases} c^2te^{-ct} & 0 < t \le \tau \\ c^2\tau e^{-ct} + c^3\dfrac{(t-\tau)^2}{2}e^{-ct}, & t \ge \tau. \end{cases}$$

One can see that the heuristics mentioned earlier do indeed hold. For example, if c has a prior gamma (α, β) distribution, the posterior distribution of c after observing $T = t$ would be a gamma $(\alpha + 2, \beta + t)$ distribution if $t \le \tau$. If $t > \tau$, c has a posterior distribution given by a mixture of gamma distributions, specifically with probability $p = \tau/\{\tau + (\alpha + 2)(t - \tau)^2/[2(\beta + t)]\}$, it is gamma $(\alpha + 2, \beta + t)$, and with complementary probability $1 - p$ it is gamma $(\alpha + 3, \beta + t)$. The posterior mean, $E(c|T = t)$, is given by

$$E(c|T = t) = \frac{\alpha + 2}{\beta + t}, \quad t \le \tau$$

$$p\left(\frac{\alpha + 2}{\beta + t}\right) + (1 - p)\left(\frac{\alpha + 3}{\beta + t}\right), \quad t > \tau.$$

The conditional mean is thus larger than $E(c) = \alpha/\beta$ for small $T = t$, but smaller for large t. This shows that the individuals should not be placed on a common time scale but analyzed separately using this hierarchical approach. One can update the prior distribution on c, π, and estimate all the individual c's. These can then be compared with the empirical arrest records subsequent to intervention to gain some insight into program effectiveness.

SUMMARY AND SUGGESTIONS FOR FURTHER RESEARCH

This paper has introduced two innovations to the quantitative modeling of criminal justice problems: a general structure of hierarchical models and a new stochastic model of a criminal career. These models allow one to distinguish variation between individual offenders and variations within an individual career. This is important given the very large variability in the offender population. In addition, the hierarchical approach allows one to correct for natural biases in a data set. Biases can arise because the sampling is not at random from the offender population but rather is conditional on some event. For example, one might consider a set of arrestees or prisoners. This group tends to contain higher rate offenders than would be seen in the general population. The new stochastic model of a criminal career offers three advantages over the standard renewal-process models in common use. First, it introduces a two-state approach in which there are periods of high and low activity. Second, the "active crime set" approach results in a natural age effect in which an offender's average crime-commission rate diminishes over time. Third, the model allows for some decision making on the part of the offender.

There are a number of ways in which one could consider extending the stochastic-process model. The major need is to include imprisonment and behavioral changes that arise from imprisonment. Indeed, this author would like to include explicitly a parameter or parameters that allow for a change in the F_t and active-crime-set distributions depending on the fact of and length of sentencing.

It appears that the next step is to fit this new class of models with data, after first correcting natural biases in the data. This should enable us to learn about the explanatory power in this class of models and to determine to what class of phase distributions the interevent (crime or arrest) times can be restricted. Data are also needed to begin to determine an appropriate class of superpopulation distributions, not only for the parameters that determine the phase distributions but also for the other behavioral parameters and the initial active-crime set. Finally, the possibility of combining the hazard-function approach of Flinn and Heckman with the phase-distribution approach given in this paper should be explored.

REFERENCES AND BIBLIOGRAPHY

Avi-Itzhak, B., and Shinnar, R.
1973 Quantitative models in crime control. *Journal of Criminal Justice* 1:185–217.

Barton, R. R., and Turnbull, B. W.
1981 A failure rate regression model for the study of recidivism. Pp. 81–101 in J. A. Fox, ed., *Models in Quantitative Criminology*. New York: Academic Press.

Chaiken, J. M., and Rolph, J. E.
1980 Selective incapacitation strategies based on estimated crime rates. *Operations Research* 28:1259–1274.

Copas, J. B.
1983 Regression, prediction and shrinkage. *Journal of the Royal Statistical Society B* 45:311–354.

Deely, J. J., and Lindley, D. V.
1981 Bayes, empirical Bayes. *Journal of the American Statistical Association* 76:833–841.

Dempster, A. P., Rubin, D. B., and Tsutakawa, R. K.
1981 Estimation in covariance components models. *Journal of the American Statistical Association* 76:341–353.

Flinn, C. J., and Heckman, J. J.
1982a Models for the analysis of labor force dynamics. *Advances in Econometrics* 1:35–95.
1982b New methods for analyzing individual event histories. Pp. 99–140 in S. Leinhardt, ed., *Sociological Methodology*. San Francisco: Jossey-Bass.
1983 The Likelihood Function for the Multistate-multiepisode Model in "Models for the Analysis of Labor Force Dynamics." Discussion Paper Series 83–10, Economic Research Center. Chicago, Ill.: National Opinion Research Center.

Harris, C. M., and Moitra, S. D.
1979 Improved statistical techniques for the measurement of recidivism. *Journal of Research in Crime and Delinquency* 16:194–213.

Harris, C. M., Kaylan, A. R., and Maltz, M. D.
1981 Recent Advances in the Statistics of Recidivism Measurement. Pp. 61–79 in J. A. Fox, ed., *Models in Quantitative Criminology*. New York: Academic Press.

Harville, D. A.
1977 Maximum likelihood approaches to variance components estimation and to related problems. *Journal of the American Statistical Association* 72:320–340.

Holden, R. T.
1983 Failure Time Models for Criminal Behavior. Department of Sociology, Yale University.

James, W., and Stein, C.
1961 Estimation with quadratic loss. Pp. 361–379 in *Proceedings of the Fourth Berkeley Symposium*. Vol. 1. Berkeley: University of California Press.

Karlin, S., and Taylor, H. M.
1975 *A First Course in Stochastic Processes*. 2nd ed. New York: Academic Press.

Kelly, F. P.
1979 *Reversibility and Stochastic Networks*. New York: John Wiley & Sons.

Maltz, M. D., and McCleary, R.
1977 The mathematics of behavioral change: recidivism and construct validity. *Evaluation Quarterly* 1:421–438.

Maltz, M. D., and Pollack, S. M.
1980 Artificial inflation of a delinquency rate by a selection artifact. *Operations Research* 28: 547–559.

Morris, C. N.
1983 Parametric empirical Bayes inference: theory and applications. *Journal of the American Statistical Association* 78:47–65.

Murray, C. A., and Cox, L. A., Jr.
1979 *Beyond Probation*. Vol. 94. Sage Library of Social Research. Beverly Hills, Calif.: Sage Publications.

Neuts, M. F.
1981 *Matrix Geometric Solutions in Stochastic Models: An Algorithmic Approach*. Baltimore, Md.: Johns Hopkins University Press.

Peterson, M. A., and Braiker, H. B., with Polick, S. M.
1981 Who Commits Crimes: A Survey of Prison Inmates. Cambridge, Mass.: Oelgeschlager, Gunn, and Hain.

Pollack, S. M., and Farrell, R. L.
1984 Past intensity of a terminated Poisson process. *Operations Research Letters* 2:261–263.

Rolph, J. E., Chaiken, J. M., and Houchens, R. E.
1981 Methods for Estimating Crime Rates of Individuals. Report R-2730-NIJ. Santa Monica, Calif.: Rand Corporation.

Stollmark, S., and Harris, C. M.
1974 Failure-rate analysis applied to recidivism data. *Operations Research* 22:1192–1205.

Tierney, L.
1983 A selection artifact in delinquency data revisited. *Operations Research* 31:852–865.